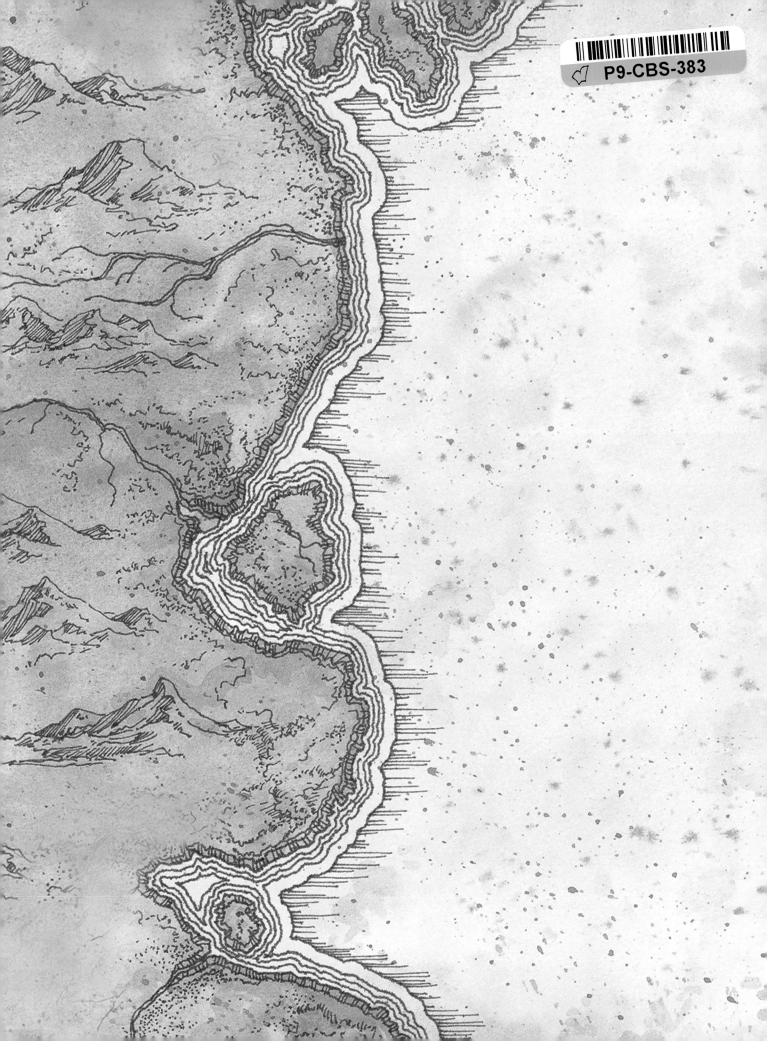

AMERICA'S STORY

Series Authors

Dr. Richard G. Boehm

Claudia Hoone

Dr. Thomas M. McGowan

Dr. Mabel C. McKinney-Browning

Dr. Ofelia B. Miramontes

Series Consultants

Dr. Alma Flor Ada

Dr. Phillip Bacon

Dr. W. Dorsey Hammond

Dr. Asa Grant Hilliard, III

HARCOURT BRACE & COMPANY

Orlando Atlanta Austin Boston San Francisco Chicago Dallas
New York Toronto London

SERIES AUTHORS

Dr. Richard G. Boehm
Professor
Department of Geography and Planning
Southwest Texas State University
San Marcos, Texas

Claudia Hoone
Teacher
Ralph Waldo Emerson School #58
Indianapolis, Indiana

Dr. Thomas M. McGowan
Associate Professor
Division of Curriculum and Instruction
Arizona State University
Tempe, Arizona

Dr. Mabel C. McKinney-Browning
Director
Division for Public Education
American Bar Association
Chicago, Illinois

Dr. Ofelia B. Miramontes
Associate Professor
School of Education
University of Colorado
Boulder, Colorado

SERIES CONSULTANTS

Dr. Alma Flor Ada
Professor
School of Education
University of San Francisco
San Francisco, California

Dr. Phillip Bacon
Professor Emeritus of
Geography and Anthropology
University of Houston
Houston, Texas

Dr. W. Dorsey Hammond
Professor of Education
Oakland University
Rochester, Michigan

Dr. Asa Grant Hilliard, III
Fuller E. Callaway Professor of Urban
Education
Georgia State University
Atlanta, Georgia

MEDIA AND LITERATURE SPECIALISTS

Dr. Joseph A. Braun, Jr.
Professor of Elementary Social Studies
Department of Curriculum and Instruction
Illinois State University
Normal, Illinois

Meredith McGowan
Youth Librarian
Tempe Public Library
Tempe, Arizona

GRADE-LEVEL CONSULTANTS AND REVIEWERS

Dr. Ira Berlin
Professor
Department of History
University of Maryland
at College Park
College Park, Maryland

Dr. Eugene Berwanger
Professor
Department of History
Colorado State University
Fort Collins, Colorado

Efren G. Camarillo
Teacher
John R. Harris Elementary School
Houston, Texas

Dr. John Henrik Clarke
Professor Emeritus
Department of Africana &
Puerto Rican Studies
Hunter College
New York, New York

Dr. Donald L. Fixico
Professor
Department of History
Western Michigan University
Kalamazoo, Michigan

Dr. Lois Harrison-Jones
Former Superintendent of Boston,
Massachusetts, Public Schools and
Richmond, Virginia, Public Schools

Cathy M. Johnson
Children's Museum
Detroit, Michigan

Lamisa Landers
Teacher–TAAS Specialist
Griffin Elementary School and Ramey
Elementary School
Tyler, Texas

Timothy L. Mateer
Teacher
East Petersburg Elementary School
East Petersburg, Pennsylvania

Dr. Howard H. Moon, Jr.
Coordinator of Language Arts/
Social Studies
Kenosha Public Schools
Kenosha, Wisconsin

Richard Nichols
(Santa Clara Pueblo Tewa)
Vice President
ORBIS Associates
Washington, D.C.

Dr. Estelle Owens
Chairman of the Social Studies Division
and Professor of History
Wayland Baptist University
Plainview, Texas

Dr. L. Anita Richardson
American Bar Association
Chicago, Illinois

Dr. Linda Kerrigan Salvucci
Associate Professor
Department of History
Trinity University
San Antonio, Texas

Dr. Stephen L. Schechter
Director of Council for
Citizenship Education
Russell Sage College
Troy, New York

Elma Schwartz
Teacher
Ascarate Elementary School
El Paso, Texas

Carolyn Smith
Teacher
Farragut Intermediate School
Knoxville, Tennessee

Dr. Judith Smith
Coordinator of Humanities
Baltimore City Public Schools
Baltimore, Maryland

Dr. Mary Jane Turner
Senior Education Advisor
Close Up Foundation
Alexandria, Virginia

Requests for permission to make copies of any part of the work should be mailed to: Permissions Department, Harcourt Brace & Company, 6277 Sea Harbor Drive, Orlando, Florida 32887-6777.

HARCOURT BRACE and Quill Design is a registered trademark of Harcourt Brace & Company.

Acknowledgments and other credits appear in the back of this book.

Printed in the United States of America

ISBN 0-15-302042-3

5 6 7 8 9 10   032   99 98 97

CONTENTS DISCARDED

An Olmec statue

Dora Pino

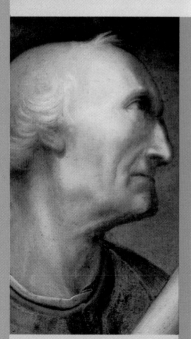

Amerigo Vespucci

Motecuhzoma

UNIT 3

OUR COLONIAL HERITAGE 154

Junípero Serra

An African in the colonies

UNIT 4

CHAPTER 7

John Adams

Mercy Otis Warren

Abigail Adams

vii

George Washington

A pioneer woman

Juan Seguín

UNIT 7

Frederick Douglass

A Confederate soldier

UNIT 8

A young immigrant

A cowhand

Theodore Roosevelt

Zora Neale Hurston

Martin Luther King, Jr.

Cinthya Guzman

F.Y.I.

LITERATURE, PRIMARY SOURCES, AND DOCUMENTS

LEARNING FROM VISUALS

GEOGRAPHY SKILLS

CHART AND GRAPH SKILLS

BUILDING CITIZENSHIP

READING AND WRITING SKILLS

THINKING SKILLS

CHARTS, GRAPHS, DIAGRAMS, TABLES, AND TIME LINES

ATLAS

CONTENTS

180° 160° W 140° W 120° W 100° W 80° W 60° W

80° N

ARCTIC OCEAN

Greenland
(DENMARK)

ALASKA
(U.S.)

60° N

CANADA

**NORTH
AMERICA**

40° N

UNITED STATES

Azores
(PORTUGAL)

Area of inset

Bermuda
(U.K.)

ATLANTIC
OCEAN

*Midway
Islands
(U.S.)*

Tropic of Cancer

20° N

MEXICO

CAPE VERDE

HAWAII
(U.S.)

PACIFIC
OCEAN

VENEZUELA GUYANA SURINAME

COLOMBIA

FRENCH GUIANA
(FRANCE)

Equator

*Galápagos
Islands
(ECUADOR)*

ECUADOR

BRAZIL

*Tokelau
(N.Z.)*

KIRIBATI

PERU

**SOUTH
AMERICA**

WESTERN
SAMOA

*American
Samoa
(U.S.)*

*Cook
Islands
(N.Z.)*

*French
Polynesia
(FRANCE)*

20° S

BOLIVIA

TONGA

PARAGUAY

*Niue
(N.Z.)*

*Pitcairn
(U.K.)*

Tropic of Capricorn

CHILE

*Easter Island
(CHILE)*

URUGUAY

ARGENTINA

40° S

PACIFIC
OCEAN

*Falkland
Islands
(U.K.)*

*South
Georgia
(U.K.)*

60° S

Antarctic Circle

80° S

180° 160° W 140° W 120° W 100° W 80° W 60° W

UNITED STATES

Gulf of Mexico

100° W

ATLANTIC
OCEAN

BAHAMAS

Tropic of Cancer

MEXICO

20° N

20° N

CUBA

*Turks and
Caicos (U.K.)*

*Puerto
Rico
(U.S.)*

Anguilla (U.K.)

St. Martin (FRANCE AND NETH.)

HAITI

DOMINICAN
REPUBLIC

ANTIGUA AND BARBUDA

*Cayman
Islands
(U.K.)*

Montserrat (U.K.)

BELIZE

JAMAICA

*Virgin Islands
(U.S. AND U.K.)*

Guadeloupe (FRANCE)

ST. KITTS
AND NEVIS

DOMINICA

GUATEMALA HONDURAS

Caribbean Sea

Martinique (FRANCE)

ST. LUCIA

EL SALVADOR

NICARAGUA

*Aruba
(NETH.)*

*Netherlands
Antilles
(NETH.)*

BARBADOS

ST. VINCENT AND
THE GRENADINES

GRENADA

PACIFIC OCEAN

*Panama
Canal*

TRINIDAD AND
TOBAGO

10° N

10° N

A2

0   200   400 Miles

0   200   400 Kilometers
Azimuthal Equal-Area Projection

COSTA
RICA

PANAMA

VENEZUELA

GUYANA

COLOMBIA

90° W

80° W

70° W

60° W

ARCTIC OCEAN

20° W 0° 20° E 40° E 60° E 80° E 100° E 120° E 140° E 160° E 180°

80° N

Arctic Circle

60° N

ICELAND

Area of inset

RUSSIA

ASIA

EUROPE

KAZAKHSTAN

MONGOLIA

40° N

GEORGIA
ARMENIA AZERBAIJAN
TURKEY TURKMENISTAN TAJIKISTAN
CYPRUS SYRIA
LEBANON IRAQ IRAN AFGHANISTAN
ISRAEL
JORDAN KUWAIT
Canary Is. MOROCCO TUNISIA
(SPAIN)
ALGERIA LIBYA EGYPT BAHRAIN QATAR
SAUDI U.A.E.
WESTERN ARABIA
SAHARA OMAN
(MOROCCO)

UZBEKISTAN
KYRGYZSTAN

NORTH
KOREA
SOUTH
KOREA

JAPAN

PACIFIC
OCEAN

CHINA

BHUTAN
PAKISTAN NEPAL
BANGLADESH

TAIWAN

20° N

MAURITANIA MALI NIGER CHAD SUDAN
ERITREA YEMEN
SENEGAL
GUINEA BURKINA NIGERIA
FASO BENIN
SIERRA CÔTE AFRICA DJIBOUTI
LEONE D'IVOIRE CENTRAL
LIBERIA GHANA EQU. AFRICAN REPUBLIC ETHIOPIA
GUINEA- TOGO GUINEA CAMEROON
BISSAU GABON CONGO UGANDA
THE SÃO TOMÉ RWANDA KENYA
GAMBIA AND PRÍNCIPE ZAIRE BURUNDI
CABINDA TANZANIA
(ANGOLA)
ANGOLA MALAWI
ZAMBIA
MOZAMBIQUE
NAMIBIA ZIMBABWE MADAGASCAR
BOTSWANA

INDIA BURMA LAOS
(MYANMAR)
THAILAND VIETNAM PHILIPPINES
CAMBODIA

SOMALIA

MALDIVES

SRI
LANKA

BRUNEI

MALAYSIA

SINGAPORE

SEYCHELLES

COMOROS

MAURITIUS

Reunion
(FRANCE)

INDONESIA

INDIAN
OCEAN

Northern
Mariana Islands
(U.S.)

Guam (U.S.)

PALAU

FEDERATED
STATES OF
MICRONESIA

MARSHALL
ISLANDS

0°

NAURU KIRIBATI

TUVALU

PAPUA
NEW GUINEA

SOLOMON
ISLANDS

VANUATU FIJI

New
Caledonia
(FRANCE)

20° S

AUSTRALIA

ATLANTIC
OCEAN

SWAZILAND
SOUTH LESOTHO
AFRICA

N
W E
S

Kerguelen
Archipelago
(FRANCE)

0 1,000 2,000 Miles
0 1,000 2,000 Kilometers
Scale accurate at equator
Robinson Projection

NEW
ZEALAND

40° S

ANTARCTICA

80° S

EUROPE

20° W 0° 20° E 40° E 60° E 80° E 100° E 120° E 140° E 160° E 180°

60° S

Arctic Circle

FINLAND

60° N

NORWAY

SWEDEN

ESTONIA

RUSSIA

0 200 400 Miles
0 200 400 Kilometers
Azimuthal Equal-Area Projection

LATVIA

UNITED
KINGDOM

North
Sea

DENMARK

LITHUANIA
KALININGRAD
(RUSSIA)

BELARUS

IRELAND

N
W E
S

NETHERLANDS

BELGIUM

GERMANY

POLAND

50° N

UKRAINE

─── National border

ATLANTIC
OCEAN

50° N

LUXEMBOURG

LIECHTENSTEIN

CZECH
REPUBLIC

SLOVAKIA

MOLDOVA

SWITZERLAND

AUSTRIA HUNGARY

ROMANIA

FRANCE

SLOVENIA
SAN CROATIA
MARINO BOSNIA AND
HERZEGOVINA

Black
Sea

BULGARIA

Abbreviations

EQU. GUINEA	EQUATORIAL GUINEA
NETH.	NETHERLANDS
N.Z.	NEW ZEALAND
U.A.E.	UNITED ARAB EMIRATES
U.K.	UNITED KINGDOM
U.S.	UNITED STATES

MONACO
ANDORRA Corsica
(FRANCE) ITALY

40° N

PORTUGAL

SPAIN

VATICAN
CITY
Sardinia
(ITALY)

Balearic Islands
(SPAIN)

Mediterranean Sea

GIBRALTAR
(U.K.)

10° W

Sicily
(ITALY)

10° E

MALTA

YUGOSLAVIA

MACEDONIA

ALBANIA

Adriatic Sea

TURKEY

GREECE

A3

Crete
(GREECE)

20° E

ARCTIC OCEAN

180° 160° W 140° W 120° W 100° W 80° W 60° W

80° N

Beaufort Sea

Queen Elizabeth Islands

Greenland

Baffin Island

Great Bear Lake

Great Slave Lake

Hudson Bay

NORTH AMERICA

Mt. McKinley 20,320 ft. (6,194 m)

Yukon R.

Mt. Logan 19,524 ft. (5,951 m)

Bering Sea

Mackenzie R.

ROCKY MOUNTAINS

GREAT PLAINS

Aleutian Islands

Gulf of Alaska

Vancouver Island

Columbia R.

Missouri R.

Mississippi R.

Ohio R.

Great Lakes

Newfoundland

APPALACHIAN MTS.

Azores

40° N

Mt. Whitney 14,494 ft. (4,418 m)

Colorado R.

Bermuda

ATLANTIC OCEAN

Hawaiian Islands

20° N

Tropic of Cancer

Gulf of Mexico

Bahamas

Cuba

Hispaniola

PACIFIC OCEAN

Citlaltepetl 18,701 ft. (5,700 m)

Yucatán Peninsula

West Indies

Cape Verde Islands

Caribbean Sea

Equator

Galápagos Islands

Orinoco River

Guiana Highlands

AMAZON

Amazon R.

Polynesia

BASIN

SOUTH AMERICA

ANDES MOUNTAINS

Brazilian Highlands

20° S

Tropic of Capricorn

Atacama Desert

Gran Chaco

Paraná River

Mt. Aconcagua 22,831 ft. (6,959 m)

Pampa

40° S

Patagonia

Falkland Islands

Strait of Magellan

Tierra del Fuego

Cape Horn

60° S

Antarctic Circle

Antarctic Peninsula

80° S

Ross Sea

180° 160° W 140° W 120° W 100° W 80° W 60° W

NORTHERN POLAR REGION

ASIA

Sea of Okhotsk

EUROPE

Kamchatka Peninsula

Severnaya Zemlya

Novaya Zemlya

New Siberian Is.

Barents Sea

Baltic Sea

0 400 800 Miles
0 400 800 Kilometers
Azimuthal Equidistant Projection

Wrangel Island

ARCTIC OCEAN

Svalbard

Norwegian Sea

North Sea

Bering Sea

North Pole

Bering Strait

Brooks Range

Beaufort Sea

North Magnetic Pole

Queen Elizabeth Islands

Greenland

Iceland

British Isles

ATLANTIC OCEAN

Baffin Bay

Arctic Circle

A4

NORTH AMERICA

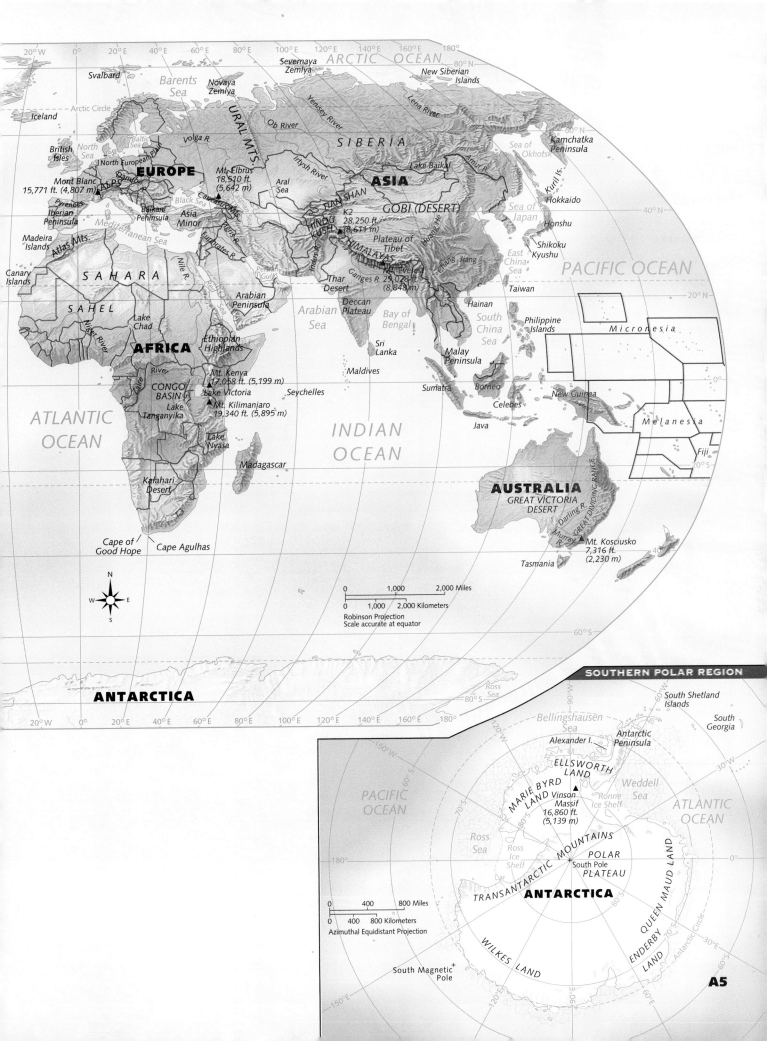

20°W | 0° | 20°E | 40°E | 60°E | 80°E | 100°E | 120°E | 140°E | 160°E | 180°

ARCTIC OCEAN

Svalbard
Barents Sea
Novaya Zemlya
Severnaya Zemlya
New Siberian Islands

Iceland
Arctic Circle

British Isles
North Sea
Baltic Sea
North European Plain
EUROPE
Mont Blanc 15,771 ft. (4,807 m)
ALPS
Pyrenees
Iberian Peninsula
Danube R.
Balkan Peninsula
Black Sea
Asia Minor
Caucasus Mts.
Mt. Elbrus 18,510 ft. (5,642 m)
Caspian Sea
Aral Sea
Tigris R.
Euphrates R.
Persian Gulf

URAL MTS.
Ob River
Irtysh River
Yenisey River
SIBERIA
Lena River
Amur R.
Sea of Okhotsk
Kamchatka Peninsula

ASIA
TIAN SHAN
K2 28,250 ft. (8,611 m)
HINDU KUSH
GOBI (DESERT)
Lake Baikal
Plateau of Tibet
HIMALAYAS
Mt. Everest 29,028 ft. (8,848 m)
Huang He
Chang Jiang
Kuril Is.
Hokkaido
Sea of Japan
Honshu
Shikoku
Kyushu
East China Sea
Taiwan

PACIFIC OCEAN

Madeira Islands
Atlas Mts.
Mediterranean Sea
Canary Islands
SAHARA
SAHEL
Nile R.
Red Sea
Arabian Peninsula
Arabian Sea
Deccan Plateau
Thar Desert
Ganges R.
Bay of Bengal
Hainan
South China Sea
Philippine Islands

Lake Chad
Niger River
AFRICA
Ethiopian Highlands
Congo River
Mt. Kenya 17,058 ft. (5,199 m)
Lake Victoria
Mt. Kilimanjaro 19,340 ft. (5,895 m)
CONGO BASIN
Lake Tanganyika
Lake Nyasa
Sri Lanka
Maldives
Seychelles
Malay Peninsula
Sumatra
Borneo
Celebes
Java
New Guinea

Micronesia
Melanesia
Fiji

ATLANTIC OCEAN

INDIAN OCEAN

Madagascar
Kalahari Desert
Cape of Good Hope
Cape Agulhas

AUSTRALIA
GREAT VICTORIA DESERT
GREAT DIVIDING RANGE
Darling R.
Murray R.
Mt. Kosciusko 7,316 ft. (2,230 m)
Tasmania

N
W   E
S

0   1,000   2,000 Miles
0   1,000   2,000 Kilometers
Robinson Projection
Scale accurate at equator

ANTARCTICA

20°W | 0° | 20°E | 40°E | 60°E | 80°E | 100°E | 120°E | 140°E | 160°E | 180°
60°S
80°S
Ross Sea

PACIFIC OCEAN

Bellingshausen Sea
Alexander I.
South Shetland Islands
Antarctic Peninsula
South Georgia
ELLSWORTH LAND
MARIE BYRD LAND
Vinson Massif 16,860 ft. (5,139 m)
Ronne Ice Shelf
Weddell Sea

ATLANTIC OCEAN

Ross Sea
Ross Ice Shelf
TRANSANTARCTIC MOUNTAINS
POLAR PLATEAU
South Pole
ANTARCTICA
QUEEN MAUD LAND
ENDERBY LAND
Antarctic Circle

WILKES LAND
South Magnetic Pole

0   400   800 Miles
0   400   800 Kilometers
Azimuthal Equidistant Projection

90°W
150°W
180°
120°W
60°W
30°W
0°
30°E
60°E
90°E
120°E
60°S
70°S
80°S

A5

ARCTIC OCEAN

Beaufort Sea

Viscount Melville Sound

Baffin Bay

Greenland
(DENMARK)

Bering Strait

Mackenzie River

Foxe Basin

Arctic Circle

ALASKA
(U.S.)

Yukon River

Fairbanks

Great Bear Lake

Davis Strait

Anchorage

Whitehorse

Yellowknife

Great Slave Lake

Hudson Strait

Gulf of Alaska

Juneau

Liard River

Peace River

CANADA

Hudson Bay

Labrador Sea

Bering Sea

60° N

Athabasca R.

Lake Athabasca

James Bay

Edmonton

Saskatchewan R.

Lake Winnipeg

Calgary

Saskatoon

Vancouver

Regina

Winnipeg

Thunder Bay

St. Lawrence River

St. John's

Puget Sound

Seattle

UNITED STATES

Great Lakes

Ottawa

Québec

St. John

Gulf of St. Lawrence

Portland

Columbia R.

Montreal

Halifax

Boise

Missouri R.

Toronto

Albany

Boston

Salt Lake City

Detroit

Cleveland

New York City

Great Salt Lake

Chicago

Reno

Denver

St. Louis

Indianapolis

Philadelphia

Washington, D.C.

San Francisco

Colorado R.

Richmond

Norfolk

Las Vegas

Memphis

Atlanta

Raleigh

ATLANTIC OCEAN

Los Angeles

Phoenix

Rio Grande

Dallas

Charleston

San Diego

Tucson

El Paso

Houston

New Orleans

Savannah

30° N

Hermosillo

San Antonio

Jacksonville

Tampa

Honolulu

Chihuahua

Gulf of Mexico

Miami

BAHAMAS

HAWAII
(U.S.)

MEXICO

Monterrey

Nassau

Tropic of Cancer

Durango

Havana

PACIFIC OCEAN

León

Tampico

CUBA

HAITI

Port-au-Prince

Guadalajara

Mexico City

JAMAICA

Santo Domingo

Puebla

Veracruz

BELIZE

PUERTO RICO (U.S.)

Acapulco

Belmopan

Kingston

DOMINICAN REPUBLIC

GUATEMALA

Guatemala

HONDURAS

Caribbean Sea

San Salvador

Tegucigalpa

EL SALVADOR

Managua

Maracaibo

NICARAGUA

San José

Caracas

GUYANA

COSTA RICA

Panama City

SURINAME

PANAMA

VENEZUELA

Georgetown

Paramaribo

Medellín

Cayenne

Cali

Bogotá

FRENCH GUIANA (FRANCE)

Quito

COLOMBIA

Equator

Galápagos Islands
(ECUADOR)

Guayaquil

Rio Negro

Belém

ECUADOR

Manaus

Amazon R.

Iquitos

Fortaleza

Trujillo

Tapajós River

Xingu R.

Recife

PERU

Tocantins

FRENCH POLYNESIA
(FRANCE)

Lima

Cuzco

BRAZIL

São Francisco R.

Salvador

Papeete

Lake Titicaca

La Paz

Brasília

Arequipa

BOLIVIA

Goiânia

Belo Horizonte

Sucre

Campo Grande

Rio de Janeiro

Tropic of Capricorn

Antofagasta

PARAGUAY

Asunción

São Paulo

San Miguel de Tucumán

Salta

Paraná R.

Curitiba

CHILE

Córdoba

Pôrto Alegre

30° S

Valparaíso

Rosario

URUGUAY

Santiago

Buenos Aires

Montevideo

Concepción

La Plata

Rio de la Plata

Mar del Plata

Valdivia

Bahía Blanca

ARGENTINA

| 0 | 1,000 | 2,000 Miles |
| 0 | 1,000 | 2,000 Kilometers |

Miller Cylindrical Projection

—— National border

⊛ National capital

• City

N
W E
S

A6

Falkland Islands
(U.K.)

South Georgia
(U.K.)

Punta Arenas

150° W

120° W

90° W

60° W

30° W

ARCTIC OCEAN

North Magnetic Pole +

Queen Elizabeth Islands

Ellesmere Island

Greenland

Melville island

Viscount Melville Sound

Devon Island

Point Barrow

Beaufort Sea

Banks Island

Victoria Island

Baffin Bay

Brooks Range

Mt. McKinley 20,320 ft. (6,194 m) ▲

Yukon River

Mackenzie Mts.

Great Bear Lake

Mackenzie River

Baffin Island

Arctic Circle

Alaska Range

Yukon

Liard River

Great Slave Lake

Foxe Basin

Cape Farewell

60° N

Mt. Logan 19,524 ft. (5,951 m) ▲

Plateau

Peace River

Lake Athabasca

Hudson Strait

Davis Strait

Gulf of Alaska

Coast Mountains

Athabasca R.

Hudson Bay

Labrador Sea

Kodiak Island

Alaska Peninsula

Queen Charlotte Islands

Cascade Range

C A N A D I A N

Saskatchewan River

Lake Winnipeg

James Bay

S H I E L D

Labrador

Aleutian Islands

Vancouver Island

Puget Sound

R O C K Y

G R E A T

M O U N T A I N S

Great Lakes

St. Lawrence R.

Newfoundland

Gulf of St. Lawrence

Nova Scotia

Bay of Fundy

Coast Ranges

Snake River

Black Hills

Missouri R.

Mississippi River

APPALACHIAN MTS.

Sierra Nevada

Great Salt Lake

GREAT BASIN

Platte R.

Arkansas R.

INTERIOR PLAINS

Ozark Plateau

Ohio R.

Cape Cod

Long Island

Mt. Whitney 14,494 ft. (4,418 m) ▲

Colorado R.

Cape Hatteras

Death Valley (lowest point in N.A.) -282 ft. (-86 m) ▼

Sonoran Desert

Rio Grande

COASTAL PLAIN

ATLANTIC OCEAN

30° N

Baja California

Gulf of California

Sierra Madre Occidental

Sierra Madre Oriental

Gulf of Mexico

Bahamas

Hawaiian Islands

Tropic of Cancer

Cuba

Greater Antilles

Hispaniola

Puerto Rico

Yucatán Peninsula

Citlaltépetl 18,701 ft. (5,700 m) ▲

Lesser Antilles

PACIFIC OCEAN

Lake Nicaragua

Caribbean Sea

Lake Maracaibo

Orinoco R.

Guiana Highlands

Isthmus of Panama

Llanos

Chimborazo 20,561 ft. (6,267 m) ▲

Galápagos Islands

Rio Negro

Amazon R.

Cape São Roque

Equator

Line Islands

Marquesas Islands

A M A Z O N

B A S I N

Tapajós R.

Xingu R.

Tocantins R.

São Francisco River

Huascarán 22,205 ft. (6,768 m) ▲

Mato Grosso Plateau

Brazilian Highlands

Cook Islands

Tuamotu Archipelago

Society Islands

Lake Titicaca

A N D E S

Paraguay R.

Tropic of Capricorn

Gran Chaco

Atacama Desert

Pilcomayo R.

Paraná R.

Iguazú Falls

Uruguay R.

Mt. Aconcagua 22,831 ft. (6,959 m) ▲

Pampa

Rio de la Plata

30° S

Patagonia

Valdés Peninsula (lowest point in S.A.) -131 ft. (-40 m) ▼

| 0 | 1,000 | 2,000 Miles |
| 0 | 1,000 | 2,000 Kilometers |

Miller Cylindrical Projection

▲ Mountain peak
▼ Point below sea level
— National border
≈ Waterfall

N
W E
S

Falkland Islands

South Georgia

Strait of Magellan

Tierra del Fuego

Cape Horn

150° W   120° W   90° W   60° W   30° W

A7

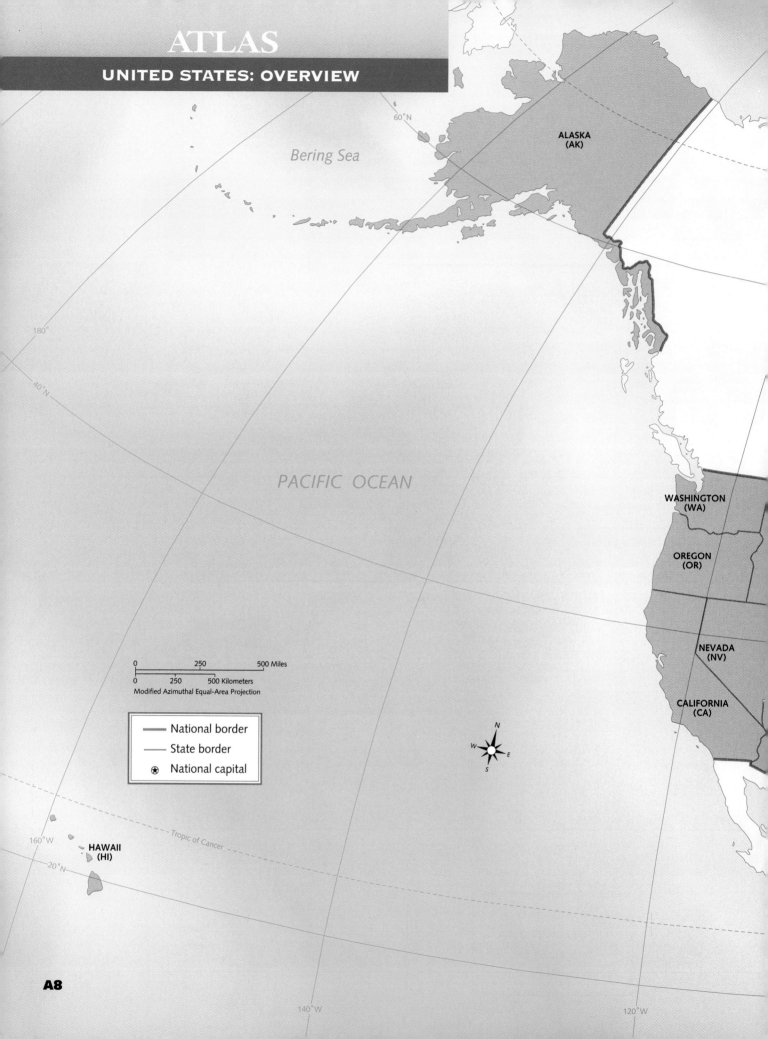

ALASKA
(AK)

Bering Sea

60°N

180°

40°N

PACIFIC OCEAN

WASHINGTON
(WA)

OREGON
(OR)

NEVADA
(NV)

CALIFORNIA
(CA)

0   250   500 Miles

0   250   500 Kilometers
Modified Azimuthal Equal-Area Projection

―――――― National border
―――――― State border
⊛ National capital

N
W   E
S

160°W

Tropic of Cancer

HAWAII
(HI)

20°N

140°W

120°W

ATLAS

UNITED STATES: POLITICAL

RUSSIA

ARCTIC OCEAN

70°N

ALASKA

120°W

Arctic Circle

Yukon River

CANADA

170°E

Fairbanks

Bering
Sea

Anchorage

60°N

180°

Juneau

PACIFIC
OCEAN

0   250   500 Miles
0   250   500 Kilometers

170°W   160°W   150°W   140°W   130°W

50°N

40°N

CANADA

120°W   110°W

Seattle
Tacoma
Olympia   Spokane

WASHINGTON

Great Falls

Portland   Columbia River   Helena   MONTANA

Salem   Billings

Eugene

OREGON   IDAHO

Boise

Snake River

WYOMING

Pocatello   Casper

Cheyenne

NEVADA   Great Salt Lake   Ogden

Reno   Salt Lake City

Sacramento   Carson City   Provo

San Francisco   Oakland   UTAH

San Jose

Denver

Colorado Springs

Fresno   COLORADO   Pueblo

CALIFORNIA   Las Vegas

Bakersfield   Colorado River

PACIFIC
OCEAN

30°N

Los Angeles   San Bernardino   Flagstaff

Santa Fe

Albuquerque

San Diego   ARIZONA   NEW MEXICO

130°W   Phoenix

Roswell

Tucson

El Paso

Rio Grande

MEXICO

	Northeast	⊛	National capital
	Southeast	★	State capital
	Middle West	•	Major city
	Southwest	—	National border
	West	—	State border

N
W   E
S

160°W   PACIFIC   155°W
OCEAN

Honolulu

HAWAII

Hilo   20°N

0   125   250 Miles
0   125   250 Kilometers

0   250   500 Miles
0   250   500 Kilometers
Albers Equal-Area Projection

20°N

120°W   110°W

A10

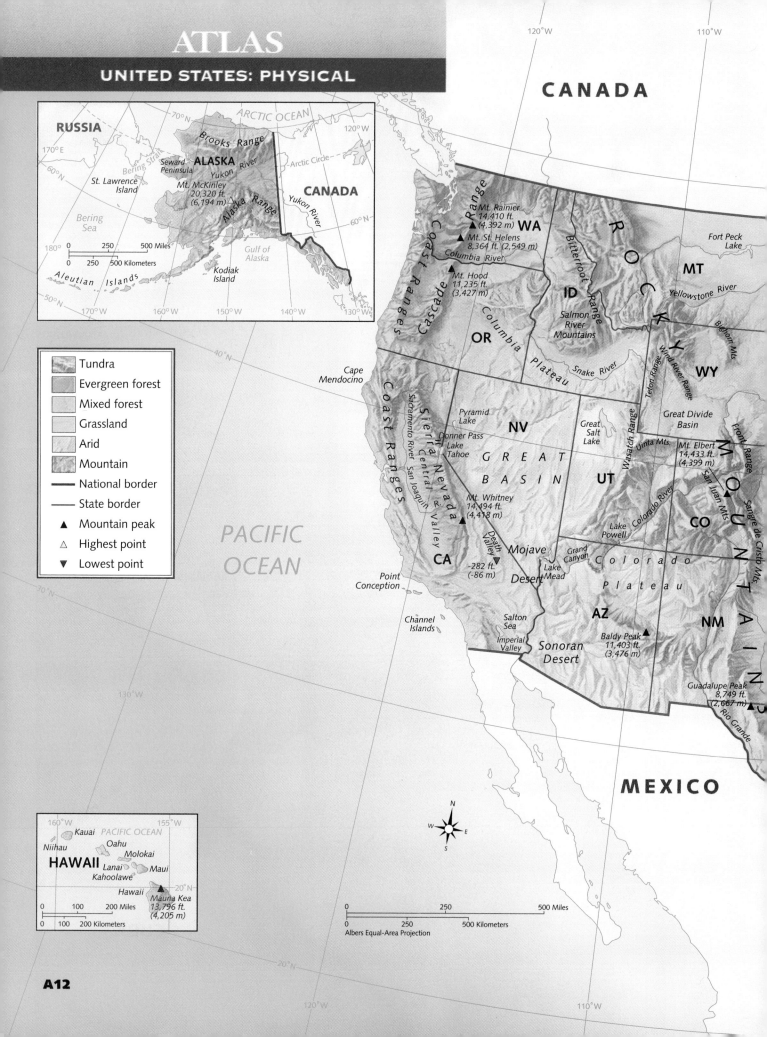

CANADA

RUSSIA

ARCTIC OCEAN

Brooks Range

Seward
Peninsula
St. Lawrence
Island
Bering
Sea

ALASKA
Mt. McKinley
20,320 ft.
(6,194 m)

Yukon
River

Alaska Range

Arctic Circle

CANADA

Yukon River

Gulf of
Alaska
Aleutian Islands
Kodiak
Island

	Tundra
	Evergreen forest
	Mixed forest
	Grassland
	Arid
	Mountain
▬	National border
—	State border
▲	Mountain peak
△	Highest point
▼	Lowest point

**PACIFIC
OCEAN**

Cape
Mendocino

Coast Ranges

Sacramento River

San Joaquin

Sierra Nevada

Central Valley

Donner Pass
Lake
Tahoe

Pyramid
Lake

NV

**GREAT
BASIN**

Mt. Whitney
14,494 ft.
(4,418 m)

Death
Valley
-282 ft.
(-86 m)

Mojave
Desert

Point
Conception

Channel
Islands

CA

Salton
Sea
Imperial
Valley

Sonoran
Desert

Mt. Rainier
14,410 ft.
(4,392 m)
Mt. St. Helens
8,364 ft. (2,549 m)
Columbia River

WA

Cascades Range

Mt. Hood
11,235 ft.
(3,427 m)

OR

Columbia
Plateau

Bitterroot Range

ID

Salmon
River
Mountains

Snake River

ROCKY

Fort Peck
Lake

MT

Yellowstone River

Bighorn Mts.

Teton Range

Wind River Range

WY

Great
Salt
Lake

Wasatch Range

Uinta Mts.

Great Divide
Basin

Mt. Elbert
14,433 ft.
(4,399 m)

Front Range

**M
O
U
N
T
A
I
N
S**

UT

Lake
Powell

Colorado River

San Juan Mts.

CO

Sangre de Cristo Mts.

Grand
Canyon

Lake
Mead

**Colorado
Plateau**

AZ

Baldy Peak
11,403 ft.
(3,476 m)

NM

Guadalupe Peak
8,749 ft.
(2,667 m)

Rio Grande

MEXICO

HAWAII

PACIFIC OCEAN

Kauai
Niihau
Oahu
Molokai
Lanai Maui
Kahoolawe
Hawaii
Mauna Kea
13,796 ft.
(4,205 m)

N
W   E
S

500 Miles
500 Kilometers

Albers Equal-Area Projection

CANADA

ME
▲ Mt. Katahdin
5,267 ft.
(1,605 m)

Lake of
the Woods

Upper
Red Lake

Lower
Red Lake

Lake Superior

Isle
Royale

Keweenaw
Peninsula

Leech
Lake

Mesabi
Range

Mille
Lacs
Lake

Upper Peninsula

Lake Champlain

VT

Adirondack
Mountains

NY

▲ Mt. Washington
5,288 ft.
(1,917 m)

Green Mts.

White Mts.

NH

Cape Ann

MA

Cape
Cod

ND

G
R
E
A
T

P
L
A
I
N
S

MN

WI

Wisconsin River

Lake
Winnebago

Lake Michigan

Lower Peninsula

MI

Lake
St. Clair

Lake Huron

Finger
Lakes

Connecticut R.

Hudson R.

CT

RI

Lake
Oahe

SD

Black
Hills

Missouri River

Mississippi River

Niagara
Falls

Lake Ontario

Lake Erie

PA

NJ

Long
Island

Sand Hills

IA

North Platte R.

NE

Platte River

South Platte R.

I
N
T
E
R
I
O
R

P
L
A
I
N
S

Illinois River

IL

Wabash River

IN

OH

CENTRAL PLAINS

Ohio River

WV

Allegheny Mts.

Potomac R.

MD

DE

Delaware
Bay

A
P
P
A
L
A
C
H
I
A
N

M
O
U
N
T
A
I
N
S

VA

James R.

Cape
Charles

Chesapeake
Bay

Smoky Hills

KS

Missouri River

MO

Lake of
the Ozarks

Harry S. Truman
Reservoir

O
z
a
r
k

P
l
a
t
e
a
u

Lake
Barkley

KY

Cumberland
Gap

Mt. Mitchell
6,684 ft.
(2,037 m) ▲

Roanoke R.

Albemarle
Sound

NC

Cape
Hatteras

Red Hills

Mississippi River

Cumberland R.

Tennessee R.

TN

Cape Fear River

SC

Cape
Fear

Arkansas River

OK

Canadian
River

Ouachita
Mountains

AR

P
I
E
D
M
O
N
T

Stone
Mountain ▲

Savannah River

Llano
Estacado

Red River

Tombigbee R.

MS

Alabama R.

AL

Chattahoochee R.

Ocmulgee R.

Oconee R.

GA

Altamaha R.

C
O
A
S
T
A
L

P
L
A
I
N

Okefenokee
Swamp

Pecos River

Brazos River

Sabine River

Colorado River

TX

Edwards
Plateau

Sam
Rayburn
Reservoir

Toledo
Bend
Reservoir

LA

Lake
Pontchartrain

Galveston
Bay

Mobile
Bay

Mississippi
Delta

St. Johns River

Cape
Canaveral

FL

Lake
Okeechobee

Tampa
Bay

Everglades

Cape
Sable

Florida Keys

Straits of Florida

ATLANTIC
OCEAN

BAHAMAS

Gulf of Mexico

CUBA

A13

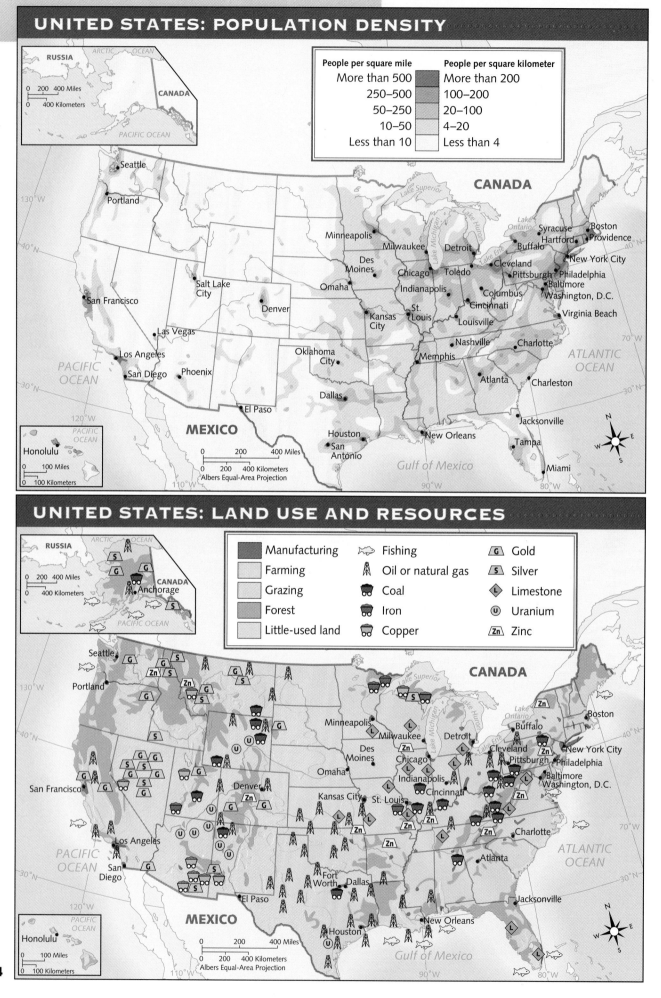

UNITED STATES: POPULATION DENSITY

People per square mile
More than 500
250–500
50–250
10–50
Less than 10

People per square kilometer
More than 200
100–200
20–100
4–20
Less than 4

RUSSIA
ARCTIC OCEAN
CANADA
PACIFIC OCEAN
0 200 400 Miles
0 400 Kilometers

CANADA
Lake Superior
Lake Michigan
Lake Huron
Lake Ontario
Lake Erie

Seattle
Portland
Minneapolis
Milwaukee
Detroit
Syracuse
Boston
Hartford
Providence
Buffalo
New York City
Des Moines
Chicago
Toledo
Cleveland
Pittsburgh
Philadelphia
Salt Lake City
Omaha
Indianapolis
Columbus
Baltimore
Washington, D.C.
San Francisco
Denver
St. Louis
Cincinnati
Kansas City
Louisville
Virginia Beach
Las Vegas
Nashville
Charlotte
Los Angeles
Oklahoma City
Memphis
Atlanta
Charleston
San Diego
Phoenix
Dallas
PACIFIC OCEAN
ATLANTIC OCEAN
El Paso
MEXICO
Jacksonville
Houston
New Orleans
Tampa
San Antonio
Gulf of Mexico
Miami

Honolulu
PACIFIC OCEAN
0 100 Miles
0 100 Kilometers

0 200 400 Miles
0 200 400 Kilometers
Albers Equal-Area Projection

130°W 120°W 110°W 90°W 80°W 70°W
40°N 30°N

UNITED STATES: LAND USE AND RESOURCES

Manufacturing
Farming
Grazing
Forest
Little-used land

🐟 Fishing
Oil or natural gas
Coal
Iron
Copper

G Gold
S Silver
L Limestone
U Uranium
Zn Zinc

RUSSIA
ARCTIC OCEAN
CANADA
Anchorage
PACIFIC OCEAN
0 200 400 Miles
0 400 Kilometers

CANADA
Lake Superior
Lake Michigan
Lake Huron
Lake Ontario
Lake Erie

Seattle
Portland
Minneapolis
Milwaukee
Detroit
Buffalo
Boston
Des Moines
Chicago
Cleveland
New York City
San Francisco
Omaha
Indianapolis
Pittsburgh
Philadelphia
Denver
Kansas City
St. Louis
Cincinnati
Baltimore
Washington, D.C.
Los Angeles
Charlotte
San Diego
Atlanta
Fort Worth
Dallas
El Paso
PACIFIC OCEAN
ATLANTIC OCEAN
MEXICO
Jacksonville
Houston
New Orleans
Gulf of Mexico

Honolulu
PACIFIC OCEAN
0 100 Miles
0 100 Kilometers

0 200 400 Miles
0 200 400 Kilometers
Albers Equal-Area Projection

130°W 120°W 110°W 90°W 80°W 70°W
40°N 30°N

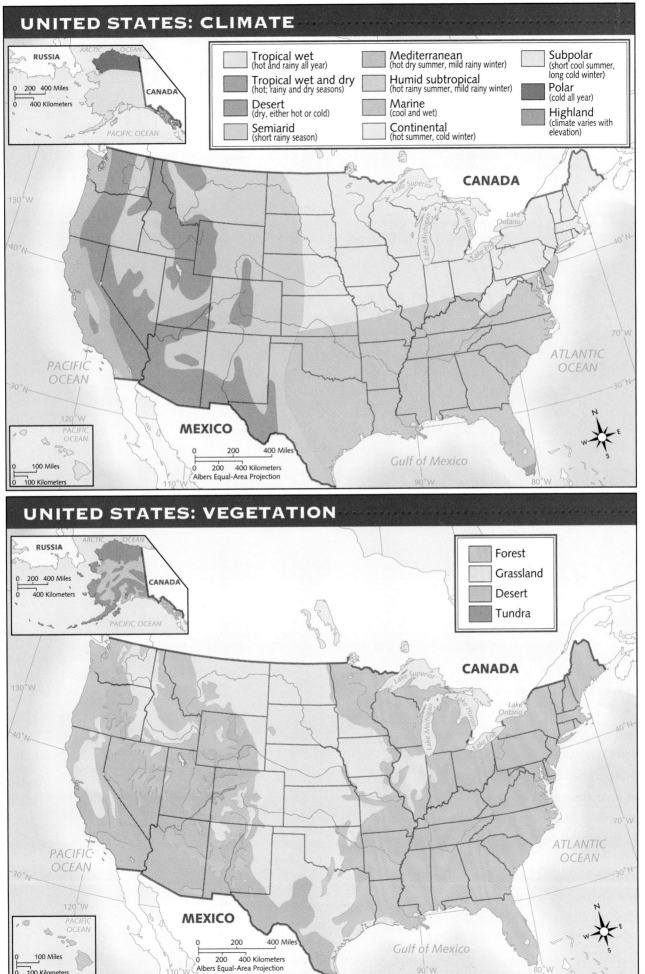

UNITED STATES: CLIMATE

Tropical wet
(hot and rainy all year)

Tropical wet and dry
(hot; rainy and dry seasons)

Desert
(dry, either hot or cold)

Semiarid
(short rainy season)

Mediterranean
(hot dry summer, mild rainy winter)

Humid subtropical
(hot rainy summer, mild rainy winter)

Marine
(cool and wet)

Continental
(hot summer, cold winter)

Subpolar
(short cool summer, long cold winter)

Polar
(cold all year)

Highland
(climate varies with elevation)

RUSSIA

CANADA

ARCTIC OCEAN

PACIFIC OCEAN

0 200 400 Miles
0 400 Kilometers

130°W

40°N

40°N

70°W

PACIFIC OCEAN

30°N

30°N

120°W

MEXICO

0 200 400 Miles
0 200 400 Kilometers
Albers Equal-Area Projection

110°W

90°W

80°W

Gulf of Mexico

ATLANTIC OCEAN

CANADA

Lake Superior
Lake Michigan
Lake Huron
Lake Ontario
Lake Erie

N
E
S
W

PACIFIC OCEAN

0 100 Miles
0 100 Kilometers

UNITED STATES: VEGETATION

Forest

Grassland

Desert

Tundra

RUSSIA

CANADA

ARCTIC OCEAN

PACIFIC OCEAN

0 200 400 Miles
0 400 Kilometers

130°W

40°N

40°N

70°W

CANADA

Lake Superior
Lake Michigan
Lake Huron
Lake Ontario
Lake Erie

PACIFIC OCEAN

30°N

30°N

ATLANTIC OCEAN

120°W

MEXICO

0 200 400 Miles
0 200 400 Kilometers
Albers Equal-Area Projection

110°W

90°W

80°W

Gulf of Mexico

N
E
S
W

PACIFIC OCEAN

0 100 Miles
0 100 Kilometers

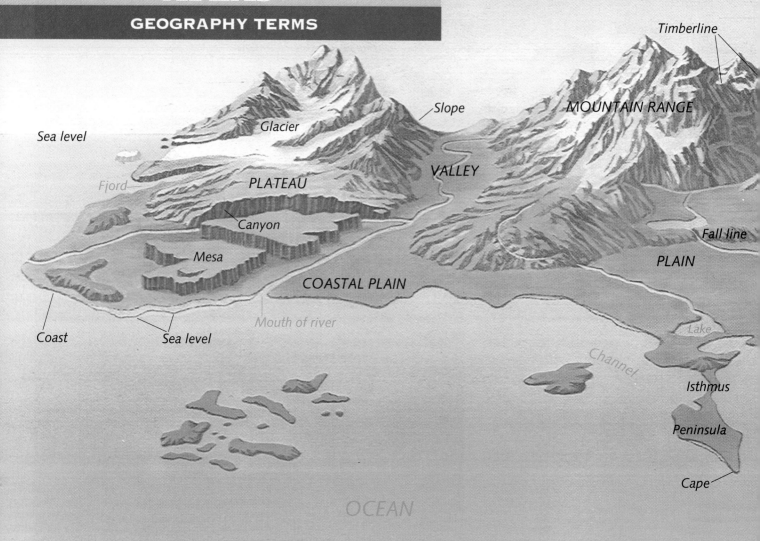

basin bowl-shaped area of land surrounded by higher land

bay body of water that is part of a sea or ocean and is partly enclosed by land

bluff high, steep face of rock or earth

canyon deep, narrow valley with steep sides

cape point of land that extends into water

channel deepest part of a body of water

cliff high, steep face of rock or earth

coast land along a sea or ocean

coastal plain area of flat land along a sea or ocean

delta triangle-shaped area of land at the mouth of a river

desert dry land with few plants

dune hill of sand piled up by the wind

fall line area along which rivers form waterfalls or rapids as the rivers drop to lower land

fjord deep, narrow part of a sea or ocean, between high, steep banks

floodplain flat land that is near the edges of a river and is formed by the silt deposited by floods

foothills hilly area at the base of a mountain

glacier large ice mass that moves slowly down a mountain or across land

gulf body of water that is partly enclosed by land but is larger than a bay

harbor area of water where ships can dock safely near land

hill land that rises above the land around it

island land that has water on all sides

isthmus narrow strip of land connecting two larger areas of land

lake body of water with land on all sides

marsh lowland with moist soil and tall grasses

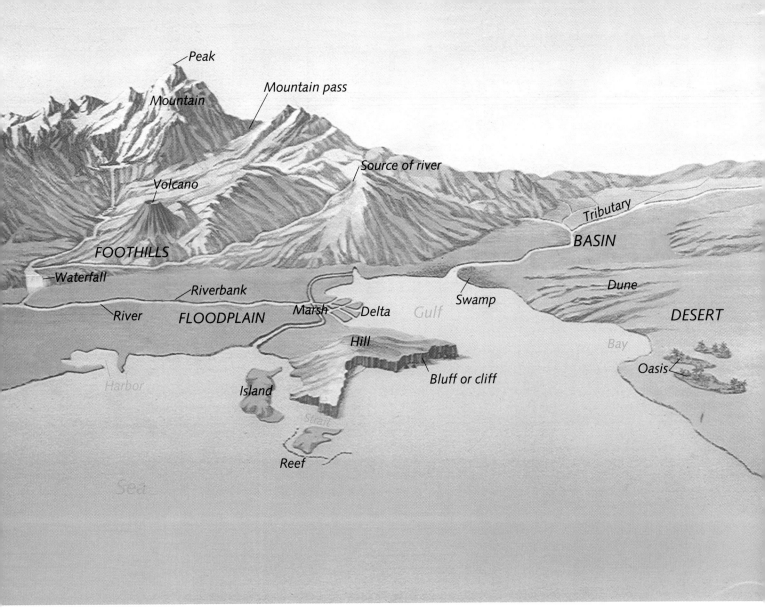

mesa flat-topped mountain with steep sides

mountain highest kind of land

mountain pass gap between mountains

mountain range row of mountains

mouth of river place where a river empties into another body of water

oasis area of water and fertile land in a desert

ocean body of salt water larger than a sea

peak top of a mountain

peninsula land that is almost completely surrounded by water

plain flat land

plateau area of high, flat land with steep sides

reef ridge of sand, rock, or coral that lies at or near the surface of a sea or ocean

river large stream of water that flows across the land

riverbank land along a river

sea body of salt water smaller than an ocean

sea level the level that is even with the surface of an ocean or sea

slope side of a hill or mountain

source of river place where a river begins

strait narrow channel of water connecting two larger bodies of water

swamp area of low, wet land with trees

timberline line on a mountain above which it is too cold for trees to grow

tributary stream or river that empties into a larger river

valley low land between hills or mountains

volcano opening in the Earth, often raised, through which lava, rock, ashes, and gases are forced out

waterfall steep drop from a high place to a lower place in a stream or river

A17

Why Study SOCIAL STUDIES?

66 Every one of you already holds the important office of citizen. Over time you will become more and more involved in your community. You will need to know more about what being a citizen means. Social studies will help you learn about citizenship. That is why social studies is important in your life. 99

The authors of *Stories in Time*

THE POWERFUL IDEAS OF SOCIAL STUDIES

*T*hink about the many groups you are a part of. Your family, your class, and your community are each a different kind of group, and you are a member of each one. You are also a member—or **citizen**—of your town or city, your state, and your country. Citizens work to improve the many groups they belong to and to make their world a better place.

To help you think, feel, and act as a citizen, *Stories in Time* begins every lesson with a question. That question connects you to one or more of five powerful ideas that citizens need to understand in order to make decisions. Each question also links you to the lesson's story, helping you see how the story relates to your own life. The lesson helps you learn about being a citizen by letting you see how people from many places and times have thought, felt, and acted.

Each lesson will help you organize your thinking around one or more of the five powerful ideas of social studies.

POWERFUL IDEA NUMBER *1*

COMMONALITY AND DIVERSITY

In some ways people everywhere are alike. We all have basic needs for things like food, clothing, and shelter. We all laugh, get angry, and have our feelings hurt. These are examples of our commonality, or what we all share. At the same time, we need to understand that each person is different from everyone else. We each have our own ways of thinking, feeling, and acting. That is our diversity. An understanding of commonality and diversity can help you see that every person deserves respect.

POWERFUL IDEA NUMBER *2*

CONFLICT AND COOPERATION

Because people are not exactly alike, they sometimes have conflicts, or disagreements. People can often overcome their conflicts by cooperating, or working together. In social studies you will learn about the disagreements people have had in the past and about many of the ways people have found to settle their disagreements. You will also learn ways to cooperate and to resolve conflicts in your own life.

In this painting by Howard Chandler Christy, American leaders are shown signing the Constitution, the plan of government for the United States. By taking part in government, these leaders were carrying out the office of citizen.

POWERFUL IDEA NUMBER **3**

CONTINUITY AND CHANGE

While some things change over time, other things stay the same. Many things have stayed the same for years and will probably stay the same in the future. This means that they have continuity. Understanding continuity and change can help you see how things in the world came to be as they are. You will learn that past events have helped shape your life and that present events can help you make better decisions about the future.

POWERFUL IDEA NUMBER **4**

INDIVIDUALISM AND INTERDEPENDENCE

Citizens can act by themselves to make a difference in the world. Their actions as individuals may be helpful or they may be harmful to other citizens. But much of the time, people do not act alone. They depend on others to help them. People depend on their families, their schools, their religious groups, their governments, and other groups and organizations. Such interdependence connects citizens with one another and affects their lives.

POWERFUL IDEA NUMBER *5*

INTERACTION WITHIN DIFFERENT ENVIRONMENTS

People's actions affect other people. People's actions also affect their surroundings, or environment. This is true of their physical environment as well as their home environment, their school environment, or the other environments they may be a part of. Understanding such interactions is important to understanding why things happened in the past and why things happen today.

Understanding interaction is also key to understanding social studies. The subjects that make up social studies are all interconnected. You will learn, for example, that history—the study of people's past—is related to geography—the study of the Earth's surface and its people. Civics and government, or the study of how people live together in a community, is related to economics, or the study of how people use resources. And all of these subjects are related to the study of culture. Culture is people's ways of life, including their customs, ideas, and practices. These subjects interact with one another to tell a story. Together they tell a story of how people have lived over time and how they have made contributions as citizens. Understanding this story will help you learn how to hold the office of citizen.

 What are the five powerful ideas of social studies?

When you take part in student government or other groups, you are also carrying out the office of citizen. Understanding each of the powerful ideas is important to making decisions as a citizen.

HISTORY

History helps you see the links between the past and the present. It also helps you better understand how what happens today can affect the future. History is about what happened last month and last year as well as in the ancient past.

As you read about the past, ask yourself the questions below. They will help you think more like a historian, a person who studies the past.

- **What happened?**
- **When did it happen?**
- **Who took part in it?**
- **How and why did it happen?**

WHAT HAPPENED?

To find out what really happened in the past, you need proof. You can find proof by studying two kinds of sources—primary sources and secondary sources. Historians use these kinds of sources in writing history.

Primary sources are the records made by people who saw or took part in an event, or something that happened. They might have written down their thoughts in a journal. They might have told their story in a letter or a poem. They might have taken a photograph, made a film, or painted a picture. Each of these records is a primary source, giving the people of today a direct link to a past event.

A **secondary source** is not a direct link to an event. It is a record of the event written by someone who was not there at the time. A magazine article, newspaper story, or book written at a later time by someone who did not take part in an event is a secondary source.

"All the News That's Fit to Print"

The New York Times.

LATE CITY EDITION
Cloudy with showers today. Partly cloudy and cooler tomorrow.
Temperature Yesterday—Max. 64; Min. 49
Sunrise today, 5:43 A.M.; Sunset, 7:59 P.M.

Copyright, 1945, by The New York Times Company.

NEW YORK, TUESDAY, MAY 8, 1945.

THREE CENTS NEW YORK CITY

VOL. XCIV..No. 31,881.

Entered as Second-Class Matter, Postoffice, New York, N. Y.

THE WAR IN EUROPE IS ENDED!
SURRENDER IS UNCONDITIONAL;
V-E WILL BE PROCLAIMED TODAY;
OUR TROOPS ON OKINAWA GAIN

ISLAND-WIDE DRIVE | The Palitzer Awards For 1944 Announced | GERMANY SURRENDERS: NEW YORKERS MASSED UNDER SYMBOL OF LIBERTY

GERMANS CAPITULATE ON ALL FRONTS
American, Russian and French Generals Accept Surrender in Eisenhower

When there are no written records of an event, historians gather proof through oral histories. An **oral history** can be either a primary or a secondary source, depending on the events a person describes. Oral histories tell the experiences of people who did not have a written language or who did not write down what happened. Oral histories can be recorded by writing down an interview with someone. Today they also can be recorded by making an audio or video tape of the interview.

As you read this book, you will read many kinds of primary and secondary sources. The stories told in each lesson contain the words and photographs of people in the past—primary sources—as well as descriptions by historians—secondary sources. Maps and graphs also help tell the story.

WHEN DID IT HAPPEN?

One way to build a story of the past is to put events related to that story in the order in which they happened. This order is called **chronology**. As you read this book, you will notice that it is organized by chronology. The events described at the beginning of the book happened before those described at the end of the book.

You will see many time lines in this book. They will help you understand each story's chronology. A time line is a diagram that shows the events that took place during a certain period of time, in the order in which those events happened. Some time lines show a period of a month or a year. Others show a period of 10 years, 100 years, or 1,000 years.

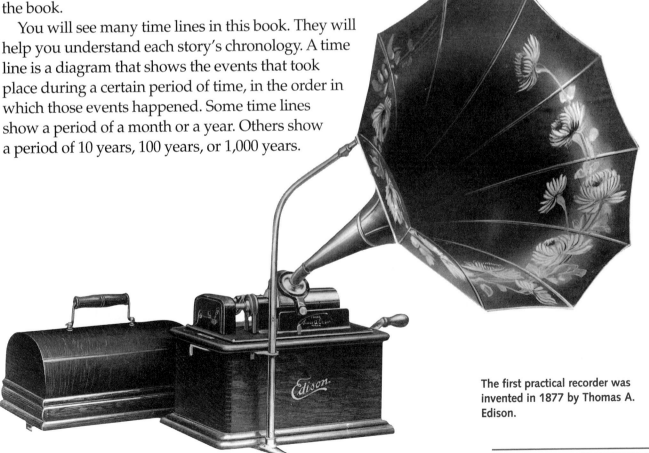

Old photographs are primary sources. When you take a photograph of a person or an event today, it is also a primary source.

The first practical recorder was invented in 1877 by Thomas A. Edison.

Time lines can help you understand how one event may have led to another.

WHO TOOK PART IN IT?

To understand the stories of the past, you need to know about the people in the stories and the times in which they lived. In this way you can understand the actions and feelings of people from other times and other places. This understanding is called **historical empathy**.

By reading the words of people of the past, you can come to understand their **perspective**, or point of view. A person's perspective is a set of beliefs that have been shaped by factors such as whether that person is old or young, a man or a woman, or rich or poor. A person's perspective is also shaped by culture and race. Your understanding of history will grow when you study the many perspectives of the people who took part in the story. This also will help you see that other people, even those living in other places and other times, are a lot like you.

HOW AND WHY DID IT HAPPEN?

Many events in history are linked to other events. To find the links between events, you will need to identify causes and effects. A cause is any action that makes something happen. What happens because of that action is an effect. Historians have found that most events have many causes and many effects.

To understand an event, you need to analyze its causes and effects. **Analyzing** is a thinking process in which you break something down into its parts and look closely at how those parts connect with each other. Once you have analyzed an event, you can summarize it or draw a conclusion about how or why it happened.

 What questions can you ask yourself when you read about the past?

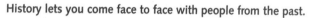

History lets you come face to face with people from the past.

24

HowTo

Read Social Studies

Why Is This Skill Important?

Social studies is made up of stories about people and places. Sometimes you read these stories in library books. Other times you read them in textbooks, like this one. Knowing how to read social studies in a textbook can make it easier to study and do your homework. It will help you identify main ideas and important people, places, and events.

Understand the Process

Follow these steps to read any lesson in this book:

1. Preview the whole lesson.

   • Look at the title and headings to find out the topic of the lesson.

   • Look at the pictures, captions, and questions for clues to what is in the lesson.

   • Answer the Link to Our World question at the beginning of the lesson to find out how the lesson relates to life today.

   • Read the statement labeled Focus on the Main Idea. It gives you the key idea that the lesson teaches.

   • Look at the Preview Vocabulary list to see what new terms will be introduced.

2. Read the lesson for information on the main idea. As you read, you will come to a number of checkpoint questions. Be sure to find the answers to these questions before you continue reading the lesson.

3. When you finish reading the lesson, say in your own words what you have learned.

4. Look back over the lesson. Then answer the review questions—from memory, if possible. The lesson review will help guide you in checking your understanding, thinking critically, and showing what you know.

Think and Apply

Use the four steps in Understand the Process each time you are asked to read a lesson in *Stories in Time*.

GEOGRAPHY

The stories you will read in this book all have a setting. The setting of a story includes the place where it happens. Geography is the study of the many different settings around the world. Studying geography helps you answer these questions about a place:

- **Where is it?**
  (location)

- **What is it like there?**
  (place)

- **Who lives there, and what do they do?**
  (human-environment interactions)

- **How did they get there?**
  (movement)

- **How is the place like other places?**
  How is it different?
  (regions)

The answers to these questions tell you what you need to know in order to understand a setting. These five questions are so important that many people call them the five themes, or key topics, of geography.

1. LOCATION

Everything on the Earth has its own location. Knowing your location helps you tell other people where you are. It also helps you become more aware of the world around you.

To tell exactly where you live in your town or city, you can use the names and numbers of your home address. To find your **absolute location**, or your exact location, on Earth, you can use the numbers of your "global address." These numbers appear on a pattern of imaginary lines drawn around the Earth. You will read more about these lines on pages 28 and 29 when you review how to read a map.

The location of a place can also be described in relation to the location of other places. You describe the **relative location** of a place when you say what is near it or what is around it. You might say that the nearest bus stop is on the corner by the gas station. Or you might also say that the city of New Orleans is south of the city of St. Louis.

2. Place

Every location on the Earth has a place identity made up of unique features that make it different from all other locations. A place can be described by its **physical features**—landforms, bodies of water, climate, soil, plant and animal life, and other natural resources. Many places also have **human features**—buildings, bridges, farms, roads, and the people themselves. People's cultures, or ways of life, also help form a place's identity.

3. Human-Environment Interactions

Humans and the environment interact, or behave in ways that affect each other. People interact with their environment in different ways. Sometimes they change it. They clear land to grow crops. They build cities and towns. Sometimes people pollute the environment. The environment can also cause people to change the way they act. People who live in cold places wear warm clothing. Sometimes things that happen in nature, such as hurricanes, tornadoes, and earthquakes, cause great changes in people's lives.

4. Movement

Each day, people in different parts of the country and different parts of the world interact with one another. These kinds of interactions involve movement. People, products, and ideas move by transportation and communication. Geography helps you understand the causes and effects of this movement. It also helps you understand how people came to live where they do.

5. Regions

Areas on the Earth whose features make them different from other areas are called **regions**. A region can be described by physical features, such as mountains or dry climate, that exist all over the region. A region can also be described by its human features, such as the language most of its people speak or the way they are governed.

Regions are sometimes divided into smaller regions that are easier to compare. Some geographers who study the Earth's surface and its people divide the United States into regions named for their relative locations—the Northeast, Southeast, Middle West, Southwest, and West. This makes the geography of the United States easier to understand.

 What are the five themes of geography?

How To
Read a Map

Why Is This Skill Important?

To answer questions you may have about the world around you, you need information. You can get this information by reading the stories in this book, by looking at its pictures and charts, and by studying its maps. Knowing how to read a map is an important skill both for learning social studies and for taking action as a citizen.

Understand the Process

Maps are drawings of places on the Earth. To help you read maps, mapmakers include certain elements on most maps they draw. These are a title, a key, a compass rose, and a scale. Mapmakers often put a grid of numbered lines on their maps to help people locate places more easily.

1. The **map title** tells the subject of the map. The title may also help you understand what kind of map it is. Physical maps show land-forms and bodies of water. Political maps show cities and national boundaries, or borders. Many of the maps in this book are historical maps that show the United States as it

THE UNITED STATES

⊛ National capital
★ State capital
— National border
— State border

was in the past. Historical maps often have dates in the title. When you look at any map, look for information in the title to find out what the map is about.

2. The **map key**, which is sometimes called a map legend, explains what the symbols on the map stand for. Symbols may be colors, patterns, lines, or other special marks, such as circles, triangles, or squares. According to the map key for the map on page 28, stars are used to show state capitals. A circle with a star inside it stands for a national capital.

3. The **compass rose**, or direction marker, shows the main, or cardinal, directions— north, south, east, and west. A compass rose also helps you find the intermediate directions, which are between the cardinal directions. Intermediate directions are northeast, northwest, southeast, and southwest.

4. The **map scale** compares a distance on a map to a distance in the real world. A map scale helps you find the real distance between

places on a map. Each map in this book has a scale that shows both miles and kilometers.

Map scales are different, depending on how much area is shown. On the map of the United States on page 28 are two smaller maps, one of Alaska and one of Hawaii. A small map within a larger map is called an **inset map**. Inset maps have their own scales. Inset maps make it possible to show places in greater detail or to show places that are beyond the area covered on the main map.

5. The north-south and east-west lines on a map cross each other to form a pattern of squares called a **grid**. The east-west lines are lines of latitude. The north-south lines are lines of longitude. The global address, or absolute location, of a place can be found where a line of latitude and a line of longitude cross.

Think and Apply

Look at the map of Texas below. Identify the parts of the map. Discuss with a partner what information you find.

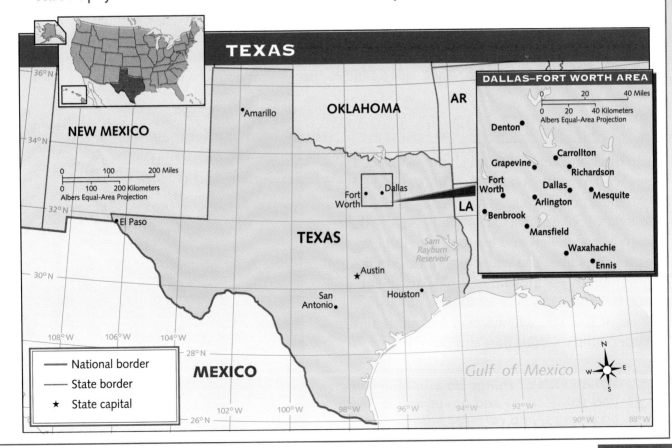

CIVICS AND GOVERNMENT

Civics and government is the study of citizenship and the ways in which citizens govern themselves. A government is the system of leaders and laws that helps people live together in their community, state, or country. In the United States, citizens have an important part in making the government work. The laws that guide the actions of people are written and carried out by citizens.

In *Stories in Time* you will learn how the United States government works today. You will learn about the people and events that shaped the government in the past. You will also learn about citizenship and the rights and responsibilities of citizens. These rights and responsibilities make the government work, and they are important parts of life in the United States.

ECONOMICS

The **economy** of a country is the ways its people use its resources to meet their needs. The study of how people do this is called economics. In *Stories in Time* you will read about how people in the past made, bought, sold, and traded goods to get what they needed or wanted. You will learn how the economy of the United States—an economy in which businesses are free to offer for sale many kinds of goods and services—came to be what it is today.

CULTURE

In this book you will learn about people of the past who have shaped the present. You will learn who these people were, what they looked like, and how they spoke and acted. You will explore their customs and beliefs and their ways of thinking and expressing ideas. You will look at their families and communities. All these things make up their culture. Each human group, or society, has a culture. In *Stories in Time* you will discover the many cultures in our country's story, past and present.

 What kinds of things do you learn when you study civics and government, economics, and culture?

Work Together in Groups

Why Is This Skill Important?

Learning social studies is sometimes easier when you work with a partner or in a group. Many projects would be difficult for one person to do. If you work with other students, each of you can work on part of the project. For a group project to succeed, each member needs to cooperate with the others. Knowing how to work together is an important skill for students and for all citizens.

Understand the Process

Suppose your group was asked to do a project, such as presenting a short play about everyday life long ago. You might find it helpful to follow a set of steps.

1. Organize and plan together.
  • Set your goal as a group.
  • Share your ideas.
  • Cooperate with others to plan your work.
  • Make sure everyone has a job.

2. Act on your plan together.
  • Take responsibility for your jobs.
  • Help one another.
  • If there are conflicts, take time to talk about them.
  • Show your group's finished work to the class.

3. Talk about your work.
  • Discuss what you learned by working together.

Think and Apply

Follow these steps for working together as you take part in the activities in *Stories in Time*.

These students are rehearsing for a class play about life in the American colonies.

UNIT 1

The ANCIENT AMERICAS

14,000 years ago	12,000 years ago	10,000 years ago	8,000 years ago

By 12,000 years ago
Early peoples move into the Americas

11,600 years ago
Hunters begin to use Clovis points

10,000 years ago
Giant Ice Age animals die out

*T*he story of the earliest peoples to come to what is known today as the Americas begins thousands of years ago. In many ways the story is filled with mystery. No one knows exactly where the first peoples of the Americas came from or when they arrived.

One thing, however, is certain. After early peoples arrived, they slowly moved throughout North and South America. Over time they developed many different ways of life. They built different kinds of villages, and some built large cities. They wore different kinds of clothing and spoke many different languages. Today we know them by many different names, such as Cree, Zuni (ZOO•nee), Iroquois (IR•uh•kwoy), and Aztec (AZ•tek). Together they are known as Native Americans or American Indians. They were the first Americans.

← Indian peoples trading in the Southwest, about the year 1500

6,000 years ago

4,000 years ago

2,000 years ago

Present

7,000 to 4,700 years ago
Early Americans begin to farm

5,000 years ago
People continue to settle the Americas

3,500 years ago
Olmec civilization develops

800 years ago
40,000 people live in the city of Cahokia

550 years ago
Iroquois League forms

THE PEOPLE SHALL CONTINUE

by Simon Ortiz

When they tell their stories, Indian storytellers open and close this Kwakiutl (KWAH•kee•oo•tel) mask by pulling a string.

Native Americans have a long, long history in North and South America. Many of their stories tell of the beginnings of the Earth as well as their beginnings as a people. Read now how one writer, an Acoma poet named Simon Ortiz, describes the earliest years of American history, when the first Native Americans—who called themselves the People—settled throughout the land.

MANY, many years ago, all things came
   to be.
The stars, rocks, plants, rivers, animals.
Mountains, sun, moon, birds, all things.
And the People were born.
Some say, "From the ocean."
Some say, "From a hollow log."
Some say, "From an opening in the ground."

Some say, "From the mountains."
And the People came to live
in the Northern Mountains and on the
   Plains,
in the Western Hills and on the Seacoasts,
in the Southern Deserts and in the Canyons,
in the Eastern Woodlands and on the
   Piedmonts.
Some People fished, others were hunters.
Some People farmed, others were artisans.
Their leaders were those who served the
   People.
Their healers were those who cared for the
   People.
Their hunters were those who provided for
   the People.
Their warriors were those who protected the
   People.

The teachers and the elders of the People
all taught this important knowledge:
    "The Earth is the source of all life.
    She gives birth.
    Her children continue the life of the Earth.
    The People must be responsible to her.
    This is the way that all life continues."
The People of the many Nations visited each
    other's lands.
The People from the North brought elk meat.
The People from the West gave them fish.
The People from the South brought corn.
The People from the East gave them hides.
When there were arguments,
their leaders would say,
    "Let us respect each other.
    We will bring you corn and baskets.
    You will bring us meat and flint knives.
    That way we will live a peaceful life.

We must respect each other, and the
    animals,
    the plants, the land, the universe.
    We have much to learn from all the
      Nations."
Nevertheless, life was always hard.
At times, corn did not grow and there was
    famine.
At times, winters were very cold and there
    was hardship.
At times, the winds blew hot and rivers
    dried.
At times, the People grew uneasy among
    themselves.
The learned men and women talked with
    each other
about what to do for their People,
but it was always hard.
They had to have great patience
and they told their People,
    "We should not ever take anything for
      granted.
    In order for our life to continue,
    we must struggle very hard for it."

Artworks such as this Navajo sand painting (left)
and this Bella Coola sun mask (below) help tell
the story of Indian peoples' long history.

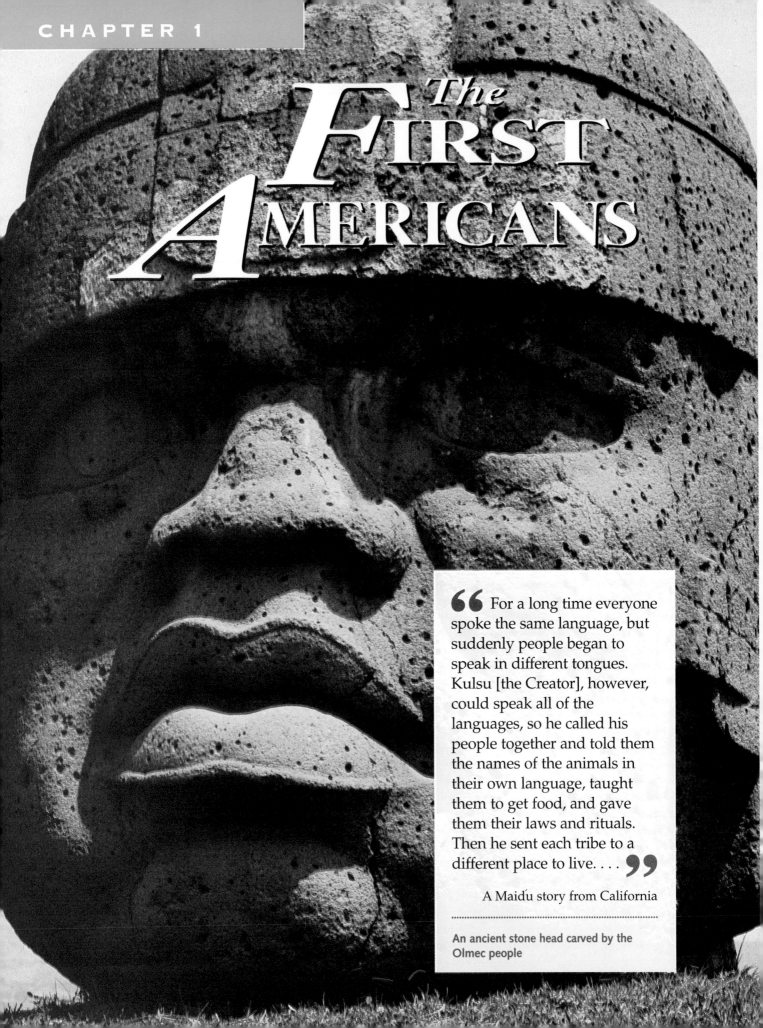

CHAPTER 1

The FIRST AMERICANS

66 For a long time everyone spoke the same language, but suddenly people began to speak in different tongues. Kulsu [the Creator], however, could speak all of the languages, so he called his people together and told them the names of the animals in their own language, taught them to get food, and gave them their laws and rituals. Then he sent each tribe to a different place to live. . . . 99

A Maidú story from California

An ancient stone head carved by the Olmec people

THE SEARCH FOR EARLY PEOPLES

LESSON 1

*L*nk to Our World

How does the environment affect the ways people today move from place to place?

Focus on the Main Idea
As you read, think about how the environment affected the ways early peoples moved from place to place.

Preview Vocabulary

migration	culture
glacier	archaeologist
band	artifact
nomad	evidence
theory	origin story

Humans have always been on the move. From earliest times until today, people have wandered the globe. Sometimes their journeys are fast-moving, exciting adventures. Other times their movements are so slow that they are hard to notice. It was in just this way—very, very slowly—that early peoples first moved from place to place on the Earth.

OVER THE LAND BRIDGE

At a number of times in its history, the Earth has had long periods of bitter cold. During these periods, known as the Ice Ages, all but the places near the equator shivered through long, hard winters.

Life could not have been easy in those wintry times. Days, even weeks, were spent inside small shelters made of animal skins. Fires inside helped keep people warm while icy winds blew outside. The weather was not as cold during the short summers, but melting ice turned the frozen ground into fields of mud.

Yet many groups of people still set out into these cold lands. During hundreds of thousands of years, their ancestors had traveled from Africa into Europe and Asia. Now some in this great **migration**, or movement, turned northward to the vast area of Asia known today as Siberia.

These early peoples did not travel alone. They followed huge Ice Age animals that they hunted for food. One such animal was the mammoth—a giant, hairy elephant. The hunters depended on these animals to survive. They ate the meat and used the fur, skins, and bones to make clothing, shelters, and tools.

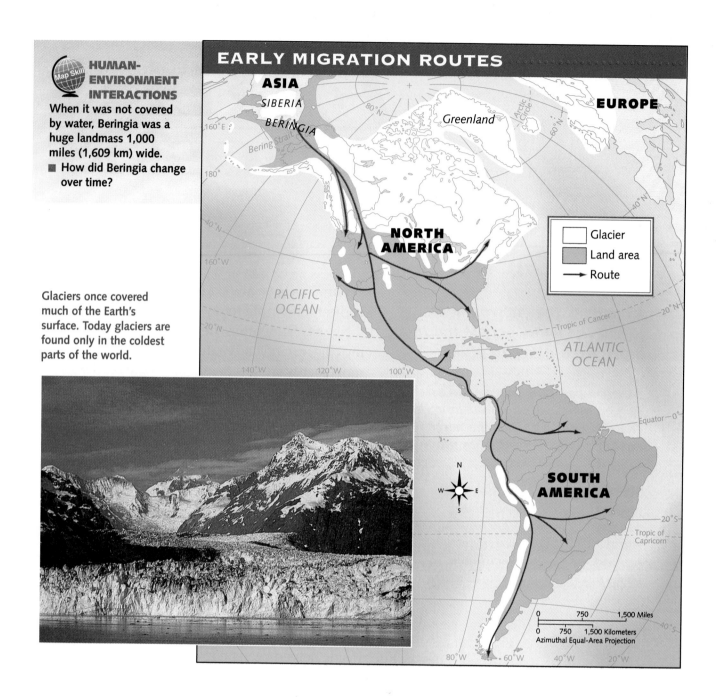

Map Skill — HUMAN-ENVIRONMENT INTERACTIONS

When it was not covered by water, Beringia was a huge landmass 1,000 miles (1,609 km) wide.

■ How did Beringia change over time?

Glaciers once covered much of the Earth's surface. Today glaciers are found only in the coldest parts of the world.

ASIA
SIBERIA
BERINGIA
Bering Strait
Greenland
EUROPE
Arctic Circle

NORTH AMERICA

PACIFIC OCEAN

ATLANTIC OCEAN

Tropic of Cancer

Equator — 0°

SOUTH AMERICA

Tropic of Capricorn

Glacier
Land area
→ Route

0   750   1,500 Miles
0   750   1,500 Kilometers
Azimuthal Equal-Area Projection

The last Ice Age started about two million years ago and ended about 10,000 years ago. At times it was so cold that huge sheets of ice called **glaciers** formed over much of the land. So much water was locked up in the glaciers that the oceans became shallower.

The Bering Strait, a narrow strip of water that today separates Siberia and Alaska, also became shallower. Over time, hundreds of miles of land that had been under water were uncovered. The land connected Asia and North America. This land bridge joining the two continents is known as Beringia (bair•IN•gee•uh).

Most scientists believe that the first humans to find Beringia were bands of hunters from Siberia. A **band** is a small group of people who work together to do things, such as hunting. At this time, bands were probably made up of one or two families.

The bands crossed Beringia slowly. They traveled only a few miles in an entire lifetime. Wanderers like these hunters, who have no settled home, are called **nomads**.

Finally, after thousands of years, the hunters reached what is today Alaska. But there they—and the animals they followed—had to stop. Huge glaciers blocked their path. They could go no farther.

Then, about 12,000 years ago, the climate changed. The Earth began to warm up. Some of the ice in the glaciers started to melt. The oceans began to rise, once again covering Beringia. At the same time a narrow path opened between two melting glaciers that covered what is now Canada. It was as if one door behind the hunters closed as another one in front of them opened. The animals followed the path between the glaciers. The hunters followed the animals, slowly making their way farther and farther into the Americas. These hunters became the first Americans.

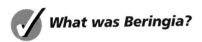 **What was Beringia?**

NEW DISCOVERIES

If this theory (THEE•uh•ree), or explanation, about the land bridge is correct, the first people arrived in the Americas about 12,000 years ago. But could they have been here earlier? Many scientists today say yes.

Once early peoples moved into the Americas, they settled all over both continents, in time reaching the southern tip of South America. Each native group developed its own culture, or way of life. Some groups lived in cities. Others were nomads who roamed the plains. Some made their clothing of furs and skins, while others made theirs of cotton. They lived in large wooden lodges, grass huts, tents made of skins, and steep cliff dwellings. They spoke thousands of different languages.

To build such different cultures must have taken a great deal of time, some scientists argue. It must have taken much longer, they say, than 12,000 years.

But how could people have arrived earlier? It turns out that Beringia was uncovered at another time during the last Ice Age—from 45,000 to 75,000 years ago. Asian hunters could have crossed then into North America on dry land. It is also possible that the first Americans did not cross the land bridge at all. Instead, they could have traveled along the coast of Beringia to the Americas by boat.

Scientists who study the cultures of people long ago are known as archaeologists (ar•kee•AH•luh•jists). In recent years archaeologists have made discoveries that seem to prove the "early arrival" theory. One of the most important was in southwestern Pennsylvania. There, archaeologists discovered an Ice Age campsite they called the

These archaeologists are searching for ancient objects at a "dig" in southwestern Pennsylvania. White tags identify the different layers of earth they have uncovered.

Meadowcroft Rock Shelter. At the campsite they found a number of objects that early people had left behind. These objects, called **artifacts**, are 14,000 to 15,000 years old. A few are more than 19,000 years old.

Other discoveries also support the early arrival theory. In Monte Verde (MOHN•tay VAIR•day), Chile, archaeologists uncovered stone tools and animal bones that are 13,000 years old. And in Brazil they found stone chips that may have been made by early people. Some believe these artifacts are 30,000 years old.

Although the number of artifacts found is growing, many archaeologists are still not convinced. They believe that there is not enough **evidence**, or proof, that people arrived in the Americas any earlier than 12,000 years ago. Some so-called artifacts, they say, are not artifacts at all. What one person believes is a stone tool shaped by humans could really be a stone shaped by nature—by wind or water.

Archaeologists today continue to search for more evidence from the past. Each new discovery brings new information about the first Americans.

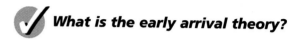 **What is the early arrival theory?**

ORIGIN STORIES

The Indian peoples themselves have many different stories about the origins of their lands and their own beginnings long ago. These stories tell of the peoples' beliefs about the world and their place in it. Such stories are called **origin stories**.

Some origin stories are much like the story of creation in the Bible that tells how the world was made. The Blackfoot people, for example, tell a story of how Old Man the Creator made the animals and plants and formed the prairies and mountains. He made a woman and her child from clay and brought them to life.

These ancient stone tools (left) were found at Monte Verde, Chile. Notice their shapes. What do you think each tool could have been used for? Archaeologists found this piece of bowl (below) at the Meadowcroft Rock Shelter in Pennsylvania. The bowl was made from a tortoise shell.

This Pueblo clay figure (above left) shows the importance of storytellers to their listeners. In some origin stories, animals like the elk (above right) are able to talk to humans.

Animals and natural surroundings such as mountains, rivers, rocks, and trees play an important part in many origin stories. The Huron (HYUR•ahn) people tell a story that says in the beginning the Earth was covered with water. Dry land was formed from a bit of soil taken from under the claws of a turtle. The turtle had picked up the soil after diving to the bottom of the ocean. Because of this story, some Indian people today still use the name Turtle Island for the Americas.

Even though no one knows exactly when the first people arrived in the Americas, all agree that it was thousands of years ago. It was so long ago that the descendants of the first Americans—the American Indians— have no memories of distant homelands. They do not tell stories of faraway places where their ancestors once lived. They tell stories of the Americas—the only home they have known.

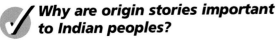 **Why are origin stories important to Indian peoples?**

LSSON 1 REVIEW

Check Understanding

1. **Recall the Facts**   In what ways did the Ice Ages change the Earth's environment?
2. **Focus on the Main Idea**   How did the environment affect the ways early peoples moved from place to place?

Think Critically

3. **Think More About It**   What skills do you think would have been important to help people survive during the Ice Ages?
4. **Explore Viewpoints**   What evidence do people give to support the early arrival theory? the late arrival theory?

Show What You Know

 Diorama Activity   Make a diorama of an Ice Age scene that includes people or giant mammals. Display the diorama in your classroom.

Use a Map to Show Movement

Why Is This Skill Important?

Some information is easiest to understand when it is shown in a drawing. One way to understand the movement of people over time is to use a map. Look at the maps on these two pages. They show the movement of early peoples as they migrated into North America and, over time, settled throughout the continent. Maps like these can help you understand the ways in which geography affects the movement of people. Learning to read these maps will help you understand other maps like them as you learn more about the story of the Americas.

Think About Direction and Movement

To use a map to describe movement, you first need to understand direction. A direction marker called a compass rose is found on most maps. The compass rose shows the cardinal directions, or main directions, of north, south, east, and west. It also shows the intermediate directions, or in-between directions, of northeast, northwest, southeast, and southwest.

The compass rose on Map A is located at the bottom of the map. The compass rose shows the arrow with the N for north pointing toward the top of the map. This means that south is toward the bottom of the map, east is toward the right, and west is toward the left.

The north arrow on a compass rose points to what is called true north. True north is in the direction of the North Pole. On some maps the compass rose may be placed so that the north arrow is not pointing straight up toward the top of the map. On Map B the north arrow of the compass rose is pointing toward the upper right part of the map. However, the arrow is still pointing north, toward the North Pole. And south is still opposite north, and east is still opposite west.

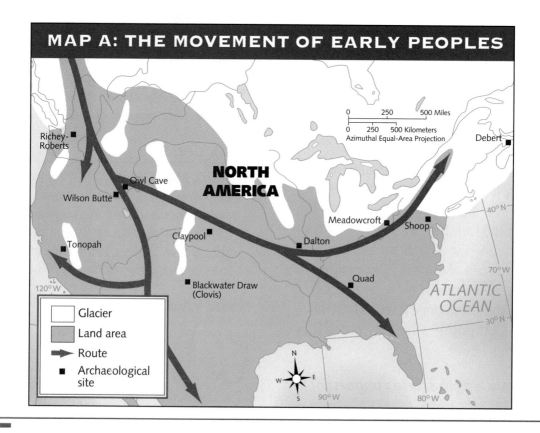

MAP A: THE MOVEMENT OF EARLY PEOPLES

On both Map A and Map B, the red route arrows show the directions in which early peoples traveled. The arrows do not stand for the exact routes taken. They show only the general direction people might have followed. It is important to remember how slowly early people moved from place to place. Bands traveled only a few miles in a lifetime, so the migration took many generations.

Understand the Process

Now that you know about the use of the compass rose and route arrows in showing movement on a map, you can answer these questions.

1. On Map A, find the archaeological site of Owl Cave. With your finger, trace the route from Owl Cave to Quad. In what direction did you move your finger?
2. Now trace the same route from Owl Cave to Quad on Map B. In what direction did you move your finger this time? It should be the same direction as you described using Map A.
3. On Map A, trace the route that goes to Meadowcroft. In what direction did people

most likely travel to get to Meadowcroft from what is now the middle of the United States?

Climate, landforms, and other physical features affected the movement of early people. As they encountered barriers to travel, they often changed the direction of their migration.

4. Why do you think early people did not travel farther east into what is now Canada before they moved south?
5. Why do you think one route in what is now the western part of the United States turned northwest?

Think and Apply

Use the information on Map A or Map B and what you already know about the geography of the United States to write a paragraph about the movement of early people. Describe a route in what is now the United States. Explain the directions in which the people moved and the physical features they might have seen along the way. Share your paragraph with a classmate.

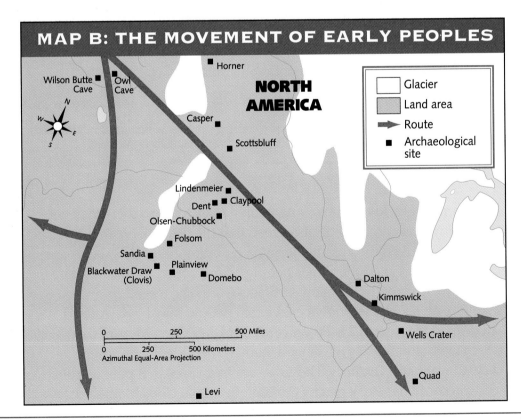

MAP B: THE MOVEMENT OF EARLY PEOPLES

How Long
Have People Lived
in the
Americas?

The walls and ceiling of a cave at Pedra Furada, Brazil, are covered with paintings of animals. Archaeologists disagree about how old some of the artifacts found there really are.

No one really knows how long people have lived in the Americas. For many years archaeologists agreed that the first people in the Americas arrived by crossing Beringia no more than 12,000 years ago. These people, called the Clovis people, were named for the place in New Mexico where their stone artifacts were discovered.

Some archaeologists now believe that people may have reached the Americas around 25,000 years ago. Jacques Cinq-Mars of the Archaeological Survey of Canada studied the Bluefish Caves in Canada's Yukon Territory. The caves are in an area that people from Siberia could have reached by crossing Beringia. Cinq-Mars said:

66 I found a bone flake in one of the caves, and two years later I found the mammoth bone from which the flake was chipped, both dating around 24,000 B.P. [before the present]. . . . It's good evidence for human presence . . . certainly at 25,000 B.P. **99**

Clovis points like this one are evidence that people lived in the Americas nearly 12,000 years ago.

But not all archaeologists agree. Many still think that the Clovis people were the first to migrate to the Americas. Vance Haynes, a professor at the University of Arizona, studied evidence in layers of rock in the ground. The layers on top are the newest. Layers below are older. Haynes said:

66 I've spent a good part of a lifetime as a geologist, as well as an archaeologist, and from Clovis up I've seen one layer after another with artifacts, while from Clovis down there's nothing human. . . . Hardly a year goes by that there isn't a new site that's claimed to be old, but they all fall away . . . unless you're a believer. **99**

Glenn Morris works for the American Indian Anti-Defamation Council in Colorado. He believes that the Indian peoples did not come to the Americas from Siberia or anywhere else. He believes they have *always* been in the Americas.

66 The problem with the Bering Strait theory is that it is wrong, not only according to indigenous [native] peoples' creation stories and histories, it is also wrong according to a growing body of Western research. . . .

Digs at Lewisville, Texas; San Diego, California; and Pedejo Cave, New Mexico, have revealed human remains at 38,000, 44,000, and 48,000 years old. . . .

By contrast, the oldest human remains found in the Siberian region of northern Asia . . . are a mere 20,000 years old! Other scientific evidence . . . indicates that a migration did occur, but the footprints went in the other direction, from the Americas to Asia! **99**

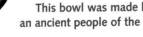

This bowl was made by the Anasazi, an ancient people of the Southwest.

COMPARE VIEWPOINTS

1. What evidence does Cinq-Mars have for his view? Why does Haynes disagree?

2. What evidence does Morris have for his view? How does his view differ from those of Cinq-Mars and Haynes?

3. A Yakima Indian once said, "I . . . did not come here. I was put here by the Creator." Which of the three views would this person most likely support?

THINK –AND– APPLY

Historians and scientists often use physical evidence, such as artifacts that have been found, to support their views. However, people do not always agree on what the evidence means. Use newspapers or magazines to identify some disagreements today that are based on the meaning of physical evidence.

BUILDING CITIZENSHIP

ANCIENT INDIANS

Link to Our World

What do people today do when their environment changes?

Focus on the Main Idea
Read to find out what the ancient Indians did when their environment changed.

Preview Vocabulary

technology	religion
extinct	tribe
agriculture	surplus
maize	specialize

As early peoples made their way across the Americas, the climate of the Earth continued to change. Over thousands of years, it became drier and warmer. In some places, lakes slowly dried up. In other places, grassy meadows turned to sand. Without water and food, the huge Ice Age animals began to disappear. Many early Americans had depended on the animals for food, clothing, and shelter. Now they had to find new ways to survive.

GIANT-MAMMAL HUNTERS

Compared to the mighty mammoth, standing 14 feet (4.3 m) high at the shoulder and weighing about 5 tons, early hunters seemed small and weak. Their spears were little more than sharpened sticks. In time they tied sharpened stones to the ends as spear points. Some hunters carried clubs and axes. Yet they survived mainly by tracking the mammoths and other giant Ice Age mammals and killing them when they could.

The earliest native hunters were nomads who lived in small bands. As they trailed behind the giant animals, they gathered fruits, nuts, and roots for food. They lived in caves or in tents made from animal skins. Their tools and weapons were made mostly from sticks, animal horns, and bones. From time to time, different peoples invented new tools, such as the atlatl (AHT•lah•tuhl), or spear-thrower. They also found new ways of sharpening stones or of leading animals into a trap. But such improvements came slowly.

This skeleton of a saber-toothed tiger shows the animal's head and fangs.

Then, about 11,600 years ago, something very important happened. Someone found a way to make a spear point by a process called flaking. First, a piece of bone or stone was used to knock off flakes, or thin pieces, from flint or another type of stone. The flakes were knocked off until the stone formed a sharp point. The point was then fluted, or hollowed out, on one or both sides. This made it easier to fasten the point tightly to a spear.

These delicate yet deadly spear points are called Clovis (KLOH•vuhs) points. They are named after the town of Clovis, New Mexico, where they were first found. Archaeologists call the early Indians who made these spear points the Clovis people. Other artifacts of the Clovis people have been found in places from Alaska to the Andes Mountains.

Clovis points were one of the important improvements in technology for early people. **Technology** is the use of scientific knowledge or tools to make or do something. You may not think of sharpened stones as technology. But these spear points were just as important to the Clovis people as computers are to us today. Clovis points were razor-sharp,

making them the best weapons early hunters had ever had.

Imagine one band of early people, moving closely behind a herd of mammoths they have been tracking for weeks. Finally the hunters see what they are looking for! In the shallow water of a small lake is a giant woolly mammoth, drinking its fill.

Looking over the area, the hunters quickly realize that they are not the only ones interested in the mammoth. A saber-toothed tiger, eager to sink its 8-inch (20.3-cm) teeth into the animal, is also watching, waiting to make its move.

What?

Atlatl

The atlatl, or spear-thrower, was an important weapon used by early hunters. Although archaeologists are not certain when it was invented, they do know that it was used in North America at least 10,000 years ago. Atlatls were spear holders 2 to 3 feet (61 to 91.4 cm) long and made of wood. The spear rested in a groove, against a base at the end. The hunter held on to the atlatl and snapped it forward with a whiplike motion to send the spear toward its target. The motion of the atlatl made the spear travel with much greater speed and force than it would have had alone.

Atlatl is an Aztec word meaning "spear-thrower." The atlatl allowed hunters to throw a spear with deadly force while staying a safe distance away from the target.

Small Clovis points like this one (right) were used to hunt the mighty mammoths (above). Clovis points were 1.5 to 5 inches (3.8 to 12.7 cm) long and were very sharp.

The hunters move in quickly and quietly. On a signal from their leader, they throw their spears. The Clovis points easily pierce the mammoth's thick skin. After wounding the animal, the hunters close in to finish the job, driving spears into the giant's heart and neck.

The band then sets to work. The people waste little of the fallen animal. From this one kill, they get about 2 tons of meat—enough to feed the band for months. Much of the meat will be dried and saved for later. The mammoth's hide will be used to make clothing and shelters. Its bones will become tools and weapons.

Even so, the Clovis people cannot carry everything with them as they move on. Some of the kill must be left behind. This does not seem important to them. After all, there is always another herd of mammoths or other animals just ahead.

But the Clovis people did not know that the giant mammals were becoming **extinct** (ik•STINGT), or dying out. The drier climate was drying up lakes and rivers and killing the tall, lush grasses that the animals ate. By about 10,000 years ago, most of the animals weighing 100 pounds (45.4 kg) or more, such as mammoths, horses, camels, and saber-toothed tigers, were gone from the Americas.

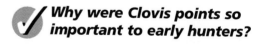 **Why were Clovis points so important to early hunters?**

FOOD GATHERERS

As the environment changed and the huge Ice Age animals died out, early peoples had to change their ways of life. Life no longer centered around the hunting of giant mammals. People began to fish and to hunt more of the smaller animals. They also began to gather more plants for food. These changes in the way people lived took place from about 9,000 years ago to 3,000 years ago.

Because they did not follow herds of large animals, food gatherers stayed in places a little longer than hunters. In time they learned where certain plants grew best and at what time of year they became ripe. Their bands then traveled to these places each season to gather food.

Picture one band of food gatherers, moving from their winter camp to their summer camp. After days of walking, they finally reach the rocky meadow near the small stream where they will spend the summer. The people set up camp in the shelter of a great rock along a hillside. Then both the women and the men begin to prepare food for their evening meal.

First, the women empty their willow baskets of the seeds and nuts they have gathered

American Indians used these decoys about 3,000 years ago to hunt ducks. The decoys are made of reeds—water plants that grow along the shores of lakes and rivers.

along the way. Then, they use flat stones to grind the food into flour. Next, they mix the flour with water and put the dough in a cooking basket. They put the basket on stones that have been heated in the fire and wait for the dough to cook.

While the women make the bread, the men skin the animals they have killed that day. They often hunt raccoons, deer, antelope, and otters, but today's meal will be rabbits. The men then heat up more stones in the fire and place the rabbits on them to roast.

After the meal the women check and repair the knives and baskets they will use to gather plants the next day. The men check and repair the spears and nets they will use to hunt and fish. Finally, they lie down in their shelters to sleep. At dawn they will be up again, ready to begin another day of searching for food.

To this day some native peoples gather foods that grow wild in nature. Some Ojibwa (oh•jib•WAY), for example, gather wild rice that grows near the Great Lakes.

 What changes did early peoples make when the giant Ice Age animals became extinct?

EARLY FARMERS

Some groups of American Indians kept to their way of life as food gatherers for thousands of years. Others, however, took the first steps toward a new technology that would change their lives forever. They began to plant seeds and grow some of their own food. This was the beginning of **agriculture**, or farming, in the Americas.

Indian peoples in Central America were among the first to develop agriculture in the Americas. Some of the earliest farmers lived in the Tehuacán (tay•wuh•KAHN) Valley in central Mexico. There archaeologists have found evidence of farming that dates from 7,000 years ago to 4,700 years ago. The early farmers of the valley harvested at least 12 kinds of corn, as well as avocados, squash, pumpkins, and beans.

Corn, or **maize** (MAYZ), was the most important food grown in the Americas. Corn gave early peoples more food than any other crop. For this reason they thought of corn as a gift from their gods. This idea was part of the Native American peoples' **religion**, or beliefs about God or gods. The religion of many early peoples centered around a number of gods connected with nature. Among these were a sun god and a rain god.

For some Native American groups, growing their own food meant that they no longer had to move from camp to camp. They could settle in one place, build stronger homes, and form villages. With more food, people lived longer and their numbers grew. In time, bands of people joined together to form tribes. A **tribe** is a group of people with a shared culture and land.

Agriculture also meant that people no longer had to spend all their time searching for food. For once, they had a food **surplus**, or more than was needed. Now people could spend more time doing other things to help the tribe. Soon they began to **specialize**, or work on one job they could do well. No longer were some early people only hunters, gatherers, or farmers. They were also potters, weavers, builders, and traders.

✓ **What changes did farming bring about in the lives of some ancient Indian peoples?**

Ears of corn appear on this carving of a god (above) believed to bring good harvests. Early corn, or maize (right), was much smaller than the corn grown today.

L SSON 2 REVIEW

Check Understanding

1. **Recall the Facts** Why did the giant Ice Age mammals become extinct?
2. **Focus on the Main Idea** What did the ancient Indians do when their environment changed?

Think Critically

3. **Personally Speaking** Would you rather have lived as a hunter, a food gatherer, or a farmer? Explain your answer.
4. **Cause and Effect** What effect did Clovis points have on the lives of early Indians?
5. **Past to Present** List five changes in technology that are important to our lives today.

Show What You Know

Collage Activity Choose one of the changes in technology that you listed for Question 5. Make a collage, using pictures from newspapers or magazines, that shows how that change affects your life today. Share your collage with your family.

Recognize Time Patterns on a Time Line

Why Is This Skill Important?

Think about some of the things you did last week. The order in which events happened is usually easy to follow over such a short time. When you think about history, however, it is different. There are a great many events, and they took place over a very long time. An easy way to understand events in history is to look at a time line. Knowing how to read a time line can help you understand the order in which events happened in the past.

Understand the Process

A **time line** is a diagram that shows the events that took place during a certain period of time. It looks something like a ruler. Instead of inches, however, dates are shown. Like inches marked on a ruler, the dates on a time line are equally spaced. The earliest date is on the left end of the time line. The most recent date is on the right. To read the events in the order in which they happened, you read from left to right.

Time lines can show events that took place during any period of time. Some time lines, for example, show events that took place over a **decade**, or a period of 10 years. Others show events that took place over a **century**, or a period of 100 years. Some even show events that took place over a **millennium**, or a period of 1,000 years.

The time line below shows dates from the ancient past to today. Notice the letters *B.C.* and

A.D. in the middle of the time line. Many people today identify years by whether they took place before or after the birth of Jesus Christ. Years that took place before the birth of Christ are labeled *B.C.* This stands for "before Christ." Years that took place after the birth of Christ are labeled *A.D.* This stands for the Latin words *Anno Domini*, which mean "in the year of the Lord."

An event that happened in 100 B.C. took place 100 years before the birth of Christ. An event that happened in A.D.100 took place 100 years after the birth of Christ. What year is it now? What letters would be used with this year? The answer is *A.D.*, but because every year in modern times is A.D., the letters are usually not used.

You may also see the letters *B.C.E.* or *C.E.* with dates. The abbreviation *B.C.E.* stands for "before the common era." It is sometimes used instead of *B.C.* The abbreviation *C.E.*, which stands for "common era," is sometimes used in place of *A.D.*

Think and Apply

Make a time line that shows some of the important events in your life. Start with the year you were born. Then add other years in which something important happened, such as the year you started school, the year you learned to ride a bicycle, or the year you moved to a new apartment or a new house.

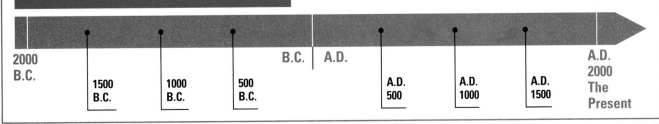

B.C. AND A.D. TIME LINE

| 2000 B.C. | 1500 B.C. | 1000 B.C. | 500 B.C. | B.C. | A.D. | A.D. 500 | A.D. 1000 | A.D. 1500 | A.D. 2000 The Present |

EARLY CIVILIZATIONS

Link to Our World

How are the lives of people today different in different parts of the world?

Focus on the Main Idea
Read to learn about the different ways of life of early peoples living in different parts of the Americas.

Preview Vocabulary

civilization   adobe
temple   mesa
pyramid   drought
cultural   kiva
   diffusion
earthwork
pueblo

This Olmec mask was found in a temple near what is today Mexico City. It is a little over 4 inches (10.2 cm) high.

With farming and settled life, Indian cultures grew and changed. Over time, people in different cultures came to hold different beliefs, speak different languages, and live in different ways. Three of these early peoples were the Olmecs (AHL•meks), the Mound Builders, and the Anasazi (ah•nuh•SAH•zee).

THE OLMECS

For hundreds of years the artifacts of a people called the Olmecs lay hidden beneath thick jungle growth. When the artifacts were finally found, archaeologists learned that the Olmecs had built one of the earliest civilizations in the Americas. A **civilization** is a culture that has well-developed forms of government, religion, and learning.

The Olmecs lived in the green river valleys along Mexico's east coast as early as 1500 B.C. So many later groups learned so much from the Olmec culture that it has become known as the "mother civilization" of the Americas.

Powerful priests governed the Olmecs, and many parts of daily life centered around religion. The Olmecs believed in many gods. One of the most important was the rain god. The Olmecs believed that the rain god appeared as a jaguar (JA•gwar), a large, spotted cat. To honor the gods, the Olmecs built great stone **temples**, or places of worship. Some temples were built on top of pyramids. A **pyramid** is a building with three or more sides shaped like triangles. The sides slant upward toward a point at the

The Olmecs carved giant stone heads from basalt (buh•SAWLT), a kind of volcanic rock. They moved the statues from miles away by floating them down rivers on rafts.

top. The Olmecs made the tops of their pyramids flat and built temples there.

Near the temples were paved streets that led to nearby buildings and a marketplace. Government leaders lived in this central area. Most other people lived in nearby villages. Huge stone faces looked out over the villages. Some weighed as much as 20 tons each. Olmec artists may have carved the faces to look like their rulers or priests.

Religious services held in the temples were important to the people. The priests standing before the crowds wore bright-red robes covered with jaguar skins. On their heads they wore bright bird feathers and flowers.

The Olmecs developed their own number system, calendar, and writing system. They wrote using pictures that stood for words or ideas. They also traded with people hundreds of miles away in present-day Mexico and Central America and along the coast of the Gulf of Mexico. Trade gave people a chance to meet and exchange ideas. In this way Olmec culture spread to other places. This process is called **cultural diffusion**.

No one knows how the Olmec civilization came to an end. We do know, however, that by A.D. 300 the Olmec civilization was gone. Yet Olmec ideas, spread through trade, lived on in other cultures.

 Why is the Olmec culture called the "mother civilization" of the Americas?

THE MOUND BUILDERS

About the same time that the Olmec people were building a civilization in Central America, a people called the Adenas (uh•DEE•nuhz) were building a civilization in North America. The Adenas lived in the Ohio River valley from about 1000 B.C. to A.D. 200.

The Adenas were the first of several ancient civilizations known as Mound Builders. The Mound Builders lived in the eastern half of what is today the United States. They got their name because of the large mounds, or hills of earth, that the people built. These mounds are called **earthworks**.

One of the most famous Adena earthworks is about 5 feet (1.5 m) high, 20 feet (6.1 m) across, and 1,330 feet (405.4 m) long. It does not look like much from the ground, but when you look at it from the air, you can see that it forms the shape of a coiled snake with jaws and a tail.

Nobody knows why the Adenas built the snake-shaped Serpent Mound, as it is called. Perhaps it was built for religious purposes. Archaeologists do know that many smaller mounds were built to bury the dead.

The most important people were given the fanciest mound burials. First, the Adenas covered the body of the person who had died with a kind of red paint. Red was the color of

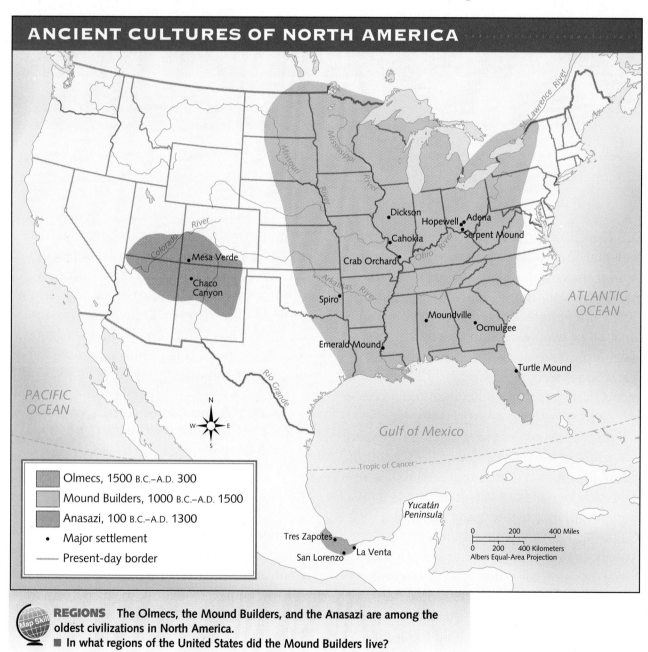

ANCIENT CULTURES OF NORTH AMERICA

Olmecs, 1500 B.C.–A.D. 300
Mound Builders, 1000 B.C.–A.D. 1500
Anasazi, 100 B.C.–A.D. 1300
• Major settlement
— Present-day border

REGIONS The Olmecs, the Mound Builders, and the Anasazi are among the oldest civilizations in North America.
■ In what regions of the United States did the Mound Builders live?

The snake-shaped Serpent Mound (right) is found near Cincinnati, Ohio. Other Adena mounds are shaped like birds, tortoises, and people. A Hopewell artist made this eagle in flight (below) out of copper. Such beautiful treasures often were placed with the dead in burial mounds.

blood and of life. They believed the red paint would allow the person's spirit to live on after death. Then they laid the body on a bed of bark strips set in the floor of a small house.

To help the dead enjoy their life after death, people placed jewelry, clay pipes, beads, and other goods around the body. Then they went outside and set the house on fire. After the house had burned down, they covered the tomb with earth. Over time more people would be buried there, and the mound would rise higher and higher.

About 300 B.C. a second, larger mound-building civilization began to take shape in the middle of what is now the United States. This was the culture of the Hopewells. Hopewell culture grew to be the strongest in the region for nearly 500 years.

The Hopewells had great skill at arts and crafts. They made beautiful pots, finely woven mats, and figures carved from bone, wood, and metal. They made spear points and knives from obsidian (uhb•SIH•dee•uhn),

a hard, shiny black stone. They wore clothing made of fur and skins and jewelry made from pearls, copper, and shells.

Like Olmec goods and ideas, Hopewell goods and ideas spread far and wide through trade. This trade reached from the Atlantic Ocean to the Great Plains and from Lake Superior to the Gulf of Mexico. Hopewell traders were often away from home for weeks at a time, visiting trading centers hundreds of miles away.

The greatest mound-building civilization was that of the Mississippians. It developed in the Mississippi River valley about A.D. 800. The Mississippians lived in hundreds of towns and several large cities. They built huge mounds, some nearly as big as a football field. Some of these high, box-shaped mounds had large temples built on top.

The largest Mississippian city was near where East St. Louis, Illinois, stands today. By A.D. 1200 as many as 40,000 people lived in this city, called Cahokia (kuh•HOH•kee•uh).

Picture the large city of Cahokia, dotted with 85 different mounds, as it looked one autumn morning. The powerful chief, who is both priest and ruler, has just come out of his house on the flat top of the huge main temple mound. He and the other priests are getting ready to greet the sun god and ask his blessing on the corn harvest.

Monk's Mound, where Cahokia's chief is standing, is 110 feet (33.5 m) high and covers 16 acres. It took the people more than 300 years to build it. They had to carry soil to the mound one basket at a time.

Below Monk's Mound is the large town square. It is already filling up with thousands of people gathering for worship. Later, the square will be used as a marketplace.

Looking over his lands, the chief looks past the square to the smaller mounds that have houses on top, where other important people live. Outside the large wooden fence around the city he sees the houses of the farmers, hunters, and workers. The people are hurrying toward the temple, and the chief's thoughts return to the religious service that is about to begin.

By about A.D. 1500 the great Mississippian civilization began to break down. War, hunger, or sickness may have played a part. Whatever the reason was, the Mississippian culture, the last of the great mound-building civilizations, ended.

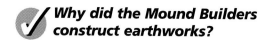
Why did the Mound Builders construct earthworks?

THE ANASAZI

From about 100 B.C. to A.D. 1300, another early civilization grew up in the dry lands of what is today the southwestern United States. This was the civilization of the Anasazi, or "Ancient People."

The Anasazi lived in groups of houses that Spanish people later described as **pueblos** (PWEH•blohs). *Pueblo* is the Spanish word for "town" or "village." Pueblos were made of adobe (ah•DOH•bay) bricks and sandstone.

Adobe is a kind of sandy clay that can be dried into bricks. The Anasazi had to carry wood for roof beams from miles away, but adobe and sandstone were near at hand.

Most pueblos were built on top of **mesas**, or high, flat-topped hills. The buildings had few windows or doors on the lower levels. People entered rooms or moved from one level to another by using ladders.

One great Anasazi settlement was Pueblo Bonito, or "beautiful town." Pueblo Bonito was built beneath the towering rock walls of Chaco (CHAH•koh) Canyon, in what is today New Mexico. It was made up of 800 rooms and housed more than 1,200 people. Nearly 5,000 people lived in smaller villages nearby. The villages were connected by paved roads, which also served as trade routes.

The Anasazi built some pueblos into the sides of high cliffs, far out of the reach of enemies. One, the pueblo at Mesa Verde (MAY•sah VAIR•day), in present-day Colorado, is known as the Cliff Palace. Rising three stories high, the pueblo has 200 rooms. Up to 1,000 people may have lived there.

The Cliff Palace of the Anasazi (left), found in southwestern Colorado, was built around A.D. 1100. It was unknown to many Americans until two cowhands came upon it, abandoned, in 1888. This pottery jar and pair of sandals (below) are artifacts of Anasazi life.

Even though their land was very dry, the Anasazi grew fields of corn, squash, and beans. They planted their seeds deep in the ground to get the most water out of the soil. They also dug holes and ditches to store water for use in drier times. In case a long dry spell, or **drought**, should come, they saved enough dried corn in clay jars to feed the people for up to two years.

Religion was an important part of Anasazi life. Religious services were held in special underground rooms called **kivas** (KEE•vuhs). Chiefs, their faces and bodies painted white, led the people in giving thanks to the Earth Mother, the sun god, and the rain god.

The Anasazi civilization came to an end about A.D. 1300, after a 22-year drought in the high mesa lands. The Anasazi people left the great pueblos and moved into the valleys of rivers such as the Rio Grande. There they built smaller pueblos or joined other groups in small farming villages.

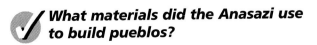 **What materials did the Anasazi use to build pueblos?**

LESSON 3 REVIEW

Check Understanding

1. **Recall the Facts**   List three of the earliest civilizations found in the Americas.
2. **Focus on the Main Idea**   What different ways of life did the peoples of early civilizations develop in the Americas?

Think Critically

3. **Think More About It**   In what ways did the environment affect the lives of the Anasazi?
4. **Past to Present**   How do ideas spread from one culture to another today?

Show What You Know

Art Activity   Imagine that you have written a book about one of the civilizations described in this lesson. Now create a cover for your book. First, choose a title for the book. Then draw a cover picture that shows the lives of the people you describe. Use your book cover in a bulletin board display.

CONNECT MAIN IDEAS

Use this organizer to show that you understand how the chapter's main ideas are connected. Copy the organizer onto a separate sheet of paper. Then complete it by writing three details to support each main idea.

The First Americans

The environment affected the ways early peoples moved from place to place.

1. _____
2. _____
3. _____

The Environment

The ancient Indians coped with changes in their environment.

1. _____
2. _____
3. _____

Early peoples living in different parts of the Americas had different ways of life.

1. _____
2. _____
3. _____

WRITE MORE ABOUT IT

1. **Write a Letter**   Imagine that you are an archaeologist searching for evidence of the first Americans. Write a letter to a friend or family member that tells what it is like to work at a "dig." Explain the kinds of artifacts or other evidence you hope to find.

2. **Write a Menu**   Write a menu that lists the kinds of foods a giant-mammal hunter might have eaten on a typical day. Then write a menu for a food gatherer and a menu for an early farmer. How are the three menus different? How are they alike?

USE VOCABULARY

Write the term that correctly matches each definition. Then use each term in a complete sentence.

adobe   band
agriculture   nomad
archaeologist

1. a small group of people who work together to do things, such as hunting

2. a wanderer who has no settled home

3. a scientist who studies the cultures of people of long ago

4. farming

5. a kind of sandy clay that can be dried into bricks

CHECK UNDERSTANDING

1. Why did Ice Age hunters move from place to place?

2. What is the name of the land bridge that once linked Asia and the Americas?

3. Why are artifacts from the Meadowcroft Rock Shelter important?

4. How did agriculture change the ways of life of early peoples?

5. What was the most important food crop grown in the Americas?

6. Why was the Olmec culture so important to the early history of the Americas?

7. What was the largest mound-building civilization?

8. What was a kiva? What was it used for?

THINK CRITICALLY

1. **Cause and Effect**   Why did the oceans become shallow during the last Ice Age?

2. **Past to Present**   In what ways do people in your community specialize in jobs today?

3. **Think More About It**   The cultures of the Olmecs, the Mound Builders, and the Anasazi developed in very different ways. Explain how this fact could be used to support the early arrival theory.

4. **Personally Speaking**   How does the environment affect your life today?

APPLY SKILLS

How to Use a Map to Show Movement   Draw a map of your school. Show places such as your classroom, the cafeteria, the office, and the library. Find out which way is north, and add a compass rose to your map. (Hint: Use the sun to help you. In which direction have you watched the sun rise in the morning? That direction is east.) Now draw a line on your map to show a route from one room to another. Use the compass rose to help you describe which directions the route follows.

How to Recognize Time Patterns on a Time Line   Draw a time line, and label the year A.D. 2000 in the center. Now label the year one decade before A.D. 2000 and the year one decade after it. Label the year one century before A.D. 2000 and one century after it. Label the year one millennium before A.D. 2000 and one millennium after it.

READ MORE ABOUT IT

The Memory String by Chester G. Osborne. Atheneum. Darath and his sister live on the Siberian Peninsula, part of present-day Russia, 30,000 years ago. They are about to take an amazing trip to what is now North America.

Science of the Early American Indians by Beulah Tannenbaum and Harold E. Tannenbaum. Franklin Watts. The authors explore the scientific achievements of the early Americans.

INDIAN LIFEWAYS
in North America

> 66 May it be delightful my house;
> From my head may it be delightful;
> To my feet may it be delightful;
> Where I lie may it be delightful;
> All above me may it be delightful;
> All around me may it be delightful. 99
>
> A Navajo house blessing

Dora Pino, a Navajo woman of Magdalena, New Mexico

INDIANS OF THE NORTHWEST COAST

Link to Our World

How does living near an ocean affect the lives of people in coastal communities today?

Focus on the Main Idea
Read to find out how living near an ocean affected the lives of the Northwest Coast Indians.

Preview Vocabulary
diversity   clan
cultural region   barter
dugout   potlatch
pit house   totem pole

Over hundreds of years, as old Indian civilizations gave way to new cultures, different tribes with different ways of life slowly settled the continent. North America became a land of great **diversity**—a land of great differences among its peoples. By the 1400s people from hundreds of different tribes lived in North America.

Often peoples living in the same area share some ways of life. Such an area is called a **cultural region**. People living in a place with cold weather, for example, wear heavy clothing. People living in a place with rich soil farm the land. Yet in North America, there were great differences even among the people of the same cultural region. Think about these differences as you read about the Indians of one cultural region—the Northwest Coast.

THE GREAT NORTHWEST

High in the Cascade Mountains between what are today the states of Washington and Oregon, the Columbia River passes through a narrow gap in the cliffs. For 15 miles (24.1 km) the river thunders through waterfalls and rapids. This area is known as The Dalles (DALZ). For hundreds of years, it was one of the greatest trading centers in North America.

People came to The Dalles from hundreds of miles away. Dozens of tribes, some speaking languages as different from each other as English is from Chinese, took part in the trading through the warm summer months.

The Dalles was part of the area known as the Northwest Coast. The Northwest Coast is a narrow strip of land that stretches about 2,000 miles (3,219 km) along the Pacific

EARLY CULTURES OF NORTH AMERICA

Legend:
- Arctic
- Subarctic
- Northwest Coast
- Plateau
- California
- Great Basin
- Southwest
- Plains
- Eastern Woodlands
- Middle America
- Caribbean
- Present-day border

0   300   600 Miles
0   300   600 Kilometers
Azimuthal Equal-Area Projection

REGIONS Many of our names for cities, states, rivers, and regions come from Indian languages.

■ Do you see any connections between the names of the Indian cultures on the map and the names of places today?

Ocean from present-day southern Alaska to northern California.

The Indians of the Northwest Coast lived between the ocean and rugged mountain ranges, in a land of rivers and forests filled with fish and game. The growing season was short, and the climate was too wet for much agriculture. But there were plenty of fish, especially salmon. There were also plenty of deer, bears, and other animals. There was wood to build houses and make tools. And if tribes could not get something by themselves, they could get it by trade.

It might seem surprising that trade was common in an area where travel was so hard. Because mountains made travel by land difficult, people traveled by water—by river. The Columbia River was the "highway" of the

Northwest, carrying people from place to place in wooden dugouts. **Dugouts** are boats made from large, hollowed-out logs.

 What foods were available to the peoples of the Northwest?

THE CHINOOKS

The Chinooks (shuh•NUKS) were the best-known traders of the Northwest Coast. This Indian tribe lived near the coast, at the mouth of the Columbia River. Chinook villages were made up of rows of long wooden houses. The houses were built of wooden boards and had no windows. The Chinooks built each house partly over a hole dug in the earth so that some of its rooms were under the ground. Such a house is called a **pit house**.

Several families belonging to the same clan lived in each house. A **clan** is a group of families that are related to one another. Like many other tribes, the Chinooks traced their clans through the mother's line. In other words, the people of the clan had the same mother, grandmother, or great-grandmother. Children belonged to their mother's clan, not to their father's.

This Chinook carving of a mother and child (left) shows the importance of the mother's position in a clan. The statue was carved in the "X-ray" style used by many Northwest Coast tribes, showing the bones of people and animals. Chinook pit houses (below) were made of split wood. These houses usually had no windows and only one door.

The Chinooks controlled the Columbia from the coast all the way to The Dalles. They even made other peoples pay them for the right to travel the river. So many different peoples, speaking different languages, traded at The Dalles that it could be difficult to talk. To help solve the problem, the Chinooks developed a special language for trading. It was made up of Chinook words and words borrowed from other languages. This trading language made it easier for different peoples to talk to each other and to **barter**, or exchange goods.

And what a lot of different goods there were! People traded dried fish, shells, furs, whale products, seal oil, cedar, dugouts, masks, jewelry, baskets, copper, and even prisoners.

Wealth was very important to the people in the Northwest Coast area. Tribes often attacked one another to gain wealth and, in turn, respect. Prisoners, a sign of wealth, were frequently taken during the many wars. Only very important people could use prisoners as servants.

To show off the things they owned, the Chinooks and other tribes who lived along the coast held **potlatches**. These were special gatherings with feasting and dancing. During a potlatch, the hosts gave away valuable gifts as a sign of their wealth. Members of some clans spent years preparing hundreds of gifts to be given away at the next potlatch.

 What role did the Chinooks play in the Northwest Coast trade?

THE MAKAHS

The waters of the Northwest helped give the peoples who lived there plenty of food. Salmon and other fish, sea otters, and whales were in good supply. Most coastal tribes captured only beached whales—whales that had come up on shore. The Makahs (mah•KAWZ), however, built canoes to hunt the huge mammals at sea.

Makah whale hunters often spent months preparing for a whale hunt. They fasted and prayed to their gods to favor them. They made new wooden harpoons—long spears with sharp shell points. And they repaired their canoes and paddles. Made of tree bark, the canoes were 6 feet (1.8 m) wide and carried up to 60 people. They were built for the open ocean. However, they still could be toppled by an angry whale.

Imagine one group of whale hunters setting out to sea. The chief harpooner leads the hunters. His father and grandfather held the same job before him. After several hours the hunters spot a gray whale. They follow the animal for about 20 miles (32 km) out into the open ocean, slowly closing in. Along the way the chief harpooner shows his respect for the huge animal by singing a special song promising to give it gifts if it allows itself to be killed.

Finally the chief harpooner sees his chance and throws his harpoon. The whale is hit! Sealskin floats tied to the harpoon make it hard for the whale to dive. Harpooners from other canoes throw their weapons, too. When the whale dies, the hunters start towing it to shore.

Many Northwest Coast Indians place carved totem poles outside their houses. Symbols on the pole often tell a family's history. This totem pole was made by a member of the Haida (HY•duh) tribe.

A chief harpooner prepares to throw his weapon at a whale. Whale hunting was important for the Makahs' survival.

After hours of paddling, the Makah hunters are glad to see their village. Wooden houses line the narrow beach between the water and the forest. Outside each house stands a wooden post called a **totem pole**. Each totem pole is beautifully carved with shapes of people and animals. The carvings show each family's history and importance. As the hunters draw near, the people on shore rush to greet them.

Little of the prized whale is wasted. The chief harpooner receives the best piece of blubber, or fat. The rest is stored for later. The people will eat the whale's meat and skin. They will make ropes and bags from different parts of the animal's body. They also will melt some of the fat for oil to burn as fuel.

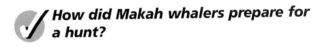 **How did Makah whalers prepare for a hunt?**

LESSON 1 REVIEW

Check Understanding

1. **Recall the Facts**   What resources were available on the Northwest Coast?
2. **Focus on the Main Idea**   How did living near an ocean affect the lives of the Northwest Coast Indians?

Think Critically

3. **Think More About It**   How do you think people from different tribes learned the special trading language used at The Dalles?

4. **Explore Viewpoints**   Why were potlatches important to people of the Northwest Coast?

Show What You Know

 Art Activity   Draw a scene showing part of daily life for one of the tribes of the Northwest Coast. Work with your classmates to put all of your scenes together to form a bulletin board display. Label the display *Lifeways of the Northwest Coast Indians.*

LESSON 2

INDIANS OF THE SOUTHWEST

L ink to Our World

What steps do people take today to help themselves live in a dry environment?

Focus on the Main Idea
As you read, think about what the Indians of the Southwest did to help themselves live in a dry environment.

Preview Vocabulary

arid	hogan
kachina	shaman
ceremony	

The Southwest is a mostly dry land of rocky mesas, deep canyons, steep cliffs, and beautiful mountains. Fierce heat during the day can be followed by sharp cold at night. Months can go by without a drop of rain. Then a sudden storm can bring so much rain that flash floods race through normally dry canyons.

It is difficult to survive in such a land. But the many peoples of the Southwest found ways not only to survive but to live well.

THE HOPIS

"Up the ladder and down the ladder." In the Southwest, these words meant "to enter a house." Like the Anasazi before them, many peoples of the Southwest lived in pueblos—adobe houses of many rooms built next to or on top of one another. To enter a home or to reach other levels, people climbed ladders. In time all of the tribes who lived in pueblos, peoples such as the Hopis (HOH•peez), the Zunis, and others, became known as the Pueblo peoples.

The name *Hopi* means "Peaceful One." The early Hopis lived in present-day northeastern Arizona, just as many Hopis do today. In early times most of their villages were built on top of high, flat mesas. Steep, narrow trails cut into the rocks led from the mesas down to the fields. There the men grew corn, beans, squash, and cotton. The climate was very dry, or **arid**, so they used water from springs under the ground and from rain showers to water their crops.

While the men worked in the fields, the women ground corn into flour, using flat, smooth stones. Women spent hours each day grinding corn, often singing songs as they worked. Part of every home was filled with jars of corn and flour. A surplus of food meant survival during times of drought.

Like other Pueblo peoples, the Hopis believed in gods of the sun, rain, and earth. Spirits called **kachinas** (kuh•CHEE•nuhz) were also an important part of their religion. They remain important today. The Hopis believe that kachinas visit the world of living people once a year and enter their bodies. On Earth, these spirits are believed to take the form of kachina dancers. The dancers are Hopi men wearing painted masks and

dressed as kachinas. Kachina dancers take part in many Hopi **ceremonies**, or special services. Some of these ceremonies are held in kivas underground and others are held in large meeting places outside.

 Why was storing extra food important to the Hopis?

DAILY LIFE

Here is how Charlotte and David Yue describe the daily lives of the early Hopis and other Pueblo peoples in their book *The Pueblo*.

❝Pueblo families lived in one room, but most of their daily activities were

A kachina dancer performs during a ceremony. The dance is not for show but is part of the Hopis' religion.

What?

Kachina Figures

Pueblo families taught their children the names and special powers of the kachinas by giving them kachina figures. Fathers and grandfathers carved and painted the wooden figures to look like the different kachinas. By studying the figures, children learned what the spirits stood for. Kachina figures were not for play. They were meant to be treasured and passed on to each child's own children.

Each Pueblo family lived together in a single room. Married couples lived with the wife's family. When one house became too crowded, part of the clan moved to a house nearby. More rooms were added to the pueblo when more space was needed.

out of doors. Their homes were used mainly for sleeping and for being sheltered from bad weather. The terrace was an outdoor kitchen and sitting room. The women went up and down ladders to outside ovens on the terrace or down on the ground. The outdoor drying racks had to be tended, and baskets and pottery were often worked on outside.

The workday began at the first light of dawn. Pueblo people hung up their bedding and everyone washed up. They worked first and ate later. The men would start off to the fields, and the women would sweep the floor and begin preparing the day's food.

Children learned by helping. Boys worked with their fathers and uncles. They would go together to the fields. Younger boys scared away crows or gathered up brush. When a boy was old enough, his father might let him work a plot by himself. Girls worked with their mothers and aunts, grinding beside them at the grinding stones. Even small children would be asked to bring some sticks of firewood. Grandfathers worked on their weaving and often taught the children, giving instruction in what was right and wrong and why. Or the wisdom of their years might entitle them to a ceremonial office or a place in the town council. Grandmothers might still do some of the pottery work. They also gave advice and helped take care of the children.

The men took leftover bread with them to eat in the fields, and the women might have some leftovers for a late morning meal. The workday ended in the late afternoon. The men returned from the fields, and the family sat on the floor and shared the main meal of the day. The evenings were spent talking, laughing, and visiting neighbors. At dark the blankets were again rolled out on the floor for sleeping. **"**

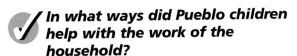 **In what ways did Pueblo children help with the work of the household?**

THE NAVAJOS

Not all the people of the Southwest were Pueblo Indians. Some had different ways of life. Often, however, other tribes learned from the success of the Pueblos and took on some of their lifeways. This was true, for example, of the Navajos (NA•vuh•hohz).

The Navajos moved into the Southwest about A.D. 1100. They settled in an area known today as the Four Corners. This is the place where the corners of the states of Arizona, New Mexico, Utah, and Colorado meet. Many Navajo people still live in the Four Corners area today.

The early Navajos were nomads. They used brushwood, animal skins, and leaves to make new shelters in each place where they stopped to hunt and gather food. Imagine their wonder when they first saw the great pueblos of the Hopis, built high on the mesas and surrounded by fields of corn!

To the Navajos, Hopi villages were filled with treasures—treasures that the Navajos wanted. For years the Navajos attacked the Hopis and stole baskets, weaving looms, pottery, blankets, and farm tools. In time, however, the Navajos learned Hopi ways. Soon they, too, were growing crops and weaving cotton clothing, as the Hopis did.

The Navajos lived in houses called hogans. A **hogan** (HOH•gahn) is a cone-shaped house built by covering a log frame with mud or grass. Rather than building their hogans together to form villages, the Navajos built

The wood of Navajo hogans is held together by mud. A hogan is always built so that the doorway faces east.

them in small, family-sized groups miles apart from one another.

The Navajos believed in gods they called the Holy People. Some gods, such as the Earth Mother, were kind. Others, such as the sun god, could cause crops to dry up and die. The Navajos believed that they needed to keep praising the gods so that the gods would not use their powers against the people.

As in other Indian cultures, Navajo ceremonies were led by a religious leader and healer called a **shaman** (SHAH•muhn). Shamans called upon the gods to give the people special favors.

Navajo shamans made beautiful sand paintings, also called dry paintings, that were believed to hold healing powers. First, the shaman created a pattern of religious symbols on the ground, using colored sand. Then, the sick person sat or lay on the sand painting while the shaman held a special ceremony believed to help him or her feel its healing powers. The painting was always rubbed away after the ceremony.

✓ **What lifeways did the Navajos learn from the Hopis?**

A Navajo shaman creates a sand painting. The shaman uses charcoal, sandstone, gypsum, and ocher ground up into powders. The powders give the shaman different colors for the painting.

LESSON 2 REVIEW

Check Understanding

1. **Recall the Facts**   Why were tribes such as the Hopis known as the Pueblo peoples?
2. **Focus on the Main Idea**   What did the Indians of the Southwest do to help themselves live in their dry environment?

Think Critically

3. **Past to Present**   In what ways were early pueblos like modern-day apartment buildings? In what ways were they different?

4. **Think More About It**   Why do you think the Navajos decided to end their nomadic way of life?

Show What You Know

Model Activity   Use several small boxes to build a three-dimensional model of a Pueblo village. Use toothpicks, straws, or other things to make ladders, and place the ladders in the model. Display your Pueblo village in the classroom.

LEARN with LITERATURE

Focus on Indians of the Great Plains

1492: THE YEAR ◆ of the ◆ NEW WORLD

by Piero Ventura

This Mandan shield has an image of a turtle painted on it.

Imagine looking out over miles and miles of flat land, marked here and there by rolling hills. The land is covered with tall, green grasses moving slowly in the breeze. What looks like a sea of grass is broken by a circle of tepees (TEE·peez) on top of a far-off hill. The tepees are cone-shaped tents made of poles covered with buffalo skins. They are the homes of the Indian peoples of this region, called the Great Plains.

The grassy lands of the Great Plains gave the buffalo—one of the area's most abundant resources—plenty to eat. The buffalo moved in huge herds made up of thousands of animals. The peoples of the Plains hunted the buffalo for food and used other parts of the animal to make clothing, tools, and weapons.

Some Plains tribes, such as the Kiowas (KY·uh·wahz), were nomads who followed the buffalo from place to place. Others, such as the Mandans, lived in villages the year round. But twice a year the Mandan villages emptied out as men, women, and children took part in a great buffalo hunt.

Read now about a Mandan boy named Fast Deer and his experiences on a summer buffalo hunt. As you read, think about how the many different people of his community worked together to reach their goal.

It is almost sunset; the summer evening is calm and warm. At the fires in front of the tepees, the women are roasting buffalo meat. Fast Deer leaves the group of youngsters running from one end of the camp to the other, still excited by the hunt; he prefers to stand by the fire and smell the cooking meat. He is thinking that his friends will make fun of him—almost old enough to become a warrior, here he is among the squaws, like a little boy!

But the real reason he is by the fire is that this is the only place he can avoid the smell of blood coming from the soaked earth, from the skinned carcasses and the hides already hanging on poles to dry. Fast Deer has a very keen sense of smell, exceptional even for the people of his tribe—the Mandans, hunters, farmers, and warriors living on the Great Plains—who have always relied on their sharp senses to survive in this boundless territory. Their land has an abundance of food but is also fraught[1] with danger in the form of nature and hostile tribes. "We should have named you Buffalo Nose," his father once told him. But that sensitive nose, which in a few years will help him hunt and "sense" the presence of enemies, now only torments[2] him with the odor of buffalo blood. . . .

While waiting for his portion of roast meat, Fast Deer goes over the events of the last few days and hours. He can still hear the thunderous trampling of the buffalo running toward the trap the tribe set for them, the men shouting to frighten them and direct them toward a gorge,[3] and the furious barking of the dogs. Everything had been planned very carefully: first of all choosing the site, a hilly area on the northeastern edge of the plains, ideal because of the many

gorges; then setting up camp a short distance from the bottom of the precipice[4] chosen as the trap; and last, finding the herd to be hunted.

Two evenings ago the men held a meeting to decide the strategy for the hunt. Yesterday evening there was a propitiatory[5] dance, a sort of simulated[6] battle between the hunters and the animals, the latter impersonated by men wearing buffalo heads. And this morning at dawn the hunt began. The herd

---

[4] **precipice:** steep cliff
[5] **propitiatory:** done to win favor
[6] **simulated:** imitation

---

[1] **fraught:** full of
[2] **torments:** causes suffering
[3] **gorge:** deep, narrow valley

selected for the hunt was outflanked[7] and almost surrounded. The hunters crawled toward the buffalo downwind; they wore fresh buffalo hides, because these animals, with an even keener sense of smell than Fast Deer's, can detect the odor of humans from far away. The women, children, and adolescent boys—including Fast Deer—who are not allowed to take part in the hunt, watched silently from a nearby stretch of high ground. Everything was quiet. Then the men shouted all together and the herd, skillfully directed

[7] **outflanked:** closed in

by the hunters, began to run toward the gorge. The buffalo fell headlong down the rocky ravine,[8] where the hunters finished them off with bows and arrows and axes. The boys and women helped drag the carcasses to the camp, and for the rest of the day the entire tribe was busy skinning and cutting the huge beasts.

The Mandans use every part of the buffalo they catch. The meat not eaten fresh is dried for the winter; the hide is transformed into tepees, boats, blankets, and moccasin soles;

[8] **ravine:** small, deep valley

Two hunters hiding under wolf skins crawl slowly toward a herd of buffalo (left). After a successful hunt, Indian peoples used the buffalo for food and to make shelters, clothing, and other goods. These skins (above) were stretched around a wooden frame and made into a boat.

the mane and tail hair is twisted into strong cord; the bones become arrowheads, needles, and other useful objects; and perhaps some hardy warrior will convert the powerful horns into a bow. Buffalo will be hunted until the tribe has all it can carry with it. To return from the grassy summer hunting areas to the wooded winter lands where they have fields of corn and tobacco, the Mandans must walk for days.

If the buffalo did not go south during the winter, Fast Deer thinks, toboggans could be used for transport, since they carry a much larger load. The round earthen dwellings in the winter village are spacious, each accommodating a family and its possessions, and dozens of people besides. It would really be comfortable, Fast Deer reflects, to have soft hides spread all over the floor, not just where they sleep.

His mother hands him a piece of meat, and Fast Deer looks around while chewing on it. A splendid white-feathered peace pipe is being handed around among a group of elders seated in a circle. A young warrior, so proud of the eagle feather that has recently been put in his hair, plays the flute for a girl wearing a dress of soft deerskin decorated with porcupine needles and colored patterns. . . .

Now the shaman moves toward the center of the camp. Of all the men in the tribe, he is the one who has the most extraordinary visions and dreams; he is able to foresee the future and cure diseases. He will now do a solo dance to thank the invisible, all-present spirit that protects the tribe, and afterward everyone will sing and dance through the night.

Yes, Fast Deer thinks, this is a great day!

This painted Mandan robe was made from the whole skin of a buffalo. The triangles on the robe stand for the feathers of a war bonnet.

Literature Review

1. How did the different members of the Mandan tribe work together during the buffalo hunt?
2. Why was careful planning for the buffalo hunt so important?
3. Make a poster that shows the many ways the Mandans used the buffalo in their daily lives. At the top of the poster, draw a buffalo. Then fill your poster with pictures of items that the Mandans made from different parts of the buffalo. Share your poster with the class.

INDIANS OF THE EASTERN WOODLANDS

Link to Our World

How does conflict affect the lives of people today?

Focus on the Main Idea
As you read, think about the ways conflict affected the lives of the peoples of the Eastern Woodlands.

Preview Vocabulary
legend
Iroquois League
confederation
council
longhouse

The figures of two people appear at the top part of this Iroquois comb, which was carved out of bone.

66 We return thanks to our mother, the earth, which sustains us. We return thanks to the rivers and streams, which supply us with water. We return thanks to all herbs, which furnish medicines for the cure of our diseases. We return thanks to the corn, and to her sisters, the beans and squashes, which give us life. We return thanks to the bushes and trees, which provide us with fruit. . . . 99

With this prayer, the Haudenosaunee (hoh•dee•noh•SAW•nee), known later as the Iroquois, gave thanks for the many resources of their land. The Iroquois lived in what is today the eastern part of the United States. This cultural region was called the Eastern Woodlands. It got its name from the many forests that covered the land. The forests were so thick that in some places sunlight could barely reach the ground.

The Eastern Woodlands was a huge region of great diversity. It had rugged, snow-covered mountains in the north and hot, wet swamps in the south. It also was home to hundreds of different peoples. So many lived there, in fact, that some places became quite crowded, with different tribes often fighting each other for room.

THE IROQUOIS

The Iroquois lived in the northeastern part of the woodlands. They were among the most powerful peoples of the region. The Iroquois

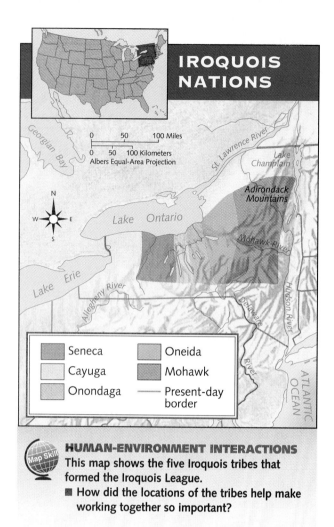

IROQUOIS NATIONS

0 50 100 Miles
0 50 100 Kilometers
Albers Equal-Area Projection

Seneca
Cayuga
Onondaga
Oneida
Mohawk
— Present-day border

Georgian Bay
St. Lawrence River
Lake Champlain
Adirondack Mountains
Lake Ontario
Mohawk River
Lake Erie
Allegheny River
Hudson River
Delaware River
ATLANTIC OCEAN

HUMAN-ENVIRONMENT INTERACTIONS
This map shows the five Iroquois tribes that formed the Iroquois League.
■ How did the locations of the tribes help make working together so important?

were not one tribe but a group of several tribes that lived near each other and spoke similar languages. These tribes were the Seneca (SEN•uh•kuh), Cayuga (ky•YOO•guh), Onondaga (ah•nuhn•DAHG•uh), Oneida (oh•NY•duh), and Mohawk.

For many years the Iroquois fought with each other and with the neighboring Algonkins (al•GON•kins). The fighting often began over land. Over the years farmers had cleared more and more forest land to raise crops to feed their people. This meant that hunters had to go farther away to find animals, often entering other tribes' lands. But the fighting that began over land continued out of revenge.

Think about this story of a Seneca woman who had lost her son in a battle with the Cayugas. Sad and angry, she asked the men of her clan to attack the Cayugas and pay

them back for her son's death. The Seneca leaders agreed, and their warriors acted quickly. They attacked a Cayuga village, killing many people and taking others prisoner. One of the Cayuga men was given to the Seneca woman in place of her lost son. But now there was likely to be a return attack, and the fighting would go on.

Like many native people, the Iroquois often used **legends**, or stories handed down over time, to explain the past. One legend says that a holy man named Dekanawida (deh•kahn•uh•WIH•duh) was one of the first to speak out against all the fighting. He said that the Iroquois must come together "by taking hold of each other's hands so firmly and forming a circle so strong that if a tree should fall upon it, it could not shake nor break it, so that our people and grandchildren shall remain in the circle in security, peace, and happiness."

An Onondaga chief named Hiawatha (hy•uh•WAH•thuh) shared Dekanawida's hopes for peace. Hiawatha visited the Iroquois tribes, asking for an end to the fighting. Tired of war, they finally agreed. They decided to work together in what became known as the **Iroquois League** (LEEG).

The members of the Iroquois League formed what is called a **confederation** (kuhn•feh•duh•RAY•shuhn), or loose group of governments. Each tribe governed itself. But matters that were important to all, such as war and trade, were decided by a Great Council. A **council** is a group that makes laws.

Men from each of the five Iroquois tribes, together called the Five Nations, served on the Great Council. The eldest women of each tribe chose the council members. Each member had one vote. All had to agree before anything was done.

The Iroquois said that their confederation was like a big **longhouse**. A longhouse is a long wooden building in which several

Iroquois longhouses could be 50 to 150 feet (15.2 to 45.7 m) in length. They had no windows, only a door at each end and small holes in the roof to let air in.

Iroquois families lived together. It was made of elm bark and had a large door at each end. Just as several families shared a longhouse, the five tribes shared the confederation. They thought of the confederation as a longhouse as big as their land, with the Mohawks guarding the eastern door and the Senecas guarding the western door.

 **What problems led the Iroquois to form a confederation?**

THE CHEROKEES

Far to the south of the Iroquois lived another people of the Eastern Woodlands—the Cherokees (CHAIR•uh•keez). The Cherokees made their homes in the rich river valleys of the southern Appalachian Mountains. There they grew corn, beans, squash, pumpkins, sunflowers, and tobacco. They gathered wild plants from the forests. They also fished, and they hunted squirrels, rabbits, turkeys, bears, and deer.

As in other tribes of the Southeast, most Cherokee families had two houses. One kept them warm in the winter, and the other kept them cool in the summer. Winter houses were small, cone-shaped pit houses made of wooden poles covered with earth. Summer houses were larger box-shaped houses with grass or clay walls and bark roofs. In both winter and summer houses, several families of the same clan lived together.

Cherokee houses—often as many as 300 to 400—were built close together to form villages. At the center of each village was an open square with a temple built high on a flat-topped mound. There the shamans led ceremonies for the hunters and farmers. The most important was the Green Corn ceremony, held at the end of the summer to give thanks for a good harvest. Shamans also led healing ceremonies. Like other Indian peoples, the Cherokees made many medicines from the plants of the forest.

Leaders called chiefs governed each village, telling the people what to do on

Cherokees play a game of Little War (above), an early version of today's lacrosse. To control the ball, each player carried two sticks like those shown here (left). Because there were few rules and no protective clothing, Little War was a dangerous game.

day-to-day matters. But the villages were also part of a larger Cherokee confederation. From time to time, chiefs from as many as 100 villages came together to discuss important matters—especially matters of war. As in other places in the Eastern Woodlands, wars with neighboring tribes took place often. High wooden fences made of logs were built around the villages to keep out enemies.

In most villages the chief in charge of matters of war was also in charge of a game called Little War. It was something like today's game of lacrosse, but it had more players and fewer rules and was much rougher. The idea was to throw a small ball between two posts, using a special stick with a net on the end. People came from miles around to watch these games.

What did the Cherokees and other Indian peoples use as natural medicines?

L SSON 4 REVIEW

Check Understanding

1. **Recall the Facts**   What were the main causes of war in the Eastern Woodlands?
2. **Focus on the Main Idea**   In what ways did conflict affect the lives of the peoples of the Eastern Woodlands?

Think Critically

3. **Past to Present**   How was the Iroquois Confederation like governments today? How was it different?
4. **Think More About It**   Why do you think the Cherokee chief who was in charge of matters of war was also in charge of a ball game?

Show What You Know

Simulation Activity   Create a conversation between Hiawatha and members of an Iroquois tribe. In the conversation Hiawatha should try to get the people to stop fighting and join the confederation. With your classmates, put your conversations together to write a scene about the formation of the Iroquois League.

Identify Causes and Their Effects

Why Is This Skill Important?

Something that makes something else happen is a cause. What happens is the effect. To find the links between events in history, you will need to identify causes and effects. Knowing about causes and effects is also important in your own life. It can help you predict likely outcomes for your actions so that you can make more thoughtful decisions.

Remember What You Have Read

Before the Iroquois League was formed, tribes often fought one another. Most of the time the fighting happened because of disagreements over land. As populations grew, farmers needed to clear more land to grow crops. This meant that hunters had to go farther away to hunt—sometimes into other tribes' lands. The fighting that was first caused by conflicts over land often continued out of revenge.

The Iroquois leaders Dekanawida and Hiawatha feared that all the fighting would destroy their people. They led the tribes to end their fighting and work together, forming the Iroquois League.

Understand the Process

Many events in history have more than one cause and more than one effect. Follow the arrows on the chart on this page to help you understand the causes and the effects of the formation of the Iroquois League.

1. What first caused the fighting among the Iroquois tribes?
2. What effect of that fighting caused more fighting?
3. What caused Dekanawida and Hiawatha to work to end the fighting? What was the effect of their work?
4. What were the effects of the formation of the Iroquois League?

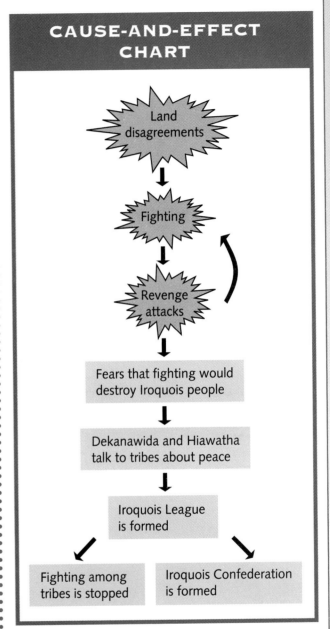

CAUSE-AND-EFFECT CHART

Land disagreements

↓

Fighting

↓

Revenge attacks

↓

Fears that fighting would destroy Iroquois people

↓

Dekanawida and Hiawatha talk to tribes about peace

↓

Iroquois League is formed

↙ ↘

Fighting among tribes is stopped

Iroquois Confederation is formed

Think and Apply

Suppose that you are hurrying to school. It is raining, and there are wet leaves on the sidewalk. You slip on the leaves and fall, hurting your leg. As a result, you are late for school and miss an important test. Draw a cause-and-effect chart to show the causes and effects of your fall.

BUILDING CITIZENSHIP

LESSON 5

INDIANS OF MIDDLE AMERICA

Link to Our World

How do people today meet their needs by borrowing ideas from others?

Focus on the Main Idea
As you read, think about how Indian peoples of Middle America met their needs by borrowing ideas from other peoples.

Preview Vocabulary

city-state	empire
class	emperor
noble	tribute
slavery	

The cultural region of Middle America includes most of the present-day country of Mexico as well as several countries of Central America. This region was home to one of the oldest civilizations in the Americas—that of the Olmecs. The Indian peoples who came after the Olmecs learned much from this "mother civilization." Two groups who borrowed ideas from the Olmecs and from other peoples of Middle America were the Mayas (MY•uhz) and the Aztecs.

THE MAYAS

From far off, it looked as if the whole city were made of stone. There were temple pyramids reaching high into the sky. There was a round-topped building where priests studied the stars. There were palaces, towers, ball courts, and bridges, all connected by roads paved with stones. This was Tikal (tih•KAHL), one of the cities built by a people known as the Mayas.

Mayan civilization began to take shape about 500 B.C., during the time of the Olmecs. Building on what the Olmecs had done, the Mayas slowly created their own culture. In time Mayan culture took Olmec ways of life to even greater heights.

The Mayas built more than 100 stone cities in Middle America. Each city had its own ruler and its own government. For this reason each was called a **city-state**. Tikal, in what is today the country of Guatemala, was the largest. Up to 100,000 people lived there.

Like the Olmecs and some other Indian peoples, the Mayas were divided into social **classes**. These are groups

This colorful plate is covered with drawings and patterns of the Mayan culture.

of people treated with different amounts of respect in their society. At the top were the all-powerful priests. Next were the **nobles**, or people from important families. The nobles ruled along with the priests. Below the nobles were traders and craftspeople—artists who worked with wood, stone, leather, gold, and clay. Near the bottom were the farmers, whose corn fed the other classes and made

Mayan civilization possible. The only people treated with less respect than the farmers were the slaves.

The Mayas, like some other Indian peoples, enslaved other people. **Slavery** is the practice of holding people against their will and making them carry out orders. Most Mayas who held slaves were nobles. They were thought of as slave owners. The

At Mayan temples priests held religious ceremonies and studied the stars. Most temples looked like this one (above) at Chichén Itzá (chih•CHEHN it•SAH). This clay figure (left) shows the clothing and jewelry worn by men of the Mayan upper classes.

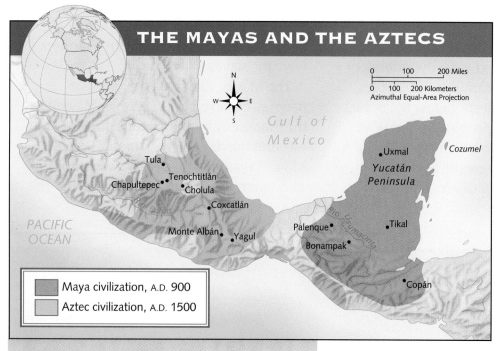

THE MAYAS AND THE AZTECS

Gulf of Mexico

0 100 200 Miles
0 100 200 Kilometers
Azimuthal Equal-Area Projection

Tula

Chapultepec • Tenochtitlán
• Cholula

• Coxcatlán

PACIFIC OCEAN

Monte Albán • • Yagul

Uxmal • • Cozumel

Yucatán Peninsula

Río Usumacinta

Palenque • • Tikal

Bonampak •

• Copán

Maya civilization, A.D. 900
Aztec civilization, A.D. 1500

This is a Mayan figure of a woman weaving at a loom. The loom is fastened to a pole, probably a tree trunk.

Map Skill **REGIONS** The Mayas and the Aztecs lived in parts of what are today Mexico and Central America.
■ Why do you think this cultural region is called Middle America?

enslaved people were thought of as an owner's property. Most slaves were people accused of crimes. Their punishment was slavery.

The priests and nobles lived in luxury in the cities. But everyday life for most Mayas, who lived in the countryside, meant hard work. Think about the members of one farm family, beginning their day when it is still dark outside. Rising first, the mother lights a fire in the family's small hut, which is made of mud. There are no windows and no furniture. The family eats and sleeps on mats laid on the dirt floor. The mother prepares tortillas (tor•TEE•yahz), or thin corn pancakes. She bakes them over the fire for her husband and son. At dawn both will leave for the fields. It takes hard work to keep the thick jungle from taking over the land where they grow corn, beans, and squash.

When father and son have left, the mother cares for her new baby and begins her own work. Today she will weave cloth and begin

to make extra baskets to store corn. The harvest this season should be good. There should be enough corn to feed the family. They might even have some left over to trade at the market in the city.

Mayan markets were busy places. Traders from many miles around bought and sold honey, cotton cloth, cocoa, feathers, copper bells, gold dishes, pearls, salt, and dried fish. All of these goods were carried to and from the markets on the backs of slaves.

The Mayas believed in gods of the sun, rain, and other parts of nature. Mayan priests not only led religious ceremonies but also spent many hours studying the stars. From watching the movement of the stars and working out long mathematical problems, the Mayas made several different calendars. One of their calendars had 365 days, as our calendar does today. To help keep track of time, the Mayas used a way of counting that had the idea of zero—a very important idea in mathematics. And they recorded what they learned using their own form of picture writing.

 How was the Olmec civilization important to the Mayas?

THE AZTECS

Another culture that developed in Middle America was that of the Mexicas, a tribe later known as the Aztecs. For many years the Aztecs were nomads, moving from place to place in search of food. About A.D. 1200 they began to settle in the Valley of Mexico.

The Aztecs built their capital, Tenochtitlán (tay•nohch•teet•LAHN), on two islands in the middle of Lake Texcoco (tes•KOH•koh). Today Mexico City, the capital of Mexico, stands on this same spot. Legend says that the Aztecs built their capital where they saw a sign from the gods—an eagle with a snake in its mouth, sitting on a cactus. Today the eagle with the snake appears on the Mexican flag.

From their capital at Tenochtitlán, the Aztecs built a great civilization. They did this by conquering other Indian peoples. By about A.D. 1500 the Aztecs ruled 200,000 square miles (518,000 sq km) and more than five million people in their huge empire. An **empire** is a conquered land of many people and places governed by one ruler. That ruler is called an **emperor**.

This drawing tells the story of the Aztecs' search for a place to build their capital. The name Tenochtitlán means "cactus rock." The blue lines in the picture stand for the waters of Lake Texcoco.

W here?

Tenochtitlán

Tenochtitlán, the capital of the Aztec Empire, was built on the swampy islands of Lake Texcoco in what is today the middle of Mexico. Under the Aztecs, the city grew to have hundreds of buildings and 300,000 people. The city has been growing and changing for hundreds of years. Today it is Mexico's capital, Mexico City.

Just as the Mayas had learned from the Olmecs, the Aztecs learned from the Mayas. The Aztecs also borrowed new ways of doing things from new peoples they conquered. In this way the Aztec Empire became one of the greatest of the time.

To have more land for farming, the Aztecs built small islands in Lake Texcoco. To do this, they tied large baskets to the lake's bottom and filled them with mud. Then they planted corn and other crops in the new soil. Canals and paved roads connected the many islands to the shore.

In the city's most important square were royal palaces with hundreds of rooms. There were also gardens and a large zoo. The palaces were the homes of the all-powerful Aztec emperor.

Near the emperor's palaces were huge warehouses piled high with tribute. **Tribute** is the name for payments a ruler demands from his or her people. Each year the people had to send goods such as cloth, jewelry, feathers, gold, and corn to Tenochtitlán. If they refused, the emperor would send Aztec soldiers to make them pay.

......

This is the lake city of Tenochtitlán, as painted by Mexican artist Diego Rivera. The city and nearby land were joined by bridges.

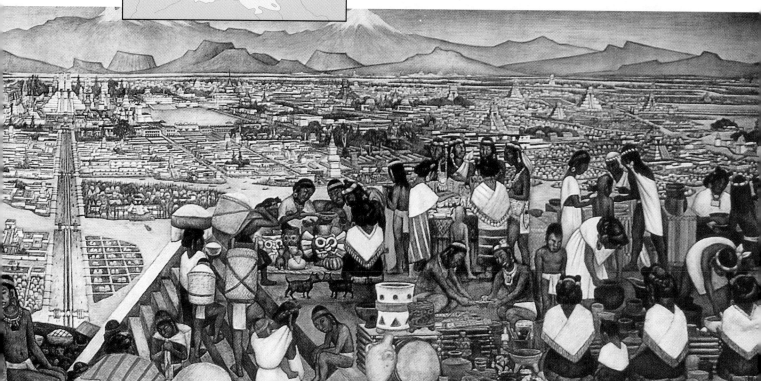

This feathered headdress belonged to Motecuhzoma (maw•tay•kwah•SOH•mah), an Aztec emperor.

Boom! Boom! Boom! An Aztec leader beat the great drum on top of the war god's temple to call the Aztec army. The soldiers moved at once to prepare for war and join their fighting groups in front of their clan's temple. Most Aztec soldiers wore special outfits. An Eagle Knight, for example, wore a wooden helmet shaped like an eagle's head. The soldier's quilted cotton armor was covered with eagle feathers. In 24 hours the Aztec army would be 200,000 strong and ready to go to war.

In the very center of Tenochtitlán, white flat-topped pyramids rose toward the sky. On top of the pyramids stood the great stone temples built to honor the Aztecs' gods.

Past the temples was a large, open area where the daily market was held. Each morning canoes crowded the lake, bringing goods from all over the empire and from places outside of it. People quickly set up their stalls, eager to do business. More than 60,000 people—from the highest nobles to the lowest farmers—came to the marketplace each day to exchange goods. At the same time they exchanged ideas, often adding new ways of life to Aztec culture.

From whom did the Aztecs learn many of their lifeways?

LESSON 5 REVIEW

Check Understanding

1. **Recall the Facts** What was the "mother civilization" of the Americas?
2. **Focus on the Main Idea** How did the Indian peoples of Middle America meet their needs by borrowing ideas from other peoples?

Think Critically

3. **Think More About It** Why do you think the idea of zero is important in mathematics?
4. **Cause and Effect** How did the Aztecs change their environment when they built the city of Tenochtitlán?

Show What You Know

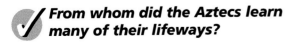 **Art Activity** Create a travel brochure inviting people today to visit the sites of either the Mayan or the Aztec civilization. Your brochure should include a map showing where the civilization was located as well as a short introduction to the people's history. Include pictures of famous sites. Present your brochure to the class.

REVIEW

CONNECT MAIN IDEAS

Use this organizer to show that you understand how the chapter's main ideas are connected. Copy the organizer onto a separate sheet of paper. Then complete it by writing three examples for each cultural region to show the diversity of Indian peoples.

Indian Lifeways in North America

Indians of the Northwest Coast

1. _____
2. _____
3. _____

Indians of the Great Plains

1. _____
2. _____
3. _____

Diversity

Indians of the Southwest

1. _____
2. _____
3. _____

Indians of the Eastern Woodlands

1. _____
2. _____
3. _____

Indians of Middle America

1. _____
2. _____
3. _____

WRITE MORE ABOUT IT

1. **Write an Invitation** Imagine that you are a wealthy Chinook getting ready to hold a potlatch. Write an invitation to a friend, describing your plans for the feast.

2. **Write a Story** Write a story entitled *A Day in the Life of an Aztec Family*. Include the conversations of friends and family members in your story.

USE VOCABULARY

Write a term from this list to complete each of the sentences that follow.

barter   empire
city-state   shaman
clan   slavery

1. A _____ is a group of families that are related to one another.

2. At The Dalles, Indians from many different Northwest Coast tribes met to _____, or exchange goods.

3. A religious leader and healer called a _____ led many Navajo ceremonies.

4. Tikal, a Mayan _____, had its own ruler and its own government.

5. _____ is the practice of holding people against their will and making them carry out orders.

6. A government in which one ruler governs many lands and peoples is known as an _____.

CHECK UNDERSTANDING

1. Why were dugouts especially important to the Indians of the Northwest Coast?

2. What do the carvings on totem poles show?

3. What are kachina figures?

4. How did Pueblo people prepare for times of drought?

5. In what ways did the tribes of the Great Plains use the buffalo they hunted?

6. What was the Iroquois League? What was its purpose?

7. What group was in the highest class in Mayan society? What group was in the lowest class?

8. What was the capital of the Aztec Empire? What city stands there now?

THINK CRITICALLY

1. **Past to Present**   Many Indian clans traced their families through the mother's line. How is that different from the way many people today trace their families?

2. **Think More About It**   How were the lifeways of the Makahs and the Mandans similar, even though they lived in different cultural regions?

3. **Cause and Effect**   How did the environment affect the ways the Hopis, Mandans, and Cherokees built their homes?

4. **Personally Speaking**   What do you think made the Aztec Empire so strong?

APPLY SKILLS

How to Identify Causes and Their Effects
Think again about the busy trading center at The Dalles. Draw a cause-and-effect chart that traces the development of the special trading language that was used there. Show the causes that led the Indians to make up the language, and show its effects.

READ MORE ABOUT IT

Children of the Earth and Sky by Stephen Krensky. Scholastic. This collection of five stories of Native American children from different cultural regions shows the diversity of Indian life in the Americas.

Dancing Tepees: Poems of American Indian Youth selected by Virginia Driving Hawk Sneve. Holiday House. Poems that have been passed down from the old to the young are presented with poems from today's tribal poets.

Indians by Edwin Tunis. HarperCollins. Drawings and descriptions help you learn about the everyday lives of Indians from various tribes in different cultural regions.

RELEVANT

A MULTICULTURAL COUNTRY

If a huge quilt could show you what life was like in the Americas in the late 1400s, it would have hundreds of different patches. Their different colors and designs would stand for the many different Indian cultures.

The United States is still a patchwork of many cultures—American Indian, Hispanic, European, African, Asian, Pacific Island, Alaska Native, and others. The people from these many backgrounds are united by being Americans. Yet they also have kept alive their own cultural traditions. This has made the United States a multicultural country—a country of many cultures.

Many people believe that our country's diversity of cultures adds to the richness of American life. Most Americans experience this diversity every day. You hear it in the languages people speak and in the music they play. You see it on signs and in the ways people dress. You taste it in the foods they make. You feel it at times of special celebration.

THINK AND APPLY

Think about the many ways people express their culture. Design a colorful patch that shows a part of your cultural heritage. Then combine your patch with those of your classmates to create a quilt that shows the cultures in your classroom community.

BUILDING CITIZENSHIP

STORY CLOTH

Study the pictures shown in this story cloth to help you review the events you read about in Unit 1.

Summarize the Main Ideas

1. One of the greatest trading centers in North America was located in the Northwest Coast. On trading days at The Dalles, people from dozens of tribes came in dugout canoes to barter.

2. Many of the peoples of the Southwest lived in pueblos. Drying and storing surplus food helped the people survive during times of drought.

3. The Mandans and other peoples of the Great Plains depended on the buffalo. After a buffalo hunt, the people worked to use every part of the animals.

4. To help end the fighting among peoples of the Eastern Woodlands, the Iroquois formed a confederation. Leaders from each of the five Iroquois tribes served on the Great Council, which decided matters that concerned them all.

5. The Aztec capital of Tenochtitlán was one of the largest cities of Middle America. The city center had palaces, warehouses, temple pyramids, and a huge market.

Illustrate the Story   Choose one of the Indian peoples described in Unit 1 but not shown in this story cloth. Draw a picture that shows a scene of daily life for the group you chose. Then write a paragraph that explains the scene. Tell where the scene should be placed in the story cloth.

COOPERATIVE LEARNING WORKSHOP

Remember
- Share your ideas.
- Cooperate with others to plan your work.
- Take responsibility for your work.
- Show your group's work to the class.
- Discuss what you learned by working together.

Activity 1
Make a Cave Wall Painting

Imagine that you and your classmates are Clovis people. You want to draw pictures of a mammoth hunt on a cave wall so your children will learn from your experiences. Tape large pieces of paper to your classroom wall. Form several groups, with each group responsible for a different part of the hunt. Using paint, colored chalk, or markers, draw scenes of the hunt. One scene should show the weapons that were used, including Clovis points and the atlatl. Another scene should show how people used the fallen animal.

Activity 2
Draw a Map

Working with your classmates, draw a large outline map of North America. Show the locations of the Indian tribes of the Northwest Coast, the Great Plains, the Southwest, the Eastern Woodlands, and Middle America. To show how the cultures were alike and how they were different, add symbols or pictures to stand for houses, temples, crops, or other items that were important to each culture.

Activity 3
Draw a Scene of Daily Pueblo Living

To show how the environment helps shape the way people live, draw a scene from the daily life of the early Hopis. Add your scene to a classroom display.

USE VOCABULARY

Write a word from this list to complete each of the sentences that follow.

culture   kivas
dugouts   maize
earthworks   origin stories

1. The way of life of a group of people is called its _____.

2. _____ tell of Indian peoples' beliefs about the world and their place in it.

3. _____ was the most important crop grown in the Americas.

4. The mounds built by early peoples for burying their dead or for religious purposes are called _____ .

5. The Anasazi and later Pueblo peoples held religious services in special underground rooms called _____ .

6. The Chinooks traveled the Columbia River in _____ , or canoes made from large, hollowed-out logs.

CHECK UNDERSTANDING

1. Why is the Olmec culture known as the "mother civilization" of the Americas?

2. What is cultural diffusion?

3. In what ways did the Indians of the Great Plains depend on the buffalo?

4. What problems led the Iroquois to form a confederation?

5. How did the Aztecs build a large empire?

THINK CRITICALLY

1. **Cause and Effect** How did the lives of early peoples change after the giant Ice Age mammals became extinct?

2. **Think More About It** What changes in technology brought changes to the lives of early Americans?

3. **Past to Present** Give three examples that show that North America in ancient times was a land of great diversity. Give three examples that show that North America today is a land of great diversity.

APPLY GEOGRAPHY SKILLS

How to Use a Map to Show Movement Chaco Canyon, in what is today New Mexico, was a center of Anasazi culture. About 400 miles (644 km) of roads ran between pueblos in the area. Use the map below to answer the questions.

1. In which direction would a person travel to follow the road from Salmon to Pueblo Bonito?

2. In which direction would a person travel to follow the road from Pueblo Pintado to Pueblo Bonito?

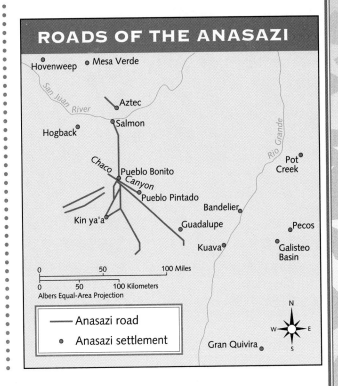

ROADS OF THE ANASAZI

Hovenweep • Mesa Verde
San Juan River
Aztec
Hogback • Salmon
Chaco Canyon Pueblo Bonito
Pueblo Pintado
Kin ya'a Guadalupe
Kuava
Pot Creek
Rio Grande
Bandelier
Pecos
Galisteo Basin
Gran Quivira

0   50   100 Miles
0   50   100 Kilometers
Albers Equal-Area Projection

—— Anasazi road
• Anasazi settlement

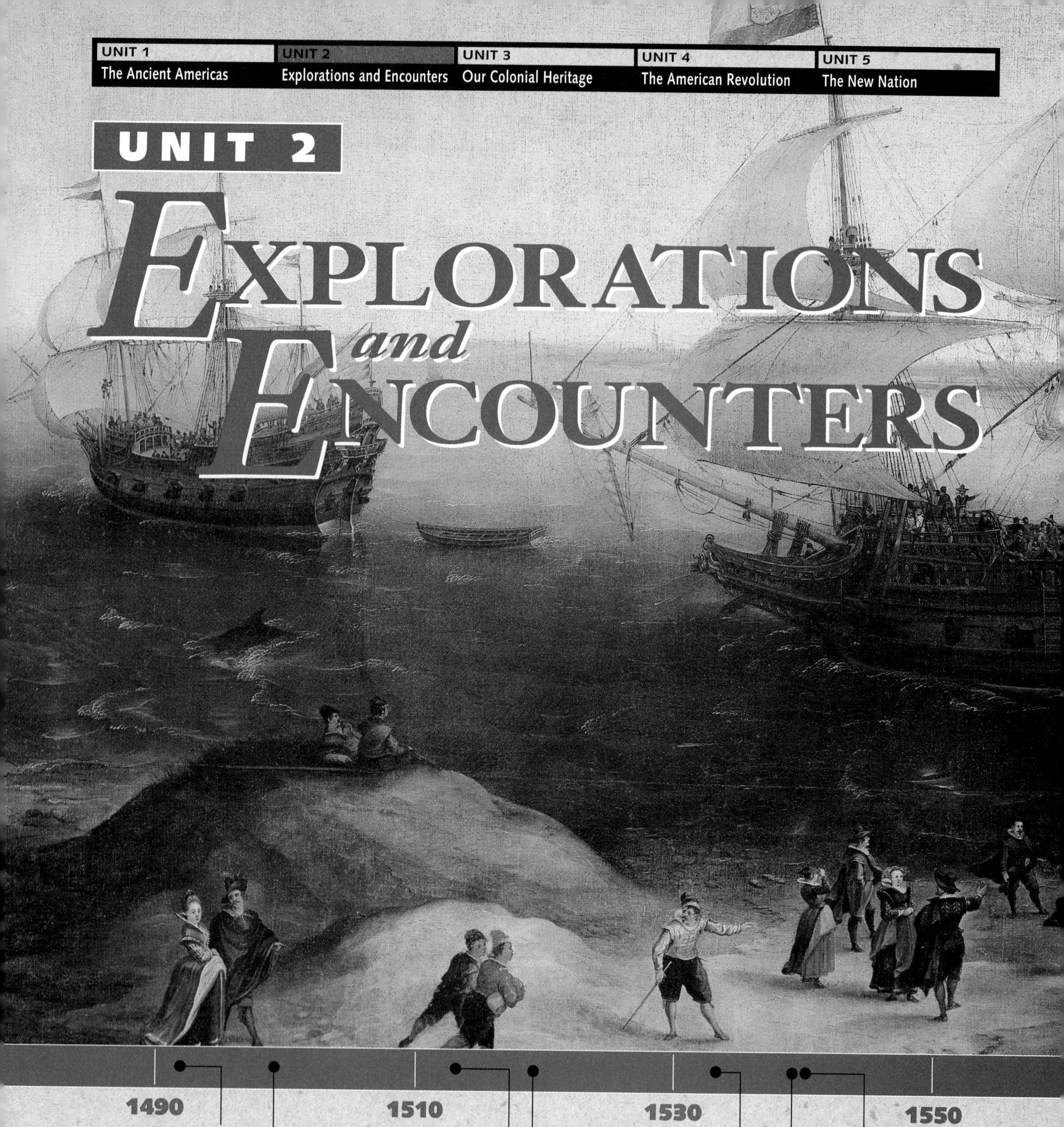

UNIT 2

EXPLORATIONS and ENCOUNTERS

1490

1492
Columbus lands in the Americas

1499
Vespucci sails to South America

1510

1513
Ponce de León explores Florida

1519
Cortés conquers the Aztecs

1530

1533
Pizarro conquers the Incas

1539
De Soto explores the Southeast

1550

1540
Coronado explores the Southwest

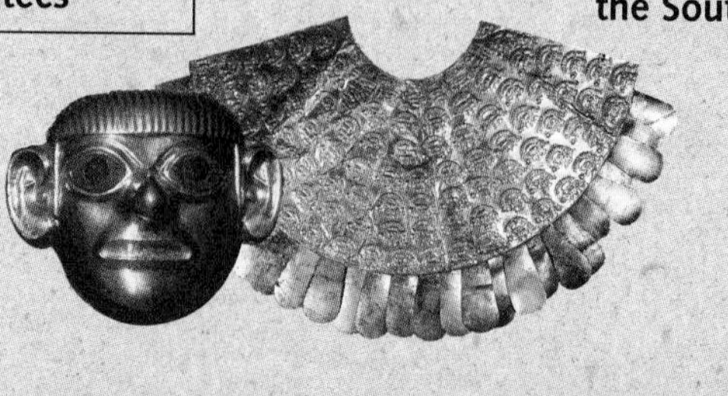

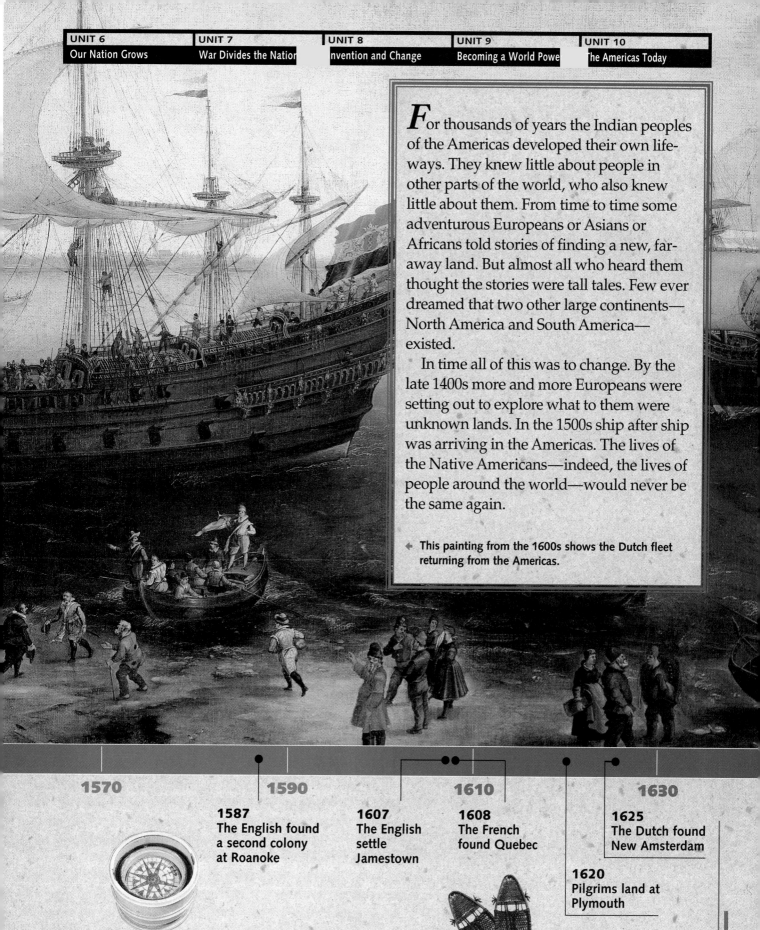

*F*or thousands of years the Indian peoples of the Americas developed their own life-ways. They knew little about people in other parts of the world, who also knew little about them. From time to time some adventurous Europeans or Asians or Africans told stories of finding a new, far-away land. But almost all who heard them thought the stories were tall tales. Few ever dreamed that two other large continents—North America and South America—existed.

In time all of this was to change. By the late 1400s more and more Europeans were setting out to explore what to them were unknown lands. In the 1500s ship after ship was arriving in the Americas. The lives of the Native Americans—indeed, the lives of people around the world—would never be the same again.

← **This painting from the 1600s shows the Dutch fleet returning from the Americas.**

1570

1590

1587
The English found a second colony at Roanoke

1607
The English settle Jamestown

1608
The French found Quebec

1610

1620
Pilgrims land at Plymouth

1625
The Dutch found New Amsterdam

1630

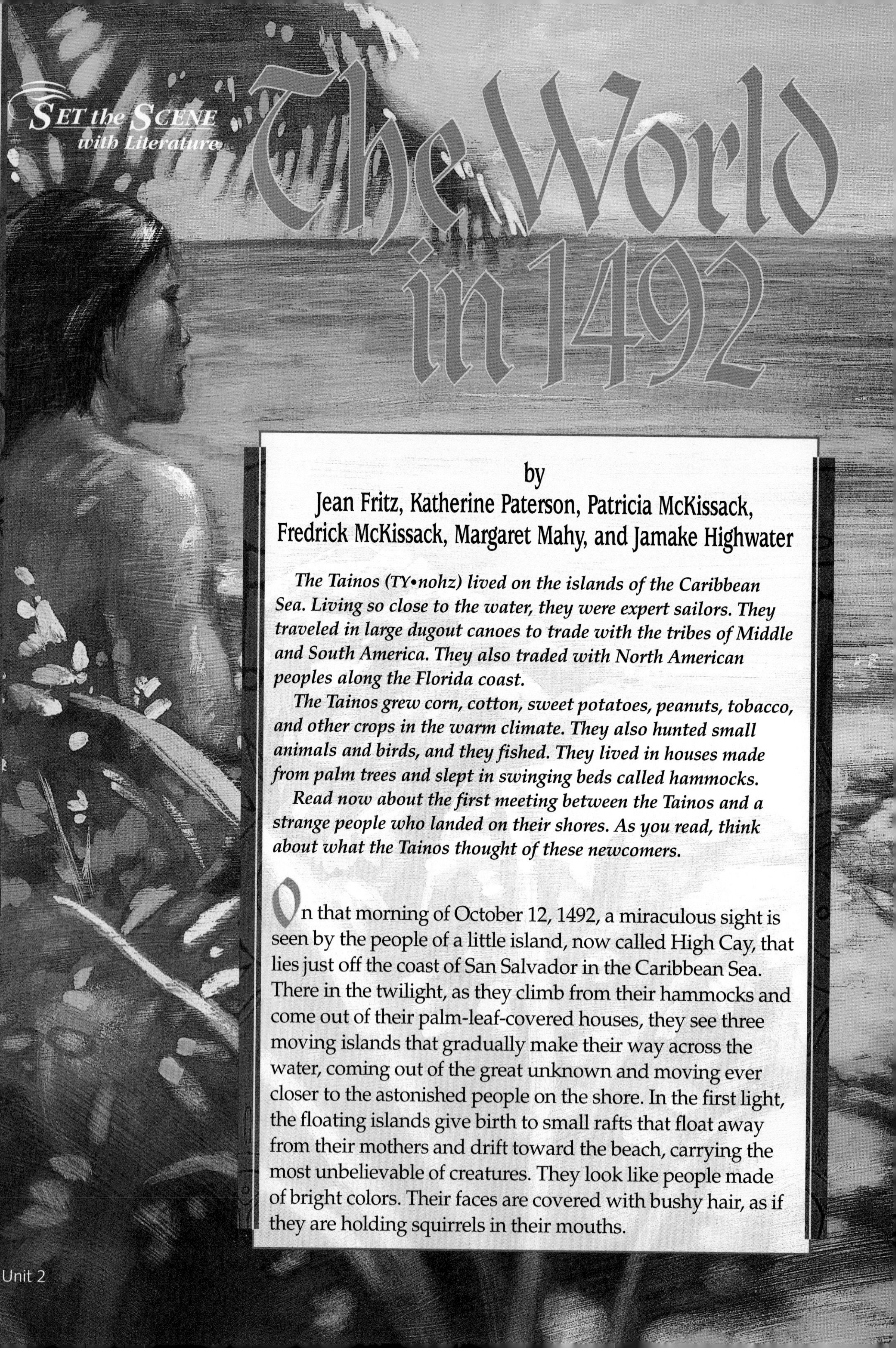

The World in 1492

by
Jean Fritz, Katherine Paterson, Patricia McKissack,
Fredrick McKissack, Margaret Mahy, and Jamake Highwater

The Tainos (TY•nohz) lived on the islands of the Caribbean Sea. Living so close to the water, they were expert sailors. They traveled in large dugout canoes to trade with the tribes of Middle and South America. They also traded with North American peoples along the Florida coast.

The Tainos grew corn, cotton, sweet potatoes, peanuts, tobacco, and other crops in the warm climate. They also hunted small animals and birds, and they fished. They lived in houses made from palm trees and slept in swinging beds called hammocks.

Read now about the first meeting between the Tainos and a strange people who landed on their shores. As you read, think about what the Tainos thought of these newcomers.

On that morning of October 12, 1492, a miraculous sight is seen by the people of a little island, now called High Cay, that lies just off the coast of San Salvador in the Caribbean Sea. There in the twilight, as they climb from their hammocks and come out of their palm-leaf-covered houses, they see three moving islands that gradually make their way across the water, coming out of the great unknown and moving ever closer to the astonished people on the shore. In the first light, the floating islands give birth to small rafts that float away from their mothers and drift toward the beach, carrying the most unbelievable of creatures. They look like people made of bright colors. Their faces are covered with bushy hair, as if they are holding squirrels in their mouths.

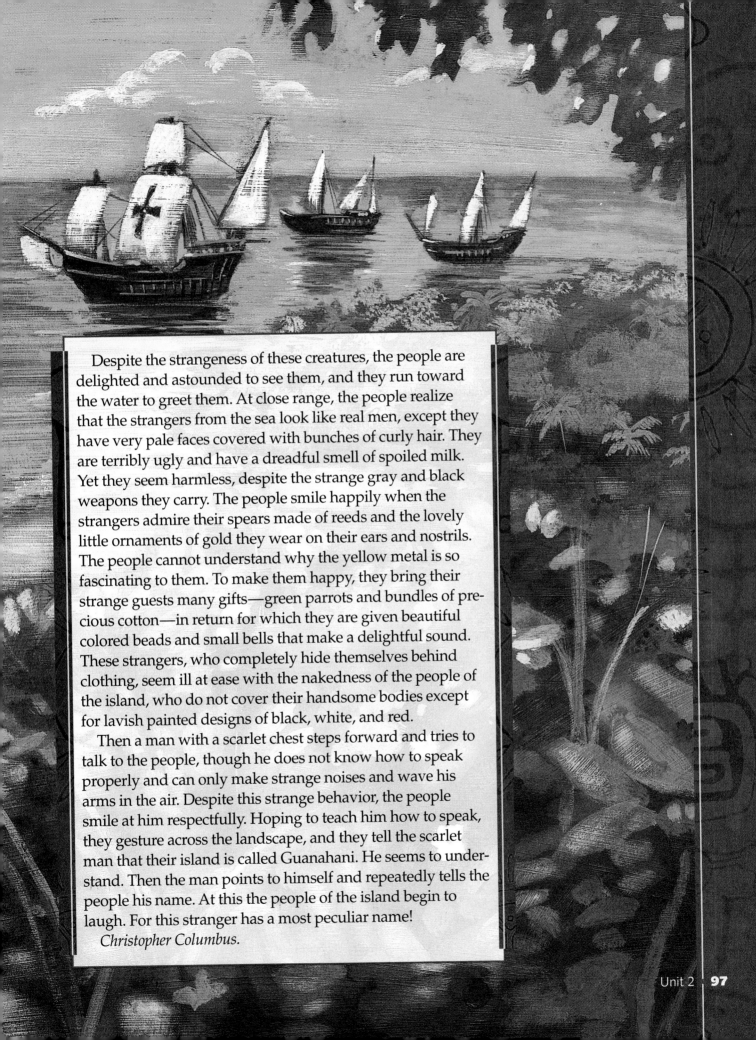

Despite the strangeness of these creatures, the people are delighted and astounded to see them, and they run toward the water to greet them. At close range, the people realize that the strangers from the sea look like real men, except they have very pale faces covered with bunches of curly hair. They are terribly ugly and have a dreadful smell of spoiled milk. Yet they seem harmless, despite the strange gray and black weapons they carry. The people smile happily when the strangers admire their spears made of reeds and the lovely little ornaments of gold they wear on their ears and nostrils. The people cannot understand why the yellow metal is so fascinating to them. To make them happy, they bring their strange guests many gifts—green parrots and bundles of precious cotton—in return for which they are given beautiful colored beads and small bells that make a delightful sound. These strangers, who completely hide themselves behind clothing, seem ill at ease with the nakedness of the people of the island, who do not cover their handsome bodies except for lavish painted designs of black, white, and red.

Then a man with a scarlet chest steps forward and tries to talk to the people, though he does not know how to speak properly and can only make strange noises and wave his arms in the air. Despite this strange behavior, the people smile at him respectfully. Hoping to teach him how to speak, they gesture across the landscape, and they tell the scarlet man that their island is called Guanahani. He seems to understand. Then the man points to himself and repeatedly tells the people his name. At this the people of the island begin to laugh. For this stranger has a most peculiar name!

Christopher Columbus.

CHAPTER 3

The AGE of EXPLORATION

> 66 I have found a continent, more full of people and animals than our Europe or Asia or Africa. 99
>
> Amerigo Vespucci, 1503

This portrait of the Italian explorer was painted in the sixteenth century.

A LEGENDARY LAND

Link to Our World

In what ways do we learn today about the world around us?

Focus on the Main Idea
As you read, think about ways early Europeans learned new information about the world around them.

Preview Vocabulary
saga
knoll
encounter
exploration
cartographer

Vikings wore bronze helmets like this one, made about A.D. 500, to protect themselves and to frighten their enemies.

The Tainos welcomed Christopher Columbus to the island of Guanahani (gwahn•uh•HAHN•ee) in 1492. Like most other Europeans of the time, Columbus knew little about Asia and Africa. He knew nothing about the Americas. Columbus thought he had sailed to Asia. He never knew that he had reached an unknown land.

STORIES OF AN UNKNOWN LAND

For a very long time, people had told stories about an unknown land in the ocean between Europe and Asia. The Irish said that a Catholic monk named Brendan had sailed to this land in the A.D. 500s. The Chinese told a story about Huishen, a Buddhist monk. He was said to have sailed to this unknown land at about the same time.

No one knows if these stories are true. Sailors from many different places, blown off course by stormy winds, may have landed on the coast of North or South America for hundreds of years. So many stories were told that it became hard to know what was fact and what was not.

Only one early landing has been proved true. It was made by a people known as the Vikings. The Vikings lived in a place that is today the countries of Norway, Sweden, and Denmark. From these lands the Vikings sailed west and built settlements in Iceland and Greenland.

The earliest stories about Vikings visiting an unknown land are found in Viking sagas (SAH•guhz). A **saga** is an adventure story that tells about the brave deeds

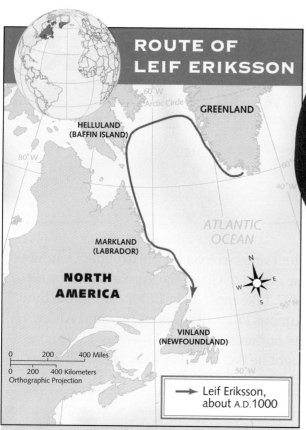

ROUTE OF LEIF ERIKSSON

GREENLAND

HELLULAND (BAFFIN ISLAND)

ATLANTIC OCEAN

MARKLAND (LABRADOR)

NORTH AMERICA

VINLAND (NEWFOUNDLAND)

0   200   400 Miles
0   200   400 Kilometers
Orthographic Projection

→ Leif Eriksson, about A.D. 1000

PLACE Leif Eriksson went to places he named Helluland, or "land of flat rocks," and Markland, or "forest land," before settling in Vinland.
■ What are the names used today for Helluland, Markland, and Vinland?

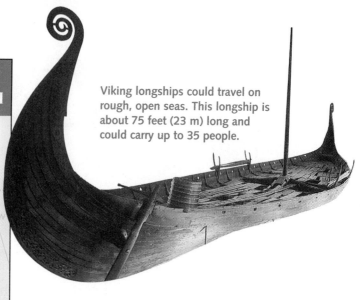

Viking longships could travel on rough, open seas. This longship is about 75 feet (23 m) long and could carry up to 35 people.

of people long ago. A story called the *Greenlanders' Saga* told of the travels of the Vikings from settlements in Greenland to the Americas. Archaeologists have since found evidence proving that much of the *Greenlanders' Saga* is true.

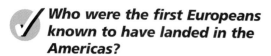
Who were the first Europeans known to have landed in the Americas?

THE GREENLANDERS' SAGA

About the year A.D. 1000, a Viking named Leif Eriksson (LAYV AIR•ik•suhn) hired a crew and set sail from Greenland, heading west. He was looking for a land he had heard about since he was a boy. It was a land "not

mountainous, well-timbered, and with small knolls upon it." A **knoll** is a small, round hill.

The land Eriksson reached was part of what is now Canada. Moving south along the coast, Eriksson soon found a place to spend the winter. The sailors went ashore and built houses of mud and grass. They called the settlement *Vinland*, or "vine land," for the many grape vines that grew there.

Eriksson and his crew returned to Greenland in the spring. During the next several years, the Vikings sailed many times to Vinland. They used it as a base for fishing and hunting.

Leif's brother Thorvald led one trip back to Vinland. When the Vikings arrived, they saw what looked like three knolls on the beach. They walked up to them and, instead, found nine people sleeping under boats. The Vikings attacked. They killed all but one person, who escaped. Later during that same trip, many boats filled with people came to Vinland and attacked the Vikings. Thorvald was wounded and later died.

After this **encounter**, or meeting, the Vikings soon ended their trips to North America. The stories of their adventures, however, were kept alive over the years in the *Greenlanders' Saga*.

What and where was Vinland?

EUROPEANS AND EXPLORATION

Five hundred years passed before Europeans returned to the Americas. During these years most Europeans did not want to go into unknown places. They believed the world outside the place they lived was very dangerous. They thought horrible sea monsters waited beneath the ocean, ready to swallow ships whole. They thought the sun was so hot in some places that it made the sea boil.

Another problem was that the Europeans' square-sailed ships were slow and could sail only with the wind. This would have made a long ocean trip very hard. Even worse, there were not many maps. Those that could be found were so different from one another that no one knew which were correct.

In any case few European rulers were willing to spend their time or money on sailing trips past their borders. Until the 1400s Europe had no strong central governments. Instead, it was made up of many small kingdoms and villages. Each was ruled by a noble. These nobles spent too much time fighting each other to care about **exploration**, or searching the unknown.

 **What kept Europeans from searching for unknown lands?**

THE KNOWN WORLD

In 1492, the year the Tainos greeted Christopher Columbus, a group of people in Germany paid Martin Behaim (BAY•hym) an amount equal to $75 to make a new kind of map. The map was in the shape of a ball. It was the first globe ever made in Europe. Behaim called it his "Earth apple." He made it from pieces of leather stitched together.

Behaim's globe showed what he and other European **cartographers**, or makers of maps,

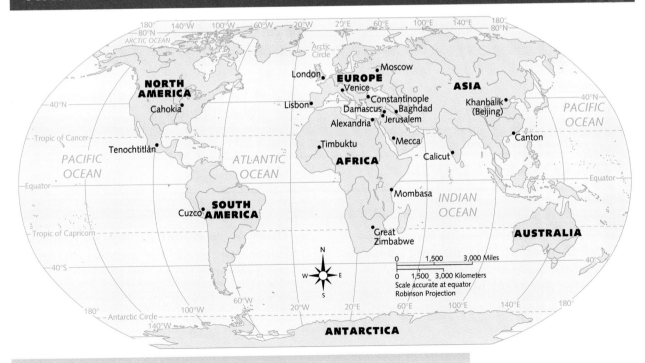

MAJOR CITIES OF THE 1400s

 HUMAN-ENVIRONMENT INTERACTIONS In the 1400s many people lived in cities, but most people had never heard of cities in faraway parts of the world.
■ Which of these cities have you heard of today?

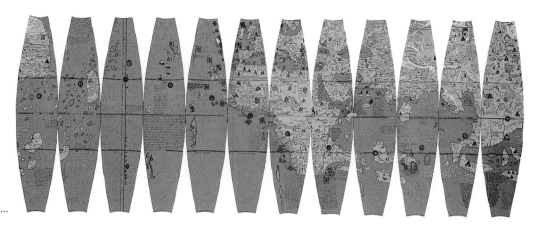

This is Martin Behaim's globe taken apart and laid flat. Which continents can you identify?

thought the Earth was like. Behaim wanted his globe to show the Earth as it really was, but he did not know enough to make it so. Behaim's globe showed the Earth much smaller than it really is. This made it seem as if sailing west from Europe to Asia would be easy. The globe made the trip look as if it would be only about 3,000 miles (4,828 km) long. Today's globes show that the trip is about 10,000 miles (16,093 km) long. More important, North and South America block the way. Behaim had no idea that these two continents were there. He did not know about Australia or Antarctica, either. And his globe showed Africa too small and the wrong shape.

But Behaim knew a lot more than other Europeans of his time. Some Europeans had heard about the riches in Asia. But few knew about China's cities, highways, and art. Most Europeans had never heard of the great African empires, such as Mali (MAH•lee) and Songhai (SAWNG•hy). They had no idea that the African city of Timbuktu (tim•buhk•TOO) was a center of learning, where people studied subjects from mathematics to medicine. And most Europeans knew nothing of the Chinooks, Hopis, Mandans, Iroquois, Cherokees, or other Indian cultures of North and South America. They didn't even know that two other continents lay across the Atlantic Ocean. Even the Atlantic Ocean, which the Europeans called the Ocean Sea or the Green Sea of Darkness, was largely unknown.

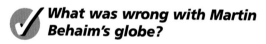 **What was wrong with Martin Behaim's globe?**

 LESSON 1 REVIEW

Check Understanding

1. **Recall the Facts**   What did most Europeans know about the Americas in the late 1400s?

2. **Focus on the Main Idea**   In what ways did early Europeans learn about the world around them?

Think Critically

3. **Personally Speaking**   Why do you think the Vikings attacked the people in Vinland?

4. **Think More About It**   Why do you think Europeans explained the unknown with ideas about monsters living in the seas?

Show What You Know

 Mapping Activity   Without looking at a map, draw the world and label the continents and oceans. Compare your drawing with the world map in this lesson. What lands or oceans are unknown to you?

BACKGROUND TO EUROPEAN EXPLORATION

Link to Our World

What conditions might lead people to explore the unknown today?

Focus on the Main Idea
As you read, think about the conditions that led Europeans to begin exploring unknown lands in the 1400s.

Preview Vocabulary
monarch   navigation
compass

Marco Polo liked to tell stories. He often told of the faraway places Europeans called Cathay and the Indies. Marco Polo had been to Cathay, as China was then called, and to the Indies, the islands off the China coast. He told of meeting Kublai Khan (KOO•bluh KAHN), China's ruler, and seeing amazing things—white bears, black stones that burned, and a place where night lasted all winter and day lasted all summer.

People laughed and called him Marco Millions because he told so many tales. Few Europeans had ever been to Asia, so they could not prove he was wrong. They just thought that the stories he told could not be true. But many were.

MARCO POLO

In 1271 Marco Polo left his home in Venice, Italy, to go to Asia with his father and uncle. Niccolò and Maffeo Polo were traders who first heard of the riches of this far-off land from fellow traders. Marco was just 17 years old when they set out. Four years later, after riding on horses and camels and walking thousands of miles through mountains and deserts, the Polos reached China. There they saw the palace of Kublai Khan. They described it as having walls "all covered with gold and silver and decorated with pictures of dragons and birds and horsemen and . . . scenes of battle." One hall was so big that "a meal might well be served there for more than 6,000 men." The Polos went on to other places in Asia, such as India and Persia. Marco never reached

Marco Polo's fantastic descriptions of Asia made many Europeans curious about life there. Many of Polo's stories were about what is today Beijing, China.

Kublai Khan, the ruler of China during Marco Polo's visit

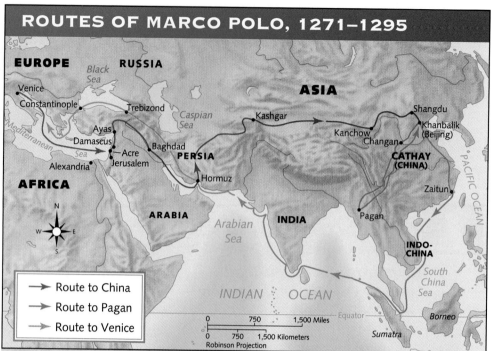

ROUTES OF MARCO POLO, 1271–1295

EUROPE

Venice
Constantinople

Black Sea

RUSSIA

Trebizond

Caspian Sea

ASIA

Kashgar

Shangdu

Khanbalik (Beijing)

Kanchow
Changan

CATHAY (CHINA)

Ayas
Damascus
Acre
Alexandria
Jerusalem
Baghdad

PERSIA

Hormuz

MOVEMENT Marco Polo spent 24 years traveling in Asia.
■ What lands did he visit on his way to China? on his way home to Venice?

Pagan

Zaitun

PACIFIC OCEAN

AFRICA

ARABIA

Arabian Sea

INDIA

INDO-CHINA

Route to China
Route to Pagan
Route to Venice

INDIAN OCEAN

0   750   1,500 Miles
0   750   1,500 Kilometers
Robinson Projection

Equator

South China Sea

Borneo

Sumatra

Japan, but he described it from stories he had heard. In Japan, he said, there was so much gold that whole palaces were built of it.

Twenty-four years after leaving Venice, Marco Polo returned home with his pockets full of jewels. In time someone wrote down

This drawing appears on a world map made in 1375. The map was based in part on Marco Polo's travels. The three people shown are Marco Polo, his father, and his uncle.

his stories. But it would be nearly 200 years before *The Travels of Marco Polo* would appear as a printed book. When it did, Europeans read it in amazement. Wanting to share in this great wealth, more and more traders took the long land route from Europe to Asia.

✔ **What information did Marco Polo take back to Europe?**

TRADE ROUTES TO THE EAST

For hundreds of years Europeans carried on a busy trade with people from Asia. The goods Europeans wanted most were gold, jewels, silk, perfumes, and spices—especially spices. In the days before refrigerators, Europeans prized spices such as pepper, cloves, cinnamon, and nutmeg. They used these spices to make their food taste better and to hide the bad taste of spoiled meat.

For most European traders, however, travel to Asia and back was too hard and took too much time. So instead of going to "the Far East," as they then called Asia, most Europeans traveled only part of the way. They went to cities in North Africa and Southwest Asia, which the Europeans called "the Middle East." The cities they went to included Alexandria (a•lig•ZAN•dree•uh), Constantinople (kahn•stan•tuhn•OH•puhl), Damascus (duh•MAS•kuhs), and Baghdad (BAG•dad). European traders exchanged their goods for goods that traders from the Middle East had gotten in Asia. The Europeans then made the journey back home, where they sold the Asian goods at the highest prices people were willing to pay. The goods cost a lot. But at least Europeans could get them.

Then suddenly the trade with Asia stopped. In 1453 the Turks, a people from a huge land called the Ottoman Empire, captured the city of Constantinople and took control of the Middle East. This closed the trade routes between Europe and Asia. There would be no more spices or gold or silk unless someone found another way to get to these treasures.

✓ **Why was trade with Asia important to Europeans?**

CHANGES IN EUROPE

By the time Constantinople was captured, many changes had taken place in Europe. One of the most important was that the lands ruled by warring nobles had become

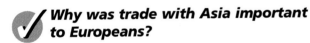

This Italian compass from 1580 is similar to those that Columbus and other early explorers used on their voyages.

countries. Portugal, Spain, France, and England were now ruled by **monarchs**, or kings and queens. Most monarchs were strong leaders who kept close watch over their countries and the countries' money.

Over the years Europeans also had made great advances in technology. They had learned how to build faster ships. They made a new kind of sail that allowed ships to sail against the wind. They also had made a better compass. A **compass** is an instrument used to find direction. It has a needle that always points north.

All of these changes helped set the stage for European exploration. And, with Constantinople closed to most traders, Europeans now had a good reason to set out into the unknown to find a new route to Asia.

✓ **What major changes set the stage for European exploration?**

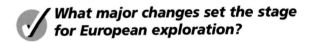

*W*hat?

The Compass

At about the same time in the 1100s, Chinese and European sailors discovered how to make and use a compass. The early compasses were just pieces of magnetic iron floating on straw or cork in a bowl of water. The magnetic iron always pointed north and south, following the direction of the Earth's magnetic field. By finding which way was north, sailors could then find any other direction. By the 1400s they were using a magnetic needle and had found other ways to make the compass more accurate.

PORTUGAL LEADS THE WAY

Portugal took the lead in the search to find the first water route to Asia. Portugal's monarch, King John, decided to spend as much money as was needed to reach that goal. The trade with Asia was important to him and his people, and they did not want to lose it. King John asked Henry, a prince of Portugal, to direct his country's search.

Prince Henry set up the first European school for training sailors in navigation (na•vuh•GAY•shuhn). **Navigation** is the study of how to plan and control the course of a ship. Because the rewards of finding a water route to Asia would be great, lessons taught at Prince Henry's school were kept secret. Anyone caught taking a map or chart from the school was sentenced to death.

Prince Henry later became known in the English-speaking world as Prince Henry the Navigator. He organized more than 50 voyages of exploration, but he did not go on any of them. For this reason he is sometimes called "the explorer who stayed at home."

Prince Henry (above left) led Portugal's search for a water route to Asia. During the late 1400s Europeans used a kind of ship called the caravel (above right) for exploration. With three masts and a triangular lateen sail, the caravel could sail against the wind.

Prince Henry thought that the most direct way to reach Asia by sea was to go south around Africa and then sail east. Under his direction dozens of Portuguese ships made their way down Africa's west coast. There they found new markets, where they could trade European goods for nuts, fruit, gold, and slaves.

Africans and others had been taking prisoners of war as slaves for hundreds of years. Often people sold these slaves to others. European traders quickly saw that they could make money by buying slaves in Africa and taking them to Europe to be sold as servants. By the time of Prince Henry's death in 1460, Portuguese traders were buying about 800 slaves from African traders each year.

At the same time, the search for a water route to Asia went on. Finally, in 1488,

Bartholomeu Dias (DEE•ahsh) sailed all the way around the southern tip of Africa—around what is today called the Cape of Good Hope. But fierce storms battered the ship. The sailors grew hungry, sick, and frightened. Dias wanted to sail on to India, but his sailors made him return home.

About ten years later Vasco da Gama (dah GA•muh) sailed around the Cape of Good Hope to India. Soon afterward he sailed back to Portugal with his ship full of spices. Da Gama had finally found a sea route to Asia, showing the way for others.

✓ **Who did King John ask to lead Portugal's drive to explore new lands?**

ROUTES OF DIAS AND DA GAMA

→ Dias, 1487–1488
→ Da Gama, 1497–1499

EUROPE
PORTUGAL
40°N   SPAIN
Lisbon
ASIA
AFRICA
INDIA
Cape Verde Islands
Calicut
Equator   0°
ATLANTIC OCEAN
INDIAN OCEAN
Tropic of Capricorn
N W E S
0   1,000   2,000 Miles
0   1,000 2,000 Kilometers
Robinson Projection
Cape of Good Hope
40°S
0°   40°E   80°E

MOVEMENT Both Dias and da Gama sailed around the Cape of Good Hope.
■ These voyages helped link the people of what continents?

L SSON 2 REVIEW

Check Understanding

1. **Recall the Facts** How did the capture of Constantinople affect Europeans?
2. **Focus on the Main Idea** What conditions led Europeans to explore in the 1400s?

Think Critically

3. **Cause and Effect** What effects did Marco Polo's travels have on Europeans?
4. **Think More About It** Why were strong monarchs important to European exploration?
5. **Personally Speaking** What places would you like to explore and why?

Show What You Know

Chart Activity Make a chart with four rows and two columns. Draw or glue a different spice in each of the four rows of the first column. In the next column, identify the spice, some of its uses today, and the place where it comes from. Present your chart to the class.

LEARN *with* **LITERATURE**

Focus on Exploration

I, Columbus
MY JOURNAL

1492-1493

edited by Peter Roop
and Connie Roop

illustrated by
Peter E. Hanson

Christopher Columbus had been a sailor almost all his life. Born and raised in Italy, he had sailed all over the known world—to England and the Canary Islands, across the Mediterranean Sea, and along the coast of Africa. He had read The Travels of Marco Polo again and again. He was fascinated by the stories he had heard of the wealth of Asia—especially the Indies.

For years Columbus had asked Spain's monarchs, King Ferdinand and Queen Isabella, to support his plan to reach Asia by sailing west instead of going around Africa. Columbus believed that sailing west was a quicker, more direct route.

Spain's king and queen, however, were more concerned about life at home. They believed that true unity would come to Spain only if it were a completely Catholic country. For this reason, they drove out the Muslims living in Spain. By 1492 the monarchs had claimed all the land that the Muslims once ruled. That same year they forced the Jews to leave Spain. Spain was now united under one religion and one government.

In 1492 Columbus once again asked Ferdinand and Isabella to support his voyage of exploration. He promised them great wealth and new lands. He also said he would take the Catholic faith to the people of Asia. This time, the king and queen agreed.

On August 3, 1492, Columbus set forth with 89 sailors and three ships—the Niña (NEEN•yuh), the Pinta (PEEN•tuh), and the Santa Maria. After two months at sea, Columbus made the following entries in his log, or ship's journal. As you read them, think about the challenges people face when exploring the unknown.

Wednesday, 10 October, 1492

Between day and night I made one hundred seventy-seven miles. I told the crew one hundred thirty-two miles, but they could stand it no longer. They grumbled and complained of the long voyage. I told them that, for better or worse, they had to complete the voyage. I cheered them on, telling them of the honors and rewards they would receive. I told them it was useless to complain. I had started to find the Indies and would continue until I had.

Thursday, 11 October, 1492

I sailed to the west-southwest. The crew of the *Pinta* spotted reeds and a small board. A stick was found that looks man-made, perhaps carved with an iron tool. These made the crew breathe easier; in fact, the men have even become cheerful. A special thanksgiving was offered to God for giving us renewed hope through the many signs of land.

About ten o'clock at night I saw a light to the west. It looked like a wax candle bobbing up and down. It had the same appearance as a light or torch belonging to fishermen or travellers who raised and lowered it. I am the first to admit I was so eager to find land I did not trust my own senses so I called Gutierrez and asked him to watch for the light. After a few moments, he too saw it. I then summoned Rodrigo Sanchez. He saw nothing, nor did any other member of the crew. It was such

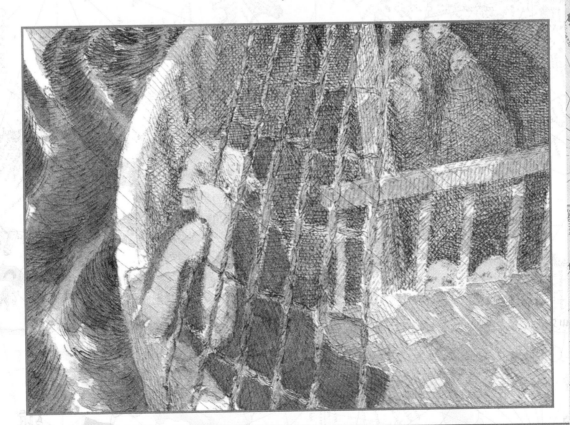

an uncertain thing I did not feel it was adequate proof of land. Then, at two hours after midnight, the *Pinta* fired a cannon, my signal for the sighting of land.

I now believe the light I saw was truly land. When we caught up with the *Pinta*, I learned Rodrigo de Triana, a seaman, was the first man to sight land. I lay-to till daylight. The land is about six miles to the west.

Friday, 12 October, 1492

At dawn we saw naked people. I went ashore in the ship's boat, armed, followed by Martin Pinzon, captain of the *Pinta*, and his brother Vincente Pinzon, captain of the *Niña*. I unfurled the royal banner and the captains brought the flags. After a prayer of thanksgiving, I ordered the captains to witness I was taking possession of this island for the King and Queen. To this island I gave the name San Salvador, in honor of our Blessed Lord. No sooner had we finished taking possession of the island than people came to the beach.

The people call this island Guanahani. Their speech is very fluent, although I do not understand any of it. They are a friendly people who bear no arms except for small spears. They have no iron. I showed one my sword, and through ignorance he grabbed it by the blade and cut himself.

I want the natives to develop a friendly attitude toward us because I know they are a people who can be converted to our Holy Faith more by love than by force. I think they can easily be made Christians, for they seem to have no religion. I will take six of them to Your Highnesses when I depart, in order that they may learn our language.

I gave some red caps to some and glass beads to others. They took great pleasure in this and became so friendly it was a marvel. They traded and gave everything they had with good will, but it seems to me that they have very little and are poor in everything. I warned my men to take nothing from the people without giving something in exchange.

This afternoon the people came swimming to our ships and in boats made from one log. They brought parrots, balls of cotton thread, spears, and many other things. We swapped them little glass beads and hawks' bells.

Saturday, 13 October, 1492

I have tried very hard to find out if there is gold here. I have seen a few natives wear a little piece of gold hanging from a hole made in the nose. By signs, if I interpret them correctly, I learned by going south I can find a king who possesses great containers of gold. I tried to find some natives to take me, but none want to make the journey.

This island is large and very flat. It is green, with many trees. There is a very large lagoon in the middle of the island. There are no mountains. It is a pleasure to gaze upon this place because it is all so green, and the weather is delightful.

In order not to lose time I want to set sail to see if I can find Japan.

Literature Review

1. What problems did Columbus face on his journey of exploration?
2. What did Columbus first think about the people of Guanahani? Compare this view with the Tainos' view of Columbus you read about at the beginning of this unit.
3. Suppose that you are a sailor on one of Columbus's ships. Write a journal entry for the day you finally see land and encounter new people.

HowTo

Use Latitude and Longitude

Why Is This Skill Important?

Just as the numbers of your home address describe where you live in your town, the numbers of your global address tell where your town is located on the Earth. The numbers in a global address stand for lines of latitude and lines of longitude. You can use these lines to help you describe the absolute, or exact, location of any place on the Earth.

Lines of Latitude

Mapmakers use a system of imaginary lines to form a grid on maps and globes. The lines that run east and west are the **lines of latitude**. Lines of latitude are also called **parallels** (PAIR•uh•lelz). This is because they are parallel, or always the same distance from each other. Parallel lines never meet.

Lines of latitude are measured in degrees north and south from the equator, which is labeled 0°, or *zero degrees.* The parallels north of the equator are marked *N* for *north latitude.* This means they are in the Northern Hemisphere. The parallels south of the equator are marked *S* for *south latitude.* This means they are in the Southern Hemisphere. The greater the number of degrees marking a parallel, the farther north or south of the equator it is.

Lines of Longitude

The lines that run north and south on a map are the **lines of longitude**, or **meridians**. Each meridian runs from the North Pole to the South Pole. Unlike parallels, which never meet, meridians meet at the poles. Meridians are farthest apart at the equator.

Meridians are numbered in much the same way as parallels are numbered. The meridian marked 0° is called the **prime meridian**. It runs north and south through Greenwich, near the

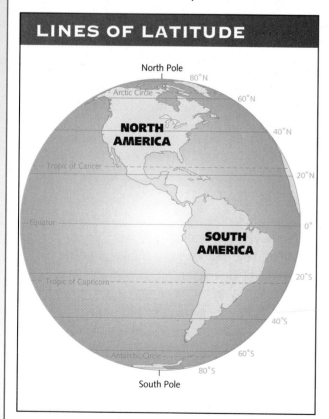

LINES OF LATITUDE

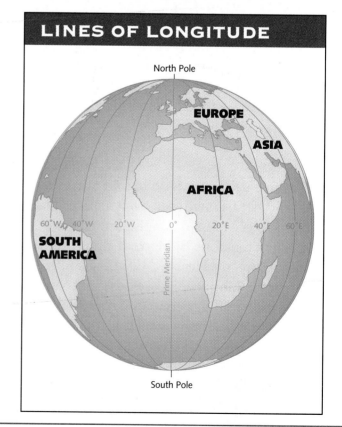

LINES OF LONGITUDE

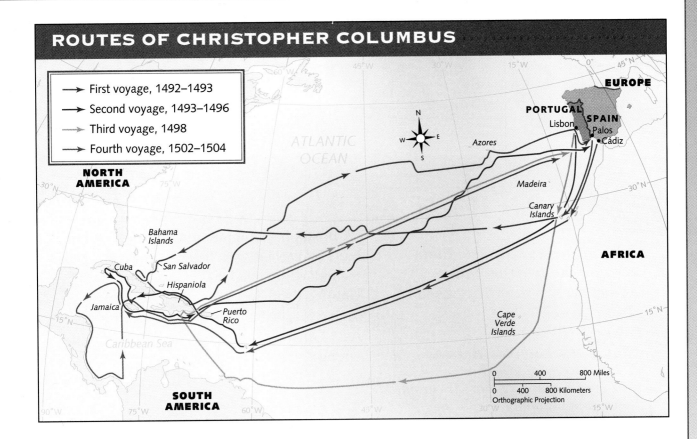

ROUTES OF CHRISTOPHER COLUMBUS

→ First voyage, 1492–1493
→ Second voyage, 1493–1496
→ Third voyage, 1498
→ Fourth voyage, 1502–1504

city of London in Britain. Lines of longitude to the west of the prime meridian are marked *W* for *west longitude*. They are in the Western Hemisphere. The meridians to the east of prime meridian are marked *E* for *east longitude*. They are in the Eastern Hemisphere.

Understand the Process

The map above shows the four voyages of Christopher Columbus to the Americas. The map has a grid of lines of latitude and longitude drawn over it. The crossing lines of latitude and longitude make it possible to describe absolute location.

Like most maps, this one does not show every parallel and meridian. Every fifteenth parallel is shown from 15°N to 45°N, and every fifteenth meridian is shown from 0° to 90°W.

Now that you know about lines of latitude and longitude, you can use them to find some locations. At either side of the map, find 30°N. At the top or bottom, find 15°W. Use a finger of each hand to trace these lines to the point where they cross each other. The Canary Islands

are not far from this point. So you can say that the location of the Canary Islands is near 30°N, 15°W.

Look for the latitude and longitude that describe the location of Columbus's first landing in the Americas. The closest parallels are 15°N and 30°N. The closest meridian is 75°W. So you can say that the location of the first landing is about 22°N, 75°W.

Think and Apply

Think about what you just learned about latitude and longitude. Use the map to answer these questions.

1. What line of latitude is closest to Hispaniola?
2. What line of longitude is closest to the Bahama Islands?
3. What islands are located near 15°N, 30°W?
4. Which location is farther north, 45°N, 60°W or 30°N, 90°W?
5. Which location is farther east, 45°N, 60°W or 30°N, 90°W?

LESSON 4

EARLY VOYAGES OF EXPLORATION

Link to Our World

In what ways can new facts change the way we think about events that happened in the past?

Focus on the Main Idea
In what ways did the facts gathered by later explorers change how people thought about the voyages of Columbus?

Preview Vocabulary

conclusion   expedition
isthmus   scurvy

Explorers used an astrolabe (AS•truh•layb) to help determine their location, based on the positions of the stars.

Christopher Columbus never knew that he had not reached Asia. Believing he had reached the Indies, he called the people he met Indians. Until his death in 1506, Columbus kept on saying that he had found a new water route to Asia. Other explorers, however, proved him wrong.

VESPUCCI CHALLENGES COLUMBUS

News of Columbus's voyages spread quickly through Europe. It stirred an excitement not felt since the days of Marco Polo. Soon every monarch in Europe wanted to send ships across the Ocean Sea to find the great riches of the Indies.

In 1497 an Italian named Giovanni Caboto sailed across the Ocean Sea on a voyage paid for by England. Caboto landed in present-day Newfoundland, which is part of Canada. When he returned to England, however, Caboto told everyone that he had found Cathay, the land of the Great Kublai Khan. The English made Caboto a hero. They even gave him an English name, John Cabot.

But not everyone in Europe really believed that Columbus had found the Indies or that Caboto had landed in China. Amerigo Vespucci (uh•MAIR•ih•goh veh•SPOO•chee) from the Italian city-state of Florence was one of those who did not believe it. In 1499, under orders from the king of Spain, Vespucci sailed to a place south of where Columbus had landed. Two years later the king of Portugal sent Vespucci on another voyage. This time he sailed down the coast of South America from present-day Venezuela to Argentina.

On these voyages Vespucci looked for signs that he had reached Asia, as Columbus believed this land to be. Like Columbus, Vespucci had read books by Marco Polo and others who had visited Asia. Yet Vespucci saw nothing that fit what Marco Polo and the others had seen. He saw no cities of gold and marble. He saw no people wearing jewels and cloth of gold.

Something else didn't make sense. Years earlier Vespucci had studied the work of Claudius Ptolemy (TAH•luh•mee), an astronomer in ancient Egypt. From Ptolemy's work, Vespucci had learned that the Earth was larger and Asia was smaller than most people had thought. If Asia were as far east as Columbus claimed, it would have to cover half the Earth. Vespucci knew that could not be true.

Vespucci also thought about the distance he had traveled. Most sailors of the time could judge how far north or south they had sailed by using instruments such as the cross-staff. But they still had trouble measuring how far east or west they had sailed. Vespucci had found a new way of measuring distances east and west. Using his new way, Vespucci figured he had sailed 6,500 miles (10,460 km) from Europe. This figure was more than three times as far as Columbus thought he had sailed.

Based on all the information he now had, Vespucci formed a conclusion. A **conclusion** is a decision or idea reached by thoughtful study. Vespucci concluded that he and Columbus and Caboto had not sailed to Asia. He concluded that the land they had found had to be another continent—the "new

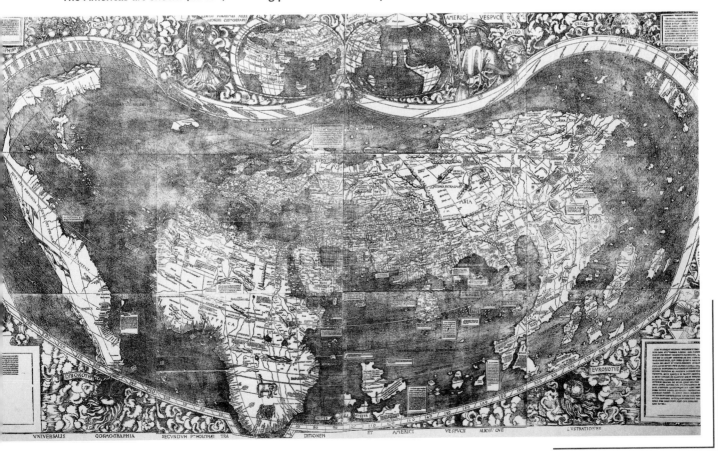

This map, drawn by Martin Waldseemüller, shows Ptolemy (top left) and Vespucci (top right). The Americas are shown (far left) as a long piece of land in two parts.

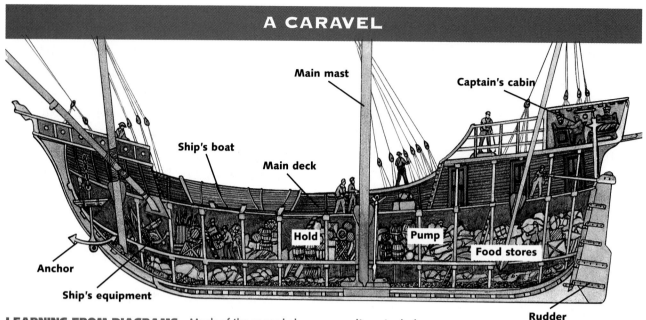

A CARAVEL

Main mast

Captain's cabin

Ship's boat

Main deck

Anchor

Hold

Pump

Food stores

Ship's equipment

Rudder

LEARNING FROM DIAGRAMS Much of the space below a caravel's main deck was used to store equipment, food, and other supplies. At night, sailors slept in the open on the main deck. A sailor steered the ship by swinging its large, flat rudder to the left or right.
■ What member of the crew had separate quarters?

world" that some Europeans thought might be there.

Soon a German cartographer named Martin Waldseemüller (VAHLT•zay•mool•er) drew a map of the new continent, using Vespucci's findings. He decided to name the new land for Amerigo Vespucci. In 1507 *America* appeared on a map for the first time.

 **What conclusion did Vespucci form?**

BALBOA REACHES THE PACIFIC

On September 25, 1513, a group of explorers made the hard climb up a mountain. It was on the west coast of what today is called the Isthmus of Panama. An **isthmus** (IHS•muhs) is a narrow strip of land that connects two larger land areas. The Isthmus of Panama connects the continents we know today as North America and South America. The group of explorers, made up of Spanish and African soldiers and Native American

guides, had landed on the east coast and walked west until they reached the mountain.

Moving ahead of the rest, Vasco Núñez de Balboa (NOON•yes day bal•BOH•ah) quickly climbed the last few feet to the mountain peak. Before him lay a huge blue sea. Falling to his knees, Balboa said that the sea—what would later be called the Pacific Ocean—belonged to Spain. A few days later Balboa and the others reached the ocean and explored the coast.

Columbus had believed that Asia stretched from near the eastern edge of Europe all the way around the world. He thought that if he sailed west from Europe across a very narrow Atlantic Ocean, he would reach it. Now Balboa had come upon a huge ocean on the western side of what Columbus had said was Asia. This proved that Vespucci was right. Columbus was wrong. He had not reached Asia but had reached a new continent instead.

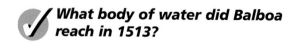 **What body of water did Balboa reach in 1513?**

AROUND THE WORLD

On a September day in 1519, cannons boomed as five ships and 242 sailors set out from Spain into the Atlantic. Ferdinand Magellan (muh•JEH•luhn), a Portuguese explorer, led the fleet. Magellan had convinced the king of Spain to pay for his expedition (ek•spuh•DIH•shuhn). An **expedition** is a journey taken for a special reason. The reason for Magellan's expedition was to find a way to reach Asia by sailing west around the Americas.

Magellan sailed to what is now Brazil and then south along South America's eastern coast. For months he sailed up rivers into the middle of the continent, hoping to find one that would go all the way to the ocean on the other side. But he never did, and each time he sailed the rivers back to the coast. As the ships fought their way through huge, pounding waves and against howling winds, one ship and many of its crew were lost.

Finally, in the fall of 1520, the remaining ships sailed through what is now called the Strait of Magellan, near the southern tip of South America. The sailors found themselves in the same ocean Balboa had seen. Magellan named it *Pacific*, which means "peaceful," because it seemed so still and quiet compared with the Atlantic.

For more than three months, the ships sailed across the Pacific. As the months passed, the small amount of food that was left quickly spoiled. There was no place to stop for fresh food. One sailor later said this:

> ❝We ate biscuit which was no longer biscuit, but powder of biscuit swarming with worms, for they had eaten the good. We drank yellow water that had been putrid for many days.❞

ROUTES OF VESPUCCI, BALBOA, AND MAGELLAN

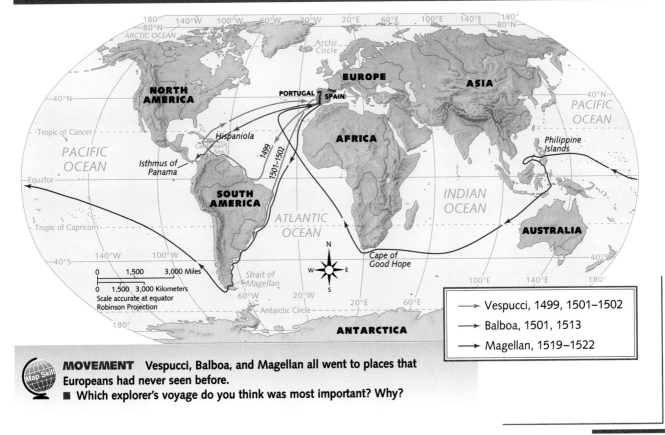

MOVEMENT Vespucci, Balboa, and Magellan all went to places that Europeans had never seen before.
■ Which explorer's voyage do you think was most important? Why?

When the food was gone, the sailors ate rats, sawdust, and leather. Some died of hunger. Others died of **scurvy**, a sickness caused by not getting enough Vitamin C, which is found in fresh fruit and vegetables. As the bodies of more and more dead sailors were thrown into the ocean, sharks began to follow the ships.

In March 1521 the ships reached what are today called the Philippine Islands. Magellan and his crew stayed in the Philippines for several weeks. Then, on April 27, while taking part in a battle between the people of one of the islands, Magellan was killed. His crew soon sailed for home. In September 1522, three years after the 242 sailors had set out, the 18 who were left finally returned to Spain.

One of Magellan's ships had sailed around the world. What Columbus had dreamed of was true. Europeans could reach Asia by sailing west. But first they had to go around the Americas and across the Pacific Ocean in what proved to be a long and dangerous trip.

 What did Magellan's crew accomplish?

Magellan used instruments for navigation. However, like most explorers of his time, he made mistakes in figuring distances. He and other explorers often found places by accident.

 # LESSON 4 REVIEW

Check Understanding

1. **Recall the Facts**   For whom was America named?
2. **Focus on the Main Idea**   In what ways did the facts gathered by Vespucci, Balboa, and Magellan change people's ideas about the place where Columbus landed?

Think Critically

3. **Think More About It**   How do you think the findings of Vespucci, Balboa, and Magellan affected the Europeans' goal of reaching Asia?
4. **Cause and Effect**   In what ways did food supplies affect early expeditions?

5. **Personally Speaking**   How might you have reacted to the hardships of sailing around the world with Magellan?

Show What You Know

Mobile Activity   You are responsible for ordering the supplies for a voyage like Magellan's. The ship will be on the ocean for a month, with no refrigeration. Find pictures in magazines or newspapers of foods and other supplies you would take aboard. Cut out the pictures and paste them on cutouts of a sailing ship. Make a mobile with your pictures. Hang your mobile in the classroom.

How To

Form a Logical Conclusion

Why Is This Skill Important?

A conclusion is a decision or idea reached by thoughtful study. A logical conclusion is one that is thought out carefully, based on the evidence.

To form a logical conclusion, you must be able to separate facts from opinions. A **fact** is a statement that can be proved true. An **opinion** is a statement that tells what a person thinks or believes. Unlike a fact, an opinion cannot be proved true. To form a logical conclusion you also must be able to put new facts together with those you already know. This will help you see why things happened in the past, as well as why things happen in your own life today.

Remember What You Have Read

You have read that Christopher Columbus formed the conclusion that he had landed in

Amerigo Vespucci, using an astrolabe

Asia. But Columbus was wrong. When Amerigo Vespucci looked at the facts and gathered new information, he formed a different conclusion—that Columbus had landed on another continent.

Think about the explorers' conclusions as you answer the following questions:

1. Why did Columbus form the conclusion that he had landed in Asia?
2. What evidence did Vespucci have that supported Columbus's conclusion?
3. What evidence did Vespucci have that did not support Columbus's conclusion?
4. How did Vespucci get his new information?
5. What conclusion did Vespucci form about where Columbus had landed?

Understand the Process

There are many ways to form a conclusion. One way is to follow these steps, as Vespucci might have done.

- Form a question about the subject or the situation, such as *Did Columbus land in Asia?*
- Think about evidence you already have that might help you answer the question.
- Gather new evidence that might help you answer the question.
- Form a conclusion based on the strongest evidence.

Think and Apply

Write a list of clues that would lead to a certain place in your school, such as the cafeteria, the office, or the library. Read the clues one by one to a partner. Can your partner form a conclusion about where the mystery place is, based on only one or two clues? Why is it important to have as many facts as possible before reaching a conclusion?

BUILDING CITIZENSHIP

CONNECT MAIN IDEAS

Use this organizer to show that you understand how the chapter's main ideas are connected. Copy the organizer onto a separate sheet of paper. Then complete it by writing three examples to support each main idea.

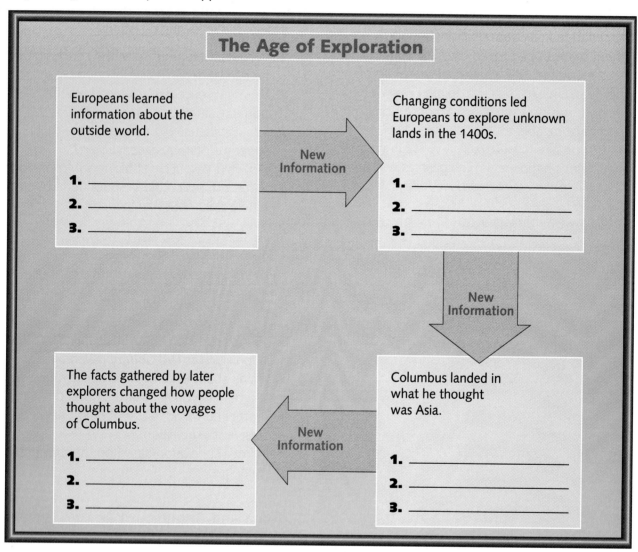

The Age of Exploration

Europeans learned information about the outside world.

1. _____
2. _____
3. _____

New Information

Changing conditions led Europeans to explore unknown lands in the 1400s.

1. _____
2. _____
3. _____

New Information

The facts gathered by later explorers changed how people thought about the voyages of Columbus.

1. _____
2. _____
3. _____

New Information

Columbus landed in what he thought was Asia.

1. _____
2. _____
3. _____

WRITE MORE ABOUT IT

1. **Write a Saga** Imagine that you are a Viking who has traveled with your family to Vinland. You are living in a base camp for the summer, hunting and fishing. Write a short saga about your adventures.

2. **Write a Ship's Log Entry** Imagine that you are one of the surviving members of Ferdinand Magellan's crew. Write an entry in the ship's log, giving your thoughts and feelings as you near the end of your journey.

USE VOCABULARY

Write a term from this list to complete each of the sentences that follow.

compass   isthmus
conclusion   knoll
encounter   navigation
exploration   scurvy

1. A small round hill is sometimes called a _____.

2. An _____ is a meeting.

3. Searching for unknown lands is called _____.

4. A _____ is a tool with a needle inside that always points north.

5. _____ is the planning and directing of a ship's course.

6. A _____ is a decision or idea reached by thoughtful study.

7. An _____ is a narrow strip of land that connects two larger land areas.

8. _____ is an illness caused by not eating enough fresh fruit.

CHECK UNDERSTANDING

1. Who was Leif Eriksson?

2. How did Marco Polo's reports about his travels affect people living in Europe?

3. What goods from Asia did Europeans want to buy?

4. What did Columbus hope to find when he began his expedition in 1492?

5. What conclusion did Vespucci draw about the lands that he, Columbus, and Caboto had reached?

6. What does the Isthmus of Panama connect?

7. What did Balboa reach in 1513?

8. What did Magellan's crew accomplish?

THINK CRITICALLY

1. **Think More About It**   Why do you think the maps and charts from Prince Henry's school were guarded so closely?

2. **Cause and Effect**   How did the fall of Constantinople affect trade between Europe and Asia?

3. **Past to Present**   What unknown places might people be interested in exploring today?

APPLY SKILLS

How to Use Latitude and Longitude Look at the map on page 117. Use the grid formed by the lines of latitude and the lines of longitude to describe the following locations: the Cape of Good Hope, the Strait of Magellan, and the part of South America that Vespucci first reached in 1499.

How to Form a Logical Conclusion   How did historians form the conclusion that the Vikings were the first Europeans to visit North America? Use encyclopedias or other books from the library to find information about the Viking settlement in Vinland. What evidence supports the historians' conclusion?

READ MORE ABOUT IT

Accidental Explorers: Surprises and Side Trips in the History of Discovery by Rebecca Stefoff. Oxford. A look at the many important discoveries made by chance in the Americas and around the world.

The Discoverers of America by Harold Faber. Scribner's. The author describes the voyages of the Vikings and other early explorers.

Forgotten Voyager: The Story of Amerigo Vespucci by Ann Fitzpatrick Alper. Carolrhoda. This story tells of the travels of the explorer for whom America was named.

ENCOUNTERS in the AMERICAS

> 66 We are crushed to the ground;
> we lie in ruins.
> There is nothing but grief
> and suffering in Mexico
> and Tlatelolco,
> where once we saw beauty
> and valor. 99
>
> Unknown Aztec poet,
> about 1523

A European artist painted this portrait of the Aztec emperor Motecuhzoma.

THE CONQUEST OF THE
AZTECS and INCAS

Link to Our World

What might cause people of different cultures to fight with one another today?

Focus on the Main Idea
Read to learn what led to fighting between the Spanish and the Aztecs and the Spanish and the Incas during the 1500s.

Preview Vocabulary
conquistador
civil war

Quetzalcoatl was sometimes shown as a snake with feathers. He was believed to control land and sky.

After Columbus, others from Spain—Balboa and Magellan among them—went on to explore the Americas. Driven by their desire for gold and other riches, they pushed deep into North and South America. This was new land to the Spanish. But it was home to the people already living there.

FALL OF THE AZTECS

The year was 1519, and the Aztec king Motecuhzoma (maw•tay•kwah•SOH•mah) stood at his palace at Tenochtitlán, looking out at the night sky. The king watched for signs that would tell him what was to happen.

In the last two years, some odd things had taken place in the grand Aztec capital. The Earth had shaken. The lake had flooded the city. Comets had been seen in the sky. Aztec priests had studied these natural wonders and decided they were signs that the Aztec Empire was coming to an end.

One day people came to the palace, bringing news of another strange happening. Men who had white skin and black beards and who rode deer without antlers were coming to Tenochtitlán. The news startled the king. The Aztecs believed that the light-skinned god Quetzalcoatl (keht•zahl•koo•WAH•tahl) would one day return to rule his people. Could it be that this god of old was coming back?

The person the Aztecs thought might be Quetzalcoatl was Hernando Cortés (kawr•TEZ). He had been sent by the Spanish government to look for gold. With Cortés were more than 500 soldiers, 14 cannons, 16 horses, and several dogs. The horses were the first in the Americas for thousands of years.

Cortés had heard stories about the great wealth of the Aztec Empire. Before setting out, he told his soldiers:

> 66We are waging a just and good war which will bring us fame. Almighty God, in whose name it will be waged, will give us victory. I offer you great rewards, although they will be wrapped about with great hardships. If you do not abandon me, as I shall not abandon you, I shall make you the richest men who ever crossed the seas.99

In the spring of 1519, Cortés landed on the east coast of Mexico. He defeated the Indians there, then set out for Tenochtitlán. The journey covered 200 miles (322 km)—

from the tropical coast, through snowy mountains, and into the Valley of Mexico.

After marching for 83 days, Cortés and his soldiers, joined by large numbers of the Aztecs' Indian enemies, finally reached Tenochtitlán. Thinking that Cortés might be Quetzalcoatl, Motecuhzoma welcomed him, offering housing and gifts of gold. When they saw the gold, the Spanish were overjoyed. They "grinned like little beasts and pounded each other with delight," the Aztecs reported.

Cortés took Motecuhzoma prisoner. Within two years the Aztec ruler was dead and his capital city was in ruins. Spanish weapons and European diseases, which were new to the American Indians, had destroyed the Aztec civilization.

Conquering the Aztecs won for Cortés both wealth and glory. He and his soldiers captured the Aztecs' treasures. Among the Europeans they soon became known as **conquistadors** (kahn•KEES•tah•doors), the Spanish word for "conquerors."

Spain now ruled Mexico. On the ashes of the Aztec capital, the Spanish built Mexico City. Mexico City became the capital of Spain's new empire in the Americas.

✔ **How did the Spanish acquire Mexico for their empire?**

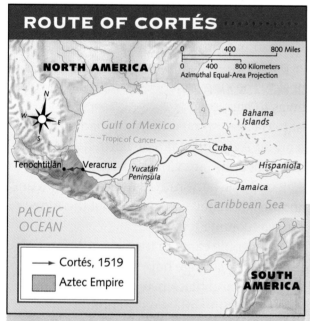

ROUTE OF CORTÉS

NORTH AMERICA

0 400 800 Miles
0 400 800 Kilometers
Azimuthal Equal-Area Projection

Bahama Islands

Gulf of Mexico
~Tropic of Cancer~

Cuba

Tenochtitlán • Veracruz
Yucatán Peninsula

Hispaniola

Jamaica

Caribbean Sea

PACIFIC OCEAN

→ Cortés, 1519
☐ Aztec Empire

SOUTH AMERICA

LOCATION Cortés sailed west from Cuba to what is now Mexico.
■ How did the location of Tenochtitlán make it hard for Cortés to conquer the Aztecs?

Motecuhzoma (seated at left) meets with Cortés (seated at right) in Tenochtitlán. With Cortés is Malintzin, an Aztec who helped translate for the Spaniards. ➡

Tenochtitlan.

ROUTE OF PIZARRO

Panama

ATLANTIC
OCEAN

Quito

Amazon River

Equator

Tumbes

Chachapoyas

SOUTH
AMERICA

Cajamarca

Lima

Machu Picchu
Cuzco

Nazca

Lake Titicaca

Tiahuanaco

0   400   800 Miles

Potosi

0   400   800 Kilometers
Modified Chambers Trimetric Projection

Tropic of Capricorn

PACIFIC
OCEAN

→ Pizarro,
   1531–1533

   Inca Empire

   Inca road

⬆ In this drawing the Inca ruler Atahuallpa is being carried to meet Pizarro. Like the Aztecs, some Incas thought their Spanish visitor was a god.

MOVEMENT Pizarro traveled south from Panama to the Inca capital of Cuzco (KOOS•koh). Along the way he found stone-paved roads built by the Incas.
■ Why do you think these roads were important to the Incas?

FALL OF THE INCAS

Other conquistadors soon followed Cortés to the Americas. Sixty-year-old Francisco Pizarro (pee•ZAR•oh) was one of them. He had heard stories of an Indian people whose empire was far richer and more powerful than that of the Aztecs. These people were called the Incas.

In 1531 Pizarro and a group of 180 Spanish and African soldiers sailed from Panama and landed on the west coast of South America. For the next two years, they wandered about the Andes Mountains, stealing gold and riches from the people they found. Then one day they came across a large Inca camp.

One of Pizarro's soldiers described the camp as "beautiful." He said there were so many tents that the sight filled the Spanish with fear. "We never thought the Indians could occupy such a proud position, nor so many tents, so well set up. It filled us all . . . with confusion and fear. But we dared not show it."

The Spanish would soon learn that the empire of the Incas was even larger and more powerful than they had heard. It had 9 million people and covered parts of the present-day countries of Peru, Ecuador, Bolivia, Argentina, and Chile.

But when Pizarro and his soldiers arrived, the Inca Empire was not at peace. It was being torn in two by a civil war. A **civil war** is a war between people of the same country. The war was being fought between the followers of two brothers, Atahuallpa (ah•tah•WAHL•pah) and Huascar (WAHS•kar). Both said they had the right to the throne. The war finally ended when Atahuallpa killed his brother and became emperor. But the fighting had weakened the empire.

Offering friendship to the new emperor, Pizarro invited Atahuallpa to the Spanish camp. The emperor arrived the next day with several thousand of his people. They carried him on a golden throne lined with parakeet feathers. Around his neck he wore a necklace

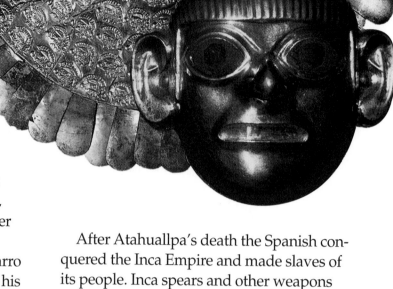

This Inca ceremonial collar (right) and mask (far right) are made of solid gold. The art of the Incas made the Spanish even more eager to capture Inca treasures.

of giant green emeralds. He wore gold ornaments in his hair.

Pizarro's priest asked Atahuallpa to give up his own religion and accept Christianity. He also asked him to accept the king of Spain as his master.

When Atahuallpa refused, Pizarro took the emperor prisoner. To buy his freedom, Atahuallpa promised Pizarro enough silver and gold to fill a whole room. Atahuallpa kept his promise, but Pizarro did not. Pizarro took the silver and gold and then ordered his soldiers to kill the Inca emperor.

With the loss of their leader, the Incas lost heart. One Inca wrote about how they felt:

66 He with the heart of a puma,
The adroitness of a fox,
They killed as if he were a llama. 99

After Atahuallpa's death the Spanish conquered the Inca Empire and made slaves of its people. Inca spears and other weapons were no match for Spanish guns and crossbows. For the Spanish, the conquest brought riches and power. But for the Incas, the encounter ended a once-great civilization.

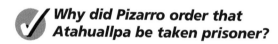 **Why did Pizarro order that Atahuallpa be taken prisoner?**

LESSON 1 REVIEW

Check Understanding

1. **Recall the Facts** What was the goal of the conquistadors Cortés and Pizarro?
2. **Focus on the Main Idea** What was the major reason for the fighting between the Spanish and the Aztecs and the Incas?

Think Critically

3. **Explore Viewpoints** Compare the viewpoints of Pizarro and Atahuallpa about who should control land in the Americas. List the reasons each leader might have given to support his ideas.

4. **Past to Present** Why do some countries today try to conquer other countries? Compare and contrast these reasons with the reasons the Spanish conquistadors had for conquering the Aztecs and the Incas.

Show What You Know

Journal Writing Activity
Imagine that you are a soldier traveling with Cortés or Pizarro. Write a journal entry that describes what you see as you arrive in the Aztec or Inca Empire.

THE SEARCH FOR GOLD and RICHES

THE SEARCH FOR

Link to Our World

What are some reasons people take actions that involve risk and danger?

Focus on the Main Idea
As you read, think about why the Spanish risked the unknown to explore North America in the 1500s.

Preview Vocabulary
grant   claim
mainland   desertion
rumor

Eager to add to their growing empire, Spain's rulers wanted conquistadors to explore the lands north of Mexico. The Spanish king offered **grants**, or gifts of money, to explorers who would lead expeditions into the northern continent. Believing that North America held riches far greater than the treasures already taken in Middle America and South America, many were quick to set out.

THE SPANISH MOVE INTO FLORIDA

One of the explorers who received a grant was Juan Ponce de León (PAHN•say day lay•OHN). Ponce de León had sailed with Columbus on his second voyage. He lived for a time on the island of Hispaniola (ees•pah•NYOH•lah), which today is made up of the countries of Haiti and the Dominican Republic. He later explored and conquered what has become Puerto Rico and was named governor of the island. There he heard a story about a fountain whose waters were said to make old people young again. This "Fountain of Youth" was supposed to be on an island to the north called Bimini (BIH•muh•nee). Ponce de León decided to find it.

He sailed north but did not find Bimini. Instead, in April 1513 he landed on the **mainland**, or the main part of the continent, near what is now the city of St. Augustine. He named the mainland *La Florida*, the Spanish word for "filled with flowers." When he tried to start a settlement in Florida, the Calusa Indians, who

A conquistador's helmet

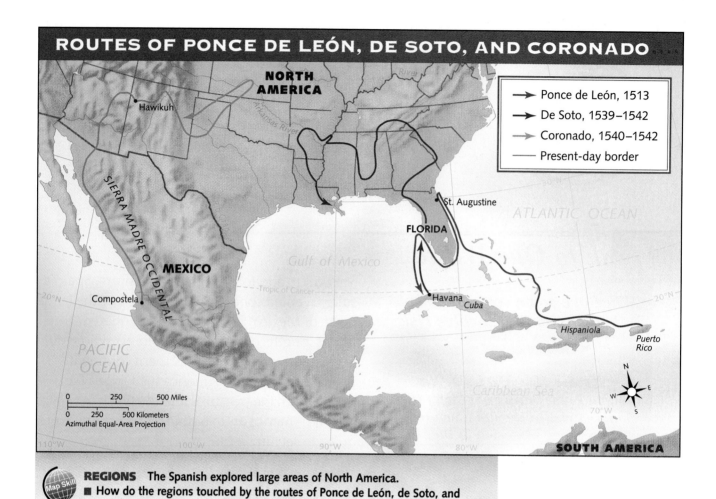

ROUTES OF PONCE DE LEÓN, DE SOTO, AND CORONADO

NORTH AMERICA

Hawikuh

SIERRA MADRE OCCIDENTAL

MEXICO

Compostela

PACIFIC OCEAN

Arkansas River

Gulf of Mexico

Tropic of Cancer

St. Augustine

FLORIDA

Havana

Cuba

Hispaniola

Puerto Rico

ATLANTIC OCEAN

Caribbean Sea

SOUTH AMERICA

→ Ponce de León, 1513
→ De Soto, 1539–1542
→ Coronado, 1540–1542
— Present-day border

0   250   500 Miles
0   250   500 Kilometers
Azimuthal Equal-Area Projection

20°N   20°N

N W E S

70°W

110°W   100°W   90°W   80°W

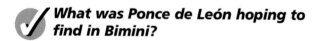

REGIONS The Spanish explored large areas of North America.
■ How do the regions touched by the routes of Ponce de León, de Soto, and Coronado reflect the Spanish culture today?

lived there, attacked. Ponce de León was wounded and died.

Though he did not discover a fountain of youth, Ponce de León was the first Spaniard to set foot on what is today the United States. Others soon followed.

> **What was Ponce de León hoping to find in Bimini?**

THE SEVEN CITIES OF GOLD

Stories about treasure sparked more expeditions into the lands north of Mexico. These stories were only **rumors**—stories without proof. But many people believed them. One of the most exciting was about seven cities believed to be built all of gold.

In 1536 four ragged men arrived in Mexico City. They were Álvar Núñez Cabeza de Vaca (kah•BAY•sah day VAH•kuh), two other Spaniards, and a North African named Estéban (ehs•TAY•bahn). They had lived through a shipwreck off the coast of what is today Texas. During their long journey to Mexico, they had heard from the people they met along the way about seven cities rich in gold, silver, and jewels.

The four men told their story to Spanish leaders in Mexico City, who listened carefully. In 1539 the leaders sent Estéban and a priest named Marcos de Niza (day NEE•sah) to see if the rumor was true. During the expedition Estéban was killed by Zuni people who believed he had been sent by an enemy tribe. But de Niza returned safely, saying he had seen a golden city.

After hearing de Niza's report, Francisco Vásquez de Coronado (kawr•oh•NAH•doh) and more than 1,000 soldiers set out to find the seven cities. They moved north out of Mexico and through the present-day states of Arizona, New Mexico, Texas, and Oklahoma into Kansas. They marched through the Zuni village of Hawikuh (hah•wee•KOO) and other Pueblo towns, but nowhere did they find any trace of the "Seven Cities of Gold." Bitterly disappointed, Coronado began the long trip home. The route he took would later become the Santa Fe Trail.

In June 1542 Coronado arrived back in Mexico with only 100 of his soldiers. Some had died. Others had run away. Coronado had not found the Seven Cities of Gold. But he had claimed many new lands for Spain, declaring that Spain owned them.

✓ **What were the results of Coronado's expedition?**

DE SOTO MOVES AHEAD

About the same time Coronado started his expedition, the king of Spain gave Hernando de Soto (day SOH•toh) a grant for an expedition to the northern continent. De Soto put together an army of 600 soldiers and sailed to the west coast of Florida in May 1539. The conquistadors moved north and reached what is now Georgia by winter. Finding no gold there, they went on through parts of present-day South Carolina and North Carolina, into the Smoky Mountains of Tennessee, and south into Alabama.

De Soto encountered many Indian peoples during his expedition. These encounters often ended in death, with de Soto's soldiers attacking the Indians in search of treasures. One of the worst battles took place in Alabama.

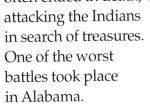

This horseshoe (right) is from de Soto's expedition of 1539. De Soto and his men (below), along with other Spanish explorers, brought horses to the Americas. What might Native Americans have thought when they first saw people riding horses?

SPANISH CONQUISTADORS

EXPLORER	DATES OF EXPLORATION	AREA EXPLORED
Juan Ponce de León	1513	Puerto Rico and Florida
Hernando Cortés	1519–1536	Eastern and central Mexico and California
Francisco Pizarro	1531–1535	The western coast of South America
Hernando de Soto	1539–1542	Southeastern North America and the Mississippi River
Francisco Vásquez de Coronado	1540–1542	Southwestern North America

LEARNING FROM TABLES This table lists several Spanish conquistadors who explored North America during the early 1500s.
■ What lands did each conquistador explore?

There the Spanish encountered some of the descendants of the Mississippians, the Mobile people, who were led by Tascalusa (tus•kah•LOO•sah). People who saw the battle later wrote that the number of Indians killed ranged from 2,500 to 11,000. They had fought, as a Spanish soldier later wrote, "with the desire to die" rather than be defeated. The Spanish lost only 20 men, but most of their supplies were destroyed in the fighting.

By this time de Soto's army was in poor condition. It had been reduced in size by deaths and **desertions**, in which soldiers ran away from their duties. Yet de Soto and what remained of his army marched on, reaching the banks of the Mississippi River in May 1541. They were the first Europeans to see the great river. The Spanish hurried to build rafts to cross it so they could search for gold on the other side. In Arkansas and Louisiana they faced more fights with the Indians they encountered.

For three years the Spanish searched for gold without finding any. Then, in 1542, de Soto died of fever. "Many of his men did not mourn his passing," one soldier noted, "for he was a stern man." The soldiers buried their leader in the Mississippi River to hide his death from the Indians. Then the Spanish finally made their way back to Mexico.

Though he found no gold, de Soto claimed much of the land he explored for Spain. The Spanish now claimed all of what is today the southeastern United States.

 What lands did de Soto claim for Spain?

 **LESSON 2 REVIEW**

Check Understanding

1. **Recall the Facts** Describe what took place when the groups led by Ponce de León, Coronado, and de Soto encountered different Indian peoples during their travels.
2. **Focus on the Main Idea** Why did the Spanish risk the unknown to explore North America?

Think Critically

3. **Personally Speaking** How would you react if outsiders arrived to explore and take over your neighborhood?
4. **Think More About It** In their battle with the Mobiles, what do you think gave the Spanish a military advantage?

Show What You Know

Information-Gathering Activity Make a table of Spanish explorers and the Indian peoples they encountered. Start with the table on this page. Use databases or reference books to add the names of the Indians each explorer met. Add other conquistadors who explored North America to your table. Display your table in the classroom.

SETTLERS —and— SLAVES

LESSON 3

Link to Our World

What brings people to a new place to live?

Focus on the Main Idea
As you read, think about what brought the Spanish and the Africans to the Americas to live.

Preview Vocabulary
missionary
colony
colonist
plantation

The conquistadors changed the history of Spain in the Americas. Up to the time of the Spanish conquests, very few Spanish people had settled in the Americas. Most were either soldiers or missionaries. **Missionaries** are people who teach their religion to others. Spanish soldiers searched for gold. Spanish missionaries worked to make the native peoples Christians.

In time, other people came to the Americas to live. Some came for the wealth they had heard about. Others were made to come as slaves.

BUILDING NEW SPAIN

The Spanish government rewarded many conquistadors by giving them large areas of land that had been taken from the Native Americans. Most of the land was in Mexico, which the Spaniards called New Spain. It became Spain's first colony in the Americas. A **colony** is a settlement ruled by another country. People who live in a colony are called settlers, or **colonists**.

Many colonists worked in gold and silver mines. Others set up **plantations**, or huge farms, to grow sugarcane, tobacco, coffee, cocoa, cotton, and other crops to be sold in Spain. The colonists brought with them oxen and plows to work the land and horses to ride. They brought cattle and sheep, fruit trees, grain, and vegetable seeds. Soon they built new cities, and tens of thousands more colonists came to these cities to work.

The Spanish needed many workers to grow their crops, to mine their gold and silver, and to build and take care of their cities. Most colonists, however, did not want to do this hard work by themselves. They wanted others to do it for them.

Spanish coins like this doubloon were made of pure gold from mines in South America.

Under Spanish rule, Indians were forced to mine gold and silver as slaves (right). Bartolomé de Las Casas (below) was among the first Europeans to call for an end to Indian slavery. He often spoke out against cruelty toward Indian peoples in the colonies.

So they made the Indian peoples their slaves. They put the enslaved people to work on the plantations and in the mines. The Indians had to work day and night with little food or rest. They had no freedom.

The Indians fought against being enslaved. Many were killed for doing so. Thousands of Indians had already died fighting the Spanish. Now thousands more died from hunger, overwork, and disease. The native peoples had never had the diseases the settlers brought from Europe, such as measles, influenza, smallpox, and scarlet fever. Because of this, their bodies could not fight these diseases. Sometimes whole tribes became ill and died.

Not all the Spanish colonists believed the Indians should be enslaved. One, a friar named Bartolomé de Las Casas (bar•toh•luh•MAY day lahs KAH•sahs), spent many years of his life trying to help the Indians. He spoke out so strongly that the king of Spain, Charles I, agreed to pass laws to protect the native peoples. These laws, however, were not always carried out, and Indians continued to die.

As the number of Indians fell sharply, the Spanish colonists who depended on slaves faced a problem. Who would do all the work?

 Who did much of the work building New Spain?

DEMAND FOR LABOR

For many years people in Europe had been trading goods for slaves with several West African kingdoms. People in the kingdom of Benin (buh•NIN), for example, carried on a large trade in slaves. They also traded ivory and gold for goods such as tools and guns.

Slavery had been practiced in Africa for a very long time. Most slaves were people taken as prisoners in war. In some parts of Africa slaves could rise to positions of honor and trust. After a time, they could be given their freedom. Africans who traded slaves to Europeans may have believed that they would treat slaves the same way.

At first, enslaved people were treated almost the same in Europe as in Africa. They often worked as house servants. Few owners thought of making slaves do hard work on farms or in mines. Some slaves in Europe became free after a time and worked at jobs they chose. Some even joined European expeditions and armies in the Americas. West African soldiers were with Cortés in Mexico and Pizarro in Peru. And 30 Africans were with Balboa when he first saw the Pacific Ocean.

Little by little, however, life for Africans in Europe and the Americas began to change. One of the most important reasons for this change was that there were not enough workers in the Americas.

As more and more Indians died from diseases and overwork, Spanish colonists looked for other workers. In time they turned to Africans held as slaves. Even Bartolomé de Las Casas, trying to help the Native Americans, thought that Africans could be used to do the hard work of building the colony. It was an idea Las Casas deeply regretted. For soon Africans were working under the same terrible conditions as the Indians had. Even those Africans who came to the Americas as servants or as free people were made to do the work of slaves. Africans were first used as slaves in large numbers on sugarcane and tobacco plantations on the Caribbean islands. Later they were put to work on the plantations and in the mines on the mainland.

 **Why did life for Africans in the Americas change?**

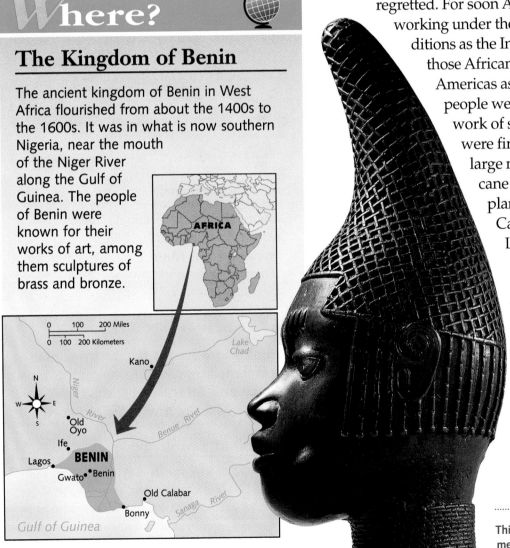

The Kingdom of Benin

The ancient kingdom of Benin in West Africa flourished from about the 1400s to the 1600s. It was in what is now southern Nigeria, near the mouth of the Niger River along the Gulf of Guinea. The people of Benin were known for their works of art, among them sculptures of brass and bronze.

AFRICA

0 100 200 Miles
0 100 200 Kilometers

Lake Chad

Kano

Niger River

Old Oyo

Ife

Benue River

Lagos

BENIN

Gwato • Benin

Old Calabar

Bonny

Sanaga River

Gulf of Guinea

This bronze statue of a member of Benin's royal family was made during the 1500s.

This painting by a British naval officer in 1846 shows the terrible conditions on slave ships. This ship, the *Albanez*, was Spanish.

THE SLAVE TRADE

As the demand for African slaves grew, more and more traders sailed to the west coast of Africa. There they emptied their ships of European goods and filled them with slaves. No longer were most slaves prisoners of war. To meet the growing demand, slave traders raided village after village, kidnapping people to sell as slaves. So many slaves were traded that part of Africa's west coast became known as the Slave Coast.

On the ships, enslaved people faced terrible conditions. Many died before they reached the Americas. Some died fighting against the chains and the cruel treatment. Others died of diseases that quickly passed from person to person on the crowded, dirty ships. Still others jumped into the ocean and drowned rather than live as slaves.

For those who survived the journey, life in the Americas was harsh. Slaves were forced to work long hours in the fields and in the mines. Their work helped raise money for the Spanish government—money that for a time made Spain the most powerful country in Europe.

✓ **How did traders meet the growing demand for African slaves?**

LESSON 3 REVIEW

Check Understanding

1. **Recall the Facts**   How did the Spanish get workers to help build New Spain?
2. **Focus on the Main Idea**   What brought Spanish people to the Americas? What brought African people?

Think Critically

3. **Think More About It**   Did the Spanish treat the Indians fairly? the Africans? Explain.
4. **Cause and Effect**   What effects did European diseases have in the Americas?

Show What You Know

Research Activity   Find out what life had been like in West Africa for the people who were made slaves in New Spain. Use an encyclopedia and other books for this research. Share your findings with classmates and members of your family.

ENCOUNTERS WITH THE FRENCH — and — DUTCH

Link to Our World

How can trade between cultures have both advantages and disadvantages?

Focus on the Main Idea
As you read, think about how the fur trade had both advantages and disadvantages for Europeans and Native Americans in North America.

Preview Vocabulary
Northwest Passage
trade network
agent

While the Spanish were growing rich and powerful from their colonies in Middle and South America, the French and the Dutch were making their own claims in North America. They found good fishing waters along the northeast coast, and they began to trade with the Native Americans. In time the trade brought the French and the Dutch new wealth. This was because they traded for something that became nearly as valuable as gold—fur.

THE FRENCH IN NORTH AMERICA

When French fishers set up camps on shore to dry their fish, they began to barter for animal furs with Indians who lived nearby. The Indians traded beaver furs and other furs for European goods. The furs the Europeans wanted most were beaver furs, which they made into hats. The goods the Indians wanted most were iron tools, pots, pans, and guns.

The French and Indian fur trade grew following the voyages of a French explorer named Jacques Cartier (ZHAHK kar•TYAY). Cartier sailed into the Gulf of St. Lawrence in 1534. The next year he sailed up the St. Lawrence River. Cartier thought that by sailing up the river, he might find a water route cutting through North America to Asia. European traders did not know if there was such a route, which they called the **Northwest Passage**, but they hoped so. Finding the Northwest Passage would mean finding a much faster way to reach Asia.

The beaver was hunted for its valuable fur.

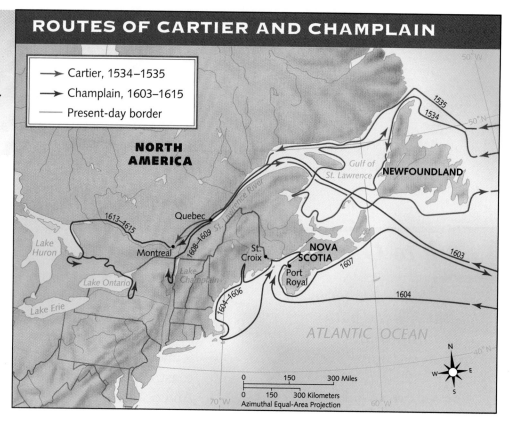

PLACE
Cartier and Champlain explored along waterways in North America.
■ On which major bodies of water did they travel?

Jacques Cartier did not find the Northwest Passage, but he did begin to trade with an Indian people known as the Hurons. The Hurons were as eager for European goods as the French were eager for furs.

By 1600 trade with the Indians was very important for many Europeans, and for the French more than most. Business people in France competed with each other to control the trade. The French monarch, King Henry IV, wanted to build colonies in North America. He said that any company that wanted to trade with the Indians in North America would first have to start a colony there.

French business people jumped at the chance for riches. Several of them formed a company to start a colony in America. They sent a cartographer there to map the places where beavers were found. The person they sent was Samuel de Champlain (sham•PLAYN). Champlain made his first trip to North America in 1603. At the time no Europeans had settled along the east coast north of the Spanish settlements in Florida.

Champlain spent three months exploring the forests of what is now eastern Canada, which he called New France. When Champlain returned to Europe, his reports about the wonderful country across the ocean made many more people want to go to New France. Champlain himself went again, this time as the king's geographer.

For the next five years, Champlain explored the lands along the St. Lawrence River and in what is today Nova Scotia and the state of New York. The search for a place to build a settlement took Champlain back to the St. Lawrence. There he chose a place that the Hurons called *Rebuc*, meaning "a narrowing of the waters." In 1608 Rebuc became Quebec, the first important French settlement in the Americas. Three years later Champlain founded a trading post at Montreal, where an Indian village called Hochelaga (hahsh•uh•LAG•uh) had once stood.

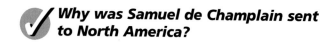

Why was Samuel de Champlain sent to North America?

THE STRUGGLE FOR THE FUR TRADE

The fur trade brought wealth to the French and to their Huron trading partners. Huron traders learned how to use a **trade network**, or system of trading, among the American Indian tribes in eastern Canada. At first the network was good for all the groups that took part in it.

The Hurons acted as **agents**—that is, they did business for other Indian groups. The Hurons traded food for beaver furs with these groups. Then they took the furs to Quebec or Montreal to trade with the French for European goods. The Hurons took home guns, kettles, and metal tools. They then returned to the other tribes to trade some of these goods for more beaver furs.

The Huron trade network lasted until the middle 1600s, when the Iroquois began to trade in the same way as the Hurons. The Iroquois at the time were trading partners with the Dutch. The Dutch had begun building settlements after 1609, when explorer Henry Hudson claimed the land along what is now the Hudson River. The capital of the Dutch colony of New Netherland was New Amsterdam, at the mouth of the Hudson River, where New York City is today. Founded in 1625, New Amsterdam quickly became a center for trade in North America and also with countries around the world.

The Hurons and the Iroquois soon quarreled over trade with the French and the Dutch. The two Indian groups began to fight for control of the fur trade. Control of the trade would give the winner power over other Indian peoples.

The fighting made both the Hurons and the Iroquois weaker and weaker.

To survive, many French and Dutch fur trappers lived with Indian tribes (below) and learned their ways of life. Indian snowshoes (right) helped people walk on deep snow.

This French trading post (above right) was built at Fond du Lac in present-day Wisconsin. Trading posts were places to live, as well as places for trading with Indians. The French traded iron goods such as pots (above left) for beaver furs.

The Europeans did nothing to stop the fighting and sometimes even tried to keep it going. In time they were able to take away the warring Indians' land with all its furs.

The trade and the wars that went with it changed the lifeways of many Eastern Woodlands Indians. The more they wanted European goods, the less they lived in their traditional ways. They changed the ways in which they farmed, hunted, cooked, and even dressed. Many stopped using the skills that had helped them live in the woodlands. Instead, they spent their time hunting for furs and fighting each other over the trade with the Europeans.

 How was fighting between Indian groups good for the Europeans?

LESSON 4 REVIEW

Check Understanding

1. **Recall the Facts** What groups took part in the fur trade?

2. **Focus on the Main Idea** What were the advantages and disadvantages of the fur trade for the Europeans? What were the advantages and disadvantages for the Indians?

Think Critically

3. **Past to Present** How is trade today both an advantage and a disadvantage for some people?

4. **Cause and Effect** How did the market for furs in Europe affect the lives of people living in North America?

Show What You Know

Diagram Activity Create a diagram that shows how the Hurons acted as agents in the fur trade. Your diagram should show who the Hurons traded with and the goods they exchanged. Compare your diagram with those of your classmates.

LESSON 5

The ENGLISH in the AMERICAS

Link to Our World

In what ways is cooperation better than conflict?

Focus on the Main Idea
As you read, think about the ways cooperation helped the English colonists at Jamestown and Plymouth.

Preview Vocabulary
armada
profit
pilgrim
compact
Mayflower Compact
interpreter

Queen Elizabeth I of England encouraged people to build colonies in North America.

By the 1600s English people, too, were coming to the Americas. Some came looking for wealth, as many of the Spanish, the French, and the Dutch did. Others came hoping to start a new and better life. Many were nobles and adventurers who had heard rumors of great riches. But most were just ordinary people—men and women, young and old. There were skilled workers, such as carpenters, tailors, and blacksmiths. There were farmers who wanted cheap or free land. And there were people who wanted the freedom to follow their own religion.

THE MYSTERY OF ROANOKE

English explorers had been sailing across the Atlantic Ocean since the mid-1500s. Sometimes they explored the eastern coast of North America. Other times they attacked Spanish treasure ships carrying gold and other riches from the Americas to Spain. England's most famous explorer was Francis Drake. On an expedition that began in 1577, Drake attacked a Spanish ship, stole its treasure, and sailed around the world to escape Spanish warships.

England's monarch, Elizabeth I, encouraged exploration. In 1584 the queen said that Sir Walter Raleigh (RAH•lee), an English noble, could set up England's first colony in North America. In July 1585 Raleigh's colonists landed on an island just off the coast of what is today North Carolina. The Hatteras Indians called the island Roanoke (ROH•uh•nohk). The English called their colony Virginia. In less than a year, however, the colony had failed. The colonists did not know how to survive in their new environment. When Francis Drake stopped by the colony in 1586, he found the colonists starving and took them back to England.

In July 1587 Raleigh sent a second group to settle Roanoke Island. Raleigh had chosen John White to lead the new colony. In August, after White helped the colonists get settled, he went back to England for supplies. At this time England needed all its ships for war with Spain, so White could not get back to the people he had left on Roanoke Island.

Three years later, after England had defeated Spain's **armada**, or fleet of war ships, John White returned to Roanoke—only to find that everyone was gone. All that remained were some books with their covers torn off, maps ruined by rain, and weapons covered with rust. White found the letters *CRO* carved on a nearby tree and the word *CROATOAN* carved on a wooden post. White and the people who were with him fired shots into the air. They searched but found nothing. They shouted but no one answered.

Nothing was ever found of the people of Roanoke Island. Many people believe they went to live with the Croatoan Indians, who later became known as the Lumbee Indians. Many Lumbee Indians today still have the last names of people from the "lost colony."

 What happened to the English colony on Roanoke Island?

SUCCESS AT JAMESTOWN

On May 24, 1607, three English ships sailed into the deep bay now called the Chesapeake. The ships and the 105 men and boys aboard had been sent to North America by the English business people who formed the Virginia Company of London. The company planned to build a trading post and colony in North America to make a profit. A **profit** is the money left over after everything has been paid for. Despite the company's plans, however, most of the colonists came looking for gold.

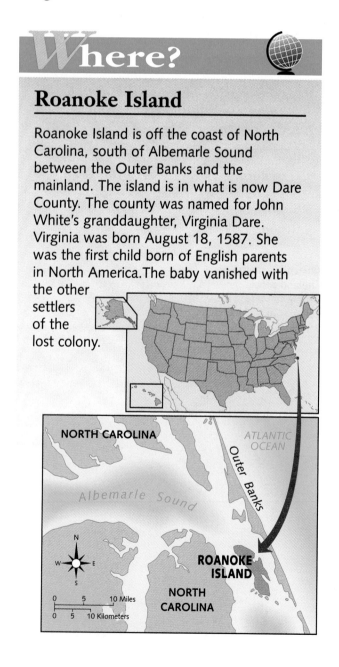

Where?

Roanoke Island

Roanoke Island is off the coast of North Carolina, south of Albemarle Sound between the Outer Banks and the mainland. The island is in what is now Dare County. The county was named for John White's granddaughter, Virginia Dare. Virginia was born August 18, 1587. She was the first child born of English parents in North America. The baby vanished with the other settlers of the lost colony.

NORTH CAROLINA

ATLANTIC OCEAN

Outer Banks

Albemarle Sound

N W E S

ROANOKE ISLAND

NORTH CAROLINA

0 5 10 Miles
0 5 10 Kilometers

The three ships sailed up a river that the men named the James, to honor King James of England. They landed on a little peninsula and decided to start a settlement there. However, the place where they built Jamestown, as they called the settlement, turned out to be a poor choice. The men dug wells, but the water was bad. The land was low and wet and full of disease-carrying mosquitoes. The way the colonists behaved toward the Indians who lived nearby—taking Indian lands and destroying their crops—also put them in danger of attack.

> 66 **OUR MEN WERE DESTROYED** *with cruel diseases, . . . burning fevers, and by wars.* 99
>
> A Jamestown colonist

By the end of the first year, half the colonists had died. One colonist later wrote, "Our men were destroyed with cruel diseases, . . . burning fevers, and by wars." They had come to the Americas to get rich. No one had bothered to plant or gather food for the winter, so many colonists starved.

Life in the colony changed when Captain John Smith became its leader. He probably saved Jamestown from becoming another lost colony. Smith's first act was to make one unbreakable rule: Anyone who did not work did not eat. Soon

Captain John Smith (above left) led the colony of Jamestown (above right) and kept its settlers from starving. In time, Smith maintained peace with the nearby Algonquian Indians. This drawing of an Algonquian village (left) was made by John White, a leader of the colony at Roanoke Island.

The Mayflower Compact

In the name of God, Amen. We, whose names are underwritten, the Loyal Subjects of our dread Sovereign Lord, *King James*, by the Grace of God, of *Great Britain*, *France* and *Ireland*, King, *Defender of the Faith*, etc.

Having undertaken for the Glory of God, and Advancement of the Christian Faith, and the Honour of our King and Country, a voyage to plant the first colony in the northern Parts of Virginia; do by these Presents, solemnly and mutually in the Presence of God and one of another, covenant and combine ourselves together into a civil Body Politick, for our better Ordering and Preservation, and

Furtherance of the Ends aforesaid; And by Virtue hereof to enact, constitute, and frame, such just and equal Laws, Ordinances, Acts, Constitutions and Offices, from time to time, as shall be thought most meet and convenient for the General good of the Colony; unto which we promise all due Submission and Obedience.

In Witness whereof we have hereunto subscribed our names at *Cape Cod* the eleventh of *November*, in the Reign of our Sovereign Lord, King *James* of *England*, *France* and *Ireland*, the eighteenth, and of *Scotland* the fifty-fourth. *Anno Domini, 1620*.

---

the colonists were planting gardens, building shelters, and putting up fences to protect the settlement from attack.

More than 30 tribes of Eastern Woodlands Indians lived in Virginia during the early 1600s. Most were members of a confederation led by Chief Powhatan (pow•uh•TAN). One day, while exploring the lands around Jamestown, Captain Smith was captured by Indians. A legend says that the chief's daughter, Pocahontas (poh•kuh•HAHN•tuhs), saved his life. Because of this act Captain Smith made peace with Chief Powhatan. Whether or not this story is true, it is known that fighting continued between the settlers and the Indians.

Despite Jamestown's many troubles, the colony survived and, in time, did well. Five years after the first colonists had sailed up the James River, they found the "gold" that would make the colony rich. It was tobacco.

Why did colonists go to Jamestown?

THE FOUNDING OF PLYMOUTH COLONY

On a cold day late in 1620, a ship called the *Mayflower* set sail from England for the Americas. The 102 colonists on board had agreed to work for the Virginia Company. The company's owners would pay for the voyage. In return, the settlers would send them furs, fish, and lumber.

Among the settlers was a group of families going to the Americas for a special reason. They were Separatists, or people who had separated from the Church of England. At the time, everyone in England had to belong to this church. Those who refused were not safe. So these Separatists decided to go to the Americas, where they hoped to find the freedom to follow their own religion. In time they became known as Pilgrims. A **pilgrim** is a person who makes a journey for a religious reason.

The colonists had planned to settle near the Hudson River. But the *Mayflower* was blown off course by terrible storms and reached the coast of what is today Massachusetts. The settlers were not sure where they were, but they knew that they were not in the lands governed by the Virginia Company. To keep order, the 41 men aboard the *Mayflower* signed an agreement, or **compact**. They agreed to make laws for the good of the colony and to obey those laws. This agreement became known as the **Mayflower Compact**. It is the first example of self-rule by colonists in the Americas.

On December 21, 1620, the Pilgrims landed at a place they called Plymouth. The first winter was hard. The weather was cold, there was not enough food, and many settlers became ill. About half died.

But help came in the spring. To the surprise of the Pilgrims, an Indian walked into their village one day and said "Welcome, Englishmen." The Indian was a Wampanoag (wahm•puh•NOH•ag) named Samoset. He had learned English from sailors who fished along the coast. Several days later Samoset returned to the settlement with an Indian who spoke English better than he did. This was Tisquantum, or Squanto. Tisquantum had been kidnapped years before and sold as

What?

Thanksgiving Day

In the fall of 1621, the Pilgrims gathered their first harvest. To celebrate, they held a feast with the Wampanoags and gave thanks to God. This is what many people today think of as the first Thanksgiving. Thanksgiving celebrations, however, have been held in the Americas for thousands of years. During celebrations such as the Green Corn ceremony, Indian peoples gave thanks for a good harvest. Some people think the first European Thanksgiving in the Americas took place in 1598 when Spanish settlers gave thanks for safely reaching the Rio Grande. Thanksgiving became a national holiday in 1863 when President Abraham Lincoln declared the last Thursday in November as "a day of thanksgiving and praise to our beneficent Father."

The Pilgrims' first Thanksgiving was a feast that lasted for three days.

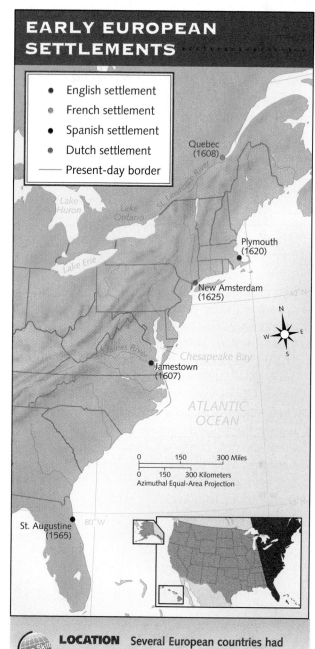

EARLY EUROPEAN SETTLEMENTS

- ● English settlement
- ● French settlement
- ● Spanish settlement
- ● Dutch settlement
- —— Present-day border

Quebec (1608)

Lake Huron

Lake Ontario

Lake Erie

Plymouth (1620)

New Amsterdam (1625)

Chesapeake Bay

Jamestown (1607)

ATLANTIC OCEAN

St. Augustine (1565)

0   150   300 Miles
0   150   300 Kilometers
Azimuthal Equal-Area Projection

LOCATION Several European countries had established American colonies by 1625.
■ Why were all the earliest European settlements located near water?

a slave in Spain. He had escaped and spent several years in England before returning to his own land.

Tisquantum stayed with the Pilgrims and became their interpreter. He translated the Indians' language and explained their lifeways. He showed the Pilgrims where to fish and how to plant squash, pumpkins, and corn. He helped keep the Pilgrims alive.

For a time the Pilgrims lived in peace with the Wampanoags, who were led by their chief, Massasoit (ma•suh•SOYT). However, as more and more English colonists came to settle in Massachusetts, things changed. The new people were not friendly toward the Indians and took their lands. Quarrels between the Wampanoags and the English became fights that grew into terrible wars.

During these wars the Wampanoags and other tribes were forced off their lands. Soon very few Native Americans lived along the eastern coast. Those who were not driven away were killed or captured, or they died from disease.

 **How did the Indians help the Pilgrims survive in their colony?**

LESSON 5 REVIEW

Check Understanding

1. **Recall the Facts**   How was life different for the English colonists in Roanoke, Jamestown, and Plymouth?
2. **Focus on the Main Idea**   How did cooperation help the settlers at Jamestown and Plymouth?

Think Critically

3. **Think More About It**   Why did the Pilgrims think it was important to write the Mayflower Compact?
4. **Personally Speaking**   Would you rather have been a Jamestown colonist or a Pilgrim at Plymouth? Explain.

Show What You Know

 **Questioning Activity**   Prepare a list of questions you might ask people who wanted to join you in starting a colony. As you write the questions, think about the personal qualities of people you would want to be colonists.

Read a Vertical Time Line

Why Is This Skill Important?

Time lines are an important tool in studying history. By studying a time line, you can find out when certain events happened. You can see the order in which events took place and how one event may have led to another. A time line can also help you see how much time passed between two events.

But not all time lines look the same or are read in the same way. Most time lines run horizontally, or across the page from left to right. But some run vertically, or from top to bottom. To be able to use time lines, it is important to know how to read those that are vertical, as well as those that are horizontal.

Understand the Process

Horizontal time lines are read from left to right. The earliest date on a horizontal time line is on the left end, and the most recent date is on the right end. The time line shown on this page is a vertical time line. It is read from top to bottom. The earliest date on a vertical time line is at the top, and the most recent date is at the bottom.

Now use the information on the vertical time line to answer the following questions about European settlement in the Americas.

1. Which European nation was the first to build a settlement in the Americas?
2. In what year was Mexico City founded?
3. How many settlements did the English build on Roanoke Island?
4. Which settlement was built first, Jamestown or Plymouth? In what year was each settlement built?
5. When was the first French settlement built in the Americas?
6. How many years passed between the building of Mexico City and the founding of New Amsterdam?

Think and Apply

Use some of the events of your school year to make your own vertical time line. These events might include a class field trip, a special program, or a holiday party. After you have finished your time line, share it with a friend or a family member.

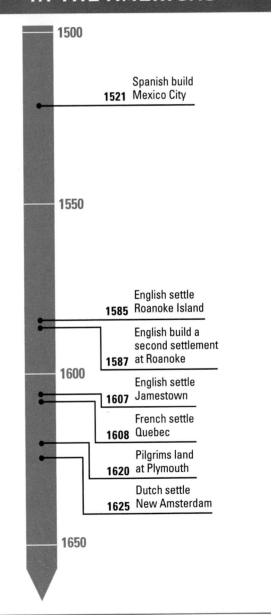

EUROPEAN SETTLEMENT IN THE AMERICAS

1500

1521 Spanish build Mexico City

1550

1585 English settle Roanoke Island

1587 English build a second settlement at Roanoke

1600

1607 English settle Jamestown

1608 French settle Quebec

1620 Pilgrims land at Plymouth

1625 Dutch settle New Amsterdam

1650

REVIEW

CONNECT MAIN IDEAS

Use this organizer to show that you understand how the chapter's main ideas are connected. Copy the organizer onto a separate sheet of paper. Then complete it by writing the main idea of each lesson.

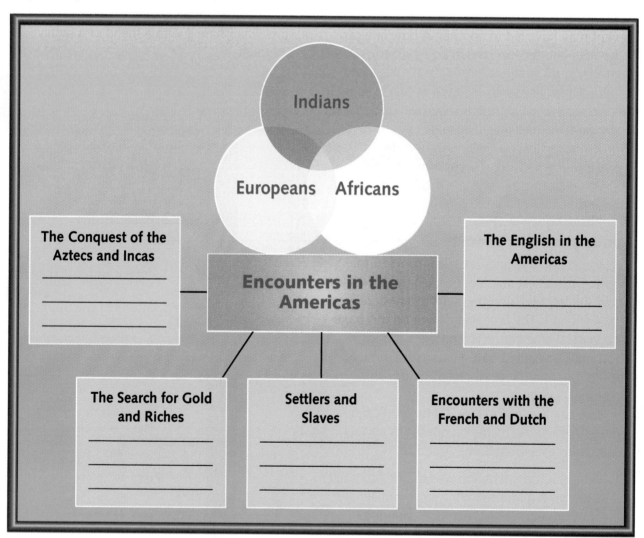

Indians

Europeans   Africans

The Conquest of the
Aztecs and Incas
_____
_____
_____

Encounters in the
Americas

The English in the
Americas
_____
_____
_____

The Search for Gold
and Riches
_____
_____
_____

Settlers and
Slaves
_____
_____
_____

Encounters with the
French and Dutch
_____
_____
_____

WRITE MORE ABOUT IT

1. **Write a Script for a Play** Write the script for one scene of a play that tells the story of an African child who was kidnapped by a slave trader, put on board a slave ship, and taken to the Americas.

2. **Write a Classroom Compact** The Pilgrims agreed to make laws for the good of the colony. Write a classroom compact that lists rules for your class. Explain how this compact will be good for members of your class.

USE VOCABULARY

For each group of terms, write a sentence or two that explains how the terms are related.

1. conquistador, claim

2. grant, mainland

3. colony, colonist, plantation

4. Northwest Passage, trade network, agent

5. pilgrim, Mayflower Compact

CHECK UNDERSTANDING

1. Why did Motecuhzoma welcome Cortés to the Aztec Empire?

2. Why did the Spanish government send Cortés to Mexico?

3. Where was the Inca Empire?

4. How did Pizarro conquer the Incas?

5. What was Coronado searching for on his journey across what is today the southwestern United States? Did he find what he was looking for?

6. Who were the first Europeans to see the Mississippi River?

7. Why did Spanish missionaries come to the Americas?

8. Why did the Spanish enslave Native Americans? Why did the Spanish enslave Africans?

9. What was the Northwest Passage?

10. How did the Hurons run their trade network?

11. How did trade with the Europeans change the lifeways of the Eastern Woodlands Indians?

12. Why did the Virginia Company want to build a colony in North America?

THINK CRITICALLY

1. **Cause and Effect**   What effects do you think the Inca civil war had on the Inca Empire?

2. **Think More About It**   Why do you think some soldiers exploring the Americas deserted their expeditions?

3. **Personally Speaking**   What skills and abilities do you think early explorers needed? Why were their explorations important?

4. **Explore Viewpoints**   How might an Indian have viewed the fighting over control of the fur trade? How might a European settler have viewed it?

APPLY SKILLS

How to Read a Vertical Time Line   Make a vertical time line showing important events in the early settlement of the Americas by the Spanish, the French, the Dutch, or the English.

READ MORE ABOUT IT

Against All Opposition: Black Explorers in America by James Haskins. Walker. The author tells of the travels of African explorers in the Americas.

From Coronado to Escalante: The Explorers of the Spanish Southwest by John Miller Morris. Chelsea. This book looks at Spanish exploration in Mexico and the American Southwest.

The Very First Thanksgiving: Pioneers on the Rio Grande by Bea Bragg. Harbinger House. This thanksgiving feast was held near present-day El Paso 23 years before the *Mayflower* landed at Plymouth Rock.

The Wampanoag by Laurie Weinstein-Farson. Chelsea. This book tells about the Wampanoag Indians of New England.

RELEVANT

THE GREAT EXCHANGE CONTINUES

Christopher Columbus's first encounter with the Tainos began a worldwide exchange of plants, animals, people, and ideas that we call the Columbian Exchange or the Great Exchange. In many ways the Great Exchange has never stopped. Products, people, and ideas continue to move all over the world. Today, however, the exchange takes place faster than ever before.

With modern transportation, people and products can reach any location in the world in less than a day. Telephones, fax machines, television, and computers—especially the World Wide Web—have made it possible for people to communicate within minutes or even seconds. The World Wide Web is a network of computers that helps people exchange information from across the country and around the world. News that took months to cross the ocean five centuries ago as the Great Exchange began now takes almost no time at all!

THINK AND APPLY

What benefits does the World Wide Web offer? Do you think it has drawbacks as well? Hold a classroom debate about how electronic communication can change the way we live today.

BUILDING CITIZENSHIP

STORY CLOTH

Study the pictures shown in this story cloth to help you review the events you read about in Unit 2.

Summarize the Main Ideas

1. Viking explorers were the first Europeans known to land in the Americas, arriving about A.D. 1000.

2. New maps, faster ships, and other advances in technology helped set the stage for European exploration in the late 1400s.

3. Christopher Columbus, leading an expedition of three ships, landed in the Americas in 1492. Believing he had reached the Indies, he called the people he met Indians.

4. The Aztec king Motecuhzoma welcomed Hernando Cortés with food, housing, and gifts of gold. The Aztecs, like the Incas, were conquered by Spanish conquistadors.

5. The demand for workers in the Americas led many colonists to enslave Indians and then Africans. Slave traders kidnapped Africans and took them to the Americas in slave ships.

6. By 1600 trade with Indian peoples in the Americas was very important to many Europeans. The fur trade brought wealth to French and Huron traders.

7. Jamestown was settled in 1607. It was the first lasting English settlement in North America.

Write a Diary Entry Imagine that you are living during the time of an event shown in this story cloth. Write a diary entry that explains what is taking place. Share your work with a classmate.

UNIT 2
REVIEW

COOPERATIVE LEARNING WORKSHOP

Remember
- Share your ideas.
- Cooperate with others to plan your work.
- Take responsibility for your work.
- Show your group's work to the class.
- Discuss what you learned by working together.

Activity 1
Make a Globe

Work with a group to make a globe that shows the routes of explorers such as da Gama, Dias, Columbus, and Magellan. Use an inflated balloon for your globe. Draw the continents in one color. Draw the routes of each explorer in another color. You may want to use a string to hang your globe from the classroom ceiling.

Activity 2
Draw a Ship

Work together to find out more about one of these ships: the *Santa Maria,* the *Golden Hind,* or the *Mayflower.* Draw a picture of the ship on a large sheet of paper. Then write a report that gives information about the ship and its history.

Activity 3
Write a Play

Work with other members of your group to write a short play about what you think happened to the settlers of the second colony on Roanoke Island. Include Sir Walter Raleigh and John White as characters. Be sure to explain in your play why you think the settlers carved the word *Croatoan* on a post.

USE VOCABULARY

Write the term that correctly matches each definition.

cartographer   expedition
colony   Mayflower Compact
conquistador   monarch

1. a maker of maps

2. a king or queen

3. a journey taken for a special reason

4. the Spanish word for *conqueror*

5. a settlement ruled by a faraway country

6. the first written plan for self-rule by colonists in the Americas

CHECK UNDERSTANDING

1. What was Vinland?

2. What changes in technology helped set the stage for European exploration?

3. What empire did Cortés conquer? What empire did Pizarro conquer?

4. Why were Africans brought to the Spanish colonies?

5. In what ways did the fur trade change the lives of many Eastern Woodlands Indians?

6. Why was Jamestown founded?

7. Why did the Pilgrims come to the Americas?

THINK CRITICALLY

1. **Cause and Effect** How did the European demand for spices, silk, and other Asian goods lead to the exploration of the Americas?

2. **Personally Speaking** Do you think the voyages of Columbus were more important than the voyages of other explorers? Why or why not?

3. **Think More About It** Why do you think John Smith started a "no work, no food" policy in the Jamestown colony?

4. **Past to Present** What are the advantages of contact between different cultures today? What are the disadvantages?

APPLY GEOGRAPHY SKILLS

How to Use Latitude and Longitude
Use the map below to answer the questions.

1. Does the map show an area in the Northern Hemisphere or the Southern Hemisphere? in the Eastern Hemisphere or the Western Hemisphere? How can you tell?

2. What line of latitude is closest to St. Augustine? to Havana?

3. What island is located near 20°N, 70°W?

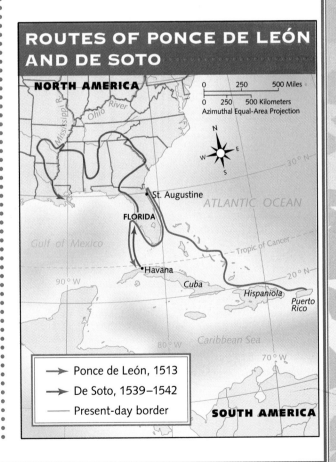

ROUTES OF PONCE DE LEÓN AND DE SOTO

NORTH AMERICA

Mississippi R.

Ohio River

0   250   500 Miles
0   250   500 Kilometers
Azimuthal Equal-Area Projection

St. Augustine

ATLANTIC OCEAN

FLORIDA

30°N

Gulf of Mexico

Havana

90°W

Cuba

Tropic of Cancer

20°N

Hispaniola

Puerto Rico

80°W

Caribbean Sea

70°W

→ Ponce de León, 1513
→ De Soto, 1539–1542
— Present-day border

SOUTH AMERICA

UNIT 3

OUR COLONIAL HERITAGE

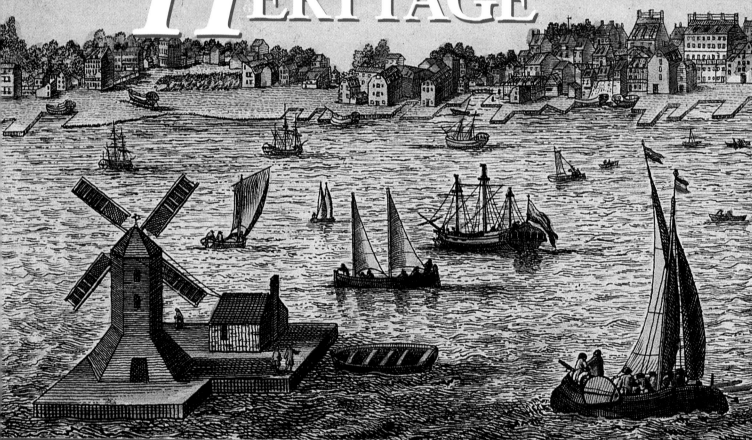

1560

1565
Spanish settlers found St. Augustine

1600

1607
Virginia colonists build Jamestown

1625
The Dutch found New Amsterdam

1630
Puritans land in Massachusetts

1632
The Maryland colony is chartered

1640

1636
Colonists settle Connecticut and Rhode Island

1638
New Sweden is founded

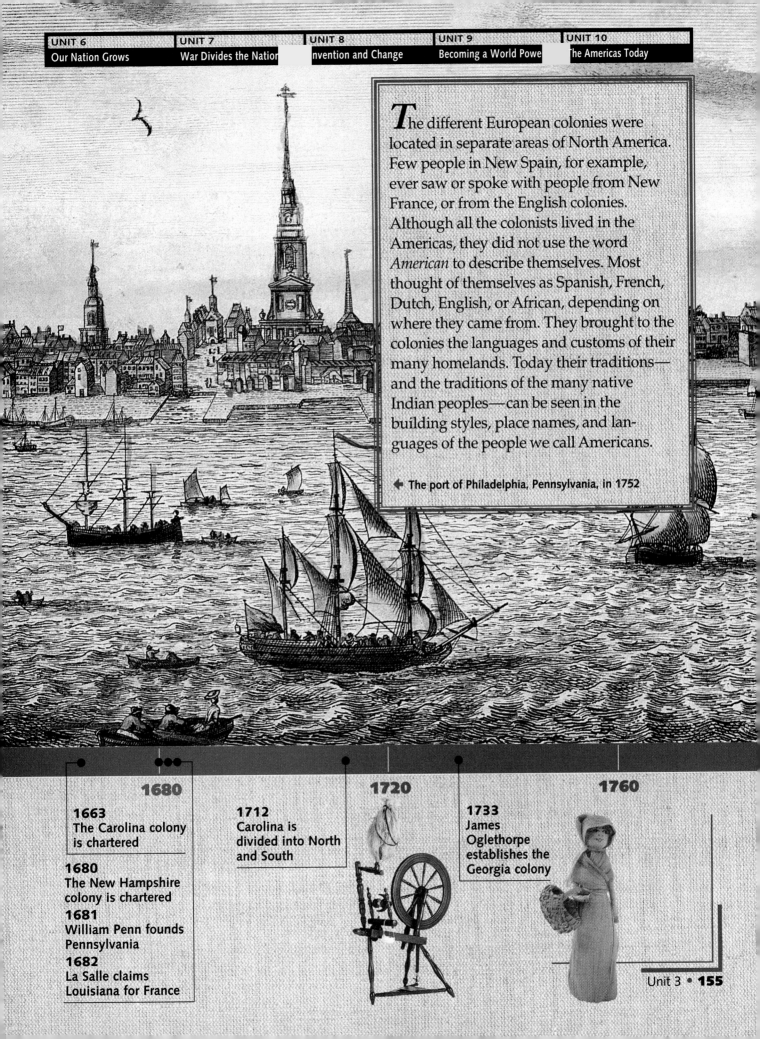

The different European colonies were located in separate areas of North America. Few people in New Spain, for example, ever saw or spoke with people from New France, or from the English colonies. Although all the colonists lived in the Americas, they did not use the word *American* to describe themselves. Most thought of themselves as Spanish, French, Dutch, English, or African, depending on where they came from. They brought to the colonies the languages and customs of their many homelands. Today their traditions—and the traditions of the many native Indian peoples—can be seen in the building styles, place names, and languages of the people we call Americans.

◄ The port of Philadelphia, Pennsylvania, in 1752

1680

1663
The Carolina colony is chartered

1680
The New Hampshire colony is chartered

1681
William Penn founds Pennsylvania

1682
La Salle claims Louisiana for France

1712
Carolina is divided into North and South

1720

1733
James Oglethorpe establishes the Georgia colony

1760

NOVA BRITANNIA.
OFFERING MOST
Excellent fruites by Planting in
VIRGINIA.

Exciting all such as be well affected
to further the same.

LONDON
Printed for SAMVEL MACHAM, and are to befold at
his Shop in Pauls Church-yard, at the
Signe of the Bul-head.
1609.

Companies seeking the wealth of
the Americas promised colonists
good land and riches.

Men used razors like this one to
trim or shave their beards.

GOING
TO THE
COLONIES

Few Europeans going to North America as colonists knew what to expect when they arrived. To help them prepare for the experience, one group in England published the following list of things to take when moving to North America. The list was based on the experiences of other colonists. It shows what many colonists brought from Europe to begin their new lives in North America.

Printed at London for Fylke Clifton in 1630

PROPORTION OF PROVISIONS NEEDFUL FOR SUCH AS INTEND TO PLANT themselves in New England, for one whole year.
Collected by the Adventurers, with the advice of the Planters.

Victual
Meal, one Hogshead.
Malt, one Hogshead.
Beef, one hundred weight.
Pork pickled, 100. or Bacon, 74 pound.
Peas, two bushels.
Greates, one bushel.
Butter, two dozen.
Cheese, half a hundred.
Vinegar, two gallons.
Aquavita, one gallon.
Mustard seed, two quarts.
Salt to save fish, half a hogshead.

Apparel
Shoes, six pair.
Boots for men, one pair.

Leather to mend shoes, four pound.

Irish stockings, four pair.

Shirts, six.

Handkerchiefs, twelve.

One Sea Cape or Gown, of coarse cloth.

Other apparel, as their purses will afford.

Tooles, which may also serve a family of four or five persons.

One English Spade.

One steele Shovel. Two Hatchets.

Axes 3. one broad axe, and 2. felling axes.

One Wood hook.

Hoes 3. one broad of nine inches, and two narrow of five or six inches.

One Wimble, with six piercer bits.

One Hammer.

Other tools as men's several occupations require, as Hand saws, Whip saws, Thwart saws, Augers, Chisels, Frowes, Grind stones, etc.

For Building

Nails of all sorts.

Locks for Door and Chests.

Gimmows for Chests.

Hooks and twists for doors.

Arms

One Musket, Rest, and Bandeliere.

Powder, ten pound.

Shot, sixteen.

Match, six pound.

One Sword.

One Belt.

One Pistol. With a mold.

For Fishing

Twelve Cod hooks.

Two Lines for fishing.

One Mackerel line, and twelve hooks.

28 pound of Lead for bullets and fishing lead.

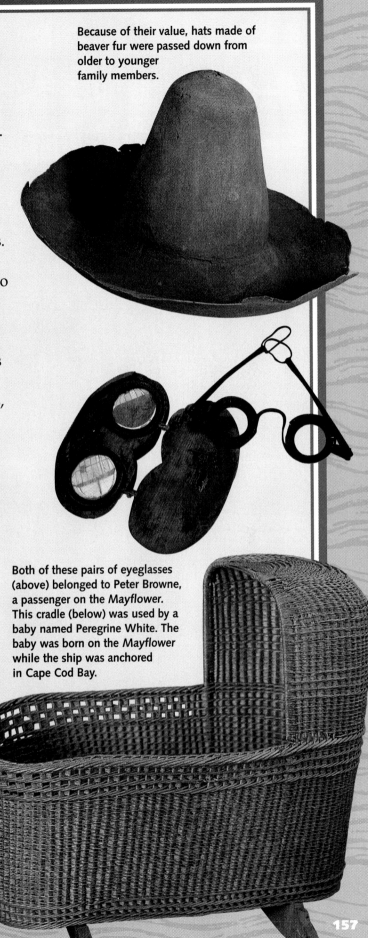

Because of their value, hats made of beaver fur were passed down from older to younger family members.

Both of these pairs of eyeglasses (above) belonged to Peter Browne, a passenger on the *Mayflower.* This cradle (below) was used by a baby named Peregrine White. The baby was born on the *Mayflower* while the ship was anchored in Cape Cod Bay.

CHAPTER 5

EUROPEANS SETTLE

THROUGHOUT NORTH AMERICA

66 Even if I die on the road, I will not go back, but you can bury me here and I shall very gladly remain among these . . . people if such be the will of God. 99

Junípero Serra, a Spanish missionary, during a journey to San Diego in 1769

158

The SPANISH BORDERLANDS

Link to Our World

Why might a government today decide to expand its lands?

Focus on the Main Idea
As you read, look for reasons the Spanish government decided to expand its lands in North America.

Preview Vocabulary

buffer	scarce
borderlands	hacienda
presidio	self-sufficient
permanent	mission

The Spanish conquistadors who explored the Americas found what they were looking for—gold and silver. Mining for these treasures became the most important money-making activity in Spain's American colonies. To protect its gold and silver mines from the other European countries that were building colonies in North America, the Spanish created a buffer. A **buffer** is an area of land that serves as a barrier. The buffer north of New Spain protected it from New France, New Netherland, and the English colonies. It came to be known as the Spanish **borderlands**. The borderlands stretched across what are today northern Mexico and the southern United States from Florida to California.

PRESIDIOS

Spanish soldiers led the way into the borderlands north of New Spain. Once they found a good place to settle, their first duty was to build a fort, called a **presidio** (pray•SEE•dee•oh), and shelters for the settlers. The largest and most important presidio in the borderlands was St. Augustine. It was located on the Atlantic coast of Florida on a bay first explored by Juan Ponce de León in 1513.

Pedro Menéndez de Avilés (meh•NEN•dehs day ah•vih•LAYS) and 1,500 soldiers and settlers reached the location of present-day St. Augustine in 1565. St. Augustine became the first **permanent**, or long-lasting, European settlement in what is now the United States. It was founded 42 years before the English landed at Jamestown and 43 years before the French founded Quebec.

Upon landing at St. Augustine, the Spanish soldiers quickly built small wooden houses and a wooden presidio in which the settlers could seek protection. Fearful of English pirates and Indian raiders, the Spanish soon began to strengthen the presidio by building walls of stone around the wooden fort. It took 25 years to finish this work, but the Castillo (ka•STEE•yoh) de San Marcos, as the presidio was called, was strong enough to protect Spanish settlers from any attackers.

Despite the danger of living in the borderlands, Menéndez felt that the settlement at St. Augustine held great promise. In a letter to the Spanish king, he wrote that Florida could "bring enormous profits from vineyards, sugar, cattle, ship stores, pearls, timber, silk, wheat, and endless supplies of fruit."

St. Augustine never lived up to the hopes of becoming a source of wealth for Spain. But it became important for another reason. It served as Spain's military headquarters in North America. It was one of a line of hundreds of presidios stretching from Florida to California and providing protection for settlers in the borderlands.

> ✓ **Why did Spain build presidios across the borderlands?**

RANCHES AND HACIENDAS

The Spanish realized that gold and silver were **scarce**, or not plentiful, in the borderlands. They also knew that in many places the land was so hot and dry "that even the cactus pads appeared to be toasted." But

---

The Castillo de San Marcos in St. Augustine is still standing today and attracts many visitors. It is more than 400 years old.

St. Augustine

St. Augustine is located in northeastern Florida, near the Atlantic Ocean. Spain established the city and ruled it for more than 200 years. During that time its settlers endured many invasions and attacks. In 1763 the English gained control of St. Augustine. Spain again ruled the settlement from 1783 until 1821, when Florida became a part of the United States.

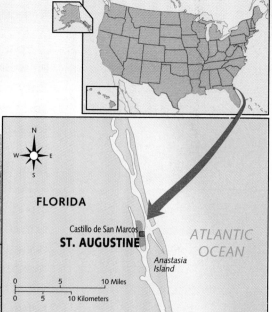

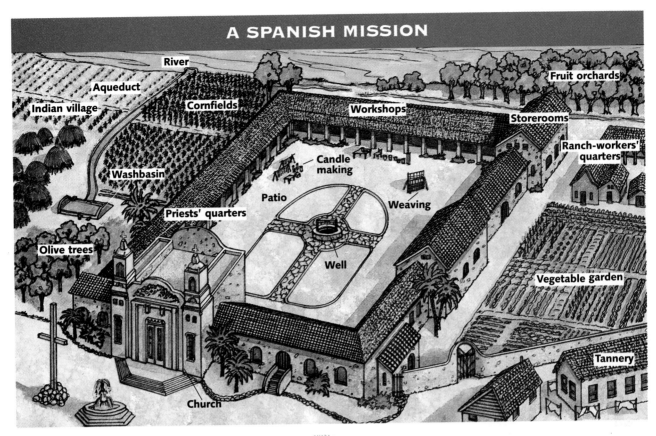

A SPANISH MISSION

River
Aqueduct
Indian village
Cornfields
Workshops
Fruit orchards
Storerooms
Candle making
Ranch-workers' quarters
Washbasin
Patio
Priests' quarters
Weaving
Olive trees
Well
Vegetable garden
Church
Tannery

LEARNING FROM DIAGRAMS The Spanish built missions to spread Christianity.
■ In what ways were missions self-sufficient?

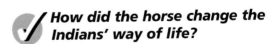

settlers moved there anyway. Most made money by raising livestock and selling the hides and animal fats to markets in the colonies and in Spain. They often traded with Indian tribes for things they needed. They traded with the Pueblos, for example, for corn, pottery, and cotton cloth.

Some ranchers in the borderlands of northern Mexico built large estates called **haciendas** (ah•see•EN•dahs), where they raised cattle and sheep by the thousands. In what are now Texas and California, cattle were the most important kind of livestock. In the drier climate of what is now New Mexico, settlers raised sheep.

Ranchers on the haciendas raised their own livestock, grew their own crops, and made most of what they needed to live. These **self-sufficient**, or self-supporting, communities developed far from the markets of Mexico City and other large cities.

As they settled throughout the borderlands, the Spanish—and the animals they brought with them—changed life for many of the Indians living there. Horses, long extinct in the Americas, once again roamed the land. The Plains Indians learned to tame horses and use them for transportation, for hunting, and for warfare. In the Southwest, the Navajos learned to raise sheep. They began weaving sheep's wool into colorful clothing and blankets.

How did the horse change the Indians' way of life?

MISSIONS

Spain's main interests in settling the borderlands were protecting its empire and expanding its economy. But the Spanish king also wanted to "bring the people of that land

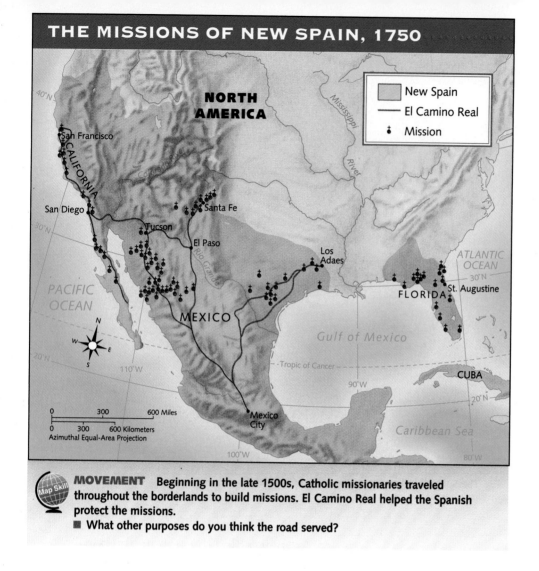

THE MISSIONS OF NEW SPAIN, 1750

Legend:
- New Spain
- El Camino Real
- Mission

NORTH AMERICA

San Francisco
CALIFORNIA
San Diego
Tucson
Santa Fe
El Paso
Los Adaes
PACIFIC OCEAN
MEXICO
FLORIDA
St. Augustine
ATLANTIC OCEAN
Gulf of Mexico
Tropic of Cancer
CUBA
Mexico City
Caribbean Sea
Rio Grande
Mississippi River

0   300   600 Miles
0   300   600 Kilometers
Azimuthal Equal-Area Projection

MOVEMENT Beginning in the late 1500s, Catholic missionaries traveled throughout the borderlands to build missions. El Camino Real helped the Spanish protect the missions.
■ What other purposes do you think the road served?

to our Holy Catholic faith." So the Spanish government sent missionaries to the borderlands to persuade the Indians to become Catholics as well as loyal Spanish subjects.

The first successful missionaries in the Spanish borderlands were the Franciscans, a group of Catholic religious workers. They built **missions**, or small religious communities, in what are now Georgia, Florida, Texas, New Mexico, Arizona, and California. The Franciscans' first mission was Nombre de Dios (NOHM•bray day DEE•ohs), "Name of God," the oldest Spanish mission in the United States. Built near St. Augustine in 1565, Nombre de Dios was the first in a

chain of missions that would link the Atlantic and Pacific coasts of North America. Father Junípero Serra helped build a string of 21 missions in California, each "one day's journey" from the next.

> ❝ **THE PUNISHMENTS RESORTED TO . . . *are the shackles, the lash, and the stocks.*** ❞
>
> A Spanish missionary

When missionaries came to the borderlands, they usually brought with them livestock, fruit trees, and seeds for crops. The missions they built included churches and ranch and farm buildings. Some missions were built near Indian villages. In other places, Indians settled around the missions.

The Spanish and the Indians learned from one another. The Indians taught the Spanish how to build adobe houses and how to use herbs as medicines. The Spanish taught the Indians how to guide a plow instead of using a stick and hoe in the Indian way. They learned to use other tools and machines the missionaries brought from Spain.

The coming of the Spanish missions changed the way many Indians lived and worked. It also changed what was even more important to the native peoples—the way they worshipped. While many Indians kept to their traditional religions, others were taught to become Catholics.

At first some Indians welcomed the advantages of living at the missions. Like the Spanish, they were learning new ways. And the Spanish missionaries and soldiers protected them from their enemies. But problems soon developed. Many Indians were forced to work on mission farms and ranches against their will. Many missionaries used cruel treatment to control the Indians. One missionary wrote, "The punishments resorted to . . . are the shackles, the lash, and the stocks." They also were forced to give up their religious traditions.

Some Indians fought back. They killed missionaries and destroyed churches and other mission buildings. To protect its missions, the Spanish government built roads linking them with nearby presidios. The longest road system was El Camino Real (ray•AHL), or "The King's Road," which stretched for more than 600 miles (966 km).

The government of New Spain, and later the Mexican government, continued to build new missions in the borderlands as late as the 1830s. Many cities in the southwestern United States, such as San Antonio, Texas, and San Diego, California, began as missions.

✓ Why did the Spanish government send missionaries to the borderlands?

LESSON 1 REVIEW

Check Understanding

1. **Recall the Facts** Name three reasons settlements were established in the Spanish borderlands.
2. **Focus on the Main Idea** Why did the Spanish government decide to expand its lands in North America?

Think Critically

3. **Explore Viewpoints** How might a Spanish missionary and an Indian mission worker each describe the benefits and problems of living at a Spanish mission?
4. **Think More About It** What effects did the Spanish have on the Indians living in the borderlands? What effects did the Indians have on the Spanish?

Show What You Know

Letter-Writing Activity
Suppose that you are a soldier sent by the Spanish government to a fort in the California borderlands. Write a letter to your family in Spain telling what you have learned about the presidios, haciendas, and missions you visited as you traveled El Camino Real. Share your letter with a classmate.

This bowl was found at a Spanish mission and shows a feathered serpent, a traditional Indian design.

THE GROWTH OF NEW FRANCE

Link to Our World

What steps do governments take today to protect their interests?

Focus on the Main Idea
As you read, think about the steps taken by the French government to protect its interests in New France.

Preview Vocabulary
royal colony
portage
tributary
proprietary colony
proprietor

In New Spain the Spanish grew wealthy from silver and gold. In New France the French grew wealthy from the fur trade. But unlike the Spanish, most French people were not interested in settling North America. From 1608 to 1763 the French built only two cities in New France—Quebec and Montreal—and some small towns across Canada and along the Mississippi River.

A SLOW-GROWING EMPIRE

The French had been fishing along the eastern coast of North America since the 1500s. In time they moved inland and established a trade in animal furs with the Hurons. The fur trade led to the founding of Quebec in 1608. But by 1625 its population had grown to only about 60 people.

In the early 1600s, civil wars kept many people from leaving France. Later, under the rule of King Louis XIV, prosperous times returned, and most people had even less reason to leave home.

Trappers dried and stretched animal skins on frames like this one, made from a tree branch.

Meanwhile, English and Dutch colonists began settling the coastal region south of New France. It was not long before conflicts over the fur trade broke out among the French, the English, and the Dutch, as well as the Iroquois and the Hurons. In time, the Iroquois defeated the Hurons, who were the main trading partners of the French. By the 1660s the French fur trade was nearly destroyed, and the French empire in North America was crumbling.

Hoping to rebuild his hold in North America, Louis XIV declared New France to be a **royal colony**. The king,

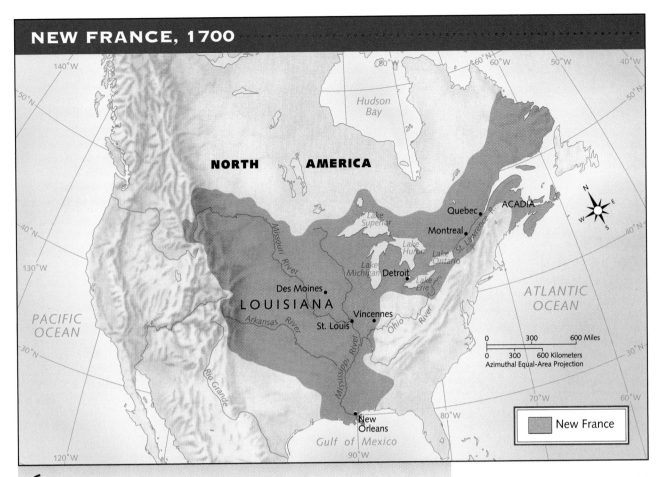

NEW FRANCE, 1700

NORTH AMERICA

Hudson Bay

ACADIA

Quebec

Montreal

Lake Superior

Lake Huron

Lake Michigan

Lake Ontario

Lake Erie

Detroit

Des Moines

LOUISIANA

Vincennes

St. Louis

Missouri River

Arkansas River

Mississippi River

Ohio River

Rio Grande

PACIFIC OCEAN

ATLANTIC OCEAN

New Orleans

Gulf of Mexico

| 0 | 300 | 600 Miles |
| 0 | 300 | 600 Kilometers |

Azimuthal Equal-Area Projection

New France

REGIONS This map shows the boundaries of New France about 1700.
■ French lands stretched across what major river valleys of North America?

rather than business people, would now rule the colony. The king appointed officials to live in New France and help him govern. The head of these officials was called the governor-general.

In 1672 King Louis XIV appointed Count de Frontenac (FRAHN•tuh•nak) governor-general of New France. The count's hot temper and stern ways often got him into trouble with the king. His friendly ways with the Indian peoples, however, helped the colony prosper.

Frontenac encouraged exploration of the West. But the way west was not easy. French ships could not travel very far inland before coming to water too shallow or dangerous for sailing. To travel the rivers, the French learned from their Indian trading partners how to build and use birchbark canoes. These boats could navigate shallow rivers. They also were light enough to be carried around waterfalls and rapids or overland between rivers. The French called this method of transportation **portage** (POHR•tij).

The Indian peoples often talked with the French about a great river, larger than all the others. The Algonkins (al•GON•kins) called it the Mississippi, which means "big river." Ever since the days of Jacques Cartier, the French had hoped to find a Northwest Passage through North America to Asia. Frontenac believed that the Mississippi River just might be the route they were looking for.

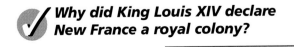

Why did King Louis XIV declare New France a royal colony?

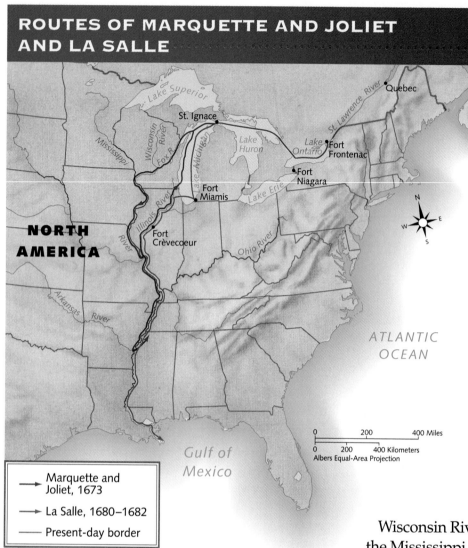

MOVEMENT
The French explorers Marquette, Joliet, and La Salle traveled on waterways in the interior of North America.

■ How far south did Marquette and Joliet travel? How far south did La Salle travel?

Legend:
→ Marquette and Joliet, 1673
→ La Salle, 1680–1682
— Present-day border

EXPLORING THE MISSISSIPPI

In 1673 Governor-General de Frontenac sent an expedition to explore the rivers and lakes that he hoped would lead French traders to the Mississippi River and then to Asia. The members of the expedition were Jacques Marquette (ZHAHK mar•KET), a Catholic missionary who knew several Indian languages; Louis Joliet (loo•EE zhohl•YAY), a fur trader; and five others.

The seven explorers set out in two birch-bark canoes from northern Lake Michigan. They crossed the huge lake, entered the Fox River, then traveled to the mouth of the Wisconsin River. There they saw the Mississippi for the first time. The explorers followed the big river but soon realized that it could not be the Northwest Passage because it flowed south.

When the explorers reached the Arkansas River, they met Indians who told them that Europeans lived farther south along the river. The explorers thought the Europeans might be Spanish or English, so they turned back. In four months Marquette and Joliet traveled about 2,500 miles (4,023 km). Their expedition opened the Mississippi to trade and settlement by the French. In time, they built trading posts that grew into towns and cities with such French names as St. Louis, Des Moines, and Louisville.

 What did Marquette and Joliet hope to find on their expedition?

FOUNDING LOUISIANA

After the Marquette and Joliet expedition, another French explorer set out to find the mouth of the Mississippi River. This explorer was René-Robert Cavelier (ka•vuhl•YAY), known as Sieur de La Salle, or "Sir" La Salle (luh•SAL). La Salle and an expedition of 20 French people and about 30 Indians paddled south from the mouth of the Illinois River on February 6, 1682. Two months later the expedition reached the mouth of the Mississippi. With shouts of "Long live the king!" the explorers fired their guns and claimed the entire Mississippi River valley, including all of its **tributaries**, or branch rivers, for France.

The region La Salle claimed was much larger than he could have imagined. It extended from the Appalachian Mountains in the east to the Rocky Mountains in the west and from the Great Lakes in the north to the Gulf of Mexico in the south. La Salle named the area Louisiana, to honor King Louis XIV.

After claiming this vast region, La Salle tried to establish a settlement. However, hardships led to disagreements, and La Salle was killed by one of the settlers. The settlement failed.

In 1698 the French king sent another expedition to Louisiana to find La Salle's river and try again to start a settlement. The leaders of this new expedition were Pierre Le Moyne (luh•MWAHN), known as Sir Iberville (ee•ber•VEEL), and his brother Jean Baptiste (ZHAHN ba•TEEST), known as Sir Bienville (bee•EN•vil).

In 1699 Iberville and Bienville reached the northern coast of the Gulf of Mexico. Their ships entered the mouth of a great river and sailed upstream. The brothers were not sure they were on the Mississippi until they met Mongoulacha (mahn•goo•LAY•chah), who was a Taensa (TYN•suh) Indian leader. Mongoulacha was wearing a French-made coat and carrying a letter addressed to La Salle. He told the Europeans his coat was a gift from Henri de Tonti (ahn•REE duh TOHN•tee). Tonti had stayed in Louisiana after traveling with La Salle years earlier. As for the letter, Mongoulacha said that Tonti had asked him to give it to a white man who would come from the sea. The explorers

The expeditions of Marquette and Joliet and of La Salle gave France claim to the Mississippi River, the longest river in North America.

Europeans used Native American birch-bark canoes to move goods and to explore waterways.

This drawing shows a French fort at the mouth of the Mississippi in 1700. Iberville is shown standing in a doorway, Bienville is sitting on the riverbank, and Tonti is walking from the riverbank into the fort.

then knew that they had found La Salle's river.

The brothers soon began to build settlements along the river and, in time, settlers began to arrive. But they faced terrible hardships, and many died.

In 1712 the French king made Louisiana a **proprietary colony**. This meant that the king gave ownership to one person, and allowed that person to rule. In 1717 John Law, a Scottish banker, became Louisiana's **proprietor**, or owner. Law formed a company to build plantations and towns. He brought in thousands of settlers. Finally Louisiana began to grow. In 1722 New Orleans, one of the colony's first towns, became Louisiana's capital.

Despite Law's efforts, however, the colony still needed more workers—especially on the plantations. Many planters began to bring in enslaved Africans to do the work. The French government soon passed laws called the Code Noir (KOHD NWAR), or "Black Code." These laws greatly restricted the ways in which the Africans in Louisiana could live.

Like the rest of New France, Louisiana failed to attract enough people for it to prosper. By 1763 there were only 80,000 French colonists in the area from Canada to Louisiana. By the same year, and in a much smaller area, there were more than 1,500,000 British colonists in North America.

 What lands did La Salle claim?

LESSON 2 REVIEW

Check Understanding

1. **Recall the Facts**   Which explorers opened the Mississippi to French trade and settlement?
2. **Focus on the Main Idea**   What steps did the French government take to protect its interests in New France?

Think Critically

3. **Think More About It**   In what ways did the environment play a role in the settlement of New France?
4. **Cause and Effect**   What were the effects of the shortage of workers in Louisiana?

Show What You Know

 **Time-Line Activity**   Construct a time line showing the French exploration and settlement of Louisiana. Compare your time line with those of your classmates.

LESSON 3

THIRTEEN BRITISH COLONIES

Link to Our World

Why might people today decide to move to a new country to live?

Focus on the Main Idea
As you read, think about why people in Europe decided to move to the colonies of North America during the 1600s and 1700s.

Preview Vocabulary

charter	Fundamental Orders
cash crop	immigrant
refuge	indigo
Puritan	debtor

The tobacco plant grew well in the warm climate of the southern colonies.

Jamestown and Plymouth were the first of many permanent British settlements in North America. By the 1730s the British had settled along the Atlantic coast from present-day Maine to Georgia. In time the area contained not one British colony, but thirteen. Each was formed in its own way and for its own purpose. And in each, the settlers had their own hopes and dreams for their new home.

THE EARLY SOUTHERN COLONIES

Virginia and Maryland were two of the earliest British colonies. Each was granted a charter by the king, allowing settlement of the Chesapeake Bay region. A **charter** is a document giving a person or group official approval to take a certain action.

Virginia began with the settlement of Jamestown in 1607. The Virginia Company of London started Jamestown as a trading post. Five years later, some colonists began growing tobacco as a **cash crop**—a crop that people raise to sell to others rather than to use themselves. The Virginia Company sold its tobacco all over Europe and made huge profits. Smoking tobacco became so popular that the company and its colony did well for a time.

At first the British king objected to the sale of tobacco. He thought using it was "a custom loathsome to the eye, hateful to the nose, harmful to the brain, [and] dangerous to the lungs." But when the Virginia Company went out of business in 1624 because of poor management, the king was quick to take back its

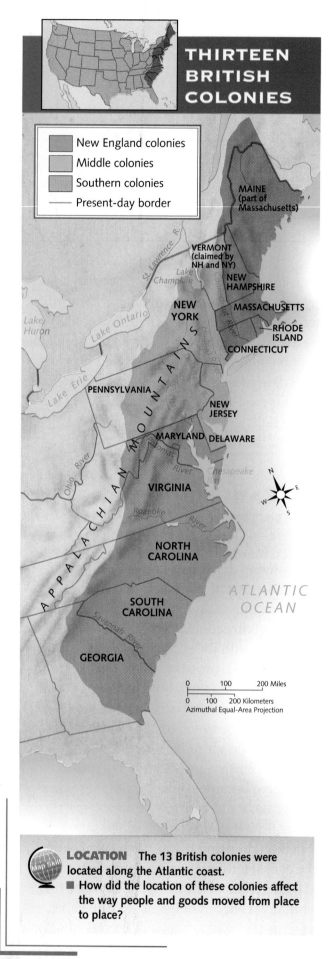

THIRTEEN BRITISH COLONIES

New England colonies
Middle colonies
Southern colonies
— Present-day border

MAINE
(part of Massachusetts)

VERMONT
(claimed by NH and NY)

NEW HAMPSHIRE

NEW YORK

MASSACHUSETTS

RHODE ISLAND

CONNECTICUT

Lake Huron

Lake Ontario

Lake Erie

PENNSYLVANIA

NEW JERSEY

MARYLAND DELAWARE

VIRGINIA

NORTH CAROLINA

ATLANTIC OCEAN

SOUTH CAROLINA

GEORGIA

APPALACHIAN MOUNTAINS

St. Lawrence R.

Lake Champlain

Ohio River

Potomac River

Chesapeake Bay

Roanoke River

Savannah River

0   100   200 Miles
0   100   200 Kilometers
Azimuthal Equal-Area Projection

LOCATION The 13 British colonies were located along the Atlantic coast.
■ How did the location of these colonies affect the way people and goods moved from place to place?

charter and make Virginia a royal colony. This meant that the king not only ruled Virginia but collected its tobacco profits for himself.

Tobacco also became an important cash crop for the Maryland colony. Maryland was founded by the Calverts, a family of wealthy business people. The Calverts wanted to build a colony not only to make money but to serve as a **refuge**, or safe place, for Catholics. Like other Catholics in England at the time, the Calverts had been treated unfairly because of their religion. The government approved of only one church—the Church of England.

> " *A CUSTOM LOATHSOME TO THE EYE, hateful to the nose, harmful to the brain, [and] dangerous to the lungs.* "
>
> King James I, describing tobacco use

In 1632 King Charles I chartered the northern Chesapeake Bay region as a proprietary colony. He made Cecilius Calvert, the second Lord Baltimore, its proprietor. One year later the first colonists left England. "I have sent a hopeful colony to Maryland," Calvert wrote. Calvert had named his colony for Queen Henrietta Maria, the king's wife.

From the beginning, Maryland's proprietors welcomed settlers of many religions. In 1649 Maryland approved the first law to guarantee religious freedom in North America. The law allowed all Christians to worship as they pleased. Sometimes, however, people of different religions had trouble getting along with one another. In time, disagreements based on people's differences affected life in all 13 British colonies.

 What was the most important cash crop in Virginia and Maryland?

THE NEW ENGLAND COLONIES

Within ten years after the Pilgrims founded their colony at Plymouth, another group of religious settlers came to North America. These settlers disliked many of the practices of the Church of England. They did not separate from the church, as the Pilgrims did, but they wanted to make it more "pure." For this reason they were called **Puritans**. The Puritans received a charter to start the colony of Massachusetts in the region that explorers from the Virginia colony had first called New England.

Beginning in 1630, Puritans built many settlements around their chief town, Boston. At the center of each town was a Puritan meetinghouse. And at the center of Puritan life in Massachusetts was religion.

Because religion was so important to the Puritans, newcomers to their colony had to share their beliefs. Those who did were given land for farming and a say in how their settlement was governed. Those who did not were not welcomed. Because of disagreements with Puritan leaders, some settlers left Massachusetts on their own. Others were forced to leave.

This portrait of a Puritan mother and her baby was made around 1674.

In 1636, settlers living in villages along the Connecticut River joined together to form the Connecticut colony. The most famous of these settlers was a minister—the Reverend Thomas Hooker. Hooker had left Massachusetts because he did not like the way that the colony's Puritan leaders controlled the lives of Massachusetts colonists.

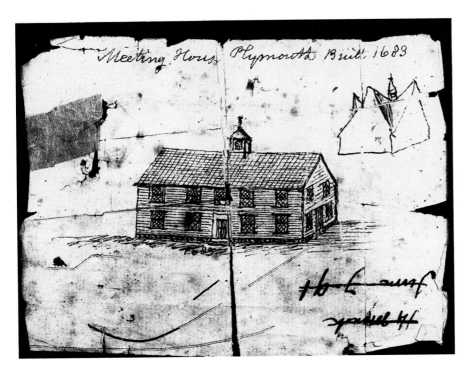

This drawing shows the Plymouth colony meetinghouse in 1683. The bell above the roof was rung to call people to meetings.

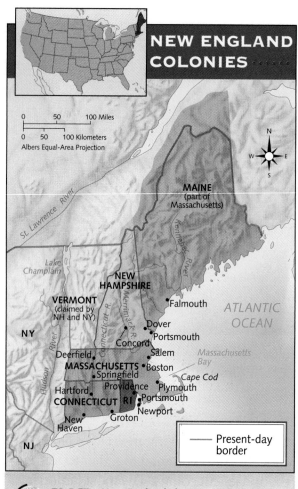

NEW ENGLAND COLONIES

0   50   100 Miles
0   50   100 Kilometers
Albers Equal-Area Projection

St. Lawrence River

MAINE
(part of
Massachusetts)

Kennebec R.

Lake
Champlain

NEW
HAMPSHIRE

VERMONT
(claimed by
NH and NY)

•Falmouth   ATLANTIC
                 OCEAN
•Dover
  •Portsmouth
Concord•
•Salem   Massachusetts
              Bay

NY

Merrimack R.

Connecticut R.

Hudson River

Deerfield•
MASSACHUSETTS •Boston
  •Springfield   Cape Cod
Hartford• •Providence •Plymouth
CONNECTICUT RI• •Portsmouth
New   •Groton Newport
Haven•

NJ

— Present-day
    border

PLACE New England changes greatly with the seasons.

■ Which season do you think was hardest for the settlers, considering New England's climate?

Like Thomas Hooker, Roger Williams did not like the way Puritan leaders governed Massachusetts. Williams spoke out time after time, asking for more freedom. Because of his views, Puritan leaders forced Williams to leave the colony. In 1636 Williams and his followers bought land from the Narraganset (nair•uh•GAN•suht) Indians and established the settlement of Providence.

No sooner were the Puritans rid of Roger Williams than they faced other attacks on their leadership. One such attack came from Anne Hutchinson. Hutchinson disagreed with some of the Puritans' religious teachings. Because of this, the Puritans declared her "a woman not fit for our society." They drove her out, too. Later, Hutchinson, her family, and followers founded a settlement on an island near Providence. Their settlement and three others, including Providence, were united under a single charter to form the Rhode Island colony.

Some settlers moved out of Massachusetts for reasons other than a desire for political or religious freedom. Settlers started the town of Strawberry Banke, now known as Portsmouth, for business reasons. The area was rich in trees, which the settlers cut and shipped as lumber to England. By 1680 Strawberry Banke was granted a charter under the name of the New Hampshire colony.

Hooker thought that a colony's government should be based on the will of its people, not its leaders. He also believed a colony should be able to elect its leaders. Other settlers in Connecticut agreed with Hooker. In 1639 the colony adopted Hooker's beliefs in the form of the **Fundamental Orders**, the first written system of government in North America. The Fundamental Orders allowed Connecticut's male colonists to elect their government leaders. They were the first colonists in North America to do so.

✓ **For what reasons did people establish colonies in New England?**

Anne Hutchinson was forced to leave Massachusetts because of her views about religion.

THE MIDDLE COLONIES

Not long after the British began establishing colonies in North America, the Dutch began to build settlements in their own colony, called New Netherland. They built their colony along the Hudson River, in parts of what are today New York and New Jersey. The Dutch, along with settlers from French-speaking Belgium, founded the city of New Amsterdam in 1625. Soon colonists moved up the river into what is now New Jersey. In 1638 colonists from Sweden established New Sweden, a string of trading posts in present-day Delaware and southern New Jersey.

The Dutch claimed New Sweden in 1655, but in 1664 British forces seized both New Sweden and New Netherland. The British king gave the colonies to his brother James, Duke of York. The land was split up and given its present-day names of New York and New Jersey. New York City grew from the Dutch capital of New Amsterdam.

In addition to settling Delaware and southern New Jersey, Swedish colonists also established trading posts in what is now Pennsylvania. In 1681, after the British had taken control of New Sweden, the British king gave William Penn a charter that made him proprietor of Pennsylvania. Penn was a member of the Society of Friends, a religious group also called the Quakers. British Quakers, like British

Peter Stuyvesant was the last Dutch leader of New Amsterdam. He lost his leg during a battle in the West Indies.

This drawing shows New Amsterdam—what is today New York City— as it was in 1651. What do you think the windmill was used for?

Catholics, often were treated unfairly because of their beliefs. William Penn, like the Calverts of Maryland, wanted to create a refuge where people could worship as they pleased. Quakers and other settlers who wanted religious freedom soon came to Pennsylvania, a name that means "Penn's woods."

William Penn carefully planned the settlements in his colony. One of them, the town of Philadelphia, had the look of a checkerboard, with straight streets that formed squares. Philadelphia's location was excellent for shipping and trading. It became the colony's main port for receiving not only goods but also immigrants. **Immigrants** are people who come to live in a country from another country.

Drawn by Penn's ideas of religious freedom, immigrants came to Pennsylvania and the other middle colonies from all over Europe. They included Irish Catholics, German Lutherans, and Jews from many countries. Many settled on small farms and raised fruits, vegetables, and wheat. So much wheat was produced in the middle colonies that they were soon called the "breadbasket" colonies.

✔️ **What countries built early settlements in the middle colonies?**

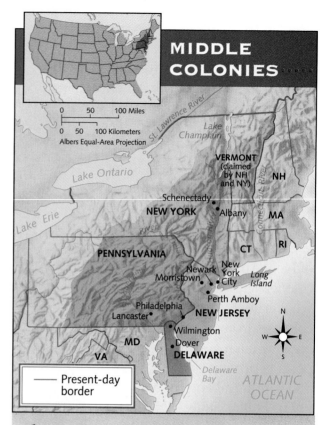

MIDDLE COLONIES

REGIONS The middle colonies were between the New England colonies and the southern colonies.
■ How do you think the location of the middle colonies affected contact with the other colonies?

Quakers gave Native Americans this necklace. It was a sign of the strong friendship between Native Americans and the colonists of Pennsylvania.

Unlike many Europeans, William Penn treated Native Americans fairly when purchasing land. This helped avoid conflicts with the Indian tribes.

THE SOUTHERN COLONIES

The southern colonies of Virginia and Maryland continued to grow during the 1600s. Then, in 1663, King Charles II granted a charter for establishing another colony in the area. The new colony would be south of Virginia, in the lands between Virginia and Spanish Florida. The charter divided the colony, known as Carolina, among eight proprietors.

Even before the charter was granted, colonists from Virginia had been building villages and farming in the northern part of Carolina. After 1663, colonists from England and the Caribbean, as well as French Protestants called Huguenots (HYOO•guh•nahts), came to settle there.

But the colonists could not survive just by owning land. They needed a cash crop. They tried tobacco, silk, grapes, and cotton. They had more success raising cattle, collecting furs, and making tar from pine trees. Only when they "found out the true way of raising and husking rice" did the colony begin to prosper.

In 1712 the northern two-thirds of the chartered area was divided into two colonies, North Carolina and South Carolina. North Carolina continued to develop as a colony of small farms. In South Carolina, landowners established huge farms in the style of the Spanish plantations of New Spain.

The main cash crop on many of South Carolina's plantations was rice. On land where rice would not grow, planters found they could grow indigo. **Indigo** is a plant from which blue dye is made.

Indigo became an important cash crop after 17-year-old Eliza Lucas experimented with the plant in the 1740s. Lucas was in charge of three South Carolina plantations owned by her father. Using seeds from the Caribbean, she spent several years growing different kinds of indigo. In 1743 samples of the dye made from her plants were judged to be of the best quality. Lucas gave indigo seeds to her neighbors and friends. Within a few years South Carolina planters were selling a million pounds of indigo a year.

The plantations of South Carolina required many workers. Many landowners filled this need by buying enslaved Africans. The coastal settlement of Charles Towne, later Charleston, South Carolina, became the most important seaport, social center, and slave market in the southern colonies.

The southern one-third of what had originally been Carolina was not settled by the British until 1733. A year earlier James Oglethorpe was given a charter to settle Georgia, a colony named for King George II.

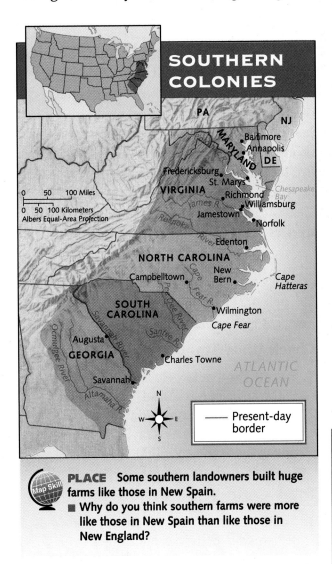

SOUTHERN COLONIES

PLACE Some southern landowners built huge farms like those in New Spain.
■ Why do you think southern farms were more like those in New Spain than like those in New England?

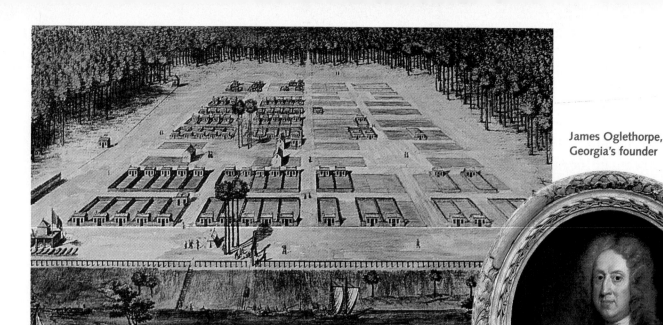

James Oglethorpe,
Georgia's founder

This 1734 engraving of Savannah, Georgia, was used to attract settlers to the colony. Present-day Savannah has the same rectangular street plan.

Oglethorpe had the idea of bringing over **debtors**, people who had been in prison for owing money, to settle the colony. Oglethorpe offered each settler 50 acres of land plus a bonus of 50 acres for every debtor the settler brought along to help work these small farms. But his plan did not work, because few people took advantage of Oglethorpe's offer.

Georgia's original charter did not allow traders to bring enslaved Africans to the colony. As a result, there were no plantations at first. After 1750, when Georgia law was changed to allow slavery, plantations soon developed.

 What three colonies were formed from the lands originally called Carolina?

LESSON 3 REVIEW

Check Understanding

1. **Recall the Facts** How was each of the 13 British colonies established?
2. **Focus on the Main Idea** Why did people in Europe decide to move to the colonies during the 1600s and 1700s?

Think Critically

3. **Think More About It** Do you think most settlers were better off in their new homes or in the places they came from? Explain.

4. **Past to Present** What reasons might people have today for coming to the United States to live?

Show What You Know

 Planning Activity Read again the list of items on pages 156 to 157. Suppose that you are going to a British colony to live. First, select a colony. Then list the ten most important items you would take with you. Compare your list with those of your classmates.

How To

Use a Table to Classify Information

Why Is This Skill Important?

Imagine looking through a drawer full of clothes. The socks, shirts, and jeans are all together in a jumble. It is hard to find things.

The same problem can happen with information. Like clothing, information is easier to find if it is **classified**, or sorted. Knowing how to classify information can make it easier to find facts.

Remember What You Have Read

When you read about the British colonies in the Americas, you were given a lot of information. You learned about where the colonies were built and when they were settled. This and other information can be classified by using a table.

Understand the Process

The tables below classify information about the 13 colonies in two different ways. In Table A, the colonies are classified according to when they were founded. Which colony was the first to be founded? Which was the last?

Table B gives the same information as Table A, but the information is classified differently. In Table B, the colonies are classified according to their location. The New England colonies are listed first, the middle colonies second, and the southern colonies third. Was New York a New England colony or a middle colony? What was the location of Massachusetts? of Virginia?

Think and Apply

Make your own table to show information about the Spanish, French, and British colonies. Choose some headings under which to classify the information by topic. Share your table with a classmate.

TABLE A: THE THIRTEEN COLONIES

Date Founded	Name	Location
1607	Virginia	Southern colony
1624	New York	Middle colony
1630	Massachusetts	New England colony
1632	Maryland	Southern colony
1636	Connecticut	New England colony
1636	Rhode Island	New England colony
1638	Delaware	Middle colony
1663	North Carolina	Southern colony
1664	New Jersey	Middle colony
1680	New Hampshire	New England colony
1681	Pennsylvania	Middle colony
1712	South Carolina	Southern colony
1733	Georgia	Southern colony

TABLE B: THE THIRTEEN COLONIES

Location	Name	Date Founded
New England colony	Massachusetts	1630
New England colony	Connecticut	1636
New England colony	Rhode Island	1636
New England colony	New Hampshire	1680
Middle colony	New York	1624
Middle colony	Delaware	1638
Middle colony	New Jersey	1664
Middle colony	Pennsylvania	1681
Southern colony	Virginia	1607
Southern colony	Maryland	1632
Southern colony	North Carolina	1663
Southern colony	South Carolina	1712
Southern colony	Georgia	1733

BUILDING CITIZENSHIP

CONNECT MAIN IDEAS

Use this organizer to show that you understand how the chapter's main ideas are connected. Copy the organizer onto a separate sheet of paper. Then complete it by writing details about each main idea.

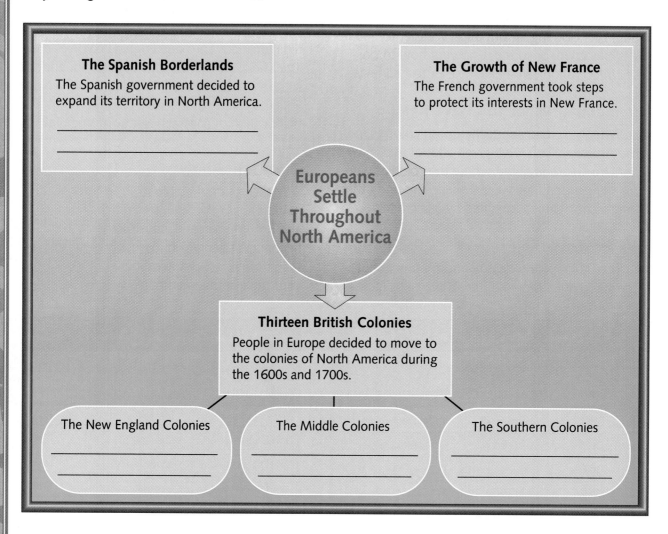

The Spanish Borderlands
The Spanish government decided to expand its territory in North America.

_____
_____

The Growth of New France
The French government took steps to protect its interests in New France.

_____
_____

Europeans Settle Throughout North America

Thirteen British Colonies
People in Europe decided to move to the colonies of North America during the 1600s and 1700s.

The New England Colonies
_____
_____

The Middle Colonies
_____
_____

The Southern Colonies
_____
_____

WRITE MORE ABOUT IT

1. **Write a Travelogue** It has been more than 300 years since Marquette and Joliet explored the Mississippi River. Use a map of the United States, your textbook, and library books to describe the route these French explorers followed.

2. **Write "Who Am I?" Questions** Choose three of the people who helped build the British colonies. For each person, write a question that gives clues about his or her identity and ends with "Who am I?" Exchange your questions with those of a classmate.

USE VOCABULARY

Write the term that correctly matches each definition.

buffer
charter
immigrant
indigo
mission

proprietary colony
refuge
royal colony
scarce
self-sufficient

1. an area of land that serves as a barrier

2. not plentiful

3. self-supporting

4. a small religious community

5. a colony ruled by a king

6. a colony owned and ruled by one person who is not the king

7. a document giving a person or group the official approval to take a certain action

8. a safe place

9. a person who comes to live in a country from another country

10. a plant from which blue dye is made

CHECK UNDERSTANDING

1. What is the oldest permanent European settlement in North America?

2. How did conflicts over the fur trade change the way New France was ruled?

3. What town became the capital of the Louisiana colony?

4. What cash crop was important to the early British colonies? Why?

5. Who were the Puritans, and where did they first settle?

6. What were the Fundamental Orders?

7. Why were there no plantations in Georgia before 1750?

THINK CRITICALLY

1. **Explore Viewpoints**   What reasons did the Spanish king give for wanting to build missions in the borderlands? How might the Indians have viewed those reasons?

2. **Past to Present**   Why do many large cities in the Middle West region of the United States have French names?

3. **Think More About It**   Thomas Hooker, Roger Williams, and Anne Hutchinson all spoke out about their beliefs. Why are some people more willing to speak out on issues than other people are?

APPLY SKILLS

How to Use a Table to Classify Information
The following figures give the estimated population for each of the 13 British colonies in 1750. Use this information to make a table that shows which colonies had more than 100,000 people and which ones had fewer than 100,000 people.

Connecticut	111,280	New York	76,696
Delaware	28,704	North Carolina	72,984
Georgia	5,200	Pennsylvania	119,666
Maryland	141,073	Rhode Island	33,226
Massachusetts	188,000	South Carolina	64,000
New Hampshire	27,505	Virginia	231,033
New Jersey	71,393		

READ MORE ABOUT IT

Fur Trappers and Traders: The Indians, the Pilgrims, and the Beaver by Beatrice Siegel. Walker. This book tells the story of the fur trade and its influence on the people of the 1600s.

Giants in the Land by Diana Karter Applebaum. Houghton Mifflin. This book describes how trees in colonial New England were cut down and used as masts for ships.

PEOPLE OF THE
BRITISH COLONIES

> **66** Such a medley!
> Such a mixed multitude
> of all classes and
> complexions. **99**
>
> Charles Woodmason, a
> minister, describing the
> people of a Carolina
> settlement in the 1760s.
>
> John Singleton Copley painted
> this portrait of an African in the
> 1770s.

LESSON 1

LIFE IN TOWNS and CITIES

Link to Our World

What different kinds of towns and cities are found in the United States today?

Focus on the Main Idea
As you read, think about the different kinds of towns and cities found in the British colonies.

Preview Vocabulary
town meeting	county
common	export
militia	triangle trade
farm produce	route
import	apprentice
Conestoga	
county seat	

During the late 1600s and early 1700s, more and more immigrants arrived in the British colonies. In time, some of the early settlements grew into towns and cities. Life in the towns and cities varied from place to place, depending on where they were built and on who settled there.

NEW ENGLAND TOWNS

Many settlers in the New England colonies lived in towns where, as one settler wrote, "every man . . . has a vote, . . . lives in a tidy warm house, has plenty of good food and fuel, with whole clothes, from head to foot [made by] his family." Most New England towns were self-sufficient communities in which the people grew or made most of what they needed.

The earliest New England towns were built around a single lane, or narrow road. Each of the town's families had a house on this lane. Families had their own gardens and planted rows of fruit trees. They also had pens for cows, sheep, chickens, or pigs. In the fields near the town, the people grew crops to sell to others and to use for themselves.

A meetinghouse stood at the center of most New England towns. In many places people came to the meetinghouse several times a week to worship. The meetinghouse was also used for town meetings. At a **town meeting** male landowners could take part in government. They voted on laws and chose workers for the town.

Two of the most important town workers were the herder and the constable. The herder was the person who took care of the animals on the town's **common**, an open area where sheep and cattle grazed. The constable was a police officer

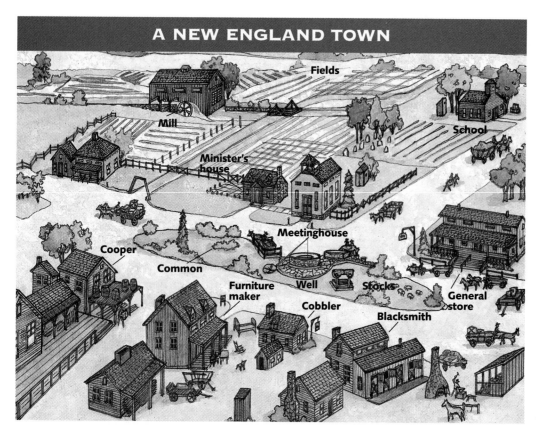

A NEW ENGLAND TOWN

Fields

Mill

Minister's house

School

Cooper

Common

Furniture maker

Well

Meetinghouse

Cobbler

Stocks

Blacksmith

General store

who made sure people obeyed the town's laws. Another important worker was the leader of the town's **militia**, or volunteer army. At least once a year, the men and boys of the town gathered on the common to train and drill.

 What gatherings were held at a meetinghouse?

MARKET TOWNS

Another kind of town developed in many places, especially in the middle colonies. This was the market town. Farmers traveled to market towns to trade their **farm produce** —grains, fruits, and vegetables—for goods and services.

In most market towns a general store sold **imports**, or goods brought into the colonies from other countries. The imports included tea, sugar, spices, cloth, shoes, stockings, and buttons. Near the general store was the shop of a

cobbler, who made and repaired shoes. There was often a blacksmith's shop, where iron was made into horseshoes, hinges, and nails. Most market towns also had a gristmill, where grain was made into flour and meal, and a sawmill, where logs were made into lumber.

Market towns often had more than one church. A Lutheran church might be a block away from a Quaker meetinghouse or just down the street from a Methodist church.

To carry their produce to market towns, many Pennsylvania farmers used big covered wagons called **Conestogas**. Conestogas were much larger than

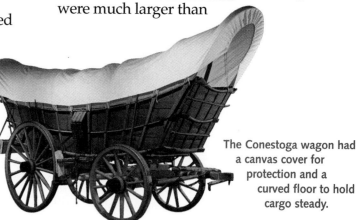

The Conestoga wagon had a canvas cover for protection and a curved floor to hold cargo steady.

regular wagons. When a visitor from Europe first saw them, he called them "huge moving houses."

When market towns grew along rivers, farmers carried their produce to the towns by boat instead of by wagon. It was easier and cheaper to ship heavy goods by water. After unloading their produce, farmers returned home, their boats filled with goods from the general store.

 What kinds of goods were bought and sold in market towns?

COUNTY SEATS

In the colonies that depended on cash crops, especially the southern colonies, there were few towns. But several times a year, plantation families would pack their bags, dress in their finest clothes, and travel to the **county seat**. This was the main town for each **county**, or large part of a colony. People went to church, held dances, and traded crops for goods at the county seat. Some plantation owners bought and sold slaves there. Along with a church and a general store, most county seats had a courthouse and a jail.

White men who owned land and other property met at the county seat to make laws and vote for government leaders. This meant that women, Africans, and Native Americans had no voice in how the colony was run.

 Why was the county seat important for people living on plantations?

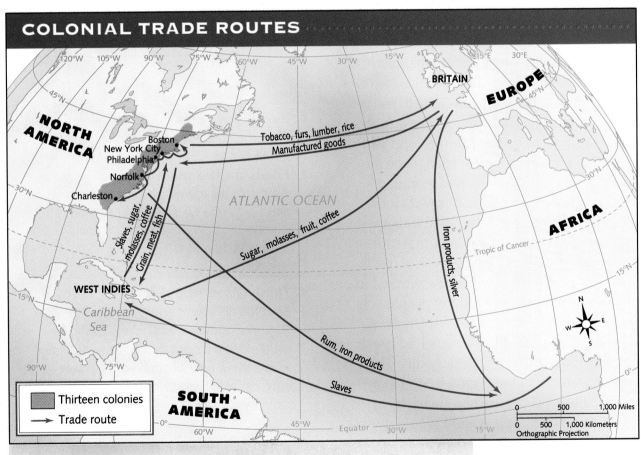

COLONIAL TRADE ROUTES

Tobacco, furs, lumber, rice
Manufactured goods
Sugar, molasses, fruit, coffee
Iron products, silver
Slaves, sugar, molasses, coffee
Grain, meat, fish
Rum, iron products
Slaves

NORTH AMERICA
Boston
New York City
Philadelphia
Norfolk
Charleston
ATLANTIC OCEAN
BRITAIN
EUROPE
AFRICA
Tropic of Cancer
WEST INDIES
Caribbean Sea
SOUTH AMERICA
Equator

Thirteen colonies
Trade route

0   500   1,000 Miles
0   500   1,000 Kilometers
Orthographic Projection

 MOVEMENT Many colonial traders traveled between Britain and the 13 colonies and between the 13 colonies and the British colonies in the West Indies. Some followed triangular routes between Britain, Africa, and the British colonies.
■ What was traded at each point of a triangular trade route?

CITIES

By the middle of the 1700s, several towns along the Atlantic coast had grown into cities. Among these were New York City, Philadelphia, and Charleston. They all had good harbors, and they grew because of trade. Ship after ship arrived at these cities, carrying new settlers and imported goods. After a few weeks in port, the ships sailed away loaded with **exports**, or goods to be sold in other countries. Exports from the colonies included raw materials such as furs, lumber, and dried fish, as well as cash crops.

Many ships followed a direct trade route between Britain and the 13 colonies. This was because the British government wanted the colonies to send their exports only to Britain or to other British colonies. The government also wanted the colonists to buy manufactured goods only from Britain.

Some ships followed what came to be known as **triangle trade routes**. These routes linked Britain, the British colonies, and Africa as the three points of a great triangle on the Atlantic Ocean. Traders carried manufactured goods from Britain and raw materials from the 13 colonies and the West Indies. They carried enslaved people from Africa.

Most coastal cities grew because of trade. However, people in the cities also worked in other kinds of businesses. Many people made their living from the sea—by fishing, whaling, or shipbuilding. Others sold goods that they made by using special skills. There were hatmakers, tailors, printers, and many others. Young people learned such jobs by becoming **apprentices**. A child would move in with the family of a skilled worker and help in the family's business for several years.

✓ Why were the first colonial cities located along the Atlantic coast?

This harbor scene shows the city of Charleston, South Carolina, in the 1730s. Charleston was one of the busiest port cities in colonial America.

LESSON 1 REVIEW

Check Understanding

1. **Recall the Facts** In colonial times, where were the different kinds of towns and cities located?
2. **Focus on the Main Idea** In what ways were colonial towns different from one another? How were the towns different from the cities?

Think Critically

3. **Think More About It** What needs of the colonists did towns and cities meet?
4. **Explore Viewpoints** People who lived on plantations did not often visit towns. How would living on a plantation have been different from living in or near a town? Where would you rather have lived? Why?

Show What You Know

Diorama Activity Create a scene showing everyday life in a colonial town or city. Display your diorama in the classroom.

Read a Circle Graph

Why Is This Skill Important?

Suppose you are writing a report on the British colonies. You want to show in a simple, clear way that the population of the colonies was made up of people from many different places. One way to show the information is by making a graph. A graph is a diagram for showing numbers. Graphs make it easier to see and compare large amounts of information.

Understand the Process

One kind of graph is a circle graph. A circle graph is often called a pie graph because it is round and divided into pieces, or parts. A circle graph compares amounts and makes it easy to see how much each part is of the whole. The circle graph on this page shows the population of the British colonies in 1775. The graph's parts are the many different ethnic groups that made up the population at that time.

You will see that a percent, shown by the symbol % in the graph, is given in each part of the graph. Suppose you cut a giant pie into 100 pieces. Those 100 pieces together equal the whole pie, or 100 percent of it. Fifty pieces would be one-half of the pie, or 50 percent of it. Ten pieces would be one-tenth of the pie, or 10 percent of it.

Find the English on the graph. The English made up about 49 percent of the population of the British colonies in 1775. That "slice" is almost 50 percent, or one-half, of the "pie."

Like other graphs, a circle graph can help you make comparisons. You can compare the parts to one another or to the whole. To be useful, however, a circle graph should have only a few parts. If it has too many, it will be crowded and hard to read.

Think and Apply

Use information from the circle graph on this page to write a paragraph about the people of the British colonies. First, compare the sizes of the different ethnic groups. Then, use the information to form a conclusion about the cultures of the British colonies. Compare your conclusion with the conclusions formed by classmates. How are the conclusions similar and different?

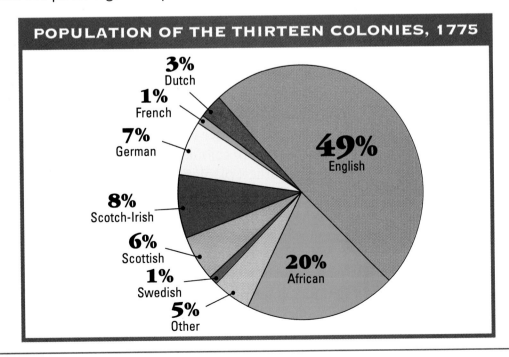

POPULATION OF THE THIRTEEN COLONIES, 1775

- **3%** Dutch
- **1%** French
- **7%** German
- **8%** Scotch-Irish
- **6%** Scottish
- **1%** Swedish
- **5%** Other
- **49%** English
- **20%** African

LIFE on PLANTATIONS

Link to Our World

How do societies today separate people into different groups?

Focus on the Main Idea
As you read, think about the ways that plantation life separated people into different groups.

Preview Vocabulary
planter
broker
indentured servant
auction

As towns and cities grew in many of the British colonies, plantations also grew—especially in the South. Settlements in Virginia, Maryland, the Carolinas, and Georgia became successful because the plantations there were able to grow more and more cash crops. Plantation owners were known as **planters**. Many planters bought as much land as they could. With bigger plantations, they could grow more crops to sell.

Plantations needed many hands to do the work. Most planters hired farm workers as well as servants to help out. Before long they added other workers—enslaved Africans. Over time slaves had a major impact on life in the southern colonies.

A SOUTHERN PLANTATION

From the time the Jamestown settlers began growing tobacco, plantations became important to the economies of the South. Planters soon learned to grow other cash crops as well, such as rice and indigo, and plantations spread to other southern colonies.

The earliest plantations were usually built along waterways. The main building was the planter's house. Servants and slaves lived in small buildings nearby. Because of the danger of fire, kitchens were in a separate building. There were sheds for storing crops and barns for livestock. There also might be a carpenter shop, a blacksmith shop, and a laundry. If the plantation was on a river, it most likely had its own dock. Plantations that were not on a waterway were connected by roads to another planter's dock.

Rice was an important cash crop in the southern colonies. This rice is ready for harvest.

A SOUTHERN PLANTATION

Tobacco fields

Dock

Slave cabins

Smoke-house

Cattle pen

Kitchen

Storage

Tobacco barn

Well

Brick making

Carpenter

Laundry

Main house

Stable

Black-smith

Office

Vegetable garden

LEARNING FROM DIAGRAMS Like a Spanish hacienda, a plantation was mostly self-sufficient. Field hands grew food and skilled workers produced many needed goods. Goods that could not be made on a plantation were brought in through trade.
■ Why were many plantations built near waterways?

Money was rarely used in the plantation economy. Instead, crops were used to trade. Crop buyers would travel up and down southern waterways, their boats filled with British-made goods such as shoes, lace, thread, farm tools, and dishes. The planters traded tobacco, rice, and indigo for these goods.

Owners of the largest plantations most often sold their crops through a British broker. A **broker** is a person who is paid to buy and sell for someone else. Planters sent their crops to Britain with a list of things they wanted the broker to buy for them. The broker then sold the crops, bought what the planter wanted, and sent the goods back to the colonies.

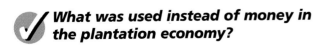

What was used instead of money in the plantation economy?

SERVANTS AND SLAVES

On small plantations, everyone in the planter's family worked. As plantations grew, planters added more workers. In time, the main job of the planter's family was to help watch over the work of others—both servants and slaves.

Many of the earliest workers in the Americas came as indentured servants. An **indentured servant** was a person who agreed to work for another person without pay for a certain length of time. Many indentured servants were Europeans who had wanted to move to the colonies but had no money. A planter or other business owner paid for the trip, and the person agreed to work without pay for anywhere from two to seven years. Once this time was over, the indentured servant was free.

Not all indentured servants had come willingly to the British colonies. Some had been sent by British courts to work in the colonies as punishment to pay for their crimes. Others were people who had been kidnapped and then sold in the colonies.

Among the first indentured servants to be sold in the British colonies were kidnapped Africans. By the middle 1600s, however, traders were bringing thousands of Africans to the British colonies not as indentured servants but as slaves. Slaves had no hope of gaining freedom after a certain length of time. They were enslaved for life. In time laws were passed saying that the children of enslaved people were slaves, too.

Olaudah Equiano (OHL•uh•dah ek•wee•AHN•oh) was 11 years old when he was stolen from his village in Africa. He described what happened this way:

> 66 *IN A MOMENT THEY SEIZED US both, and without giving us time to cry out, they stopped our mouths and ran off with us into the nearest woods.* 99
>
> Olaudah Equiano

66One day, when all our people were gone to the fields to work, and only I and my dear sister were left to mind the house, two men and a woman got over our walls. In a moment they seized us both, and without giving us time to cry out, they stopped our mouths and ran off with us into the nearest woods.99

Equiano was soon parted from his sister and sold at an **auction**, or public sale. Like other enslaved Africans, he had no choices about his future. The British colonies meant freedom for many Europeans, but they meant slavery for Africans.

✓ *What kinds of workers were there on plantations?*

Iron shackles (below) were sometimes used to prevent slaves from escaping. Olaudah Equiano (far right) was freed from slavery and later wrote a book about his life.

Charlestown, July 24th, 1769.

TO BE SOLD,

On THURSDAY the third Day of AUGUST next,

A CARGO

OF

NINETY-FOUR

PRIME, HEALTHY

NEGROES,

CONSISTING OF

Thirty-nine MEN, Fifteen BOYS, Twenty-four WOMEN, and Sixteen GIRLS.

JUST ARRIVED,

In the Brigantine DEMBIA, *Francis Bare*, Master, from SIERRA-LEON, by

DAVID & JOHN DEAS.

Advertisements for enslaved people (above) were given out before auctions. Slaves who were sick were often forced to hide their illnesses long enough to be sold.

Most plantation owners and their families lived in large houses with expensive furnishings. Many had ballrooms, music rooms, and libraries. The home of plantation owner William Byrd had the largest private library in the colonies. It had about 4,000 books.

EVERYDAY LIFE

Plantations in the southern colonies were often far from one another and far from any towns. Weeks or months could go by without visitors and without news about the latest happenings. For this reason company was always welcome.

Although slaves did most of the work, life for a planter was not always easy. A planter had to see that the crops were planted, harvested, stored, and shipped. Careful records had to be kept in order to run the plantation as a successful business.

One of the most famous early Virginia planters was William Byrd II. We know much about him because he kept a diary. Byrd's diary shows how difficult life on plantations could be. Many of his diary entries are about sickness and death. Some are about financial worries. More than once Byrd learned that the ships carrying his cash crops to Britain had sunk at sea. Even his neighbors gave him problems.

66In the evening I took a walk about the plantation and found that some of my good neighbors had dug down the bank of my ditch to let their hogs into my pasture, for which I was out of humor.99

A planter's wife had the same responsibilities as other colonial women caring for a household. She had to clothe and feed her family. Her household—family, servants, and slaves—sometimes numbered in the hundreds. It was up to her to see that all these people had food, clothing, and medical care.

There were few schools in the southern colonies because people lived so far apart. Large plantations had their own small schools for children to learn basic reading and writing. Planters often hired teachers from Europe for their children. When they were about 12 or 13 years old, the young people might attend special town schools. After that, boys often went to college in Britain or in the colonies. By age 12 or 13,

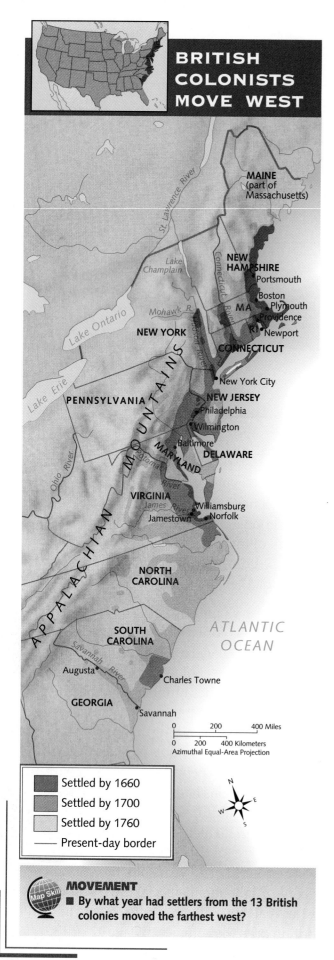

BRITISH COLONISTS MOVE WEST

MAINE (part of Massachusetts)

St. Lawrence River

Lake Champlain

NEW HAMPSHIRE
Portsmouth
Boston
Plymouth
Providence
MA
RI Newport
CONNECTICUT

Lake Ontario

Mohawk R.

NEW YORK

Lake Erie

New York City

PENNSYLVANIA

NEW JERSEY
Philadelphia
Wilmington
Baltimore
MARYLAND
DELAWARE

APPALACHIAN MOUNTAINS

Ohio River

Potomac River

VIRGINIA
James River
Williamsburg
Jamestown Norfolk

NORTH CAROLINA

SOUTH CAROLINA

ATLANTIC OCEAN

Savannah River

Augusta
Charles Towne

GEORGIA
Savannah

0   200   400 Miles
0 200 400 Kilometers
Azimuthal Equal-Area Projection

Settled by 1660
Settled by 1700
Settled by 1760
—— Present-day border

MOVEMENT
■ By what year had settlers from the 13 British colonies moved the farthest west?

girls stopped going to school. Planters' daughters were supposed to learn only "to read and sew with their needle."

There were no schools for servants or for the African slaves on the plantations. Laws in the colonies did not allow slaves to learn to read and write. By the age of 10, most young Africans were working alongside the adults.

Enslaved people were expected to spend their days working. At any time, they could be whipped for falling behind in their work or, as William Byrd wrote, for "a hundred faults." But at night, when their work was finished, the Africans often told stories and sang songs about their homeland. They found ways to keep their heritage alive.

 **Why were there so few schools in the southern colonies?**

*L*SSON 2 REVIEW

Check Understanding

1. **Recall the Facts** Describe life on a typical plantation in the southern colonies.
2. **Focus on the Main Idea** In what ways were people on southern plantations separated into different groups?

Think Critically

3. **Think More About It** Describe the differences between being an indentured servant and being a slave.
4. **Explore Viewpoints** How do you think Olaudah Equiano and William Byrd each viewed life on the plantations?

Show What You Know

 **Diary Activity** Suppose that you are living on a plantation in colonial times. Take on a role, and write an entry in a diary to show what a day on the plantation is like. Share your entry with a classmate.

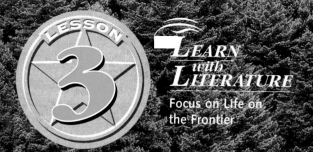

LEARN
with
LITERATURE

Focus on Life on
the Frontier

GREENHORN ON THE
FRONTIER

by Ann Finlayson

The history of the British colonies, like the entire history of the United States, is the story of people on the move. People left settled areas to claim what they saw as open land. They hoped to make a piece of wilderness into a farm, to build a house, and to raise a family. They saw land as an opportunity to better their lives.

Living on the **frontier***, the western border of settlement, was dangerous and difficult. Frontier farmers were always in danger of attack. They had to protect themselves from wild animals as well as human enemies. The Indian tribes were angry that farmers were moving into their homelands. The French and the Spanish did not want the British moving into land they themselves had claimed. Every day, frontier settlers had to meet challenges with few supplies and little or no help from other people.*

As you read this story, think about why Harry and Sukey, a brother and sister whose parents had died, would work so hard to build a farm they could call their own.

Harry started clearing at dawn, Sukey working at his side. By the end of the day, they had removed brush and small trees from a good acre on both sides of the brook. The big trees would remain until next winter, when Harry could burn them off.

The following day they planted corn—Indian fashion, with corn, beans, and squash all in the same mound. The corn would provide a stake up which the beans could twine, and the squash would spread out on the ground between the mounds. Later when the rich forest mold had lost some of its fertility, they would bury a fish in each mound for fertilizer.

His two years with the Wertmüllers had given Harry a healthy respect for Indian corn. It had a dozen uses. When fresh, it could be roasted in the ear and eaten with butter and salt like a vegetable. (The first time it was served to him, Harry had politely tried to eat the cob.) When dried, it could be hulled and ground and used as a grain—for pudding and cake and pone and mush and quick bread. The husks of the ear made excellent mattress stuffing, and the stripped cob could be turned into a smoking pipe or a child's doll, or burned as fuel. The stalk and leaves that were left could then be dried out in shocks and used as animal fodder. Corn had only one drawback: It could not be sown like other grains but had to be planted individually in mounds. But in a stump-filled field, there was no other way to plant anyway.

After corn, they rough-cleared another two acres and put in barley and rye, . . . and then Sukey's herbs and some vegetables. By the end of the second week, all the seeds were in the ground. It would be a small crop but enough . . . to keep them over winter. Harry felt good and gave himself an afternoon off to go hunting.

After that, Harry sharpened up the felling ax and got at the business of cutting timber for the cabin. He chose trees at least a foot thick and fourteen feet long, felled them, lopped off the tops and lower branches. He then squared them with the broadax and notched the ends (squared logs sat closer on one another than round ones and made a warmer house). By working hard, he could finish three logs in two days.

Making dolls like this one from corn husks was a craft that settlers learned from Native Americans.

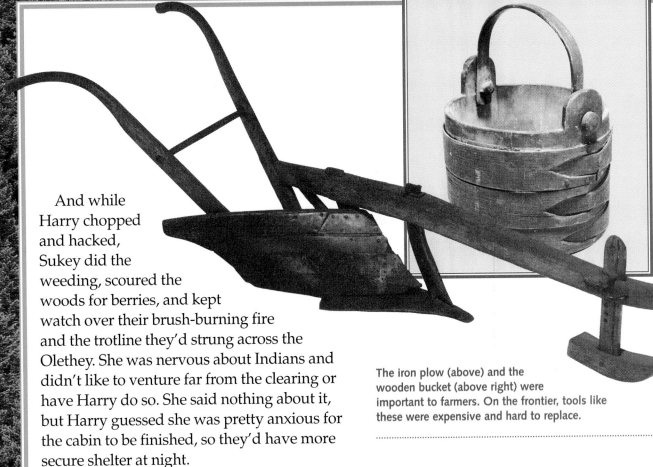

And while Harry chopped and hacked, Sukey did the weeding, scoured the woods for berries, and kept watch over their brush-burning fire and the trotline they'd strung across the Olethey. She was nervous about Indians and didn't like to venture far from the clearing or have Harry do so. She said nothing about it, but Harry guessed she was pretty anxious for the cabin to be finished, so they'd have more secure shelter at night.

When the sun was high, the two would meet by the brookside, dangle their feet in the cold rushing water, and eat whatever Sukey had found and prepared for dinner. They had plenty of fish—bass and trout mostly—and soon there were carrots and beets to pull. After the meal, it was back to work until near sundown, when Harry always knocked off to hunt something for the pot—and sometimes succeeded. After supper, they'd sit hugging their knees in the evening cool, companionable.

Sometimes it didn't seem real to Harry that they could actually be here, on their own land, working for themselves, making a farm out of the forest. It was exhausting labor. Harry went to sleep at night dead weary and aching. And yet it wasn't like plain work. You did that mechanically and then collected your pay and your keep in return, and that was that. Working like this to make a farm—well, you won your keep,

The iron plow (above) and the wooden bucket (above right) were important to farmers. On the frontier, tools like these were expensive and hard to replace.

of course, but you won something more, something that didn't get spent up. You had your farm, and it was yours in a way that a farm you bought—supposing you were rich and could just buy a farm—could never be.

Their deed was important, but that was for other people. What made the farm truly theirs was their labor.

Literature Review

1. Why did Harry and Sukey work so hard day after day?
2. Would you have joined Harry and Sukey on the frontier? Why or why not?
3. Search newspapers and magazines for stories about people like Harry and Sukey, people risking everything for a place of their own. Share these stories with classmates.

Use a Product Map to Make Generalizations

Why Is This Skill Important?

Symbols provide people with helpful information every day. If you see the symbol of a telephone receiver on a sign, for example, you know that a telephone is nearby. Map symbols also provide helpful information. They tell you such things as what cities are state capitals or where certain battles were fought.

Like other maps, product maps can help give you an overall, or general, picture of a place. Symbols for products tell you where certain products are made or grown. This can help you understand more about the kinds of work people in those places do. This, in turn, can help you to better understand the economic activities of a place.

This general picture of a place can help you make generalizations. A **generalization** is a statement based on facts. It is used to summarize groups of facts and show relationships between them. A generalization tells what is true most of the time but not always. It may contain words such as *often, many, most, generally,* or *usually.*

Think About Map Symbols

Notice that this map of colonial products has two map keys. The key in the lower right part of the map uses colors as symbols. The one in the upper left part of the map uses pictures.

The map key that uses colors shows the division of the British colonies into three regions. These regions are identified as the New England colonies, the middle colonies, and the southern colonies. The colonies within each region are shown in the same color. This map key also tells you that the borders shown on the map are those of the present-day states, not those of the colonies.

In the other map key, pictures stand for the important goods produced in the colonies. These

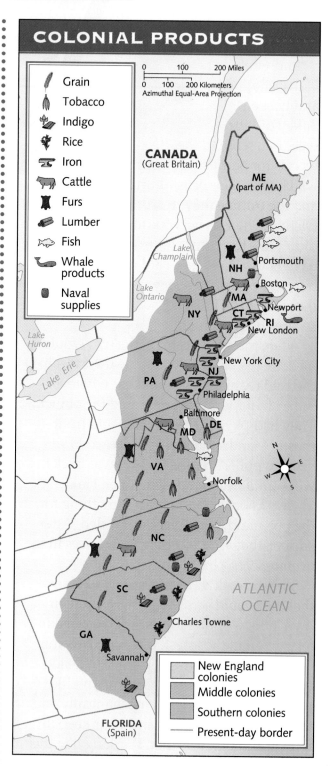

COLONIAL PRODUCTS

Grain
Tobacco
Indigo
Rice
Iron
Cattle
Furs
Lumber
Fish
Whale products
Naval supplies

0   100   200 Miles
0   100   200 Kilometers
Azimuthal Equal-Area Projection

CANADA
(Great Britain)

ME
(part of MA)

Lake Champlain

NH
Portsmouth

Lake Ontario

Boston
MA
NY
CT
Newport
RI
New London

Lake Huron

Lake Erie

New York City
NJ
PA
Philadelphia

Baltimore
DE
MD

VA
Norfolk

NC

ATLANTIC OCEAN

SC
Charles Towne

GA
Savannah

FLORIDA
(Spain)

New England colonies
Middle colonies
Southern colonies
Present-day border

THE NEW ENGLAND COLONIES

Connecticut

Massachusetts

New Hampshire

Rhode Island

THE MIDDLE COLONIES

Delaware

New Jersey

New York

Pennsylvania

THE SOUTHERN COLONIES

Georgia

Maryland

North Carolina

South Carolina

Virginia

goods were important not only because they were sold in the colonies, but also because they were exported for sale in Britain. The map does not show every good produced in the colonies, because there are too many to show on one map. The map shows only some of the most important ones.

Some of the map symbols stand for certain products and raw materials, such as tobacco, indigo, iron, and lumber. Others stand for groups of products. Naval supplies, for example, are products such as tar and rope that are used to build and repair ships. Whale products include the oils used for making lamp fuel and candles.

Understand the Process

Now that you know more about the symbols in the map keys, you can use these questions as a guide for making generalizations about the colonial economy.

1. What color is used to show the New England colonies? the middle colonies? the southern colonies?
2. What products appear most often on the map in the New England colonies?
3. What generalization can you make about the kinds of work most people did in the New England colonies?
4. What generalization can you make about the economy of the New England colonies?
5. What products appear most often on the map in the middle colonies?
6. What generalization can you make about the kinds of work most people did in the middle colonies?
7. What generalization can you make about the economy of the middle colonies?
8. What products appear most often on the map in the southern colonies?
9. What generalization can you make about the kinds of work most people did in the southern colonies?
10. What generalization can you make about the economy of the southern colonies?
11. What generalization can you make about the kinds of work most people did in all 13 colonies?
12. What generalization can you make about the economy of the 13 colonies?

Think and Apply

 Draw a product map of your state. Use an encyclopedia, atlas, or almanac to gather the information you will need. Use colors to show the different regions of your state, and then use pictures to show the products that are important there. Also include labels for cities and nearby states. Have a classmate use your map to make some generalizations about the economy of your state.

REVIEW

CONNECT MAIN IDEAS

Use this organizer to show that you understand how the chapter's main ideas are connected. Copy the organizer onto a separate sheet of paper. Then complete it by writing details about each main idea.

Life in Towns and Cities

Different kinds of towns and cities were found in the British colonies.
1. New England towns _____
2. market towns _____
3. county seats _____
4. coastal cities _____

The People of the British Colonies

Life on Plantations

Plantation life separated people into different groups.
1. planters _____
2. indentured servants _____
3. slaves _____

Life on the Frontier

Living on the frontier was dangerous and difficult.
1. dangers _____
2. hard work _____

WRITE MORE ABOUT IT

1. **Write a Description** The people who lived in market towns depended on one another for different goods and products. Imagine that you are visiting a colonial market town for the first time. Describe the sights, sounds, and smells around you.

2. **Write a Dialogue** After a hard day's work on the frontier, Harry and Sukey had time to talk before going to sleep. Write a dialogue that might have taken place between them. Have them tell about the work they did that day and about their hopes for the future.

USE VOCABULARY

For each pair of terms, write a sentence or two that explains how the terms are related.

1. town meeting, common

2. farm produce, Conestoga

3. import, export

4. county seat, county

5. apprentice, indentured servant

CHECK UNDERSTANDING

1. What were the purposes of the meetinghouse in most New England towns?

2. What kind of goods did general stores sell?

3. Who made the laws and voted for government leaders in the colonies?

4. What was the triangle trade route?

5. What effect did trade have on coastal cities?

6. How did planters get their indentured servants?

7. How were indentured servants different from slaves?

8. Why were there few schools in the southern colonies?

9. Why did African slaves not go to school?

THINK CRITICALLY

1. **Explore Viewpoints** One early settler in New England wrote, "every man . . . has a vote, . . . lives in a tidy warm house, has plenty of good food and fuel, with whole clothes, from head to foot [made by] his family." Do you think every colonist living in New England would have agreed with this viewpoint? Explain why or why not.

2. **Past to Present** Town meetings are still held in many towns in the New England states today. Why do you think this tradition continues?

3. **Cause and Effect** What effect did the triangle trade route have on the people of the British colonies?

4. **Think More About It** How were southern waterways important to plantation life?

5. **Personally Speaking** Would you have been willing to become an indentured servant in order to move to the colonies? Explain.

APPLY SKILLS

How to Read a Circle Graph Use the circle graph on page 185 to answer these questions.

1. Who made up the second-largest group of people in the 13 colonies?

2. Were there more German or French settlers in the 13 colonies?

How to Use a Product Map to Make Generalizations Use the map on page 194 to list the major products of the southern colonies. Then write a generalization about which products were related to the rise of slavery.

READ MORE ABOUT IT

Huskings, Quiltings, and Barn Raisings: Work-Play Parties in Early America by Victoria Sherrow. Walker. This book explores some of the ways that colonists helped each other while having fun.

The Jamestown Colony by Carter Smith. Silver Burdett. This book tells how Jamestown was founded and how the colonists worked to survive.

The Picture Story of Colonial Living by Edward Tunis. HarperCollins. The author describes and shows colonial clothing, tools, and furniture.

"Give me your tired, your poor, Your huddled masses yearning to breathe free..."

Coming to the United States Today

Since colonial times people from all over the world have come to the Americas, especially to the United States. In the past many were forced to come as slaves and prisoners. Others chose to come to start new lives or because of hard times in their homelands.

An American named Emma Lazarus wrote a poem in 1883, a time when hundreds of thousands of people were immigrating to the United States each year. The poem is now on the base of the Statue of Liberty, which stands in New York Harbor. Part of it says:

"Give me your tired, your poor, Your huddled masses yearning to breathe free . . ."

Today immigrants continue to come to the United States in large numbers. Some who cannot legally enter the country risk their lives to enter illegally. People have tried to enter the United States hidden in tanker ships and in the trunks of cars. Others, from Haiti and Cuba, have built their own small boats to cross the dangerous waters of the Straits of Florida to reach the United States. The United States remains a magnet for people from all over the world who hope to find better lives and more freedom.

THINK AND APPLY

Think about why people come to the United States today. Collect magazine and newspaper articles about present-day immigrants, and compare their reasons for moving to the Americas with those of the European colonists hundreds of years ago. Report your findings to the class.

BUILDING CITIZENSHIP

STORY CLOTH

Study the pictures shown in this story cloth to help you review the events you read about in Unit 3.

Summarize the Main Ideas

1. The Spanish built many missions in their borderlands. Roads such as El Camino Real connected the missions with haciendas and presidios.

2. In the borderlands north of Mexico, Spanish settlers raised large herds of livestock. Their haciendas were self-sufficient communities.

3. The French grew wealthy by trading with Indian peoples for furs.

4. The French explored the middle of North America. La Salle followed the Mississippi River to the Gulf of Mexico. He claimed the whole Mississippi River valley for France.

5. The British had 13 colonies along the Atlantic coast. Many New England settlers lived in small towns. Most towns had a meetinghouse for town meetings and for worship.

6. On plantations in the southern British colonies, planters grew cash crops such as tobacco, rice, and indigo. Enslaved Africans did much of the work.

7. People who moved west from the British colonies lived on the frontier. These people worked to clear the land and build farms.

Write a Story   Imagine that you are one of the people in a picture on this story cloth. Write a story about yourself. Tell who you are and where you came from or where you are going. Describe where you live. Tell about a problem you had in the place shown on the story cloth. How did the problem work out?

UNIT 3
REVIEW

COOPERATIVE LEARNING WORKSHOP

Remember

- Share your ideas.
- Cooperate with others to plan your work.
- Take responsibility for your work.
- Show your group's work to the class.
- Discuss what you learned by working together.

Activity 1
Draw a Map

Work in a group to draw an outline map of the 13 British colonies on a large sheet of paper. Maps in your textbook and in encyclopedias can help you. Label the colonies and their largest cities. Also label large bodies of water. Then draw symbols to show each colony's major products. Point out places on the map as you take the rest of the class on a "tour" of the colonies.

Activity 2
Make a Poster

You have learned about the ways in which Spanish settlers changed the lives of Indians in the border-lands. Work in a group to make a poster that shows at least three of these ways. Display the poster in your classroom.

Activity 3
Make a Model

Work in a group to make a model of either a New England town or a plantation. The model of a New England town should have a common, a general store, a blacksmith's shop, a mill, a meet-inghouse, and a school. The model of a plantation should include the planter's house, a kitchen, barns and sheds, buildings for servants and slaves, and fields.

Activity 4
Plan a Presentation

Enslaved Africans found ways to keep their traditions alive. Some told stories and sang songs they remembered from Africa. Work in a group, using reference books and other books from the library, to find a traditional African story or song. As a group, decide how you will present the story or song to your classmates and invited guests. You may want to perform a story as a play or do a dramatic reading of it. You may want to sing a song as a group or invite the whole class to take part.

USE VOCABULARY

Use each term in a sentence that will help explain its meaning.

1. presidio
2. permanent
3. tributary
4. debtor
5. militia
6. apprentice
7. broker
8. auction

CHECK UNDERSTANDING

1. What was the most important money-making activity in Spain's American colonies?

2. Why did the Spanish government build roads linking Spanish missions to presidios?

3. What convinced Iberville and Bienville that they had found La Salle's river?

4. What attracted European immigrants to the middle colonies?

5. What was the triangle trade route? What was carried on each part of the route?

6. What different groups of people worked on southern plantations? What work did each group do?

THINK CRITICALLY

1. **Cause and Effect**   How did the beliefs of the Puritans lead to the founding of other colonies in New England?

2. **Past to Present**   Describe how religious freedom affects people in the United States today.

3. **Personally Speaking**   Would you rather have been a planter or a planter's broker? Explain your answer.

4. **Think More About It**   Why do you think there were laws against slaves' learning to read and write?

APPLY GEOGRAPHY SKILLS

How to Use a Product Map to Make Generalizations   The map below shows some important colonial industries. What industries were found in the New England colonies? What generalizations can you make about New England's economy?

COLONIAL INDUSTRIES

Legend:
- Fishing
- Ironworks
- Silversmith
- Sugar refinery
- Shipbuilding

0   100   200 Miles
0   100   200 Kilometers
Azimuthal Equal-Area Projection

CANADA (Great Britain)

ME (part of MA)

Lake Champlain

NH — Portsmouth
Boston
MA
CT — Newport
NY   RI
New London
New York City
NJ
PA
Philadelphia
MD • Baltimore
DE
VA
• Norfolk
NC
SC
• Charles Towne
GA
Savannah
ATLANTIC OCEAN
FLORIDA (Spain)

Lake Huron
Lake Ontario
Lake Erie

Legend:
- New England colonies
- Middle colonies
- Southern colonies
- Present-day border

UNIT 4

The AMERICAN REVOLUTION

1760

1765

1770

1763
The French and
Indian War ends

1765
The Stamp Act
Congress

1770
The Boston
Massacre

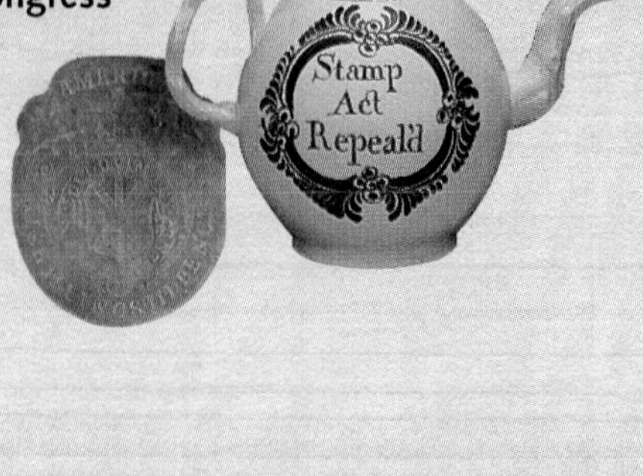

Stamp
Act
Repeald

*T*he colonists who moved to North America continued to be citizens of the European lands they came from. They were still expected to obey the laws of those lands. Over the years, however, many British colonists grew unhappy with British rule. They had little voice in a government thousands of miles away. They also believed that their far-off rulers did not understand life in the colonies. In time the British colonies in North America decided to break away from their homeland. They won their freedom, but only after a long and bitter fight.

← **The Battle of Princeton, 1777**

1775

1780

1785

1773
The Boston Tea Party

1774
The First Continental Congress

1775
The War for Independence begins

The Second Continental Congress

1776
The Declaration of Independence

1781
Battle of Yorktown

1783
The Treaty of Paris

GUNS FOR GENERAL WASHINGTON

by Seymour Reit

Crack! Crack! Crack!

The sound of musket fire cut through the stillness of the sleeping camp. Colonial soldiers, bleary-eyed, tumbled out of their shelters with their weapons ready and raced toward the palisade.[1] One of these men was a trooper named William Knox, who had been hoping to see action. Excited, he joined the others on the firing line and peered into the gray mist.

The news spread quickly among the waiting men. Hidden by morning fog, a British patrol had slipped across Mill Creek in an attempt to probe the rebel defenses. But an alert sentinel had spotted them in the marshes and opened fire. Others had joined in and the redcoats, giving up, had raced to their barge and escaped. The immediate crisis was over.

With shrugs and yawns, the soldiers trudged back to their warm beds. But Will Knox was too keyed up to go back to sleep. Unloading his musket, he walked across the drill grounds and climbed a rise called Prospect Hill. From here he could see his beloved Boston, locked in the hands of the enemy to the southeast. The city was only a few miles away, but it could well have been a thousand; the British had thrown a tight blockade around the city, and nobody could get in or out.

On this frosty morning in October of 1775, a sharp wind was blowing, but William was warmly dressed. Some weeks earlier a regiment of Pennsylvania frontiersmen had come marching into camp. Tough, hardy men, they wore long homespun shirts of butternut brown, fringed leather tunics, leggins, and Indian-style moccasins. Will had traded his best hunting knife, plus half a pound of sugar, for a long shirt and tunic. He'd also fancied one of the fine coonskin caps worn by the Pennsylvania

---

[1]**palisade:** fence of wooden stakes

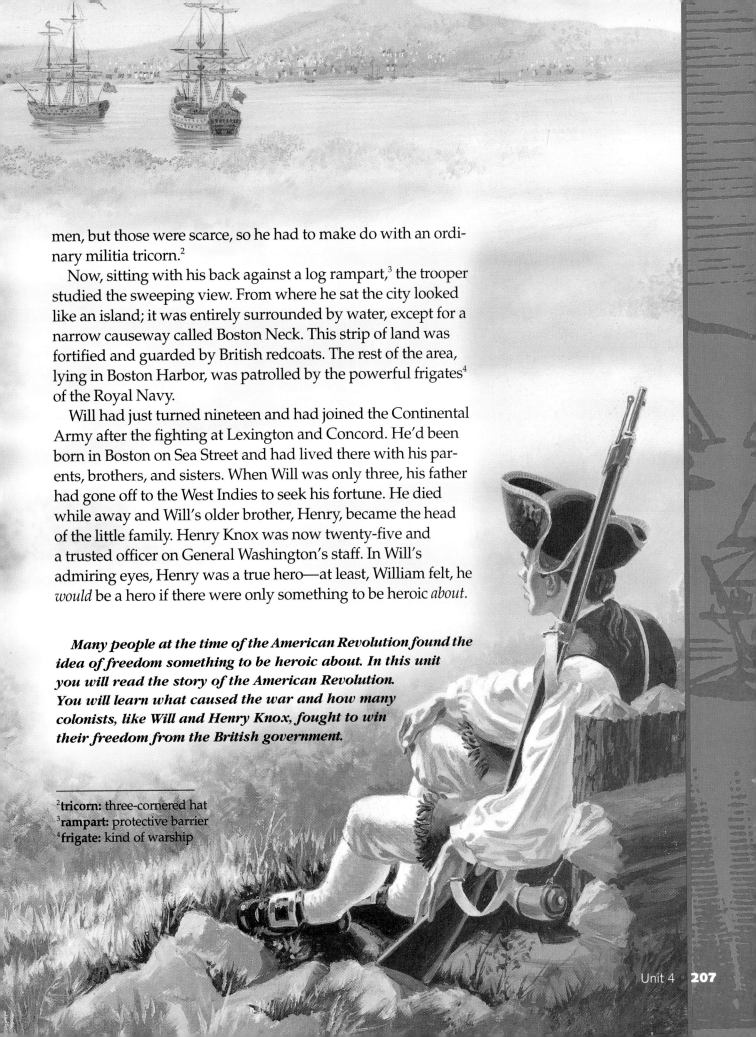

men, but those were scarce, so he had to make do with an ordinary militia tricorn.[2]

Now, sitting with his back against a log rampart,[3] the trooper studied the sweeping view. From where he sat the city looked like an island; it was entirely surrounded by water, except for a narrow causeway called Boston Neck. This strip of land was fortified and guarded by British redcoats. The rest of the area, lying in Boston Harbor, was patrolled by the powerful frigates[4] of the Royal Navy.

Will had just turned nineteen and had joined the Continental Army after the fighting at Lexington and Concord. He'd been born in Boston on Sea Street and had lived there with his parents, brothers, and sisters. When Will was only three, his father had gone off to the West Indies to seek his fortune. He died while away and Will's older brother, Henry, became the head of the little family. Henry Knox was now twenty-five and a trusted officer on General Washington's staff. In Will's admiring eyes, Henry was a true hero—at least, William felt, he *would* be a hero if there were only something to be heroic *about.*

Many people at the time of the American Revolution found the idea of freedom something to be heroic about. In this unit you will read the story of the American Revolution. You will learn what caused the war and how many colonists, like Will and Henry Knox, fought to win their freedom from the British government.

---

[2]**tricorn:** three-cornered hat
[3]**rampart:** protective barrier
[4]**frigate:** kind of warship

DIFFERENCES DIVIDE
*B*RITAIN *and Its*
*C*OLONIES

66 The Revolution was effected before the war commenced. . . . The Revolution was in the minds and hearts of the people. 99

John Adams

John Adams, colonial leader from Massachusetts

LESSON 1 · GOVERNMENT in the COLONIES

L ink to Our World

Why might people today become unhappy with their government?

Focus on the Main Idea
As you read, look for reasons the British colonists became unhappy with British rule.

Preview Vocabulary
Parliament   ally
self-government   tax
democracy   authority
legislature

At the beginning of American colonial times, the monarchs of Spain and France ruled their colonies in the Americas. Sometimes the king or queen asked a small council of advisers to help make the laws. More often the monarch ruled alone, making all of the laws for the colonies. In Britain and in the British colonies, however, the government ruled in a different way.

BRITISH RULE

The British monarch made some of the laws. But some of the people in Britain also took part in deciding what laws were made. British citizens elected leaders to speak for them in the part of the government called **Parliament**. The members of Parliament passed the laws for all British people.

The monarch and Parliament governed not only Britain but also the British colonies in North America. But the people living in the colonies were not allowed to vote in British elections. So, unlike other British citizens, the colonists could not elect lawmakers to speak and act for them in Parliament.

Some of the American colonists thought they should have **self-government**. That is, they thought they should be able to make their own laws. They felt that people in Britain did not understand life in the colonies. After all, the colonies were more than 3,000 miles (4,828 km) from London, Britain's capital city. What worked for Britain did not always work for the colonies, where ways of life were different.

As the colonies developed in the 1600s and 1700s, the monarch and Parliament let the colonists make some of the laws that affected them. Government in the British colonies

NORTH AMERICA IN 1750

ALASKA

Hudson
Bay

NORTH
AMERICA

NEW FRANCE

PACIFIC
OCEAN

LOUISIANA

BRITISH
COLONIES

FLORIDA ATLANTIC
OCEAN

NEW
SPAIN

Gulf of
Mexico

Caribbean
Sea

British
French
Spanish
Russian
Disputed

0   600   1,200 Miles
0   600   1,200 Kilometers
Azimuthal Equal-Area Projection

SOUTH
AMERICA

REGIONS This map shows the lands in North America that were claimed by Europeans in 1750. Notice that the British claimed much of the Atlantic coast.
■ What advantages would control of the coast give to the British?

Parliaments, made most of the decisions. The first of these colonial legislatures was known as the House of Burgesses. It was established in the Virginia colony in 1619.

The 13 colonial legislatures were made up of wealthy male property owners—women, people who did not own property, and slaves could not be members. People were elected to the legislatures by the property owners in each colony. The legislatures made laws for ruling their own colonies and set up local militias for protection.

Besides its legislature, each colony had a governor. The king chose the governor of a royal colony. In proprietary colonies, the proprietor named the governor. The governor made sure that the laws the colonists made were ones the British government would agree to. He also made sure that the colonists obeyed the laws passed in Britain.

 How were laws made for governing the British colonies?

THE FRENCH AND INDIAN WAR

British colonists ruled themselves without problems for many years. Then, little by little, things began to change. In 1753 the French in Canada began building forts on lands in the Ohio River valley claimed by both France and Britain. The British colonists viewed this move as an attack.

In the fighting that followed, both the French and the British colonists were helped by their Indian **allies**, or friends in war. But the British colonists could not fight off the French and their Indian allies with just the help of their own Indian allies. So the British

became more like a **democracy**, a government in which the people take part. But Parliament was quick to remind the colonists that they were British subjects. Parliament had to agree to the laws the colonists made. And the colonists still had to follow the laws made by Parliament.

The colonists welcomed the chance for self-government. In New England, towns had been making laws from the beginning. Soon every colony began making its own laws. People serving in **legislatures**, which were like small, local

This horn, used to carry gunpowder, was given to a British officer during the French and Indian War. It is engraved with a map showing some of the areas where the heaviest fighting took place.

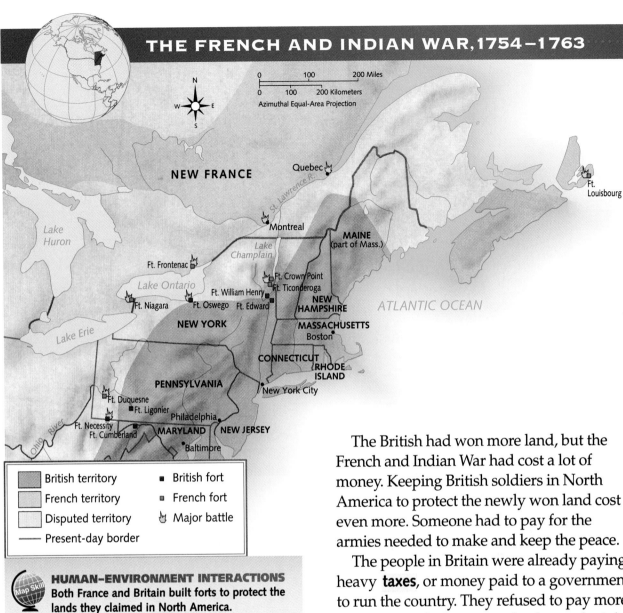

0   100   200 Miles
0   100   200 Kilometers
Azimuthal Equal-Area Projection

NEW FRANCE

Quebec

Ft. Louisbourg

St. Lawrence R.

Montreal

Lake Huron

Lake Champlain

MAINE (part of Mass.)

Ft. Frontenac

Lake Ontario

Ft. Crown Point
Ft. Ticonderoga

Ft. William Henry

NEW HAMPSHIRE

ATLANTIC OCEAN

Ft. Niagara   Ft. Oswego   Ft. Edward

Lake Erie

NEW YORK

MASSACHUSETTS
Boston

CONNECTICUT
RHODE ISLAND

PENNSYLVANIA

New York City

Ft. Duquesne
Ft. Ligonier

Philadelphia

Ohio River

Ft. Necessity
Ft. Cumberland

MARYLAND   NEW JERSEY

Baltimore

	British territory	■	British fort
	French territory	▪	French fort
	Disputed territory	♨	Major battle
——	Present-day border		

HUMAN–ENVIRONMENT INTERACTIONS
Map Skill Both France and Britain built forts to protect the lands they claimed in North America.
■ Where were most of the major battles of the French and Indian War?

government sent its army to help the colonists fight what came to be called the French and Indian War. With the help of the British army and of their Indian friends, especially the Iroquois, the British colonists defeated the French and their Indian allies in 1763.

After the French and Indian War, French Canada became a British colony. The British also gained French lands in North America between the Appalachian Mountains and the Mississippi River. Many British colonists were eager to settle these new western lands.

The British had won more land, but the French and Indian War had cost a lot of money. Keeping British soldiers in North America to protect the newly won land cost even more. Someone had to pay for the armies needed to make and keep the peace.

The people in Britain were already paying heavy **taxes**, or money paid to a government to run the country. They refused to pay more to take care of what seemed to be a colonial problem. So the king, George III, and Parliament decided that the colonists would have to pay for part of the cost of the war. They would also have to pay for the cost of keeping British soldiers in North America.

The colonists agreed to this plan, but many were angry about it. The colonial legislatures had been making their own tax laws. Now Parliament was telling them what taxes they had to pay. Then the British king took steps that angered the colonists even more.

First, he gave an order stating that the colonists were to stop settling the western lands just won from France. This order, called the Proclamation of 1763, reserved these

In this scene from 1704, France's Indian allies attack the town of Deerfield, Massachusetts. Why do you think some Indians fought for the French and others fought for the British?

lands for the Native Americans as their "hunting grounds." The king hoped this order would prevent more wars between the colonists and the Indians. But the colonists were furious.

Then, to make matters worse, the king gave his colonial governors greater **authority**, or control, over the colonies. The colonists were allowed to keep their legislatures. However, the governor could order the legislatures to change any laws he did not like.

The colonists did not expect these changes. They had hoped to gain more authority to govern themselves. Now they were reminded that they had to obey laws made in London. The colonists felt that the king knew little or nothing about their lives in North America. But what could they do?

 How did the lives of the British colonists change after the French and Indian War?

L SSON 1 REVIEW

Check Understanding

1. **Recall the Facts** What were the causes of the French and Indian War?
2. **Focus on the Main Idea** Why did the colonists become unhappy with British rule after the French and Indian War?

Think Critically

3. **Think More About It** Why do you think only wealthy male property owners were allowed to serve in colonial legislatures?

4. **Explore Viewpoints** Explain how each of the following people might have felt about the Proclamation of 1763: a member of Parliament, a colonist, and a Native American.

Show What You Know

 Speech Activity Plan a speech in favor of colonial self-government to give to the British Parliament. Present your speech to the class.

How To

Use a Historical Map

Why Is This Skill Important?

A historical map gives information about a place as it was in the past. It can show where past events took place. It can also show the way cities and countries looked at a particular time. Knowing how to use a historical map can help you gather information about a time long ago.

Understand the Process

Many atlases and history books contain historical maps. The title of a historical map usually tells you the subject of the map and the time period the map shows. The map on this page shows North America in 1763, at the end of the French and Indian War.

NORTH AMERICA IN 1763

Hudson Bay
50°N   50°W
140°W
PACIFIC OCEAN
NORTH AMERICA
LOUISIANA
30°N   30°N
NEW SPAIN
13 COLONIES
FLORIDA
ATLANTIC OCEAN
Gulf of Mexico
Caribbean Sea
80°W
10°N
SOUTH AMERICA

N
W E
S

- British
- British (reserved for Indians)
- French
- Spanish
- Russian
- Disputed
— Proclamation Line of 1763

0   600   1,200 Miles
0   600   1,200 Kilometers
Azimuthal Equal-Area Projection

Look at the map key to learn what each symbol means. Then use these questions to guide you in gathering information.

1. What color is the land controlled by the British in 1763? by the French? by the Spanish?
2. What land did the Russians control in North America at this time?
3. Which country controlled more land in North America in 1763, Britain or France?
4. Which European country claimed Florida in 1763?

One of the boxes in the map key has a pattern of diagonal stripes, called hatch lines, instead of a solid color. Hatch lines are often used on historical maps to indicate land that was claimed by two different countries or land that had a special purpose. In this case the map key tells you that land shown by hatch lines was controlled by the British—that is why one of the colors of the hatch lines is the same as the color for the British. It also tells you that the British reserved this land for another group—the American Indians.

You have read that in 1763 the British drew an imaginary line through North America called the Proclamation Line of 1763. Find the line on the map. The map shows that the Proclamation Line of 1763 served as the border between the land of the 13 colonies and the land that the British reserved for the Indians.

Think and Apply

Use an atlas to find a historical map of the United States. The map can be from any time period in the country's history. Then write a paragraph about what the map shows. What time period is shown? What special symbols are used to show information? How was the country different then from the way it is today? Share your paragraph with a classmate, and use it to explain why historical maps are useful.

BRITISH RULE OR SELF-GOVERNMENT?

Official buildings in the colonies displayed the British Royal Arms, shown here.

After the French and Indian War, Britain and the colonies began to disagree on matters of government. People had different ideas about what colonies were for and who should govern them. Here are five opinions on British rule and colonial self-government.

Joseph Fish was a minister in Connecticut. Like most colonists, he did not talk much about public affairs. But in this case he had very strong feelings. In a letter to his daughter Mary, he wrote:

66 They [the British] seem determined to distress us to the last degree, if not destroy us, unless we submit to the yoke of slavery they have prepared for us. 99

John Appleton was a merchant in Charleston, South Carolina. He traded tobacco, rice, and lumber for tea from China and cloth from India. This was his opinion:

66 We were doing fine here in the colonies when they [Parliament and the king] left us alone. Now I find taxes on everything I bring into the colonies to sell. It is bound to hurt business. 99

In a letter to a friend, a member of Parliament told how he felt about the colonies. Here is part of his letter:

66 Certainly, you don't think we are going to let all these colonies make whatever rules they want. English authority must be obeyed wherever the English flag flies. 99

A committee of Parliament wrote a report on the purpose of the colonies. Part of the report said:

66 We must remind all members of Parliament that colonies were set up for the good of England, not for the good of the colonists. These settlements can provide us with many needed things—tobacco, lumber, whale oil, fish, grain, and furs. And they also provide England with a place to sell our manufactured goods. 99

In a speech to Parliament, Prime Minister George Grenville explained why new rules were being made for the colonies. Here is part of what he said:

66 So it is only right and just that the colonists help to pay for the protection we are giving them. Clearly, Parliament and the King have authority over the colonies. It is in the name of that authority that we suggest new rules which will make the colonists pay taxes to the English government. 99

Boston, Massachusetts, in the mid-1700s

COMPARE
VIEWPOINTS

1. What views about government did each person or group hold? How do you know?

2. Why do you think each held those views?

THINK
-AND-
APPLY

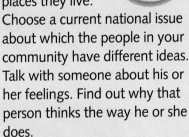

People often hold different views about issues because of their jobs or backgrounds or the places they live. Choose a current national issue about which the people in your community have different ideas. Talk with someone about his or her feelings. Find out why that person thinks the way he or she does.

LESSON 2

QUARRELS OVER TAXES and GOVERNMENT

Link to Our World

How do individuals and groups today work to make changes in their government?

Focus on the Main Idea
As you read, think about how individuals and groups in the British colonies worked to make changes in their government.

Preview Vocabulary
tariff   liberty
Loyalist   boycott
representation   congress
treason   repeal
petition   massacre

The people in the 13 British colonies had to buy many goods they could not grow or make themselves. They bought sugar, molasses, paper, glass, lead, paint, and tea from Britain, the British colonies in the Caribbean, and other countries. To pay for these goods, the colonists sold furs, fish, wood, tobacco, rice, wheat, corn, cattle, and other products to the British and people in other countries. Quarrels over these imports and exports were among the first to come between the colonists and their British rulers.

NEW TAXES FOR THE COLONISTS

When Parliament decided that the colonists should help pay the cost of the French and Indian War, it also decided how the payment would be made. In 1764 Parliament passed a law that came to be known as the Sugar Act. This law said the colonists must pay a tax on many goods coming to the colonies from other places. When colonists bought a pound of sugar, for example, they had to pay an extra amount on top of the item's price. The extra they paid was a **tariff**, a tax on goods brought into a country.

This tariff angered the colonists. But what bothered them most was that they had had no part in making this tax law. The king and Parliament had taxed the colonists without their consent.

Two of the first colonists to speak out against the new taxes were Mercy Otis Warren and her brother, James Otis, of Massachusetts. She called the British "stupid" and "greedy," while he called the tariff "unjust" and "a burden."

Barrels like this were used to ship goods during colonial times.

Some colonists made cartoon stamps (below) to show how they felt about the Stamp Act.

Under the Stamp Act, colonists had to pay for stamps (above and left) to be attached to printed goods of all kinds. The tax money collected for the stamps was sent to the British government.

But not all the colonists agreed with Warren and Otis. Some held the British view. These people were called **Loyalists** or Tories. Loyalist Martin Howard of Rhode Island felt that the colonists should be more grateful to the king and Parliament than they were. After all, he and other Loyalists argued, without British help, France or even Spain might have ruled the colonists. As Howard said,

> ❝Yet for a moment I wish that those unworthy subjects of Britain could feel the iron rod of a Spanish inquisitor or a French tax agent. This would indeed be a punishment suited to their ungrateful feelings.❞

 What did the colonists think of the new taxes on sugar and other goods?

THE STAMP ACT

Less than a year after the Sugar Act went into effect, Parliament made another tax law.

This one angered the colonists more than the first had. It was called the Stamp Act. Almost everything written or printed on paper in the colonies—from newspapers to playing cards—had to have a special stamp on it to show that a tax had been paid.

In the case of the Stamp Act, as with the other tariffs, the money was not what the colonists minded most. What really bothered them was that they had not agreed to the taxes. They had no **representation** in Parliament—no one acting or speaking for them.

James Otis asked his fellow colonists not to buy paper goods that had been stamped. He told a crowd in Boston that they should refuse to pay the taxes. Colonists began repeating Otis's words, *no taxation without representation.*

Other colonists also dared to speak out against the Stamp Act. In Virginia, Patrick Henry told the members of the House of Burgesses that they alone could say what taxes were ordered. Henry said that Parliament did not represent the colonies.

The colonies had their own legislatures to represent them.

Some Loyalist Virginia lawmakers shouted "Treason!" By accusing Patrick Henry of **treason**, they were saying that he was working against the government. "If this be treason, make the most of it," Henry answered. The Virginia legislature listened to Patrick Henry. It voted against paying any new British taxes unless the colonists agreed to them.

What James Otis and Patrick Henry had said about the Stamp Act spread through the colonies. More and more people decided not to buy goods that had been stamped. Everywhere people repeated the words *no taxation without representation*.

> " **IF THIS BE TREASON,**
> *make the most of it.* "
>
> Patrick Henry, 1765

 Why were many colonists angry at the British government about the Stamp Act?

PEOPLE PROTEST IN DIFFERENT WAYS

Word of the colonists' anger over the Stamp Act soon reached King George III and the British Parliament. Some members of Parliament said that James Otis and Patrick Henry should be thrown in prison for speaking out against the government. But no harm came to the two men.

Some colonists wrote letters to Parliament about the law. Others held public meetings and sent long **petitions**— signed requests for action—asking King George III to change the Stamp Act. But the king paid little attention to the colonists.

Throughout the 13 colonies, people met in groups to talk and act against the new taxes. In Massachusetts they called themselves the Sons of Liberty and the Daughters of Liberty. *Liberty* was the word heard over and over again. To most colonists, **liberty** meant freedom to make their own laws.

Crowds often gathered to hear Patrick Henry's fiery speeches. Henry, shown here arguing a court case, was a lawyer and a member of the House of Burgesses. In his most famous speech, Henry protested British rule and said, "Give me liberty or give me death!"

Members of these groups told other colonists that they should stop buying stamped goods. They even asked the people to **boycott**, or refuse to buy, any British goods. In Boston the Daughters of Liberty knitted, spun, and wove cloth so that colonists could boycott British-made cloth. People sang this song:

66Young ladies in town and those that
live 'round,
Wear none but your own country linen,
Of economy [saving money] boast,
let your pride be the most,
To show clothes of your own make and
spinning.99

Some of the Sons of Liberty protested in more violent ways. They attacked the homes of tax collectors, breaking their windows and stealing their property. They beat some tax collectors and chased several out of the Massachusetts colony.

Other colonists tried peaceful ways of protest. They decided to talk directly to the British lawmakers. The Pennsylvania legislature sent representatives to ask Parliament to think about the colonists' wish for representation. Among those sent was Benjamin Franklin of Philadelphia.

Franklin represented his colony well. Over the course of 50 years he had helped change Philadelphia from a simple colonial town to one of the best-planned cities in North America. He had organized the volunteer fire department, started Philadelphia's first hospital, and directed street lighting and paving projects. He had organized the town watch, a group of volunteers that protected Philadelphia's citizens. Benjamin Franklin was his city's and his colony's most respected scientist, business leader, and citizen.

Franklin warned the British lawmakers that the colonists would fight if Parliament sent the British army to make them pay the new taxes. He said, "The seeds of liberty are

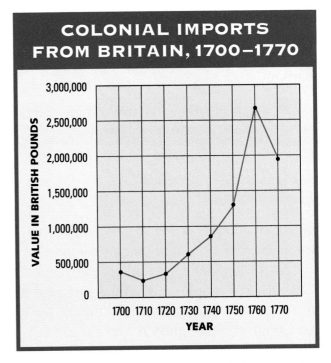

COLONIAL IMPORTS FROM BRITAIN, 1700–1770

LEARNING FROM GRAPHS This graph shows the value of the goods imported from Britain to the 13 colonies between 1700 and 1770. The amounts are measured in British pounds, the money used in both Britain and the colonies.
■ Why did British imports drop between 1760 and 1770?

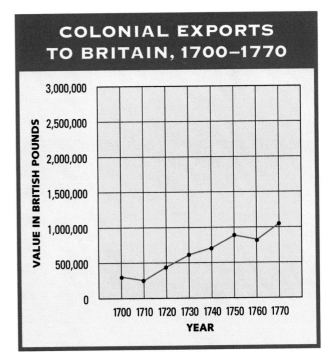

COLONIAL EXPORTS TO BRITAIN, 1700–1770

LEARNING FROM GRAPHS This graph shows the value of the goods exported from the 13 colonies to Britain between 1700 and 1770.
■ Why do you think that in most years the colonists imported more goods than they exported?

universally sown there [in Pennsylvania], and nothing can eradicate [destroy] them." But British leaders did not listen to Franklin's warning.

✓ *In what different ways did colonists act against the new taxes?*

THE STAMP ACT CONGRESS

Benjamin Franklin, James Otis, and other leaders had long thought that the colonies should work together instead of acting separately. In 1765 people who felt this way held a meeting in New York City called the Stamp Act Congress. A **congress** is a meeting of representatives who have the authority to make decisions. Nine colonies sent representatives to the Stamp Act Congress. They discussed

Benjamin Franklin was an inventor and a scientist as well as a colonial leader. Among his inventions were bifocal reading glasses and the lightning rod. He built his first invention, the Franklin stove (below right), in 1740.

the problems that the new tax laws had caused. The congress decided to ask people in all the colonies to refuse to buy stamped goods.

When Parliament heard about the Stamp Act Congress and the anger of the colonists, it **repealed** the Stamp Act. This meant that the Stamp Act was no longer a law. But while Parliament repealed one law, it added some new ones that affected trade in the colonies. By passing these new laws, the British government wanted to show that it still could make laws for the colonists.

To show clearly its authority over the colonists, Parliament sent more soldiers to North America. By 1770 there were more than 9,000 British soldiers in the 13 colonies. The colonists were told that the soldiers were there to protect the far-off western lands won in the French and Indian War. But the soldiers were in the cities along the coast!

Having British soldiers in their cities angered many of the colonists. The soldiers seemed like a police force. Sometimes this anger led to rock-throwing and name-calling. The colonists called the British soldiers "redcoats" and "bloodybacks," making fun of their red uniforms. The British soldiers paid them back by destroying colonial property and doing other damage—by riding their horses through churches and other buildings, for example.

As the anger between the British soldiers and the colonists grew stronger, fights broke out more and more often. Some of the worst fighting took place in Boston on March 5, 1770. In the evening a crowd gathered near several British soldiers. Some in the crowd shouted insults at the soldiers and began to throw rocks and snowballs. As the crowd moved forward,

This engraving (left) by American colonist Paul Revere shows his view of the Boston Massacre. The British, however, claimed that they were attacked first. Crispus Attucks (above) and four other colonists were killed in the fighting.

the soldiers opened fire. Three colonists were killed, and two died later. Among the dead was a 47-year-old runaway slave named Crispus Attucks (AT•uhks). Attucks had led the charge against the soldiers.

The events of that day have become known as the Boston Massacre. A **massacre** is the killing of people who cannot defend themselves. After the Boston Massacre took place, an uneasy calm settled over the thirteen colonies.

 What was the purpose of the Stamp Act Congress?

LESSON 2 REVIEW

Check Understanding

1. **Recall the Facts**   Why did the colonists decide to hold the Stamp Act Congress?
2. **Focus on the Main Idea**   In what ways did the colonists show they were unhappy with the British government for trying to control the colonies?

Think Critically

3. **Past to Present**   What do you think the words *no taxation without representation* might mean to people today?

4. **Cause and Effect**   Why did the British want to make new tax laws for the colonies? What happened when they did?

Show What You Know

 **Collage Activity**   Look through magazines and newspapers to find stories about present-day boycotts or other forms of peaceful protest. Ask members of your family to help you cut out the stories and paste them onto posterboard for display in class.

Chapter 7 • **221**

The COLONISTS UNITE

Link to Our World

What brings people together in difficult times?

Focus on the Main Idea
As you read, think about what brought the colonists together as they protested British rule.

Preview Vocabulary
Committee of Correspondence
consequence
blockade
quarter
Continental Congress
right
Minuteman
Patriot

In the months following the Boston Massacre, King George III received report after report of continued fighting and boycotts in the 13 British colonies. Petitions, too, poured in to the king from the colonists. When the king chose not to act on them, the colonists chose to act on their own.

THE COMMITTEES OF CORRESPONDENCE

The Stamp Act Congress had shown that the colonists could work together. But when their representatives were not meeting, it was not as easy for them to work together or even to communicate from day to day. This was because news traveled slowly. It could take weeks for people in one colony to find out what was happening in the other colonies.

Samuel Adams of Massachusetts found an answer to this problem. Adams was one of his colony's leaders. He had spoken out many times against British rule. Adams's answer was to set up a Committee of Correspondence in Boston. Then he got cities and towns in other colonies to do the same.

These **Committees of Correspondence** corresponded with, or wrote letters to, one another. Writers told what was being done in their colonies to protest the latest British laws. The letters were then delivered by riders on horseback. In this way anything that happened in one colony quickly became known in all the others.

 Why were the Committees of Correspondence set up?

Quill pens used during colonial times were made from feathers. The person using a pen dipped the tip in a small bottle of ink.

Samuel Adams of Massachusetts led many colonists in protesting British rule. He helped form the Sons of Liberty and organized the Committees of Correspondence.

THE BOSTON TEA PARTY

In 1773 Parliament passed another new law. This law allowed a British company to sell tea in the colonies for a very low price. This would hurt colonial merchants. And colonists would still have to pay a tax on tea.

People in every colony soon decided to boycott British tea. In Pennsylvania and New York, colonists did not allow ships carrying British tea to enter their ports. In Massachusetts, however, ships' captains refused to be turned away. Angry colonists showed their feelings in what later became known as the Boston Tea Party.

British ships carrying tea arrived in Boston Harbor in December 1773. Late one night, members of the Sons of Liberty, disguised as Mohawk Indians, boarded the ships, broke open all the chests of tea, and dumped the tea into the harbor. As they threw the tea overboard, they sang:

> **"**Rally, Mohawks! bring out your axes,
> And tell King George we'll pay no taxes.**"**

The colonists knew that their actions could have very serious **consequences** (KAHN•suh•kwens•ihz), or results. They were right. After hearing about the Boston Tea Party, Parliament decided to punish the colony of Massachusetts. A law was passed saying that no ship carrying colonial goods could leave Boston Harbor until the colonists paid for all the tea that was destroyed. To enforce the new law, Parliament ordered the Royal Navy to blockade Boston Harbor. To **blockade** is to use warships to prevent other ships from entering or leaving a harbor. The punishment was not just a matter of paying for the tea. The British government wanted to show the colonists that they had to obey its laws.

To further prove its authority, the British government ordered the colonists to **quarter** British soldiers, or pay for their housing. The colonists had to pay to feed the soldiers as well as give them a place to sleep. The king also

More than 300 chests of tea were dumped into Boston Harbor during the Boston Tea Party. Legend says that this chest washed ashore the next morning.

made General Thomas Gage the new colonial governor of Massachusetts. Gage was head of the British army in North America. "Intolerable acts!" shouted the colonists in response to the new laws.

People acted against the tax on tea in other colonies, too. In Edenton, North Carolina, a colonist named Penelope Barker led 51 women in a "tea party" of their own. They agreed to do everything they could to help with the tea boycott. They declared that they could not "be indifferent to whatever affected the peace and happiness of the country." The Edenton Tea Party has been called by one historian "the earliest known instance of political activity on the part of women in the American colonies."

 Why did colonists hold the Boston and Edenton tea parties?

THE CONTINENTAL CONGRESS

Many of the colonists believed that the British government would do anything, even use its army, to make them obey the laws. So the Committees of Correspondence called a meeting of representatives of all the colonies to decide what to do. The meeting took place in Philadelphia in September 1774. Because it was the first meeting of its kind on the North American continent, the colonists called it the

Continental Congress. Representatives from every colony except Georgia came to the meeting.

Members of the Continental Congress agreed to stop all trade with Britain. Imports would stop immediately. Exports would stop in one year. The Congress also said that the colonies would no longer obey British laws when the laws took away their liberty as citizens. The colonists told Parliament, "We are *for the present* only resolved to pursue . . . peaceable measures." The Congress agreed that if the demands for colonial **rights**, or freedoms, were not met, they would meet again in May 1775 to decide what to do next.

✓ *Why did the Continental Congress meet?*

FIGHTING AT LEXINGTON AND CONCORD

By the end of the Continental Congress, anger against the British government had turned Massachusetts into an armed camp. Members of the colony's militia companies became **Minutemen**, fighters who could be ready in a minute to defend Massachusetts. The British, too, kept their soldiers and their weapons ready.

The colonists who were against the British now called themselves **Patriots**. In April 1775 British General Thomas Gage, the new governor of Massachusetts, heard that the Patriots were storing weapons in the town of Concord near Boston. Gage also heard that John Hancock and Samuel Adams, two leaders of the Sons of Liberty,

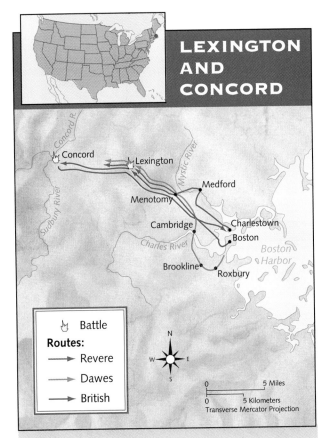

LEXINGTON AND CONCORD

MOVEMENT The battles at Lexington and Concord were the first of the Revolutionary War.
■ What cities did Revere and Dawes ride through to warn of the British approach?

were staying nearby, in the village of Lexington. The general sent 700 British soldiers to find the weapons and arrest the Patriot leaders.

But Paul Revere and William Dawes, members of the Sons of Liberty, went on a night ride on April 18 to warn Hancock and Adams that British soldiers were on their way. When the British arrived in Lexington on

"One if by land, two if by sea." Two lanterns hanging in a church tower signaled that the British were coming to Concord by boat across the Charles River.

Paul Revere
1735–1818

Paul Revere was one of the few people in Boston to own a horse. He kept one because he liked to spend his free time galloping through the countryside. Revere worked as a silversmith. As a Son of Liberty, Revere often carried messages from the Boston Committee of Correspondence to committees in other towns. In 1773 he rode to Philadelphia with news of the Boston Tea Party. But his most famous ride was the one he made to Lexington on the night of April 18, 1775, carrying the news "The British are coming!"

April 19, they found Minutemen waiting for them. The Minutemen were of all ages. Many owned property, but some were working men. At least five were Africans. Several were slaves. Shots were fired, and eight of the Minutemen were killed. Several others were wounded.

The British marched on to Concord, but the weapons they expected to find had been moved. As they marched back to Boston, they were shot at by Minutemen from the woods and fields beside the road. British losses for the day were 73 killed and 174 wounded. Of the 4,000 Minutemen at Lexington and Concord, 93 died or were wounded in the fighting.

The battle for colonial liberty had begun. The shots fired at Lexington and Concord marked the beginning of a long, bitter war between Britain and its American colonies.

 **Why did the British go to Lexington and Concord?**

# LESSON 3 REVIEW

Check Understanding

1. **Recall the Facts**   How did the Committees of Correspondence help bring the colonies together?
2. **Focus on the Main Idea**   What brought the colonists together as they protested British rule?

Think Critically

3. **Explore Viewpoints**   Describe how people in each of these groups might have viewed the Boston Tea Party: Parliament, Loyalists, Patriots.
4. **Think More About It**   Why do you think the first shot fired at Lexington and Concord has been called "the shot heard round the world"?
5. **Personally Speaking**   Do you think the Minutemen had any advantages over the British soldiers? Explain.

Show What You Know

Letter-Writing Activity   It is the spring of 1775, and you are a member of the Committee of Correspondence in Boston. Write a letter to a member of the committee in Philadelphia, telling what is taking place in your city.

Make Economic Choices

Why Is This Skill Important?

When you buy something at the store or decide what to order at a restaurant, you are making economic choices. Sometimes these choices are difficult. In order to buy or do one thing, you have to give up buying or doing something else. This is called a **trade-off**. What you give up is the **opportunity cost** of what you get. Knowing about trade-offs and opportunity costs can help you make thoughtful economic choices.

Remember What You Have Read

Like people today, the colonists had to make many economic choices. They, too, faced trade-offs and opportunity costs. Their economic choices, however, were made even more difficult by the continuing protests against British rule.

You have read that in 1773 Parliament passed a new law that affected the tea trade in the colonies. How did many colonists show their anger over the new law?

Understand the Process

Imagine that you are a colonist living in Annapolis, Maryland, in 1774. Like many other colonists, you like to drink tea. You have to make a choice. Should you buy British tea? Or should you buy sassafras, a local tea?

1. Think about the trade-offs. To do this, you must balance the advantages and disadvantages of your choices. British tea tastes much better than sassafras, but it is more expensive. And by buying British tea, you would not be taking part in the boycott. While sassafras tea does not cost as much, it tastes spicy. But buying sassafras tea would show that you support the boycott.
2. Think about the opportunity costs. You do not have enough money to buy both teas, so you have to give up one. If you buy the

The tea used in the colonies was not grown in Britain. It was imported from India and China to Britain, and then sold to the colonies.

British tea, you give up the sassafras and the extra money you would have left over. You also give up taking part in the boycott. If you buy the sassafras, you give up the good taste of the British tea. What choice would you make?

Because you usually cannot have everything you want, there will be opportunity costs as you trade off one product for another. This does not mean that the product you give up has no value. It means that at this time, another product or another action has more value to you.

Think and Apply

Imagine that a family member has given you $25 for your birthday, and you are trying to decide how to spend it. You may want to buy some compact discs or take some friends out for pizza. You do not have to spend all your money on one thing. You can choose some of one thing and some of another. Explain to a partner the trade-offs and opportunity costs of your choices.

BUILDING CITIZENSHIP

CONNECT MAIN IDEAS

Use this organizer to show that you understand how the chapter's main ideas are connected. Copy the organizer onto a separate sheet of paper. Then complete it by writing three details to support each main idea.

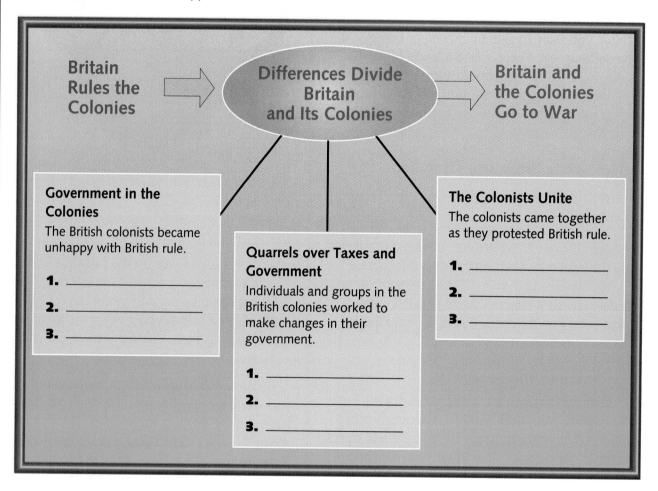

Britain Rules the Colonies

Differences Divide Britain and Its Colonies

Britain and the Colonies Go to War

Government in the Colonies
The British colonists became unhappy with British rule.

1. _____
2. _____
3. _____

Quarrels over Taxes and Government
Individuals and groups in the British colonies worked to make changes in their government.

1. _____
2. _____
3. _____

The Colonists Unite
The colonists came together as they protested British rule.

1. _____
2. _____
3. _____

WRITE MORE ABOUT IT

1. **Write a Persuasive Letter**   Imagine that you are living in one of the British colonies in 1770. Write a letter in which you try to persuade a member of Parliament to help American colonists gain self-government.

2. **Write a Report**   Choose one of the colonists you read about in this chapter. Then write a report on his or her life. Explain the person's role in the events leading to the American Revolution.

3. **Write a Descriptive Letter**   Imagine that it is the spring of 1774. You are a member of the Committee of Correspondence in Boston. Write a letter to a Committee member in North Carolina, describing events taking place in Boston.

 **SE VOCABULARY**

For each group of terms, write a sentence or two that explains how the terms are related.

1. tax, tariff

2. Parliament, congress

3. Loyalist, Patriot

4. self-government, democracy

5. boycott, petition

6. representation, legislature

 HECK UNDERSTANDING

1. How were laws made in the British colonies?

2. Who fought on each side in the French and Indian War?

3. What was the purpose of the Proclamation of 1763? How did most colonists react to it?

4. Why were some colonists unhappy with the Sugar Act?

5. What was the Stamp Act?

6. Why was the Stamp Act repealed?

7. How did the colonists' problems with Britain help unite them?

8. What was the purpose of the Committees of Correspondence?

9. Why did the "Intolerable Acts" make the colonists so angry?

10. Who were the Minutemen?

11. What was the effect of the fighting at Lexington and Concord?

 HINK CRITICALLY

1. **Think More About It** Why did colonists think they should have self-government?

2. **Personally Speaking** Do you think it was fair for King George III and Parliament to ask the colonists to pay for the French and Indian War? Explain.

3. **Explore Viewpoints** What do you think members of Parliament thought about the idea of taxation without representation?

4. **Cause and Effect** What were some of the causes and effects of the Boston Tea Party?

5. **Past to Present** How might Committees of Correspondence send news to one another today?

 PPLY SKILLS

How to Use a Historical Map
Compare the map on page 213 with a present-day political map of the United States. What states have been formed from the British land between the Appalachian Mountains and the Mississippi River?

How to Make Economic Choices Imagine that you need to choose between buying an apple or an orange at lunch. How would you make this economic choice? Identify the trade-offs and the opportunity costs.

 EAD MORE ABOUT IT

The Colonial Wars by Alden R. Carter. Franklin Watts. This book tells the history of the French and Indian War, which gave the British control over much of North America.

Concord and Lexington by Judy Nordstrom. Dillon. Photographs and stories bring to life the events of the first battle of the American Revolution.

Story of the Boston Massacre by Mary K. Phelan. HarperCollins. This book describes the major events leading to fighting between British soldiers and the colonists in Boston.

The WAR for INDEPENDENCE

> 66 In Freedom we're born, and like Sons of the brave, Will never surrender, . . . 99
>
> Mercy Otis Warren

American writer Mercy Otis Warren

At WAR with the HOMELAND

LESSON 1

Link to Our World

What might give one side an advantage over the other in a war today?

Focus on the Main Idea
As you read, think about what gave the British army an advantage over the Continental army as the war began.

Preview Vocabulary
olive branch
Continental
mercenary
enlist

The Committees of Correspondence quickly spread the news of the fighting at Lexington and Concord. A second Continental Congress was called, and it met in Philadelphia in May 1775. Some of the most important colonial leaders went to the meeting to decide what to do now that a battle had been fought. Pennsylvania sent Benjamin Franklin. Massachusetts sent John Hancock, Samuel Adams, and John Adams. Virginia sent George Washington and the fiery Patrick Henry.

THE SECOND CONTINENTAL CONGRESS

The Second Continental Congress moved carefully. The Patriots sent a letter called the Olive Branch Petition to King George III, telling him of their desire for peace and asking him to repeal the Intolerable Acts. An **olive branch** has stood for peace since ancient times. But in case the king refused to repeal the laws, the Second Continental Congress decided to form a colonial army.

The Congress asked all the colonies to send soldiers to Massachusetts. It chose George Washington of Virginia to lead this new Continental army. Washington, who had fought in the French and Indian War, came to the meeting in uniform to show that he would like to be the army's general. But it was Washington's understanding of soldiers and war that helped him to be chosen instead of such leaders as Artemas Ward, Charles Lee, or John Hancock.

The Second Continental Congress asked each colony to give money to support the new army. The money was

This scene of colonial Philadelphia shows the intersection of Second and Market. Thomas Jefferson wrote the Declaration of Independence here in a room he rented on the corner.

Philadelphia

Philadelphia calls itself "The Most Historic City in America"—and with good reason. It first earned its place in history in 1774, when the Continental Congress met in Carpenters' Hall, in the city's center. Over the next 30 years, many of the most important events in American history took place in Philadelphia.

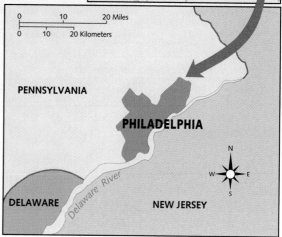

0   10   20 Miles
0   10   20 Kilometers

PENNSYLVANIA

PHILADELPHIA

DELAWARE

Delaware River

NEW JERSEY

needed to pay full-time soldiers and buy guns, bullets, food, and uniforms. The Congress also voted to print its own paper money, which came to be known as Continental currency.

In everything it did, the Congress seemed to believe the words of Patrick Henry. "The distinctions between Virginians, Pennsylvanians, New Yorkers are no more," he said. "I am not a Virginian but an American." The Second Continental Congress came to stand for the new unity of the 13 colonies.

> **❝ I AM NOT A VIRGINIAN but an American. ❞**
>
> Patrick Henry, 1775

 Why did colonial leaders call a second meeting of the Continental Congress?

THE CONTINENTAL ARMY

George Washington left Philadelphia right away to take charge of his army, which had already fought its first major battle. The Battle of Bunker Hill, which took place in Boston on June 17, 1775, was among the fiercest battles of the whole war. It was so fierce that to save bullets, the colonists were ordered, "Don't fire until you see the whites of their eyes." The colonists drove back the British twice before running out of bullets.

Washington arrived in Massachusetts to meet his army less than three weeks after this battle. The 14,000 soldiers, mostly from the northern colonies, wore no uniforms—only their ordinary clothes. Those who had guns carried flintlock muskets, which could not be used to shoot very far. Many of the soldiers had no guns at all. Instead, they carried spears and axes as weapons.

Some of Washington's soldiers had fought on the frontier and in the French and Indian War. They had learned to fight the way the Native Americans did—in irregular lines and from hiding—not the way a European army would. In fact, they had never fought as an army. Washington made rules for them and trained them. He punished soldiers who did not obey his orders. Slowly, Washington created the beginning of an army whose soldiers were proud to be called **Continentals**.

With little money and not much training, the Continentals went to war against the most powerful army in the world. Later, an officer would report, "It is incredible that soldiers composed of men of every age, even children of fifteen, of whites and blacks, almost naked, unpaid, and rather poorly fed, can march so well and withstand fire so steadfastly."

 What was the Continental army like when Washington took charge?

THE BRITISH ADVANTAGE

Unlike George Washington's army of mostly first-time soldiers, the British army was made up of professional soldiers. They had the best training, the most experienced officers, and the newest weapons. They also had help. The British used **mercenaries**, or hired soldiers, to fight on their side. These soldiers were Hessians, from the Hesse

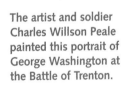

The artist and soldier Charles Willson Peale painted this portrait of George Washington at the Battle of Trenton.

Timothy Pickering of the Salem militia created this plan to show Continental soldiers basic marching steps. Unlike the British force, the Continental army had little formal training.

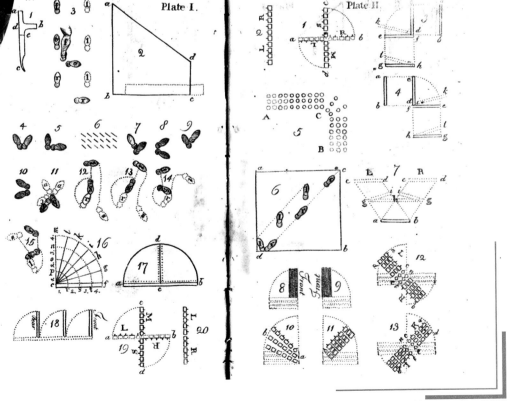

This scene at the Battle of Bunker Hill in 1775 was painted by Howard Pyle. Although the British eventually took the hill, their way of marching in straight lines during an attack caused more than 1,000 British soldiers to be killed or wounded.

region of Germany. The British also had Indian allies. Many tribes hated the colonists because settlers had taken over Indian lands.

But the British had problems, too. It was hard to fight a war 3,000 miles (4,828 km) from home. They had trouble getting supplies across the Atlantic Ocean. They also had political problems at home.

In the early days of the war, the British used their greater numbers and experience as fighters to take the advantage. While the British had 50,000 soldiers, General Washington usually had no more than 10,000 soldiers in his army at any one time. Most of the Americans **enlisted** in, or joined, the army for one year at a time. They might stay that long or longer, or they might not. When harvest time came, some of the Continentals would go home to their farms. If they did not get their pay as soldiers, they could not stay in the army. Washington did his best to keep his army together.

 How was the British army different from the Continental army?

LESSON 1 REVIEW

Check Understanding

1. **Recall the Facts**   What actions did the Second Continental Congress take?
2. **Focus on the Main Idea**   What gave the British army an advantage over the Continental army as the war began?

Think Critically

3. **Personally Speaking**   What do you think might have happened if the British king had accepted the Olive Branch Petition?
4. **Think More About It**   George Washington overcame many problems in leading his soldiers against the British army. What qualities should a good leader have?

Show What You Know

Poster Activity   Make a poster calling for soldiers to join the Continental army to fight the British. Compare your poster with those of your classmates.

Read a Political Cartoon

Why Is This Skill Important?

Cartoons can make you laugh. They can tell a story. They also can have deeper meanings behind their humor. Many cartoons give opinions about something. Cartoons that express opinions about politics or government are called **political cartoons**. Political cartoons are most often found in newspapers and magazines. Knowing how to read a political cartoon will help you understand its humor and its meaning.

The First American Political Cartoon

Benjamin Franklin drew the cartoon shown on this page. It may have been the first American political cartoon. It appeared in the *Pennsylvania Gazette* in 1754. Franklin was representing the Pennsylvania colony at the Albany Congress in New York. At this meeting he presented a "Plan of Union" for the colonies. He hoped his cartoon would make colonial leaders want to unite.

Franklin used his cartoon to urge colonists to support his plan for a union. The snake in the cartoon stands for all of the colonies. Each piece of the snake represents one of the colonies. The saying "Join, or Die" was based on an old tale about snakes. This story said that a snake that was cut into pieces would come to life again if it was put back together before sunset. Benjamin Franklin wanted the pieces of the snake—the colonies—to come together to survive.

Understand the Process

In his cartoon, Benjamin Franklin used the snake as a symbol. Symbols are a good way to show ideas that are sometimes hard to draw in a picture—ideas such as unity among the colonies. The use of symbols can make the message of a political cartoon easier to understand.

Animals are often used as symbols for ideas in political cartoons. The eagle is often used to represent the idea of freedom. The dove stands for the idea of peace. The hawk stands for war. The snail is used as a symbol of slowness.

To understand the meaning of a political cartoon, you first need to identify the symbols that are used. Then you need to think about the ideas that the symbols stand for.

Think and Apply

Make a booklet of symbols used in political cartoons both past and present. Draw each symbol, and write a short paragraph to explain its meaning. Make up a symbol of your own to add to the booklet.

BUILDING CITIZENSHIP

Franklin hoped this cartoon would help unite the colonies. It represents all the colonies except Delaware and Georgia.

The Decision for INDEPENDENCE

Link to Our World

Why is it important for leaders today to explain the reasons for their decisions?

Focus on the Main Idea
As you read, think about why it was important for colonial leaders to explain their decision to break free from British rule.

Preview Vocabulary
revolution declaration
independence grievance
allegiance

In Britain, Thomas Paine lost his job as a tax collector after asking for a raise. Benjamin Franklin, who was in London at the time, suggested that Paine go to America.

Although they were already at war, many colonists still believed that their problems with the British government could be settled without more fighting. They hoped the king and Parliament would let them take part in making the laws. By 1776 that thinking began to change, and the colonists prepared for a longer war.

THE FIRST STEPS

One of the Patriots who did the most to change the colonists' way of thinking was Thomas Paine. In January 1776 Paine published a pamphlet he called *Common Sense.* In it he attacked King George III as a bully and questioned the idea of one person having all the authority to rule. Paine felt that people should rule themselves. He called for a sudden, complete change of government—a **revolution** (rev•uh•LOO•shuhn). The colonies should cut their ties with the British government, he said, and set up their own government.

Everyone in the colonies talked about *Common Sense.* After nearly a year of war, the idea of **independence**, or freedom to govern on one's own, sounded good to many colonists. It also sounded good to many members of the Second Continental Congress. The time to act had come.

On June 7, 1776, Richard Henry Lee of Virginia gave a speech to Congress. He said that "these United Colonies are and of right ought to be free and independent States." He went on to say that the colonies no longer owed **allegiance** (uh•LEE•juhnts), or loyalty, to the king.

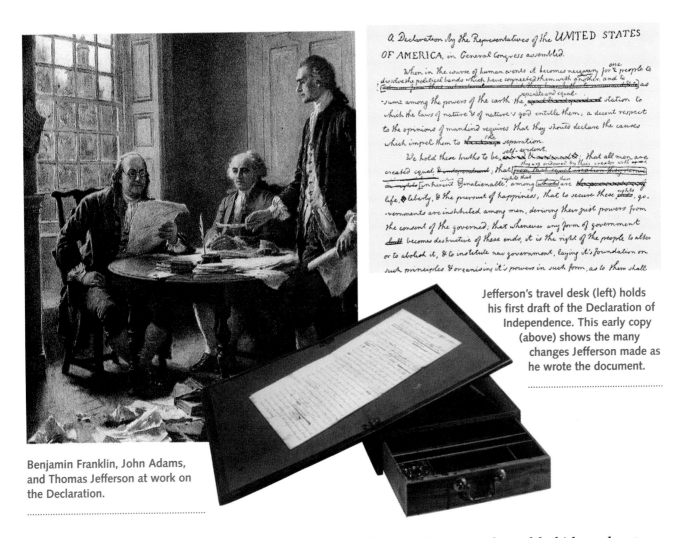

Jefferson's travel desk (left) holds his first draft of the Declaration of Independence. This early copy (above) shows the many changes Jefferson made as he wrote the document.

Benjamin Franklin, John Adams, and Thomas Jefferson at work on the Declaration.

The Congress waited almost a month before voting on the idea of cutting ties with the British government. Not all of the colonies were ready for independence. The representatives of seven or eight of the colonies would have voted for the idea in June. But at least three of the colonies would have voted against it, and one or two others were unsure. They needed more time before taking such a dangerous step. The leaders of the Congress hoped that a month's wait would help all 13 colonies decide in favor of independence. In the meantime, they formed a committee to draw up a **declaration**, or official statement, of independence.

The members of the committee were Benjamin Franklin of Pennsylvania, John Adams of Massachusetts, Robert R. Livingston of New York, Roger Sherman of Connecticut, and Thomas Jefferson of Virginia. Each member added ideas about what the Declaration should say. But Jefferson did most of the writing.

Only 33 years old, Thomas Jefferson was a leader of the Patriots in Virginia. He was a lawyer, he had studied government, and he had already written about the problems with British rule. Two years before, he had written *A Summary View of the Rights of British America,* in which he had listed for the first Continental Congress the changes the colonies wanted in their government. When the Declaration committee was selected, Jefferson began work at once. Every evening for the next 17 days, Jefferson wrote—and rewrote—the document that would become the Declaration of Independence.

Why did Congress wait before voting on independence?

WRITING THE DECLARATION

Thomas Jefferson wanted his words to help the colonists win their war for freedom. He wrote very carefully. He had to state the facts so that people would agree that the cause for independence was right, and that it was worth fighting for.

Jefferson planned the Declaration in several parts. In the introduction, he stated why the Declaration was needed. He said that sometimes a group of people must cut themselves off from the country they once belonged to. They find they have no choice but to form a new nation with the same authority as other independent countries. Jefferson said that when people do this, they must have good reasons. And, he said, they must explain their reasons so there is no doubt about why such a step is taken.

In the second part of the Declaration, Jefferson listed the colonists' main ideas about government. The words he wrote in 1776 are among the most famous in American history. Jefferson said:

> ❝ **WE HOLD THESE TRUTHS TO BE SELF-EVIDENT, *that all men are created equal.* ❞**
>
> Thomas Jefferson, 1776

❝We hold these truths to be self-evident, that all men are created equal, that they are endowed [provided] by their Creator with certain unalienable Rights, that among these are Life, Liberty and the pursuit of Happiness.❞

In the third and longest part of the Declaration, Jefferson listed the colonists' **grievances** (GREE•vuhns•es), or complaints, about the unfair things that the king and Parliament had done. He also listed the ways

John Trumbull's painting of the signing of the Declaration of Independence shows 48 members of the Second Continental Congress. The delegates met in Pennsylvania's State House, known today as Independence Hall.

What?

Independence Day

On July 4, 1776, the Second Continental Congress approved the Declaration of Independence. After the vote, the president of the Congress, John Hancock, signed his name to the document in large, bold writing. John Adams, writing home to his wife, Abigail, said that the event should be remembered with shows, games, sports, guns, bells, bonfires, and fireworks "from this time forward forever more." Americans have celebrated the Fourth of July, or Independence Day, as a national holiday ever since.

On July 8, 1776, Patriots rang the Liberty Bell in Philadelphia's State House to celebrate the adoption of the Declaration of Independence. The bell was rung each year after that until it cracked in 1835. The words written on the bell, "Proclaim Liberty throughout all the land unto all the inhabitants thereof," are from the Bible.

the colonists had tried to settle their differences with the British government peacefully. But, he noted, the king had refused to listen to the colonists. Such a king, Jefferson wrote, was "unfit to be the ruler of a free people."

Then, in the last part of the Declaration, Jefferson wrote that for all of the reasons he had described, the 13 colonies were no longer a part of Great Britain.

❝ We, therefore, . . . in the Name, and by Authority of the good People of these Colonies, solemnly publish and declare, That these United Colonies are, and of Right ought to be Free and Independent States. . . . ❞

When he finished writing, Jefferson gave the Declaration to Congress, and on June 28 it was read aloud. Then the members returned to Richard Henry Lee's idea of cutting ties with Britain. On the morning of July 2, 1776, Lee's idea was approved without a single no vote. The Congress spent the next two days talking about the Declaration. After several small changes were made, it was approved on July 4, 1776. The 13 colonies had declared independence.

 What did Jefferson describe in the longest part of the Declaration of Independence?

LESSON 2 REVIEW

Check Understanding

1. **Recall the Facts**   What were the main parts of the Declaration of Independence? What was the purpose of each part?
2. **Focus on the Main Idea**   Why was it important for colonial leaders to explain their decision to break free from British rule?

Think Critically

3. **Think More About It**   Why do you think Jefferson was asked to write the Declaration of Independence?
4. **Personally Speaking**   What do you think Jefferson meant when he wrote, "all men are created equal"?
5. **Past to Present**   Why do you think the Declaration is still important today?

Show What You Know

Simulation Activity   With a partner, act out a conversation between two colonists discussing the Declaration of Independence. The first colonist is a Loyalist. The second is a Patriot. Try to make each side of the argument as real as you can. Discuss your conversation with classmates.

AMERICANS TAKE SIDES

L ink to Our World

How do people's experiences affect the decisions they make?

Focus on the Main Idea
As you read, think about how people's experiences affected their decisions to take sides in the American Revolution.

Preview Vocabulary
neutral   encroach
pacifist   regiment
movement

After the Declaration of Independence was signed, people had to decide if they would support the rebelling colonies or the British king. Some chose to be **neutral** (NOO•truhl), taking neither side. Those who were neutral were willing to accept the outcome of the revolution, whichever way it went.

About a third of the colonists were Loyalists, and another third were Patriots. The last third remained neutral. Friends, neighbors, and families were sometimes torn apart by the need to choose sides. The fighting became as much a civil war as it was a war with the British.

REVOLUTION AND THE CHURCHES

Many things affected people's views on independence. One was religion. "There is a time to pray and a time to fight," Peter Muhlenberg, a young Lutheran minister, told his followers. Then, before their eyes, he tore off his church robes to show the uniform of a militia officer. His father, the colonies' Lutheran leader, was shocked—he was a Loyalist. The Lutherans, like the people of other church groups, were divided between Patriots and Loyalists.

Taking sides was especially hard for Anglican Church members. The British king was the head of the Anglican Church, as the Church of England was called in the colonies. Many Anglicans in the northern and middle colonies supported the king, while many of those in the southern colonies worked for independence.

Button molds were used to make metal buttons for Continental army uniforms.

Most Congregationalists, members of the largest church group in the colonies, worked for independence, as did many northern Presbyterians and Baptists. Many southern Presbyterians, however, were Loyalists.

Members of the Society of Friends, also called Quakers, would not fight in the war for independence. Quakers are against all wars, because they believe that violence for any reason is wrong. These **pacifists**, or believers in peaceful settlement, published pamphlets calling for an end to the war. Loyalists and Patriots both saw pacifists as their enemies.

 How did some people's religious beliefs affect the way they felt about independence?

WOMEN AND THE WAR

Many women in the colonies took part in the **movement**, or effort by many people, to gain freedom. When Patriot leaders asked the colonists to boycott British-made goods, women in Boston and other colonial towns banded together to make their own goods. Many women worked for independence in other ways.

Some women formed groups to raise money for the war and collect clothing for the soldiers. In Lancaster, Pennsylvania, women formed a group called the Unmarried Ladies of America. Its members promised that they would never give their hand in marriage to any gentleman until he had first proved himself a Patriot.

Women also took part in the fighting. Like some women, Mary Ludwig Hays traveled with her husband after he joined the

Mary Ludwig Hays earned the name Molly Pitcher by bringing water to the troops during the long, hot Battle of Monmouth, fought in June 1778.

Who?

Phillis Wheatley 1753?–1784

When she was only five or six years old, a young African girl, probably born in the country of Senegal, was kidnapped and enslaved. She was taken to Boston and in 1761 was sold to John Wheatley. Unlike many other slaveowners, Wheatley educated the young girl and then freed her. Phillis Wheatley, who took the last name of her owner, was one of the earliest American poets.

Continental army. When her husband fell during the Battle of Monmouth, Hays took over the firing of his cannon. Mary Slocumb rode through thick forests at night to join her husband and other members of the North Carolina militia. She fought with them in the Battle of Moore's Creek Bridge.

In Boston, Phillis Wheatley wrote poems that were praised by George Washington. She used her mind to champion the independence movement. So did Mercy Otis Warren. She wrote a play that made fun of the British and supported the Patriots.

Patriot Abigail Adams wanted to be sure that independence would be good for women as well as men. She wrote to her husband, John:

> 66 If particular care and attention are not paid to the ladies we are determined to foment [start] rebellion and will not hold ourselves bound to obey any laws in which we have no voice or representation. 99

Not all women were Patriots. There were Loyalist women in every colony. Some of them fought for the British. Many others brought them food and supplies.

 How did women on both sides take part in the Revolution?

NATIVE AMERICANS AND THE WAR

"We have heard of the unhappy differences and great contention betwixt you and Old England," an Oneida chief is said to have told a Patriot. "We cannot meddle in this dispute between two brothers. . . . Should the great king of England apply to us for aid, we shall decline him; if the colonies apply to us, we shall refuse."

Over the years native peoples had grown angry with both the American colonists and the British. Settlers from both sides continued to **encroach** on traditional Indian lands, moving onto them without asking. By 1776 the land between the Appalachian Mountains and the Mississippi River was being taken over by Europeans, despite the Proclamation of 1763, which forbid settlement there.

Francis Marion, known as the "Swamp Fox," led Continental soldiers through southern swamps as they defended the South against the British. Africans fought in Marion's militia and other companies during the war.

Yet many Native Americans had come to depend on Europeans as trading partners. For this reason the Patriots hoped that the Indians would at least stay out of the war, even if they would not fight for them. The British, however, promised to give the Indians guns and other European goods if they agreed to help the British army. Many tribes in the Ohio River valley, so often at war with each other, made peace in order "to assist His Majesty's troops." Other tribes, however, were divided. In the Hudson River valley, some of the Iroquois fought for the Patriots. Others decided to fight for the British.

Most Indians, however, stayed out of the fighting. When asked to take sides, one Cherokee chief is said to have told both the colonists and the British that the Great Spirit "has given you many advantages, but he has not created us to be your slaves. We are a separate people!"

 What view did most Indians take about the fighting?

AFRICANS AND THE WAR

At the start of the war, free Africans were as quick to take sides as their European neighbors. Peter Salem was among at least five Africans who fought at Concord with the Minutemen. A few weeks later he and other Africans, both free and enslaved, fought at the Battle of Bunker Hill in Boston. More than 5,000 Africans fought in the Continental army during the Revolutionary War.

Enslaved Africans who enlisted in the Continental army were promised freedom after the war as a reward. Many were so filled with ideas of freedom and liberty that they changed their names. Among the names listed in army records are Cuff Freedom, Dick Freedom, Ned Freedom, Peter Freeman, Cuff Liberty, Jeffrey Liberty, and Pomp Liberty.

The royal governor of Virginia, John Murray, Earl of Dunmore, also promised to give enslaved Africans their freedom if they ran away from their owners and were "able and willing to bear arms" for the British government. In a few weeks nearly 300 runaway slaves were enlisted in the Ethiopian Regiment of the British army. A **regiment** is a troop of soldiers. These soldiers wore uniforms that had patches reading *Liberty to Slaves.*

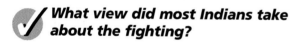 **What promise helped some enslaved Africans decide to take sides?**

LESSON 3 REVIEW

Check Understanding

1. **Recall the Facts** Why was the American Revolution as much a civil war as it was a war with Britain?
2. **Focus on the Main Idea** How did people's experiences affect their decisions to take sides in the American Revolution?

Think Critically

3. **Explore Viewpoints** Imagine that you were a Loyalist and your best friend was a Patriot during the American Revolution. List the reasons each of you might have had to take the sides you did.
4. **Past to Present** How might people who are pacifists view conflicts that are taking place around the world today?

Show What You Know

Chart Activity Draw a chart showing the colonial groups that worked for independence and those that remained loyal to the British government. Do some research on one group to find out why it chose the side it did.

Samuel's Choice

BY **Richard Berleth**
ILLUSTRATED BY **James Watling**

Taking the side of the Patriots was a difficult decision for many people, but especially for enslaved Africans. Thomas Jefferson had written in the Declaration of Independence that "all men are created equal." Yet he and many other Patriot leaders owned slaves. Even if the Patriots won their freedom from Britain, enslaved people knew that they would not win freedom from slavery.

Read now about the choice made by a 14-year-old boy named Samuel Abraham, who was held as a slave in Brooklyn, New York. Samuel, his friend Sana, and other slaves worked on the farm of a Loyalist named Isaac van Ditmas. It was Samuel's job to care for Farmer Isaac's boat and to take him and his family from place to place on New York Harbor.

In the summer of 1776, George Washington and the Continental army were forced to retreat from Brooklyn as the British approached. In the fighting that followed, Samuel chose to help the Patriots, carrying dozens of Patriots to safety in his boat. One of the people he helped was Major Mordecai Gist.

When I tied the boat to the dock below the Heights, Major Gist clapped his hands on my shoulders and looked me in the eyes. "Samuel," he said, "out in that creek you did more than many a free man for your country. I'd take it as a privilege if you'd consent to be my orderly and march beside me. And General Washington may need handy boatmen like you soon enough."

The next day it rained and rained. A thick sea fog covered the land. I looked everywhere for Sana. Many soldiers crowded into the camp, but they could tell me nothing. Alone and frightened, I mended the holes in my sail, pushing the big needle through the canvas, drawing it back again. Then, I heard voices nearby.

Major Gist stood there with an officer in a fine blue uniform. They asked me how deep the water was at this point between Brooklyn and Manhattan. They wanted to know if a British ship could sail between the two places. I told them that most ships could. Only the fog was keeping the British men-of-war from trapping Washington's army on Long Island.

The officer in the blue uniform thanked me. He and Major Gist walked away, looking thoughtful.

The next day the heavy rains continued. I spread the sail over the boat and slept snug and dry. Then I heard the voice I missed more than any in the world calling, "Samuel, Samuel Abraham!" Sana had found me! It was not a dream. "You chose, Samuel," she said. "You did it right. You chose our new country." From under her cloak she took a hot, steaming loaf wrapped in a napkin—her freedom bread, the sweetest I ever tasted. While we ate, she told me that Toby and Nathaniel were safe.

But this new country was in danger. Major Gist came to me again and explained that every boat was needed to carry Washington's army from Brooklyn to Manhattan. The army had to retreat that night. I was going to help save the army with Farmer Isaac's boat. Wouldn't he be surprised?

On the night that General Washington's army left Brooklyn, the worst storm I'd ever seen blew in from the Northeast. The wind howled. It drove the rain, stinging, into our eyes. It shook buildings and knocked down chimneys. And it whipped the water at Brooklyn Ferry into a sea of foam.

Down from the Heights in file marched Washington's army. The men entered the boats Major Gist and others had gathered at the ferry landing.

"What we need is a rope to cling to," someone said in the dark. "A rope stretching from here to Manhattan to guide us against the wind and current."

"There's rope here in the shipyard," a soldier remembered. "Buoys to float the rope

across, too. But who can cross this flood in the dark?"

"Can you do it, Samuel?" Major Gist asked. "Can you get across with the rope?"

"I can do it, Major," I shouted, the wind tearing the words out of my mouth. But I wasn't sure. Even if the rope were fed out from shore slowly, the sail might split or the rope might tear down the mast. But the British ships were sure to force their way between Brooklyn and Manhattan. I had to try.

When the rope was ready, I tied it to the foot of the mast. Sana jumped into the boat. I shouted at her to stay behind, but she wouldn't move. There was no time to lose. I shoved off into the swirling current.

My only hope was to let the shore current carry me out into midstream, and then, as the wind and tide thrust the boat toward the other shore, raise the sail and race for the Manhattan landing.

Fighting the rudder, I heard Sana's voice in my ear. "Will we make it, Samuel?" Water crashed over the side. Sana was bailing as fast as she could. "I can't swim, Samuel!" she cried into the wind. We were halfway across to Manhattan, and the boat was filling with sea. The gale was spinning us around. The rope was pulling us backward. I heaved at the sail, praying the mending wouldn't tear.

Then, as the sail filled, the boom swung around with a crack, and we were darting forward at last. On the Manhattan landing, by lantern light, we could see people waiting. Over the roar of the storm, we heard them cheering us on. But Isaac's boat was sinking. The rope was tearing the mast out of the bottom. With a terrible crash, the mast broke and was carried over the side. A second later the bow smashed into the side of a wharf, and I found myself in the water swimming with one arm, clinging to Sana with the other.

We stumbled ashore on Manhattan Island, where kind people wrapped us in blankets. They were smiling—the rope was across! The boats full of Washington's soldiers would follow. We had done it, together.

All through the night Washington's men followed that rope, boat after boat, across the water. In the stormy darkness, every soldier escaped from Long Island.

And so the fight for freedom would go on. It would take many long years before we would beat the British king, but never again did I wonder what freedom was, or what it cost. It was people pulling together. It was strong hands helping. It was one person caring about another.

And where was Washington? Many times that night Sana and I hoped to see him.

"Why, Samuel," Major Gist told us later, "he was that officer in the blue coat who asked you how deep the water was between Brooklyn and Manhattan. Last night the general arrested a farmer in Brooklyn for helping the British. That farmer, Isaac van Ditmas, turned all of his property over to the Army of the Continental Congress in exchange for his freedom. It seems now that you and Sana have no master."

From that day forward, we and Isaac's other slaves were to be citizens of a new nation.

Literature Review

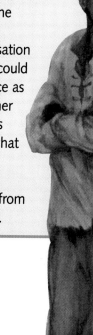

1. How did Samuel help the Continental army?
2. Why do you think Samuel chose to help the Patriots?
3. Write a conversation that you think could have taken place as Samuel and other slaves on Isaac's farm decided what to do as they watched the Americans flee from the British army.

LESSON 5

THE PUSH FOR VICTORY AND INDEPENDENCE

Link to Our World

How do people meet difficult challenges today?

Focus on the Main Idea
As you read, look for ways Americans met the challenges of their war for independence.

Preview Vocabulary
siege
treaty
negotiate

The Badge of Merit was designed by George Washington and given to soldiers who showed special bravery. Today this award is known as the Purple Heart.

After General Washington's retreat following the Battle of Long Island, Continental troops moved into New Jersey. There, they won important battles at Trenton and Princeton. But victory was still far from certain. In December 1777 Washington set up headquarters at Valley Forge, Pennsylvania, near Philadelphia. That winter his ragged army was almost destroyed by cold and hunger. By Washington's own count, 2,898 of his men had no boots. Many were ill, and many died. The Patriots had declared their independence, but would their army be strong enough to win it?

HELP FROM OTHER LANDS

The Patriots got some help from soldiers of other countries. Among them were two Polish officers, Casimir Pulaski (puh•LAS•kee) and Thaddeus Kosciuszko (kawsh•CHUSH•koh). Later Kosciuszko returned to Poland to lead a revolution there. Among others who came from Europe were the German soldiers Johann de Kalb and Friedrich von Steuben (vahn STOO•buhn). The Marquis de Lafayette (lah•fee•ET), a 20-year-old French noble, came from France to fight along with the Americans.

At Valley Forge during the winter of 1777, von Steuben took on the job of drilling the Continental army so that the soldiers would be ready to move quickly. By spring 1778 the soldiers were marching well.

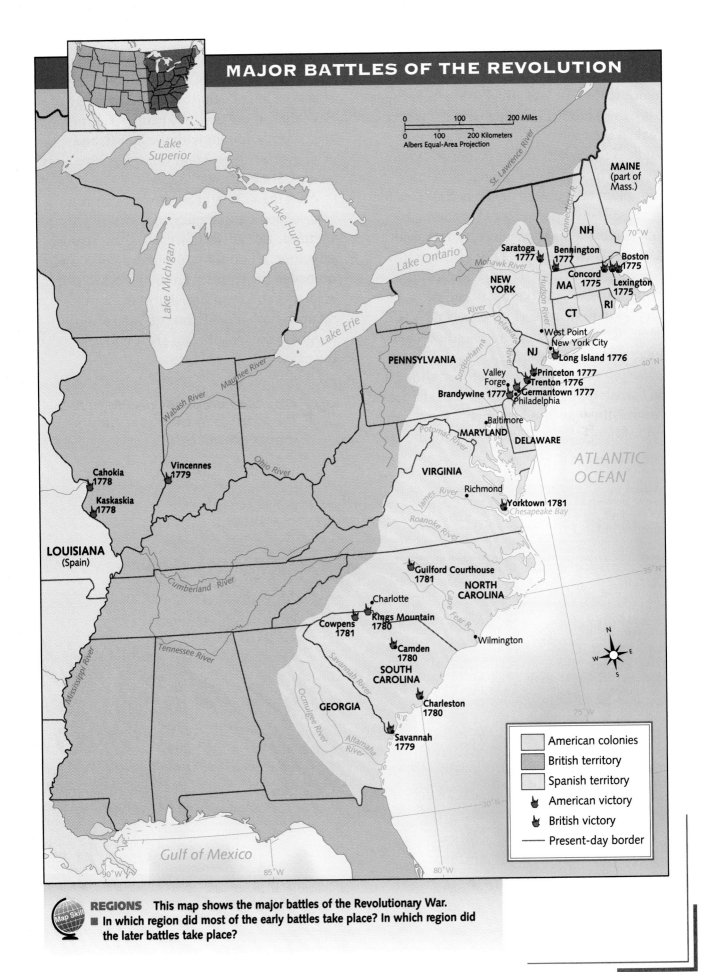

MAJOR BATTLES OF THE REVOLUTION

0   100   200 Miles
0   100   200 Kilometers
Albers Equal-Area Projection

Lake Superior

Lake Michigan

Lake Huron

Lake Ontario

Lake Erie

St. Lawrence River

MAINE
(part of Mass.)

NH

70°W

Saratoga 1777

Bennington 1777

Boston 1775

Mohawk River

Concord 1775

Lexington 1775

NEW YORK

MA

CT

RI

Hudson River

West Point
New York City

NJ

Long Island 1776

40°N

PENNSYLVANIA

Delaware River

Susquehanna River

Valley Forge

Princeton 1777
Trenton 1776
Germantown 1777

Brandywine 1777

Philadelphia

Baltimore

MARYLAND

DELAWARE

Potomac River

ATLANTIC OCEAN

VIRGINIA

James River

Richmond

Yorktown 1781

Chesapeake Bay

Roanoke River

Cahokia 1778

Vincennes 1779

Wabash River

Maumee River

Ohio River

Kaskaskia 1778

LOUISIANA
(Spain)

Cumberland River

35°N

Guilford Courthouse 1781

NORTH CAROLINA

Tennessee River

Charlotte

Cape Fear R.

Kings Mountain 1780

Cowpens 1781

Wilmington

Camden 1780

SOUTH CAROLINA

Savannah River

Charleston 1780

GEORGIA

Ocmulgee River

Altamaha River

Savannah 1779

Mississippi River

75°W

N
W   E
S

Gulf of Mexico

90°W   85°W   80°W

30°N

American colonies

British territory

Spanish territory

American victory

British victory

Present-day border

REGIONS This map shows the major battles of the Revolutionary War.
■ In which region did most of the early battles take place? In which region did the later battles take place?

In the meantime, the Continental Congress had sent Benjamin Franklin to Paris to ask the French to join the war. The French were eager to see the American colonies win the war and weaken their long-time enemy, the British. But the French felt that the colonists did not have much chance of winning.

Franklin talked with the French leaders for months. Then came news of the colonists' great victory at Saratoga in New York. More than 5,700 British soldiers under General John Burgoyne (buhr•GOYN) had moved south from Canada, hoping to cut the colonies in two. Instead, on October 17, 1777, the British lost to Continental soldiers led by General Horatio Gates.

The colonists' victory at Saratoga showed the French that the colonists stood a chance of winning the war. The French sent guns, ships, and soldiers to help. With the help of the French, the colonists fought more battles, including the siege of Savannah in 1779. A **siege** is a long-lasting attack. At the siege of Savannah, more than 800 Haitians, 80 of them slaves, fought with the French and American soldiers. Haiti was a French colony in the Caribbean.

After the victory at Saratoga, other countries helped the colonists, too. In 1779 Bernardo de Gálvez (GAHL•ves), the Spanish governor of Louisiana, sent guns, food, and money to the Patriots. Later he led his own soldiers in taking a British fort in Florida. Spanish-born Jorge Farragut (FAIR•uh•guht) fought in the Continental army and also the navy.

 Why did Europeans decide to help the Patriots in their war for independence?

General Friedrich von Steuben helped train Continental soldiers at Valley Forge. After learning how to march and move together on the battlefield, soldiers were able to attack and retreat faster.

VICTORY AT YORKTOWN

When the British government learned that France had joined the American side, British army leaders moved their attack from the northern colonies to the southern. The British hoped that the greater Loyalist support in the south would help defeat the Patriots once and for all. With the help of Loyalists, the British army captured Charleston, South Carolina, in 1780. Pushing north from South Carolina, the British then charged through North Carolina and into Virginia.

During 1781 the fighting centered in Virginia. For several weeks Benedict Arnold, a former Continental army officer, attacked colonial towns in Virginia for the British. Arnold was a traitor—he acted against his country. Earlier, he had turned over the plans to the American fort at West Point, New York, in exchange for money and a high rank in the British army.

By late summer of 1781, British General Charles Cornwallis had set up at Yorktown, a small Virginia town on Chesapeake Bay, where it was easy for British ships to land supplies. The French and the Continentals moved quickly to defeat the British at Yorktown. The French joined the Continentals near New York City, and together the two armies marched to Virginia and surrounded Yorktown. At the same time, the French navy took over Chesapeake Bay. Now the British navy could not get supplies to the British army at Yorktown. The British army was trapped.

In late September Cornwallis sent word to his commander in the north. "If you cannot relieve me very soon," he said, "you must be prepared to hear the worst."

The worst happened. Surrounded and under siege for two weeks from both land and sea, Cornwallis had to give up. A person who was there wrote, "At two o'clock in the evening Oct. 19th, 1781, the British army, led by General O'Hara, marched out of its lines, with colors cased [flags folded] and drums beating a British march." When the French

When?

1775–1783

The American Revolution took place mainly on the east coast of North America. During that time, however, other things were happening on the western part of the continent. Spanish-speaking people were settling traditional Indian lands in the area that stretched from the Mississippi River to the Pacific Ocean—the present-day Southwest. They were building towns and giving names to places that later would become part of the United States. In Hawaii, whaling ships from all over the world were stopping for supplies. In Alaska, Russian fur traders were setting up trading posts.

LEARNING FROM TIME LINES This time line lists key battles and other important events of the American Revolution.
■ How long after the war began was independence declared?

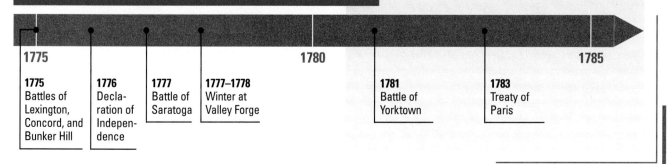

KEY EVENTS OF THE REVOLUTION

| 1775 | | | | 1780 | | | 1785 |

1775
Battles of Lexington, Concord, and Bunker Hill

1776
Declaration of Independence

1777
Battle of Saratoga

1777–1778
Winter at Valley Forge

1781
Battle of Yorktown

1783
Treaty of Paris

and American soldiers heard the drums, they stopped their fire. The British and Hessian soldiers then marched out of Yorktown and laid down their weapons in a field.

Though fighting dragged on in some places for more than two years, it was clear that victory had been decided at Yorktown in 1781. The Patriots had won after a long and hard fight.

 How did the French help the Americans win the Battle of Yorktown?

THE TREATY OF PARIS

The Battle of Yorktown did not end the Revolutionary War. The Treaty of Paris did that. A **treaty** is an agreement between countries.

Work on the treaty began in April 1782 when the British sent Richard Oswald, a wealthy merchant, to Paris to talk with Benjamin Franklin. Franklin gave Oswald the American terms—that is, what Americans wanted in the treaty. One of the terms was that the British had to accept American independence and remove British soldiers from American soil. Franklin told Oswald that Americans might feel better toward the British if Parliament paid those whose towns had been destroyed in the war.

In return, the British asked that the Loyalists who remained in the United States be treated fairly. Many Loyalists fled to Nova Scotia, New Brunswick, and Upper Canada. Those who returned to Britain were sorry they did. Most could not find jobs and soon became very poor. Instead of being grateful

In John Trumbull's painting of the surrender at Yorktown, American General Benjamin Lincoln (center, on the white horse) receives the surrender from an aide to British General Cornwallis. George Washington is in front of the American flag.

for their support, the British government ignored them.

The British and Americans **negotiated**, or talked with one another to work out an agreement. After more than a year of such talks, the Treaty of Paris was signed by British and American representatives on September 3, 1783.

The Treaty of Paris named the United States of America as a new nation and described its borders. The United States would reach to Florida on the south, a line through the Great Lakes on the north, and the Mississippi River on the west. The fact that much of the land between the Appalachian Mountains and the Mississippi River was the home of many different American Indian tribes was of little or no interest to the leaders who signed the treaty.

The Treaty of Paris was a victory just as much as winning at Yorktown had been. Independence was now a fact. But the Americans faced many problems. They had formed a new country, yet the 3 million people in the 13 new states were far from united.

 What were the terms of the Treaty of Paris?

NORTH AMERICA IN 1783

United States

British

French

Spanish

Russian

0   600   1,200 Miles
0   600   1,200 Kilometers
Azimuthal Equal-Area Projection

REGIONS This map shows the United States and the North American lands claimed by European countries in 1783, following the Treaty of Paris.

■ What were the boundaries of the new nation called the United States?

LESSON 5 REVIEW

Check Understanding

1. **Recall the Facts** How was help from the people of France and other countries important to the colonists in winning the war?

2. **Focus on the Main Idea** How did the colonists meet the challenges of war against the British?

Think Critically

3. **Think More About It** Why do you think the colonists did not give up when it looked as if they would not win the war?

4. **Past to Present** What can Americans today learn from the Patriots?

Show What You Know

 Research Activity Because the Revolution was so important, many places are named after people who fought on the Patriots' side. Use an atlas to locate as many places as you can that are named for Washington, Franklin, Gálvez, Lafayette, and others. Compare your list with that of a classmate.

REVIEW

CONNECT MAIN IDEAS

Use this organizer to show that you understand how the chapter's main ideas are connected. Copy the organizer onto a separate sheet of paper. Then complete it by writing the main idea of each lesson.

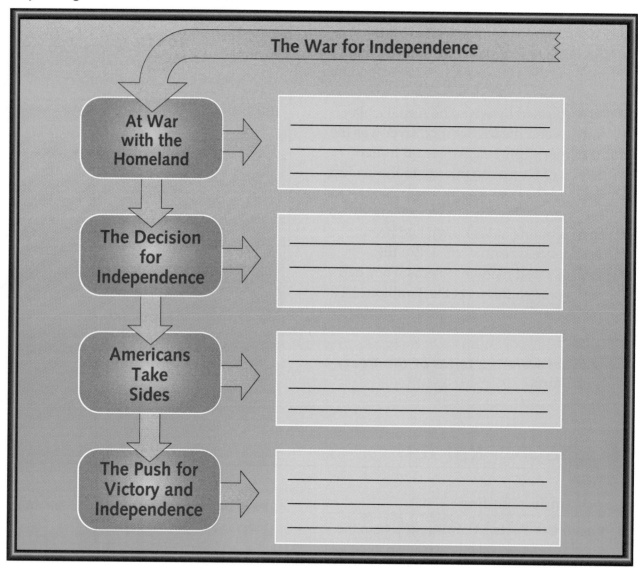

The War for Independence

At War with the Homeland →

The Decision for Independence →

Americans Take Sides →

The Push for Victory and Independence →

WRITE MORE ABOUT IT

1. **Write a Pamphlet** Take the role of a Loyalist or a Patriot. Write a short pamphlet that explains your point of view about British rule. Explain why you have chosen your side.

2. **Write a Newspaper Article** Imagine you are a reporter who witnessed the British surrender at Yorktown. Write a newspaper article describing what you saw.

USE VOCABULARY

Use each term in a sentence that helps explain its meaning.

1. allegiance
2. declaration
3. enlist
4. grievance
5. mercenary
6. movement
7. negotiate
8. neutral
9. olive branch
10. pacifist

CHECK UNDERSTANDING

1. How did the Second Continental Congress try to make peace with Britain?

2. What were George Washington's strengths as a general?

3. What was the importance of Thomas Paine's *Common Sense*?

4. What did the Declaration of Independence tell the world?

5. How did people who did not fight in the war show their support for independence?

6. How was help from other countries important to the American victory?

7. What was the important result of the Battle of Saratoga?

8. Put these events in the proper order: the Treaty of Paris, the Declaration of Independence, Valley Forge, the Battle of Bunker Hill, the Battle of Yorktown.

THINK CRITICALLY

1. **Think More About It** Many leaders of the Revolution, such as George Washington and Thomas Jefferson, were successful and wealthy. Why would they risk everything they had to take part in a revolution?

2. **Personally Speaking** Imagine that you were a delegate to the Second Continental Congress. Do you think you would have signed the Declaration of Independence? Explain your answer.

3. **Past to Present** How do American citizens today let their government know about their grievances?

4. **Explore Viewpoints** Explain how Patriots and Loyalists viewed the American Revolution.

5. **Cause and Effect** How did the military training of Continental soldiers affect the war?

APPLY SKILLS

How to Read a Political Cartoon Look through newspapers and magazines for a political cartoon about a subject that interests you. Cut out the cartoon and paste it to a piece of paper. Below the cartoon, write a brief paragraph that explains its meaning.

READ MORE ABOUT IT

The American Revolutionaries: A History in Their Own Words 1750–1800 edited by Milton Meltzer. HarperCollins. This book explores the events of the Revolution as told in people's letters, speeches, and other primary sources.

Black Heroes of the American Revolution by Burke Davis. Harcourt Brace. The author describes the actions of soldiers, sailors, scouts, spies, and others who contributed to the colonies' struggle for freedom.

The Fighting Ground by Avi. J.B. Lippincott. In this story 13-year-old Jonathan seeks the glories of war and finds that he must fight several battles within himself.

Heroines of '76 by Elizabeth Anticaglia. Walker. The author tells about the brave deeds of 14 women during the Revolutionary War.

MAKING SOCIAL STUDIES
RELEVANT

TIANANMEN SQUARE

In 1776 the American Patriots struggled for freedom. Today people in some parts of the world are doing the same. In April 1989, college students in China wanted their country to be more like a democracy. The students gathered at Tiananmen (TYAHN•AHN•MEN) Square in the center of Beijing (BAY•JING), the capital city, to express their views in a public demonstration.

Thousands of people, young and old, came to the square every day to show their support for the students. One group made its own Statue of Liberty out of plastic foam. Other people made posters. One poster quoted the Declaration of Independence, calling for "life, liberty and the pursuit of happiness" for all Chinese people. Another recalled Patrick Henry's famous words, "Give me liberty or give me death."

The democracy demonstration in Tiananmen Square ended violently on June 4, 1989. That morning hundreds of Chinese soldiers poured into the square, killing many of the demonstrators. Government leaders had ordered the attack.

Like the British king in 1776, the Chinese rulers feared losing their authority.

Shen Tong, a Beijing University student speaking at an Independence Day celebration in Boston on July 4, 1989, compared the Tiananmen Square massacre with the Boston Massacre. "People died," Shen said of the Boston Massacre, "but it sparked the American struggle for independence. I do not believe that the Tiananmen Square massacre was the end of the democracy movement in China. It was the beginning." Today many people in China continue the struggle for freedom.

THINK AND APPLY

Think about what happened at Tiananmen Square. Find examples of people today struggling for freedom or independence. Select the example that interests you the most. Use a Venn diagram to compare and contrast the present-day events with those of the American Revolution. Share your findings with a classmate.

BUILDING CITIZENSHIP

STORY CLOTH

Study the pictures shown in this story cloth to help you review the events you read about in Unit 4.

Summarize the Main Ideas

1. The colonists were forced to pay taxes to Britain even though they had no representation in Parliament. They especially hated the tax law called the Stamp Act.

2. The colonists united to protest British taxes. At the Boston Tea Party, colonists dumped tea from British ships into Boston Harbor.

3. As anger grew, both the colonists and the British prepared for fighting. Paul Revere and William Dawes went on a night ride to warn of approaching British soldiers.

4. Minutemen faced British soldiers at Lexington and Concord in April 1775. This was the start of the War for Independence.

5. On July 4, 1776, the Declaration of Independence was approved by members of the Continental Congress.

6. The war went on for years, and soldiers in the Continental army faced many hardships. Yet they continued to receive support from many people in the colonies.

7. The American victory at Yorktown in 1781 forced the British to surrender. In 1783 the Treaty of Paris named the United States as a new nation.

Show More of the Story Draw pictures that show more about the American Revolution. Label the pictures, and tell where they should go on the story cloth.

COOPERATIVE LEARNING WORKSHOP

Remember
- Share your ideas.
- Cooperate with others to plan your work.
- Take responsibility for your work.
- Show your group's work to the class.
- Discuss what you learned by working together.

Activity 1
Make a Time Line
Work with three or four classmates. Make a time line showing the important events of the American Revolution. Begin with the Stamp Act, and end with the signing of the Treaty of Paris. Be sure to label the date of each key event on the time line.

Activity 2
Present a Dramatic Reading
After the Declaration of Independence was signed in 1776, copies of it were sent to all the colonies. In many towns the Declaration was read aloud at public meetings. The readers showed the importance of the document by adding drama to their reading. Your class should work in four groups, each responsible for preparing a dramatic reading of one part of the Declaration of Independence. Each group member should help read his or her group's part.

Activity 3
Give a Speech
The actions of many individuals affected the outcome of the American Revolution. With other students, choose one such individual and write a speech for that person as though he or she were coming to visit your class. Be sure to tell in the speech how this person's actions affected the outcome of the Revolution. Select one member of your group to present the speech to the class.

Activity 4
Make a Model
Imagine that you are taking part in a Fourth of July celebration. With three or four of your classmates, build a model for a parade float that shows an important event of the American Revolution. Display your model in the classroom.

USE VOCABULARY

Write the term that correctly matches each definition.

Continental   tax
pacifist   treaty
self-government

1. a believer in peaceful settlement

2. making one's own laws

3. money paid to a government for running it

4. an agreement between countries

5. a soldier in George Washington's army

CHECK UNDERSTANDING

1. What actions by the British king angered the colonists?

2. Why did some enslaved Africans join the British side, while others fought on the side of the colonies?

3. How did the actions of Thomas Paine, Crispus Attucks, Paul Revere, and Benedict Arnold affect the outcome of the American Revolution?

4. What battle made the French believe the colonists could really defeat the British?

5. Who were Charles Cornwallis and Thomas Gage?

THINK CRITICALLY

1. **Past to Present** What does the Declaration of Independence mean to Americans today?

2. **Explore Viewpoints** People in the British colonies were divided in their views about self-government and independence. What were these different views? Why did people hold them?

3. **Personally Speaking** What person who took part in the American Revolution do you admire most? Why?

4. **Think More About It** Why do you think the small Continental army was able to defeat the powerful British army?

APPLY GEOGRAPHY SKILLS

How to Use a Historical Map The Treaty of Paris described the borders of the new nation. However, disputes over land remained between former colonies and between the United States and Britain. Use the map below to answer the questions.

1. What year does this map show?

2. How are disputed lands shown on the map?

3. Which two former colonies claimed the same land?

4. Describe the location of the land claimed by both the United States and Britain.

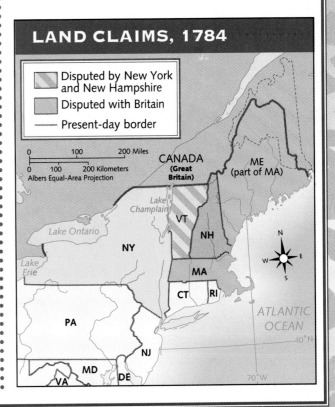

UNIT 5

The NEW NATION

1775

1776
Declaration of
Independence

1780

1781
Articles of
Confederation

1783
Treaty of Paris

1785

1787
Shays's Rebellion

Northwest
Ordinance

Constitutional
Convention

*W*hen the American people won their independence, they had to decide what kind of government they should form. Their leaders had to answer many questions as they decided how to live free from British rule. Should the former colonies have a single government and not divide into states? Should the colonies become 13 separate states with no central government? Should there be a king or queen of the United States? One thing was certain. The newly independent country had to give its people the chance to take part in government.

← *Signing the Constitution,* a painting by Howard Chandler Christy

1790

1795

1800

1788
The Constitution becomes law

1789
George Washington becomes the first President

The first Congress under the Constitution meets

The first Supreme Court is appointed

1797
John Adams takes office as the second President

Shh! We're Writing the Constitution

by Jean Fritz
pictures by Tomie dePaola

The job of turning the 13 former British colonies into a single country was not easy. The biggest problem was getting people to think of themselves as citizens of a new country—the United States of America. Until this time most people thought of themselves as citizens of their state rather than of their country.

After the Revolutionary War most people in America were glad that they were no longer British. Still, they were not ready to call themselves Americans. The last thing they wanted was to become a nation. They were citizens of their own separate states, just as they had always been: each state different, each state proud of its own character, each state quick to poke fun at other states. To Southerners, New Englanders might be "no-account Yankees." To New Englanders, Pennsylvanians might be "lousy Buckskins." But to everyone the states themselves were all important. "Sovereign states," they called them. They loved the sound of "sovereign" because it meant that they were their own bosses.

George Washington, however, scoffed at the idea of "sovereign states." He knew that the states could not be truly independent for long and survive. Ever since the Declaration of Independence had been signed, people had referred to the country as the United States of America. It was about time, he thought, for them to act and feel united.

Once during the war Washington had decided it would be a good idea if his troops swore allegiance to the United States. As a start, he lined up some troops from New Jersey and asked them to take such an oath. They looked at Washington as if he'd taken leave of his senses. How could they do that? they cried. New Jersey was their country!

So Washington dropped the idea. In time, he hoped, the states would see that they needed to become one nation, united under a strong central government.

But that time would be long in coming.

CHAPTER 9

The CONSTITUTION

> " In the new code of laws, which I suppose it will be necessary for you to make, I desire you would remember the ladies, and be more generous and favorable to them than [were] your ancestors. "
>
> Abigail Adams, in a letter to her husband, John, March 31, 1776

Abigail Adams in a portrait from the 1780s

The ARTICLES of CONFEDERATION

L nk to Our World

What problems might be caused by a weak government?

Focus on the Main Idea
As you read, look for problems that were caused by the weaknesses of the first government of the United States.

Preview Vocabulary
constitution   territory
republic   township
ambassador   ordinance
inflation

John Dickinson headed the committee that wrote the first draft of the Articles of Confederation.

Before the war with Britain had ended, the Continental Congress decided to set up a national government for the 13 former colonies. The newly independent states had already started to write their own **constitutions**, or plans of government. But leaders believed that the country also needed a national government with its own constitution. Then all 13 states could act together as one nation.

"A FIRM LEAGUE OF FRIENDSHIP"

Most people did not want a powerful national government for the country. After all, they had just fought a war to get rid of one. They were afraid that a strong national government would make laws for their states just as the British king and Parliament had made laws for the colonies. Now that they finally had won their independence, they did not want to give it away to a national government.

In 1781 the states accepted the plan for a central government approved by the Continental Congress. The plan, written mostly by representative John Dickinson, united the states in a confederation. The confederation would be something like the Iroquois League, which brought together different Indian tribes. The Confederation of the United States of America would bring together 13 independent states in "a firm league of friendship." This first plan of government for the new country was called the Articles of Confederation.

The Articles of Confederation created a **republic**, a form of government in which people elect representatives to run the country. Under the Articles, voters of each state elected leaders who, in turn, chose representatives. These representatives met in a national legislature—a Congress—where each state had one vote. Congress could do only certain things. Most important, it could declare war, make treaties, and settle serious disagreements between states.

For Congress to make a law or decide important questions, at least 9 of the 13 states had to agree. However, the states seldom agreed on anything. Each wanted its own way. No state wanted to be under the control of the other states.

No state wanted to be under the rule of one person, either. That is why the Articles did not allow a single leader to control the government. The states were afraid of giving one person too much authority. That person might become like a monarch. So a committee of representatives kept the government running when Congress was not meeting.

The Articles also did not plan for a national court system. Congress acted as a court for settling disagreements between states. But most often the states did not obey Congress anyway. People who had disagreements with their state governments had no national court where they could settle their differences.

✔️ **How did the Articles limit the authority of Congress?**

PROBLEMS FROM THE START

Under the Articles of Confederation, the national government did not work well. It was, as George Washington called it, "a half-starved, limping government."

Often there were not enough representatives present to allow Congress to meet. Even when there were, the legislature had no place of its own to hold meetings. Congress met sometimes in Philadelphia and sometimes in Annapolis, Maryland. It also met in Princeton or in Trenton, New Jersey. Most Americans did not know where or when Congress was meeting. Foreign **ambassadors**, representatives from one country to another, did not know either. When the first Dutch ambassador arrived in the United States, he spent ten days looking for Congress. He finally found it in Princeton, where it had been chased by soldiers demanding their pay for fighting in the Revolutionary War.

Even when Congress met, however, it could do only what the Articles of Confederation allowed. The Articles did not allow Congress to raise a national army without the states' permission. State leaders were afraid the national government would use such an army to make them obey national laws. This rule let the states keep their authority, but it also meant there would be no army to defend the nation if Spanish troops should attack from Florida or British troops should attack from Canada.

The Articles did not allow Congress to make laws about trade or about taxes. To get the money needed to run the national government, Congress had to ask each state to pay its share. But Congress did not have the authority to make the states pay what they owed. For three years Congress did not even have enough money to pay its members!

This staff was used to list the members of the League of the Haudenosaunee, a confederation of five Iroquois tribes. The pegs in the staff stood for each tribe's representatives. How was the early government of the United States like the Iroquois League?

Before he was stopped by government troops, Daniel Shays (left, on porch) led attacks on courthouses like this one. The courts were making judgments against debtors.

The paper money printed by Congress, called continentals, had little value due to inflation. The phrase *not worth a continental* was used to describe things that were worthless.

Congress did have the authority to print and to coin money. But when it tried to pay its debts from the war, it printed too much and caused terrible inflation. When there is **inflation**, more and more money is needed to buy the same goods. During this time, for example, a twenty-dollar bill could buy only two cents' worth of goods.

Many people, such as the soldiers who had not been paid, soon had money problems. Most of these people were farmers. They already had to pay state taxes—taxes they thought were too high. But they also had to buy tools and seeds for planting. Many had

> **"THAT CROWD IS TOO WEAK to act!"**
>
> Daniel Shays, 1787

to go into debt or borrow money. Some states made debtors pay back what they owed right away. If they did not, the state could take away their land or send them to prison. Many farmers protested to their state governments. Some protests, such as Shays's Rebellion, became violent.

In the fall of 1786, Daniel Shays, a former captain in the Continental army, and about 1,200 other poor farmers wanted to show their anger toward their state, Massachusetts. In January 1787 they attacked a building used for storing weapons in the western part of the state. The weapons belonged to the national government, not to Massachusetts, but the

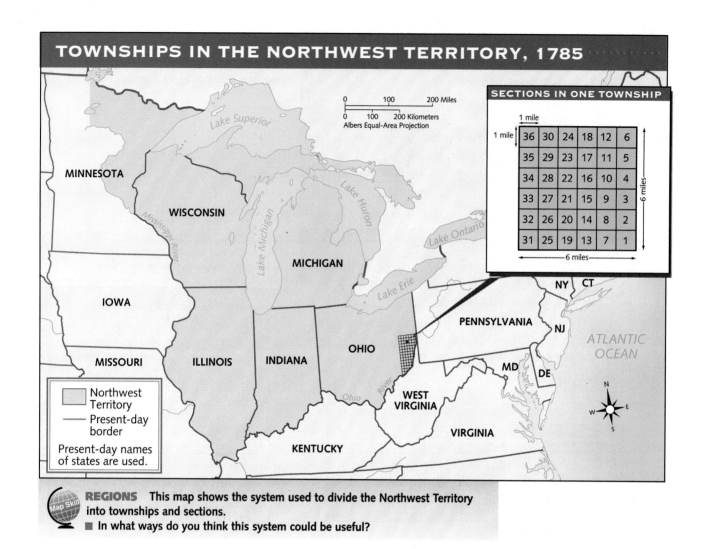

TOWNSHIPS IN THE NORTHWEST TERRITORY, 1785

SECTIONS IN ONE TOWNSHIP

36	30	24	18	12	6
35	29	23	17	11	5
34	28	22	16	10	4
33	27	21	15	9	3
32	26	20	14	8	2
31	25	19	13	7	1

1 mile

6 miles

0   100   200 Miles
0   100   200 Kilometers
Albers Equal-Area Projection

REGIONS This map shows the system used to divide the Northwest Territory into townships and sections.
■ In what ways do you think this system could be useful?

protesters did not care. "That crowd [the members of Congress] is too weak to act!" said Shays. But the governor of Massachusetts was not. He called out the state militia to end the rebellion. Four protesters died in the fighting.

Shays's Rebellion was quickly put down, but it showed that people were not happy with their government. Under the Articles of Confederation, Congress could do little to help them. Congress did not even have the money or the authority to defend national property—like the weapons in western Massachusetts. Many people feared that unrest would spread to other states.

 What problems did people face under the Articles of Confederation?

THE WESTERN LANDS

Under the Articles of Confederation, Congress did make some important decisions on how to divide and govern the country's western lands. These lands stretched from the Appalachian Mountains to the Mississippi River.

After the French and Indian War, Britain had refused to allow new settlement west of the Proclamation Line of 1763, near the Appalachian Mountains. This land was reserved for the Indians. Once the new United States was independent, however, it opened the frontier to settlement. Settlers poured into the Ohio River valley. The land north of the river was called the Northwest Territory. A **territory** is land that belongs to a national government but is not a state.

In 1785 Congress set up a system to survey, or measure, the western lands. The land was divided into squares called **townships**. Each side of a township measured 6 miles (9.7 km). Each township, in turn, was divided into 36 squares, or sections. This system of surveying by townships and sections can still be seen in parts of the United States.

In 1787 Congress passed the Northwest Ordinance. The **ordinance**, or set of laws, set up governments in the Northwest Territory and described the steps by which new states would be formed. The Northwest Ordinance also had other provisions. It did not allow people to keep slaves in the Northwest Territory. It said that Indian peoples should be treated fairly. And it encouraged townships to help build schools.

The Northwest Ordinance was a good plan for the growth of the United States. It showed what could be done when members of Congress worked together. But since this did not happen often, many people thought that Congress was not important.

✔ *What were the states able to do when they worked together?*

LESSON 1 REVIEW

Check Understanding

1. **Recall the Facts**   What was the first plan for governing the 13 states after the Revolutionary War?
2. **Focus on the Main Idea**   What problems were caused by the weaknesses of the United States government under the Articles of Confederation?

Think Critically

3. **Explore Viewpoints**   What might the Indians who lived in the western lands have said about the Northwest Ordinance? Why?
4. **Personally Speaking**   Do you think Daniel Shays and his followers were right to break the law? Explain why you feel as you do.

Show What You Know

Speech Activity   Plan a speech explaining how the 13 former colonies settled the question of governing themselves. Deliver your speech to a classmate.

George Washington was once a surveyor. He owned this bronze compass.

A NEW PLAN OF GOVERNMENT

*L*nk to Our World

How can people cooperate to make changes in their nation?

Focus on the Main Idea
As you read, look for ways people worked together to change the government of the United States.

Preview Vocabulary
convention
delegate
Preamble

This United States flag was made in 1781. How is today's flag different?

Just after the Revolutionary War, the former colonists had been afraid of a national government that was too strong. Now the people had a government that was too weak to work well. The confederation was really 13 separate and independent states rather than one nation. The country was not really united. The British, in fact, called it the "Disunited States."

"A ROPE OF SAND"

James Madison was a member of Congress under the Articles of Confederation. In 1779 Madison had been elected to represent Virginia. Jemmy, as his friends called him, was 29 years old and Congress's youngest member. He was to spend the rest of his life in public service. Madison became a student of government. He read everything he could find about ancient and modern ways of governing.

Madison was worried about the weaknesses of the Articles of Confederation. Congress had little authority over the states. Madison said he was afraid that Congress had become "a rope of sand."

Such leaders as George Washington, Thomas Jefferson, and John Adams agreed with Madison. Once, while traveling in Britain, John Adams had been asked, "Do you represent one nation or thirteen?" Madison and the other leaders began to argue for a stronger national government. Only a strong national government could keep the confederation from breaking apart, Madison said.

Others did not agree. Patrick Henry of Virginia was one of many who preferred the Articles of Confederation. These leaders were afraid of a strong national government. A rope of sand, they said, was better than a rod of iron.

✓ Why did Madison call Congress "a rope of sand"?

AGREEING TO WORK TOGETHER

The states argued and argued among themselves over such things as borders and trade. Maryland and Virginia quarreled over who had the right to control travel on the Potomac River, which ran between them. Both states wanted to control the middle of the river because it was a good, deep shipping lane.

The states argued about money, too. Each state printed its own paper money in addition to the money printed by the national government. States quarreled about whose money would be used when people from one state bought goods in another state. Some states even placed a tariff on goods brought in from other states.

Things became so difficult that a **convention**, or an important meeting, was held in Annapolis, Maryland, in September 1786. Alexander Hamilton of New York and James Madison of Virginia called the meeting to give the states a chance to talk out their problems. However, representatives from only five states—New York, New Jersey, Pennsylvania, Delaware, and Virginia—attended. The representatives, or **delegates**, talked for days before deciding that the country needed a stronger national government. This meant that the Articles of Confederation had to be changed.

Led by Hamilton and Madison, the delegates to the Annapolis Convention sent a letter to Congress asking it to call a second convention. Delegates from all the states could meet there to discuss their problems and whether changing the Articles might help solve them.

At first Congress did not want to call a convention, but after Shays's Rebellion it agreed to do so. Each state was asked to send delegates to a convention to be held in Philadelphia in the spring of 1787. Only Rhode Island refused the invitation.

The delegates to the convention began to gather in Philadelphia in May 1787. When Thomas Jefferson saw the list of those attending, he wrote to John Adams, "It really is an assembly of demigods [heroes]."

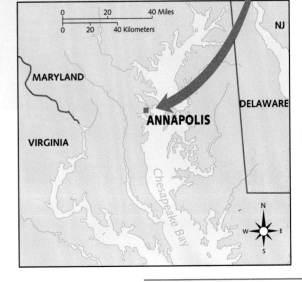

here?

Annapolis

From November 26, 1783, to June 3, 1784, Annapolis, Maryland, was the capital of the United States. Congress met in the State House where the Annapolis Convention was held in 1786. Today Annapolis is the capital of the state of Maryland.

One of the first to arrive was George Washington of Virginia. In 1787 Washington was 55 years old and the most honored hero of the American Revolution. He traveled to Philadelphia in a great black carriage pulled by six high-stepping horses. The first thing the delegates did was elect Washington president of the convention.

The most colorful arrival was made by Benjamin Franklin, then 81 years old and governor of Pennsylvania. Unable to walk far or to ride in a bumpy carriage, Franklin arrived in a Chinese sedan chair carried by prisoners from the Philadelphia jail.

In all, 55 delegates from 12 states met in the Pennsylvania State House. The delegates were mostly lawyers, planters, business people, and judges. Some had signed the Declaration of Independence, and almost all were members of Congress. Many owned slaves. Most shared the desire to do what was best for their state and their country.

Some famous people were not delegates. Thomas Jefferson, who had written the Declaration of Independence, was in Paris as ambassador to France. John Adams was in London as ambassador to Britain. His cousin Samuel Adams was in ill health, and John Hancock was too busy as governor of Massachusetts to attend. Patrick Henry refused to take part because he did not believe that a stronger national government was a good idea.

Most ordinary people did not take part, either. Daniel Shays and other frontier farmers did not attend. Women did not sit at the convention tables. There were no representatives from any of the Indian tribes at the meeting. Nor were there any Africans, slave or free, though they made up one-fifth of the new nation's population.

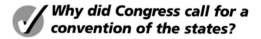 **Why did Congress call for a convention of the states?**

THE CONVENTION BEGINS

From the beginning the delegates agreed to meet in secrecy. They believed this would help them make the best decisions. Windows were covered and sealed shut. Guards watched the doors and hallways.

As the meeting was called to order, many of the delegates offered ideas they thought would make the Articles of Confederation better. But they soon saw that there was no way to simply fix up the old plan of

This drawing from 1799 shows Iroquois leaders outside the Pennsylvania State House, now called Independence Hall.

government. Only a new plan—a new constitution—would do. They agreed to unite the nation under a strong central government instead of through a "firm league of friendship."

The delegates to this Constitutional Convention wrote the new rules of government, which they called the Constitution of the United States of America, with great care. Gouverneur (guh•vuh•NIR) Morris of Pennsylvania spent long hours working out each sentence. The delegates gave Morris the job of writing down all the ideas that had been approved during the convention.

In the **Preamble**, or introduction to the Constitution, Morris began with the words *We the people of the United States. . . .* He had originally written *We the people of the States of New Hampshire, Massachusetts, ...* But Morris changed the words because he wanted the American people to know that the Constitution would make them citizens of a nation first and citizens of separate states second.

Morris went on to explain in the Preamble that the purpose of the Constitution was to

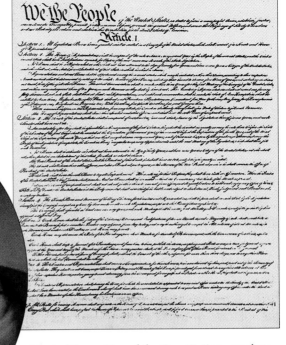

Most of the writing of the Constitution was done by members of two committees. Gouverneur Morris (left) was in charge of the final wording.

create a better plan of government. This government would work toward justice and peace. It would allow the nation to defend itself against enemies. It would promote the country's well-being. And it would provide "the blessings of liberty" for its citizens.

✓ **What was the purpose of the Constitution?**

LESSON 2 REVIEW

Check Understanding

1. **Recall the Facts**   Why did Gouverneur Morris change the opening of the Preamble?
2. **Focus on the Main Idea**   In what ways did American leaders work together to change the plan of government?

Think Critically

3. **Personally Speaking**   Would you have gone to the Constitutional Convention? Why?

4. **Explore Viewpoints**   How might Patrick Henry have felt about the way Gouverneur Morris wrote the Preamble? Why?

Show What You Know

Research Activity   Gather information about a convention delegate from encyclopedias and biographies. Write a report and describe the person for the class.

Figure Travel Time and Distance

Why Is This Skill Important?

"How much longer will it take to get there?" Have you ever heard these words on a car trip with your family or friends?

When planning any trip, it is important to know the travel time, or how long the trip will take to complete. Travel time can be affected by many things, including the weather in a place or the speed limit if you are traveling by car. But two of the most important things that affect travel time are the distance you will travel and the method of transportation you will use. As you know, traveling by jet airplane is much faster than traveling by car or train.

Understand the Process

In the 1700s, however, there were no cars, trains, or airplanes. Roads, when they existed at all, were often little more than dirt paths winding across the countryside. This made travel much slower and more difficult than it is today.

Imagine that you are a delegate planning your trip to the Constitutional Convention in Philadelphia, Pennsylvania. You will start out in Charleston, South Carolina, in a horse-drawn carriage. You have been told that the roads are bad north of New Bern, North Carolina, so you will continue from there on horseback. To save money, you will travel from Annapolis,

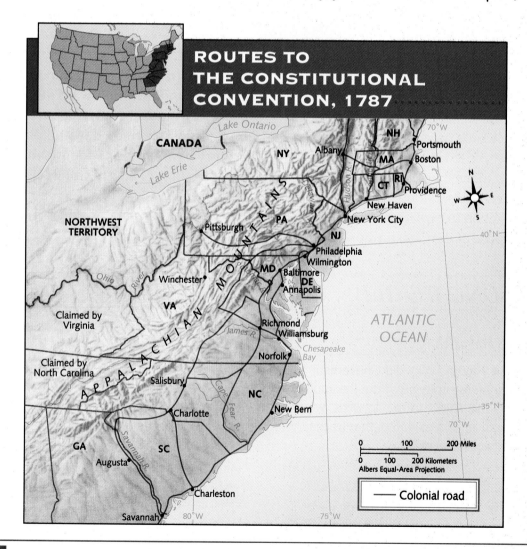

ROUTES TO THE CONSTITUTIONAL CONVENTION, 1787

Colonial road

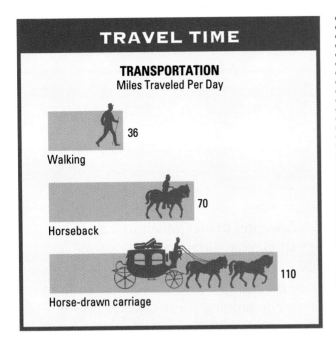

TRAVEL TIME

TRANSPORTATION
Miles Traveled Per Day

Walking 36

Horseback 70

Horse-drawn carriage 110

Maryland, on foot. How long will it take you to get from Charleston to Philadelphia? To answer this question you will need to figure out the distance between the cities. You will also need to know the travel rates for different forms of transportation used in the late 1700s.

The map on page 276 shows the routes that some of the delegates to the Constitutional Convention might have taken to reach Philadelphia in 1787. The map scale can help you figure out the distances on these routes. The map scale shows distance in both miles and kilometers. In this skill exercise, you will use only miles to measure distance.

Use a ruler to measure the map scale. What length on the ruler equals 200 miles? To measure a curving route, you can use a string. Hold the string on the map, and use a pencil or pen to make a mark on the string, at the starting point. Then lay the string along the route. Make another mark on the string, at the ending point. Place the string against the map scale. You can measure the distance by making a mark at every length of 200 miles.

The chart on this page shows travel rates for different forms of transportation. People at the time of the convention often traveled in horse-drawn carriages. They could go about 110 miles

a day. How many days did it take to get from Providence, Rhode Island, to Philadelphia by carriage? To figure this out, divide the total number of miles by the rate of travel. The total number of miles between Providence and Philadelphia is about 240. If you divide that number by 110, you get 2 with a remainder of 20. So it took about 2 days to get from Providence to Philadelphia by carriage.

Now use the map and the chart to answer the questions that follow.

1. About how many miles is it from Pittsburgh, Pennsylvania, to Philadelphia?
2. How long might it have taken a delegate traveling in a horse-drawn carriage to get from Pittsburgh to the convention in Philadelphia?
3. How long might it have taken a delegate from New York, such as Alexander Hamilton, to travel on horseback from New York City to Philadelphia?
4. How long might it have taken a delegate from Wilmington, Delaware, to walk from Wilmington to Philadelphia?
5. How long would it take the delegate from Charleston, South Carolina, to get to the convention by carriage, on horseback, and on foot? First, figure the time to travel by carriage from Charleston to New Bern, North Carolina. Next, figure the time to travel on horseback from New Bern to Annapolis, Maryland. Finally, figure the time to walk from Annapolis to Philadelphia. Add all three travel times together to get the total time it would take the delegate from Charleston to reach the convention.

Think and Apply

Measure the distance between two cities on a present-day highway map, using the map scale. Find the shortest highway distance between the two cities, using string. Then, using a travel rate of 55 miles per hour, figure out how long it would take to travel by car between those two cities.

LESSON 3

DEBATES AND COMPROMISES

Link to Our World

How can people with different ideas reach agreement?

Focus on the Main Idea
As you read, think about how delegates to the Constitutional Convention reached agreement on a new plan of government.

Preview Vocabulary
compromise   debate
federal system   Union
bill

The delegates to the Constitutional Convention often did not agree with one another. The Constitution came into being only because the delegates were willing to compromise. To **compromise** means to give up some of what you want in order to reach an agreement. As compromises were made, decisions were written down and the Constitution took shape.

A FEDERAL SYSTEM OF GOVERNMENT

The convention delegates first talked about the relationship between the states and the new national government. Few of the delegates agreed with George Read of Delaware, who thought that the states "must be done away [with]." Even those who wanted a strong national government said that getting rid of the states would be going too far.

But the delegates knew that the Articles of Confederation—with strong state governments and a weak national government—must be changed. So they agreed to create a **federal system** in which the authority to govern would be shared. The states would keep some authority, give away some authority, and share some authority with the national, or federal, government.

The states would *keep authority* over their own affairs. They would set up schools and local governments, for example. They would make laws for businesses and set rules for state and local elections.

This sketch from 1789 shows the original design for the Great Seal of the United States. The Great Seal is used on important government documents.

THE FEDERAL SYSTEM OF GOVERNMENT

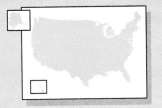

POWERS OF THE NATIONAL GOVERNMENT

Control trade between states and with foreign countries

Create an army and a navy

Print and coin money

Admit new states

Declare war and make peace

Make laws for immigration and citizenship

SHARED POWERS

Collect taxes

Set up court systems

Charter banks

Borrow money

Make laws to provide for public health and welfare

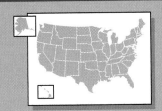

POWERS OF THE STATE GOVERNMENTS

Set up public schools

Set up local governments

Conduct elections

Control trade within the state

Make laws for marriage and divorce

Set qualifications for voting

LEARNING FROM DIAGRAMS Under a federal system, some powers are given to the national government and others are given to the states. Certain powers are shared by both levels of government.
■ Which level of government can print money? Which can set up public schools?

The states would *give away authority* to the national government over matters that affected the whole country. The states would no longer print money, raise armies and navies, or make treaties with other countries, for example. Under the Articles of Confederation, each state had done these things as if it were a country.

The states would *share authority* with the national government, too. Both would be able to raise money by taxing citizens, for example.

The states and the national government might not always agree, however. In that case the national government would have authority over the state governments. The delegates made it clear that under this new federal system, the Constitution would be "the supreme law of the land."

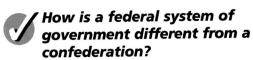
How is a federal system of government different from a confederation?

THE GREAT COMPROMISE

One of the first important disagreements among the delegates to the Constitutional Convention was about how each state would be represented in Congress, the new national legislature. Most delegates agreed that the Congress should have two parts, or houses. But they disagreed about how representatives should be chosen.

Edmund Randolph and the other Virginia delegates, including James Madison, thought the number of representatives a state would have in Congress should be based on the number of people living in that state. Under this plan, called the Virginia Plan, more people in a state would mean more representatives and more votes in Congress. This plan would help the large states with large populations, such as Virginia, Pennsylvania, and New York.

Edmund Randolph (above left) and William Paterson (above right) were on opposite sides of the struggle between large and small states at the Constitutional Convention. Randolph's Virginia Plan (far right), which called for representation to be based on population, favored the large states.

"Not fair!" shouted delegates from the small states. William Paterson of New Jersey said he "had rather submit to a monarch, to a despot, than to such a fate." Paterson offered his own plan for representation, called the New Jersey Plan. Under the New Jersey Plan, the new Congress would have one house rather than two. Each state would have one vote. This plan would help the small states by giving them the same representation as the large states.

The delegates argued for weeks about representation. Which plan would be fairer? The larger states wanted the Virginia Plan. The smaller states wanted the New Jersey Plan. Neither side would give in. "We are now at full stop," said Roger Sherman of Connecticut.

As president of the convention, George Washington chose a committee with one member from each state to work out a compromise. Roger Sherman, a member of the committee, offered a new plan, based on the idea of a two-house Congress. In one house, representation would be based on the number of people in each state, as in the Virginia Plan. In the other house, each state

would have an equal vote, as in the New Jersey Plan. Either house could present a **bill**, or an idea for a new law. But the other house would have to agree to it before it could become a law.

Large-state delegates on the committee did not like Sherman's plan because they felt it gave too much authority to the small states. So the committee added another idea. The house in which representation was based on the number of people in each state would have the authority to tax. Bills having to do with money could come only from this house. The house in which each state had an equal vote could then agree to the bill or not.

The committee presented its compromise plan to the whole convention. The delegates **debated**, or argued, the good and bad points of the compromise. At first, supporters of the Virginia and New Jersey plans held firm. But they came to understand that if they did not compromise, they would not have a new government. Because Sherman's compromise kept the plan for the Constitution alive, some people called it the Great Compromise of the convention.

 What was the Great Compromise?

THE THREE-FIFTHS COMPROMISE

More compromises were made before the convention was over. One had to do with a problem that had long divided the northern and southern states—slavery. Delegates from the two regions argued about whether enslaved Africans should be counted in determining how many representatives a state should have.

At the time of the convention, nearly 4 million people lived in the United States. Almost 2 million lived in the southern states. Of that number, about 667,000 were slaves.

Because the northern states had fewer enslaved Africans than the southern states had, the northern states did not want slaves to be counted for representation. After all, the delegates argued, slaves were not citizens under the Articles of Confederation and they would not become citizens under the Constitution. Delegates from the southern states wanted slaves to be counted. That way the southern states could count more people and get more representatives—and votes— in Congress.

The delegates also debated how much each state should pay in taxes to support the national government. They agreed that each state's share should be based on the number of people in the state. For taxes, the delegates from the southern states did not want slaves counted, while the delegates from the northern states did.

Once again, the delegates reached a compromise. Three-fifths of the total number of slaves would be counted when figuring both representation and taxes. For every five slaves, a state could count three.

The delegates agreed to the Three-fifths Compromise to move closer to forming a

Enslaved people working on this South Carolina plantation lived in small shacks near the fields. Arguments over slavery nearly brought the Constitutional Convention to a halt.

new government. But there were still problems to solve and more compromises to make before the delegates' work was done.

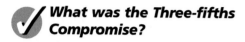 **What was the Three-fifths Compromise?**

SLAVERY AND THE CONSTITUTION

The delegates did not find it easy to compromise on every subject they debated. The subject of slavery nearly broke up the convention—and the United States of America.

More than one-fourth of the delegates, even the convention president, George Washington, owned slaves. These men decided not to use the word *slave* in the Constitution. Instead, they described enslaved people as "such persons" or "all other persons." The words *person held to service or labor* came closest to describing slaves. But even though the delegates did not use the word *slave*, they could not get around the problem of slavery. If the Constitution was to stand for liberty, how could it allow slavery?

The subject of slavery came up most often in the debate over the authority of Congress to control trade with other countries. Some delegates from both northern and southern states did not want Congress to have the authority to end the slave trade. But other delegates from both regions wanted the slave trade stopped.

George Mason of Virginia, an owner of more than 200 slaves, tried to end the trade of enslaved people. "I hold it essential," said Mason, "that the general government should have power to prevent the increase of slavery." He believed that over time all slaves should be set free.

John Rutledge of South Carolina did not agree. Plantation owners in his state and other southern states depended on enslaved workers to grow their cash crops. The slave problem was so important to Rutledge that he questioned "whether the Southern states shall or shall not be parties to the Union" if the slave trade were stopped.

Fearing that the southern states would break away from the **Union**—the United States of America—the delegates compromised. They gave Congress the authority to make laws controlling trade. But Congress could not stop the slave trade for at least 20 years. In the meantime, the delegates took no steps to end slavery in the states.

 What compromise did the delegates reach on the slave trade?

*L*SSON 3 REVIEW

Check Understanding

1. **Recall the Facts** What debates almost ended the Constitutional Convention?
2. **Focus on the Main Idea** How did the delegates reach agreement on a new plan of government?

Think Critically

3. **Past to Present** How do government leaders today use compromise to reach agreement?

4. **Cause and Effect** How would the southern states have been affected if the Constitution had put an end to the slave trade?

Show What You Know

Simulation Activity With a classmate, role-play a debate between delegates at the Constitutional Convention. As representatives of a large and a small state, tell what you think of the Virginia Plan and the New Jersey Plan.

Compromise to Resolve Conflicts

Why Is This Skill Important?

Disagreements can be upsetting. However, there are many ways to handle a disagreement. You can walk away and let the strong feelings fade over time. You can talk about it and explain your way of thinking. You also can compromise. Knowing how to compromise gives you another way to resolve, or handle, conflicts.

Remember What You Have Read

Many people believe that if the delegates to the Constitutional Convention had not been willing to compromise, the Constitution would never have been written. You have read that one of the most serious disagreements at the convention was over representation in the new legislature. Delegates from the large states wanted representation in Congress to be based on population. This would give the large states more

Roger Sherman

representatives—and more votes—than the small states. Delegates from the small states wanted each state to have one representative. This would give all the states equal representation.

Roger Sherman helped resolve this disagreement by suggesting what later became known as the Great Compromise. Congress would be made up of two houses. In one house, representation would be based on population. In the other house, each state would have two representatives and two votes. Both sides got some of what they wanted, but both sides also had to give up other things they wanted.

Understand the Process

To resolve a conflict through compromise, you can follow steps similar to the ones below.

- Before you begin to talk with the person you disagree with, be aware that you may have to give up some things you would like.
- Tell the other person clearly what you want.
- Decide which of the things you want are most important to you.
- Present a plan for a possible compromise. Let the other person present his or her plan.
- Talk about any differences in the two plans.
- Present another plan for a compromise, this time giving up one of the things that is not most important to you. Continue talking until the two of you agree on a compromise plan.
- If either of you becomes angry, take a break and calm down before you go on talking.
- If there are many people on each side of the disagreement, each side should choose one or two people to do most of the talking.

Think and Apply

With your classmates, choose an issue that you do not all agree on, such as a school rule. Form sides to discuss the issue, using the steps in Understand the Process.

A GOVERNMENT OF THREE BRANCHES

Link to Our World

How can people make sure that no part of the government holds too much authority?

Focus on the Main Idea
As you read, look for ways the delegates made sure that no branch of the United States government held too much authority.

Preview Vocabulary

legislative
  branch
executive
  branch
judicial branch
separation of
  powers
majority
census

electoral
  college
veto
impeach
justice
override
unconstitutional
checks and
  balances

This early gavel, used in the Senate to open and close meetings, had no handle.

Under the Articles of Confederation, Congress made the laws, approved the laws, and acted as a court to settle disagreements between the states. But having only one branch of government had created problems. So the delegates to the Constitutional Convention decided there would be three branches of government instead of one. Each would have its own authority. A **legislative branch** would make the laws. An **executive branch** would carry out the laws. A **judicial branch** would settle differences about the meaning of the laws. Once the delegates agreed to this **separation of powers**, they had to decide how the three branches would work together.

THE LEGISLATIVE BRANCH

Like the Congress under the Articles of Confederation, the Congress under the Constitution would make laws. But the new Congress was to have more authority than the old one. The new Congress, for example, could make laws to raise taxes, control trade with other countries, print and coin money, raise an army and a navy, and declare war.

The new Congress would have two houses, the House of Representatives and the Senate. Either house could propose most bills. For a bill to become a law, the **majority**, or the greater part, of each house would have to vote for it.

The number of members each state sent to the House of Representatives would depend on the state's population.

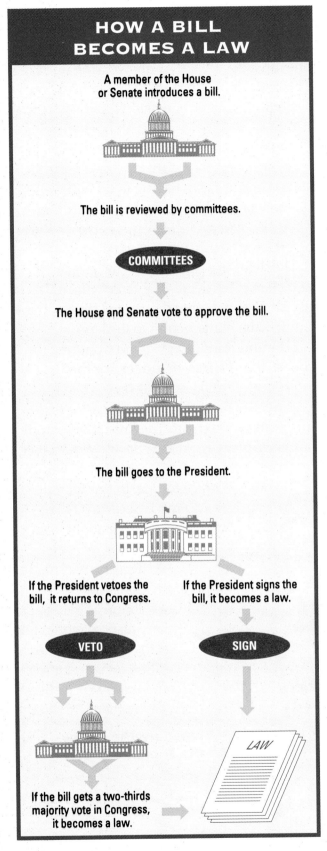

HOW A BILL BECOMES A LAW

A member of the House or Senate introduces a bill.

The bill is reviewed by committees.

COMMITTEES

The House and Senate vote to approve the bill.

The bill goes to the President.

If the President vetoes the bill, it returns to Congress.

If the President signs the bill, it becomes a law.

VETO

SIGN

If the bill gets a two-thirds majority vote in Congress, it becomes a law.

LAW

LEARNING FROM DIAGRAMS Under the Constitution, a bill must follow the steps shown in this diagram to become a law.
■ What part does the President play in this process?

A **census**, or population count, would be taken every ten years to determine the number of people in each state. Today the number of members in the House of Representatives is limited to 435. In the Senate, each state has two senators, as originally planned.

James Madison thought that the members of both houses of Congress should be elected by the voters of each state. Other delegates, however, disagreed. Many felt that most people were not educated enough or informed enough to have a say in government. After a long debate, a compromise was worked out. The delegates agreed that citizens should vote directly for members of the House of Representatives. Senators would be elected by their state legislatures. Today, however, citizens vote directly for members of both houses of Congress, as Madison wanted.

The delegates also decided on other rules for Congress, which are still in effect. Members of the House of Representatives serve for two years. Senators serve for six years. To qualify, members of the House of Representatives must be at least 25 years old, must be citizens of the United States for at least seven years, and must live in the state they represent. Senators must be at least 30 years old, must be citizens of the United States for nine years, and must live in the state they represent.

 **What are the duties of Congress?**

THE EXECUTIVE BRANCH

Once Congress makes the laws, it is the job of the executive branch to carry them out. In doing so, the executive branch runs the day-to-day business of government.

The delegates had many long debates about the executive branch. One of the most heated was about whether it should be headed by one person or a group of people.

James Wilson of Pennsylvania felt that one person should be the chief executive. He thought that a single executive would govern more effectively than a committee. Even though some delegates feared that a single executive would be too much like a monarch, most agreed with Wilson. They decided on a single chief executive, called the President. The President serves for four years.

It also was Wilson's idea to choose the President by having citizens vote for electors, who in turn would vote for the executive. This group of electors is called the **electoral college**.

The delegates also had long debates about how much authority the President should have. Many thought the President should be able to **veto**, or reject, bills passed by Congress.

George Mason disagreed. Such authority, he thought, was too much like that held by a king or queen. But most of the other delegates were willing to take a chance on a strong executive. The delegates counted on the other branches to keep the executive branch under control.

The debates went on and on, but finally the executive branch began to take shape. It was decided that the President would represent the nation in dealing with other countries and would head the nation's military forces. The President's chief responsibility, however, would be to "take care that the laws be faithfully executed." If these duties were not carried out, Congress could **impeach** the President. This means it could accuse the President of wrongdoing. The President then could be tried and removed from office.

✓ **What are the duties of the President?**

THE JUDICIAL BRANCH

Once laws are made and carried out, someone must decide if they are working fairly. This is the job of the judicial branch, or court system. The states had always had their own courts. But the delegates to the Constitutional Convention agreed on the need for a national court system. The courts in this system would decide cases having to do with national laws, treaties, or the Constitution. They also would decide cases between states or between citizens of different states.

The delegates did not plan the judicial branch in great detail. They made the most decisions about what they called the Supreme Court—the highest court in the land.

Edmund Randolph wanted Congress to choose the **justices**, or judges, for the Supreme Court. James Wilson wanted the President to have this authority. A compromise was worked out. The President would name the justices, and the Senate would vote on them. It was decided that a justice would stay in office for life. In this way, justices could reach decisions fairly without worrying about losing their jobs.

No decision was made at the Constitutional Convention as to how many justices would be on the Supreme Court. Congress decided on that number later. At first there were six justices on the court. Today there are nine.

✓ **What are the duties of the Supreme Court?**

The scales of justice stand for fair treatment.

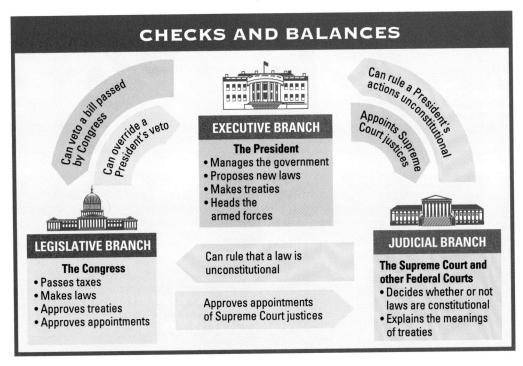

CHECKS AND BALANCES

EXECUTIVE BRANCH

The President
• Manages the government
• Proposes new laws
• Makes treaties
• Heads the armed forces

Can veto a bill passed by Congress

Can override a President's veto

Can rule a President's actions unconstitutional

Appoints Supreme Court justices

LEGISLATIVE BRANCH

The Congress
• Passes taxes
• Makes laws
• Approves treaties
• Approves appointments

Can rule that a law is unconstitutional

Approves appointments of Supreme Court justices

JUDICIAL BRANCH

The Supreme Court and other Federal Courts
• Decides whether or not laws are constitutional
• Explains the meanings of treaties

LEARNING FROM DIAGRAMS This diagram shows the checks and balances among the three branches of government.
■ How can the President check the authority of Congress? How can Congress check the authority of the Supreme Court?

HOW THE BRANCHES WORK TOGETHER

None of the delegates wanted any one branch of government to have too much authority. So they gave each branch some ways to check, or limit, the authority of the others.

Congress, for example, can check the authority of the President by overriding the President's veto. To **override** a veto means to vote to cancel it. The Supreme Court can check the authority of Congress by ruling that a law is **unconstitutional**, or does not follow the Constitution. The President can check the authority of the Supreme Court by choosing its justices.

The delegates set up these checks to keep a balance of authority among the three branches. The **checks and balances** keep any one branch from using its authority wrongly. They help all three branches work together as equal partners.

 What is the purpose of checks and balances among the three branches?

 # LESSON 4 REVIEW

Check Understanding

1. **Recall the Facts** What are the duties of each branch of the national government?
2. **Focus on the Main Idea** How did the delegates to the Constitutional Convention make sure that no branch of the government would have too much authority?

Think Critically

3. **Cause and Effect** What might happen if one branch of the government became too powerful?
4. **Think More About It** How do the separation of powers and the checks and balances help the national government work well?

Show What You Know

Diagram Activity Show your understanding of the separation of powers and the checks and balances by making a flowchart or a diagram. Share your work with a family member or a classmate.

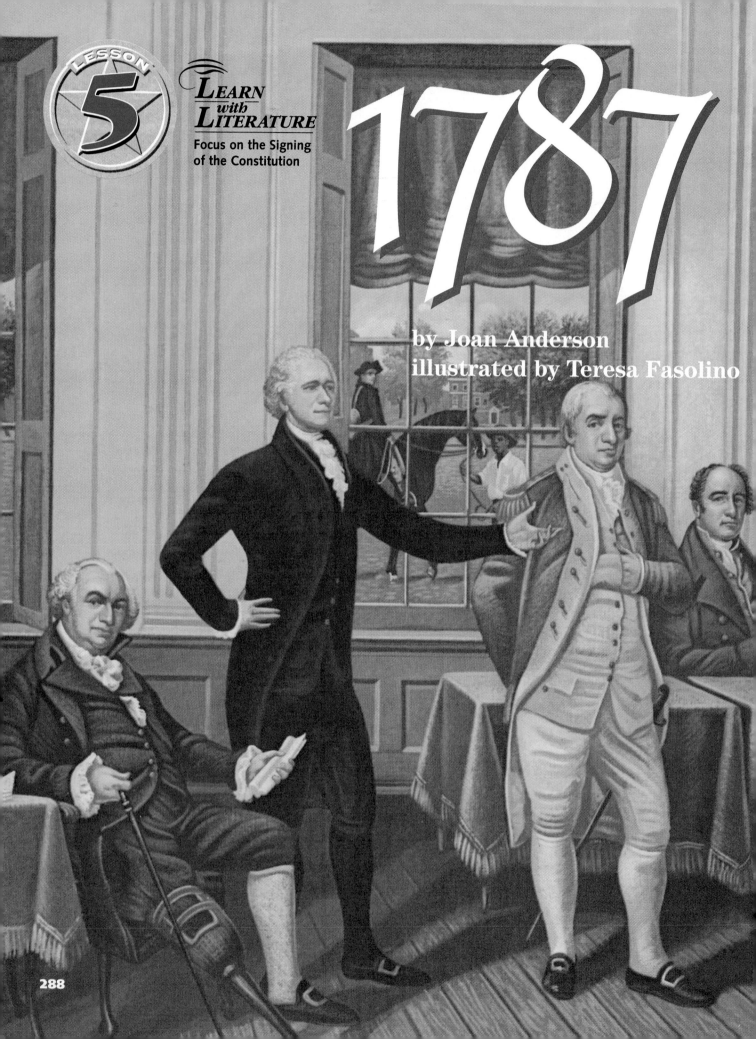

LEARN with LITERATURE

Focus on the Signing
of the Constitution

1787

by Joan Anderson
illustrated by Teresa Fasolino

During the hot and humid summer of 1787, the 55 delegates to the Constitutional Convention worked at writing a new plan of government. In the seven parts, or Articles, of their plan, they described the duties of each branch of government and the relations among the states. They also wrote rules for making changes to the Constitution. Finally the time came for the delegates to sign their names to show they agreed with what had been written.

Read now about the last day of the convention in this story of historical fiction. Jared Mifflin, the boy who tells the story, is James Madison's helper. As Jared listens to the delegates debate, he wonders if the Constitution will ever be signed.

Teresa Fasolino

WE, THE PEOPLE OF THE UNITED STATES, in order to form a more perfect Union, Establish Justice, insure domestic Tranquillity, provide for the common defense, promote the general Welfare, and secure the Blessings of Liberty to ourselves and our Posterity, do ordain and establish this Constitution for the United States of America . . .

*A*s Secretary Jackson continued to read, Jared stood in the back of the East Room gazing upon the delegates, none of whom moved a hair as they listened to the words they had labored so hard to formulate[1] into a sturdy document. *Another hour or so, and the whole thing will be over,* Jared thought, a tinge of

---

[1]**formulate:** state in an exact way

sadness stirring his soul as he realized his unique experience was coming to an end.

The windows of the East Room had finally been opened, allowing an unfamiliar cool breeze to descend upon the delegates at this, their last official meeting. . . .

"And so, let it be Done," General Jackson began the final phrase that now was familiar to Jared because he had read and reread Uncle Thomas's first draft, ". . . in convention by the unanimous[2] consent of the states present, the seventeenth day of September in the year of our Lord, One Thousand Seven Hundred and Eighty Seven and of the Independence of the United States of America the Twelfth. In witness whereof we have hereunto subscribed[3] our names."

Jared gazed about the room, wondering what would happen next. He focused on General Washington, assuming that he would make the next move. There were some stirrings from the Virginians. *They're probably thinking up last-minute suggestions*, Jared surmised.[4] Suddenly, George Mason asked for the floor. Everyone was sitting on the edge of their chairs.

"Gentlemen," he said in a strong, bold tone, "after much soul-searching I must inform you that since this Constitution does not yet contain a Bill of Rights I cannot, in all

HAMILTON

PINCKNEY

good conscience, subscribe to the document that lays waiting."

Jared was stunned. Mr. Mason's attendance during the summer had been almost perfect, and he'd sat on many committees. How could he not sign? No sooner had he taken his seat than Virginia's Governor Randolph rose—to agree with George Mason. "I will gladly present this Constitution to the legislature in Virginia but cannot, at this time, find it in my heart to put name to paper."

Now the room was full of rumblings. Governor Randolph had been one of the early arrivals and the first to speak at the opening of the Convention. He was the one who presented the Virginia Plan, Jared recalled—the paper on which the new Constitution drew some of its ideas! The various states were now huddled together in discussion and General Washington had to bang the gavel several times to bring order to the room. *How many others would follow suit?* Jared wondered.

"I must inform my colleagues that I, too, will not sign this Constitution in its present form," Elbridge Gerry of Massachusetts announced from his seat at the back of the room.

Here we go, Jared thought. *Divisiveness spreading once again from state to state.*

"Mr. President," the voice of Alexander Hamilton rose from the other side of the room. "May I speak?"

---

[2]**unanimous:** in complete agreement
[3]**subscribed:** written below
[4]**surmised:** guessed

Washington nodded, not a trace of emotion on his stoic[5] face.

Jared turned to look at Mr. Hamilton, the man responsible for calling the meeting at Annapolis, where the writing of a Constitution was first discussed. More than anyone else, it seemed that Alexander Hamilton cared about nationhood. He had written numerous articles and papers advocating[6] a strong federal government. Ironically he'd had to endure a delegation that completely disagreed with him throughout this Convention.

"I must express my deepest anxiety that every member should sign," he said with an urgency in his voice. "If a few characters of consequence refuse to sign, their actions could do infinite mischief by kindling latent sparks which lurk under the general enthusiasm for this Constitution." He sat down, but did not take his eyes off Governor Randolph, to whom he was obviously delivering these brief but firmly stated remarks.

There was momentary silence. Jared wished that General Washington would rise and simply commence the signing. Instead, yet another delegate took the floor. *Oh no,* Jared thought, *another Massachusetts man. Will he also dissent?*

Nathaniel Gorham instead moved that the stipulation for representation in the House be changed from one representative per forty thousand citizens to one per thirty thousand. *How could they change anything now?* Jared wondered, as he gazed over at the beautifully printed pieces of parchment that were spread out on the table. *With this latest diversion, the Convention will surely trail on for days,* he sighed. Knowing how meticulously[7] these men had worked over this document, clause by clause, article by article, Jared resigned himself to the delay and took a seat on the stool provided for him by the door.

Rufus King seconded the motion, and Jared got set to watch yet another debate on representation. But instead, General Washington rose from his seat to make a statement. "Being the presiding member," he informed the group, "I know I am not at liberty to comment one way or another and have not done so until this moment. However, I must agree with my colleagues," he continued. "It has always appeared to me that an exceptional plan would be to have one representative for every thirty thousand citizens, and it would give me much satisfaction to see it adopted."

That did it. Everyone agreed to vote with the man considered to be the foremost of all Americans. With the representation issue finally put to rest and no one else jumping up with final objections, Dr. Franklin asked for the floor.

MADISON

WASHINGTON

---

[5]**stoic:** calm
[6]**advocating:** speaking for

---

[7]**meticulously:** very carefully

Finally! Jared said to himself. *Not many men here are going to disagree with Benjamin Franklin, no matter what he says.*

"Due to a weakened voice, gentlemen," he began, "I have asked my friend James Wilson to read you my sentiments on this momentous day." He nodded for Wilson to begin:

"Mr. President, I confess that there are several parts of this Constitution which I do not at present approve, but I am not sure I shall ever approve them. For having lived a long time, I have experienced many instances of being obliged by better information or fuller consideration to change opinions even on important subjects which I once thought right, but found to be otherwise.

It is, therefore, that the older I grow, the more apt I am to doubt my own judgment, and to pay more respect to the judgment of others.

In these sentiments, sir, I agree to this Constitution with all its faults, if they are such. . . . I doubt, too, whether any other convention we can obtain, may be able to make a better Constitution.

For when you assemble a number of men to have the advantage of their joint wisdom, you inevitably assemble with those men all their prejudices, their passions, their errors of opinion, their local interest, and their selfish views. From such an assembly can a perfect production be expected?

It, therefore, astonishes me, sir, to find this system approaching so near to perfection as it does; and I think it will astonish our enemies. . . .

Thus I consent, sir. I cannot help expressing a wish that every member of the Convention who may still have objections to it, would with me, on this occasion, doubt a little of his own infallibility,[8] and to make manifest our unanimity, put his name to this instrument."

FRANKLIN

❦

When Franklin's speech was over, the signing began. George Washington was first to write on the cream-colored parchment. Delegates from each state followed. In the end, all but 16 of the 55 delegates signed the new United States Constitution on September 17, 1787. Mason, Randolph, and Gerry did not sign. The 13 others had already left the convention and returned home.

As Benjamin Franklin left the convention hall, he was asked by the wife of Philadelphia's mayor what kind of government the new nation would have. "A republic," he told her, "if you can keep it." Franklin's words were meant for all the people of the United States.

Literature Review

1. Why did the delegates decide to stop debating and sign the Constitution?
2. Why do you think Benjamin Franklin believed that a "perfect" Constitution was not possible?
3. Write a short scene about the closing of the Constitutional Convention. With classmates, act out your scene for the class.

---

[8]**infallibility:** inability to make a mistake

CHAPTER 9

CONNECT MAIN IDEAS

Use this organizer to show that you understand how the chapter's main ideas are connected. Copy the organizer onto a separate sheet of paper. Then complete it by writing the main idea of each lesson and by listing the three branches of government.

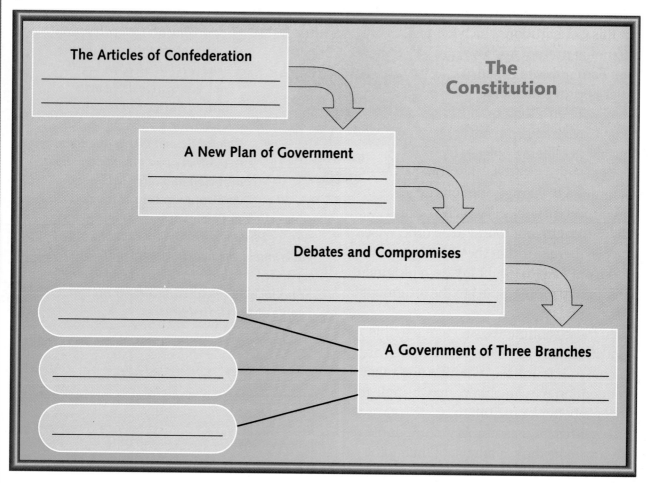

The Articles of Confederation
_____
_____

The Constitution

A New Plan of Government
_____
_____

Debates and Compromises
_____
_____

_____

_____

_____

A Government of Three Branches
_____
_____

WRITE MORE ABOUT IT

1. **Write a Persuasive Letter** Imagine that you are living in one of the 13 states during the time delegates were meeting to discuss the Articles of Confederation. Write a letter to the editor of your newspaper, telling why you think the Articles of Confederation should or should not be changed.

2. **Report a News Event** Suppose that you are a newspaper reporter who has been asked to cover the Constitutional Convention. Write a short newspaper article in which you explain the Great Compromise. Be sure to tell how its passage will affect the outcome of the convention.

USE VOCABULARY

Write one or two sentences for each pair of terms to explain how the terms are related.

1. constitution, republic

2. convention, delegate

3. compromise, debate

4. federal system, Union

5. veto, override

CHECK UNDERSTANDING

1. How was the United States under the Articles of Confederation like the Iroquois League?

2. What powers did Congress have under the Articles of Confederation? What powers did it not have?

3. What was the purpose of the Northwest Ordinance?

4. Why did some people call the United States under the Articles of Confederation the "Disunited States"?

5. Where was the Constitutional Convention held?

6. How are power and authority shared in a federal system?

7. What were the differences between the New Jersey Plan and the Virginia Plan?

8. What are the three branches of the United States government? Describe the duties of each branch.

9. How does the United States census affect the number of members each state has in the House of Representatives?

10. How are justices on the Supreme Court chosen? How long do they serve?

11. What is the system of checks and balances?

THINK CRITICALLY

1. **Explore Viewpoints** While most delegates to the Constitutional Convention thought the chief executive should be paid, Benjamin Franklin thought the President should serve without pay. If you had been a delegate to the convention, which view would you have supported? Why?

2. **Past to Present** Is compromising still important for government leaders today? Explain your answer.

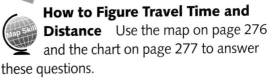

APPLY SKILLS

How to Figure Travel Time and Distance Use the map on page 276 and the chart on page 277 to answer these questions.

1. How many days might it have taken to travel by horse from Charleston to Philadelphia?

2. How many days might it have taken to walk from Boston to Philadelphia?

3. How many days might it have taken to get from New York to Philadelphia by carriage?

How to Compromise to Resolve Conflicts
Think of something that you and a friend disagree about. Then list the steps that you might follow to resolve your conflict. What things are you willing to give up to reach a compromise?

READ MORE ABOUT IT

If You Were There When They Signed the Constitution by Elizabeth Levy. Scholastic. This nonfiction book traces the events leading up through the signing of the Constitution.

Our Constitution by Linda Carlson Johnson. Millbrook. This book tells the history of the United States Constitution and how the Constitution has changed over time.

CHAPTER 10

A NEW GOVERNMENT BEGINS

66 The basis of our political systems is the right of the people to make and to alter their constitutions of government. 99

George Washington, in his farewell speech as President, 1796

A portrait of George Washington by Gilbert Stuart

APPROVING THE CONSTITUTION

Link to Our World

What would make the people of a country want to support its plan of government?

Focus on the Main Idea
As you read, think about what made the people of the United States want to support the Constitution.

Preview Vocabulary
ratify
Federalist
Anti-Federalist

James Madison had taken careful notes all through the Constitutional Convention. The day his fellow delegates signed their approval for the new plan of government, Madison wrote in his notebook,

66 Whilst the last members were signing it Doctor Franklin looking towards the President's Chair, at the back of which a rising sun happened to be painted, observed to a few members near him, that Painters had found it difficult to distinguish in their art a rising sun from a setting sun. I have, said he, often and often in the course of the Session . . . looked at that behind the President without being able to tell whether it was rising or setting: But now at length I have the happiness to know that it is a rising and not a setting Sun. 99

Despite Franklin's words, the new plan of government that he and the other delegates had approved was not yet the law of the land. According to Article VII of the Constitution, 9 of the 13 states had to **ratify**, or agree to, the Constitution before it would become law.

STATE RATIFYING CONVENTIONS

Once the delegates signed the Constitution on September 17, 1787, George Washington ordered it sent to Congress. Congress in turn sent copies to the states. To decide about the new plan of government, the states held their own ratifying conventions. In each state, the people elected delegates

The chair that Washington used during the Constitutional Convention (right) is still on display inside Independence Hall in Philadelphia. The top part of the chair (above) shows the "rising sun."

to go to the state convention and vote for or against the Constitution.

At the state conventions debate began all over again. Some delegates, such as Patrick Henry in Virginia and George Clinton in New York, told their conventions that the new national government was too strong. Samuel Adams told delegates in Massachusetts that he did not like the way the Preamble began with *We the People.* He thought it should say *We the states.*

There was one point, however, on which the delegates to just about every state convention agreed. They felt the Constitution needed to list the things the government could *not* do. This would protect the rights of the states and the people.

The state delegates wanted to protect freedoms such as the right to tell the government if it was doing something wrong. They remembered that Patrick Henry and James Otis had almost been sent to prison for

speaking out against the British government. The delegates did not want the new national government to have the authority to do the same thing.

The delegates to the state ratifying conventions said they would be more willing to agree to the Constitution if a list of rights were added to it. So supporters of the Constitution promised that after it was ratified, a bill of rights would be added.

 Why were many delegates not willing at first to agree to the new Constitution?

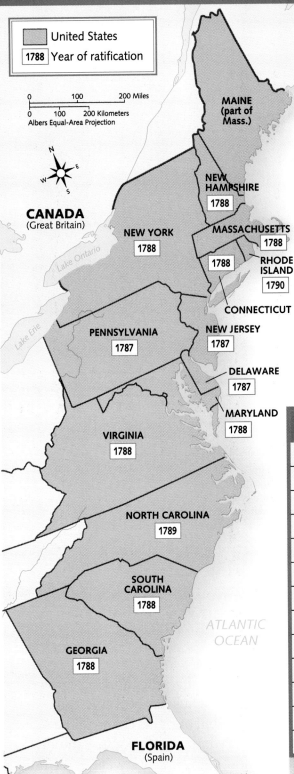

RATIFICATION OF THE CONSTITUTION

Legend:
- United States
- 1788 Year of ratification

0   100   200 Miles
0   100   200 Kilometers
Albers Equal-Area Projection

CANADA
(Great Britain)

Lake Ontario

Lake Erie

MAINE
(part of Mass.)

NEW HAMPSHIRE
1788

NEW YORK
1788

MASSACHUSETTS
1788

1788

RHODE ISLAND
1790

CONNECTICUT

PENNSYLVANIA
1787

NEW JERSEY
1787

DELAWARE
1787

MARYLAND
1788

VIRGINIA
1788

NORTH CAROLINA
1789

SOUTH CAROLINA
1788

GEORGIA
1788

ATLANTIC OCEAN

FLORIDA
(Spain)

THE VOTE

The first state to call for a vote on the Constitution was Delaware. On December 7, 1787, all the state delegates voted to ratify. Later that month, delegates in Pennsylvania and New Jersey also voted to ratify. In January 1788, delegates in Georgia and Connecticut voted to ratify. But several states still had not voted. Among those were New York and Virginia. People wondered how the new government could possibly work if the country's largest states voted against it.

From January to June 1788, people who were for the new Constitution and people who were against it both tried to get the support of people in the states that had not yet voted. Those who wanted the Constitution came to be called **Federalists**. Those who did not want it became known as **Anti-Federalists**. Federalists wanted the plan's strong national government.

STATE	DATE	VOTES FOR	VOTES AGAINST
Delaware	December 7, 1787	30	0
Pennsylvania	December 12, 1787	46	23
New Jersey	December 18, 1787	38	0
Georgia	January 2, 1788	26	0
Connecticut	January 9, 1788	128	40
Massachusetts	February 6, 1788	187	168
Maryland	April 28, 1788	63	11
South Carolina	May 23, 1788	149	73
New Hampshire	June 21, 1788	57	47
Virginia	June 25, 1788	89	79
New York	July 26, 1788	30	27
North Carolina	November 21, 1789	194	77
Rhode Island	May 29, 1790	34	32

PLACE The map and the table show when the Constitution was ratified in each state.
■ Which state took the longest to ratify the Constitution? In which state was the vote closest?

This banner was carried by members of the Society of Pewterers in a parade held in 1788 to celebrate New York's ratification of the Constitution. Pewterers made plates, pitchers, and other items out of pewter, a metal.

Anti-Federalists did not want a strong national government unless a bill of rights was added to the plan.

In New York, Federalists and Anti-Federalists used the newspapers to tell how they felt and why. Alexander Hamilton, James Madison, and John Jay wrote letters to the newspapers, defending the Constitution. These letters were later published as a book called *The Federalist*.

Those who could read followed the debate in the newspapers. Others heard the arguments at community meetings and even at church services. Some people saw the new Constitution as the work of "lawyers and men of learning, and moneyed men that talk so finely . . . to make us poor illiterate people swallow down the pill." But others thought that having a government with three branches and a Congress with two houses was a good idea. They also liked the promise of a bill of rights.

Alexander Hamilton wrote most of the letters published in *The Federalist*. Many people think this book provides the best description ever written of the ideas behind the American plan of government.

No one was sure how all the arguing would affect the ratifying conventions. In Massachusetts, however, the promise of a bill of rights changed the minds of some very important people. Samuel Adams and John Hancock went to the ratifying convention as firm Anti-Federalists. They returned home as Federalists. Massachusetts easily ratified the Constitution in February 1788.

TOWARD A NEW PLAN OF GOVERNMENT

1775

1775
The Revolutionary War begins

1776
Declaration of Independence

1777
The Articles of Confederation are written

1780

1781
The Articles of Confederation are ratified

1783
The Revolutionary War ends

1785

1787
Shays's Rebellion

The Constitution is written

1788
The Constitution is ratified

1790

1789
Government under the Constitution begins

When?

1789

The new government of the United States went to work early in 1789. That same year, in France, another change in government began. The French Revolution was a long, terrible conflict that took many lives. But when the revolution was over, the French had overthrown their monarchy.

In many ways what was important to the Americans during the American Revolution was also important to the French. The leaders of the French Revolution believed in democratic ideas such as liberty. Even the colors of the French Revolution were red, white, and blue, like those of the United States flag.

Maryland and South Carolina soon followed Massachusetts. Then, on June 21, 1788, New Hampshire became the ninth state to ratify. That was enough for the Constitution to become law. That summer Virginia and New York voted for the Constitution. By early 1789 the new government was at work. North Carolina ratified later that year. The last state to ratify the Constitution, Rhode Island, finally gave its approval in 1790.

✓ **Why was The Federalist important?**

LEARNING FROM TIME LINES This time line lists key events of the nation's early history, leading toward ratification of the Constitution.
■ How many years were the Articles of Confederation in effect as the nation's plan of government?

LESSON 1 REVIEW

Check Understanding

1. **Recall the Facts** What were the differences between the Federalists and the Anti-Federalists?
2. **Focus on the Main Idea** How did the new Constitution gain support?

Think Critically

3. **Think More About It** Why do you think winning ratification in large states such as New York was so important?
4. **Cause and Effect** What effect did the promise of a bill of rights have on the debate over ratification?

Show What You Know

Cartoon Activity Choose one side in the debate over the ratification of the Constitution. Draw a political cartoon showing your point of view. Ask a family member or a classmate to interpret your political cartoon.

For or Against a BILL *of* RIGHTS?

James Madison

Thomas Jefferson

James Madison and Thomas Jefferson liked and respected one another. Both men were important leaders who were born and grew up in Virginia. Both served in Virginia's legislature. Jefferson took part in writing the Declaration of Independence, and Madison helped write the Constitution. But Jefferson and Madison disagreed about many things, too, such as the need for a bill of rights to be added to the Constitution.

Shortly after the Constitutional Convention ended, Madison sent Jefferson a copy of the Constitution along with a long letter about the convention. Jefferson wrote back, explaining why he felt a bill of rights was needed. At first, Madison saw little need for a bill of rights and felt that any changes to the Constitution would just prolong the debate and threaten ratification. Read the following parts of Jefferson's and Madison's letters.

Jefferson to Madison
December 20, 1787

66 Let me add that a bill of rights is what the people are entitled to against every government on earth, general or particular, & what no just government should refuse. . . . 99

Madison to Jefferson
April 22, 1788

66 Should this [the demand for a bill of rights] be carried in the affirmative, . . . I think the Constitution, and the Union will be both endangered. 99

Jefferson to Madison
July 31, 1788

66 I hope therefore a bill of rights will be formed to guard the peoples against the federal government, as they are already guarded against their state governments in most instances. 99

Madison to Jefferson
October 17, 1788

66 I have never thought the omission [of a bill a rights] a material defect, nor been anxious to supply it even by subsequent amendment. . . . A bill of rights will be good ground for an appeal to the sense of the community. . . . Where the power, as with us, is in the many not in the few, the danger can not be very great that the few will be thus favored. It is much more to be dreaded that the few will be unnecessarily sacrificed to the many. 99

Jefferson to Madison
March 15, 1789

66 I am much pleased with the prospect that a declaration of rights will be added: and hope it will be done in that way which will not endanger the whole frame of the government, or any essential part of it. 99

COMPARE
VIEWPOINTS

1. What viewpoint about the Bill of Rights did Jefferson hold? How do you know?
2. What viewpoint about the Bill of Rights did Madison hold at first? How do you know?
3. How did Madison's viewpoint change over time?

THINK
–AND–
APPLY

BUILDING CITIZENSHIP

People often change their views about things over time. You have read that James Madison changed his view about the need for a bill of rights. Can you think of times when you changed your views on a subject? What caused you to change your views? Was it talking to friends, some new information you learned, or something else?

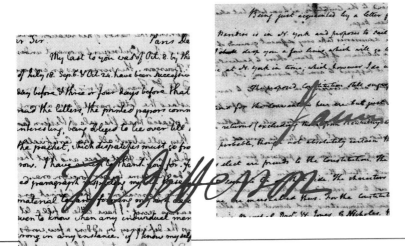

LESSON 2 — THE PEOPLE'S RIGHTS and RESPONSIBILITIES

Link to Our World

Why do citizens have responsibilities to their nation as well as individual rights?

Focus on the Main Idea
As you read, look for citizens' responsibilities and individual rights that come from the Constitution.

Preview Vocabulary
amendment
Bill of Rights
due process of law
human rights
jury
patriotism

As promised, not long after the states ratified the United States Constitution, it was changed. Ten **amendments**, or changes, were added to protect the rights of the people. These ten amendments, called the **Bill of Rights**, describe freedoms that the government cannot take away and list actions that the government is not allowed to take.

The British had long had a Bill of Rights. But the British monarch and Parliament could ignore it or change it any time they wanted. The American Bill of Rights became part of the Constitution in 1791. There was only one way it could be changed—by another amendment.

THE BILL OF RIGHTS

The First Amendment in the Bill of Rights is perhaps the most famous because the freedoms it guarantees are so much a part of our daily lives. The First Amendment says that people have the freedom to follow any religion they want, or no religion at all. It protects freedom of speech and freedom of the press. It also says that people can hold meetings to discuss problems and that they can ask the government to hear their complaints.

The Second Amendment protects people's right to carry arms, or weapons. It says, "A well-regulated militia, being necessary to the security of a free state, the right of the people to keep and bear arms shall not be infringed."

The Third Amendment says that the government cannot force citizens to pay for quartering, or housing, soldiers.

On this 1795 coin, Lady Liberty wears the type of cap that former slaves in ancient Rome wore to show they had been freed.

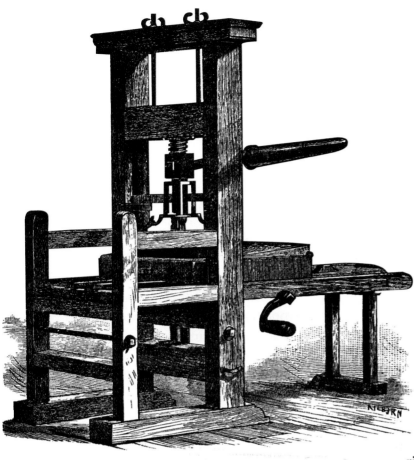

During the late 1700s, the printing press was the main tool for spreading news and opinions. Why do you think the Bill of Rights includes freedom of the press?

Before the Revolutionary War, many colonists had to spend their own money to house and feed British soldiers. Under the Fourth Amendment, the government cannot order that a person's home be searched or property taken away without good reason.

The Fifth through Eighth Amendments have to do with **due process of law**. This means people have the right to a fair, public trial. They do not have to speak against themselves. They have the right to have a lawyer speak for them in court. They cannot be put on trial twice for the same crime or be given "cruel or unusual" punishment.

The Ninth Amendment says that people have many other rights that are not listed in detail in the Constitution. Among these are **human rights**—the freedoms that all people should have. The Declaration of Independence calls them "unalienable rights" and lists them as "Life, Liberty and the pursuit of Happiness."

As a final protection for citizens, the Tenth Amendment says that the national government can do only those things listed in the Constitution. All other authority belongs to the states or to the people.

 Why is the Bill of Rights an important part of the Constitution?

CITIZENS' RESPONSIBILITIES

With the first ten amendments, the American people made it clear that their rights are important. Government must protect these rights. But the people also have a role to play. Certain responsibilities go along with the rights of citizens. For the United States to remain free and strong, its citizens have to take an active part in its government.

The responsibilities of citizens are not written in the Constitution. They are implied, or suggested. The Constitution says, for example, that the laws of the United States are the highest laws in the nation. This implies that citizens should respect and obey the laws. The Constitution gives citizens the right to elect representatives to govern them. This implies that citizens should take part in government by voting in elections.

The Constitution gives Congress the authority to raise an army. This means that citizens should be ready to defend the country. The Constitution says that every person charged with a crime will be judged by a **jury**—a group of citizens who decide a

Symbols on craftwork, such as this quilt from the late 1700s, show the patriotic spirit of the people.

This would depend on good citizens—"a virtuous citizenry," as the writers of the Constitution described it. Past republics, like that of ancient Rome, broke up when the people grew greedy and selfish. To stay strong, the American people had to keep alive the spirit that had given the country its independence and its Constitution.

The writers of the Constitution felt that a love of country is important. But **patriotism**, or love of country, is more than simply waving the American flag at special times. Americans have to be virtuous citizens all the time.

 Why is love of country important?

case in court. So citizens must be willing to be members of a jury when called to do so. The Constitution also gives Congress the authority to raise money to run the country. Citizens must be willing to pay taxes if the country is to run smoothly.

 Why should citizens take an active part in government?

"A VIRTUOUS CITIZENRY"

The writers of the Constitution were not sure their new government would last. They looked to other countries and other times in history. No other nation had a government quite like the one described by the Constitution. No other people had the kinds of freedoms that American citizens now enjoyed. But would the people be able to keep their government going and protect their freedoms over time?

*L*SSON 2 REVIEW

Check Understanding

1. **Recall the Facts**   What important freedoms are protected by the Bill of Rights?
2. **Focus on the Main Idea**   What are the main responsibilities of American citizens?

Think Critically

3. **Think More About It**   Can American citizens have rights without responsibilities? Why or why not?
4. **Personally Speaking**   What do you think is the most important right described in the Bill of Rights? Explain your view.

Show What You Know

 **Art Activity**   Make a collage by cutting out drawings, photographs, and cartoons that show the importance of the Bill of Rights today.

LESSON 3

PUTTING THE NEW GOVERNMENT to WORK

This pitcher from 1789 marks the election of George Washington as the nation's first President.

Link to Our World

Why must a nation's leaders be willing to compromise for government to work well?

Focus on the Main Idea
As you read, look for ways the nation's leaders compromised to make the new plan of government work.

Preview Vocabulary
Cabinet
political party
campaign

In early 1789, elections were held for the first time under the new government. Property-owning male citizens all over the United States elected members of the House of Representatives. Legislatures of the 13 states each chose two senators. The electoral college chose the nation's first President.

NEW LEADERS

Fourteen years after Congress had chosen George Washington to lead the Continental army, the electoral college elected him as the nation's first President. John Adams, the runner-up to Washington in the voting, became the first Vice President. His job was to help President Washington with his duties.

On April 30, 1789, George Washington stood on the balcony of Federal Hall in New York City, where the new Congress was to meet for the first time. There he recited the President's oath of office:

❝I do solemnly swear (or affirm) that I will faithfully execute the Office of President of the United States, and will to the best of my ability, preserve, protect, and defend the Constitution of the United States.**❞**

The new President and the first Congress helped the government make a good start. Congress decided on the number of justices who would serve on the Supreme Court. The President named John Jay as the first chief justice. Washington chose new leaders, too, for important jobs in the executive branch. These were the secretaries, or heads, of the departments of state, the treasury, and war. These departments would carry out the main responsibilities of the executive branch.

President Washington asked Thomas Jefferson to help him deal with other countries. He made Jefferson the nation's first secretary of state. Jefferson worked to set up ties with the leading world powers of that day—Spain, France, and the former enemy of the United States, Britain.

Alexander Hamilton was given the important job of secretary of the treasury. The national government badly needed money. Hamilton worked with Congress to set up a new banking system and pass new tax laws. He also ordered the printing and coining of money.

George Washington chose Henry Knox, who had been a general in the Revolutionary War, as secretary of war. Knox began building a national army of 1,000 soldiers to defend the nation's western border.

Edmund Randolph became the President's legal adviser, now called the attorney general. He told the President what the Constitution and the nation's other laws would and would not allow him to do.

Jefferson, Hamilton, Knox, and Randolph together were known as the **Cabinet**, a group of the President's most important advisers. Every President since Washington has relied on a Cabinet for help in carrying out the duties of the executive branch. Under later Presidents, the number of Cabinet members grew as the executive branch gained more responsibilities.

 How did George Washington organize the work of the executive branch?

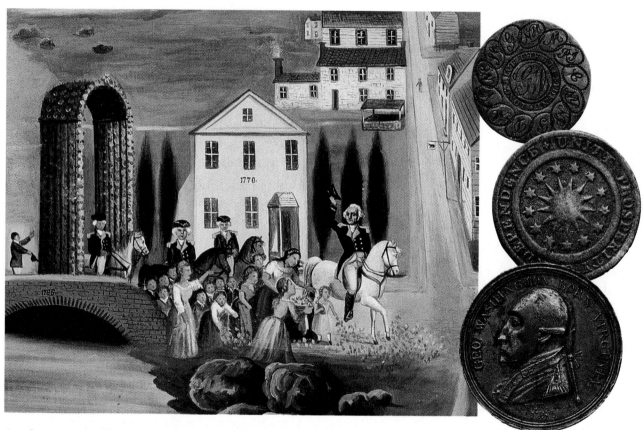

People wore special buttons (right) to honor Washington when he became President. After the election, Washington rode from Virginia to New York, where he took the oath of office. This painting (left) shows children giving him flowers as he passes through Trenton, New Jersey.

What?

Presidents' Day

George Washington's Birthday was first celebrated as a holiday in the late 1700s. Washington was born on February 22, 1732, according to the calendar we use today. However, by the calendar used during Washington's time, he was born on February 11. For this reason the holiday was celebrated on different days by different people.

Another great President, Abraham Lincoln, was born on February 12, 1809. His birthday is also celebrated. Starting in the 1970s some states combined the birthday celebrations for Washington and Lincoln on a holiday called Presidents' Day. This day is the third Monday of February each year.

NEW DISAGREEMENTS

Almost as soon as the new government got started, President Washington's two top advisers began to quarrel. Thomas Jefferson and Alexander Hamilton disagreed on almost every problem facing the new nation.

One of the main differences between the two leaders had to do with the authority of the states and the national government. Jefferson worked for the rights of the states. He did not trust a strong national government. Hamilton liked a strong national government and did not trust the states to act on their own.

Jefferson and Hamilton also disagreed about what some parts of the Constitution meant. Jefferson said the national government had only the authority described in the Constitution. He said all other authority belonged to the states. Hamilton said that the Constitution allowed the national government far greater authority over many more

areas than those it listed. He felt that the government should be active in all parts of American life.

There were other differences. Jefferson wanted Americans across the country to spread out and live on farms. "When we get piled upon one another in large cities," Jefferson argued, "we shall become corrupt." Hamilton wanted the United States to be a nation of cities. He thought the national government should build ports and factories.

Jefferson thought the United States should have close ties with France. France, after all, had been an ally of the United States in the Revolutionary War. Hamilton wanted the United States to become friendlier with Britain to make use of Britain's trading network, which covered much of the world.

What were the main differences between Jefferson and Hamilton?

THE FIRST POLITICAL PARTIES

Representatives and senators in Congress began to take sides in the Jefferson-Hamilton quarrel. They even started voting together as groups. These groups formed the nation's first **political parties**. Party members tried to get others to agree with their ideas and chose leaders who shared the party's points of view.

Hamilton's followers formed what became known as the Federalist party. The party's members were some of the same people who had supported the Constitution during the state ratifying conventions. John Adams, John Jay, and Henry Knox all became members of the Federalist party.

Many Anti-Federalists took Jefferson's side in the quarrel. Patrick Henry, George Clinton, and others formed the Democratic-Republican party. They were sometimes called simply Republicans. Jefferson's Republican party was not today's Republican party, which was formed much later. In fact, it was the beginning of the present-day Democratic party.

Most often Federalists and Republicans had to compromise so that laws could get passed. In one compromise, they agreed that a national capital would be built as a permanent home for the new government. But the capital would not be part of any one state. Maryland and Virginia would both give up some of their land to create the District of Columbia (D.C.). George Washington himself chose the location for the capital city that came to carry his name.

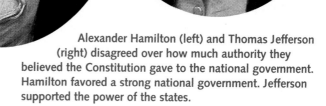

Alexander Hamilton (left) and Thomas Jefferson (right) disagreed over how much authority they believed the Constitution gave to the national government. Hamilton favored a strong national government. Jefferson supported the power of the states.

 What were the main differences between Federalists and Republicans?

A PEACEFUL CHANGE IN LEADERSHIP

In 1792 the electoral college chose George Washington as President, just as it had done in 1789. Many people hoped Washington would remain President even longer than eight years. They said two 4-year terms were not enough—the country needed his leadership. In 1796, however, Washington turned down the chance to run again and went home to Mount Vernon, his plantation in Virginia. In leaving after two terms, Washington set an example that many other Presidents would follow. Later the Constitution would be changed so that no President could serve more than two terms in office.

But by 1796 the growth of political parties had changed the way the electoral college

chose the President. Instead of making its own list of people to choose from, the electoral college was given lists made by each party's leaders. The electoral college chose from these lists when it voted for the President.

When George Washington left office, the Federalist party backed John Adams, Washington's Vice President. Thomas Jefferson was the Republicans' choice.

As they had done with their quarrel over the Constitution, the Federalists and the Republicans took their fight to the people through the newspapers. This fight was less polite, though. Instead of arguing about problems, the political parties called one another names.

The **campaign**, or race for office, was bitter. Yet the election was peaceful. In the end John Adams won by three electoral votes over Jefferson, who became the Vice President.

On March 4, 1797, John Adams took the President's oath of office in Philadelphia's Congress Hall, next door to the more famous Independence Hall. This was an important day in history. It marked one of the first times in the history of the world that a nation had changed leaders by means of a peaceful election.

John Adams started his term as President in Philadelphia, where Congress met. By the end of his term, in November 1800, the government had moved to the District of Columbia. When John Adams and his family moved to the new capital city, they lived in a special house built for the President. It has had several names, among them the President's House, the Executive Mansion, and the White House—the name by which it is known today.

Abigail Adams, the President's wife, was impressed by her new home. She wrote to her daughter in Massachusetts that the house was "built for ages to come." Could the same be said for the nation's new government and its Constitution?

✓ **What was important about the way John Adams became President?**

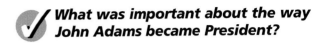 **W**here?

The District of Columbia

President Washington selected a place for the capital city a few miles up the Potomac River from his plantation, Mount Vernon. Two former clockmakers, Andrew Ellicott and Benjamin Banneker, surveyed the land. An engineer, Pierre Charles L'Enfant, planned the buildings and the streets. L'Enfant's plan for the capital city called for wide streets reaching out from two main centers. In these centers stand the offices of the President and Congress today.

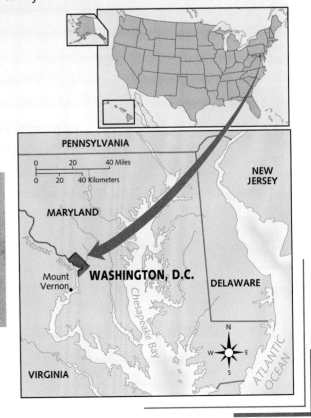

Benjamin Banneker, a free African, taught himself mathematics and astronomy. Among his many accomplishments were surveying the land for the nation's capital and making scientific calculations for his own almanacs.

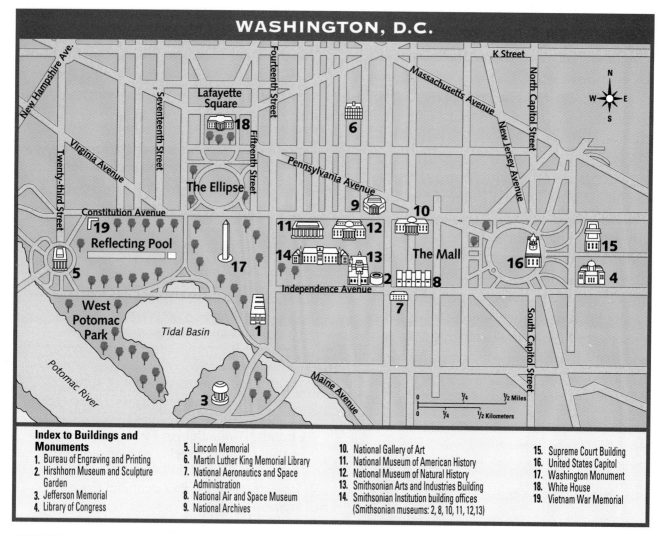

WASHINGTON, D.C.

K Street

New Hampshire Ave.

Seventeenth Street

Virginia Avenue

Twenty-third Street

New Jersey Avenue

Massachusetts Avenue

North Capitol Street

Fourteenth Street

Fifteenth Street

Lafayette Square 18

6

Pennsylvania Avenue

The Ellipse

9

10

Constitution Avenue

19

Reflecting Pool

11 12

14 13

The Mall

15

16 4

5

17

2 8

Independence Avenue

7

West Potomac Park

Tidal Basin

1

South Capitol Street

Potomac River

Maine Avenue

3

0   ¼   ½ Miles
0   ¼   ½ Kilometers

Index to Buildings and Monuments

1. Bureau of Engraving and Printing
2. Hirshhorn Museum and Sculpture Garden
3. Jefferson Memorial
4. Library of Congress

5. Lincoln Memorial
6. Martin Luther King Memorial Library
7. National Aeronautics and Space Administration
8. National Air and Space Museum
9. National Archives

10. National Gallery of Art
11. National Museum of American History
12. National Museum of Natural History
13. Smithsonian Arts and Industries Building
14. Smithsonian Institution building offices (Smithsonian museums: 2, 8, 10, 11, 12, 13)

15. Supreme Court Building
16. United States Capitol
17. Washington Monument
18. White House
19. Vietnam War Memorial

LEARNING FROM DIAGRAMS The streets of Washington, D.C., today reflect the original plan laid out by Pierre Charles L'Enfant.

■ Where do the leaders of each of the three branches of government meet?

LESSON 3 REVIEW

Check for Understanding

1. **Recall the Facts** What caused political parties to form? How did they change government?

2. **Focus on the Main Idea** How did the country's early leaders compromise to make the Constitution and the government work?

Think Critically

3. **Past to Present** Why is the President's Cabinet larger today than in Washington's time?

4. **Personally Speaking** If you were a member of the electoral college in 1796, which leader would you have chosen as President? Explain your answer.

Show What You Know

Newspaper Activity Imagine a problem George Washington is facing as the first President of the United States. Then write a newspaper article telling how Alexander Hamilton and Thomas Jefferson feel about the problem.

Learn from a Document

Why Is This Skill Important?

You have already studied many documents that are important to American history, such as the Mayflower Compact and the Declaration of Independence. In the study of history, a document is any photograph, recording, or written or printed paper that gives information. Maps, letters, drawings, and journals are all documents. So is money, such as the paper money shown below.

Historical documents are primary sources that give important information about the past. They tell us things that many books cannot. Knowing how to gather information from a historical document can help you learn more about life in the past.

Understand the Process

In 1790 Secretary of the Treasury Alexander Hamilton asked Congress to set up the Bank of the United States. The bank would be a safe place to store the money the government collected in taxes. It would also loan money to merchants and manufacturers, which would speed the growth of business. One way the bank would loan money would be by printing paper money called banknotes.

In 1796 the Bank of the United States printed the banknote shown here. This is an important document because it gives information about the time in which it was printed.

Sometimes you have to look hard to find information on a document. Study the document by using these questions as a guide:

1. How do you know this banknote was printed by the Bank of the United States?
2. What tells you how much the banknote is worth?
3. At the bottom of the banknote, the name of the holder and the date have been written by hand. What might this tell you about how this banknote was used?

Think and Apply

With a partner, compare the 1796 banknote with a dollar bill of today. What can you learn from each one that you cannot learn from the other? Share your observations with classmates.

BUILDING CITIZENSHIP

CONNECT MAIN IDEAS

Use this organizer to show that you understand how the chapter's main ideas are connected. Copy the organizer onto a separate sheet of paper. Then complete it by writing the main idea of each lesson.

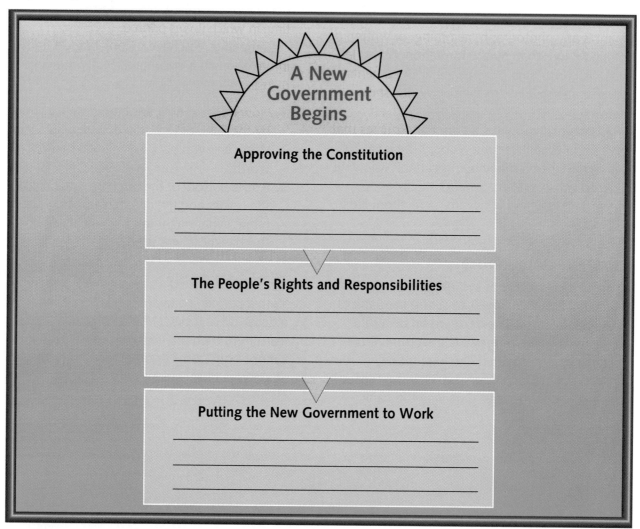

A New Government Begins

Approving the Constitution

_____

_____

_____

The People's Rights and Responsibilities

_____

_____

_____

Putting the New Government to Work

_____

_____

_____

WRITE MORE ABOUT IT

1. **Write a Persuasive Letter** Suppose that you are either an Anti-Federalist or a Federalist. Write a letter to the newspaper describing your views about the ratification of the Constitution. Tell in the letter how you feel about adding a Bill of Rights to the document.

2. **Write an Explanation** Imagine that you are an adviser to President Washington. He asks you to explain the differences that divide Thomas Jefferson and Alexander Hamilton. Write what you will tell the President about the leader's disagreements.

USE VOCABULARY

For each group of underlined words, write the term from the list below that has the same meaning.

amendments	jury
Cabinet	patriotism
campaign	political parties
due process of law	ratify

1. Nine of the 13 states had to <u>agree to</u> the Constitution before it would become law.

2. Ten <u>changes</u> were added to the Constitution.

3. The Constitution guarantees <u>the right to a fair, public trial</u>.

4. A person charged with a crime is judged by a <u>group of citizens who decide a case in court</u>.

5. The writers of the Constitution felt that <u>love of country</u> was very important.

6. President Washington relied on a <u>group of the President's most important advisers</u>.

7. <u>Groups that try to get others to agree with their ideas and to choose leaders who share their points of view</u> soon formed.

8. The <u>race for office</u> between Adams and Jefferson was bitter.

CHECK UNDERSTANDING

1. What collection of letters urged people to support the Constitution?

2. What leaders were members of the first Cabinet? What offices did they hold?

3. What were the first two political parties?

4. Who was the second President of the United States? Who was his Vice President?

5. Who was the first President to live in the White House?

THINK CRITICALLY

1. **Cause and Effect** What promise helped convince states to ratify the Constitution?

2. **Personally Speaking** The First Amendment protects freedom of speech and freedom of the press. Can you think of any examples in which these rights should be limited? Explain your answer.

3. **Explore Viewpoints** Why do you think President Washington turned down the chance to serve a third term in office? Why do you think the Constitution was later changed so that no President could serve more than two terms?

4. **Think More About It** Why was the peaceful election of John Adams as President so important?

APPLY SKILLS

How to Learn from a Document Use the banner on page 300 to answer these questions.

1. Who carried this banner?

2. Why do you think they chose to include the American flag on their banner?

3. What do the words *solid* and *pure* on the banner tell you?

4. What does the banner tell you about the work of a pewterer?

READ MORE ABOUT IT

A More Perfect Union by Betsy Maestro. Lothrop, Lee & Shepard. This book tells the story of how the Constitution was drafted and ratified.

We the People: The Constitution of the United States of America by Peter Spier. Doubleday. The author explores the country's diversity in this book about the United States Constitution.

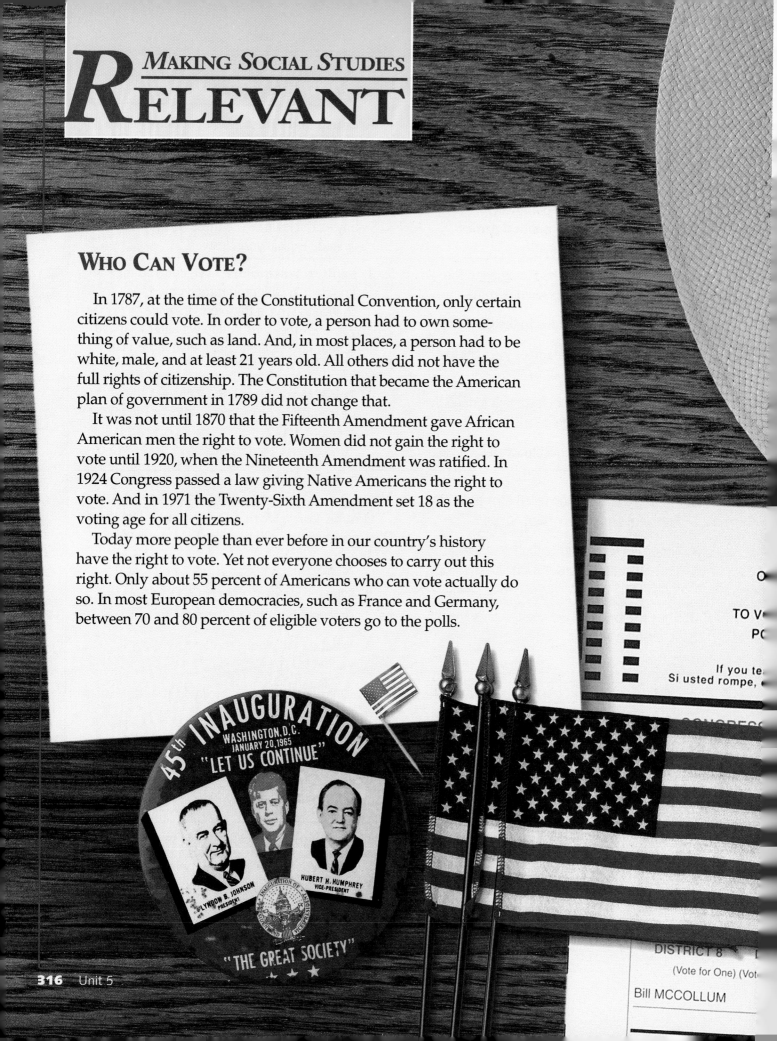

MAKING SOCIAL STUDIES
RELEVANT

WHO CAN VOTE?

In 1787, at the time of the Constitutional Convention, only certain citizens could vote. In order to vote, a person had to own something of value, such as land. And, in most places, a person had to be white, male, and at least 21 years old. All others did not have the full rights of citizenship. The Constitution that became the American plan of government in 1789 did not change that.

It was not until 1870 that the Fifteenth Amendment gave African American men the right to vote. Women did not gain the right to vote until 1920, when the Nineteenth Amendment was ratified. In 1924 Congress passed a law giving Native Americans the right to vote. And in 1971 the Twenty-Sixth Amendment set 18 as the voting age for all citizens.

Today more people than ever before in our country's history have the right to vote. Yet not everyone chooses to carry out this right. Only about 55 percent of Americans who can vote actually do so. In most European democracies, such as France and Germany, between 70 and 80 percent of eligible voters go to the polls.

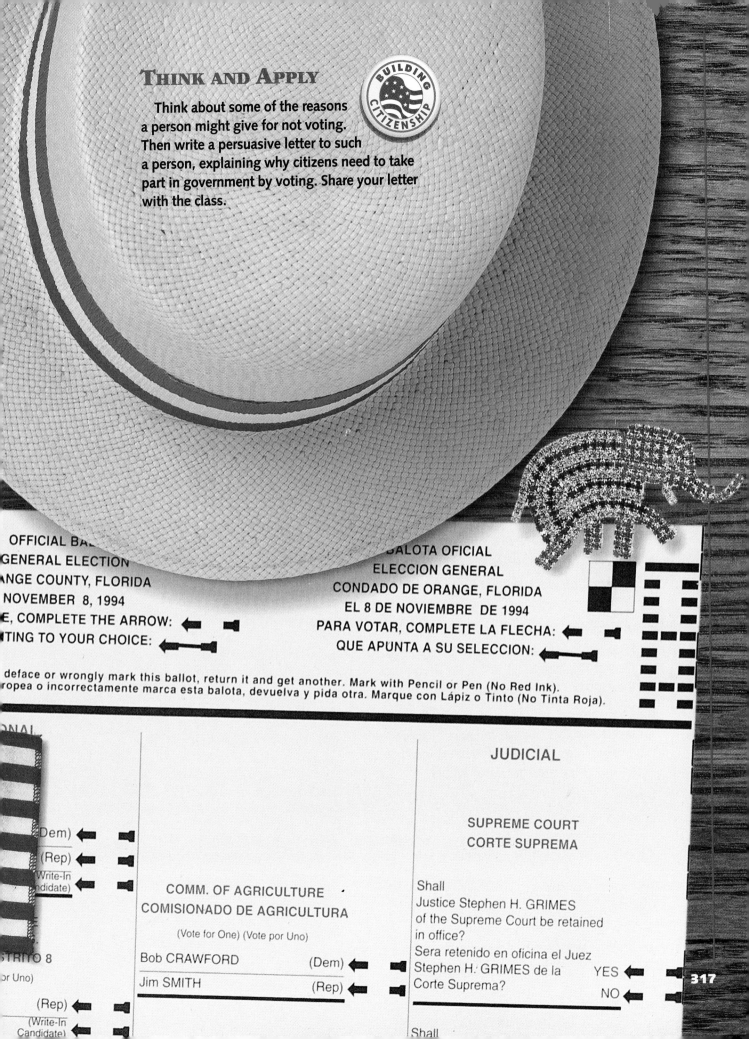

THINK AND APPLY

Think about some of the reasons a person might give for not voting. Then write a persuasive letter to such a person, explaining why citizens need to take part in government by voting. Share your letter with the class.

BUILDING CITIZENSHIP

OFFICIAL BA...
GENERAL ELECTION
...ANGE COUNTY, FLORIDA
NOVEMBER 8, 1994
...E, COMPLETE THE ARROW:
...TING TO YOUR CHOICE:

BALOTA OFICIAL
ELECCION GENERAL
CONDADO DE ORANGE, FLORIDA
EL 8 DE NOVIEMBRE DE 1994
PARA VOTAR, COMPLETE LA FLECHA:
QUE APUNTA A SU SELECCION:

...deface or wrongly mark this ballot, return it and get another. Mark with Pencil or Pen (No Red Ink).
...ropea o incorrectamente marca esta balota, devuelva y pida otra. Marque con Lápiz o Tinto (No Tinta Roja).

...ONAL

(Dem)
(Rep)
(Write-In ...ndidate)

COMM. OF AGRICULTURE
COMISIONADO DE AGRICULTURA

(Vote for One) (Vote por Uno)

Bob CRAWFORD   (Dem)

Jim SMITH   (Rep)

...TRITO 8
...or Uno)

(Rep)
(Write-In Candidate)

JUDICIAL

SUPREME COURT
CORTE SUPREMA

Shall
Justice Stephen H. GRIMES
of the Supreme Court be retained
in office?
Sera retenido en oficina el Juez
Stephen H. GRIMES de la
Corte Suprema?   YES

                        NO

Shall

STORY CLOTH

Study the pictures shown in this story cloth to help you review the events you read about in Unit 5.

Summarize the Main Ideas

1. Under the Articles of Confederation, the national government had little authority. In the late 1780s Daniel Shays led a violent rebellion in Massachusetts. People feared that the government could not handle such unrest.

2. Delegates from the states went to a convention in Philadelphia to discuss their problems. The delegates were respected leaders. Benjamin Franklin, then 81, was carried to the convention in a sedan chair.

3. The delegates met at the Pennsylvania State House. They decided that a new plan of government was needed. They described the new plan in the Constitution.

4. On September 17, 1787, the United States Constitution was signed at the convention. It was later ratified by all 13 states.

5. The Constitution says that one person—the President—is head of the executive branch. George Washington, the first President, took the oath of office on April 30, 1789.

6. Many people wanted the Constitution to protect their rights, such as freedom of speech. Ten amendments were added to the Constitution to do this. They form the Bill of Rights.

Write a Journal Imagine that you are a delegate to the Constitutional Convention. Write several journal entries that tell what you think about the events shown in this story cloth.

COOPERATIVE LEARNING WORKSHOP

Remember

- Share your ideas.
- Cooperate with others to plan your work.
- Take responsibility for your work.
- Show your group's work to the class.
- Discuss what you learned by working together.

Activity 1
Write and Perform a Class Play

Write and perform a play about the conflicts and cooperation that led to the ratification of the Constitution. As a class, decide on the people and events you want to include in your play. Give your play a title. Then form small groups. Each group will write one scene. Decide on roles and other responsibilities, such as making costumes and sets, and have at least one rehearsal. Then perform the play for invited guests from your school or community.

Activity 2
Draw a Map

Work in a group to draw a map that shows the United States at the time the Constitution was ratified. Include the 13 states, the state capitals, and the Northwest Territory. Color each state to show the year it ratified the Constitution. Use blue for 1787, red for 1788, yellow for 1789, and green for 1790. Make a key for your map. Then use the map to help explain to your classmates how the Constitution was ratified.

Activity 3
Draw a Mural

Work together to draw a large mural that shows a scene of several delegates meeting during the Constitutional Convention. Use encyclopedias, biographies, and other library books to find information about these delegates. Then fasten a large sheet of paper to a wall in your classroom. First, use pencils to sketch the scene. Then, use paint, crayons, or markers to color it. Each group member should choose a delegate shown in the mural and write a short biography of him. Present the mural and the biographies to your class.

Activity 4
Make a Book

Work in a group to write and design a book about the Bill of Rights. Your book should summarize each of the amendments in the Bill of Rights and explain how they are important to people today. To illustrate your book, draw pictures or cut out pictures from magazines and newspapers. Give your book a title, and display it where others in your school can read it.

USE VOCABULARY

Write the term that correctly matches each definition.

ambassador   impeach
census   inflation
human rights   majority

1. a representative from one country to another country

2. when more and more money is needed to buy the same goods

3. the greater part

4. a population count

5. to accuse an official of wrongdoing

6. the freedoms that all people should have

CHECK UNDERSTANDING

1. Why did some people think that the Congress under the Articles of Confederation was not very important?

2. What problems caused the delegates to the Constitutional Convention to disagree? How were the problems settled?

3. What was considered by many people to be a major problem with the Constitution after it was written? How was that problem finally solved?

4. How were Thomas Jefferson's and Alexander Hamilton's views about the role of government different?

THINK CRITICALLY

1. Explore Viewpoints James Madison said he was afraid Congress had become "a rope of sand" under the Articles of Confederation. Others, like Patrick Henry, argued that a rope of sand was better than a rod of iron. What were the meanings of these ideas?

2. Think More About It Imagine that you are a member of the House of Representatives and have just written a new bill. Describe the process your bill will take on its way to becoming a law.

APPLY GEOGRAPHY SKILLS

How to Figure Travel Time and Distance The map below shows George Washington's route from his home, Mount Vernon, to New York City, where he took the oath of office as the first President. Washington rode his horse on the journey. Use the map to answer the questions, figuring that Washington could travel about 70 miles a day.

1. How long would it have taken Washington to ride from Mount Vernon, in Virginia, to Wilmington, Delaware?

2. How long would Washington's entire journey from Mount Vernon to New York City have taken?

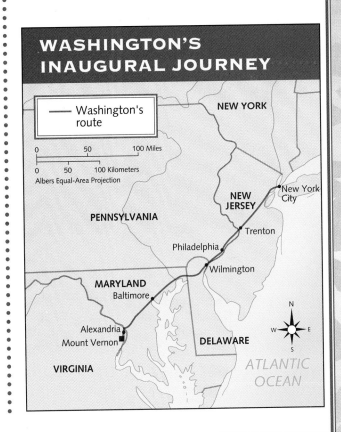

WASHINGTON'S INAUGURAL JOURNEY

UNIT 6

OUR NATION GROWS

1775

1775
Daniel Boone settles
Kentucky

1790

1790
The first American
factory is built

1805

1803
The Louisiana
Purchase

*T*he United States grew rapidly in the 50 years after the War for Independence. As more people came to live in the new country, many began to leave the 13 states to find more land. At first, settlers went only as far as the Appalachian Mountains. Later they went to the Mississippi River. By the 1840s they had crossed the continent and were building new settlements on the Pacific Coast and in the Southwest.

During those same 50 years, the United States became more important among the countries of the world. The young nation fought another war with Britain and showed itself as a leader among the countries in the Americas. The United States built a strong industrial economy, and more and more of its people demanded their rights as citizens.

← This scene of pioneers moving west was painted by Albert Bierstadt in 1867.

1820

1835

1850

1812
The War of 1812 begins

1830
American railroads begin to use steam locomotives

1836
Texas declares independence

1838
The Trail of Tears

1848
Gold is discovered in California

1846
The Mexican-American War begins

CASSIE'S JOURNEY

by Brett Harvey
illustrated by Deborah Kogan Ray

The people who settled the West came from many different places. Most came from the first 13 states, but some came from as far away as Europe and Asia. Almost everyone had read about the American West in newspapers, magazines, books, or letters. Many had heard about it in songs.

The West promised a new life to people like Cassie and her family, whom you will meet in this story. But getting to the West to enjoy its benefits was not easy. People traveling in wagon trains faced long, hard journeys. Sometimes food ran out, or water or firewood could not be found. People moving to the West faced these problems and more.

It's been raining for two days and everything is wet, wet, wet—our clothes, our bedding, even our food. Last night the rain was so heavy and the wind was blowing so hard that we couldn't make a fire. We had cold coffee and soggy bread for supper. This morning Mama cooked our breakfast under an umbrella. Today it's raining in sheets of gray so we have to stay in the wagon with the flaps tied down tight. I hate riding in the wagon—its swaying motion and the screeching noise of the wheels make me feel seasick. Mama is drilling us in our multiplication tables. I wonder if we'll ever be dry again.

Now we are dry as dust and hard as bones and all we think about is water. We are following along the Platte River, and sometimes I want to throw myself in and drink it all up. But the Platte has a bad taste, and Mama warned us not to drink it because people are getting sick and dying from the water. Papa says Platte means "flat," and that the Platte is "too thin to plow, too thick to drink, and too muddy to bathe in." We still have plenty of water in our rain barrel, but Papa says it has to last us a long time. We can only have two cups a day. Even the wheels of our wagon will dry out if we don't take them off every night and soak them in the river. There are mosquitoes, too—so

many they even got in the bread dough and turned it gray. Plato and I wouldn't eat it at first, but then we got so hungry we had to.

On this trip we see many, many graves—some of them are no more than wooden crosses with signs on them stuck in the dirt. Alice and I have been counting and so far, we've seen thirty-one. We always read the signs and think about the people who died. Especially the children. One said "Here lies Eliza Harris. Born July 7 1840, died July 1 1843 from falling out of her family's wagon." Another sign said "Here lize our onlee son, John Hanna, bit by a snake at 7 years of age." There are so many dangers on this journey. It makes me shiver to think of all the narrow escapes we've already had, and we're not yet near the end of our journey.

Today we saw our first Indians! We're camped on the Sweetwater River at South Pass [in Wyoming] now—it's called that because the easiest place to pass through the Rocky Mountains is in the south. When the Indians first came into camp at sunset, we were all frightened because they looked so strange. They wore soft animal skins with beads and feathers sewn onto them. But they let us know they didn't mean to hurt us, only to trade with us. We gave them calico cloth and bread in return for moccasins and buffalo meat. I hate buffalo meat because it's too chewy.

Today when I was riding up with Papa, we came 'round a mountain and suddenly, spread out far below us, was a soft green valley, like a velvety carpet with little hills under it. Papa says that's where we're going. We still have to go down the other side of these terrible mountains, and Papa says we have yet another river to cross. But now I can close my eyes and see a picture of that green valley, and imagine Aunt Rose and her family waiting for us in a little house with windows and doors that sits still on the ground and doesn't go anywhere.

Now I know we're going to get there!

CHAPTER 11

On the MOVE

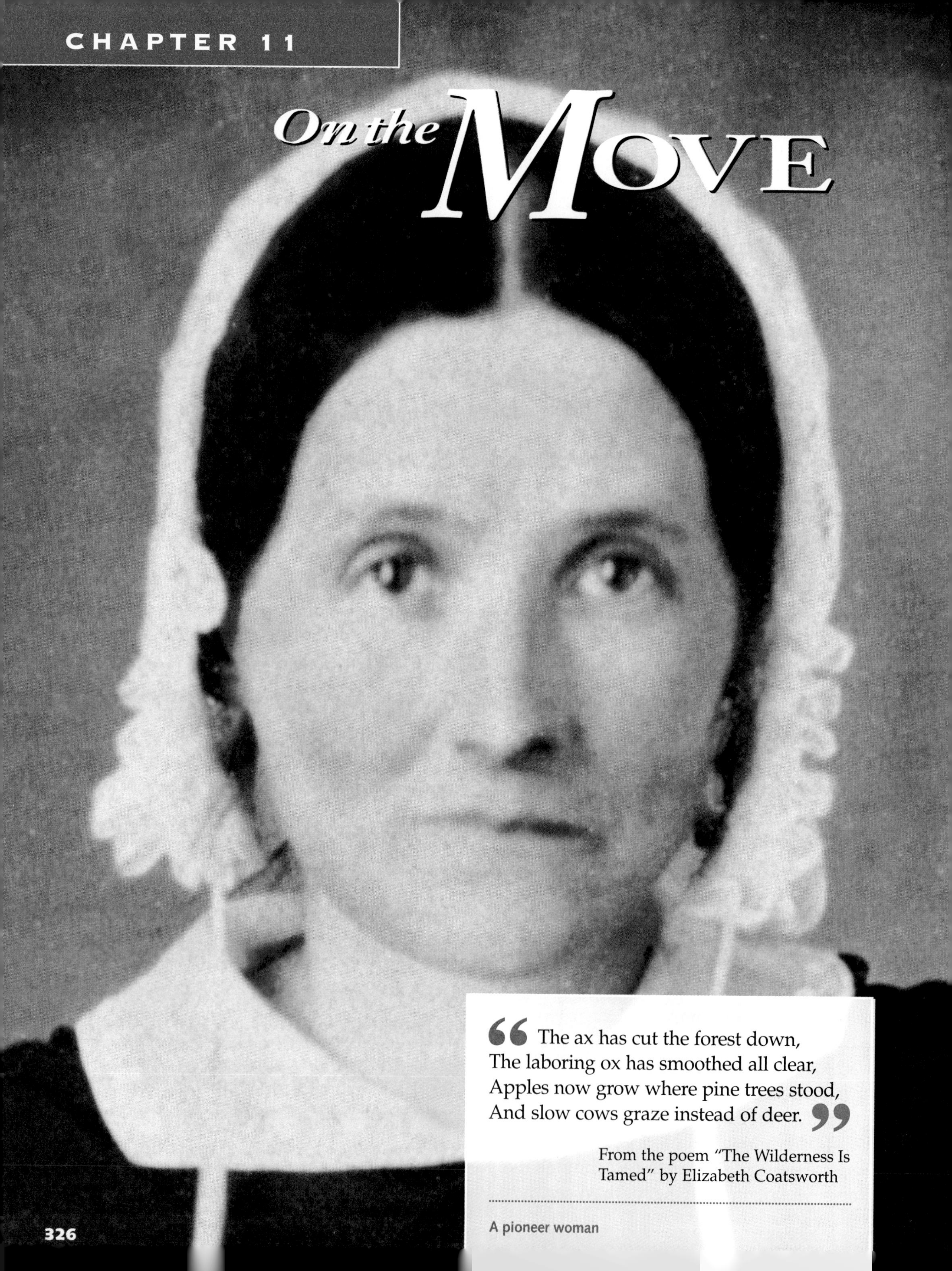

> " The ax has cut the forest down,
> The laboring ox has smoothed all clear,
> Apples now grow where pine trees stood,
> And slow cows graze instead of deer. "
>
> From the poem "The Wilderness Is
> Tamed" by Elizabeth Coatsworth

A pioneer woman

ACROSS the APPALACHIANS

Link to Our World

What problems might a person face in moving to a new place today?

Focus on the Main Idea
As you read, look for some of the problems faced by the early settlers who crossed the Appalachian Mountains.

Preview Vocabulary
pioneer

Pioneer women wore slat bonnets, which contained wooden pieces, or slats, to make the bonnets stiff.

The Treaty of Paris, which ended the Revolutionary War, set the Mississippi River as the new nation's western border. When people talked about the West in those days, they meant the land between the Appalachian Mountains and the Mississippi River. This was the American frontier.

DANIEL BOONE

Pushing the frontier west were the American pioneers. A **pioneer** is a person who first settles a new place. Daniel Boone was one of the earliest and best-known American pioneers to cross the Appalachians.

Boone was born in Pennsylvania. He was 16 years old when his family moved to the Yadkin Valley of North Carolina. Boone came to love living in the woods and hunting.

During the French and Indian War, Boone served in the army. There he met John Finley, a fur trader. Boone later remembered the stories Finley told about a wonderful land far to the west over the Appalachian Mountains. There, Finley said, green forests and meadows stretched for miles.

After the war Boone tried to find this land, now known as Kentucky. But he could not find a way over the mountains. He looked for the Warrior's Path, an Indian trail Finley had described that crossed the mountains, but he could not find it.

Soon after Boone returned home, a peddler, or seller, came to the door of the Boone house in North Carolina. The peddler was John Finley! With Finley's help, Boone again tried

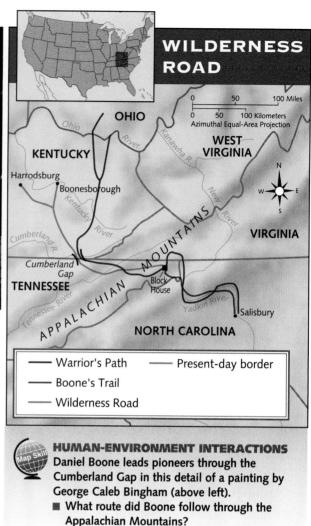

to find Kentucky. This time he found the Warrior's Path and followed it across the Appalachian Mountains through what was called the Cumberland Gap. Boone later told a friend what he had seen on the other side.

> 66 Thousands of Buffalo roamed the Kentucky hills and land that looked as if it never would become poor. 99

Both the Cherokees and Shawnees lived in settlements throughout Kentucky. Several times the Shawnees captured Boone during his visits there. Each time they let him go with a warning not to come back. But Boone did not listen. He returned again and again to Kentucky to explore and to hunt. Stories of Boone's adventures and Kentucky's rich land soon spread, making people want to settle there.

✓ **What did Daniel Boone find when he reached Kentucky?**

SETTLING KENTUCKY

As word spread about Kentucky, several families tried to make their way over the mountains. But the Cherokees and Shawnees did not want to give up their land. They fought the pioneers, who had to turn back.

HUMAN-ENVIRONMENT INTERACTIONS
Daniel Boone leads pioneers through the Cumberland Gap in this detail of a painting by George Caleb Bingham (above left).
■ What route did Boone follow through the Appalachian Mountains?

Finally, in 1774, the Virginia militia fought a battle with the Indians and won. Virginia leaders made Indian leaders sign a treaty giving up their lands in Kentucky.

As soon as the treaty was signed, a land developer hired Daniel Boone to clear a road to Kentucky. In March 1775 Boone led a group through the Cumberland Gap. Cutting down trees and bushes to make way for wagons, the workers cleared a path that came to be known as the Wilderness Road.

Once in Kentucky, Boone built a fort and named it Boonesborough. He then returned to North Carolina to lead a group of settlers back to Kentucky. In August he set out with his family and some neighbors for the new land. It was a slow, hard trip over the mountains. Getting a cow to walk 300 miles

(483 km) was not easy. Sometimes wild animals scared the horses so that they ran off in all directions. The Cherokees and Shawnees made surprise attacks, hoping to scare off the pioneers. But the settlers pushed on to Boonesborough, joining others at Kentucky's first pioneer settlement.

Over the next few years, thousands of pioneers took the Wilderness Road to the valleys beyond the Appalachian Mountains. Many more settlements were built in Kentucky and

in Tennessee to the south. By 1800, American and European settlers had moved as far west as the Mississippi River. Kentucky and Tennessee had become states. Farmers in these states shipped their crops and animals on flatboats down the Mississippi River to the port of New Orleans, then controlled by Spain. From New Orleans the goods went by ship to markets on the east coast of the United States.

How did Daniel Boone help settle the West?

W̱hat?

Log Cabins

Most pioneers in Kentucky lived in log cabins because such homes were quick and easy to build. First, a number of straight trees, all about the same size around, were chosen. Then the trees were cut down and trimmed to the right length. The logs were pulled by horses or dragged by hand to where the cabin was to be built. Notches were cut at the ends so that they would fit together. Next, the logs were lifted into place. The spaces between the logs were "chinked," or filled with mud, clay, or moss. Finally, a roof and fireplace were added. Following this plan, two people could build a cabin in about two weeks.

PIONEER LIFE

Life on the western frontier was hard for pioneer families like the Boones. After they bought their land from a land developer, they had to clear thick forest in order to build their homes and farms. Most pioneers had little food to last until their first crops were ready. One pioneer told how poor his family was when they first settled in Kentucky.

❝My Wife and I had neither spoon, dish, knife, or any thing to do with when we began life.❞

Pioneer homes were surrounded by vast areas of wilderness. Pioneers had to depend on themselves for food and goods because travel was difficult on the frontier.

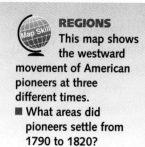

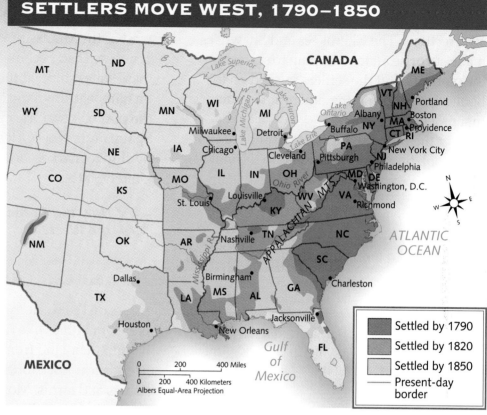

REGIONS
This map shows the westward movement of American pioneers at three different times.
■ What areas did pioneers settle from 1790 to 1820?

SETTLERS MOVE WEST, 1790–1850

Settled by 1790
Settled by 1820
Settled by 1850
Present-day border

Pioneer families had to become self-sufficient very quickly or they did not survive on the frontier. They built their own homes, grew their own food, and made their own clothes and tools. They bartered with the Indian peoples, who traded furs, tobacco, cotton, and corn for cloth and other goods.

As pioneers continued moving onto Indian lands, many banded together in forts to protect themselves. In some settlements they built their log houses close together with a high log fence all around.

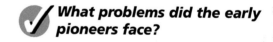
What problems did the early pioneers face?

LESSON 1 REVIEW

Check Understanding

1. **Recall the Facts**   Why did pioneers push west into the frontier?
2. **Focus on the Main Idea**   What problems did the early settlers face in crossing the Appalachian Mountains?

Think Critically

3. **Cause and Effect**   How did Daniel Boone's Wilderness Road help the settlement of Kentucky and the West?

4. **Think More About It**   Do you think the Indians and the pioneers could have lived peacefully together in the land beyond the Appalachians? Explain your answer.

Show What You Know

Simulation Activity   It is 1775, and you own a general store in North Carolina. Create a poster with pictures of some of the supplies you think a pioneer would need to take west. Display your poster in the classroom.

The LOUISIANA PURCHASE

Link to Our World

What might people today learn from the examples set by people in the past?

Focus on the Main Idea
As you read, look for things that American pioneers learned from explorers who traveled west before them.

Preview Vocabulary
purchase
pathfinder

In time some of the pioneers who had settled between the Appalachians and the Mississippi began to look beyond the mighty river. Spain and France claimed these rich lands, although it was mostly Indian peoples who lived there. In one of the largest land sales in history, the United States bought part of this region from France in 1803. The way was now open for settlers to move farther west.

THE INCREDIBLE PURCHASE

Shortly before noon on March 4, 1801, Thomas Jefferson walked through the muddy streets of Washington, D.C., to the Capitol building. The writer of the Declaration of Independence was about to become the third President of the young nation. His simple clothes seemed right for the new capital, which was only half built.

After he took the President's oath of office, Jefferson spoke of his hopes for the country. He called the United States "a rising nation, spread over a wide and fruitful land." He knew, however, that the country faced a big problem. Spain had closed the port of New Orleans to western farmers, hoping to stop the United States frontier from moving farther west.

Spain had taken over all of Louisiana, including New Orleans, after France lost the French and Indian War. The French had given this huge area to Spain to keep the British from getting control of it. In 1802 President Jefferson learned that Spain had secretly given Louisiana back to France. Now, Jefferson thought, was the time to act.

President Thomas Jefferson

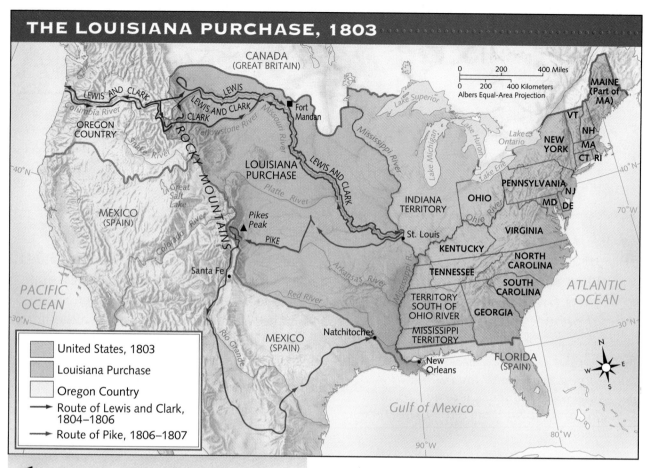

THE LOUISIANA PURCHASE, 1803

United States, 1803

Louisiana Purchase

Oregon Country

→ Route of Lewis and Clark, 1804–1806

→ Route of Pike, 1806–1807

 PLACE The huge territory of the Louisiana Purchase was later divided among 15 states.
■ What natural features of the territory made exploring it easier?

Jefferson sent two representatives to ask the French leader, Napoleon Bonaparte (nuh•POH•lee•uhn BOH•nuh•part), to sell part of Louisiana, including New Orleans, to the United States. Jefferson was willing to offer $10 million. But Bonaparte had other problems on his mind. France was preparing for war with Britain. And people in the French colony of St. Domingue (SAN duh•MAHNG) in the Caribbean had rebelled against France. Needing money to pay for two wars, Bonaparte offered to sell *all* of Louisiana to the United States. To the surprise of the Americans, the price was $15 million—for more than 800,000 square miles!

On April 30, 1803, the United States agreed to **purchase**, or to buy, the huge territory, reaching from the Mississippi River west to

Who?

Toussaint-Louverture 1743–1803

In 1791 Pierre Dominique Toussaint-Louverture (TOO•san LOO•ver•tur) helped lead a slave revolt in St. Domingue. Peace returned only after France agreed to end slavery in its colonies. An experienced soldier, Toussaint held several military positions on the island and soon became its most important leader. In 1802 the French tried to take back St. Domingue, and Toussaint was arrested. He died in prison, but the French could not defeat the rebels. On January 1, 1804, St. Domingue became the independent country of Haiti.

the Rocky Mountains and from New Orleans north to Canada. The territory became known as the Louisiana Purchase. With it the United States doubled in size and became one of the largest countries in the world.

✓ **How did the Louisiana Purchase change the United States?**

THE LEWIS AND CLARK EXPEDITION

Few people in the United States knew much about the lands of the Louisiana Purchase. It was an area that Americans had never explored. President Jefferson asked Meriwether Lewis to lead an expedition to learn all he could about the new land. Lewis was to be a **pathfinder**, someone who finds a way through an unknown region.

Lewis had been an army officer in the wilderness of the Northwest Territory. He chose William Clark, a good friend, to help him lead the expedition. Clark was an excellent cartographer. Lewis and Clark put together a group of about 30 men, most of them frontier soldiers. One member of the group was York, William Clark's African slave. York contributed to the mission through his skill in hunting and fishing.

The leaders called their group the Corps of Discovery. On a spring morning in May 1804, the group left St. Louis and traveled up the Missouri River. The pathfinders spent the summer and fall pushing deep into the Louisiana Purchase. When they reached present-day North Dakota, they built a winter camp near a Mandan village.

While there, Lewis and Clark hired a French fur trader to translate some Indian

This picture shows Sacagawea (below right) using sign language to communicate with the Chinooks during the Lewis and Clark expedition. The explorers brought many items back from their travels, including a Cree Indian robe (below left). They also made drawings of plant and animal life, such as this bitterroot flower (above left).

languages for them. The fur trader was married to a Shoshone (shoh•SHOH•nee) woman who was named Sacagawea (sak•uh•juh•WEE•uh). Sacagawea agreed to serve as a translator when the Corps of Discovery reached the land of the Shoshones.

In the spring of 1805, the Lewis and Clark expedition again moved up the Missouri River by boat. But they would need horses in order to cross the Rocky Mountains. They put their hope in Sacagawea and the Shoshones. "If we do not find them or some other nation who have horses, I fear the successful issue of our voyage will be very doubtful," Lewis wrote in his journal.

At last the expedition reached the lands of the Shoshones. Sacagawea's brother, Cameahwait (kah•MEE•ah•wayt), was now the chief. Lewis and Clark were given horses and continued their journey over the Rockies.

Who?

Sacagawea
1786?–1812?

Sacagawea, whose name in Shoshone means "Bird Woman," helped the members of the Lewis and Clark expedition survive. With her help the pathfinders completed their journey to the Pacific Ocean and back. In 1809 Clark brought Sacagawea, her husband, and her young son to St. Louis, where they settled on a farm. Little more is known about Sacagawea. One story says she died on the Missouri River as early as 1812. Others say she died and was buried on the Wind River Reservation in Wyoming in 1884.

Once over the mountains, they built more boats. They went down the Snake River to the Columbia River and on to the Pacific Ocean. In November 1805, after traveling for more than a year and more than 3,000 miles (4,828 km), Clark wrote in his journal,

> **"**Great joy in camp. We are in view of the . . . great Pacific Ocian which we have been so long anxious to see, and the roreing or noise made by the waves brakeing on the rockey shores (as I may suppose) may be heard distinctly.**"**

The Corps of Discovery returned to St. Louis in September 1806. Lewis and Clark brought back seeds, plants, and even living animals. Among these were many birds. Lewis and Clark were able to report much about the land and its people. The expedition also brought back maps showing the major rivers and mountains. Clark had carefully mapped important passes through the Rockies. In later years these maps helped pioneers on their way to the Pacific Coast.

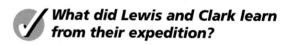 **What did Lewis and Clark learn from their expedition?**

JOURNEY TO THE SOUTHWEST

A few weeks before Lewis and Clark returned to St. Louis, another expedition set out from Missouri to explore the southwestern part of the Louisiana Purchase. A small group of pathfinders led by Captain Zebulon Pike followed the Arkansas River through the middle part of the new lands.

By the winter of 1806, Pike had reached a great prairie in present-day Kansas. He saw with wonder that the prairie was covered with thousands of buffalo.

As the expedition traveled farther west, Pike saw what he described as a "blue mountain" in the distance. Today that blue

Pikes Peak (above right) was named for Zebulon Pike, who tried to climb to the top but failed. Pike (above left) became a general in the War of 1812 and was killed in battle.

mountain is called Pikes Peak for the explorer. It is part of the Rocky Mountain range.

Pike's expedition followed the mountains south. The explorers built a small fort beside what Pike thought was the Red River. It was really the northern part of the Rio Grande. The expedition had wandered out of the Louisiana Purchase and onto Spanish land!

Spanish soldiers soon arrived and took Pike and the other explorers to Santa Fe, the capital of the Spanish colony of New Mexico. They were jailed for being on Spanish land. In Santa Fe the Spanish governor asked Pike if the United States was getting ready to invade the Spanish lands. Pike said no, but in fact the expedition did lead to an "invasion" of another kind.

When he was set free several months later, Pike described the route to the Spanish lands. He reported that the people of Santa Fe needed manufactured goods. Soon American traders were heading for New Mexico as part of a great economic invasion.

 How did Pike's expedition lead to more American settlement of the West?

LESSON 2 REVIEW

Check Understanding

1. **Recall the Facts** What were the boundaries of the Louisiana Purchase?
2. **Focus on the Main Idea** How did the Lewis and Clark expedition and the Pike expedition help later pioneers?

Think Critically

3. **Think More About It** Why do you think President Jefferson thought it was important for Lewis and Clark to explore the Louisiana Purchase?
4. **Explore Viewpoints** Why did the Spanish fear Pike's entry into their lands? What might Pike have thought of their viewpoint?

Show What You Know

 Simulation Activity Imagine that you are planning an expedition into an unknown land. List your expedition's objectives, writing what you hope to learn during your travels. Compare your objectives with the objectives of the Lewis and Clark expedition.

A SECOND *War with* BRITAIN

Link to Our World

What do you think makes people feel proud of their country?

Focus on the Main Idea
As you read, look for ways the War of 1812 helped make Americans proud of their country.

Preview Vocabulary
impressment
nationalism
annex
doctrine

The exciting stories of pathfinders such as Meriwether Lewis, William Clark, and Zebulon Pike made many people want to move to the West. But American Indians still fought with American pioneers, trying to turn them back. In the Northwest Territory, the British helped the Indians by selling them guns. Before long, trouble in the Northwest Territory helped push the United States into a second war with Britain.

TECUMSEH AND THE PROPHET

As more and more pioneers moved to the Northwest Territory, many Indians grew angry that so much of their land was being lost. The leader of these Indians was a Shawnee named Tecumseh (tuh•KUHM•suh). Tecumseh dreamed of forming a strong Indian confederation. He went from one tribe to another with his brother, Tenskwatawa (ten•SKWAHT•uh•wah), whom people called the Prophet, talking about his plan. Tecumseh called on the tribes to stop fighting each other and to unite against the Americans settling their land.

Prophetstown was the Shawnee town where Tecumseh had his headquarters. It was just below the mouth of the Tippecanoe River, near where Lafayette, Indiana, is today.

In 1809, by signing the Treaty of Fort Wayne, a group of Indian tribes agreed to sell 3 million acres of land to the United States government. "Sell a country!" Tecumseh cried upon hearing the news. "Why not sell the air, the clouds, and the great sea?"

Tecumseh said that no one tribe had the right to sell land. He warned the Americans that the Indians would fight if

A computer drawing (above) shows what Prophetstown may have looked like before it was attacked. The Shawnee chief Tecumseh (left) wanted the United States to stop forcing Indians from their homelands.

they were made to give up any more land. The warriors led by Tecumseh were eager for battle, but Tecumseh would not let them fight unless they were attacked first.

In 1811 Tecumseh decided to talk with the Creeks and other Indian tribes living in Kentucky and Tennessee about his plan for a confederation. Before he left, he told Tenskwatawa to keep the peace until he returned.

> " *SELL A COUNTRY!* *Why not sell the air, the clouds, and the great sea?* "
>
> Tecumseh, 1809

 What plan did Tecumseh have for the Indian tribes?

BATTLE OF TIPPECANOE

William Henry Harrison was governor of the Indiana Territory in 1811. Knowing that Tecumseh was away from Prophetstown, Harrison sent 1,000 soldiers to the Shawnee town. They camped nearby the night of November 6, 1811. Tenskwatawa feared that the soldiers would soon attack, so he ordered the Indians to attack first. The morning of November 7, the terrible Battle of Tippecanoe took place.

Neither side clearly won the battle. The Americans destroyed Prophetstown, but Indians went through the territory, attacking settlers.

Many people blamed the Indian attacks on Britain. They said the British were giving guns to the Indians and talking against American settlers. People in the Northwest Territory thought the answer was simple—take over Canada and drive the British out of North America.

What were the results of the Battle of Tippecanoe?

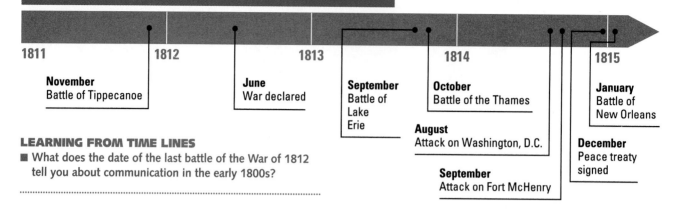

KEY EVENTS OF THE WAR OF 1812

1811

1812

1813

1814

1815

November
Battle of Tippecanoe

June
War declared

September
Battle of
Lake
Erie

October
Battle of the Thames

August
Attack on Washington, D.C.

September
Attack on Fort McHenry

January
Battle of
New Orleans

December
Peace treaty
signed

LEARNING FROM TIME LINES

■ What does the date of the last battle of the War of 1812 tell you about communication in the early 1800s?

WAR FEVER

People in the South, too, were angry with Britain. To stop Americans from trading with the French and other Europeans, the British stopped American ships at sea. They even

MAJOR BATTLES OF THE WAR OF 1812

CANADA
(GREAT BRITAIN)

Lake Superior

Fort
Mackinac
1812

INDIANA
TERR.

ILLINOIS
TERR.

Mississippi River

L. Michigan

York
(Toronto)
1813

Lake Huron

Lake Ontario

Plattsburg 1814

VT
NH

MICHIGAN
TERR.

NY

Lake Erie

The Thames 1813

MA
CT RI

MISSOURI
TERRITORY

Frenchtown
1813

Put-in-Bay
1813

PA

NJ

Fort
Dearborn
(Chicago)
1812

INDIANA
TERR.

OH

Ohio River

Fort McHenry
(Baltimore) 1814

DE
MD

ME
(Part
of MA)

KY

VA

Washington,
D.C. 1814

Mississippi River

TN

NC

MISSISSIPPI
TERRITORY

GA

SC

LA

Horseshoe
Bend 1814

ATLANTIC
OCEAN

N
W E
S

New Orleans
1815

FLORIDA
(SPAIN)

Gulf of Mexico

🔥 American
victory

🔥 British
victory

0   200   400 Miles
0   200   400 Kilometers
Albers Equal-Area Projection

 REGIONS Both sides won major battles during the War of 1812.

■ Did the British capture lands near Washington, D.C., during the war? How can you tell from the map?

took sailors off American ships and put them to work on British ships. Taking workers this way is called **impressment**.

People in the West and the South called on the United States government to declare war on Britain. Those who called the loudest were known as War Hawks. The War Hawks blamed the British in Canada for helping the Indians defend themselves against settlers in the West. They blamed the British government for stopping trade in the South. Eager for more land, the War Hawks even hoped to take Canada from Britain.

Not everyone wanted war, however. Northern merchants had made a lot of money trading with the British. They did not want a war that would end their trade. Yet the desire for war was so great all over the rest of the country that Congress voted to declare war on Britain in 1812. It seemed as if a "war fever" had swept the nation.

✓ *Which regions of the United States wanted war with Britain? Which did not?*

THE WAR OF 1812

As the fighting began, Britain had the strongest navy in the world. Yet the small 16-ship United States Navy won an important battle on Lake Erie that became a turning point in the war. Ships commanded by

American captain Oliver Hazard Perry defeated the British on September 10, 1813. After the battle, Perry sent a message to General William Henry Harrison saying "We have met the enemy and they are ours."

With British control weakened on the Great Lakes, General Harrison was able to lead American soldiers across Lake Erie into Canada. At the Battle of the Thames (TEMZ) on October 5, 1813, the Americans defeated the British. Among the dead was Tecumseh, who was fighting on the British side.

Tecumseh's plan for a strong Indian confederation died with him. From that time on, settlers in the Northwest Territory were free from attacks by Indians.

 What was a turning point in the War of 1812?

RAIDS ON WASHINGTON AND BALTIMORE

In August 1814, British troops marched on Washington, D.C., then a city of only 8,000 people. As the cracking of rifles and booming of cannons filled the air, President James Madison rode to the battle 7 miles (11.3 km) away. First Lady Dolley Madison stayed behind, racing through the White House to save what she could from the British soldiers. She narrowly escaped. When the British arrived, they set fire to the White House, the Capitol, and other buildings.

With Washington in flames, the British sailed up Chesapeake Bay to Baltimore. But Baltimore was protected by Fort McHenry. Although British ships bombed the fort for hours, the Americans refused to surrender.

Unable to defeat the Americans at Baltimore, the British sailed to New Orleans. But American soldiers under General Andrew Jackson were waiting for them.

The British laid siege to New Orleans for ten days. Fierce fighting from Jackson's soldiers finally made the British leave the city. Americans would later learn that the Battle of New Orleans had not been necessary. On December 24, 1814—two weeks before the battle—the British and Americans had signed a peace treaty in Europe. Word that the war was over had not reached New Orleans in time.

What were the results of British attacks on Washington, Baltimore, and New Orleans?

During the war the British burned eight buildings in Washington, D.C.—the White House, the Capitol, the Treasury, and five houses. Dolley Madison (left) was able to save just a few things from the White House before she was forced to flee British troops.

During a battle off the coast of Nova Scotia, British cannonballs could not break through the hard oak sides of the American warship *Constitution*. Legend says that a crew member yelled, "Her sides are made of iron!" After that the victorious *Constitution* was nicknamed Old Ironsides.

THE ERA OF GOOD FEELINGS

Neither side was clearly the winner in the War of 1812. However, Americans were proud that the United States had proved itself equal to a great European nation. A wave of **nationalism**, or pride in the country, swept the land. People began to feel for the first time that they were Americans, not Virginians, New Yorkers, or Ohioans. For this reason the years from 1817 to 1825 have been called the Era of Good Feelings.

National pride could be seen in the government's strong dealings with other countries. President James Monroe set a new border between the United States and British Canada. He also convinced Spain to give up claims in West Florida, which had been **annexed**, or added on, earlier, and to give East Florida to the United States.

President Monroe knew that if the United States wanted to keep growing, it had to stop the growth of the Spanish, French, and British colonies in the Americas. So on December 2, 1823, the President announced a **doctrine**, or government plan of action, that came to be called the Monroe Doctrine. The Monroe Doctrine declared that the United States was willing to go to war to stop European countries from expanding their American empires.

✓ How did the War of 1812 affect the United States and its people?

LESSON 3 REVIEW

Check Understanding

1. **Recall the Facts** What did Tecumseh hope to accomplish?
2. **Focus on the Main Idea** How did the War of 1812 help make Americans proud of their country?

Think Critically

3. **Explore Viewpoints** Why did people from the North, the South, and the West feel differently about going to war with Britain?
4. **Past to Present** For their actions during the War of 1812, many Americans became national heroes. Who are some heroes of today? What actions helped them become known as heroes?

Show What You Know

Research Activity Use encyclopedias to find out more about the navy's battles during the War of 1812. Draw a picture and write a report about one battle. Present your findings to the class.

How To

Predict a Likely Outcome

Why Is This Skill Important?

People often make **predictions**. This means that they look at the way things are and decide what they think will most likely happen next. When people make predictions, they are not guessing about what will happen in the future. They are using information and past experiences to predict a probable, or likely, outcome.

Remember What You Have Read

Think about what you have read about the War of 1812. In the years before the war, the British sold guns to the Indian tribes in the Northwest Territory to help them defend their lands against American settlers. Many Americans blamed the British for the Indian attacks that followed. This was one reason for the war with Britain. During the war, the British lost the Battle of the Thames. The Indian leader Tecumseh died during the battle, and Indian attacks on settlers in the Northwest Territory soon ended.

Understand the Process

You can use this information to predict what probably happened next in the westward movement of settlers after the War of 1812. Follow these steps:

- Think about what you already know about the loss of Indian lands as settlers moved west during colonial times and during the early years of the United States. Look for patterns in the events that took place.
- Review the new information you learned about Tecumseh and the War of 1812.
- Make a prediction about the westward movement of settlers following the war.
- As you read or gather more information, ask yourself whether you still think your prediction is correct.
- If necessary, go through the steps again to form a new prediction.

After going through these steps, you should have been able to predict that pioneers would continue to move west, building settlements on Indian lands.

Think and Apply

The nationalism that swept across the country after the War of 1812 led to a time called the Era of Good Feelings. During this time President Monroe announced what came to be known as the Monroe Doctrine. Follow the steps listed above to predict how the Monroe Doctrine would affect the growth of the United States. As you read the next chapter, see whether the new information you learn supports your prediction.

These pioneers moved west from Connecticut to Ohio. The trip was more than 600 miles (966 km) and took about 90 days.

By the Dawn's Early Light:

The Story of
The Star-Spangled Banner

by Steven Kroll
illustrated by Dan Andreasen

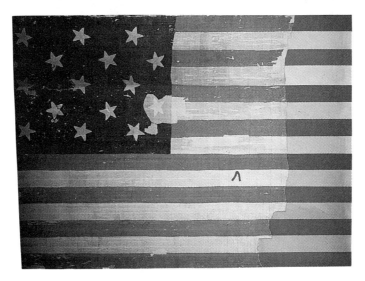

This is the flag that Francis Scott Key saw flying "by the dawn's early light" at Fort McHenry.

While the British prepared to attack Baltimore during the War of 1812, an American doctor named William Beanes was held prisoner on the warship H.M.S. Tonnant. With the permission of President Madison, Beanes's friend, Francis Scott Key, along with Colonel John S. Skinner, went to the ship to ask that he be set free. Key explained to the British commanders that Beanes had cared for many wounded British soldiers during the Battle of Bladensburg. Major General Sir Robert Ross agreed to free Beanes, but all three men would not be released until after the British had attacked Fort McHenry.

Read now about the frightening days early in September 1814 when the British fleet approached Baltimore. Key and Skinner have just been taken to see Dr. Beanes and have told him what was happening. As you read, think about how Francis Scott Key chose to describe his experiences.

"And we must sit and watch while our country is attacked?" Beanes exclaimed.

"I'm afraid so," Colonel Skinner replied.

The three Americans were put up on the frigate *Surprise*, and for three days the British fleet crept up Chesapeake Bay.

Meanwhile, Baltimore was getting ready. Though inexperienced, the militia was on call. The city was ringed by trenches and ramparts[1] built by citizens. At star-shaped Fort McHenry, out on Whetstone Point overlooking the Patapsco River, a thousand troops were under the command of Major George Armistead. They had thrown up barriers outside the moat, placed sandbags around the powder magazine,[2] and sunk many small ships and barges in the north channel of the river to slow enemy progress. They had also stationed a half-dozen small gunboats between the sunken hulls and the city.

There was a bold, new flag flying over the fort. Forty-two by thirty feet, fifteen stars and fifteen stripes, it was the work of Mary Pickersgill and her daughter, Caroline.

On Saturday, September 10th, the British fleet anchored off North Point at the mouth of the Patapsco River. Francis, Colonel Skinner, and Dr. Beanes were hustled from

[1]**rampart:** protective barrier

[2]**powder magazine:** storage area for gunpowder

the *Surprise* back to their own small boat. Admiral Cochrane had decided to take personal command of the bombardment. He wanted the smaller, faster frigate as his flagship.

Sunday morning, Baltimore's church bells called the militia to arms. Monday, boats filled with British soldiers in scarlet uniforms began leaving for shore. Francis watched grimly. Things did not look good for the Americans.

With the troops underway on land, the fleet began moving upriver. As the ships came within view of Fort McHenry, the Stars and Stripes were waving overhead.

Later that afternoon, word came from shore. The Americans had retreated to positions outside the city. General Ross had been killed.

A silence seemed to fall over the fleet, but preparations continued. Francis, Dr. Beanes, and Colonel Skinner spent a restless night as sixteen smaller British ships moved into the shallower water closer to the fort.

At dawn the bombardment began. The noise was so great and the smell of burning powder so strong that the three hostages were forced to take refuge in their cabin. When the response from the fort seemed to die away for a moment, it became clear that the Americans' thirty-six-pound shells were not reaching the ships. But then the heavy shelling and rocketing began again and went on hour after hour.

At dusk Francis crawled out onto the deck. "Can you see the flag?" Dr. Beanes called after him.

Francis squinted through the smoke and the din and the glow of the setting sun. "The flag is flying," he replied.

Soon after, it began to rain. Thunder and lightning joined the booming of the guns. Very late that night, Francis struggled out on deck again. Though he could not know it, at that moment the British were trying to land a thousand men at Ferry Branch. An American sentry discovered them and Fort McHenry began to fire. As the barges fled, every available American gun pursued them.

The rainy night sky was suddenly lit up, and in that moment Francis could see the flag again. It was soaked now and drooping from its staff, but it was there, still there.

By dawn the rain had stopped and the fight was over. Peering through the clouds, Francis, Dr. Beanes, and Colonel Skinner strained to see what flag was flying over the fort. Had the British triumphed in the night? But no, there it was, unfurling in the breeze, the Stars and Stripes!

All his life, Francis had written poetry. He reached into his pocket and found an old letter. With the tune to the song, "To Anacreon[3] in Heaven" in mind, he scribbled *O say can you see* and then *by the dawn's early light.*

He wrote a few more lines, crossed out a few, but there wasn't much time. Already redcoats were leaving for the ships. The fleet was abandoning the assault!

The sails of the little cartel boat[4] were returned to the members of its American crew. By afternoon, Francis, Dr. Beanes, and Colonel Skinner were back in Baltimore.

Cheering crowds were everywhere. The three men went straight to the Indian Queen Hotel on Baltimore Street, rested, and had supper, but later that night, Francis finished the four stanzas[5] of his poem.

The next day he went to visit his brother-in-law, Judge Joseph Nicholson, who had been at Fort McHenry. Judge Nicholson loved the new poem. "Let's get it printed," he insisted.

The judge rushed over to the *Baltimore American*, but the printers weren't back from defending the fort. A young apprentice, Samuel Sands, agreed to set the verses in type and run off the handbills. Because Francis hadn't thought of a title, Judge

---

[3]**Anacreon:** a Greek poet
[4]**cartel boat:** cargo boat
[5]**stanza:** section of a poem

Nicholson came up with "The Defense of Fort McHenry," but it wasn't long before everyone was singing what had come to be known as "The Star-Spangled Banner."

The Star-Spangled Banner

Oh, say can you see by the dawn's early light

What so proudly we hail'd at the twilight's last gleaming,

Whose broad stripes and bright stars through the perilous fight

O'er the ramparts we watch'd were so gallantly streaming?

And the rockets' red glare, the bombs bursting in air,

Gave proof through the night that our flag was still there.

Oh, say does that star-spangled banner yet wave

O'er the land of the free and the home of the brave?

Literature Review

1. How did Francis Scott Key describe his experiences during the Battle of Baltimore?
2. How did ordinary citizens help Baltimore survive the British bombing?
3. Imagine that you were part of the Baltimore militia during the British bombing. Write a letter to a friend, telling how you feel about Francis Scott Key's poem.

CONNECT MAIN IDEAS

Use this organizer to show that you understand how the chapter's main ideas are connected. First copy the organizer onto a separate sheet of paper. Then complete it by writing one or two sentences to tell about each person or pair of people or to summarize each event or idea.

On the Move

Across the Appalachians	The Louisiana Purchase	A Second War with Britain
Daniel Boone _____ _____	The Purchase _____ _____	Tecumseh and Tenskwatawa _____ _____
Settling Kentucky _____ _____ _____	Lewis and Clark _____ _____ _____	War Fever _____ _____
Pioneer Life _____ _____ _____	_____ Zebulon Pike _____ _____	The Era of Good Feelings _____ _____

WRITE MORE ABOUT IT

1. **Write a Diary Entry**   Imagine that you are a pioneer who has traveled across the Appalachians to settle in Kentucky. Write a diary entry that tells what your life is like. Describe your house and your work.

2. **Express an Opinion**   Suppose that President Jefferson has asked for your opinion about whether or not the United States should purchase the Louisiana Territory. Write what you would tell him.

3. **Write a Newspaper Article**   Imagine that you are a writer for a Baltimore newspaper. Write a headline and a short article about Francis Scott Key and the exciting events at Fort McHenry.

4. **Write a Biography**   You have read about many people in this chapter. Use encyclopedias and other library books to learn more about one of them. Then write a short biography of that person.

USE VOCABULARY

Use the terms from the list to complete the paragraphs that follow. Use each term once.

annex   pathfinders
impressment   pioneers
nationalism   purchase

When the American Revolution ended, __(1)__ pushed the frontier west. Then, in 1803, the United States decided to __(2)__ land west of the Mississippi River. __(3)__ soon found ways through this unknown region.

The United States found itself at war with Britain. Americans were upset over the __(4)__ of sailors. Although neither side was clearly the winner, a wave of __(5)__ swept the land. The United States decided to __(6)__ Spanish West Florida.

CHECK UNDERSTANDING

1. What was the Wilderness Road?

2. Why did pioneers often band together in forts?

3. What did Spain hope to do by closing the port of New Orleans to western farmers?

4. How did the size of the United States change as a result of the Louisiana Purchase?

5. What did Lewis and Clark accomplish? How did Sacagawea help them?

6. What area did Zebulon Pike explore?

7. What plan did Tecumseh hope to carry out when he visited the tribes in Kentucky and Tennessee?

8. Why did many Americans blame the British for Indian attacks on settlers?

9. Why were many northern merchants against the idea of declaring war on Britain?

10. What was the Era of Good Feelings?

THINK CRITICALLY

1. **Past to Present**   This chapter tells the stories of many pioneers. Who are the pioneers of today? What frontiers are they exploring?

2. **Think More About It**   What do you think Tecumseh meant when he said that no one had the right to sell land?

3. **Personally Speaking**   Why do you think so many pioneers chose to risk their lives to settle in Kentucky and Tennessee? Would you have made the same choice? Explain.

4. **Cause and Effect**   How did the War of 1812 affect the nation's capital?

5. **Explore Viewpoints**   How do you think Americans viewed the Monroe Doctrine? How do you think Europeans viewed the Monroe Doctrine?

APPLY SKILLS

How to Predict a Likely Outcome   Think about the events that usually take place in school on each day of the week.

- Predict the events that are likely to take place in school each day next week.
- Make a list of your predictions.
- Share your list with classmates.
- As events take place, compare them to your list. Ask yourself whether or not your predictions are correct.
- If necessary, form new predictions.

READ MORE ABOUT IT

1812: The War Nobody Won by Albert Martin. Atheneum. This book tells about memorable events of the War of 1812.

Pioneer Children of Appalachia by Joan Anderson. Clarion. The book uses photographs to help show how an Appalachian family might have lived during the early 1800s.

The WAY WEST

> ❝ I am determined to sustain myself as long as possible & die like a soldier who never forgets what is due to his own honor & that of his country—VICTORY OR DEATH. ❞
>
> The words of William Travis, describing the determination of those fighting for Texas independence
>
> Juan Seguín, fighter for Texas independence

The INDUSTRIAL REVOLUTION

LESSON 1

Link to Our World

How might a new technology change a person's life today?

Focus on the Main Idea
As you read, look for ways new technology changed life in the United States in the 1800s.

Preview Vocabulary
Industrial Revolution
textile mill
mass production
interchangeable part
transport
canal
locomotive

Before the War of 1812, the economy of the United States had been growing. This growth increased after the war. New inventions changed the way goods were made. People began using machines instead of hand tools. New transportation routes were built. This **Industrial Revolution** brought great changes in the way people lived, worked, and traveled.

INDUSTRY COMES TO THE UNITED STATES

In a factory in Britain, a young worker named Samuel Slater carefully studied the new spinning machine until he could remember exactly how each iron gear and wooden spool worked. This invention made large textile mills possible. **Textile mills** are factories where fibers such as cotton and wool are woven into cloth, or textiles. In 1789 Britain was the only country in the world that had this technology.

The British kept new inventions, such as those in the British textile mills, closely guarded secrets. Anyone caught leaving Britain with machine designs was put in jail. Samuel Slater was about to break British law.

Slater took his knowledge to the United States. Remembering each part he had studied, he made a spinning machine for a business person named Moses Brown. In 1790 Brown and Slater built a textile mill at Pawtucket, Rhode Island. It was America's first factory. Samuel Slater had brought the Industrial Revolution to the United States.

 What technology did Samuel Slater bring to the United States?

Samuel Slater (above right) was born in Britain and came to the United States in 1789. His knowledge of textile machines was used for building America's first cotton mill (above). The machines in the mill, such as this wooden spinning machine (right), ran on waterpower and made yarn quickly at low cost.

MASS PRODUCTION STARTS

Another idea changed American manufacturing forever. An inventor named Eli Whitney thought of a new way to produce large amounts of goods at one time. His idea came to be called **mass production**.

Before this time, one craftworker made each product from start to finish. Muskets, for example, were made by hand, one at a time. Because each craftworker had his or her own way of making parts and putting them together, no two muskets were exactly the same. To repair a broken musket, a craftworker had to make a new part to fit it.

Whitney thought of a way workers could make more muskets. He designed machines to make many copies of each part, all the same. Such **interchangeable parts** could be used to make or repair any musket. Whitney also made machines to put the parts together very quickly.

Mass production made it possible to use untrained workers in factories. No longer were craftworkers needed to make most products. Anyone could put together machine-made parts. Using interchangeable parts, factory workers could manufacture more goods much more quickly than craftworkers could.

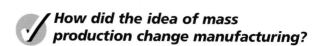 **How did the idea of mass production change manufacturing?**

THE LOWELL SYSTEM

From 1810 to 1812 Francis Cabot Lowell of Massachusetts visited textile mills and factories in Britain. As Samuel Slater had done earlier, Lowell studied the way the machines worked. He took care to remember the way the separate spinning, dyeing, and weaving mills were planned.

When Lowell returned to the United States, he started his own textile mill at Waltham, Massachusetts. But he put spinning, dyeing, and weaving together under one roof. This was a change from having a different factory for each step. In Lowell's textile mill raw cotton went into the factory and finished cloth came out. Nothing like that had ever been done before. Other manufacturers began following Lowell's lead as they built factories.

Young women and children came to work in Lowell's textile mills. When a girl named Harriet Hanson was ten years old, she began work as a "doffer." From five o'clock in the morning until seven in the evening, Harriet changed spools of thread on the spinning machines. She "wanted to earn money like the other little girls."

Though the hours were long, Harriet did not think the work was hard. She had time to read, sew, and sometimes even play. She enjoyed living in a boardinghouse with other mill workers.

Lowell took care to set up good living conditions for his workers. Other manufacturers did not show the same care. As the demand for many manufactured goods grew, more factories—and more factory workers—were needed. Many workers, both young and old, soon were working long hours in dangerous conditions.

By the 1840s thousands of immigrants were coming to the United States each year to take jobs in the new factories. The populations of manufacturing cities like New York, Boston, Philadelphia, and Baltimore grew quickly. Almost half of the immigrants were from Ireland. Others came from Germany, Poland, and other parts of northern and central Europe.

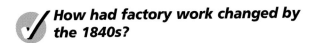

How had factory work changed by the 1840s?

Bells rang to tell Lowell's workers (left) when it was mealtime and when it was time to start work. Factory workdays were long, and it was common for children to do hard work. In this picture (right) a young girl packs cotton into containers.

THE ERIE CANAL

The new factories turned out many products. But factory owners had a problem. How could they **transport**, or carry, their products from the factories to their customers, many of whom lived in the West? The people in the West, too, needed to transport their farm products to the cities in the East.

To help solve this problem, the New York legislature voted in 1817 to build a **canal**, or human-made waterway. The Erie Canal would link Buffalo on Lake Erie with Troy on the Hudson River. It would be 363 miles (584 km) long—the longest canal in the world.

Most of the Erie Canal was dug by hand by some 3,000 Irish immigrants. The Irish came to the United States from Europe to get jobs working on the Big Ditch, as they called the Erie Canal. The workers were paid 80 cents a day and were given meals and housing. These wages were three times what the immigrants could earn in Ireland. The high wages acted like a magnet to attract thousands of Europeans to the United States.

When the Erie Canal was finished in 1825, it opened a transportation route to the heart of the young nation. The opening of this route helped make New York City the leading trade city in the United States.

✓ **Why was the Erie Canal built?**

THE NATIONAL ROAD

During the early years of the nation, Americans lacked a good system of roads. Most roads were just dirt paths that were full of tree stumps and holes. The roads turned into rivers of mud when it rained.

What?

Locks

Because Lake Erie is 572 feet (174 m) higher than the Hudson River, boats on the Erie Canal must go "uphill" or "downhill." They do this by using locks. A lock is a short part of a canal, with a gate at each end. A boat enters the lock, both gates are shut, and the water level is raised or lowered. When it matches the level of the next part of the canal, the gate at that end opens and the boat goes on its way. A lock is like an elevator for canal boats!

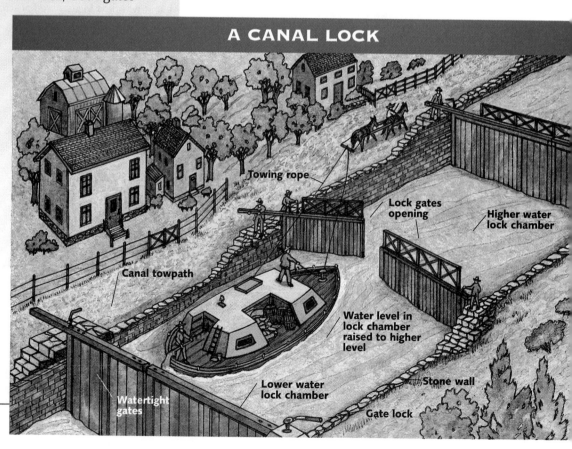

A CANAL LOCK

Towing rope

Canal towpath

Lock gates opening

Higher water lock chamber

Water level in lock chamber raised to higher level

Lower water lock chamber

Stone wall

Watertight gates

Gate lock

Just before Ohio became a state in 1803, Congress voted to build a road from the Atlantic Coast to Ohio. The road would be used to transport goods and help settlers travel to the new state. This route became known as the National Road.

Work on the National Road began on November 20, 1811. The road was built using the best technology of the day. It was wide and level, and it was paved with stones and tar. It stretched from Maryland to Pennsylvania and then on to what would become West Virginia. It passed through Ohio and Indiana and finally ended in Vandalia, Illinois. As the Erie Canal became the water route, the National Road became the land route linking East and West.

 Why was the National Road built?

STEAMBOATS AND RAILROADS

At about the same time that the National Road and the Erie Canal were being built, Americans were inventing new forms of travel. Steamboats took the place of flat-bottom barges as the main form of river transportation. Railroads changed the way people and goods moved on land.

In 1807 Robert Fulton amazed watchers by chugging up the Hudson River in his steamboat, the *Clermont*. In 1811 the *New Orleans* made the first steamboat voyage from Pittsburgh to New Orleans. By the 1820s great paddle-wheel steamboats could be seen on most large rivers and lakes in the United States. Trips that once took months by flatboat now took only a few days.

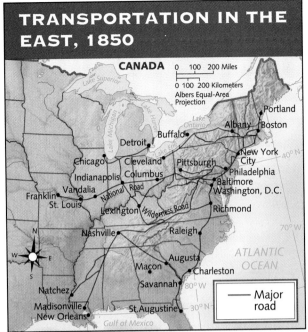

TRANSPORTATION IN THE EAST, 1850

MOVEMENT These maps show major transportation links that had been built in the United States by 1850.

■ Why do you think few links had been built west of the Mississippi River?

The *Tom Thumb* was made famous in a race with a horse. The locomotive was small, but powerful for its day. The first locomotives went about 10 miles (16.1 km) per hour.

Railroads had a slower start. At first many people had fears about traveling by train. Some did not think the trains would stay on the tracks. Some thought that fast speeds would cause human blood to boil.

One of the first **locomotives**, or railroad engines, made in the United States was the *Tom Thumb*. A manufacturer named Peter Cooper built it in 1830 for the Baltimore and Ohio Railroad. The company had been using railroad cars pulled by horses for its 13-mile (21-km) service between Baltimore and Ellicott's Mills. To prove a steam engine could pull a heavy load faster than a horse, Cooper raced his *Tom Thumb* against a railroad car pulled by a horse. The locomotive broke down before the finish line and lost the race. Even so, it was clear that the steam locomotive had better pulling power than a horse.

The number of locomotives and railroads grew quickly after 1830. By 1850 about 9,000 miles (14,484 km) of track crossed the nation, mostly near the Atlantic coast.

Railroads made it easier to move raw materials and manufactured goods to all regions of the country. As the railroads grew, so did manufacturing in the United States.

 **What inventions improved transportation in the early 1800s?**

LESSON 1 REVIEW

Check Understanding

1. **Recall the Facts**   What brought about the Industrial Revolution in the United States?

2. **Focus on the Main Idea**   How did new technology change the way people lived in the United States in the 1800s?

Think Critically

3. **Cause and Effect**   How did more factories lead to better transportation? How did better transportation lead to more factories?

4. **Past to Present**   What kinds of transportation connect the regions of the United States today?

Show What You Know

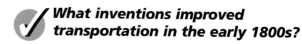 **Writing Activity**   Imagine that you work at a Lowell textile mill or another early factory. Write a letter to a friend, telling what you like and do not like about factory work. Share your letter with a classmate.

The AGE of JACKSON

LESSON 2

Link to Our World

What concerns might cause people in different parts of the country to react differently today?

Focus on the Main Idea
As you read, look for concerns Americans in different parts of the country felt differently about in the early 1800s.

Preview Vocabulary
sectionalism
states' rights
secede
ruling

On July 4, 1826, the United States was 50 years old. Americans everywhere celebrated with parades, speeches, and parties. Many hoped that the two old patriots John Adams and Thomas Jefferson would live to see the celebration. Both men did live to greet that Fourth of July, but they both died before sunset. In Philadelphia the Liberty Bell tolled at their passing. The deep sound of the bell marked the end of an age that had brought the American people independence and a new nation. But as the old age ended, a new age dawned with new leaders and new challenges for the United States.

"OLD HICKORY"

On March 4, 1829, Andrew Jackson took the oath of office as the seventh President of the United States. The Union he was about to lead had grown from the original 13 states to 24 states. Vermont, Maine, Kentucky, and Tennessee had become states. The states of Ohio, Illinois, and Indiana had been carved from the Northwest Territory. The states of Louisiana and Missouri had been formed from the Louisiana Purchase. Alabama became a state after the Creeks were forced off their land. Mississippi and the Territory of Florida had been created from land once claimed by Spain.

The Presidents before Jackson had all been property owners from either Massachusetts or Virginia. They also had all been well educated. Jackson had a different background. He had been born on the frontier of South Carolina to a poor family living in a log

President Andrew Jackson

VOTER PARTICIPATION, 1824–1840

PERCENT OF ELIGIBLE VOTERS WHO VOTED vs **ELECTION YEAR**

(Bar graph showing voter participation for election years 1824, 1828, 1832, 1836, and 1840, with percentages ranging from about 27% in 1824 rising to about 80% in 1840.)

LEARNING FROM GRAPHS This graph shows the percent of voters who actually voted in elections for President.
■ Why did the number of people who voted rise between 1824 and 1828?

cabin. Tough and stubborn, he taught himself law and became a judge. As a soldier he earned the nickname Old Hickory, hickory being a very hard wood. "He's tough," said his soldiers. "Tough as hickory."

The election that made Jackson President was the first in which all white American men could vote. Before this time, voting had been only for men who owned property. The change came about partly because of the new western states. There the vote was given to all white men, not just property owners. By the election of 1828, the eastern states were following this example. Many of the new voters chose Jackson because they felt he was a "common man," like them.

> 66 *OUR FEDERAL UNION:*
> *It must be preserved.* 99
>
> Andrew Jackson, 1830

 What change in voting helped Andrew Jackson become President?

REGIONAL DISAGREEMENTS

As President, Jackson went right on being both tough and stubborn. He vetoed a bank bill that would have helped the rich factory owners in the North. Government should not help the rich get richer, he said. Government should instead "shower its favors alike on the high and the low, the rich and the poor."

Many of Jackson's decisions were based on his background of living on the western frontier. People from the North and the South were just as interested in helping their own section, or region, rather than the country as a whole. This regional loyalty is called **sectionalism**.

Sectionalism became a problem in 1828 when Congress set a high tariff on imports. The tariff was supposed to help northern factory owners sell their manufactured goods because it made European goods cost more. However, the tariff also raised the prices southerners had to pay for goods they could get only from Europe.

Jackson's Vice President, John C. Calhoun of South Carolina, was loyal to the South. He argued against the tariff. Calhoun believed in **states' rights**, or the idea that the states have final authority over the national government. No one knew how President Jackson felt about states' rights until he spoke at a dinner in honor of the late Thomas Jefferson. Jackson looked straight at Calhoun and said, "Our federal Union: It must be preserved [kept]."

Calhoun answered, "The Union, next to our liberty, most dear." This was the beginning of a deep split between Jackson and Calhoun. Calhoun soon resigned as Jackson's Vice President.

The debate over states' rights went on. In 1832 Congress passed another tariff. South

Carolina said it would **secede**, or leave the Union, because of it. President Jackson warned South Carolina's leaders that leaving the Union was treason. South Carolina's leaders backed down, but sectionalism only grew stronger in the years to come.

 What leader spoke out for states' rights? Who spoke against it?

INDIAN REMOVAL

President Jackson's toughness also led to harsh and unfair treatment of the Indians who still lived east of the Mississippi. Pathfinders had reported that the plains west of the Mississippi were of no use to the settlers. At that time people believed that soil was good only where trees grew. They began to think that the Indians should move west to those treeless lands. Jackson put the idea into action.

In 1830 Congress passed the Indian Removal Act. This act said that all Indians east of the Mississippi must leave their land and move west. Once this bill became a law, President Jackson ordered the Creeks, Seminoles, Chickasaws, Cherokees, and other tribes to live in the Indian Territory, what is today the state of Oklahoma.

Many tribes fought against removal. Among them were the Seminoles of Florida, who were helped by runaway slaves. But, like other tribes, most of the Seminoles were killed or forced to leave their homes.

The 15,000 Cherokees made up one of the richest tribes in the United States. They had many towns and villages throughout the Southeast. Many Cherokees owned small farms, and a few had large plantations where Africans were enslaved. The Cherokees had their own government, a republic with a constitution and elected leaders who met at their capital of New Echota (ih•KOHT•uh) in Georgia.

 ## Where?

New Echota, Georgia

By the 1830s New Echota, the capital of the Cherokee republic, was a city like any other city in the United States. It had churches, businesses, and schools. It also had its own newspaper, the *Cherokee Phoenix*, which was printed in both English and Cherokee. Although spoken for hundreds of years, the Cherokee language was not written until 1821. In that year a Cherokee leader named Sequoyah (sih•KWOY•uh) created an alphabet and writing system for it.

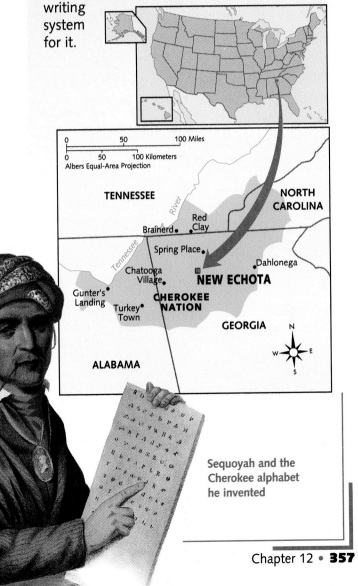

Sequoyah and the Cherokee alphabet he invented

In 1791 the United States government had agreed to the independence of the Cherokee nation by signing a treaty. However, in 1828 lawmakers in Georgia said that Cherokee laws no longer were in effect. In 1829, when gold was discovered on Cherokee lands, white settlers poured in to stake their claims.

The Cherokee nation fought back in the United States courts, and their case went all the way to the Supreme Court. In 1832 Chief Justice John Marshall gave the Court's **ruling**, or decision. He said the United States should protect the Cherokees and their lands in Georgia. Yet instead of supporting the court ruling, President Jackson ignored it.

By 1838, soldiers had forced the last large group of Cherokees to leave their lands and move to the Indian Territory. Their long, painful journey came to be called the Trail of Tears. It ended on March 26, 1839, after more than 4,000 Cherokees had died of cold, disease, and lack of food. The Trail of Tears had become a trail of death.

How did the Cherokee nation try to keep its land?

LESSON 2 REVIEW

Check Understanding

1. **Recall the Facts**   What group of voters helped Andrew Jackson win the election of 1828?
2. **Focus on the Main Idea**   What problems divided the American people in the early 1800s?

Think Critically

3. **Explore Viewpoints**   How would the Cherokees and Georgia's white settlers have viewed the Indian Removal Act?
4. **Think More About It**   How do you think life on the frontier encouraged the growth of democracy?

Show What You Know

Writing Activity   Make a list of the qualities that helped Andrew Jackson get elected President. Then write a phrase that he might have used as a campaign slogan for his elections in 1828 and 1832. Display your slogans in the classroom.

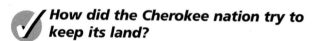

This painting, called *The Choctaw Removal*, was created by the Choctaw artist Valjean Hessing. What feelings does the artist show in the painting?

WESTWARD HO!

Link to Our World

Why might a country today want to own more land?

Focus on the Main Idea
As you read, look for reasons the United States wanted its lands to reach the Pacific Ocean.

Preview Vocabulary
manifest destiny
dictator
forty-niner

In the early 1800s Americans began to move beyond their country's borders. Wanting more land, they looked to the Spanish colony of Texas, the Oregon Country in the Pacific Northwest, and other western lands with the rallying cry, "Westward Ho!" The idea of the lands in the West being set aside for Indian peoples was soon forgotten. In 1845 the words **manifest destiny** were first used to describe what many Americans believed to be the certain future of the United States—to stretch from the Atlantic Ocean to the Pacific Ocean.

AMERICANS IN TEXAS

Stephen F. Austin began a settlement in Texas. Present-day Austin, Texas, was named for him.

Since the earliest years of European settlement, Spain had built missions and presidios all over Texas. Yet few settlers lived on this open borderland. In 1820 Moses Austin, a Missouri banker, asked Spanish leaders if he might start a colony of Americans in Texas. The Spanish agreed, but Austin died before he could carry out his plan.

Stephen F. Austin, Moses Austin's son, took up his father's work and started the colony. He chose land between the Brazos and Colorado rivers. In 1821 the first colonists began to settle there. That same year Mexico won its independence from Spain. Texas now belonged to Mexico.

Austin and the American settlers worked hard, and they soon did well in raising cotton, corn, and cattle. Encouraged by their success, the Mexican government decided to let more people settle in Texas. At first the Mexican government left the Americans in Texas alone. But in time Mexico's leaders became worried about the growing number of Americans on their land.

In 1830 the Mexican government passed a law that said no more American settlers could come to Texas. The Mexican government also said that settlers already in Texas had to obey Mexico's laws and pay more taxes. These changes angered Texans.

Then, in 1834, another change took place. General Antonio López de Santa Anna took over the Mexican government and made himself **dictator**, a leader who has total authority. When Santa Anna sent soldiers to Texas to enforce Mexican laws, fighting broke out.

 **Why did Americans first come to Texas?**

THE TEXAS REVOLUTION

Working together, a force of Americans and Mexicans living in Texas attacked the town of San Antonio on December 5, 1835. After four days of fighting, Mexican troops were driven from the center of the town. They surrendered on December 11. The defeat angered General Santa Anna. He marched on San Antonio with thousands of soldiers, planning to take back the city.

Church bells rang out a warning as the huge Mexican army came close to the city in February 1836. Texas rebels in San Antonio took shelter behind the walls of the Alamo, an old Spanish mission church. Among them were American volunteers willing to help the Texans in their fight for freedom. They included James Bowie, Davy Crockett, and William B. Travis, who served as commander. Juan Seguín and several others born in Texas also arrived to help. Some fighters were joined by their wives and children.

For 13 days the Mexican soldiers attacked the Alamo. The defenders fought to the end. Finally, on March 6, 1836, the Alamo fell. The force of about 187 Texans had been killed. Santa Anna spared the lives of the women and children.

At the Alamo fewer than 200 Texans faced more than 2,000 Mexican soldiers. In this painting Davy Crockett swings his rifle at the enemy after having run out of ammunition.

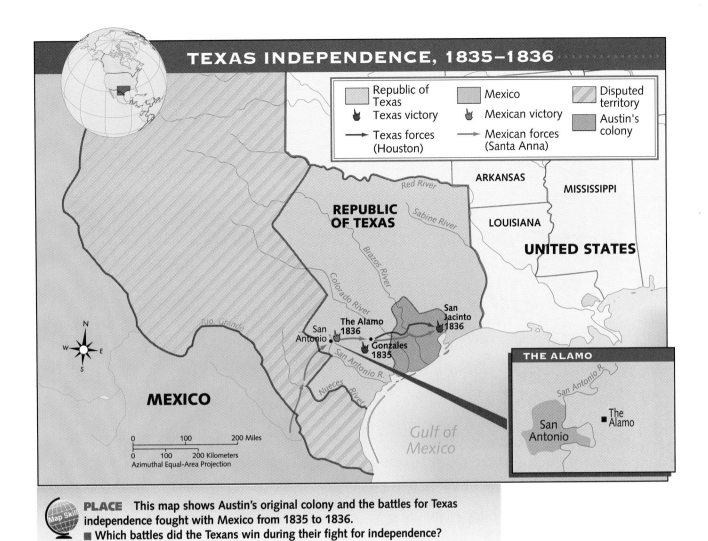

TEXAS INDEPENDENCE, 1835–1836

Legend:
- Republic of Texas
- Texas victory
- Texas forces (Houston)
- Mexico
- Mexican victory
- Mexican forces (Santa Anna)
- Disputed territory
- Austin's colony

ARKANSAS
MISSISSIPPI
Red River
REPUBLIC OF TEXAS
Sabine River
LOUISIANA
UNITED STATES
Brazos River
Colorado River
San Jacinto 1836
The Alamo 1836
San Antonio
Gonzales 1835
Rio Grande
San Antonio R.
MEXICO
Nueces River
Gulf of Mexico

THE ALAMO
San Antonio R.
San Antonio
The Alamo

0   100   200 Miles
0   100   200 Kilometers
Azimuthal Equal-Area Projection

PLACE This map shows Austin's original colony and the battles for Texas independence fought with Mexico from 1835 to 1836.
■ Which battles did the Texans win during their fight for independence?

During the attack at the Alamo, Texas leaders met. On March 2, 1836, they declared independence from Mexico and set up the Republic of Texas. They chose David G. Burnet as president and Sam Houston as commander of the army.

After the fall of the Alamo, Santa Anna moved quickly to put down the Texas revolution. On March 27 he ordered more than 300 prisoners killed at Goliad. But other Texans fought on, yelling "Remember Goliad!" and "Remember the Alamo!"

On April 21 Houston's army took the Mexicans by surprise at the Battle of San Jacinto (jah•SIN•toh) and captured Santa Anna. Houston offered to let Santa Anna live in return for Texas's independence. Santa Anna agreed, and his army returned to

Mexico. Texas remained an independent republic until it became a state of the United States in 1845. Sam Houston served twice as president of the republic and later as governor of the state of Texas.

The Texas flag, adopted in 1839, has a single white star and red, white, and blue bars. For this reason Texas was known as the Lone Star Republic. Today it is known as the Lone Star State. On April 3, 1965, the Texas State Legislature adopted the following pledge to the state flag:

66 Honor the Texas flag.
I pledge allegiance to thee,
Texas, one and indivisible. 99

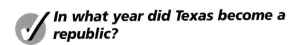

In what year did Texas become a republic?

LEARNING FROM DIAGRAMS Pioneers packed as many household goods as they could in their covered wagons. This quilt (below right) was signed by people traveling together in a wagon train.

■ Which parts of a wagon might have to be fixed right away if they broke?

Seat
Foot rest
Tool box
Tire
Cover
Brake lever
Water bucket
Feed trough
Spoke
Hub
Brake shoe
Tar pot

THE OREGON COUNTRY

American pioneers continued to push west. In 1834, Christian missionaries journeyed to the Oregon Country. This region was made up of present-day Oregon, Washington, and Idaho, and parts of Montana and Wyoming. In 1836 Marcus and Narcissa Whitman and Henry and Eliza Spalding set up a mission in the Walla Walla Valley. They hoped to teach the Indians Christianity.

The missionaries' letters to people back East told of the green valleys, wooded hills, and fertile soil of the Oregon Country—a place many began to dream of. In 1842 the first large group of pioneers headed for Oregon. Thousands more followed. The route they took came to be called the Oregon Trail. The Oregon Trail led northwest more than 2,000 miles (3,219 km) from Independence, Missouri, to the Platte River and across the Continental Divide to the Snake and Columbia rivers. The end of the trail was the Willamette (wuh•LA•muht) Valley of Oregon.

The journey took as much as six months. What a hard trip it was! Fresh water was scarce, but sudden storms soaked the travelers. Wagons broke down. Rivers had to be crossed. Many people died along the way. Yet many reached Oregon and the settlements there grew quickly.

To protect its settlements, the United States wanted a clear dividing line between its Oregon territory and nearby British land. In 1846 President James K. Polk signed a treaty with Britain fixing the 49th parallel of latitude as the boundary between the United States and the British territory in Canada. The treaty gave the United States the lands of what are now Oregon, Washington, Idaho, western Montana, and Wyoming.

How did people in the East learn about the Oregon Country?

THE MORMONS IN UTAH

In the 1840s the Mormons, or members of the Church of Jesus Christ of Latter-day Saints, joined the pioneers moving west. Under their leader, Joseph Smith, the Mormons had settled in Nauvoo (naw•VOO), Illinois. But their beliefs caused problems with other settlers, and in 1844 an angry crowd killed Joseph Smith.

When Brigham Young became the new leader of the Mormons, he decided that they should move to a place where no one would bother them. In 1846 Young and the first group of Mormons to head west set out for the Rocky Mountains.

In July 1847 the Mormons reached the Great Salt Lake valley in the Great Basin. Young chose this harsh land to settle in because he thought that no other settlers would want it. He used words from the Bible to tell his followers, "We will make this desert blossom as the rose." One of the first things the Mormons did was build irrigation canals to turn the dry land into farmland.

> 66 *WE WILL MAKE THIS desert blossom as the rose.* 99
>
> Brigham Young, 1847

The Mormons did make the land blossom with crops of grain, fruit, and vegetables. The region grew rapidly, and soon it became the Utah Territory. Brigham Young became its first governor.

 **Why did the Mormons go to Utah?**

WAR WITH MEXICO

The land the Mormons settled in the Great Basin belonged to Mexico. In 1848, only a few months later, that land became part of the United States.

Mormon pioneers get ready to move out from what is today Omaha, Nebraska. They stayed there for the winter before completing their journey westward.

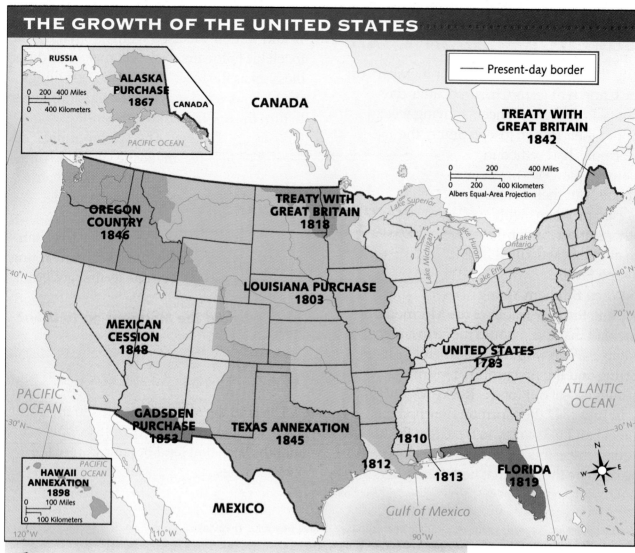

THE GROWTH OF THE UNITED STATES

— Present-day border

RUSSIA

ALASKA PURCHASE 1867

CANADA

0 200 400 Miles
0 400 Kilometers

PACIFIC OCEAN

CANADA

TREATY WITH GREAT BRITAIN 1842

OREGON COUNTRY 1846

TREATY WITH GREAT BRITAIN 1818

Lake Superior

Lake Michigan

Lake Huron

Lake Ontario

Lake Erie

0 200 400 Miles
0 200 400 Kilometers
Albers Equal-Area Projection

LOUISIANA PURCHASE 1803

40°N

40°N

70°W

MEXICAN CESSION 1848

UNITED STATES 1783

PACIFIC OCEAN

ATLANTIC OCEAN

30°N

GADSDEN PURCHASE 1853

TEXAS ANNEXATION 1845

1810

1812

1813

FLORIDA 1819

30°N

N
W   E
S

HAWAII ANNEXATION 1898

PACIFIC OCEAN

0 100 Miles
0 100 Kilometers

MEXICO

Gulf of Mexico

120°W

110°W

90°W

80°W

REGIONS By 1898 the United States had gained the land for what would become 50 states.
■ When did the United States first gain land on the Pacific Ocean?

James K. Polk was President then, and he wanted to see the United States reach to the Pacific Ocean. He thought that all the lands west of Texas should be part of the United States.

In January 1846 President Polk sent American soldiers into lands that were disputed between the United States and Mexico. In April Mexican troops crossed the Rio Grande and attacked an American patrol. Polk then asked Congress to declare war on Mexico.

In 1847 the United States invaded Mexico by sea. American soldiers led by General Winfield Scott marched from Veracruz to

Mexico City. After a year of fighting, the war was over. In 1848 Mexico and the United States signed the Treaty of Guadalupe Hidalgo (gwah•dah•LOO•pay ee•DAHL•goh). In the treaty ending the war, the United States got California—and much more. It got land that now makes up Utah and Nevada and parts of Arizona, New Mexico, Colorado, and Wyoming. The United States purchased more land from Mexico in 1853, bringing the part of the country between Canada and Mexico to its present size.

What did the United States gain in its war with Mexico?

THE CALIFORNIA GOLD RUSH

Just a few days before the treaty with Mexico was signed, gold was found in California. In January 1848 James Marshall was building a waterwheel for John Sutter's new sawmill near Sacramento. Something in the water glittered. Marshall picked it up. He held a shiny stone that was half the size of a pea. Then he saw another and another. The news flashed to the East like wildfire. Gold!

In 1849, less than a year later, more than 80,000 gold seekers came to California. They were called **forty-niners**. Most had made their way west on the Oregon Trail, cutting south across the Nevada desert to California. The longer but easier way was to travel around Cape Horn, the tip of South America, by clipper ship. Clipper ships were the fastest ships to sail the oceans. For gold seekers in a hurry to reach California and willing to pay extra to get there fast, the journey around Cape Horn took about three months.

The gold rush quickly filled California with new people. They came from Europe and Asia as well as from the United States. In 1850, only two years after Marshall's discovery at Sutter's Mill, California had enough people to become a state.

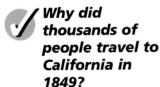

Why did thousands of people travel to California in 1849?

These forty-niners are trying to find gold among stones in a riverbed. Looking for gold was hard work, and the chances of finding any were slim.

LESSON 3 REVIEW

Check Understanding

1. **Recall the Facts** What led American settlers to move west into Texas, Oregon, Utah, and California?
2. **Focus on the Main Idea** Why did the leaders of the United States want its borders to reach the Pacific Ocean?

Think Critically

3. **Personally Speaking** What qualities do you think a pioneer needed? Why would they be important?
4. **Past to Present** Are there still pioneers and frontiers today? Why or why not?

Show What You Know

Art Activity Make a picture map of the growth of the western United States. On your map, show the Alamo, the Whitman-Spalding mission, travelers on the Oregon Trail, Mormon settlers, and forty-niners. Share your map with family members.

How To

Use Relief and Elevation Maps

Why Is This Skill Important?

When we think of traveling long distances today, we think of going by airplane, car, or train. Early pioneers, however, had to travel long distances by walking or by riding in wagons. They had to cross steep mountains and wade across wide rivers.

Certain kinds of maps can help you better understand how difficult the journeys of the pioneers must have been. Those maps show how high or how low the land is.

Relief and Elevation

A relief map helps you picture the physical features of the land. **Relief** (rih•LEEF), or the differences in height of an area of land, is often shown by shading. Heavily shaded areas on a relief map show high relief, or sharp rises and drops in the land. Lightly shaded areas show low relief, where the land gently rises or falls. Areas with no shading show land that is mostly flat.

Look at the relief map showing trails to the West. You will see that there is heavy shading in the western lands. This shows areas of high relief, such as the Rocky Mountains and the Cascade Range. In the eastern lands, there is little shading. This means that the land has low relief. That area, including the Great Plains, is mostly flat land or has gently rolling hills.

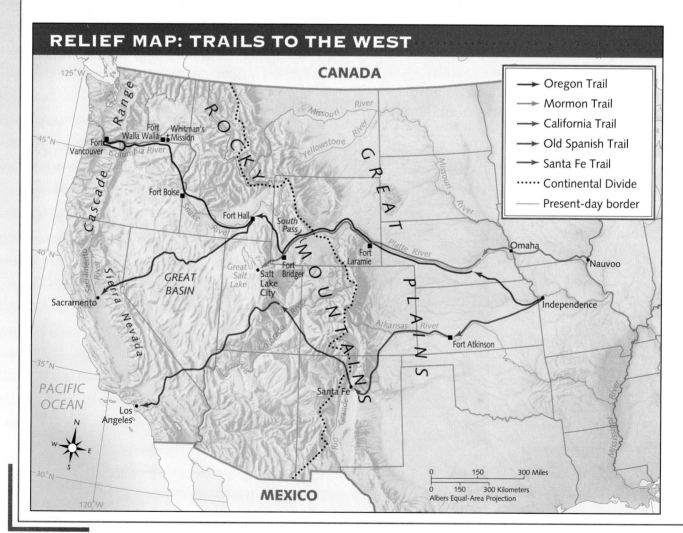

RELIEF MAP: TRAILS TO THE WEST

Legend:
→ Oregon Trail
→ Mormon Trail
→ California Trail
→ Old Spanish Trail
→ Santa Fe Trail
····· Continental Divide
— Present-day border

This picture was taken of pioneers traveling in Kansas. Using the relief map that shows trails to the West, how would you describe the land in Kansas?

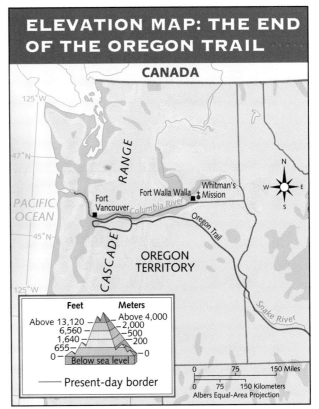

ELEVATION MAP: THE END OF THE OREGON TRAIL

Although a relief map shows you where mountains, hills, and plains are located, it does not tell you the elevation (eh•luh•VAY•shuhn) of the land. **Elevation** is the height of the land. Land that is level with the surface of the ocean is said to be at sea level. Its elevation is zero. The elevation of all other land is measured from sea level, up or down, in feet or meters. To find the elevation of a place, you must look at an elevation map.

Most elevation maps use color to show elevation. Look at the elevation map showing the end of the Oregon Trail. The map key tells you which colors are used to show different elevations. Dark green is used for the lowest land, which is between sea level and 655 feet (200 m). Brown is used for the highest land, which is above 13,120 feet (4,000 m).

Understand the Process

Now that you know more about relief and elevation, use the questions that follow as a guide for learning how to use relief maps and elevation maps.

1. What is the difference between a relief map and an elevation map?
2. To find the elevation at Fort Walla Walla, should you use a relief map or an elevation map? Why?
3. Will a relief map tell you whether western Oregon is flat or mountainous? Explain.
4. Will a relief map tell you the elevation of western Oregon? Explain.
5. How high are the highest areas in Oregon?
6. Where are the lowest areas in Oregon?
7. What is the elevation of the land at Fort Vancouver?

Think and Apply

Imagine that you are a pioneer on the Oregon Trail. On the relief map, use your finger to trace the route of the trail from Independence to Fort Vancouver. Describe the landforms you pass along the way. Once you reach Oregon, use the elevation map to describe in greater detail the final days of your journey.

An Age of R EFORM

L nk to Our World

How do people today work to make things better in their school, community, or country?

Focus on the Main Idea
As you read, look for ways people in the 1800s worked to make American society better.

Preview Vocabulary

reform	abolitionist
public school	equality
abolish	suffrage

The fast growth of the United States in the first half of the 1800s made many Americans hopeful. They saw how the nation's growth in manufacturing and in size helped many people. But they also saw the need to **reform**, or change for the better, many parts of American life.

Not everyone was helped by America's growth. Some were hurt by it. Not everyone had the freedoms promised by the Declaration of Independence and the Constitution. So many Americans were concerned about these problems that the 1830s through the 1850s became an age of reform. During this time many Americans worked to improve life for others.

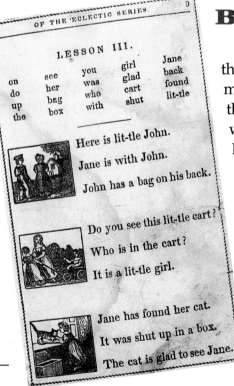

This spelling book was used in schools during the early 1800s.

BETTER SCHOOLS

Young Horace Mann was excited to see the red leaves falling from the oak and maple trees in Massachusetts. He knew that when winter put an end to farm work, he would be able to go to school. Horace's school had only one room and one teacher for children of all ages. And there were very few books.

When Horace Mann grew up, he became a reformer in education. In 1837 Mann was made secretary of the Massachusetts Board of Education. He worked to improve the state's **public schools**, the schools paid for by taxes and open to all children.

368 • Unit 6

Millions of people around the world read about the cruel conditions of slavery in the novel *Uncle Tom's Cabin*. The Webb family (right) read the novel to audiences in the North.

Horace Mann wanted laws requiring children to go to school. He called for special schools to train teachers. In Mann's day most teachers worked only part-time. They were often students in law or in the clergy. Mann wanted full-time, well-trained teachers. He also wanted new schools built. Before this time most public-school classes were held in stores or in people's homes.

By 1850 many of Horace Mann's ideas were being used in the North and West. Most white children received an elementary education and sometimes a high-school education. Free African children, however, had to go to separate schools. In the South, most boys who were white went to private schools. Girls had few

 TOO LONG *have others spoken for us.* 99

Samuel Cornish and
John Russwurm, 1827

chances for education. Enslaved children had none.

✓ **What reforms in education did Horace Mann try to make?**

THE FIGHT AGAINST SLAVERY

While Horace Mann worked to improve education during the age of reform, other reformers worked to **abolish**, or end, slavery. Since the early days of the country's history, some Americans had been deeply troubled by slavery. Soon they started working together to help enslaved people gain their freedom. Among the first to speak out were members of a religious group called the Quakers. In 1775 the Quakers formed the first group to work against slavery—an antislavery society.

People who wanted to abolish slavery were called **abolitionists** (a•buh•LIH•shuhn•ists). Some abolitionists used the written word to spread their message. In 1827 Samuel Cornish and John Russwurm started a newspaper that called for **equality**, or the same rights, for all Americans. The newspaper, *Freedom's Journal*, was the first to be owned and written by Africans in the United States. "Too long," Cornish and Russwurm wrote, "have others spoken for us."

A few years later another abolitionist, William Lloyd Garrison, founded a newspaper called the *Liberator*. In it he called for a complete end to slavery at once.

    66On this subject, I do not wish to think or speak or write in moderation. I am in earnest . . . I will not excuse. I will not retreat a single inch. AND I WILL BE HEARD.99

In 1852 abolitionist Harriet Beecher Stowe wrote a novel that turned many people against slavery. The book, called *Uncle Tom's Cabin*, told the heartbreaking story of slaves being mistreated by a cruel slave owner. The book quickly became a best-seller and was made into a play.

Large crowds came to hear Sojourner Truth. She spoke against slavery and in favor of women's rights.

While some abolitionists were writing, others were giving speeches. One of the speakers was Frederick Douglass, a runaway slave. William Lloyd Garrison asked him to speak at an abolitionist meeting. Douglass slowly rose and walked up to the stage. He shared from the heart how it felt to be free. And he told his listeners the story of his escape from slavery.

When Douglass finished speaking, everyone cheered. Before long, he had become the leading abolitionist speaker. His speeches made many people agree that slavery had to be stopped.

Like Douglass, Sojourner Truth traveled the country speaking out against slavery. Sojourner Truth was a former slave named Isabella. She believed that God had called her to "travel up and down the land" to preach. She decided to change her name to *Sojourner*, which means "traveler." She chose *Truth* as a last name.

Sojourner Truth believed that slavery could be ended peacefully. Frederick Douglass argued in his speeches that only rebellion would end it.

In the end, Douglass was proved right. The nation that grew large and strong in the 1800s would soon be divided by civil war.

 **How did abolitionists work to end slavery?**

RIGHTS FOR WOMEN

In 1840 Elizabeth Cady Stanton and Lucretia Mott went to a convention of abolitionists in London. However, they were not allowed to speak because they were women. Stanton and Mott were so angry that they decided to hold their own convention—for women's rights.

The first women's rights convention met on July 19 and 20, 1848, at Seneca Falls, New York. Those who attended wanted women to have the same political, social, and economic rights as white men. They wrote a statement saying women should have "all the rights and privileges which belong to them as citizens of the United States." The statement called for women to be able to own property, keep wages they earned, and be given **suffrage**, or the right to vote.

The reformers began to get some support. In 1850 Susan B. Anthony of New York worked for women teachers to have the same pay as men and for women to have the same property rights as men. She later became a leader of the women's suffrage movement.

Sojourner Truth used her speaking skills to help. In 1851 she was at a women's rights

Elizabeth Cady Stanton spoke at the first women's rights convention and wrote a document called the Declaration of Sentiments. The document describes women's rights by using words from the Declaration of Independence. But Stanton added some words, as in "all men *and women* are created equal."

Where?

Seneca Falls, New York

Seneca Falls is a small town in the middle of New York State, between Rochester and Syracuse. Seneca Falls was the home of Elizabeth Cady Stanton. With Lucretia Mott, she planned the first women's rights convention in the summer of 1848. Those attending the Seneca Falls Convention called for women to work together to win their rights as citizens. Today Seneca Falls has a Women's Hall of Fame.

Susan Brownell Anthony 1820–1906

For most of her life, Susan B. Anthony worked to get women the right to vote. She was once arrested and fined $100 for breaking the law by voting in an election for President. Anthony also started a weekly newspaper and wrote books to spread her message. Susan B. Anthony died 14 years before the Nineteenth Amendment to the Constitution became law. From 1979 to 1981, the United States government honored her work for women's rights by minting one-dollar coins with her picture on them. Susan B. Anthony was the first woman to have her picture on a coin in the United States.

convention in Ohio when a man said, "Women are weak." She stood up quickly and answered the man.

66 The man over there says women need to be helped into carriages and lifted over ditches and puddles, and have the best place everywhere. Nobody helps me into carriages and over puddles, or gives me the best place—and ain't I a woman?

Look at my arm! I have plowed and planted and gathered into barns, and no man could beat me—and ain't I a woman?99

Women won a few rights during this time. A few states gave women control of the money they earned and of the property they owned. Some even allowed women to vote. But it would not be until 1920 that the Nineteenth Amendment gave all women this right.

✓ *What reforms did Elizabeth Cady Stanton and others work for?*

LESSON 4 REVIEW

Check Understanding

1. **Recall the Facts**   What did reformers want to change about American society?
2. **Focus on the Main Idea**   How did reformers in the 1800s work to improve society?

Think Critically

3. **Personally Speaking**   Why do you think so many people wanted to hear Frederick Douglass tell his story?
4. **Past to Present**   Do you think Americans today live up to the idea that all people are created equal? Explain your answer.

Show What You Know

Writing Activity   Imagine that you are a reformer in the 1800s. Write a letter in which you try to persuade a member of the school board to make a change in the public schools. Be sure to give the reason the change is needed. Collect the letters in a binder for classroom display.

Use a Double-Bar Graph

Why Is This Skill Important?

People often make comparisons and look at how things have changed over time. Some parents mark their children's heights on a wall to keep a record of how much the children have grown each year. If records are kept for two children, the parents can compare how much each has grown over the years and how much each has grown compared with the other. A good way to compare such information is by making a double-bar graph. A double-bar graph allows you to compare information quickly and to see changes over time.

Understand the Process

Between 1790 and 1850 both the urban and rural populations of the United States grew at a steady pace. The double-bar graph on this page shows the differences in urban and rural populations for these years. It also shows how urban and rural populations have changed over time.

1. Look at the words and numbers along the top, bottom, and left-hand side of the graph. Years are listed along the bottom, and numbers of people are listed along the left-hand side.
2. Notice that the information on this graph is shown only for every tenth year from 1790 to 1850.
3. Notice how different colors—red and blue—are used to show the urban population and the rural population.
4. Read the graph by running your finger up to the top of each bar and then left to the population number. If the top of the bar is between numbered lines, estimate the population by selecting a number between those two numbers.
5. Compare the heights of the red bars with one another. Then compare the heights with the blue bars. How did the urban population

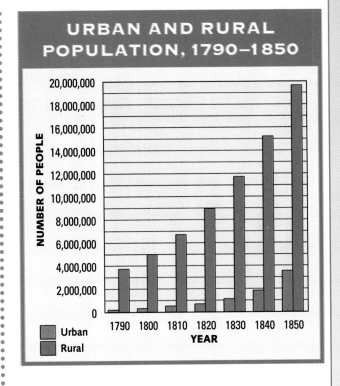

URBAN AND RURAL POPULATION, 1790–1850

change over time? How did the rural population change over time?
6. Now compare the heights of the red bar and the blue bar for each year shown. This allows you to compare urban growth with rural growth over time. How does the double-bar graph help you understand how the population of the United States grew between 1790 and 1850?

Think and Apply

Make a double-bar graph of your test scores in social studies and in another subject. Label the bottom of your graph by weeks. Along the left-hand side of your graph, list possible test scores. For example, you could mark 0 percent on the bottom and go up in 10-percent units, reaching 100 percent at the top. Each week, make a bar to represent your test scores for that week in each subject. Remember to use a different color for each subject.

REVIEW

CONNECT MAIN IDEAS

Use this organizer to show that you understand how the chapter's main ideas are connected. Copy the organizer onto a separate sheet of paper. Then complete it by writing three details to support each main idea.

The Industrial Revolution
New technology changed life in the United States in the 1800s.

1. _____
2. _____
3. _____

The Age of Jackson
Americans in different parts of the country felt differently about concerns in the early 1800s.

1. _____
2. _____
3. _____

The Way West

N
W — E
S

Westward Ho!
The United States wanted its land to reach the Pacific Ocean.

1. _____
2. _____
3. _____

An Age of Reform
People in the 1800s worked to make American society better.

1. _____
2. _____
3. _____

WRITE MORE ABOUT IT

1. **Write a Conversation** Write a conversation that could have taken place between Eli Whitney and a factory owner. Whitney and the factory owner should discuss how mass production will affect Americans.

2. **Write a Letter** Imagine that you witnessed the race between the *Tom Thumb* and a railroad car pulled by a horse. Write a letter to a friend describing the excitement of the event.

3. **Write a Scene for a Play** Susanna Dickinson and her daughter lived through the siege of the Alamo. Santa Anna chose her to tell Sam Houston and other Texas leaders about the battle. Santa Anna hoped that hearing Dickinson's sad story would make the Texans give up. Her report, however, made the Texans fight all the harder. Write a scene for a play in which Dickinson meets with Texas leaders and describes what happened at the Alamo.

USE VOCABULARY

Write a term from this list to complete each of the sentences that follow.

abolish   secede
equality   sectionalism
manifest destiny   suffrage

1. ____ is another name for regional loyalty.

2. South Carolina threatened to ____ in 1832 because Congress passed another tariff.

3. In 1845 the words ____ were first used to describe the idea that the United States would one day stretch from the Atlantic Ocean to the Pacific Ocean.

4. During the age of reform, many people worked to ____ slavery.

5. Reformers called for ____, or the same rights, for all Americans.

6. ____ is the right to vote.

CHECK UNDERSTANDING

1. How was Francis Cabot Lowell's textile mill different from earlier ones?

2. How was the National Road important to the country's growth?

3. What change in voting helped Andrew Jackson become President?

4. What was the Trail of Tears?

5. What changes made by the Mexican government angered American settlers in Texas?

6. What group settled the Utah Territory? Why did they go there?

7. What lands did the United States gain from the war with Mexico?

8. Who were Frederick Douglass and Sojourner Truth? How did they spread their messages?

THINK CRITICALLY

1. **Think More About It** How did the Industrial Revolution change life in the United States?

2. **Explore Viewpoints** How did Vice President Calhoun's view of states' rights differ from that held by President Jackson?

3. **Cause and Effect** What effect did the California gold rush have on the growth of the United States?

APPLY SKILLS

How to Use Relief and Elevation Maps Use the maps on pages 366 and 367 to answer these questions.

1. What is the elevation of the land at Whitman's Mission?

2. How would you describe the land near Ft. Laramie?

3. What cities are located in or near the most mountainous parts of the Oregon Trail?

How to Use a Double-Bar Graph Make a double-bar graph showing the high and low temperatures over the next five days. Label the bottom of the graph with the days of the week, and show the temperatures along the left side. Each day, make bars for the high and low temperatures. Remember to use different colors for the two temperatures.

READ MORE ABOUT IT

Ahyoka and the Talking Leaves by Peter and Connie Roop. Lothrop, Lee & Shepard. This story, based on truth, tells how Sequoyah developed an alphabet for the Cherokee language.

Susanna of the Alamo: A True Story by John Jakes. Harcourt Brace. This is the true story of Susanna Dickinson and her young daughter, who survived the siege of the Alamo in 1836.

MAKING SOCIAL STUDIES
RELEVANT

CHILD LABOR

By the middle of the nineteenth century, the United States was on its way to becoming an industrial nation. Much of this change happened through the work of young people, such as the young women who worked at the textile mills in Lowell, Massachusetts. More than a million children worked in the mines and factories that helped the American economy grow. They were the first of a great tide of American child-laborers.

Child labor is on the rise again in the United States. However, today it is illegal. Laws have been passed to keep business owners from hiring children under the age of 18 to work in mines, factories, or other places. Yet government figures show that many of these laws are being broken. In many large cities children younger than 10 are working in dangerous clothing industry sweatshops. In some states, children move from place to place with their parents, working in the fields to harvest crops.

As in the 1800s, some families today have come to depend on the income children bring in by working. Many children work in legal and safe jobs outside of school hours. But others do not. Whatever the causes, the effects of illegal child labor have been harmful. More than 60,000 children are injured and more than 100 are killed each year doing jobs that child labor laws say they should not do.

THINK AND APPLY

Think about the reasons some children today might have for holding an unsafe job. Write a paragraph that describes why you think they are working. Trade paragraphs with a partner, and compare what you wrote.

BUILDING CITIZENSHIP

STORY CLOTH

Study the pictures shown in this story cloth to help you review the events you read about in Unit 6.

Summarize the Main Ideas

1. The Industrial Revolution brought great changes to the United States. The nation's first factory was built in 1790.

2. In 1803 the Louisiana Purchase doubled the nation's size. Lewis and Clark explored the new territory with help from Sacagawea.

3. In the early 1800s, steamboats made travel by river much faster.

4. In 1811 work began on the National Road. It became the main land route between the East and the West.

5. The first locomotive in the nation was built in 1830. Railroads grew quickly after that.

6. By the mid-1800s, the nation had gained Texas, the Oregon Country, and other western lands. At the Alamo in 1836, Texans had fought for freedom from Mexico.

7. The Indian Removal Act of 1830 forced American Indians to leave their homes and make difficult journeys to the West.

8. The United States had grown, but many people saw the need for reform. People such as Sojourner Truth spoke out against slavery.

Make Your Own Story Cloth   Choose a topic that is illustrated in this story cloth. Then create your own story cloth about just that topic. Draw simple pictures, and label each one. Add a title to your story cloth.

ABOLISH SLAVERY

COOPERATIVE LEARNING WORKSHOP

Remember
- Share your ideas.
- Cooperate with others to plan your work.
- Take responsibility for your work.
- Show your group's work to the class.
- Discuss what you learned by working together.

Activity 1
Make a Time Line

Work in a group to draw a time line on a large sheet of paper. Show the years from 1770 to 1850, using ten-year periods. Then label the time line with events from this unit. Draw pictures to illustrate the events.

Activity 2
Write and Perform a Scene for a Play

Work with members of a group to write a scene for a play about a typical workday at an early textile mill. The scene should tell something about the workers and the working conditions at the mill. Decide who the characters in the scene will be, and write dialogue for them. Then choose roles, practice the scene, and perform it for your class.

Activity 3
Draw a Map

Work together to draw a map showing how the United States grew in the first half of the 1800s. Maps in your textbook and in encyclopedias and atlases can help you. First, draw an outline map of the country, and label major landforms and bodies of water. Then, color the boundaries of the United States in 1783, following the American Revolution. Use different colors to show the Louisiana Purchase, Florida, Texas, the Oregon Country, and the land that the United States won or bought following its war with Mexico. Add a map key to your map.

Activity 4
Make a Diorama

Work in a group to make a diorama about pioneer life on the frontier. Show the kind of work that pioneers had to do, such as clearing the land, building a log cabin, or growing their own food. Display your finished diorama in the classroom.

USE VOCABULARY

Use each term in a sentence that will help explain its meaning.

1. doctrine
2. Industrial Revolution
3. textile mill
4. interchangeable parts
5. canal
6. locomotive
7. states' rights
8. forty-niners
9. reform
10. abolitionist

CHECK UNDERSTANDING

1. How was the Cumberland Gap important to Daniel Boone and the Wilderness Road?

2. How did the Louisiana Purchase change the United States?

3. What was the purpose of the Lewis and Clark expedition?

4. Who were the War Hawks?

5. What is mass production? Who first put this idea for producing goods into practice?

6. Why was the Erie Canal built?

7. What was the result of the Indian Removal Act of 1830?

8. Who was Stephen Austin?

9. What physical features first attracted pioneers to the Oregon Country?

THINK CRITICALLY

1. **Past to Present** Technology changed life for Americans in the 1800s. How does technology change life for Americans today?

2. **Explore Viewpoints** The Supreme Court ruled that the United States should protect the Cherokees and their land. Why do you think President Jackson ignored that ruling?

3. **Personally Speaking** If you had been alive in 1849, would you have gone to California in search of gold? Explain your answer.

4. **Think More About It** What experiences do you think helped make Frederick Douglass such an effective abolitionist speaker?

APPLY GEOGRAPHY SKILLS

How to Use Relief and Elevation Maps Use the map below to answer the questions.

1. Where did the Trail of Tears lead to?

2. Which part of the Trail of Tears passed mostly through mountains? How do you know?

3. What is the elevation of the land near Murfreesboro, Tennessee? near Springfield, Missouri?

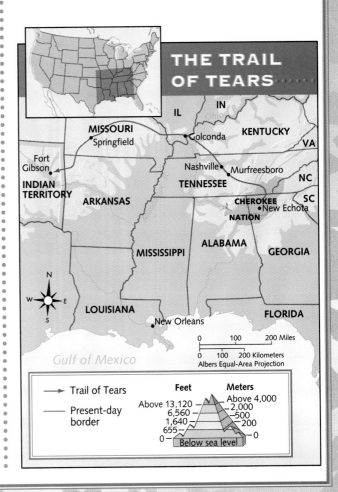

THE TRAIL OF TEARS

Trail of Tears
Present-day border

Feet	Meters
Above 13,120	Above 4,000
6,560	2,000
1,640	500
655	200
0	0
Below sea level	

UNIT 7

WAR DIVIDES the NATION

1790   1800   1810   1820   1830

1793
Eli Whitney invents
the cotton gin

1820
The Missouri
Compromise

1831
Nat Turner's
Rebellion

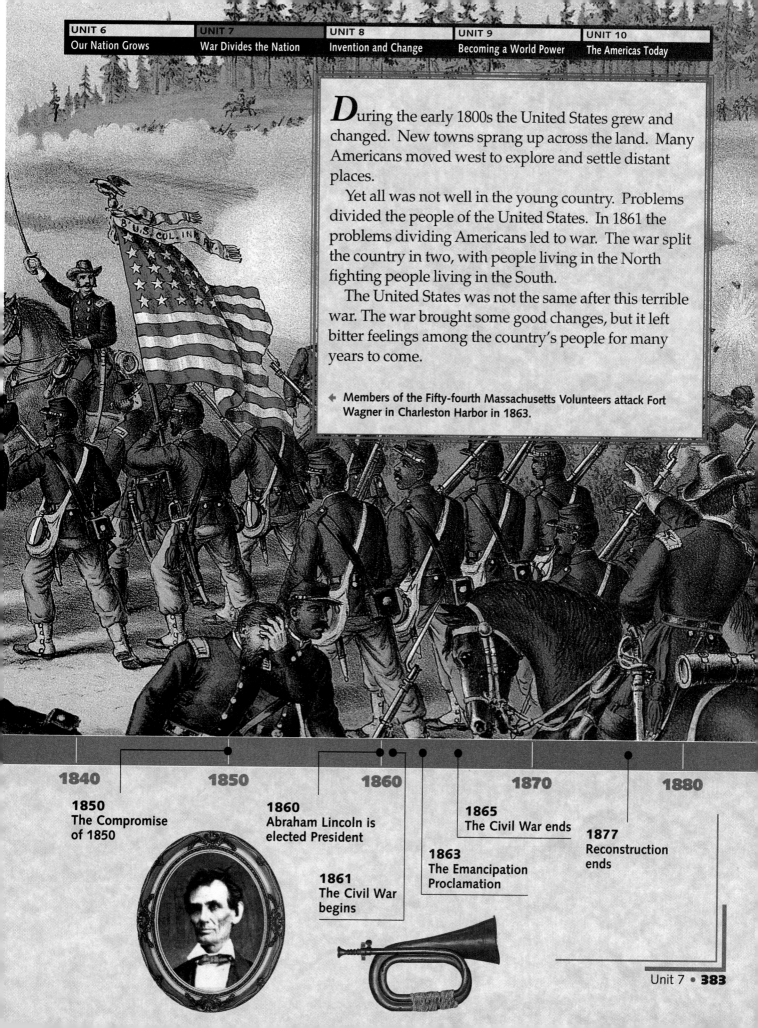

During the early 1800s the United States grew and changed. New towns sprang up across the land. Many Americans moved west to explore and settle distant places.

Yet all was not well in the young country. Problems divided the people of the United States. In 1861 the problems dividing Americans led to war. The war split the country in two, with people living in the North fighting people living in the South.

The United States was not the same after this terrible war. The war brought some good changes, but it left bitter feelings among the country's people for many years to come.

◆ Members of the Fifty-fourth Massachusetts Volunteers attack Fort Wagner in Charleston Harbor in 1863.

1840 1850 1860 1870 1880

1850
The Compromise of 1850

1860
Abraham Lincoln is elected President

1861
The Civil War begins

1863
The Emancipation Proclamation

1865
The Civil War ends

1877
Reconstruction ends

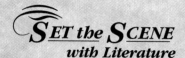
STONEWALL

by Jean Fritz

This battle drum belonged to a young New York volunteer.

In towns and cities across the country, thousands of excited young men signed up to join the army. It was 1861, and the country was at war. Northerners and Southerners alike signed up, but not to fight on the same side. They signed up to fight each other.

Most people said that it would be a quick and easy war. It would be over, they said, after only one or two battles. Most people also said that their side would win.

Read now about the war's first major battle, which took place near the small Virginia town of Manassas Junction, not far from Washington, D.C. Imagine Northern soldiers, called Yankees, lining up for the first time against Southern soldiers, called Confederates or Rebels, as crowds looked on.

As the participants gathered at Manassas, excitement mounted. At last! This was it! The war was starting! Victory was in the air as if nothing else could possibly exist. The Confederates, obviously outnumbered, were lined up in a defensive position beside a small stream known as Bull Run, but if they worried, they didn't show it. Hadn't they always believed that one rebel could beat five Yankees? As for the Yankees, they straggled down to Manassas, stopping to pick blackberries—in no hurry, for hadn't they been told that the Rebs would run once they saw how bold the Yanks were? Even the civilians in Washington, high-ranking officials and their wives, were so sure of a Union victory that they planned to picnic on the outskirts of Manassas on the Big Day. They would drink champagne and toast the army and cry "Bravo! Bravo!" What could be nicer?

Although there had been several days of initial skirmishing, the Big Day turned out to be Sunday, July 21st. A beautiful sunny day—perfect for a picnic. Carriages were drawn up on a hill overlooking Bull Run; ladies rustled under parasols; gentlemen adjusted field glasses; couriers galloped up with the latest news. Good news, all of it. Yankee advances. Confederate confusion. So it went for the first six hours.

Yet not all the Confederates had been heard from. The Army of the Shenandoah that was supposed to be held in the hills by the Union watchdog forces had eluded their enemy on July 18th and had left for Manassas. At first they'd been slow. The men didn't know where they were going or why and saw no reason to rush just because their officers told them to. Finally General Thomas Jackson, whose brigade led the march, stopped them and read an official statement. "Our gallant army under General Beauregard is now attacked by overwhelming numbers," Jackson read. He asked the troops if they would not "step out like men and make a forced march to save the country."

A battle! The men yelled their approval—a special rebel yell. . . . It was a fierce sound that a Yankee soldier once said sent a corkscrew sensation down the spine. Woh-who-ey. The yell rose to a pitch on the *who* and held there, trembling and drawn out, then fell with a thud on the *ey*. The men quickened their pace. Woh-who-ey. For eighteen hours they marched until at last, having waded waist deep through the green Shenandoah River, they dropped, exhausted. They marched and they rode a train for a few hours, and then

....

Men were supposed to be at least 18 years old to join the army, but some boys much younger—like the two shown here—still signed up. Most boys were not allowed to fight. Instead they tended horses, drove wagons, or served as drummer boys.

they marched again. But they were there now. The question was: Were they in time?

By noon on the 21st it was clear that Beauregard had positioned the major part of his army in the wrong place. While the enemy was concentrating its forces on the left, the Confederates were wasting their time on the right. In the general scramble to change positions, Jackson and his brigade found themselves in the thick of the activity. Union men were in the distance but steadily advancing; the Confederates were retreating. As one officer passed Jackson, he shook his head. "The day is going against us," he said.

"If you think so, sir," Jackson replied, "don't say anything about it."

Jackson did not plunge forward to meet the enemy, as his men might have expected. Looking over the field, he saw a plateau which he recognized as the best possible position for making a stand. Here he placed his men and artillery and when the enemy fire closed in, Jackson stood before his brigade, his blue eyes blazing, the old battle fever upon him. Walking back and forth, indifferent to bullets, he was lifted out of himself, possessed with a power he'd known only once before, in Mexico. He understood exactly how to get the most out of every man and every gun and he *willed* victory into the day. "The fight," as one officer put it, "was just then hot enough to make [Jackson] feel well." Shot in the hand as he held it up, Jackson wrapped a handkerchief around the wound and went on as if nothing had happened.

In another part of the field, General Bee, a West Point classmate of Jackson's, was desperately trying to stop a retreat. "Look yonder!" he cried to his men. "There's Jackson standing like a stone wall."

General Bee was killed almost as soon as he'd finished speaking, but retreating Confederates did see how well Jackson's line was holding and gradually they began to

rally around it. The last reinforcements from Shenandoah army, which had just arrived, were rushed to the scene. And the tide of the battle began to turn.

When the center of the Union line was in plain sight, General Beauregard ordered a charge. Jackson relayed the order.

"Reserve your fire till they come within fifty yards," he shouted, "then fire and give them the bayonet. And when you charge, yell like furies."

The orders were carried out precisely.
Woh-who-ey!
Woh-who-ey!
Suddenly the entire Union army was falling back, then turning around and hurrying off the field. A huge, confused mob mixed with panic-stricken picnickers headed pell-mell back to Washington.

The battle was over and with it some of the innocent glory was gone. For the fields were strewn with bodies—young men who only the day before had been laughing and making jokes. Two thousand Confederates killed or wounded; three thousand Union men. Stopped right in the midst of doing something. In the middle of a sentence perhaps, in mid-step, in the act of raising a rifle, at the beginning of a smile. Struck down, blown apart as if they weren't *people*. As if they weren't *young*. How could inexperienced men have imagined what death would be like on a battlefield?

In one day soldiers on both sides became veterans, but of course the victors felt better than the losers. If they could win a battle, southerners said, they could win a war.

What started out for many as an exciting adventure ended in fear, injury, and death at the Battle of Bull Run. One Union soldier, staggering from the battlefield, told an onlooker, "I know I'm going home. I've had enough fighting to last my lifetime." During the battle, Private A. P. Hubbard's pocket-sized Bible saved his life, protecting him from a bullet that ripped the book apart.

CHAPTER 13

BACKGROUND
to the
CONFLICT

> 66 I appear this evening as a thief and a robber. I stole this head, these limbs, this body from my master, and ran off with them. 99
>
> Frederick Douglass, runaway slave and abolitionist, about 1842

This photograph of Frederick Douglass, taken about 1850, is in the National Portrait Gallery in Washington, D.C.

DIFFERENCES DIVIDE
NORTH and SOUTH

Link to Our World

What might cause people living in different regions to disagree today?

Focus on the Main Idea
As you read, look for the reasons that caused people in the North and the South to disagree during the mid-1800s.

Preview Vocabulary
cotton gin

Differences among Americans help make the United States strong. Sometimes, however, differences come between people. In the mid-1800s differences became disagreements between Americans living in two regions—the North and the South. These disagreements threatened to tear the country apart.

REGIONAL DIFFERENCES

Many of the differences between the North and the South developed over time, as people in each region found different ways of making a living. In the mid-1800s most Americans still lived and worked on farms. For many people, however, life was changing.

In the North, factories seemed to be springing up everywhere, making all kinds of goods. Many people were moving from farms to towns and cities, where they hoped to work in the factories. People even came from other countries to find jobs.

Life in the South was not changing as quickly. Factories were being built and cities were growing, yet farming remained the most common way to earn a living. The biggest farms were huge plantations along the Coastal Plain and near the Mississippi River, where the soil was rich and the weather was warm. Planters there raised acres and acres of cash crops, such as cotton, rice, tobacco, and sugarcane, to sell at market.

Wealthy plantation owners were among the South's leaders. Many white Southerners copied the ways of these planters and dreamed about owning their own plantations someday. Yet few ever did. Most lived on small farms, where

Even though most people still lived on farms, many in the North were moving to cities, where they hoped to find work. This photograph of Cincinnati, Ohio, was taken in 1848.

In the South farming continued to be the center of life. This scene shows a cotton plantation along the Mississippi River.

they raised cattle, cut lumber, and grew only enough food to feed their families.

Partly because of the differences in work opportunities between the two regions, many more people lived in the North than in the South. By 1860 the population of the North had grown to more than 19 million. Only 11 million people lived in the South. Of those 11 million people, nearly 4 million were Africans held as slaves.

 How was the North different from the South?

THE SLAVE ECONOMY

Slavery had been a part of American life since colonial days. In many places, however, slavery did not last. Some people thought that slavery was wrong. Others could not make money using enslaved workers. The cost of feeding, clothing, and housing slaves was too great.

Yet slavery continued in the South, where owners had come to depend on the work of enslaved people. Slaves were made to work as miners, carpenters, factory workers, and

SOUTHERN SLAVEHOLDERS, 1860

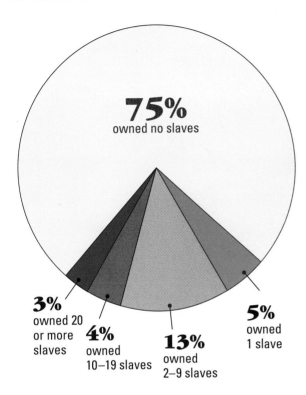

75% owned no slaves

3% owned 20 or more slaves

4% owned 10–19 slaves

13% owned 2–9 slaves

5% owned 1 slave

LEARNING FROM GRAPHS Most Northerners once thought that all Southerners owned slaves. Look at the circle graph to tell if this is true.
■ What percent of Southerners owned no slaves at all in 1860? What percent did own slaves?

house servants. Most, however, were taken to large plantations. There they worked in the fields, raising cash crops for the planters to sell.

Not every white Southerner owned slaves. In fact, most did not. By 1860 only one white Southern family in four owned slaves. Many of these families lived on small farms with one or two slaves. Only a few wealthy slave-holders lived on large plantations with many slaves. These planters together owned more than half the slaves in the South.

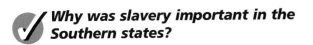

Why was slavery important in the Southern states?

"KING COTTON"

In the early years of settlement in the South, few planters grew cotton—the plant from which soft, cool cotton cloth is made. Cotton was in great demand. But before it could be sold, workers had to separate the small seeds from the white cotton fibers. This was a slow, tiring job that took too many people too much time. Inventor Eli Whitney changed this.

In 1793 Whitney invented a machine called the cotton gin, or engine. The **cotton gin** removed the seeds from the cotton fibers much faster than workers could. This one change in technology led to many other changes.

With the cotton gin, cotton could be cleaned and prepared for market in less time. Planters could then sell more cotton and make more money. They sold the cotton to textile mills in the North and in Europe.

Who?

Eli Whitney 1765–1825

Eli Whitney taught school and studied law. He also liked to fix things. While visiting a friend's Georgia plantation, he learned how hard it was to remove the seeds from cotton. Whitney invented a machine that could take care of the problem. Soon so many people wanted cotton gins that he could not make enough to keep up with the demand. Other people began to make and sell copies of his invention. Whitney had to pay lawyers to stop others from copying his work. This used up most of the money he made from inventing the cotton gin.

Turning raw cotton into cloth was a long process that led from farms and plantations to textile mills. The steps shown here are ❶ removing the seeds and cleaning the cotton with the cotton gin; ❷ shipping the cleaned cotton; and ❸ spinning the fibers into threads at a textile mill.

Worldwide demand for cotton made both Southern planters and Northern textile-mill owners rich. It also made slavery more important than ever before. Planters needed slaves to plant the seeds, weed the fields, pick the cotton, and run the cotton gins. "Cotton is King," said Senator James Henry Hammond of South Carolina, "and the African must be a slave, or there's an end of all things, and soon."

 What invention helped make slavery more important than it had been?

NORTH AND SOUTH DISAGREE

By the mid-1800s some Southerners did not like the way growth was booming in the North. As a writer for one Alabama newspaper described it,

66The North fattens and grows rich upon the South. We depend upon it for our entire supplies. . . . The slaveholder dresses in Northern goods, rides in a Northern saddle. . . . His land is cleared with a Northern axe, and a Yankee clock sits upon his mantel-piece; his floor is swept by a Northern broom, and is covered with a Northern carpet . . . and he is furnished with Northern inventions.99

Bad feelings over growth were not the worst of the troubles between the North and

the South. Far worse was the disagreement over states' rights and slavery. Northerners and Southerners had argued since colonial days about whether states should allow slavery. The argument flared up again with the rapid settlement of the western frontier.

Over the years American pioneers and soldiers had pushed many of the Indian peoples off their lands. This made it possible for more settlers to move west into territories such as Illinois, Iowa, Missouri, and Arkansas. The settlers took with them their own ways of life. For settlers from the North, this meant a way of life without slaves. For some settlers from the South, however, this meant taking their enslaved workers with them.

It was not long before the question of the spread of slavery to the frontier became one of the most argued issues in the country. Most white Northerners thought that slavery

should go no farther than where it already was—in the South. Most white Southerners believed that slave owners had the right to take their slaves wherever they wanted, including to the West.

The disagreement over slavery led to fierce arguments. Even so, the number of people held as slaves in the South continued to grow. So did the number of enslaved people who were taken west.

✓ **Why did the settlement of the western frontier bring about new arguments over slavery?**

LESSON 1 REVIEW

Check Understanding

1. **Recall the Facts** In what ways were the North and the South different?
2. **Focus on the Main Idea** What caused people living in the North and the South to disagree during the mid-1800s?

Think Critically

3. **Think More About It** How did the differences between the North and the South affect the ways of life in the two regions?
4. **Cause and Effect** How did the invention of the cotton gin affect Southern planters? How did it affect Northern textile-mill owners?
5. **Explore Viewpoints** Divide a sheet of paper into two columns. Label one column *For* and the other *Against*. List all the reasons you can that tell why people were for or against the spread of slavery to the West.

Show What You Know

Art Activity Think about how the cotton gin changed life in the 1800s. Create an advertisement for the people of that time that explains how the cotton gin affects those who make and buy cotton and cotton products. Then present your advertisement to a group of your classmates.

HowTo

Use Graphs to Identify Trends

Why Is This Skill Important?

Some graphs show information that can help you see patterns of change over time. These patterns are called **trends.** A graph showing the number of people living in the United States since 1800 would show that the number has gone up steadily over the years. The trend, then, has been for the population of the United States to increase.

Graphs can show trends that go upward, go downward, or hold steady. Some graphs show trends that change. For example, a graph could show a downward trend for a time and then an upward trend.

Understand the Process

Follow the numbered steps to identify the trends shown by the two graphs on this page. The first is a line graph that shows the amount of cotton produced in the United States from 1800 to 1860. The second is a bar graph that shows

the number of people enslaved in the United States from 1800 to 1860.

1. Look at the line graph. About how much cotton was produced in 1800? About how much cotton was produced in 1830? About how much cotton was produced in 1860? You can see that the amount of cotton produced from 1800 to 1860 went up. The trend, then, was for cotton production to go up during this period of time.

2. Look at the bar graph. About how many people were enslaved in 1800? About how many people were enslaved in 1830? About how many people were enslaved in 1860? What trend does the bar graph show?

Think and Apply

Think about the trends shown in these graphs. Write a paragraph that describes what the trends tell you about the connection between cotton production and slavery between 1800 and 1860.

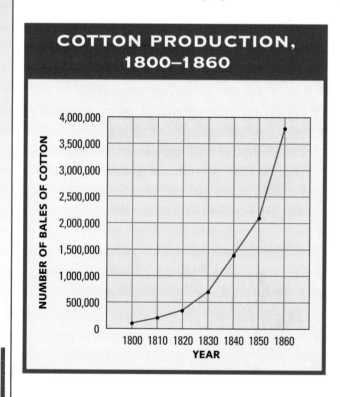

COTTON PRODUCTION, 1800–1860

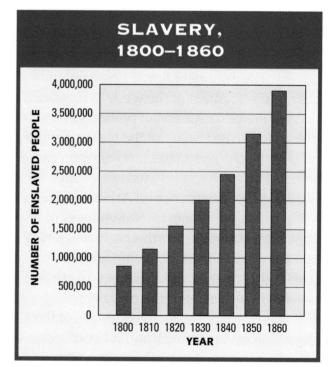

SLAVERY, 1800–1860

AFRICANS IN SLAVERY —and— FREEDOM

Link to Our World

In what ways do people today protest against unfair treatment?

Focus on the Main Idea
As you read, look for ways enslaved people protested against being held in slavery.

Preview Vocabulary
slave code
overseer
spiritual
resist
Underground Railroad

While many Americans argued about slavery, the number of enslaved people grew. In 1800 there were nearly 900,000 slaves. By 1860 there were nearly 4 million. Some Africans—both in the North and in the South—were free. Yet they did not have the rights of full citizenship. Despite the hardships, most Africans found ways to survive. Some also found ways to fight back.

LIFE UNDER SLAVERY

Most Southern states had laws that shaped the day-to-day lives of enslaved people. These laws were called **slave codes**. Under these codes slaves were not allowed to leave their owners' land. They were not allowed to meet in groups or to buy or sell goods. Most were not allowed to learn to read and write. They were treated as property—as objects that could be bought and sold.

Some slave owners hired people called **overseers** to watch the slaves as they worked and to whip them if they fell behind. Slave owners broke up families by selling husbands without their wives, and children without their parents. They punished enslaved people harshly, sometimes with death.

"No day ever dawns for the slave, nor is it looked for," one African of the time wrote. "For the slave it is all night—all night, forever."

To help themselves survive, many enslaved people formed close-knit communities. Families, friends, and neighbors helped one another, giving comfort and support. They

Many slaves had to wear identification badges sewn to their clothing.

Enslaved people were sold, usually one at a time, at auctions. Families were often separated because relatives could be bought by different slave owners.

talked of what they remembered about Africa or what they had heard about it from others. They tried to keep their traditions alive.

Religious beliefs gave many enslaved people the strength they needed to handle the miseries of life under slavery. Some slaves expressed their beliefs by singing spirituals. **Spirituals** (SPIR•ih•chuh•wuhlz) are religious songs based on Bible stories. One spiritual told the deepest feelings of those who were enslaved.

> 66 If I had my way,
> If I had my way,
> If I had my way,
> I'd tear this building down. 99

 **How did people in slave communities help one another?**

FIGHTING BACK

Most slaves did whatever they could to **resist**, or act against, slavery. Some resisted in quiet ways, secretly damaging the plantation.

They broke tools, making the damage look like an accident. They left gates open so that farm animals could escape. They let boats drift away. They hid household goods.

Such actions were dangerous, and slaves had to be very careful to escape punishment. Some acted as if they did not understand what they had been told. They said they were sorry and would try to do better. "Got one mind for the boss to see," one slave song went. "Got another mind for what I know is me."

Other slaves chose a more violent way to resist—they rebelled. One rebellion took place in Southampton County, Virginia, on a hot August night in 1831. A slave named Nat Turner led an attack that killed 57 people, among them Turner's owner and the owner's family. Slave owners trying to end the rebellion killed more than 100 slaves. Turner and the other leaders were caught, put on trial, and hanged.

Despite the dangers, the rebellions went on. On the night of October 16, 1859, a white abolitionist named John Brown and a group of followers seized a government storehouse in Harpers Ferry, in what is now West Virginia. The storehouse was filled with guns. Brown planned to give the guns to slaves so they could fight for their freedom. Like Turner, Brown was caught, put on trial, and hanged.

Such rebellions frightened many white Southerners. As one visitor to the South reported, "I have known times here when not a single planter had a calm night's rest. They never lie down to sleep without . . . loaded pistols at their sides."

In what ways did enslaved people resist slavery?

RUNNING AWAY

Over the years thousands of slaves chose another way to resist slavery. They tried to gain their freedom by running away.

Some slaves ran away alone. Others tried to escape with their families or friends. Some planned their escape carefully, slowly gathering what they would need. Others saw a sudden chance and decided quickly— they ran.

Once away from their owners' land, runaways had to find safe places to hide. Many were helped along the way by other slaves. Some were taken in by Indian peoples. Others hid in forests, swamps, or mountains—sometimes for years.

"Father got beat up so much that after a while he ran away and lived in the woods," one former slave from Virginia remembered. "Mama used to send John, my oldest brother, out to the woods with food for Father. . . . Father wasn't the only one hiding in the woods. There was his cousin, Gabriel, that was hiding and a man named Charlie."

Some runaways stayed in hiding, but others went on with their journey until they reached free land in the Northern states or in Canada or Mexico. They traveled for weeks or months, some guided only by the North Star. Others found helping hands to lead the way—the brave men and women of the Underground Railroad.

Slave owners often sent out posters (above) offering rewards for the return of runaway slaves. This painting by Eastman Johnson (left) shows one family's escape. The painting is called *A Ride for Liberty—The Fugitive Slaves.*

The Underground Railroad was not under the ground, and it was not a real railroad. The **Underground Railroad** was a system of escape routes leading to free land. Most routes led from the South to the Northern states and to Canada. Some led to Mexico and the Caribbean.

Members of the Underground Railroad were called conductors. Working at night, the conductors led runaways from one hiding place to the next along the routes. These hiding places—barns, attics, secret rooms— were called stations. There the runaway slaves could rest and eat, preparing for the next night's journey to the next station on the route.

Harriet Tubman, who had escaped from slavery herself, was one of the best-known conductors of the Underground Railroad. During the 1850s Tubman returned to the South 19 times and guided about 300 people to freedom. She proudly claimed, "I never lost a single passenger."

✓ **How did the Underground Railroad help slaves escape?**

THE UNDERGROUND RAILROAD

0 150 300 Miles
0 150 300 Kilometers
Azimuthal Equal-Area Projection

CANADA

Legend:
- Free state
- Slave state
- → Major routes of the Underground Railroad

MOVEMENT This map of the Underground Railroad shows the major routes leading to free land.
■ To what places did the routes leading north go? To what places did the routes leading south go?

Among those Harriet Tubman (below) led to freedom were her mother and father, her sister, and her two children.

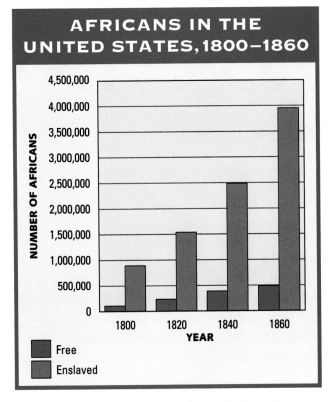

AFRICANS IN THE UNITED STATES, 1800–1860

NUMBER OF AFRICANS

YEAR

■ Free
■ Enslaved

LEARNING FROM GRAPHS This graph shows the numbers of free and enslaved Africans in the United States from 1800 to 1860.
■ What trends does the graph show?

FREE AFRICANS

Not all Africans of the time were enslaved. By 1860 nearly 500,000 free Africans lived in the United States. A few were members of families that had been free since colonial times, or at least since the American Revolution. Some were former slaves who had been freed by their owners. Others had bought their freedom or had become free by running away.

Many free Africans lived in cities, where they had a better chance of finding a job. They worked in many different professions. Some were carpenters, tailors, blacksmiths, and shopkeepers. Others became ministers, doctors, nurses, and teachers.

Some free Africans became quite wealthy. Jehu Jones, for example, owned one of South Carolina's best hotels. James Forten ran a

busy sail factory in Philadelphia, where many ships were built. Thomy Lafon made a fortune from his businesses in New Orleans.

For most Africans, however, life was very hard no matter where they lived. They were unwelcome in many places and often were attacked. State laws in both the North and the South gave them little freedom. Most were not allowed to vote or to meet in groups. They could not attend certain schools or hold certain jobs. Some free Africans were wrongly called runaway slaves. Others were taken and sold into slavery. The danger of losing the little freedom they had was very real.

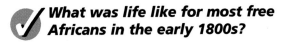 **What was life like for most free Africans in the early 1800s?**

LESSON 2 REVIEW

Check Understanding

1. **Recall the Facts**   What was the Underground Railroad?
2. **Focus on the Main Idea**   In what ways did enslaved people act against slavery?

Think Critically

3. **Personally Speaking**   Why do you think many enslaved people were willing to risk their lives to resist slavery?
4. **Past to Present**   In what ways do people today protest if they are denied freedom?

Show What You Know

Poster Activity   Chains are a symbol of slavery. Think about some symbols of freedom. Look through magazines and newspapers for pictures that express the meaning of freedom. Cut out the pictures, and use them to create a poster that shows the idea of freedom. Add your poster to a class display titled *Freedom*.

FACING A NATIONAL PROBLEM

L ink to Our World

In what ways do people today try to settle disagreements?

Focus on the Main Idea
Read to learn about the ways Northerners and Southerners tried to settle their disagreements during the early 1800s.

Preview Vocabulary
free state
slave state

As time passed, more and more Northerners wanted an end to slavery, while more and more slave owners grew angry and bitter. Americans began to understand that slavery was not just a problem between the people of two regions. It had become a problem for the whole country.

NEW COMPROMISES

One leader who worked hard to help settle the differences dividing the country was Henry Clay of Kentucky. As a member of Congress, Clay often found himself in the middle of heated arguments about slavery.

The worst arguments broke out over the spread of slavery to the West. Each time groups of settlers asked to join the Union as a new state, the same question arose. Would the new state be a free state or a slave state? A **free state** did not allow slavery. A **slave state** did. For a time there were as many free states as slave states. This kept a balance between the North and the South. Then, in 1819, settlers in the Missouri Territory, a part of the Louisiana Purchase, asked to join the Union as a slave state. If this happened, slave states would outnumber free states.

The Missouri question became a heated debate that dragged on for months. Henry Clay worked day and night to help solve the problem. Clay himself owned slaves. But he did not want to see the question of slavery tear the country apart. Finally, in 1820, he persuaded Congress to agree to a compromise—the Missouri Compromise.

Because of his work to help settle the differences between the North and the South, Henry Clay became known as the Great Compromiser.

THE MISSOURI COMPROMISE, 1820

CANADA

OREGON COUNTRY

UNORGANIZED TERRITORY

MICHIGAN TERRITORY

MEXICO

ILLINOIS

MISSOURI

ARKANSAS TERRITORY

MAINE
VT
NH
NEW YORK
MA
CT
RI
PENNSYLVANIA
NJ
INDIANA OHIO
MD DE
VIRGINIA
KENTUCKY
NORTH CAROLINA
TENNESSEE
SOUTH CAROLINA
ALABAMA GEORGIA
MISSISSIPPI
LOUISIANA
FLORIDA TERRITORY

ATLANTIC OCEAN

PACIFIC OCEAN

Gulf of Mexico

0   250   500 Miles
0   250   500 Kilometers
Albers Equal-Area Projection

Legend:
- Free state
- Free territory
- Admitted as a free state
- Missouri Compromise line
- Slave state
- Slave territory
- Admitted as a slave state

REGIONS The Missouri Compromise line divided lands that could join the Union as free states from lands that could join as slave states.
■ Which two states were admitted to the Union as part of the compromise? Were they admitted as free states or as slave states?

Under this plan Missouri would be allowed to join the Union as a slave state. Maine would join as a free state. This would keep the balance between free states and slave states. Then an imaginary line would be drawn through the rest of the lands gained in the Louisiana Purchase. Slavery would be allowed south of the line. Places north of the line would be free.

The Missouri Compromise kept the peace for nearly 30 years. During this time six new states joined the Union, but the number of free states and slave states remained equal.

Then, in 1848, the United States gained new lands after winning the war with Mexico. Settlers in California, a part of these new lands, soon asked to join the Union as a free state.

Henry Clay once again found himself in the middle of an argument in Congress over slavery. Once again he worked toward a compromise. This plan became known as the Compromise of 1850.

Under this compromise California joined the Union as a free state. The rest of the lands won from Mexico were divided into two territories—New Mexico and Utah. The people there would decide for their territory whether or not to allow slavery.

The Compromise of 1850 also had a new law dealing with runaway slaves. Under the Fugitive Slave Law, anyone caught helping slaves to escape would be punished. People who found runaway slaves—even runaways who had reached the North—had to return them to the South.

Henry Clay, who became known as the Great Compromiser, died in 1852. He never gave up hope that the country would find a peaceful way to settle its differences. On a marker by his grave in Lexington, Kentucky, are the words *I know no North—no South—no East—no West.*

 What two compromises on the spread of slavery did Congress reach?

HOPES FOR PEACE FADE

Even with the compromises, bad feelings grew between the North and the South. In 1854 harsh words turned to violence.

The problem began when Congress passed a new law called the Kansas-Nebraska Act. This law changed the rules of the Missouri Compromise. Under the compromise, slavery would not have been allowed in the territories of Kansas and Nebraska. Under the Kansas-Nebraska Act, people living in those lands were now given the chance to decide for themselves whether to allow slavery. They would decide by voting.

Kansas quickly became the center of attention. People for and against slavery rushed into the territory, hoping to help decide the vote. It was not long before fighting broke out between the two sides. More than 200 people were killed in what came to be known as Bleeding Kansas.

While fighting went on in Kansas, those against slavery suffered another defeat. In 1857 the Supreme Court decided the case of an enslaved African named Dred Scott. Scott had asked the Court for his freedom. The Court said no.

Scott argued that he should be free because he had once lived on free land. Scott's owner had often moved from place to place. When he moved, Scott went with him. For a time they lived in Illinois, a free state. Then they lived in the Wisconsin Territory, a free territory under the Missouri Compromise.

After Scott's owner died, Scott took his case to court. The case moved from judge to judge until it landed in the Supreme Court.

In 1857 the Supreme Court decided that Dred Scott (left) should not be given his freedom. Chief Justice Roger Taney (right) spoke for the Court.

There Scott lost his fight for freedom. Chief Justice Roger B. Taney (TAW•nee) said that Scott had "none of the rights and privileges" of American citizens. He was a slave, Taney said. Living on free land did not change that.

Taney had more to say. He declared that Congress had no right to outlaw slavery in the Wisconsin Territory to begin with. The Constitution protects people's right to own property. Slaves, he said, were property. The Missouri Compromise was keeping people in some places from owning property. This, he said, went against the Constitution.

Many people had hoped that the Dred Scott decision would settle the battle over slavery once and for all. Instead, it made the problem worse.

✓ **Why did the Supreme Court deny freedom to Dred Scott?**

ABRAHAM LINCOLN WORKS FOR CHANGE

The Kansas-Nebraska Act and the Dred Scott decision caused violence and anger that caught the attention of Americans across the country. Soon new leaders began to speak out. One of these leaders was Abraham Lincoln.

Abraham Lincoln had grown up on the frontier in Kentucky and Indiana. Like other pioneers, he had had a rough, hard life. He worked so many hours on the family farm that he often could not go to school. But he borrowed books and read all he could.

When Lincoln was a young man, he moved with his family to Illinois. There he held several jobs before serving in the state legislature. He studied law, and in time he became a lawyer. In the late 1840s he served a term in Congress. During these years the matter of the spread of slavery to the West became an important question.

Lincoln was against the spread of slavery. He did not think the government had the right to end slavery everywhere in the country. But he hoped that if slavery were not allowed to spread, it would one day die out.

Lincoln joined a new political party formed to fight the spread of slavery. This party was called the Republican party. He even thought about running again for government office. The Kansas-Nebraska Act and the Dred Scott decision helped him make up his mind. In 1858 Lincoln entered a race for the United States Senate. The person he ran against was Stephen A. Douglas. Douglas had written the Kansas-Nebraska Act.

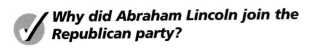 **Why did Abraham Lincoln join the Republican party?**

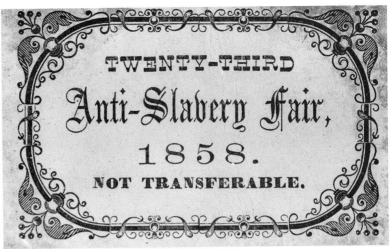

This ticket was to a fair held in 1858 where money was raised to fight slavery.

THE LINCOLN–DOUGLAS DEBATES

Few people could have been more different from each other than Lincoln and Douglas. Abraham Lincoln was a tall, thin man from the frontier. His thick, black hair looked uncombed. He wore plain, dark clothes that were a bit rumpled. He was not well known around the country. In fact, few people outside of Illinois had heard of him.

Stephen Douglas was heavy and a full foot shorter than Lincoln. He was well educated and wore fine clothes—a ruffled shirt, tailored suit, and polished boots. He was already serving in the Senate, and Americans across the country knew of him. People called him the Little Giant.

In one way, though, Lincoln and Douglas were very much alike. They were both powerful public speakers. In the summer of 1858, the two men traveled around Illinois and debated questions that were important to voters. Huge crowds turned out to listen. Everyone wanted to hear Lincoln and Douglas debate about whether slavery should be allowed in the West.

Stephen Douglas argued that each new state should decide the slavery question for

Stephen Douglas and Abraham Lincoln held seven debates in 1858. This painting shows Lincoln (standing) and Douglas (to Lincoln's right) debating in Charleston, Illinois.

itself. That was what the country's founders had allowed, he said, and that was what the new Kansas-Nebraska Act allowed.

Abraham Lincoln disagreed. He said that "the framers of the Constitution intended and expected" slavery to end. The problem, Lincoln pointed out, was more than a question of what each state wanted. It was a question of right and wrong. Slavery should not spread to the West, he said, because slavery was wrong.

"That is the real issue," Lincoln said. "That is the issue that will continue in this country when these poor tongues of Judge Douglas and myself shall be silent. It is the eternal struggle between these two principles—right and wrong—throughout the world."

Stephen Douglas won the race for the Senate. But people around the country now knew who Abraham Lincoln was.

 How did Lincoln's views differ from those of Douglas?

LESSON 3 REVIEW

Check Understanding

1. **Recall the Facts**   What events led Abraham Lincoln to speak out against slavery?
2. **Focus on the Main Idea**   In what ways did people try to settle the disagreements between the North and the South during the early 1800s?

Think Critically

3. **Think More About It**   How was the Missouri Compromise changed by the Kansas-Nebraska Act and the Dred Scott decision?

4. **Past to Present**   Do you think it is still important for leaders today to hold debates before elections? Explain your answer.

Show What You Know

 Simulation Activity   Imagine that you have been asked to interview Henry Clay, Dred Scott, Stephen Douglas, or Abraham Lincoln. Write the questions you would ask and the answers the person might give. Present your interview to the class.

A TIME FOR HARD DECISIONS

Link to Our World

When must people today make difficult decisions in their lives?

Focus on the Main Idea
Read to learn about the difficult decisions Americans had to make in 1860 and 1861.

Preview Vocabulary
Confederacy

In 1860 Americans prepared to choose a new President. They listened to speeches. They read newspapers. They watched parades. They also worried. Anger and bitterness were driving the North and the South further apart than ever. Could a new President hold the country together?

THE ELECTION OF 1860

The question of the spread of slavery to the West seemed to be all that people talked about during the election of 1860. Stephen Douglas ran as a member of the Democratic party. He argued that western settlers should decide for themselves whether to allow slavery. However, many Democrats in the South backed another leader—John Breckinridge of Kentucky. Breckinridge thought that the government should allow slavery everywhere in the West.

Abraham Lincoln ran as a member of the Republican party. He spoke out strongly against the spread of slavery. He promised not to stop slavery in the South, where it was already practiced. But he said that he hoped it would one day end there, too.

Many white Southerners worried about what would happen if Lincoln became President. They thought that the problem was far greater than the question of slavery. They believed that their whole way of life was being attacked. Some said that their states would secede from the Union if Lincoln was elected.

A supporter of Stephen Douglas wore this campaign button during the election of 1860. How do people today show their support for leaders running for office?

STEPHEN A. DOUGLAS.

On election day, November 6, 1860, Lincoln won the Presidency. Southern leaders did not wait long before carrying out their threat. On December 20, South Carolina's leaders declared that "the United States of America is hereby dissolved." With these words the state seceded from the Union.

Six other states—Mississippi, Florida, Alabama, Georgia, Louisiana, and Texas—soon followed South Carolina's example.

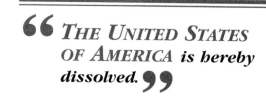

> ❝ **THE UNITED STATES OF AMERICA** *is hereby dissolved.* ❞
>
> South Carolina leaders, 1860

Together these seven states formed a new country. They called the new country the Confederate States of America, or the **Confederacy** (kuhn•FEH•duh•ruh•see). They elected a Mississippi senator, Jefferson Davis, as president. The United States was now split in two.

✓ **What did seven Southern states decide to do after Lincoln was elected President?**

FORT SUMTER

Lincoln had little time to celebrate winning the election. He wanted to save the Union—to keep the country together. Yet seven states had said that they were no longer part of the Union. What would he do about those states?

Some people told Lincoln to let the Southern states go. Others said that he should give in on the slavery question and hope that the Southern states would return. Still others felt that Lincoln should use the army to end the revolt.

Lincoln thought a great deal about his choices. He hoped to prevent a war. "We are not enemies, but friends," Lincoln told Southerners after taking the oath of office as President on March 4, 1861. "We must not be enemies." The very next day, however, Lincoln received an important message. When he read it, he knew that time was running out. The message was from Major Robert Anderson. Anderson was the commander of Fort Sumter.

When the Southern states had seceded, they had taken over post offices, forts, and other federal government property. Fort Sumter, which was located on an island off the coast of South Carolina, near Charleston,

This poster (above) urged people to vote for Lincoln and his running mate, Hannibal Hamlin. The gold ax (right) was a campaign pin. The ax reminded people of Lincoln's early years splitting logs on the frontier. The "WIDE AWAKE" on the handle meant that Lincoln's supporters were "wide awake" to dangers to the Union.

was one of the few forts in the South that remained in Union hands. The message from Major Anderson said that supplies at the fort were almost gone. If new supplies were not sent soon, Anderson would have to surrender the fort to the Confederacy.

Lincoln knew that he had an important decision to make. His goal was to keep Fort Sumter under Union control. But several problems stood in the way. The most important problem was that the fort was running out of supplies.

Lincoln thought carefully about his choices. Each had its own possible consequence. He could send supplies to the fort. If he did, the Southerners might attack. He could send troops to the fort. If he did, the Southerners would surely attack. He could choose to do nothing at all. By doing nothing, he would really be giving the fort to the

Confederacy because Major Anderson would have to surrender.

Finally, Lincoln made the choice he thought was the best. He said that he would send supply ships to the fort. Then he waited to see what would happen.

Where?

Fort Sumter

Fort Sumter was one of several forts built to protect American coastlines following the War of 1812. Building the fort was a long, difficult job. Workers first had to build the island on which the fort would stand. Then they built the fort itself, with walls 5 feet (1.5 m) thick and nearly 50 feet (15.2 m) high. Today Fort Sumter is part of the national park system.

The Confederate flag flew over Fort Sumter after the Union surrender.

407

THE UNION BREAKS APART

November 1860
Lincoln is elected President

December 1860
South Carolina secedes

January 1861
Mississippi, Florida, Alabama, Georgia, and Louisiana secede

February 1861
Texas secedes

March 1861
Lincoln is inaugurated President

April 1861
Southern troops attack Fort Sumter

Virginia secedes

May 1861
Arkansas, Tennessee, and North Carolina secede

LEARNING FROM TIME LINES This time line shows when each of 11 Southern states seceded from the Union.
■ Which state was the first to secede from the Union? Which states were the last to secede?

Now Confederate president Jefferson Davis had to make a decision. His goal was to take control of Fort Sumter for the Confederacy. His problem was that Union troops held the fort. Lincoln was now sending supplies to help those troops.

Like Lincoln, Davis thought carefully about his choices and their possible consequences. Then he made what he thought was the best choice, even though he knew that one possible result was war. Davis decided to attack the fort before the supply ships arrived. On April 12, 1861, Confederate soldiers fired on Fort Sumter. The next day Major Anderson ran out of ammunition and had to give up.

Davis had met his goal. Lincoln had not. Lincoln quickly called for Americans to join an army to stop the rebellion. Fearing that Northern armies would march into the South, the states of Virginia, Arkansas, Tennessee, and North Carolina joined the seven already in the Confederacy. Now the country was even more divided. The Civil War had begun.

✓ **What did Davis decide to do when Lincoln said he would send supplies to Fort Sumter?**

LESSON 4 REVIEW

Check Understanding

1. **Recall the Facts** What event led South Carolina's leaders to secede from the Union?
2. **Focus on the Main Idea** What difficult decisions did Americans make in 1860 and 1861?

Think Critically

3. **Think More About It** Why was Fort Sumter important to both Abraham Lincoln and Jefferson Davis?
4. **Personally Speaking** Do you think Lincoln made the right decision when he decided to send supplies to Fort Sumter? Explain your answer.

Show What You Know

Writing Activity The attack on Fort Sumter marked the beginning of the Civil War. Write two headlines that could have appeared in newspapers in the days following the attack. The first should be a headline for a newspaper in the North. The second should be a headline for a newspaper in the South. Present the headlines to your classmates.

Make a Thoughtful Decision

Why Is This Skill Important?

Did you have to make a decision today? Did you have to decide whether to go somewhere with your friends? Did you have to decide how to settle a disagreement with someone?

You make many decisions every day. Some decisions are easy. Other decisions are more difficult. The difficult ones may require more thought because your choices may have lasting consequences.

Remember What You Have Read

You have read about the difficult decisions Abraham Lincoln and Jefferson Davis had to make as supplies ran out at Fort Sumter in South Carolina. The ways in which these leaders came to their decisions show how a thoughtful decision can be made. Think again about what happened.

1. What goal did each leader have?
2. What steps did each leader follow in making a decision?
3. What choice did each leader make?
4. What were the consequences of Lincoln's choice? of Davis's choice?

Understand the Process

You can use similar steps to help make a thoughtful decision.

- Identify your goal.
- Think about problems that may keep you from reaching your goal.
- Identify actions you could take to reach your goal.
- Think about the possible consequences of each action.
- List your choices for action. Begin with those that might have the best results, and end with those that might have the worst results.
- Make the choice that seems best.
- Put your choice into action.
- Think about whether your choice helped you reach your goal.

Think and Apply

Think about a decision you made at school. What steps did you follow? What choice did you make? What were the consequences? Do you think you made a thoughtful decision? Explain.

BUILDING CITIZENSHIP

Abraham Lincoln

Jefferson Davis

UNION
OR
SECESSION?

The Union flag as it looked in 1861

An early Confederate flag

At the news of Abraham Lincoln's election as President, Americans in both the North and the South got ready for what some called the Revolution of 1860. Some hoped that the South would not carry out its threat to secede. Lincoln himself said, "The people of the South have too much sense to attempt the ruin of the government." But he and others did not understand how badly many Southerners wanted their independence. As one Southerner put it, "You might as well attempt to control a tornado as to attempt to stop them."

Not all Southerners agreed about seceding. Some were against it. Others thought that the South should first give Lincoln a chance. They would be willing to secede only if nothing else worked. Still others wanted to secede right away. "The time for compromise," Jefferson Davis said, "has now passed."

Two Southerners who made their feelings clear were Edmund Ruffin of Virginia and Sam Houston, the governor of Texas. The words of the two men, quoted in 1861, show how they felt about secession, or seceding from the Union.

Edmund Ruffin

❝ I will be out of Virginia before Lincoln's inauguration, and so . . . avoid being, as a Virginian, under his government even for an hour. I, at least, will become a citizen of the seceded Confederate States, and will not again reside in my native state, nor enter it except to make visits to my children, until Virginia shall also secede. . . . This result . . . cannot be delayed long.
     The bloodshed of South Carolinians defending their soil and their rights, or maintaining the possession of their harbor . . . will stir doubly fast the sluggish blood of the more backward Southern States into secession. **❞**

Sam Houston

❝ Let me tell you what is coming. . . . Your fathers and husbands, your sons and brothers, will be herded at the point of the bayonet. . . . You may, after the sacrifice of countless millions of treasure and hundreds of thousands of lives, as a bare possibility, win Southern independence. . . . But I doubt it. I tell you that, while I believe with you in the doctrine of States' Rights, the North is determined to preserve this Union. They are not a fiery, impulsive people as you are, for they live in colder climates. But when they begin to move in a given direction . . . they move with the steady momentum and perseverance of a mighty avalanche. **❞**

COMPARE
VIEWPOINTS

1. What viewpoint about seceding did Ruffin hold? How do you know?

2. What viewpoint about seceding did Houston hold? How do you know?

3. What other viewpoints might Southerners have held on the matter of secession? Governor Thomas H. Hicks of Maryland said, "The only safety of Maryland lies in preserving a neutral position between our brethren of the North and of the South." What view did the governor hold?

THINK
–AND–
APPLY

You have read that three Southerners—Ruffin, Houston, and Hicks—each had a different view about secession. At what other times in history have people from the same region held different views about something?

BUILDING CITIZENSHIP

CONNECT MAIN IDEAS

Use this organizer to show that you understand how the chapter's main ideas are connected. First copy the organizer onto a separate sheet of paper. Then complete it by writing three details to support each main idea.

Differences Divide North and South
People in the North and the South disagreed during the mid-1800s.

1. _____
2. _____
3. _____

Africans in Slavery and Freedom
Enslaved people protested against being held in slavery.

1. _____
2. _____
3. _____

Background to the Conflict

Facing a National Problem
Northerners and Southerners tried to settle disagreements during the 1800s.

1. _____
2. _____
3. _____

A Time for Hard Decisions
Americans had to make important decisions in 1860 and 1861.

1. _____
2. _____
3. _____

WRITE MORE ABOUT IT

1. **Write a Persuasive Letter** Imagine that you are an abolitionist trying to get new stations for the Underground Railroad. Write a letter in which you try to persuade a friend to allow his or her home to become a station. Describe the dangers your friend might face.

2. **Write a Report** Write a short report about what Henry Clay did to keep the country from being torn apart over the question of slavery.

3. **Write Your Opinion** Tell whether you think agreeing to a compromise is always a good way to settle differences. Explain.

4. **Summarize Viewpoints** Write a paragraph that summarizes Stephen Douglas's point of view about how the slavery question should be settled. Then write another paragraph that summarizes Abraham Lincoln's point of view on the same issue.

USE VOCABULARY

For each pair of terms, write a sentence or two that explain how the terms are related.

1. slave code, overseer

2. resist, spiritual

3. free state, slave state

CHECK UNDERSTANDING

1. How was life in the North changing in the mid-1800s?

2. Why did Southern planters feel they needed enslaved workers?

3. How did the invention of the cotton gin affect cotton production?

4. What kinds of laws affected the everyday lives of slaves?

5. Why was the North Star important to some runaway slaves?

6. What role did religion play in the lives of many enslaved people?

7. How did the settlement of the West add to the argument over slavery?

8. How did the Compromise of 1850 help satisfy the demands of slaveholders?

9. Why did the Kansas-Nebraska Act lead to fighting?

10. What major decisions led to the start of the Civil War?

THINK CRITICALLY

1. **Past to Present**   How do some people today protest against the things they feel are unfair? How are those ways similar to the ones used by enslaved people before the Civil War? How are they different?

2. **Personally Speaking**   What kind of person do you think a conductor on the Underground Railroad needed to be?

3. **Cause and Effect**   Why did compromises fail to settle disagreements over the issue of slavery?

4. **Explore Viewpoints**   Why did Chief Justice Roger Taney believe that Dred Scott should not be given his freedom?

5. **Think More About It**   How did the Lincoln-Douglas debates affect Lincoln's political career?

APPLY SKILLS

How to Use Graphs to Identify Trends
Look in newspapers or magazines for a bar graph or a line graph that shows a trend. Cut out the graph and tape it to a sheet of paper. Below the graph, identify the trend shown. How does the trend change over time?

How to Make a Thoughtful Decision
Imagine that a friend has asked you to allow your home to be used as a station on the Underground Railroad. What steps might you follow to come to a decision?

READ MORE ABOUT IT

Many Thousand Gone: African Americans from Slavery to Freedom by Virginia Hamilton. Knopf. This nonfiction book tells the history of slavery through the stories of those who experienced it.

A Nation Torn: The Story of How the Civil War Began by Delia Ray. Lodestar. The author uses primary source materials to help explore the events leading to the Civil War.

Who Comes with Cannons? by Patricia Beatty. Morrow. Twelve-year-old Truth becomes involved with the Underground Railroad when she goes to live with her uncle's family in North Carolina.

CHAPTER 14

CIVIL WAR and RECONSTRUCTION

> 66 I put in many hours of weary work and soon thought myself quite a soldier. . . . I was elected First Sergeant, much to my surprise. Just what a First Sergeant's duties might be, I had no idea. 99
>
> Elisha Rhodes,
> Pawtucket, Rhode Island, 1861

Confederate Private Edwin Jennison, killed at the Seven Days' Battles in 1862

The FIGHTING BEGINS

Link to Our World

Why is it sometimes difficult to choose sides in a disagreement?

Focus on the Main Idea
As you read, think about why it was difficult for many Americans to choose sides during the Civil War.

Preview Vocabulary
border state
Emancipation Proclamation

When Confederate soldiers fired on Fort Sumter, hopes for peace between the North and the South ended. Now Americans had to make some hard decisions about going to war.

TAKING SIDES

In the weeks following the attack on Fort Sumter, many people thought that the war would be short and easy. For most, the choice of which side to support was clear.

Most Northerners supported the Union. They were willing to go to war to save their flag and all that it stood for. "If it is necessary that I should fall on the battlefield for my country," wrote a soldier from New England, "I am ready. . . . I am willing—perfectly willing—to lay down all my joys in this life, to help maintain this government."

Most white Southerners supported the Confederacy. They were willing to go to war to win their independence. Whether they owned slaves or not, many felt that the North was trying to change the South. They thought that the government was taking away their rights. The only way to get those rights back, they believed, was to leave the Union.

The need to defend their land also led many Southerners to join the fight. One young soldier, caught early in the war by Union troops, told his captors, "I'm fighting because you're down here."

For some Americans, however, the choice between the Union and the Confederacy was not an easy one. People in Missouri, Kentucky, Maryland, and Delaware were torn between the two sides. These **border states** were between the North and the South. Although they allowed slavery, they had remained a part of the Union. When the time came for people in the border states to choose sides, some fought for the North. Others fought for the South.

Taking sides was also hard for people living in some parts of the South. In the mountains of eastern Tennessee and northern Alabama, there was very little slavery. Many people there sided with the North. In western Virginia, feelings for the Union were so strong that the people voted to break away from Virginia and form a new state. West Virginia joined the Union in 1863.

Taking sides was also hard for many in the Indian nations. By the time of the war, the Cherokee, Creek, Seminole, Choctaw, and Chickasaw peoples had been driven from their lands to the Indian Territory, which is today Oklahoma. When it came time to choose sides, most people in these five tribes had little reason to like either the North or the South. In the end the Choctaws and the Chickasaws fought for the South. The Creeks, Seminoles, and Cherokees were divided between the Union and the Confederacy.

The decisions people had to make in these early days of the war divided families and friends. When war finally came, four of Henry Clay's grandsons decided to join the Confederacy. Three others fought for the Union. Even President Lincoln's own family

In some of the early battles, soldiers wore the clothes they had brought from home. Later, Northern soldiers would wear blue uniforms (left). Southerners would wear gray (below).

was divided. Mary Todd Lincoln, his wife, had been born in Kentucky. Four of her brothers fought for the South.

✓ **Why was taking sides hard for people in the border states?**

LEE JOINS THE CONFEDERACY

On April 19, 1861—a week after the attack on Fort Sumter—Robert E. Lee paced his bedroom floor. It was nearly midnight. Lee was a United States Army colonel. The day before, President Lincoln had asked him to take command of a Union army. Just hours later Lee had learned that his home state of Virginia had seceded.

Lee loved his country. He was a graduate of the United States Military Academy at West Point, New York. He had fought in the war with Mexico and had served his country for 32 years. Yet Lee also loved Virginia. Could he lead an army that would fight his family and neighbors?

Robert E. Lee led Confederate troops throughout the war.

THE UNION AND THE CONFEDERACY

Union state
Border state
Confederate state
Territory

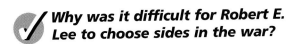 **REGIONS** This map shows the division of the nation at the start of the Civil War.
■ Which states were the border states?

The next morning Lee told Mary, his wife, what he had decided. He turned down Lincoln's offer and quit the Union army. A few days later he took command of Virginia's troops. Lee knew he would be fighting old friends who were fighting for the Union. Even so, he decided to serve Virginia. "I cannot raise my hand against my birthplace, my home, my children," he said.

✓ **Why was it difficult for Robert E. Lee to choose sides in the war?**

BATTLE PLANS

Three months after the attack on Fort Sumter, two armies of eager young men prepared for the first major battle of the war. The battle took place at Bull Run, a stream near the town of Manassas Junction, Virginia.

After hours of fighting, the South won the battle. The defeat shocked the Union. Northerners had entered the war feeling very strong. The North had nearly twice as many people as the South. It had more factories to make weapons and supplies. It had more railroads to get those supplies to the troops.

But the South had proved more powerful than most Northerners had expected. Southerners fighting to defend their own land had a very strong will to win. Stories were already being told about the bravery of officers such as Stonewall Jackson.

Lincoln quickly began to look for new officers of his own. He called for more soldiers. He also called for new battle plans.

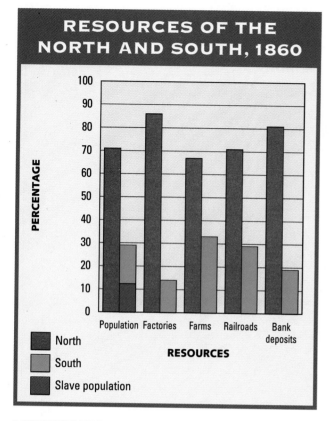

RESOURCES OF THE NORTH AND SOUTH, 1860

PERCENTAGE

RESOURCES

- North
- South
- Slave population

LEARNING FROM GRAPHS This graph compares the resources of the North and the South at the beginning of the Civil War.

■ Based on this graph, which side had greater resources?

An early Northern plan to win the war had to do with trade. The South depended on trade with the North and with other countries to buy goods such as cloth, shoes, and guns. The North hoped to cut off trade by setting up a blockade. Northern warships would stop trading ships from leaving or entering Southern ports. Without trade, the South would slowly become weaker.

Not everyone in the North liked the idea of a blockade. Some made fun of it, calling it the Anaconda (a•nuh•KAHN•duh) Plan. An anaconda is a large snake that squeezes its prey to death. But this way of killing takes time. Many Northerners wanted quicker action. They said the government should send the army to enter the South by force—to invade. "On to Richmond!" they cried. Richmond, Virginia, was the Confederate capital.

At first the most important fighting plan of the Confederate leaders was simply to protect their lands. Some Southerners compared their situation with the way things were for George Washington and the Patriots during the Revolutionary War. Southerners hoped to defend their homes against invaders and slowly wear down their enemy, just as the Patriots had worn down the British.

But many Southerners, just like many Northerners, were impatient. Cries of "On to Washington!" were soon answered with plans to invade the North.

Southerners also hoped that other countries would help them win the war. Britain and France depended on cotton to keep their textile mills running. Many thought that these countries would help the South as soon as their supplies of cotton ran low.

In both the North and the South, only men were allowed to join the army. Women, however, found many ways to help. They took over factory, business, and farm jobs that men left behind. They sent food to the troops, made bandages, and collected supplies. Many women, such as Clara Barton and Sally Tompkins, worked as nurses. A few served as spies, and some even dressed as men, joined the army, and fought in battles.

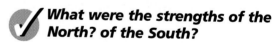

What were the strengths of the North? of the South?

THE WAR AND SLAVERY

As the fighting dragged on into 1862, Northern plans seemed to be working. The blockade brought trade to a halt, and supplies ran very low in the South. Plantations and shops were destroyed.

Even so, the North had not won yet. Thousands of Union soldiers were dying in battle. President Lincoln knew he had to find a way to push the North to victory.

To Lincoln, the purpose of the war was to keep the country together—to save the

Who?

Clara Barton
1821–1912

"While our soldiers stand and fight, I can stand and feed and nurse them." Clara Barton followed the fighting from battle to battle, caring for sick and wounded Union soldiers. Barton had always tried to help people in need. She taught school for a time and then worked as a government clerk. When the Civil War broke out, she wanted to help. Her work is still carried on by the American Red Cross. Barton founded the American branch of this world organization in 1881.

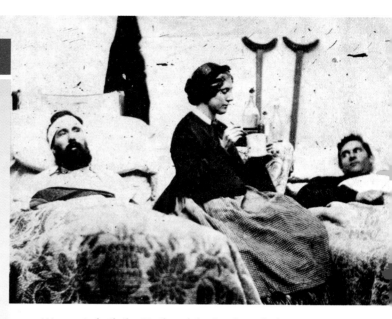

Women in both the North and the South worked as nurses on the battlefields and in hospitals. This nurse is helping wounded soldiers at a hospital in Nashville, Tennessee.

Union. Yet he knew that slavery was the issue that had divided the country. He realized that writing an order to free the slaves would greatly help the North. The loss of millions of enslaved workers would be a blow to the South. Freeing the slaves would also help in another way. It would turn the British, who needed cotton but were against slavery, away from the South.

Lincoln held back on giving an order freeing the slaves—an **Emancipation Proclamation**. He feared that such a step might turn people in the border states, as well as some states in the North, against the Union. Lincoln's waiting made the abolitionists angry. William Lloyd Garrison wrote that Lincoln was "nothing better than a wet rag."

As the war went on, Lincoln thought more and more about the question of slavery. Had the time come to write an Emancipation Proclamation? What would be the consequences of such a decision?

✓ Why did Lincoln think that an Emancipation Proclamation would help the North?

LESSON 1 REVIEW

Check Understanding

1. **Recall the Facts**   What were the battle plans of the North and the South?
2. **Focus on the Main Idea**   Why was it difficult for many Americans to choose sides during the Civil War?

Think Critically

3. **Explore Viewpoints**   Why might a person in a border state have joined the Union army or the Confederate army?
4. **Past to Present**   During the war many people told President Lincoln how they felt about slavery. How do government leaders learn about people's opinions today?

Show What You Know

Art Activity   The Civil War divided many families and friends. Make a drawing that shows how some people in the border states must have felt as family members and friends joined different sides. Use your drawing to tell about the hard decisions people had to make during the Civil War.

LESSON 2

LEARN
with
LITERATURE

Focus on the
Emancipation
Proclamation

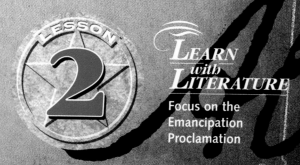

THE

SIGNATURE THAT CHANGED AMERICA

by

HAROLD HOLZER

In 1862 Abraham Lincoln faced one of his hardest decisions as President. He wanted to save the Union, but the fighting seemed to go on and on between Union and Confederate troops. Lincoln knew that an order to free the slaves could help the North. Abolitionists wanted him to sign such an order. But Lincoln also knew that an Emancipation Proclamation would make some people in both the North and the South angry.

Read now about the days when Lincoln made a decision about slavery and took action. As you read, think about why it is important for leaders to consider many points of view before making a decision.

It was January 1, 1863. The Civil War was still raging, but in Washington, D.C., this was a day of celebration. At the White House, President and Mrs. Abraham Lincoln welcomed the new year by hosting a party. For hours they greeted hundreds of visitors, just as Presidents and First Ladies had done for years.

But this was no ordinary New Year's Day at the White House. Today history would be made.

In mid-afternoon the President quietly left the party and walked upstairs to his office on the second floor. Waiting for him there were Secretary of State William H. Seward and members of Lincoln's staff. On a large table in the center of the room sat an official-looking document, written out in beautiful hand-writing by a professional "engrosser." Lincoln sat down at the table, the document spread out before him. The moment was at hand. Now, at last, the President would sign the Emancipation Proclamation.

Abraham Lincoln took pen in hand, dipped it in ink, and then, unexpectedly, paused and put the pen down. To his surprise—and to everyone else's—Lincoln's hand was trembling.

Abolitionists had long called for an end to slavery.

It was not, Lincoln later said, "because of any uncertainty or hesitation on my part." As he put it, "I never in my life felt more certain that I am doing right than I do in signing this paper."

But greeting so many guests had taken a toll. "I have been shaking hands since 9 o'clock this morning, and my hand is almost paralyzed," Lincoln explained. "If my name ever goes into history it will be for this act, and my whole soul is in it. If my hand trembles when I sign the proclamation, all who examine the document hereafter will say, 'He hesitated.'"

After a few moments Lincoln again took pen in hand. The room was quiet except for the muffled sounds of laughter and music drifting upstairs from the party below. Slowly but firmly he wrote "Abraham Lincoln" at the bottom of the document that declared all slaves in the Confederacy "forever free."

With that, Lincoln glanced at his signature, looked up, smiled, and modestly said, "That will do."

What Lincoln's proclamation did—and did not do—has been debated ever since. Some argue that the Emancipation Proclamation did little. After all, it ordered slaves freed only in the states of the Confederacy—the states where Lincoln had no authority. But in the words of one contemporary, the document struck like a second Declaration of Independence. In truth, nothing so revolutionary had happened since the Revolutionary War itself. Perhaps that is why Lincoln worried so long before finally doing what some thought he should have done the moment he became President.

Lincoln had been against slavery all his life. Seeing slaves in chains for the first time in New Orleans, he vowed: "If I ever get a chance to hit this thing, I'll hit it hard." As a young legislator in Illinois, he had been one of the few lawmakers to sign a resolution against slavery. Years later he spoke angrily against the idea that slavery should be allowed to spread to the western territories.

True, Lincoln did not then believe in equality for Africans living in the United States. He did not yet think they should be permitted to vote or sit on juries. But he differed with most citizens of the day by declaring, "In the right to eat the bread which his own hands earn," a black man "is my equal and . . . the equal of every living man."

When Lincoln was elected President in 1860, he promised to do nothing to interfere with slavery in the slave states. He still believed that slavery was wrong, but he felt that personal belief did not give him the right to act. After a year of war, however, Lincoln decided that the only way to put the Union back together was to fight not only against

Confederate armies but also against slavery itself. "We must free the slaves," he confided, "or ourselves be subdued."

Then why did he not order slaves freed immediately? Lincoln believed that the country was simply not ready for it. "It is my conviction," he said, "that had the proclamation been issued even six months earlier than it was, public sentiment would not have sustained it." The President worried that if he acted against slavery too soon, he would lose support in the important border states, which he wanted so much to keep in the Union. Lincoln could not afford to lose the slave state of Maryland, for example. If Maryland seceded, then Washington, D.C., would become a capital city inside an enemy country! Lincoln worried, too, that Northern voters might turn against Republicans and elect a new Congress unwilling to continue the war. So he waited.

Not until July 1862 did Lincoln finally decide that he could safely act. "Things had gone on from bad to worse," he said, "until I felt that we had reached the end of our rope . . . that we had about played our last card and must change our tactics, or lose the game."

On July 22, a blisteringly hot summer day, Lincoln called a meeting of the Cabinet and told the members he had an important decision to announce. He warned them that he would listen to no arguments. He had already made up his mind. Then he unfolded some papers and slowly read aloud his first draft of the proclamation. No one present dared speak against it, but Secretary of State Seward expressed a reasonable concern. With the war going so badly, wouldn't the announcement be taken by most Americans as "a cry for help—our last shriek on the retreat?" Seward wanted the President to

Abraham Lincoln (third from left) meets with members of his Cabinet to discuss the Emancipation Proclamation. Secretary of State William H. Seward is sitting across from Lincoln.

Freedom made it possible for many former slaves to attend school for the first time.

postpone the proclamation until the Union could win a victory on the battlefield. Lincoln agreed.

Over the next two months, emancipation was the best-kept secret in America. Then, on September 17, 1862, Union troops finally gave Lincoln a victory. The North defeated the South at the Battle of Antietam in Maryland. Five days later Abraham Lincoln announced the Emancipation Proclamation.

Just as Lincoln had feared, the emancipation was immediately and bitterly attacked. Some newspapers warned that it would set off riots. Union soldiers began deserting in greater numbers than ever. That fall, Lincoln's Republican party suffered losses in elections for Congress.

But Lincoln did not back down. On January 1—with his trembling hand steadied—he signed the final proclamation. He even added his hope that former slaves would now join Union armies to fight for the freedom the emancipation promised. Everyone knew that, for all its good intentions, the Emancipation Proclamation would do nothing unless Union armies could win

victories in Rebel states. That is exactly what happened. The Emancipation Proclamation freed 200,000 slaves as Union troops marched farther and farther into the Confederacy.

By the stroke of his pen, Lincoln had launched a second American Revolution. He not only had helped end the shame of human bondage in America but had guaranteed the survival of American democracy. As he put it, "By giving freedom to the slave, we assure freedom to the free."

Literature Review

1. Why was it important for Lincoln to think about all points of view before deciding to write the Emancipation Proclamation?
2. Why did some people think the Emancipation Proclamation did very little?
3. Lincoln said, "By giving freedom to the slave, we assure freedom to the free." Rewrite Lincoln's words in your own words to show classmates what you think he meant.

THE LONG ROAD TO A
*U*NION
*V*ICTORY

*L*ink to Our World

What actions might help bring a difficult conflict to an end?

Focus on the Main Idea
As you read, think about the events that helped bring the Civil War to an end.

Preview Vocabulary
Gettysburg Address
assassination

The Emancipation Proclamation did not give enslaved people instant freedom. The order was only for the states that had left the Union—not the four border states. And until Union troops were sent to the Confederate states to see that the proclamation was carried out, many people there remained enslaved. Still, it gave new hope to Africans and new spirit to the North.

In the months that followed, the North seemed to be winning the war. Yet terrible battles lay ahead, and many more soldiers would die before the war's end.

Like many other Africans in the United States, this soldier, Andrew Scott, fought for the Union.

AFRICAN REGIMENTS

Africans had fought to defend the United States since the Revolutionary War. Over the years, however, many had been kept from joining the army. By the start of the Civil War, they were not allowed to serve.

As the war went on, many Africans decided to form their own regiments to fight for the Union. While they trained, their leaders asked Congress to let them enlist. Finally, in 1862, with no end to the war in sight and fewer white soldiers joining the army, Congress agreed. More than 186,000 Africans signed up. They formed 166 regiments of artillery, cavalry, infantry, and engineers.

At first African soldiers were not paid as much as white soldiers. They were given poor equipment and often ran out of supplies. To make things worse, Confederate soldiers said that they would enslave or kill any black soldiers they captured.

Even with the hardships and the dangers, African soldiers soon proved themselves in battle. They led raids behind

Confederate lines and served as spies and scouts. They fought in almost every battle, facing some of the worst fighting of the war. More than 38,000 black soldiers lost their lives defending the Union.

✓ **How did African regiments help the Union war effort?**

GRANT LEADS THE UNION

Another boost for the North came when President Lincoln finally found a general as good as Confederate general Robert E. Lee. His name was Ulysses S. Grant.

Like Lee, Grant had been educated at West Point and had fought in the war with Mexico. When the Civil War began, Grant offered his services to the Union army. His quick decisions in battles soon led to Union victories. After one battle, when the Confederates asked for the terms of surrender, Grant replied, "No terms except an unconditional and immediate surrender can be accepted." After that, Northerners liked to say that Grant's initials, *U. S.*, stood for *Unconditional Surrender*.

One of Grant's most important battles began in May 1863, at Vicksburg, Mississippi. After two attacks Grant decided to lay siege to the city. For weeks Union guns pounded Vicksburg. The trapped Confederates, both soldiers and townspeople, soon ran out of food. They ate mules, horses, and dogs to stay alive. They tore down houses for firewood and dug caves in hillsides for shelter. Finally, on the Fourth of July, the starving people of Vicksburg gave in.

Vicksburg proved to be a key victory. It gave the Union control of the Mississippi River. This, in turn, helped weaken the Confederacy by cutting it into two parts. As one Union soldier wrote from Vicksburg, "This was the most glorious Fourth I ever

African troops played a key role in support of the Union. This photograph shows members of an artillery unit completing cannon drills.

GETTYSBURG

At about the same time that Grant won Vicksburg, other Union troops were facing the invading army of Robert E. Lee in the small town of Gettysburg, Pennsylvania. The Battle of Gettysburg ended in one of the most important Union victories of the war. But more than 3,000 Union soldiers and nearly 4,000 Confederates were killed. More than 20,000 on each side were wounded or reported missing.

The fate of the Fourteenth Tennessee Regiment tells the story. When the battle began, there were 365 men in the unit. When the battle ended, there were only 3.

On November 19, 1863, President Lincoln went to Gettysburg to dedicate a cemetery for those who had died there. A crowd of nearly 6,000 people gathered for the ceremony.

Lincoln gave a short speech that day. In fact, he spoke for less than three minutes. A photographer who was there hoped to take a picture of the President as he gave his speech. But by the time the photographer had set up his heavy camera, Lincoln had already sat down!

Lincoln's speech at Gettysburg was so short that many people in the crowd were disappointed. Lincoln himself called it "a flat failure." But people soon realized that this short speech, later known as the **Gettysburg Address**, was one of the most inspiring ever given by an American leader.

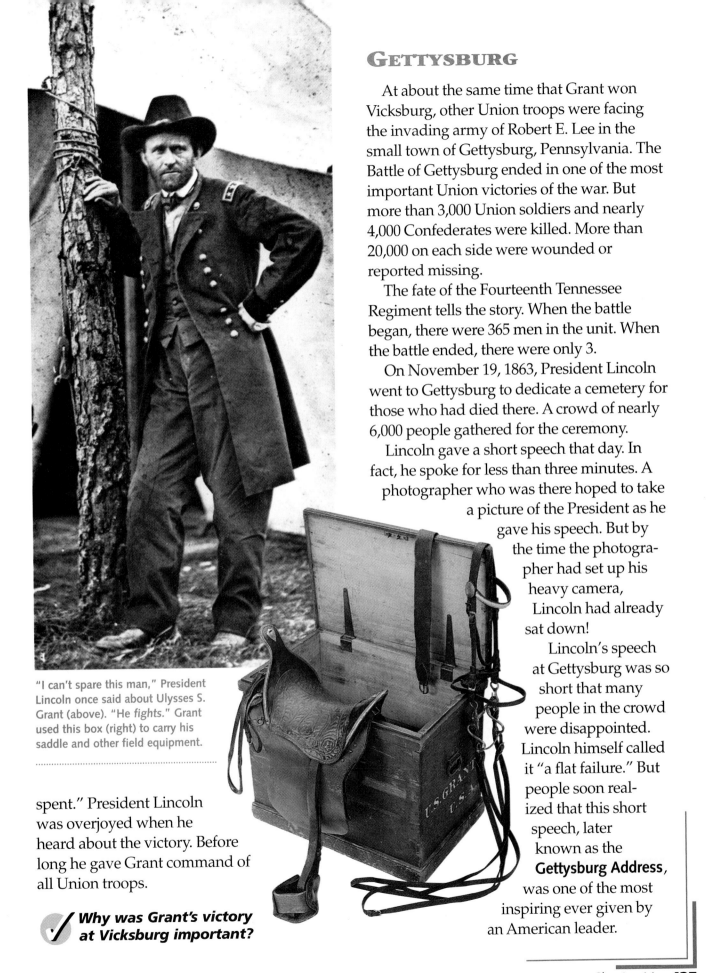

"I can't spare this man," President Lincoln once said about Ulysses S. Grant (above). "He *fights*." Grant used this box (right) to carry his saddle and other field equipment.

spent." President Lincoln was overjoyed when he heard about the victory. Before long he gave Grant command of all Union troops.

Why was Grant's victory at Vicksburg important?

The Gettysburg Address

Four score and seven years ago our fathers brought forth on this continent, a new nation, conceived in Liberty, and dedicated to the proposition that all men are created equal.

Now we are engaged in a great civil war, testing whether that nation, or any nation so conceived and so dedicated, can long endure. We are met on a great battlefield of that war. We have come to dedicate a portion of that field, as a final resting place for those who here gave their lives that that nation might live. It is altogether fitting and proper that we should do this.

But, in a larger sense, we can not dedicate—we can not consecrate—we can not hallow—this ground. The brave men, living and dead, who struggled here, have consecrated it, far above our poor power to add or detract. The world will little note, nor long remember what we say here, but it can never forget what they did here. It is for us the living, rather, to be dedicated here to the unfinished work which they who fought here have thus far so nobly advanced. It is rather for us to be here dedicated to the great task remaining before us—that from these honored dead we take increased devotion to that cause for which they gave the last full measure of devotion—that we here highly resolve that these dead shall not have died in vain—that this nation, under God, shall have a new birth of freedom—and that government of the people, by the people, for the people, shall not perish from the earth.

In the Gettysburg Address, Lincoln spoke of the ideals of liberty and equality on which the country had been founded. He honored the soldiers who had died defending those ideals. And he called on Americans to try even harder to win the struggle those soldiers had died for—to save "government of the people, by the people, for the people."

 What did President Lincoln ask Americans to do in his speech at Gettysburg?

THE MARCH TO THE SEA

More Union victories followed those at Vicksburg and Gettysburg. Then came one of the worst times for the South—the invasion of Georgia.

In 1864 Union General William Tecumseh Sherman led his army south from Tennessee into Georgia. Through heavy fighting Sherman pushed to Atlanta, the railroad center of the South. As he took the city, much of it burned to the ground.

From Atlanta, Sherman's troops headed toward Savannah, on the Atlantic coast. Their march has become known as the March to the Sea. The goal of this terrible march was to destroy everything that could help the South in the war. Sherman hoped that this would break the South's will to fight. "We cannot change the hearts of those people of the South," Sherman said, "but we can make war so terrible . . . make them so sick of war that generations would pass away before they would again appeal to it." Cutting a path of destruction 60 miles (96 km) wide and 300 miles (482 km) long, Union troops burned homes and stores, destroyed crops, wrecked bridges, and tore up railroad tracks.

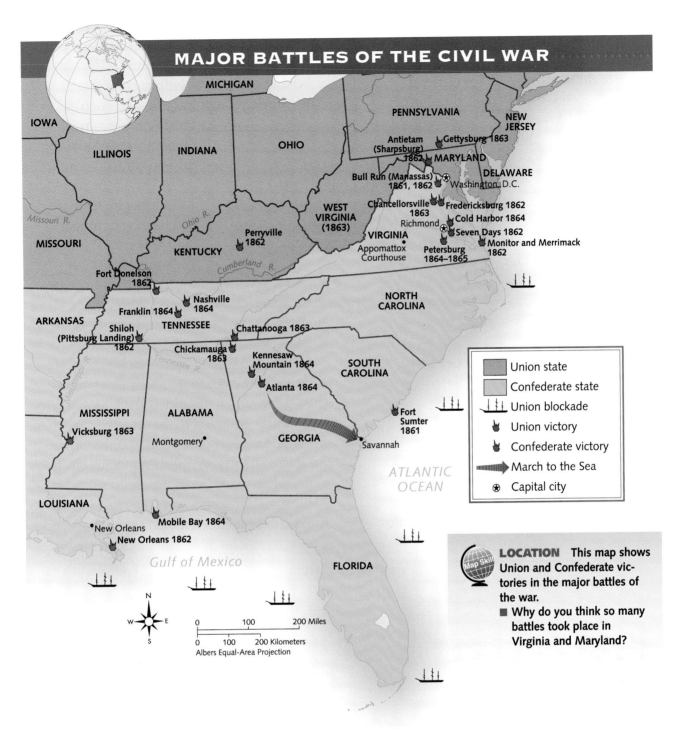

MAJOR BATTLES OF THE CIVIL WAR

MICHIGAN

IOWA

ILLINOIS

INDIANA

OHIO

PENNSYLVANIA

NEW JERSEY

Antietam (Sharpsburg) 1862

Gettysburg 1863

MARYLAND

DELAWARE

Bull Run (Manassas) 1861, 1862

Washington, D.C.

MISSOURI

Missouri R.

Ohio R.

WEST VIRGINIA (1863)

Perryville 1862

KENTUCKY

Cumberland R.

VIRGINIA

Chancellorsville 1863

Richmond

Fredericksburg 1862

Cold Harbor 1864

Seven Days 1862

Monitor and Merrimack 1862

Appomattox Courthouse

Petersburg 1864–1865

Fort Donelson 1862

ARKANSAS

Franklin 1864

Nashville 1864

NORTH CAROLINA

Shiloh (Pittsburg Landing) 1862

TENNESSEE

Tennessee R.

Chattanooga 1863

Chickamauga 1863

Kennesaw Mountain 1864

SOUTH CAROLINA

MISSISSIPPI

ALABAMA

Atlanta 1864

Montgomery

GEORGIA

Savannah

Fort Sumter 1861

Vicksburg 1863

ATLANTIC OCEAN

LOUISIANA

New Orleans

New Orleans 1862

Mobile Bay 1864

Gulf of Mexico

FLORIDA

	Union state
	Confederate state
↓↓↓	Union blockade
↓	Union victory
↓	Confederate victory
➤	March to the Sea
⊛	Capital city

N
W E
S

0   100   200 Miles
0   100   200 Kilometers
Albers Equal-Area Projection

LOCATION This map shows Union and Confederate victories in the major battles of the war.

■ Why do you think so many battles took place in Virginia and Maryland?

On December 22, 1864, Savannah fell to Union troops. That night Sherman sent a message to President Lincoln. "I beg to present you as a Christmas gift the city of Savannah." Sherman then turned north and marched through South Carolina, destroying even more than he had in Georgia.

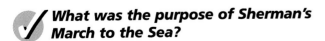 **What was the purpose of Sherman's March to the Sea?**

LEE SURRENDERS

In April 1865 Grant's Union army met Lee's Confederate army in Virginia. Lee's troops were starving, and their clothes were in rags. Grant's soldiers, who were well armed and well fed, kept pushing the Confederate troops.

Finally, Lee was trapped. He could neither fight nor retreat. He had to make another hard decision. He decided to give up the fight—to surrender. "There is nothing left for me to do but to go and see General Grant," Lee said. "And I would rather die a thousand deaths."

Lee surrendered his army to Grant at the tiny Virginia town of Appomattox Courthouse on April 9, 1865. In the next few weeks, as word of Lee's surrender reached them, other Southern generals surrendered, too. The war was finally over.

> 66 **THERE IS NOTHING LEFT FOR ME** to do but to go and see General Grant. And I would rather die a thousand deaths. 99
>
> Robert E. Lee, 1865

✔ **What problems led to Lee's surrender?**

ONE MORE TRAGIC DEATH

The war had ended, but there was still another tragedy to come. Abraham Lincoln did not live to see peace return to the Union.

On April 14, 1865, just five days after Lee's surrender, Lincoln was murdered by a man who thought he was helping the South. The murder of a political leader such as President Lincoln is called an **assassination** (uh•sa•suhn•AY•shuhn).

The President and Mary Todd Lincoln, his wife, had been watching a play at Ford's Theater in Washington, D.C. It was there that an actor named John Wilkes Booth shot the President and ran. Booth died later, during his escape.

Lincoln's assassination shocked both the North and the South. Northerners had lost the leader who had guided the Union to victory. Many gathered in the streets when they heard the news. Some cried openly. Others marched silently. People hung black cloth everywhere—on buildings, fences, and trees.

Many Southerners were also saddened by the death of the President. Lincoln had said

Robert E. Lee (seated at left) surrendered to Ulysses S. Grant (seated at right) at the home of Wilmer McLean in Appomattox Courthouse.

Memorial Day

On May 5, 1866, people in Waterloo, New York, honored those who died in the Civil War. The people closed businesses for the day and decorated soldiers' graves with flowers. This was the beginning of the holiday known as Memorial Day, or Decoration Day. On this day Americans remember those who gave their lives for their country. At Arlington National Cemetery, a wreath is placed on the Tomb of the Unknowns. Four unknown American soldiers who were killed in war are buried there. Today most states observe Memorial Day on the last Monday in May. Many Southern states also have their own days to honor Southern soldiers who died in the Civil War. This holiday is called Confederate Memorial Day or Confederate Heroes Day.

This monument on Culp's Hill honors Confederate soldiers who died at the Battle of Gettysburg.

he would treat the South fairly in defeat. He had promised to bring the country together again "with malice toward none, with charity for all." What would happen now that the President was dead?

A Southerner named Mary Chesnut feared the worst. When she learned of the assassination, Chesnut wrote in her diary, "Lincoln—old Abe Lincoln—killed . . . I know this foul murder will bring down worse miseries on us."

 Why was Lincoln's death a shock to both the North and the South?

**L**SSON 3 REVIEW

Check Understanding

1. **Recall the Facts**   What is the Gettysburg Address?
2. **Focus on the Main Idea**   What events helped bring the Civil War to an end?

Think Critically

3. **Think More About It**   In what ways did individual Americans make a difference during the war?
4. **Past to Present**   Why do you think people today still find meaning in the words of Lincoln's Gettysburg Address?

5. **Explore Viewpoints**   If you had lived in the North during the Civil War, how might you have felt about the March to the Sea? How might you have felt if you had lived in the South?

Show What You Know

Diorama Activity   Make a diorama of one of the events described in this lesson. Your diorama should show either conflict or cooperation. Take turns with a partner, telling the stories about the events each of you has shown.

HowTo

Compare Maps with Different Scales

Why Is This Skill Important?

A map scale compares a distance on a map to a distance in the real world. It helps you find the real distance between places. Map scales are different depending on how much area is shown. Knowing about different map scales can help you choose the best map for gathering the information you need.

Map Scales

Look at the map below and the map on page 433. They show the same area around Gettysburg, Pennsylvania, but with different scales. On Map A, Gettysburg looks smaller. For that reason the scale is said to be smaller. On Map B, Gettysburg appears larger, and the scale is said to be larger.

When the map scale is larger, more details can be shown. For example, note the details of the hills and woods on Map B. Also note that Map B is the larger map. It takes a larger piece

of paper to show a place on a map with a large scale than to show it on a map with a smaller scale. Although they have different scales, Maps A and B can both be used to measure the distance between the same two places.

Understand the Process

On July 2, 1863, the second day of the Battle of Gettysburg, the Union line stretched from Spangler's Spring north to Culp's Hill, on to Cemetery Hill, south along Cemetery Ridge to the hill called Little Round Top, and beyond. What was the distance between Cemetery Hill and Little Round Top? To find out, follow the steps below:

1. On Map A, use a ruler to measure the exact length of the scale, or use a pencil to mark off the length on a sheet of paper. How long is the line that stands for 1/2 mile?
2. Still using Map A, find Cemetery Hill and Little Round Top. Using the ruler or the sheet

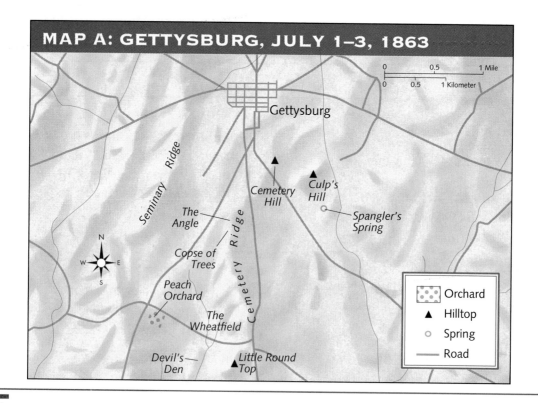

of paper you marked, measure the distance between these two hills. How many times can you fit the 1/2-mile scale length end to end between the hills? Multiply the number of scale lengths between the hills by the distance that the scale length represents. What is the real distance between Cemetery Hill and Little Round Top?

3. Now go through the same steps for Map B. How long is the scale length that stands for 1/2 mile on Earth? Use that scale length to measure the distance between Cemetery Hill and Little Round Top on the map. Are the distances you found on the two maps the same? You should see that even when map scales are different, the distances shown on the maps are the same.

4. Can you figure the distance between the Confederate line at the Peach Orchard and the Union line at Little Round Top? Which map would you use?

Think and Apply

Think about how you use maps when you travel. Find two road maps with different scales—perhaps a road map of your state and a road map of a large city within your state. Compare the actual distances between two places that are on both maps. How far apart are the two places? Are the distances the same on both maps? When would it be more helpful to use the state map, with the smaller scale? When would it be more helpful to use the city map, with the larger scale?

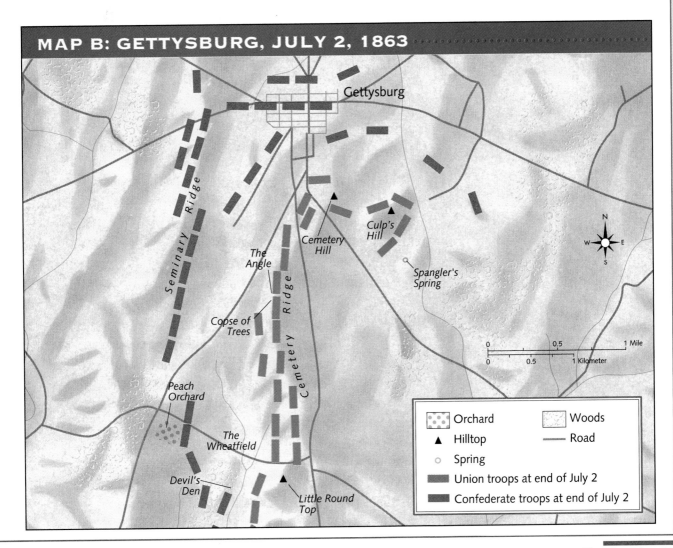

MAP B: GETTYSBURG, JULY 2, 1863

Gettysburg

Seminary Ridge

Cemetery Hill

Culp's Hill

Spangler's Spring

The Angle

Cemetery Ridge

Copse of Trees

Peach Orchard

The Wheatfield

Devil's Den

Little Round Top

0   0.5   1 Mile
0   0.5   1 Kilometer

Orchard   Woods
▲ Hilltop   ——— Road
○ Spring
▮▮▮ Union troops at end of July 2
▬▬▬ Confederate troops at end of July 2

LIFE AFTER the WAR

LESSON 4

Link to Our World

How can new laws affect the lives of citizens?

Focus on the Main Idea
Read to learn about how new laws affected the lives of Americans in the years following the Civil War.

Preview Vocabulary
sharecropping
Reconstruction
scalawag
carpetbagger
segregation

When the Civil War finally ended, it was clear that peace had not come easily. More than 600,000 soldiers had died. Many others had returned home wounded. Much of the South was destroyed. And now the President was dead. As one Southerner remembered, "All the talk was of burning homes, houses knocked to pieces . . . famine, murder, desolation."

The years following the war were hard ones. However, the end of the war brought new hope to at least one group of people—the former slaves.

A FREE PEOPLE

With the Union victory, 4 million enslaved people were freed. Most slaves were already free by the time the Civil War ended in 1865. In December of that year, the Thirteenth Amendment to the Constitution ended slavery in the United States forever. "I felt like a bird out of a cage," one former slave remembered, looking back on the day he was set free. "I could hardly ask to feel any better than I did that day."

Free Africans quickly began to form new communities. They built churches and schools. They opened stores. They formed groups to help people find jobs and to take care of people who were sick. In 1866, only one year after the war ended, one African leader proudly said, "We have progressed a century in a year."

As soon as they could, many former slaves began to search for family members who had been sold and sent away under slavery. Newspapers were filled with advertisements asking for help in finding loved ones. This ad appeared in a newspaper in Nashville, Tennessee.

"During the year 1849, Thomas Sample carried away from this city, as his slaves, our daughter, Polly, and son, George. . . . We will give $100 each for them to any person who will assist them, or . . . get word to us of their whereabouts."

Many families never found their missing loved ones. But for those that did, it was a time of great joy. "I wish you could see this people as they step from slavery into freedom," one Union soldier wrote to his wife. "Families which had been for a long time broken up are united and oh! such happiness."

Former slaves worked hard to build new lives. Yet life remained difficult. Often it was hard just to find food, clothing, and shelter. Many began to look to the United States government for help.

 How did free Africans help one another after the war?

THE FREEDMEN'S BUREAU

In 1865 Congress set up an organization to help former slaves. This group was called the Bureau of Refugees, Freedmen, and Abandoned Lands—or the Freedmen's Bureau.

The Freedmen's Bureau gave food and other supplies to freed slaves. It also helped some white farmers rebuild their farms. The most important work of the Freedmen's Bureau, however, was education. Newly freed slaves were eager to learn to read and write. To help meet this need, the Freedmen's Bureau built more than 4,000 schools and hired thousands of teachers.

The Freedmen's Bureau also wanted to help former slaves earn a living by giving them land to farm. This plan, however, did not work out. The land was to have come from the plantations taken during the war, but white Southerners wanted the land back. In the end, most former slaves were not given

What?

Juneteenth

Abraham Lincoln signed the Emancipation Proclamation on January 1, 1863. But because Union troops did not control Texas at the time, the order had little effect there. On June 19, 1865, Union soldiers landed at Galveston, Texas. On that day Union General Gordon Granger read an order declaring that all slaves in Texas were free. Today people in Texas celebrate June 19, or Juneteenth, as a day of freedom. It is a state holiday marked by picnics, parades, and family gatherings.

This photograph of people going to a Juneteenth celebration was taken in Houston about 1900.

Many former slaves, like those shown attending this Freedmen's Bureau school, were eager to learn to read and write.

free land. Without money to buy land of their own, they had to find work where they could.

 What was the purpose of the Freedmen's Bureau?

SHARECROPPING

In their search for jobs, some former slaves went back to work on the plantations. Many planters welcomed them. Fields needed to be plowed, and crops needed to be planted. Now, however, planters had to pay Africans for their work.

In the days following the war, there was not much money. Instead of paying workers in cash, many landowners paid them in shares. Under this system, known as **sharecropping**, a landowner gave a worker a cabin, mules, tools, and seed. The worker then farmed the land. At harvest time the landowner took part of the crops, plus enough to cover the cost of the worker's rent and supplies. What was left was the worker's share.

Sharecropping gave landowners the help they needed to work the fields. It also gave former slaves work for pay. Yet few people got ahead through sharecropping. When crops failed, both landowners and workers suffered. Even in good times, most workers' shares were very little, if anything at all.

 Why did landowners pay workers in shares rather than in cash?

A NEW PRESIDENT

As Americans were getting used to their new lives after the war, government leaders began making plans for bringing the country back together. This time of rebuilding was called **Reconstruction**.

After Lincoln's death the Vice President, Andrew Johnson, became the new President. Johnson tried to carry out Lincoln's promise to be fair to the South in defeat. He pardoned most Confederates who promised loyalty to the United States. They were then given back the rights of citizenship and were allowed to vote. Their states held elections, and state governments went back to work.

Johnson also said that the Confederate states must abolish slavery. This requirement was met when the Thirteenth Amendment was passed late in 1865. Johnson then said that the last of the Confederate states could return to the Union.

Such easy terms, however, made some people angry. Many Northerners felt that the Confederates were not being punished at all. White Southerners were being elected to office and taking over state governments just as they always had. Yet no one talked about the rights of former slaves. What would happen to them?

It was not long before white Southerners passed laws to limit the rights of former slaves. These laws were called black codes. The black codes differed from state to state. In most states Africans were not allowed to vote. In some they could not travel freely. They could not own certain kinds of property or work in certain businesses. They could be made to work in the fields if they could not find another job.

Many, however, faced an even worse problem. Shortly after the war ended, some white Southerners formed secret groups to keep Africans from having their rights as free persons. Most of those who joined these groups were upset about their war losses and angry about the new rights of former slaves.

One such group was the Ku Klux Klan, or the KKK. Dressed in white robes and hoods, its members delivered nighttime messages of hate. Klan members broke into homes and attacked and killed Africans. They burned schools and churches. They hurt anyone who helped former slaves. It was a time of terror for many people.

 How did some white Southerners keep Africans from having their rights as free persons?

CONGRESS TAKES ACTION

Many leaders of Congress were alarmed about the way former slaves in some Southern states were being treated. They believed that President Johnson's Reconstruction plan was not working. So they voted to change to a plan of their own—a plan that was much tougher on white Southerners.

As sharecroppers, former slaves were paid for their work. But sharecropping was a hard way to make a living, and it put many families in debt.

First, Congress did away with the new state governments and put the Southern states under the army's rule. Union soldiers kept order, and army officers were made governors. Before each Southern state could reestablish its government, it had to write a new state constitution giving all men, both black and white, the right to vote. To return to the Union, a state also had to pass the Fourteenth Amendment. This amendment gave citizenship to all people born in the United States—including former slaves.

Johnson was very angry about this plan and about other laws that Congress passed to cut back his authority. Believing that these laws were unconstitutional, Johnson refused to carry them out. Then, in 1868, the House of Representatives voted to impeach the President, or charge him with a crime. He was put on trial in the Senate. There, in a very close vote, he was found not guilty. Although he stayed in office, Johnson was no longer a strong leader.

The Southern states began to write new state constitutions and pass the Fourteenth Amendment. State elections were held once again. For the first time, African Americans

from the South were elected to Congress. They also served in state governments that took over the job of rebuilding the South.

 **Why did Congress vote to change Johnson's Reconstruction plan?**

RECONSTRUCTION ENDS

The new state governments made many important changes. They did away with the black codes. They approved the Fifteenth Amendment, which said that no citizen could be kept from voting because of race. They built hospitals and schools and repaired roads, bridges, and railroads.

Yet the work of the state governments did not make everyone happy. To pay for their projects, state leaders placed high taxes on land. These taxes hurt landowners who were trying to get their farms and plantations working again. Some were forced to sell their land because they could not pay the taxes.

Many white Southerners soon grew angry with their state leaders. They did not like the fact that African Americans were voting and taking part in government. They did not like the white Southerners who supported the government. They called them **scalawags** (SKA•lih•wagz)—people who support something for their own gain. They also did not like being told what to do by Northerners. Under military rule Northern soldiers guarded their streets. Other Northerners went to the South to try to help with Reconstruction or to make money buying

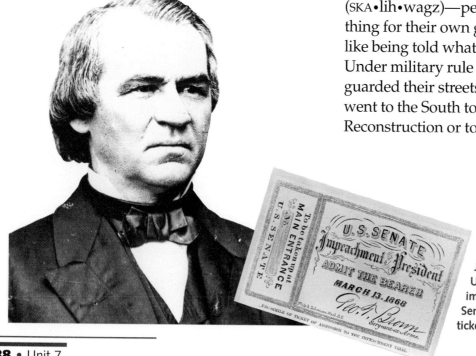

The disagreements between Congress and Andrew Johnson (far left) led to his impeachment. Johnson was the only President in United States history ever to be impeached. Johnson's trial in the Senate drew crowds of people, and tickets (left) were scarce.

The first African Americans to serve in the United States Congress (left) were elected during Reconstruction. Hiram R. Revels of Mississippi (seated at far left) was elected in 1870 to fill the Senate seat once held by Confederate President Jefferson Davis.

land or opening businesses. White Southerners called them **carpetbaggers** because many of them arrived carrying their belongings in suitcases made of carpet pieces.

Some white Southerners tried again to take authority from their state leaders. One way they did this was to control the way people voted. Groups such as the Ku Klux Klan used violence to keep African Americans from voting or to make sure they voted as they were told. Sometimes the votes of African Americans simply were not counted.

In time white Southerners once again took control of their state governments. New state laws were passed that made it very hard, if not impossible, for African Americans to vote. African Americans had to go to separate schools and churches and sit in separate railroad cars. Such laws led to the **segregation**, or separation, of black people and white people.

Reconstruction was over by 1877. In that year the last of the Union troops left the South. The rights and freedoms African Americans had just won were again taken away.

 How did white Southerners take authority back from their state leaders as Reconstruction ended?

LESSON 4 REVIEW

Check Understanding

1. **Recall the Facts** In what ways did the government try to help former slaves?
2. **Focus on the Main Idea** How did new laws affect the lives of Americans in the years following the Civil War?

Think Critically

3. **Think More About It** In what ways did life change for former slaves who became sharecroppers?
4. **Explore Viewpoints** Why do you think Lincoln wanted to be fair to the South in defeat?
5. **Cause and Effect** Why were many white Southerners angry with the state governments set up during military rule?

Show What You Know

Writing Activity Imagine that you are a news reporter writing a story about Reconstruction. Write an interview with a former slave, a Southern white landowner, a Union soldier stationed in the South, or a carpetbagger. Give both your questions and the person's answers. Present your interview to the class.

CHAPTER 14

CONNECT MAIN IDEAS

Use this organizer to show that you understand how the chapter's main ideas are connected. First copy the organizer onto a separate sheet of paper. Then complete it by writing one or two sentences to summarize each idea or event.

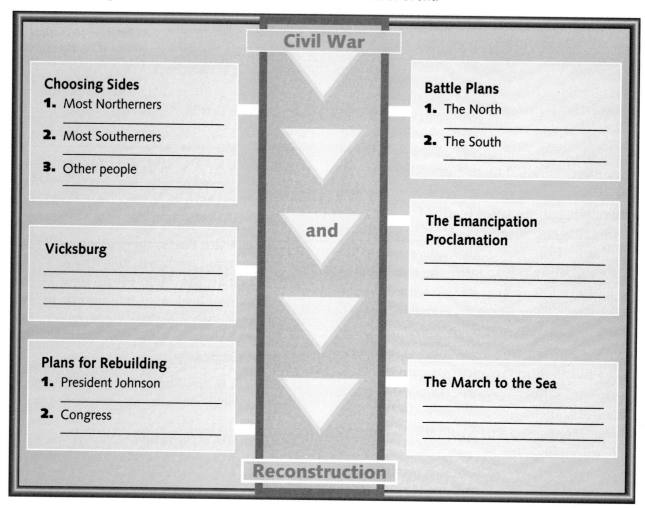

Civil War

Choosing Sides
1. Most Northerners
_____
2. Most Southerners
_____
3. Other people
_____

Vicksburg
_____
_____
_____

Plans for Rebuilding
1. President Johnson
_____
2. Congress
_____

and

Battle Plans
1. The North
_____
2. The South
_____

The Emancipation Proclamation
_____
_____
_____

The March to the Sea
_____
_____
_____

Reconstruction

WRITE MORE ABOUT IT

1. **Write a Diary Entry** Imagine that you are living in Missouri, Kentucky, Maryland, or Delaware at the beginning of the Civil War. Write a diary entry in which you tell why you think some members of your family have chosen to fight for the North while others have chosen to fight for the South.

2. **Write a News Story** Imagine that you are a newspaper reporter covering the White House in 1863. Write an article for your newspaper in which you tell readers what the Emancipation Proclamation will do, why President Lincoln decided to issue it, and how it will affect the war.

USE VOCABULARY

Use each term in a complete sentence that will help explain its meaning.

1. border state
2. assassination
3. sharecropping
4. scalawag
5. carpetbagger
6. segregation

CHECK UNDERSTANDING

1. Why did the Confederacy hope to receive help from Britain and France?

2. Why did Lincoln finally decide to issue the Emancipation Proclamation?

3. How did African soldiers help the North?

4. What ideals did President Lincoln speak about in the Gettysburg Address?

5. During the March to the Sea, why did General Sherman try to destroy everything in his path?

6. Why were some Southerners sad about Lincoln's death?

7. What was the purpose of the Freedmen's Bureau?

8. How did the black codes help bring about the end of President Johnson's Reconstruction plan?

THINK CRITICALLY

1. **Personally Speaking** If you had been in Robert E. Lee's place, would you have made the decision to join the Confederacy? Why or why not?

2. **Explore Viewpoints** Mary Chesnut wrote, "I know this foul murder will bring down worse miseries on us." What do you think she meant? Do you think she was right? Explain your answer.

3. **Think More About It** The most important work of the Freedmen's Bureau was education. Why is education important to people in a free country?

4. **Past to Present** Government leaders raised taxes to pay for rebuilding the South. Today government leaders sometimes increase taxes to pay for new projects. How can taxes both help and hurt people?

APPLY SKILLS

How to Compare Maps with Different Scales The maps of Gettysburg on pages 432 and 433 show the sites of many battles. You can visit these battle sites today at the Gettysburg National Military Park in Pennsylvania. Use either map to answer the questions.

1. How far would you have to walk to go from the battle sites of Devil's Den to the Wheatfield?

2. How far is it from the Wheatfield to the Peach Orchard?

3. Which map did you use to answer these questions? Why did you choose that map?

READ MORE ABOUT IT

The Boys' War: Confederate and Union Soldiers Talk About the Civil War by Jim Murphy. Clarion. This book includes letters, diary entries, and photographs of young Civil War soldiers.

A Separate Battle: Women and the Civil War by Ina Chang. Lodestar. This book highlights the important contributions that women made in the Civil War.

Undying Glory: The Story of the Massachusetts 54th Regiment by Clinton Cox. Scholastic. This book details the Massachusetts 54th, a regiment of African American soldiers.

THE FIGHT FOR FREEDOM GOES ON

The Civil War changed forever the way most Americans thought about one another. People who had been friends had fought as enemies. People who had been enslaved were now free. Those who had been thought of as property were now citizens of the United States.

Yet the rights that African Americans had fought so long for were still kept out of reach. In the years following the Civil War, many African Americans were kept from voting and holding office. They were made to live their lives apart from other citizens, in separate neighborhoods and schools. It would be 100 years after the Civil War before African Americans would be given the full rights of United States citizenship.

In the 1950s and 1960s, Americans across the country began to take part in the civil rights movement. This was a movement to gain the rights promised to all people in the Constitution. One of the greatest leaders of the civil rights movement was Dr. Martin Luther King, Jr. In 1963 King gave a speech about his hopes for the future. He said that he dreamed of a time when all the unfair ways of the past would end. He dreamed of a day when "the sons of former slaves and the sons of former slaveowners will be able to sit down together at the table of brother-hood." On that day, King said, all Americans will finally be able to sing together the words of an old spiritual,

"Free at last!
Free at last!
Thank God Almighty,
We are free at last!"

Think and Apply

Think about people today who are working for equal rights. Identify an individual or a group working to protect people's rights and freedoms. Gather information about the person or group, and prepare a report for the class.

BUILDING CITIZENSHIP

STORY CLOTH

Study the pictures shown in this story cloth to help you review the events you read about in Unit 7.

Summarize the Main Ideas

1. As slavery continued in the South, more and more enslaved people tried to escape by running away.

2. After Abraham Lincoln was elected President in 1860, Southern states seceded from the Union.

3. During the Civil War thousands of people in both the North and the South joined the war effort.

4. The war dragged on for four long years, destroying property and lives on both sides.

5. Robert E. Lee surrendered his Confederate forces to Union General Ulysses S. Grant at Appomattox Courthouse in 1865.

6. During Reconstruction the Freedmen's Bureau opened schools for former slaves.

7. After the war, life was difficult for former slaves, even though they were now free. Many tried to build new lives as sharecroppers.

Dramatize the Story Choose any of the people shown in the story cloth, and invent a conversation they might have with us today describing their experiences. Act out the conversation with a classmate.

COOPERATIVE LEARNING WORKSHOP

Remember
- Share your ideas.
- Cooperate with others to plan your work.
- Take responsibility for your work.
- Show your group's work to the class.
- Discuss what you learned by working together.

Activity 1
Publish a Class Magazine

You and your classmates have decided to put together a magazine about the Civil War. First, plan your magazine by preparing a table of contents. Decide what articles and illustrations you would like to include. Give your magazine a title. Then form several small groups, with each group working on a different part of the magazine. Once all the groups have finished, put the parts together. Ask permission to display the magazine in the school library.

Activity 2
Draw a Map

Work together to draw a map of the United States at the time of the Civil War. Use different colors for the states of the Union and the states of the Confederacy. Write the date on which each Southern state seceded. Draw diagonal lines on the border states. Label the capitals of the North and the South and the key battle sites. Use your map to tell classmates about one event of the Civil War.

Activity 3
Make Decision Cards

Work in a group to make decision cards. Each member of your group should choose a well-known leader—Abraham Lincoln, Jefferson Davis, Harriet Tubman, Henry Clay, Stephen Douglas, Robert E. Lee, or another person that you have read about in this unit. On a large note card, write the person's name and birth and death dates. Then write and attach a paragraph describing how that person made a decision that affected history.

Activity 4
Honor Your Hero

Choose someone you admire from the Civil War as the subject of a poster for a display called *Heroes of the Civil War*. Work together to find or draw a picture of the person or a picture of a scene showing the person in action. Then add words or phrases around the picture that tell what made that person a hero. Present your poster to the class.

USE VOCABULARY

Write the term that correctly matches each definition. Then use each term in a complete sentence.

Confederacy   segregation
Gettysburg Address   spiritual
Reconstruction

1. a religious song based on a Bible story

2. the new country formed by the Southern states after they seceded from the Union

3. a famous speech given by Abraham Lincoln

4. a time of rebuilding

5. the separation of black people and white people

CHECK UNDERSTANDING

1. In what ways had the South come to depend on the work of enslaved people?

2. How did the Underground Railroad help slaves?

3. What was the Missouri Compromise? What was the Kansas-Nebraska Act?

4. How did the Emancipation Proclamation affect the war?

5. What problems led Congress to change President Johnson's Reconstruction plan?

THINK CRITICALLY

1. **Explore Viewpoints** Lincoln once was called "the miserable tool of traitors and rebels." Today he is thought of as a great leader. Why might someone at the time have been so critical of him?

2. **Past to Present** Why is it important for Presidents today to consider different view-points before making a decision?

APPLY GEOGRAPHY SKILLS

How to Compare Maps with Different Scales The Battle of Gettysburg ended on July 3, 1863, when Pickett's Charge—led by Confederate General George Pickett—was stopped at The Angle and the Copse of Trees. Use the map below and the maps on pages 432 and 433 to answer the questions.

1. Pickett's Charge began on the east side of Seminary Ridge. What was the distance between the starting line of the charge and the Union line?

2. Compare the map on this page to Map A on page 432. Which would more clearly show Pickett's Charge or other troop movements over small distances? Explain.

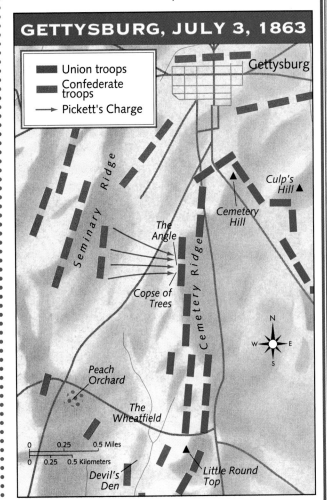

GETTYSBURG, JULY 3, 1863

Union troops
Confederate troops
→ Pickett's Charge

Gettysburg
Seminary Ridge
Cemetery Ridge
Culp's Hill
Cemetery Hill
The Angle
Copse of Trees
Peach Orchard
The Wheatfield
Devil's Den
Little Round Top

0   0.25   0.5 Miles
0   0.25   0.5 Kilometers

UNIT 8

*I*NVENTION *and* *C*HANGE

THE BOWERY SAVINGS BANK

UNIFORM SUITS AT LOW PRICES

$12

1850

1860

1870

1880

1862
Homestead Act
gives free land to
settlers

1869
Transcontinental
Railroad is
completed

1876
Battle of Little
Bighorn

1879
Thomas Edison
invents the
incandescent
light

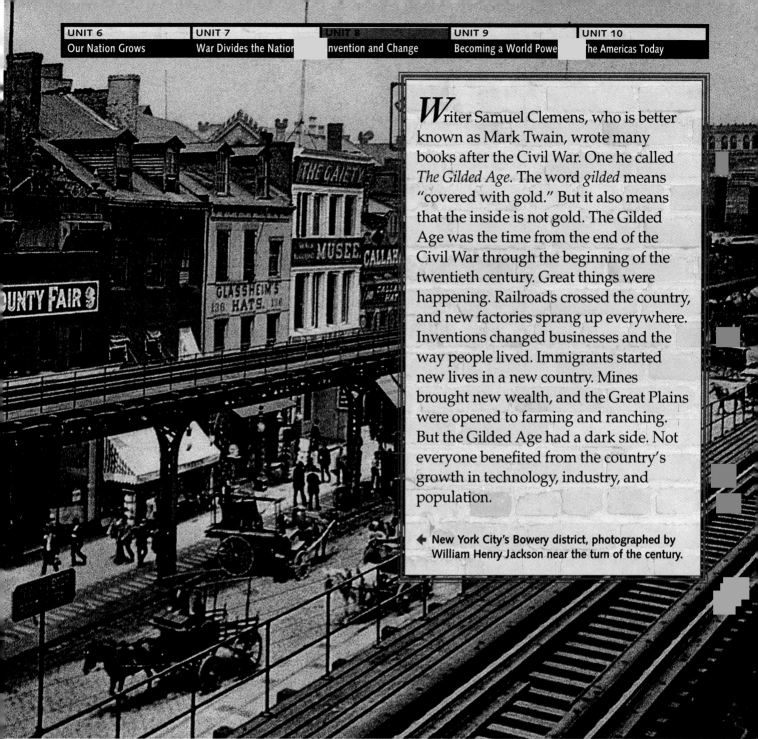

*W*riter Samuel Clemens, who is better known as Mark Twain, wrote many books after the Civil War. One he called *The Gilded Age.* The word *gilded* means "covered with gold." But it also means that the inside is not gold. The Gilded Age was the time from the end of the Civil War through the beginning of the twentieth century. Great things were happening. Railroads crossed the country, and new factories sprang up everywhere. Inventions changed businesses and the way people lived. Immigrants started new lives in a new country. Mines brought new wealth, and the Great Plains were opened to farming and ranching. But the Gilded Age had a dark side. Not everyone benefited from the country's growth in technology, industry, and population.

← New York City's Bowery district, photographed by William Henry Jackson near the turn of the century.

1890

1900

1910

1920

1889
Jane Addams starts Hull House

1892
Homestead steelworkers strike

1916
Many African Americans from the South move north to industrial cities

1886
American Federation of Labor is founded

1890
New period of immigration begins

The Story of Thomas Alva Edison

by Margaret Cousins

Thomas Alva Edison may have been the greatest inventor of all time. He invented the phonograph, the movie camera, and the microphone. But his most important invention was the electric light bulb. Can you imagine a world without electric lights?

The first electric light bulbs were called filament bulbs or incandescent bulbs because of the way they worked. Electricity flowed through a thin piece of carbon—the filament—inside a glass bulb. This filament became so hot that it was incandescent, or glowed with a white light.

After many failures and more than a few explosions, Edison finally had an electric light bulb that worked. The first public demonstration of the amazing invention was at Edison's workshop in Menlo Park, New Jersey. It was a night of great excitement.

After the news of the electric lamp was published, people swarmed to Menlo Park. Edison then announced a demonstration of the incandescent lamp for New Year's Eve. This was one of the most unusual New Year's Eve parties ever given. The Pennsylvania Railroad transported more than three thousand persons to Menlo Park on the cold, snowy last night of the year 1879. They came from both New York and Philadelphia.

Edison had put some of his lamps along two wires strung between the leafless trees on the road leading from the railway station to his laboratory. As the trains began to pull in in the winter darkness, he pulled the switch and the electric lamps glowed like golden flowers, illuminating the road with a flood of light and casting long rays across the snow.

It is hard for us to imagine how exciting this was to people who had never seen an electric light. Many of them were sophisticated city people, dressed in their New Year's Eve party clothes; but they all gasped. It was the most beautiful sight they had ever seen. It was fairyland!

Edison stood in the power house, watching the dynamo turn steam power into the electric current to light the lamps. He was wearing an old gray shirt, a flannel coat full of acid holes and some chalk-stained, dusty trousers. A broad-brimmed black felt hat sat on the back of his head. Some people took him for a coal stoker,[1] so he had a good chance to listen to what they were saying.

"It's a miracle!"

"Did you ever see anything so beautiful?"

"He's a wizard! A wizard!"

Suddenly there was a scream and a commotion. A young lady was standing near the generators with her hair down her back.

"I'm sorry," Edison said. "The generators magnetized her hairpins and pulled them out of her hair!" He apologized to the lady and gave her a silk kerchief to put on her head. "Maybe this will help," he said, but she fled back to the train.

The success of the New Year's Eve demonstration at Menlo Park created excitement all over the world. Cables, letters, telegrams and gifts descended on Edison. He was no longer just a hero, but the "American Wizard."

Thomas Edison was not the only inventor making important discoveries in the years after the Civil War. Alexander Graham Bell invented the telephone in 1876, and a revolution in communication began. The first automobiles came into use, and transportation changed forever. This growth of technology sparked the growth of industry that marks the period of history in the United States from 1865 to 1920.

---

[1] **coal stoker:** person who shovels coal into a furnace

After 72 hours of non-stop work, Thomas Edison listens to his new invention, the talking machine.

CHAPTER 15

INDUSTRY and IMMIGRATION

> 66 When we set foot on these shores, . . . we were bewildered and lost. We did not know where to turn for shelter or food. Fortunately, there were enough of us so that some set to putting up these houses while others looked for food. 99
>
> The leader of an Asian miners' organization, addressing a group of newly arrived immigrants

Many immigrants, like this Japanese girl, came to the United States in the late 1800s and early 1900s.

BIG BUSINESS AND INDUSTRIAL CITIES

LESSON 1

Link to Our World

How have new inventions changed your life?

Focus on the Main Idea
Read to learn how new inventions changed life in the United States in the years after the Civil War.

Preview Vocabulary
free enterprise
transcontinental
   railroad
capital resource
invest
stock
corporation
entrepreneur
consolidate
refinery
monopoly

The Industrial Revolution came to the United States in the early 1800s. During this time, machines took the place of hand tools, and factories took the place of craft shops. After the Civil War even greater changes happened in American industry. Inventors developed new technologies, and business owners set up new ways of running their businesses. It was an important time for **free enterprise**—an economic system in which businesses have the freedom to offer for sale many kinds of goods and services.

RAILROADS

When Abraham Lincoln ran for President in 1860, the Republican party promised to build a **transcontinental railroad**. This was to be a railroad that went across the continent, linking the Atlantic and Pacific coasts. When Lincoln was elected, he kept his promise. In 1862 Congress gave two companies the right to build the railroad. The government gave them land and loaned them money. Railroads already had been built from the Atlantic Coast west to Nebraska. The Union Pacific built west from Omaha, Nebraska. The Central Pacific built east from Sacramento, California. On May 10, 1869, the two railroads met at Promontory, Utah.

The Union Pacific–Central Pacific was not the only railroad across the West for long. By the 1890s four more railroads had been built from midwestern cities to the Pacific Coast. Railroads in the East added to their systems, too. In 1860 the United States had just over 30,000 miles (48,000 km) of track. By 1900 it had more than 193,000 miles (311,000 km) of track.

A golden spike with a prayer written on it was used to complete the first transcontinental railroad.

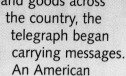 What?

The Telegraph

As railroad tracks carried people and goods across the country, the telegraph began carrying messages. An American inventor, Samuel F. B. Morse, experimented with sending electricity along iron wires during the 1830s. To send messages along the wires, Morse invented a code system in which dots and dashes stand for letters of the alphabet. The railroads quickly saw how useful Morse code and the telegraph would be, and telegraph lines were soon strung along railroad tracks. The telegraph helped railroads run their trains safely and on time. It also carried news to every part of the country in minutes. For the first time, news could travel faster than people.

One reason for the growth of railroads was the development of new inventions that improved rail transportation. George Westinghouse's air brake made trains safer by stopping the locomotive and all the cars at the same time. Inventor Granville T. Woods improved the air brake and developed a telegraph system that let trains and stations communicate with one another.

As railroads grew, their owners faced many problems. They had to buy more locomotives, cars, and tracks. They had to pay the workers who laid track and repaired it, as well as the workers who ran the trains. To do all this, they needed **capital resources**, or money to run their businesses. Railroad owners, among them Cornelius Vanderbilt and Leland Stanford, received millions of dollars from the government, but they needed more. They got the money they needed from people who invested money in the railroads. To **invest** is to buy shares of a business in the hope of making a profit. These shares are called **stocks**.

As the railroads grew, many people bought shares of stock in railroad companies. Buying stock let them own part of the railroad. When the railroad company made money, stock owners received part of the profit. Businesses that sell shares of stock to investors are called **corporations**.

People who bought stock were part owners of businesses, but they did not run them. A board of directors ran each corporation, and managers took care of the day-to-day activities. Railroads were the first kind of business to be set up as corporations on such a large scale.

 **Why did people invest money in railroads?**

THE STEEL INDUSTRY

In the early part of the Industrial Revolution, iron was used to build bridges, buildings, and railroads. In fact, the early growth of railroads depended on iron tracks. As locomotives got bigger and heavier, however, iron tracks were no longer strong enough. Many lasted only about three years.

Steel tracks were harder and lasted longer, but steel cost a great deal to make. Steel is made from iron with small amounts of other metals added. Because of its cost, steel was used only for small items, such as knives and swords.

By the 1850s inventors in both Britain and the United States had developed a way to make steel more cheaply and easily. Named after the English inventor Henry Bessemer, the new way of making steel was called the Bessemer process. The Bessemer process melted iron ore and other metals together in a new kind of furnace. The higher heat of this "blast furnace" made the steel stronger.

During the 1860s an American entrepreneur (ahn•truh•pruh•NER) named Andrew Carnegie visited Britain and saw the Bessemer process for the first time. An **entrepreneur** is a person who sets up a new business, taking a chance on making or losing money. After returning to the United States, Carnegie looked for investors to help him build a small steel mill in Pittsburgh, Pennsylvania. By the early 1870s business was good for Carnegie. With his profits he built more steel mills and made even larger profits.

Looking for ways to cut costs and, in turn, make more money, Carnegie bought mines to supply his steel mills with coal and iron. He then bought ships to carry these natural resources to his mills. All this helped him make more steel at a lower cost. He could then afford to sell his steel for less money.

This photograph of the Homestead Steel Works in Homestead, Pennsylvania, was taken about 1890. The equipment shown was used to pour melted steel into molds to make 90-ton blocks.

Other steel mills were not able to match Carnegie's low prices. Carnegie bought these other mills and **consolidated**, or joined, their businesses with his. The Carnegie Steel Company became one of the biggest steel businesses in the United States, and Andrew Carnegie became one of the richest people in the world.

 How was Carnegie able to make more steel for less money?

THE OIL INDUSTRY

Like Andrew Carnegie, John D. Rockefeller saw that he could become rich in business. Rockefeller was 23 years old in 1863 when he set up an oil refinery in Cleveland, Ohio. A **refinery** is a factory where crude oil is made into usable products. The first products made by Rockefeller's refinery were grease and kerosene for lamps. This was before Edison invented the incandescent light bulb.

Many business people were building refineries because of oil finds in Ohio, Pennsylvania, and West Virginia. The Rockefeller refinery was one of 30 in the Cleveland area. Within a few years, however, Rockefeller bought most of the other refineries. He consolidated them into one business, which he called the Standard Oil Company.

Rather than let other companies make a profit from his business, Rockefeller did something similar to what Carnegie had done. He bought forests to get his own lumber. He bought a barrel factory to make his own barrels. He bought ships and railroad cars to carry his products. Other companies soon could not match Rockefeller's low prices for oil products. Before long he had a **monopoly**, or almost complete control, of the oil business. By 1899 the Standard Oil Company controlled about 90 percent of the country's oil refining business.

After the invention of the gasoline engine, when cars came into use, Rockefeller's oil refineries produced gasoline and engine oil. Standard Oil's yearly profits zoomed to more than $45 million.

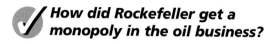 **How did Rockefeller get a monopoly in the oil business?**

THE NEW INDUSTRIAL CITIES

Before the Gilded Age the most important cities in the United States were those on good harbors near the oceans. With the growth of industries such as steel and oil, new industrial cities developed inland, far from the coast. They were built close to the natural resources needed by mills and factories.

The region west of the Appalachians and east of the Mississippi had many such resources. Because western Pennsylvania had iron ore, coal, and limestone—the natural resources needed for making iron and steel— places such as Pittsburgh were among the first iron-and-steel centers in the North. In the South, Birmingham, Alabama, which was close to iron and coal deposits, became an iron-and-steel center, too.

Iron ore deposits also were found in the hills of the Mesabi Range near Lake Superior. The ore was taken by barge across Lake Superior to Chicago and other Great Lakes cities. Trains brought coal from the Appalachian region to the same cities. So cities such as Chicago, Illinois; Gary, Indiana; Cleveland, Ohio; and Detroit, Michigan, also became industrial cities.

LEARNING FROM GRAPHS The Carnegie Steel Company, founded by Andrew Carnegie (left), produced much of the steel made in the United States during the late 1800s.
■ During which five-year period did steel production go up the most? the least?

LEARNING FROM GRAPHS John D. Rockefeller (right) controlled the oil business in the United States.
■ About how many barrels of oil were produced in 1865? in 1890?

STEEL PRODUCTION, 1865–1900

NUMBER OF TONS

12,000,000
11,000,000
10,000,000
9,000,000
8,000,000
7,000,000
6,000,000
5,000,000
4,000,000
3,000,000
2,000,000
1,000,000
0

1865 1870 1875 1880 1885 1890 1895 1900

YEAR

OIL PRODUCTION, 1865–1900

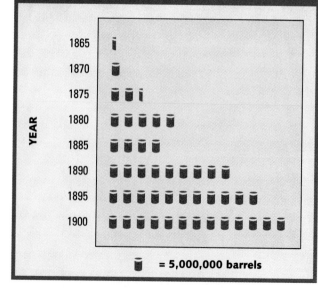

YEAR

1865
1870
1875
1880
1885
1890
1895
1900

🛢 = 5,000,000 barrels

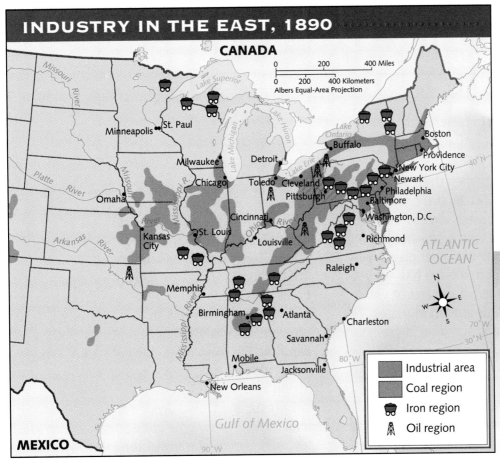

INDUSTRY IN THE EAST, 1890

CANADA

0   200   400 Miles
0 200 400 Kilometers
Albers Equal-Area Projection

ATLANTIC OCEAN

Gulf of Mexico

MEXICO

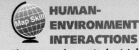

Industrial area
Coal region
Iron region
Oil region

Map Skill **HUMAN-ENVIRONMENT INTERACTIONS**
This map shows industrial areas and resource regions in the eastern part of the United States about 1890.
■ If you were going to build an oil refinery in 1890, where would you put it? Where would you put a steel mill?

Because of the railroads, businesses that used iron and steel to make their products built factories near iron-and-steel centers. Railroads brought in raw materials to the factories and carried out finished products to deliver to customers. Cities such as Chicago and Pittsburgh, as well as St. Louis, Missouri, and Atlanta, Georgia, became railroad centers.

✓ **Why did inland cities become important in the late 1800s?**

LESSON 1 REVIEW

Check Understanding

1. **Recall the Facts** Who were the important business leaders in the steel and oil industries?
2. **Focus on the Main Idea** How did new inventions change life in the United States in the years after the Civil War?

Think Critically

3. **Past to Present** What kinds of businesses do you think are the most important today?

4. **Exploring Viewpoints** How do you think other oil-refinery owners felt about Rockefeller's oil monopoly?

Show What You Know

Table Activity Make a table comparing information about Andrew Carnegie and John D. Rockefeller. Be sure to include information about their businesses. Share your table with a classmate.

Use a Time Zone Map

Why Is This Skill Important?

Years ago people used sun time—they figured time based on the sun's position. According to sun time, noon is the hour when the sun reaches its highest position in the sky. By this rule, you know it is noon when the sun is directly overhead. But when it is noon where you are, the sun is not at its highest point at other places. Because of the Earth's rotation, the sun has not yet reached its highest point at places west of you. And the sun is past its highest point at places east of you. So according to sun time, these other places have different times.

Telling time by the sun was not a problem until people began to travel long distances. When transcontinental railroads began to cross the United States and Canada, no one knew what time to use to follow train schedules. So a new time system was developed. Knowing how to use this system is just as important today as it was during the 1800s.

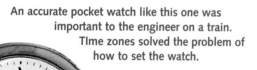

An accurate pocket watch like this one was important to the engineer on a train. Time zones solved the problem of how to set the watch.

Time Zones

As the railroads grew, managers set schedules of times when trains would arrive and depart from places along their routes. But setting schedules was difficult because of the many time differences from place to place. No one knew whose time to use. Most railroads set their own times. They called it "railroad time." By the 1880s there were about 100 different railroad times. This made things very confusing.

Finally, two men had an idea to help solve the problem. Charles Dowd of the United States and Sandford Fleming of Canada decided to divide the world into time zones. A **time zone** is a region in which a single time is used.

Fleming and Dowd divided the world into 24 time zones. A new time zone begins at every fifteenth meridian, starting at the Prime Meridian and moving west. In each new time zone to the west, the time is one hour earlier than in the time zone before it. All parts of a time zone use the same time. In the 1880s the railroads began to use this plan. Now most of the countries in the world follow it.

The United States has six time zones. From east to west, they are the eastern, central, mountain, Pacific, Alaska, and Hawaii-Aleutian time zones.

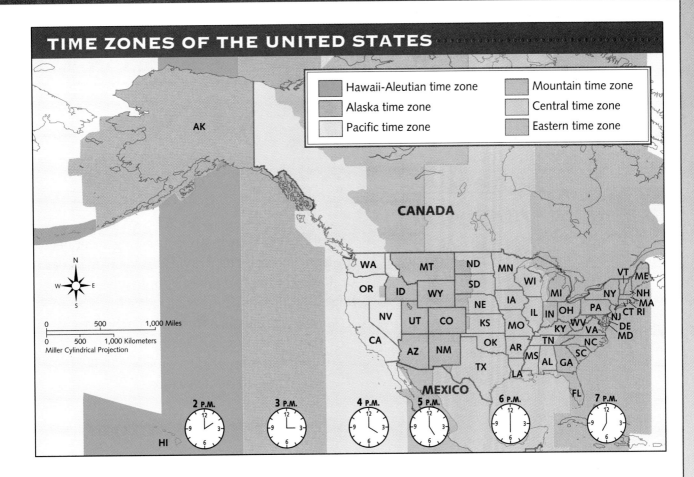

TIME ZONES OF THE UNITED STATES

Hawaii-Aleutian time zone
Alaska time zone
Pacific time zone
Mountain time zone
Central time zone
Eastern time zone

Understand the Process

How can you figure out what time it is in cities that are in different time zones? Follow the steps listed in the example below to guide you:

1. Find Maryland on the map. It is in the eastern time zone.
2. Now find Arkansas. It is in the central time zone, which is just west of the eastern time zone. The time in the central time zone is one hour earlier than in the eastern time zone. To find the time in Arkansas, subtract one hour from the time in Maryland.
3. Find Colorado on the map. It is in the mountain time zone. The time is two hours earlier in Colorado than in Maryland. To find the time in Colorado, subtract two hours from the time in Maryland.
4. Now look to the west on the map to find California. It is in the Pacific time zone. The time is three hours earlier in California than in Maryland. To find the time in California,

subtract three hours from the time in Maryland.
5. Locate the largest part of Alaska, in the Alaska time zone. The time there is four hours earlier than in Maryland. To find the time in this part of Alaska, subtract four hours from the time in Maryland.
6. Find Hawaii on the map. It is in the Hawaii-Aleutian time zone. The time is five hours earlier in Hawaii than in Maryland. To find the time in Hawaii, subtract five hours from the time in Maryland.

Think and Apply

 Use an almanac to find a world time zone map. Suppose it is 9 A.M. where you live. Find the time in each of these cities: London, England; Tokyo, Japan; and Cairo, Egypt. Help younger students understand time zones by describing how you figured out the time for each of these cities. Then explain when it would be helpful to know the time in different places.

GROWING PAINS

LESSON 2

Link to Our World

How do people today improve their working conditions?

Focus on the Main Idea
Read to find out how people fought for better working conditions in the late 1800s and early 1900s.

Preview Vocabulary
human resource
strike
labor union
federation
regulate

These boys worked in a coal mine. Young mine workers were often sent to parts of the mine that were too small for adults to crawl through.

The growth of industry caused a greater need for **human resources**, or workers, as well as natural and capital resources. People were needed to build railroads, mine coal, stoke furnaces in steel mills, refine oil, and make machines and other products. Workers by the thousands—many of them immigrants—moved to the industrial cities to fill these jobs.

WORK IN THE FACTORIES

Because there were so many people looking for work, factory owners were able to hire people willing to work for low wages. As the years passed, the number of workers went up, and wages went down. Soon many factory workers could no longer support their families. They needed more money just to buy food and pay rent. To bring in the money they needed, many parents sent their children to work.

In the 20 years between 1890 and 1910, the number of working children between ages 10 and 15 went from 1.5 million to 2 million. By 1910, children made up almost one-fifth of the workers in the United States.

Many children no longer had time for school. They worked in factories all day. In 1906, John Spargo, a reporter, described what he saw in one glassmaking factory.

66 The hours of labor for the 'night shift' were from 5:30 pm to 3:30 am. . . . Then began the work of . . . the 'carrying-in boys,' sometimes called 'carrier pigeons,' [who] took the red-hot bottles from the benches, three or four at a time. . . .
The work of these 'carrying-in boys,' several

An employer saved money by hiring children, because they could be paid much less than adults. The children shown in this photograph are working in a textile mill.

of whom were less than twelve years old, was by far the hardest of all. They were kept on a slow run all the time from the benches to the annealing [finishing] oven . . . [the trip] was one hundred feet, and the boys made seventy-two trips per hour, making the distance traveled in eight hours nearly twenty-two miles. Over half of this distance the boys were carrying their hot loads to the oven. The pay of these boys varies from sixty cents to a dollar for eight hours' work. 99

Workers of all ages had another problem, too— the machines. Workers had to be careful because many machines were not safe. Hundreds of workers were killed each year in factory accidents, and thousands more were badly hurt.

66 **THE WORK OF THESE 'CARRYING-IN BOYS,' several of whom were less than twelve years old, was by far the hardest of all.** 99

John Spargo, 1906

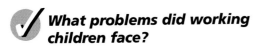
What problems did working children face?

OWNERS AGAINST WORKERS

Some workers complained about their working conditions. Others went on strike, or stopped work, as a way to get the factory owners to listen to them. Few factory owners did. They simply fired the complainers and hired new workers. Plenty of people were still looking for jobs.

As conditions grew worse, some workers started to fight back. By themselves they could do little against the power of the factory owners. Together they formed labor unions. A labor union is a group of workers who take action to protect their interests.

One early labor union leader was Samuel Gompers. When Gompers was 14 years old, he went to work in a cigar makers' shop. The cigar makers worked from dawn until sunset. Most were paid only pennies an hour. Gompers joined a cigar makers' union, and soon he was the union leader in his shop. In 1877 Gompers brought all of the separate cigar makers' unions together to form one large union. Members of the union went on strike for a shorter workday and better wages, but the strike failed. Tobacco buyers owned many of the apartment buildings where workers lived. They fired the striking workers and put them out of their apartments.

After this experience Gompers decided that cigar makers needed other workers to join them to make the labor union stronger. He believed that only skilled workers should be in this federation. If skilled workers went on strike, it would be hard to replace them. The strike might then have a better chance. Gompers began to organize groups of different skilled workers, such as carpenters, plumbers, and bricklayers along with the cigar makers, into one large federation. A **federation** is an organization made up of many member groups.

In 1886 Samuel Gompers formed the American Federation of Labor, or AFL. As the AFL got larger, business leaders began to listen to its representatives. The AFL asked for higher wages and a shorter workday. Workers sang,

> **"**Eight hours for work,
> eight hours for rest,
> eight hours for what we will.**"**

The AFL also wanted better working conditions, accident insurance, and an end to child labor. The insurance would pay the wages and medical bills for workers who were hurt on the job.

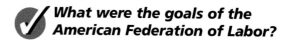 **What were the goals of the American Federation of Labor?**

LABOR UNIONS AND STRIKES

Going on strike became the labor unions' most important way to be heard by the factory owners. Sometimes, however, strikes became violent. Violence did not help the unions. In fact, some labor unions lost their power.

In 1886, workers belonging to a labor union known as the Knights of Labor went on strike against the McCormick Harvesting Machine Company. The union demanded higher wages and an eight-hour workday. During one protest meeting, strikers clashed with police at Haymarket Square in Chicago. Suddenly, someone threw a bomb. Seven police officers were killed, and many other people were hurt. No one knew who threw the bomb, but people blamed the labor union. The Knights of Labor soon lost many of its members.

LEARNING FROM GRAPHS This graph shows the number of workers who joined unions from 1898 to 1920.
■ How did union membership change during this time?

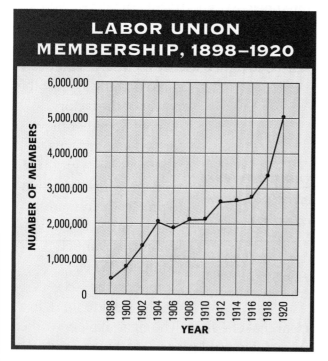

LABOR UNION MEMBERSHIP, 1898–1920

NUMBER OF MEMBERS

6,000,000
5,000,000
4,000,000
3,000,000
2,000,000
1,000,000
0

1898 1900 1902 1904 1906 1908 1910 1912 1914 1916 1918 1920

YEAR

One of the demands of these New York City clothing workers was an eight-hour workday. Many of the workers in this photograph were immigrants and carried signs in their own languages, including Italian, Yiddish, and Russian.

One of the most violent strikes during this time took place in 1892 at a Carnegie steel mill in the town of Homestead, Pennsylvania, near Pittsburgh. While Andrew Carnegie was in Scotland, one of his managers, Henry Clay Frick, announced a pay cut. In June the workers went on strike. Frick fought back. He shut down the mill and hired private police from the Pinkerton National Detective Agency to protect it.

When 300 Pinkertons, as they were called, arrived in Homestead, they were met by hundreds of angry union workers. A fight broke out, and 7 Pinkertons and 9 strikers were killed. The governor of Pennsylvania sent in soldiers from the National Guard to keep order.

The Homestead strike went on for four months. Finally the union gave up. Frick won, but many people began to think that factory owners should listen to labor unions' demands.

 What caused the Homestead strike?

GOVERNMENT AND BUSINESS

Workers used strikes in the hope of making their lives and working conditions better. But pay was still low, and many children still had to work. And more and more workers were hurt in accidents every year. Workers hoped that the government would help, but many government leaders took the side of the factory owners.

Government leaders believed that business people helped make the country's economy strong by producing goods and creating new jobs. The leaders felt that government should leave factory owners and their businesses alone. For industry to grow, they said, businesses had to be free to produce goods in the best way possible.

Business leaders also felt that government should leave their companies alone. They did not want government to start telling them what to do. They feared that government would then **regulate** their businesses, or control them by law. Business owners wanted as few laws having to do with their businesses as possible.

 Why did the government choose to leave business owners alone?

What?

Labor Day

In New York City on September 5, 1882, Americans held the first Labor Day parade. Matthew Maguire, a machine worker, and Peter McGuire, a carpenter and the founder of an early labor union, are given credit for the idea of Labor Day. It is a day to honor working people and to recognize their importance to the United States. In 1894 Congress made Labor Day a legal holiday. Today the United States and Canada celebrate Labor Day on the first Monday in September. On different days many other countries also honor workers with labor celebrations.

Crowds watch a Labor Day parade in New York City in 1926.

LESSON 2 REVIEW

Check Understanding

1. **Recall the Facts**   What were conditions like for factory workers during the late 1800s?
2. **Focus on the Main Idea**   How did people fight for better working conditions in the years between 1890 and 1910?

Think Critically

3. **Explore Viewpoints**   How do you think workers in the late 1800s felt about going on strike? How do you think business owners felt?

4. **Personally Speaking**   If you had worked in the glass factory that John Spargo described in 1906, how might you have felt about your job?

Show What You Know

Art Activity   Think about the problems that factory workers faced years ago. Draw a poster that you think a labor union might have used to get people to join. Display your poster in the classroom.

NEW IMMIGRANTS

Link to Our World

What problems do immigrants to the United States face today?

Focus on the Main Idea
Read about some of the problems that immigrants to the United States faced in the past.

Preview Vocabulary
prejudice
barrio
tenement
naturalization

About three of every four workers in the Carnegie steel mills had been born outside the United States. Carnegie himself had been born in Scotland. When he was 12 years old, he had moved to the United States with his father. Between 1860 and 1910, about 23 million immigrants arrived in the United States. Those from Asia and Mexico settled mostly in the West and Southwest. Those from Europe settled mostly in the cities on the East coast and in the growing industrial cities of the Middle West. Immigrants played an important part in the growth of agriculture and industry in the United States.

ASIAN IMMIGRANTS

Chinese people came to the United States in great numbers after the California gold rush of 1849. By 1852 about 25,000 Chinese had arrived in San Francisco and were working in the goldfields.

Like other immigrant groups, the Chinese faced prejudice from some Americans who were born in the United States. **Prejudice** is a feeling some people have against others because of their race or culture. The Chinese were made to pay a special tax to pan for gold. Some Americans tried to force the Chinese out of the goldfields by beating them and even killing them.

As less and less gold was found in the goldfields, the Chinese looked for other work. Because they wanted to stay in the United States, they were willing to work for low wages. Some Chinese immigrants worked in mining and agriculture. Thousands worked for the Central Pacific Railroad to build the transcontinental railroad.

Some immigrants, like this Chinese American, needed to carry a special certificate when they traveled so that they would be allowed to return to the United States.

Some Mexican American families had lived in the United States for many years. This photograph shows five generations of the Aguilar family of Texas in 1902.

By the 1870s many Americans wanted to stop the Chinese from coming to the United States. They also wanted Chinese people who were already here to go back to China. The Americans worried that the immigrants would take their jobs. California and other western states passed laws that made life harder for the Chinese. Chinese people could not get state jobs, for example. They had to pay higher state taxes. State courts would not hear lawsuits brought by Chinese people. Finally, in 1882 Congress passed a law that stopped all immigration by Chinese people. By this time there were about 75,000 Chinese immigrants living in the United States.

Japanese and other Asian people still were allowed to come to the United States. Most found jobs in agriculture. Many bought small farms in California and parts of the Southwest. But in time they, too, met with prejudice. By the early 1900s many Americans were calling for a stop to all immigration from Asia. But instead of passing a law to stop immigration, the United States government persuaded Japan to stop all but a few of its people from going to the United States.

 Why did many Americans want to stop Asian immigration?

MEXICAN IMMIGRANTS

Mexican Americans had lived in the Southwest for years. Many lived in places that had been part of Mexico before the Treaty of Guadalupe Hidalgo, which ended the Mexican War.

During the late 1800s, immigrants from Mexico came to many places in the south-western part of the United States. By 1900 about 80,000 Mexican immigrants had come to Texas, New Mexico, Arizona, and southern California.

Like most new immigrants to the United States, few Mexicans spoke English or knew people in the United States. Imagine how these immigrants must have felt when they first met people from their homeland. Just to be able to talk with people in their own language made them feel more at home.

Soon **barrios**, or neighborhoods of people from Mexico, sprang up in most cities in the Southwest. People in the barrios helped one another. The immigrants who had been here longer helped the new immigrants find homes and jobs. Many Mexican immigrants found jobs on farms. They spent almost 14 hours a day planting, weeding, and picking lettuce, tomatoes, and grapes. Others found factory jobs in the cities.

Like the immigrants from China and Japan, those from Mexico also met with prejudice. Some people tried to make them go back to Mexico. Many Mexicans were beaten, and some were killed. In 1910 a writer for a Mexican newspaper wondered what made "our countrymen, so attached to the land, . . . abandon the country, even at the risk of the Yankee contempt [lack of respect] with which they are treated on the other side of the Bravo [Rio Grande]."

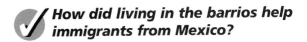 **How did living in the barrios help immigrants from Mexico?**

EUROPEAN IMMIGRANTS

European immigrants were by far the largest group to come to the United States. Between 1890 and 1920, nearly 16 million immigrants arrived from countries in Europe.

Before 1890 most European immigrants had come from northern and western Europe. They had come from countries such as Britain, Ireland, Germany, Norway, and Sweden. These were the immigrants who had helped build the Erie Canal and who had taken part in the great westward movement.

LEARNING FROM GRAPHS The number of immigrants to the United States is shown on this graph for four periods of time.

■ When were there more immigrants from eastern Europe than from northwestern Europe?

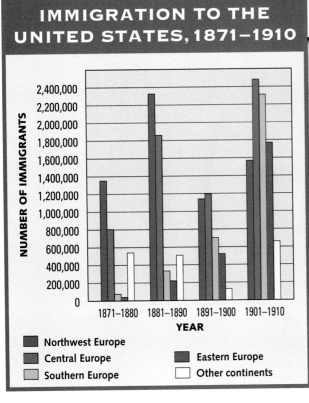

IMMIGRATION TO THE UNITED STATES, 1871–1910

NUMBER OF IMMIGRANTS

YEAR: 1871–1880, 1881–1890, 1891–1900, 1901–1910

- Northwest Europe
- Central Europe
- Southern Europe
- Eastern Europe
- Other continents

Most immigrants, like the members of this family, brought few belongings with them when they came to the United States. How might age affect learning to live in a new country?

Around 1890 a new period of immigration began. People still came from the countries of northern and western Europe, but now they also came from countries in southern and eastern Europe. They came from Italy, Greece, Poland, Austria, Hungary, Armenia, and Russia. Many of these people were poor and unhappy in their homelands. Often they did not have enough to eat. They came to the United States hoping for a better life.

Most of the ships that brought European immigrants to the United States landed at Ellis Island in New York Harbor. Many immigrants stayed in New York City. After a while some moved to the new industrial cities, where they hoped to find factory jobs. Many immigrants had lived on small farms in Europe, and they had hoped to buy land in the United States. But few were able to. Most lived with relatives or friends. Many lived crowded together in poorly built apartment houses called **tenements**. Wages were so low that everyone in the family had to work just to earn enough money for food.

Like other immigrants, the Europeans often met with prejudice. Posters about jobs sometimes said, "Irish need not apply." Some were even treated badly by immigrants who had arrived earlier. Immigrants who were already living and working

in the United States worried that the new immigrants would take away their jobs.

 From what parts of Europe did many immigrants come after the 1890s?

BECOMING A CITIZEN

No matter how hard their lives were, many immigrants felt that becoming an American citizen was very important. To be a citizen

Where?

Angel Island and Ellis Island

In the late 1800s and early 1900s, Angel Island in San Francisco Bay and Ellis Island in New York Harbor were the places where ships carrying immigrants landed in the United States. Both islands served as immigration stations. Immigrants were checked for health problems, and anyone with a serious illness was sent back to his or her country. Immigrants also had to tell about themselves, their families, and their job skills. Anyone who had been in jail was sent back. Sometimes the names of immigrants were changed by mistake because the workers filling out papers could not understand different languages.

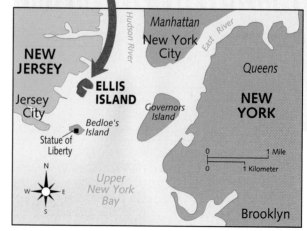

Immigrant children came from many different cultures. This diversity is shown by these children living in Gary, Indiana.

meant taking part in the government, voting, and serving on juries. To many immigrants, these rights were something new.

Immigrants could become citizens through a process called **naturalization**. They had to live in the United States for five years and then pass a test. The test asked questions about the government and history of the United States, such as *Who makes the laws in the United States?* and *Who was the first President?*

The questions on the test had to be answered in English. Thousands of immigrants went to school after work so they could learn English to take the test. Those who passed the test took an oath promising allegiance, or loyalty, to the United States.

❝I pledge allegiance to the Flag of the United States of America, and to the Republic for which it stands, one Nation under God, indivisible, with liberty and justice for all.**❞**

✔ *How did an immigrant become a citizen of the United States?*

LESSON 3 REVIEW

Check Understanding

1. **Recall the Facts**   What were some of the reasons immigrants came to the United States?
2. **Focus on the Main Idea**   What problems did immigrants to the United States face in the past?

Think Critically

3. **Personally Speaking**   How might you feel if you were the target of prejudice?
4. **Think More About It**   Why was becoming an American citizen important to many immigrants?

Show What You Know

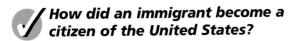

Writing Activity   Imagine that it is the late 1800s and you are an immigrant who has just arrived in the United States in search of a job. Use the information in this lesson to write a journal entry about what you might see and do. Share your writing with a classmate.

LEARN with LITERATURE

Focus on the Movement
of People from Place to Place

The Great Migration

AN AMERICAN STORY

by Jacob Lawrence

Even as immigrants moved to the United States from other countries, people within the United States moved from place to place. This was true of many different groups of native-born Americans, including African Americans.

After the Civil War, most African Americans in the South found jobs as workers on farms or as sharecroppers on plantations. Few moved into the cities. But between 1916 and 1919, many decided to move to the industrial cities in the North—to New York, Chicago, Detroit, Pittsburgh, Cleveland, and St. Louis. There they hoped to find jobs in factories. During these years factory workers were needed to fill in for those who left to fight in a war in Europe. The war would later be called World War I. As African Americans left their farms to become factory workers, their lives changed forever.

Jacob Lawrence's family took part in this great migration from the South. Read his story to learn more about the migration and about the problems African Americans shared with other newcomers to the cities during this time.

Around the time I was born, many African-Americans from the South left home and traveled to cities in the North in search of a better life. My family was part of this great migration.

There was a shortage of workers in northern factories because many had left their jobs to fight in the First World War.

The factory owners had to find new workers to replace those who were marching off to war.

Northern industries offered southern blacks jobs as workers and lent them money, to be repaid later, for their railroad tickets. The northbound trains were packed with recruits.

Nature had ravaged the South. Floods ruined farms. The boll weevil destroyed cotton crops.

The war had doubled the cost of food, making life even harder for the poor.

Railroad stations were so crowded with migrants that guards were called to keep order.

The flood of migrants northward left crops back home to dry and spoil.

For African-Americans the South was barren in many ways. There was no justice for them in the courts, and their lives were often in danger.

Although slavery had long been abolished, white landowners treated the black tenant farmers harshly and unfairly.

And so the migration grew.

Segregation divided the South.

The black newspapers told of better housing and jobs in the North.

Families would arrive very early at railroad stations to make sure they could get on the northbound trains.

Early arrival was not easy, because African-Americans found on the streets could be arrested for no reason.

And the migrants kept coming.

In the South there was little opportunity for education, and children labored in the fields. These were more reasons for people to move north, leaving some communities deserted.

There was much excitement and discussion about the great migration.

Agents from northern factories flocked into southern counties and towns, looking for laborers.

Families often gathered to discuss whether to go north or to stay south. The promise of better housing in the North could not be ignored.

The railroad stations were crowded with migrants.

Letters from relatives in the North and articles in the black press portrayed a better life outside the South.

Many migrants arrived in Chicago.

In Chicago and other cities they labored in the steel mills . . . and on the railroads.

And the migrants kept coming.

Southern landowners, stripped of cheap labor, tried to stop the migration by jailing the labor agents and the migrants. Sometimes the agents disguised themselves to avoid arrest, but the migrants were often taken from railroad stations and jailed until the trains departed.

Black and white southern leaders met to discuss ways to improve conditions to stop the flow of workers north.

Although life in the North was better, it was not ideal.

Many migrants moved to Pittsburgh, which was a great industrial center at the time.

Although they were promised better housing in the North, some families were forced to live in overcrowded and unhealthy quarters.

The migrants soon learned that segregation was not confined to the South.

Many northern workers were angry because they had to compete with the migrants for housing and jobs. There were riots.

Longtime African-American residents living in the North did not welcome the newcomers from the South and often treated them with disdain.

The migrants had to rely on each other. The storefront church was a welcoming place and the center of their lives, in joy and in sorrow.

Black professionals, such as doctors and lawyers, soon followed their patients and clients north. Female workers were among the last to leave.

Life in the North brought many challenges, but the migrants' lives had changed for the better. The children were able to go to school, and their parents gained the freedom to vote.

And the migrants kept coming.

Theirs is a story of African-American strength and courage. I share it now as my parents told it to me, because their struggles and triumphs ring true today. People all over the world are still on the move, trying to build better lives for themselves and for their families.

Literature Review

1. What events and problems caused Jacob Lawrence's family to move to the North?
2. Why do you think southern landowners wanted to stop the migration of African Americans to northern cities?
3. Imagine that you live in the North and it is the time during World War I. Write a letter to Jacob Lawrence's family describing how life in the North is different from life in the South.

THE GROWTH of CITIES

Link to Our World

What problems do people face in cities today?

Focus on the Main Idea
Read to learn about problems people faced as cities grew large and about how people worked to solve them.

Preview Vocabulary
settlement house
skyscraper

By the beginning of the twentieth century, cities in the United States were growing fast. Some people thought they were growing too fast. No one had expected it, and no one had planned for it. Millions of people were moving to American cities from the farms, and millions more were coming from other countries. There were just too many people. As cities grew, so did their problems.

CITY PROBLEMS

One problem was that of overcrowded tenements. When one person became ill, disease spread quickly. In one overcrowded Chicago tenement, three out of every five babies born in 1900 died before they were three years old. A newspaper reporter named Jacob Riis (REES) described the same kind of poor living conditions in New York City tenements. He saw that when someone died, a bow made of ribbon was hung on the tenement door—black for an adult and white for a child. Riis wrote,

❝Listen! that short hacking cough, that tiny, helpless wail—what do they mean? They mean that the soiled bow of white you saw on the door downstairs will have another story to tell—Oh! a sadly familiar story—before the day is at an end. The child is dying with measles. With half a chance it might have lived; but it had none.❞

Insects and rats in the garbage caused much of the illness. With so many people in the cities, garbage piled up. Before this time there was no regular garbage collection. Even in the largest cities, garbage was eaten by pigs in the streets.

Crime became a problem in many places as cities grew. This early police badge is from the city of Paterson, New Jersey.

The danger of fire became greater as new buildings went up. Most were made at least partly of wood. Terrible fires burned down entire city blocks. The Chicago fire of 1871 was one of the worst. It burned for 24 hours, killing at least 300 people and leaving more than 90,000 people homeless. Few cities at that time had full-time fire departments.

Crime was another problem in cities. The large numbers of people and businesses made things easy for criminals. And the crowds made it hard for the police to find lawbreakers. Sometimes a gang took over an entire neighborhood in a city, and even the police were afraid to go there.

Jacob Riis took this photograph of people living in a crowded, dirty tenement in New York City.

 What problems faced many people who were living in cities?

HELP FOR THE CITIES' POOR

Some people who lived in cities tried to solve the problems they saw around them. Jane Addams was one person who worked to help. Addams came from a wealthy family and had gone to college, something few women at that time did. She worried about the growing problems of the tenements in Chicago.

On a visit to England, Addams had heard about a place in London called Toynbee Hall. It was a **settlement house**, a community center where people could learn new skills. Addams took the idea back to Chicago.

66 *I GRADUALLY BECAME CONVINCED that it would be a good thing to rent a house in a part of the city where many . . . needs are found.* 99

Jane Addams, 1889

66 It is hard to tell just when the very simple plan . . . began to form itself in my mind. . . . But I gradually became convinced that it would be a good thing to rent a house in a part of the city where many . . . needs are found. 99

In 1889 Jane Addams started Hull House in Chicago with a friend, Ellen Gates Starr. The settlement-house workers ran a kindergarten for children whose mothers worked. They gave classes in sewing, cooking, and English. Later they did other things to help people living in cities. They worked to improve conditions in tenements. They also tried to abolish child labor and to improve health and safety conditions in the mills and factories.

Hull House became a model for other community centers. In 1890 African American teacher Janie Porter Barrett founded a settlement house in Hampton, Virginia. Three years later, Lillian Wald started the Henry Street Settlement in New York City. By 1900 almost 100 settlement houses had opened in American cities.

Why were settlement houses important in the cities?

THE CHANGING CITY

Even with their many problems, cities came to stand for all that was good in industrial America. Besides factories, stores, and tenements, cities had parks, theaters, schools, zoos, railroad stations, and tall office buildings.

Children in this New York City settlement house are attending class. Settlement houses offered help for many people living in cities.

Before this time buildings could not be taller than four or five stories because their walls were made of bricks. The bricks on the bottom had to hold up the weight of all the bricks above them. In the 1880s an engineer named William Jenney found a way to build taller buildings. Jenney used steel frames to hold up a building the way a skeleton holds up a body. In 1885 Jenney built the ten-story Home Insurance Company Building in Chicago. It was the world's first tall, steel-frame building, or **skyscraper**.

As buildings were made taller and taller—20 stories, then 50 stories, then 100 stories—fast, safe elevators were needed. The first electric elevator was put into a skyscraper in New York City in 1889.

As cities grew upward, they also grew outward. When the first cities were built in the United States, people walked to and from work. As people began moving away from the center of the city, transportation was needed to help them get to their jobs.

In this photo from 1901 (left), floors are still being added to New York City's Flatiron Building. Without elevators (far left), skyscrapers would not have been possible.

Streetcars were an important form of transportation in many cities. This streetcar had open sides that made it easy to board.

In 1865 most cities had streetcars pulled by horses. Horses could go only about 6 miles (9.7 km) an hour on flat ground, and each horse cost about $200. In San Francisco the horses had to pull the cars up very steep hills. This was hard for the horses and slow for the passengers. So in 1873 Andrew S. Hallidie invented the cable car. Cable cars were attached to a steam-powered cable running in a slot in the street. The cable pulled the cars at about 9 miles (14.5 km) an hour up and down steep hills. Fifteen cities put in cable cars. Chicago had 710!

Then, in the late 1880s, Frank Sprague built an electric streetcar that was used in Richmond, Virginia. His streetcar also ran along tracks in the street, but electricity was what made it move. A small trolley on top of the car rode along overhead electric wires. The new streetcar was called a trolley car. By 1890 more than 50 cities had trolley transportation systems.

As more trolley tracks were laid farther and farther from the center of the city, many people moved to the suburbs. They still could take trolley cars to work or to shop in the city. But they now could live farther and farther away from the inner city with its many problems.

 What inventions helped cities grow upward and outward during the late 1800s?

LESSON 5 REVIEW

Check Understanding

1. **Recall the Facts**   How did cities change in the late 1800s?
2. **Focus on the Main Idea**   What problems did people face as cities grew large, and how did people work to solve them?

Think Critically

3. **Think More About It**   In what ways do you think Jane Addams was like Samuel Gompers, the labor union leader you read about in Lesson 2?
4. **Cause and Effect**   How did the inventions discussed in this lesson affect city life?

Show What You Know

TV Report Activity   Prepare a script outline for a TV program on life in the cities in the late 1800s. List the topics you might cover in your program. Suggest possible interviews and ideas for pictures, maps, charts, and graphs. Work in a group to present a part of your outline to the class.

Solve a Problem

Why Is This Skill Important?

People everywhere face problems at one time or another. Many people face more than one problem at the same time. Think about a problem you have faced recently. How did you know you had a problem? Were you able to solve it? Did you wish you could have found a better way to solve the problem? Knowing how to solve problems is a skill that you will use your whole life.

Remember What You Have Read

You have read about the many problems that made city life difficult in the late 1800s and early 1900s. Overcrowding, disease, fire, and crime were among the problems that people faced. Jane Addams was one person who tried to help. Think again about the problems Addams saw and the way she tried to solve them.

1. What problems did Jane Addams see in Chicago?
2. What solution did Addams learn about when she visited another city?
3. What did Addams decide was one of the best ways to solve the problems in Chicago?

4. How did Addams carry out her solution?
5. How did Addams's solution help solve the problems of city life?

Understand the Process

You can use similar steps to help you solve problems.

- Identify the problem.
- Think of possible solutions.
- Compare the solutions, and choose the best one.
- Plan how to carry out the solution.
- Try your solution, and think about how well it helps solve the problem.

Think and Apply

Identify a problem in your community or school. Write a plan for solving the problem. What steps did you follow? What solution did you choose? Do you think your solution will help solve the problem? Explain.

Jane Addams founded Hull House to help Chicago's immigrants. Addams (above, with a child at Hull House) was one of the country's best known reformers.

CONNECT MAIN IDEAS

Use this organizer to show that you understand how the chapter's main ideas are connected. Copy the organizer onto a separate sheet of paper. Then complete it by writing three examples to support each main idea.

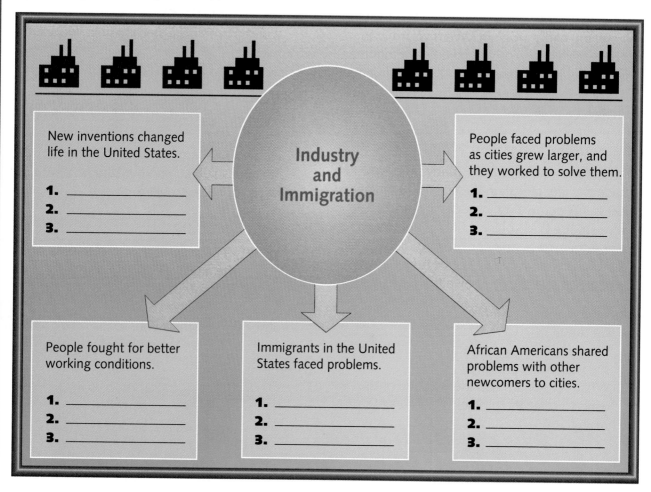

New inventions changed life in the United States.

1. _____
2. _____
3. _____

Industry and Immigration

People faced problems as cities grew larger, and they worked to solve them.

1. _____
2. _____
3. _____

People fought for better working conditions.

1. _____
2. _____
3. _____

Immigrants in the United States faced problems.

1. _____
2. _____
3. _____

African Americans shared problems with other newcomers to cities.

1. _____
2. _____
3. _____

WRITE MORE ABOUT IT

1. **Write a Description** Imagine that you have been asked to write part of a book about working conditions in the United States in the early 1900s. As part of your research, you visit several factories. Describe what you see there.

2. **Write an Explanation** Suppose that you are an immigrant who plans to become a citizen through naturalization. What would you tell someone who asks why you want to become a citizen? Write your response.

3. **Write a Letter** Imagine that you have just moved from a farm to a city in the early 1900s. Write a letter to a friend. Describe how life in the city is different from life on the farm.

For each group of underlined words in the sentences, write the term from the list below that has the same meaning.

capital resources	human resources
corporation	labor union
free enterprise	prejudice

1. The years after the Civil War were an important time for <u>an economic system that allows businesses the freedom to offer for sale many kinds of goods and services</u>.

2. Business owners need <u>money to run their businesses</u>.

3. People sometimes invest their money in a <u>business that sells shares of stock to investors</u>.

4. The growth of industry caused a greater need for <u>workers</u>.

5. Some workers joined a <u>group of workers who take action to protect their interests</u>.

6. Immigrants often faced <u>a feeling some people have against others because of their race or culture</u>.

CHECK UNDERSTANDING

1. What was the transcontinental railroad?

2. How did railroads affect the growth of inland cities?

3. What is an entrepreneur?

4. How were Angel Island and Ellis Island important to immigrants?

5. How could an immigrant become a citizen of the United States?

6. Why did many African Americans move to industrial cities in the North?

7. What invention made it possible for more people to move to suburbs?

THINK CRITICALLY

1. **Cause and Effect**   What effect did the railroad boom have on the steel industry?

2. **Think More About It**   Why do you think some factory owners in the early 1900s treated their workers poorly?

3. **Explore Viewpoints**   How do you think workers' views of labor unions might have differed from the views held by factory owners?

4. **Past to Present**   Hull House helped to improve the lives of poor people living in Chicago. What groups try to improve the lives of poor people in cities today?

APPLY SKILLS

 How to Use a Time Zone Map   Use the time zone map on page 459 to answer these questions.

1. If it is 10 A.M. in Illinois, what is the time in Ohio?

2. If it is 5 P.M. in Georgia, what is the time in New Mexico?

3. If it is 3 A.M. in North Carolina, what is the time in Colorado?

How to Solve a Problem   Identify a problem that a person you read about in this chapter faced. Use the steps listed on page 479 to write a plan that you think might help solve the problem.

EAD MORE ABOUT IT

The Factories by Leonard Everett Fisher. Holiday House. This book shows how the work of Samuel Slater set the stage for amazing industrial growth in the United States during the 1800s.

Immigrant Kids by Russell Freedman. Dutton. This book describes the everyday lives of immigrant children during the late 1800s and early 1900s.

CHAPTER 16

The LAST FRONTIER

> 66 Most of the time we were solitary adventurers in a great land as fresh and new as a spring morning, and we were free and full of the zest of darers. 99
>
> Charles Goodnight,
> Texas cattle driver and rancher

Cowhands like the one in this photograph worked on ranches throughout the West.

FARMING THE GREAT PLAINS

Link to Our World

How do people today change their ways of life to suit their environments?

Focus on the Main Idea
Read to learn how western farmers changed some of their ways to suit conditions on the Great Plains.

Preview Vocabulary
homesteader
sod
bonanza farm

The explorers of the early 1800s who first crossed the Great Plains described the region as a desert. By the 1890s, however, farmers were turning the plains into fields of wheat. The Great Plains would become the "breadbasket" of the United States and the greatest wheat-growing region in the world.

SETTLING THE PLAINS

In 1862, while the Civil War was being fought in the East, Congress passed the Homestead Act. This law opened the Great Plains to settlers by giving 160 acres of land to anyone who would live on it for five years. Between 1862 and 1900 about 80 million acres of public land on the Great Plains was settled. The people who settled the government lands, or homesteads, were called **homesteaders**.

Thousands more settlers bought western land at low prices from the railroads. Over the years the government had given the railroads millions of acres of land on the Great Plains. Railroad owners used the land to build new railroad lines. But they also wanted people to settle there because settlers would bring more business. Settlers would use the railroads for travel. Farmers would use the railroads to send their products to the cities in the Middle West and in the East.

The railroads placed advertisements for land sales in newspapers all over the United States and in other countries. Many Americans

Advertisements like this one urged settlers to buy low-cost land on the Great Plains.

jumped at the chance to buy land in the West. Most wanted to start farms or ranches. Some planned to open businesses. More than 100,000 immigrants moved to the West from northern Europe. All hoped to find better lives. By 1890 there were 5 million people living on the Great Plains.

The best lands on the Plains were quickly taken. In the Oklahoma land rush of 1889, thousands of homesteaders raced each other to claim land. By 1890 most of the territories in the Great Plains had enough people to become states. North Dakota, South Dakota, and Montana joined the Union in 1889. Wyoming joined in 1890. Oklahoma followed in 1907.

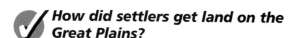 **How did settlers get land on the Great Plains?**

LIFE ON THE FAMILY FARM

Living on the Great Plains was very different from living in most other places in the United States. Trees for building homes were scarce, but there was plenty of **sod**—soil in which thick grass grows. Many settlers used sod to build their houses. Sod houses were cool in summer and warm in winter, but keeping them clean was a problem. Dirt often fell from the sod ceiling onto the furniture. Sometimes snakes did, too! Leaky roofs were common. "There was running water in our sod house," joked one Kansas girl. "It ran through the roof."

Farm families on the Plains faced other problems. In summer, sun baked the thin, dusty soil. In winter, snow and freezing

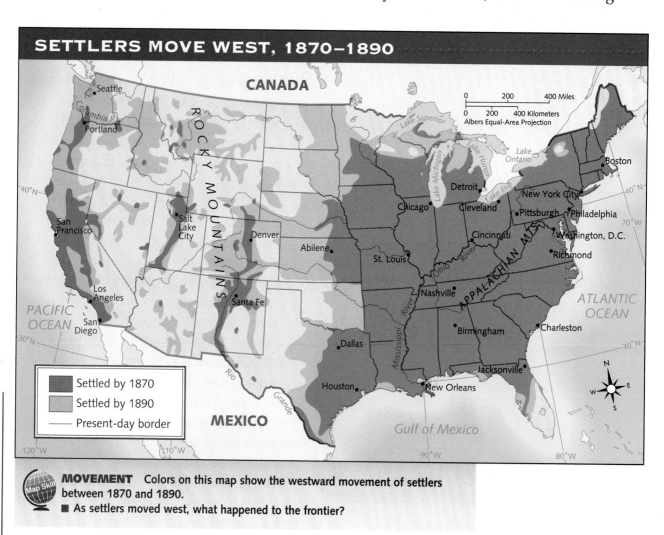

SETTLERS MOVE WEST, 1870–1890

Legend:
- Settled by 1870
- Settled by 1890
- Present-day border

MOVEMENT Colors on this map show the westward movement of settlers between 1870 and 1890.

■ As settlers moved west, what happened to the frontier?

Because few trees grew on the Great Plains, many families lived in houses made of sod. Windmills were used to pump water from wells dug in the ground.

temperatures blasted the region. In years of drought nothing grew. When crops did grow, farmers worried about prairie fires and hailstorms. One settler, Susan Orcutt, wrote that they would have had plenty to eat "if the hail hadn't cut our rye down and ruined our corn and potatoes."

Insects, too, were a problem. Grasshoppers attacked in 1874. They came by the millions, blackening the sky and eating anything that was green. Adelheit Viets was wearing a white dress with green stripes the day the grasshoppers came. "The grasshoppers settled on me and ate up every bit of green stripe in the dress before anything could be done about it," she remembered.

Changes in technology helped many farm families survive. New models of windmills let farmers pump water from hundreds of feet below the ground. Stronger plows, first invented by James Oliver of Indiana, helped homesteaders cut through the thick sod. And harvesting machines made farm work easier.

Sometimes the hardships became so great that some people left their farms. But most stayed. They built churches and schools, starting towns and cities all over the Great Plains.

 What hardships did the early Plains farmers face?

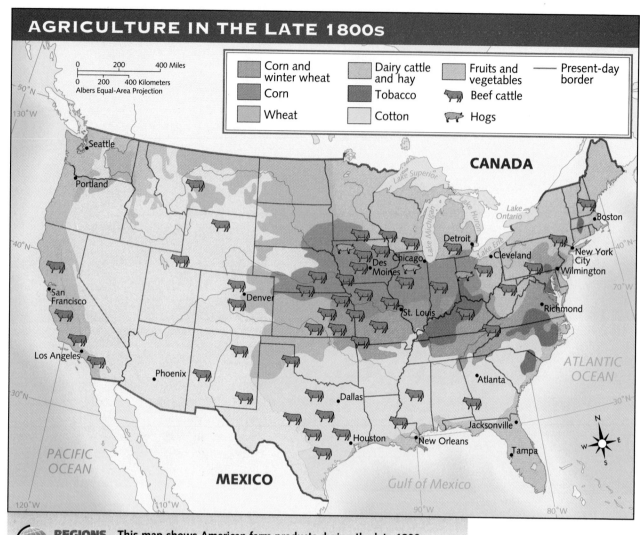

AGRICULTURE IN THE LATE 1800s

Legend:
- Corn and winter wheat
- Corn
- Wheat
- Dairy cattle and hay
- Tobacco
- Cotton
- Fruits and vegetables
- Beef cattle
- Hogs
- Present-day border

0 200 400 Miles
0 200 400 Kilometers
Albers Equal-Area Projection

REGIONS This map shows American farm products during the late 1800s.
■ If you had lived on the Great Plains during this time, what crops would you probably have grown?

"BONANZA FARMS"

Using the new technology and the railroads, some companies started large farms on the Great Plains. People in the East invested money in these **bonanza farms**. A bonanza is something that makes a good profit.

The first bonanza farms on the Great Plains grew wheat in the Red River valley of present-day North Dakota and Minnesota. By 1890 there were about 300 of these farms, each spreading over thousands of acres.

Bonanza farms were run like factories by managers. Workers had specialized jobs, and everything was done by machines. When the wheat was ripe, workers used 30-horse teams to pull reaping machines across the fields. Tons of wheat from bonanza farms were sent by railroad to feed millions in the cities of the Middle West and the East.

Bonanza farms made large profits for their investors because they could grow crops cheaply. They bought seed and equipment in large amounts, so they paid lower prices. But in times of drought and when wheat prices were low, profits fell. Because of this, many bonanza farms on the Great Plains went out of business.

How was a bonanza farm like a factory?

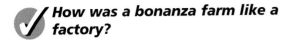

The Reaper

For hundreds of years farmers harvested crops such as wheat using a scythe (SYTH), a long, curved knife with a handle. This was very hard work. In 1831 an inventor named Cyrus McCormick built a reaping machine. Farmers could cut as much wheat in one day with McCormick's reaper as they could cut in two weeks with a scythe. In 1847 McCormick started a reaper factory in Chicago. The McCormick Harvesting Machine Company built many of the reapers used on farms on the Great Plains. In the late 1800s many farmers began to use combines (below). Combines are reapers and threshers. They cut crops and separate the grain from the straw.

Check Understanding

1. **Recall the Facts**   What hardships did the homesteaders face?
2. **Focus on the Main Idea**   What changes did western farmers make in their lives to live on the Great Plains?

Think Critically

3. **Think More About It**   Why do you think people stayed on the Great Plains despite the hardships?
4. **Personally Speaking**   How do you think you would have liked living on the Great Plains during this time?

Show What You Know

Art Activity   Draw a picture of a settlement on the Great Plains. Include a house and farm equipment. Share your picture with classmates or a family member.

487

How To

Read a Climograph

Why Is This Skill Important?

In the late 1800s, many Americans who moved from eastern cities to the Great Plains were surprised by much of what they found there. Nothing surprised them more, perhaps, than the constant wind and the extremes of temperature and precipitation. Suppose you and your family were moving to another part of the country or another part of the world. You would want to know more about the climate before you got there.

Understand the Process

One way to learn about the climate of a place is to study a climograph, or climate graph. A **climograph** shows the average monthly temperature and the average monthly precipitation for a place. Both temperature and precipitation information are shown on the same graph. The temperatures are shown as a line graph. The amounts of precipitation are shown as a bar graph. Along the bottom of a climograph, the months are labeled, from January to December.

Study the climographs on page 489. Along the left-hand side of each climograph is a Fahrenheit scale for temperature. A point is shown on the climograph for the average temperature for each month. These points are connected with a red line. By studying the line, you can see which months are hotter and which are colder.

Along the right-hand side of each climograph is a scale for precipitation. The average monthly amounts of precipitation are shown in inches. By studying the heights of the blue bars, you can see which months are usually dry and which are usually wet.

These two climographs show weather averages for Omaha, Nebraska, and Philadelphia, Pennsylvania. Omaha is on the Great Plains, and Philadelphia is near the Atlantic coast. By comparing the climographs, you can see the differences in temperature and precipitation between these two places. This might help you understand why many early settlers on the Great Plains were surprised by new climates. Use the climographs to answer the questions on page 489.

Many pioneers experienced blizzards on the northern Great Plains. A blizzard is a dangerous snowstorm with winds of 35 miles (56 km) per hour or more.

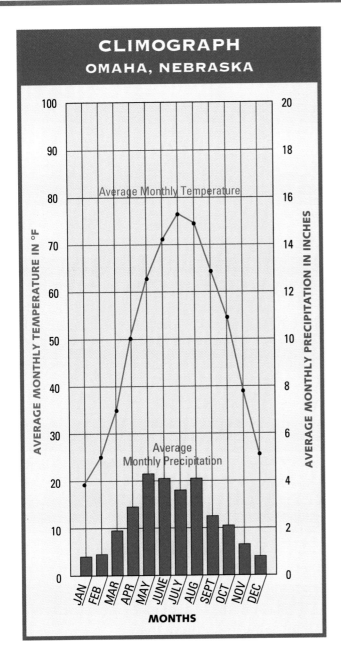

CLIMOGRAPH
OMAHA, NEBRASKA

Average Monthly Temperature

Average Monthly Precipitation

MONTHS

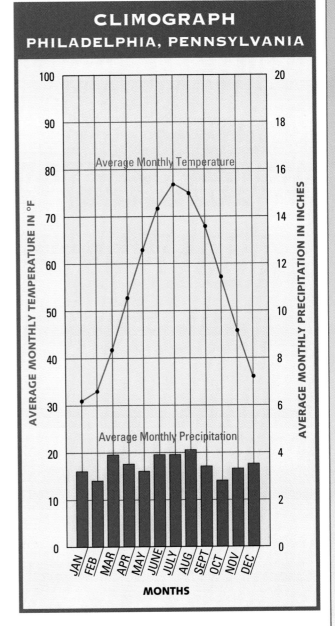

CLIMOGRAPH
PHILADELPHIA, PENNSYLVANIA

Average Monthly Temperature

Average Monthly Precipitation

MONTHS

1. Which is the warmest month in each of the cities?
2. Which is the coldest month in each place?
3. What are the wettest months in each city?
4. What are the driest months in each place?
5. Which city receives more precipitation during the year?
6. What is the average temperature for each place in January?
7. How much precipitation falls during that month in each place?

Think and Apply

Use an almanac to create a climograph for your city or for a city close to where you live. Compare your climograph with the ones on this page. Which place shows the greatest changes in temperature and precipitation? Share your findings with a family member or friend. Then discuss the importance of this information. When might people need to know this information? What does it tell you about the place where you live?

The CATTLE KINGDOM

Link to Our World

How do people build businesses today?

Focus on the Main Idea
Read to find out how ranchers built the Cattle Kingdom.

Preview Vocabulary
long drive
open range
vaquero
barbed wire
range wars

Ranching in the American West began in the 1700s in what is now Texas, when that area was a Spanish colony. These first ranches started with cattle brought from Spain. By the early 1800s settlers from the United States and Mexico had moved to Texas. Many started ranches. After the Civil War, cattle ranches spread over the Great Plains. Parts of the region came to be known as the Cattle Kingdom. In the Cattle Kingdom, ranching became a way of life.

THE RISE OF THE CATTLE INDUSTRY

Before the Civil War, cattle were raised mainly for their hides. In Texas, cattle sold for about $4 each. In northern cities, however, there was a great demand for beef. Cattle sold there for 10 times as much as they did in Texas. It was clear that ranchers could make a lot more money if they could get their cattle to northern markets.

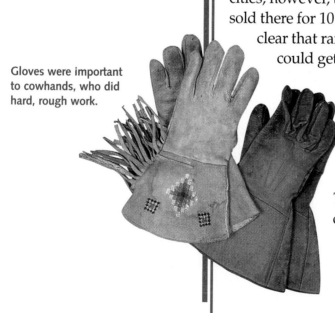

Gloves were important to cowhands, who did hard, rough work.

Railroad lines were the answer. Joseph McCoy, a cattle trader, built large cattle pens called stockyards near some railroad tracks in Abilene, Kansas. Then he sent word to ranchers in Texas that he would buy whole herds of cattle. In 1867 Texas ranchers started moving huge herds of cattle north to Abilene. Later, as the railroad was built farther west, other cities also became important "cow towns," or places where stockyards were located. These were Dodge City, Kansas; Ogallala, Nebraska; and Cheyenne, Wyoming.

Longhorn cattle are easily frightened, making a cowhand's job especially dangerous during a storm. This painting by Frederic Remington is called *Stampede by Lightning*. When cattle stampeded, cowhands tried to race ahead and make them run in a circle until the cattle became tired and slowed down.

A cattle drive was the best way to get cattle to the cow towns. It was called a cattle drive because the ranchers were making the cattle go where they wanted them to, or driving them. Between 1867 and 1890, Texas ranchers drove about 10 million head of cattle north. These trips were called **long drives**.

Each long drive took about three months. During the drive a trail boss managed a crew of 10 to 12 cowhands, who were skilled ranch workers. During a long drive a crew could move as many as 3,000 cattle.

The long drives followed several trails. One of these was the Chisholm (CHIZ•uhm) Trail. It started in southern Texas and ran all the way to Abilene. When the herds reached Abilene, the cattle were loaded onto freight cars and sent to Chicago, where they were prepared for market. Their meat was then sent in refrigerated freight cars to all parts of the East. The invention of the refrigerated freight car also allowed farmers from as far

away as California to send fruits and vegetables across the country without spoiling.

 **What were the long drives?**

THE OPEN RANGE

Ranchers soon started letting their cattle graze on the huge open grasslands of the Great Plains. The cattle ranchers did not own the grasslands, but they used millions of acres of this public land for their herds. The government allowed the ranchers to use the land as **open range**, or free grazing land.

Many of the early ranches were owned and run by families. One of the best-known ranches was started by Richard King in Texas in the 1850s. The King Ranch in South Texas covered more than 1 million acres.

While few ranches were as large as King's, most still covered thousands of acres. The ranches had to be large because the cattle

CATTLE TRAILS

MOVEMENT This map shows four of the major cattle trails used during the 1880s.
■ Why did the trails run north and south?

needed a lot of grazing land to get enough to eat. They also needed water. Rivers, lakes, and streams often determined the size and location of ranches. "Wherever there is any water, there is a ranch," said one cattle rancher.

By the 1880s large companies owned many ranches. They used the government's offer of land and money from investors to set up huge ranches. About 20 companies invested $12 million in Wyoming ranches alone.

Why were open range lands important to ranchers?

RANCH LIFE

Living on a ranch meant hard work for everyone. Women often cooked for all the cowhands and did other chores. Even children did adult jobs, caring for the horses and herding cattle.

The most important event in ranch life was the roundup. Each spring and fall ranchers and hired cowhands, then called cowboys, drove the cattle from the open range to a stockyard. There the cattle were marked with a brand. Each rancher's brand had a special shape, so it was easy to tell from the brand who owned which cattle.

Who?

Bill Pickett 1870?–1932

A ranch boss once described African American cowhand Bill Pickett as "the greatest sweat and dirt cowhand that ever lived—bar none." Pickett worked for much of his life on the 101 Ranch in what is now Oklahoma. He also was part of the 101 Ranch Wild West Show. Pickett, a rodeo rider, was said to have started bulldogging, or steer wrestling. In 1971 Pickett was elected to the Cowboy Hall of Fame. He was the first African American to receive that honor.

Cowhands learned many of their skills from Mexican **vaqueros** (bah•KAY•rohs), the first cowhands. Many familiar cowhand words, such as *lariat*, or rope, and *chaps*, or leather trousers, come from Spanish words. The word *rodeo* is the Spanish word for "roundup."

The cowhand has become a legend of the American West. People picture a rider in pointed-toe boots, wide-brimmed hat, and leather chaps. Real cowhands, however, had hard lives. They worked in all kinds of weather and made little money. The long drives and the roundups also kept them away from their families for long periods of time. Most worked as cowhands for only a few years before they settled in towns or on farms. A popular song of this time ended with these words:

> ❝Good-by, old trail boss, I wish
> you no harm;
> I'm quittin' this business to go
> on the farm.
> I'll sell my old saddle and buy me
> a plow;
> And never, no never, will I rope
> another cow.❞

 What work did cowhands do?

END OF THE CATTLE KINGDOM

On a cattle drive, cowhands ate simple food, such as beans and biscuits. Food and other supplies were carried on a chuck wagon.

The cattle industry continued to grow for about 25 years. At its peak, the Cattle Kingdom covered the West from Texas to Montana. But before long a number of problems came up. Most important, ranchers found they were sharing the land with farmers.

It was difficult for farmers to grow crops where ranchers kept cattle. The cattle wandered into the farmers' fields and trampled or ate the crops. To keep the cattle out, farmers built fences. Ranchers also built fences to keep cattle from wandering off the ranch.

In 1874 Joseph Glidden invented a new kind of wire that could be used to make fences. Glidden twisted two strands of steel wire together. He placed sharp points, or barbs, every few inches along the wire.

This kind of wire became known as **barbed wire**. A farmer or rancher could fence fields using posts with this wire strung between them. A barbed-wire fence was easier and cheaper to build than one made of rock or wood.

Not all farmers and ranchers on the Great Plains wanted open range land to be fenced. Farmers did not like having the barbed-wire fences of large cattle ranches all around them. And ranchers did not like fences that kept their cattle from getting to water. Angry farmers and ranchers soon were cutting each other's barbed-wire fences. People even started shooting one another. These fights, called **range wars**, went on through the 1880s.

Finally the ranchers were told they had to move their cattle off public land or buy it. Later, farmers began raising cattle themselves. The days of the open range and the Cattle Kingdom were over.

 How did the invention of barbed wire affect the Cattle Kingdom?

LESSON 2 REVIEW

Check Understanding

1. **Recall the Facts**   How did ranchers in Texas get their cattle to markets in the North?
2. **Focus on the Main Idea**   How did ranchers build the Cattle Kingdom?

Think Critically

3. **Cause and Effect**   What inventions affected the Cattle Kingdom?
4. **Think More About It**   Why was it important for cowhands to work together on the long drives?

Show What You Know

Diorama Activity   Think about the activities that would take place on a ranch. Use pictures, models, or computer visuals to make a diorama of a ranch scene. Display your diorama for the class.

Cowhands wore protective clothing such as these leather chaps (left). Many types of barbed wire (far left) were used in the late 1800s. This simple invention led to angry fights between farmers and ranchers.

MINING
IN THE WEST

LESSON 3

Link to Our World

How do individuals and groups both play important roles in history?

Focus on the Main Idea
Read to learn how individual miners and mining companies helped settle the West.

Preview Vocabulary
prospector
boom
bust
vigilance

While homesteaders farmed the Great Plains and cowhands worked on ranches, miners rushed to the West to get rich. After the California gold rush of 1849, there were other finds. Thousands hurried to the Colorado Territory after gold was found near Pikes Peak in 1858. Wagons with the words *Pikes Peak or Bust* painted on their sides crowded the western trails. In 1859, silver was found in the Carson River valley of present-day Nevada. Later finds in what are now Arizona, Idaho, and Montana started a mining boom in the West.

MINING BOOMS AND BUSTS

Many of the early **prospectors**—people who searched for gold, silver, and other mineral resources—worked alone. They roamed the West, leading their packhorses loaded with gear and mining tools. With luck they might find $25 worth of silver by scooping gravel in a stream.

In most places, the minerals above the ground were taken out in just a few years. The minerals were then said to be "worked out." To get to the minerals below the ground, mines had to be dug. It became harder for prospectors working alone to find and dig out the minerals. Only large companies could afford to buy heavy equipment and pay workers to dig mines deep underground.

Towns soon grew up around the mines. Some sprang up almost overnight. Miners at first made shelters out of whatever materials they could find, such

What every prospector hoped to find—a gold nugget

as blankets, old shirts, and even potato sacks. As the towns grew, refineries were built to process the minerals. Stores and other businesses moved in as the mines and refineries hired more workers. Many of these workers came from cities in the East. Others were immigrants from Asia or Europe. The hope of finding jobs brought many families to the mining towns.

Some mining towns grew quickly. During the mining **boom**, or time of quick economic growth, towns such as Denver, Colorado, and Boise, Idaho, became centers for industry and transportation as well as mining. Other mining towns were just as quickly left empty. During a **bust**, or time of quick economic decline, people left these towns as soon as the gold, silver, or, later, copper ran out. Today these deserted towns, called ghost towns, can still be seen in the West.

✔️ **What is the difference between a boom and a bust?**

LIFE IN MINING COMMUNITIES

Mining towns usually started as mining camps made up of prospectors looking for minerals in the same place. Unlike farmers and ranchers, most prospectors did not take their families with them. Fights often broke out among prospectors, and mining camps were not safe places.

Mining brought many different groups of people to the West in the 1860s. Prospectors from Mexico, the United States, Chile, and Peru each formed their own settlements. In other mining regions, the settlers were a mix of Americans born in the United States and

Many Asian immigrants, like those in this photograph (left), came to the United States to work in mining towns. Prospectors weighed gold with a balance (above) to find out how much it was worth.

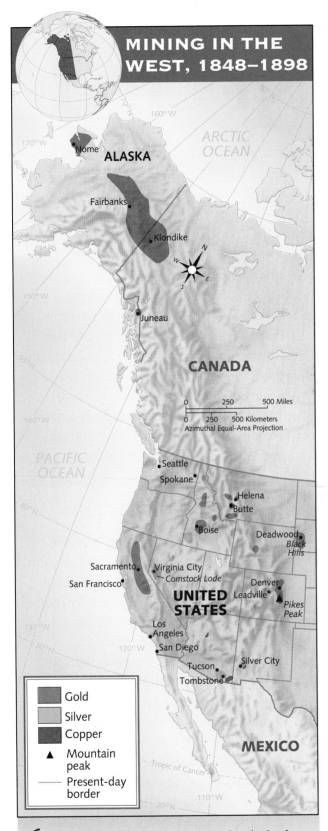

MINING IN THE WEST, 1848–1898

ARCTIC OCEAN

Nome

ALASKA

Fairbanks

Klondike

Juneau

CANADA

0   250   500 Miles
0   250   500 Kilometers
Azimuthal Equal-Area Projection

PACIFIC OCEAN

Seattle
Spokane
Helena
Butte
Boise
Deadwood
Black Hills
Sacramento
Virginia City
Comstock Lode
San Francisco
Denver
Leadville
Pikes Peak
UNITED STATES
Los Angeles
San Diego
Tucson
Tombstone
Silver City

MEXICO

Tropic of Cancer

Gold
Silver
Copper
▲ Mountain peak
— Present-day border

PLACE During the late 1800s, hundreds of thousands of people hoped to get rich by mining in the West. This map shows many of the places that had deposits of gold, silver, and copper.

■ What mineral had the largest deposits? Where was it found?

immigrants from Europe and Asia. Irish and Chinese workers who came to work on the transcontinental railroad stayed to work in the mines when the railroad was completed.

As mining camps grew into towns, some families arrived. But there was no law and little order. Without a government there were no sheriffs. "Street fights were frequent," one writer reported, " and . . . everyone was on his guard against a random shot."

In some mining communities a group of people would form a Vigilance Committee. **Vigilance** means "watching over something or someone." The Vigilance Committee watched over the town to maintain law and order. As more families came, many mining towns set up proper governments and started schools, hospitals, and churches.

 **What was a Vigilance Committee?**

 **LSSON 3 REVIEW**

Check Understanding

1. **Recall the Facts** What cities of today started as mining communities?
2. **Focus on the Main Idea** How did individual miners and mining companies help settle the West?

Think Critically

3. **Cause and Effect** What caused some mining communities to become ghost towns?
4. **Think More About It** Why do you think early mining communities were dangerous places to live?

Show What You Know

Brainstorming Activity Think about the problems in mining communities. Work with a partner to prepare a list of five laws you might make in starting a new government. Present your list to the class.

CONFLICT
IN THE
WEST

LESSON 4

*L*ink to Our World

In what ways do people today work to keep their traditions?

Focus on the Main Idea
Read to find out how Native Americans in the late 1800s worked to keep their ways of life.

Preview Vocabulary
reservation

The native peoples of the Great Plains thought the western lands would be theirs forever. The United States government had promised this in 1830. Then settlers started to arrive. At first miners and traders just crossed Indian lands on their way to California and Oregon. By 1860, however, homesteaders and ranchers were settling the Great Plains. Railroad workers arrived, too, and they began killing the Plains Indians' most important resource—the buffalo.

RAILROADS AND THE BUFFALO

The railroads made it easier for settlers to live in the West. Railroads carried people and supplies to farms, ranches, and mining towns. They took western grain, beef, and minerals to eastern cities. Yet as they made things easy for the settlers, railroads caused great problems for the Plains Indians.

The problems began when settlers started killing large numbers of buffalo. Hunters working for the railroads shot buffalo to feed the workers who were laying track. Buffalo Bill Cody killed enough buffalo to feed 1,000 workers for more than a year.

After the railroads were built, the killing continued. Many buffalo were shot for their hides, which were sold to make coats. The Indians believed this hunting was wasteful because only the animals' hides were used. When they hunted, the Indians used almost every part of the buffalo to meet their needs.

In the 1860s about 15 million buffalo lived on the Great Plains. Within 20 years, fewer than 1,000 were left. Without

In this scene from the 1870s, railroad workers shoot buffalo blocking the tracks.

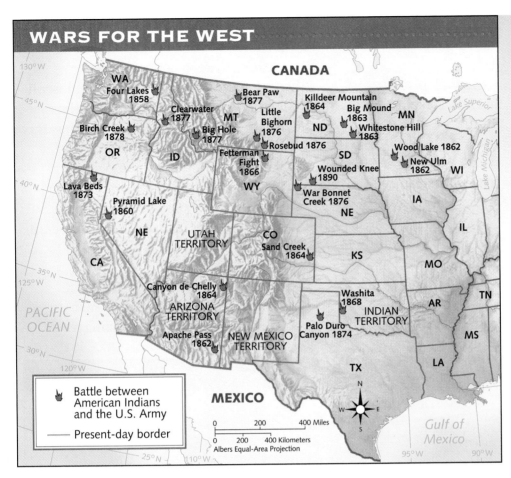

WARS FOR THE WEST

CANADA

130°W
45°N
WA
Four Lakes 1858
Bear Paw 1877
Clearwater 1877
MT
Little Bighorn 1876
Killdeer Mountain 1864
Big Mound 1863
MN
Lake Superior
Birch Creek 1878
Big Hole 1877
ND
Whitestone Hill 1863
OR
ID
Rosebud 1876
SD
Wood Lake 1862
Lake Michigan
Fetterman Fight 1866
Wounded Knee 1890
New Ulm 1862
WI
40°N
Lava Beds 1873
WY
War Bonnet Creek 1876
IA
Pyramid Lake 1860
NE
IL
NE
UTAH TERRITORY
CO
Sand Creek 1864
KS
MO
CA
35°N
125°W
Canyon de Chelly 1864
ARIZONA TERRITORY
Washita 1868
INDIAN TERRITORY
AR
TN
PACIFIC OCEAN
Palo Duro Canyon 1874
MS
Apache Pass 1862
NEW MEXICO TERRITORY
30°N
120°W
TX
LA
MEXICO
N
W E
S
Gulf of Mexico
25°N
110°W
95°W
90°W

Battle between American Indians and the U.S. Army
—— Present-day border

0   200   400 Miles
0   200   400 Kilometers
Albers Equal-Area Projection

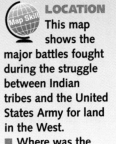

LOCATION This map shows the major battles fought during the struggle between Indian tribes and the United States Army for land in the West.
■ Where was the Battle of the Little Bighorn? Where was the last major battle between Indians and the army?

the buffalo for food, clothing, and shelter, the traditional way of life of the Plains Indians came to an end.

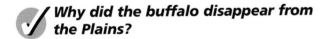
Why did the buffalo disappear from the Plains?

FIGHTING BACK

The Sioux (SOO) were a powerful tribe of the northern Plains. In 1865 the United States Army began guarding a road that passed through Sioux land and led to the gold mines of Montana. For three years the Sioux, led by Chief Red Cloud, fought miners and soldiers as they traveled through Indian lands.

Finally, in 1868, the United States government signed a treaty with the Sioux. In the treaty, the government promised that the Indians would have a reservation west of the Missouri River in the Black Hills of the Dakota Territory. A **reservation** is an area of

land set aside by the government as a home for American Indians. In the treaty, the government promised that this land would be Sioux land forever.

The treaty did not last long, however. In 1874 gold was discovered on the Great Sioux Reservation. Hundreds of miners paid no attention to the treaty and went looking for gold in the Black Hills. The government tried to buy back the land from the Sioux, but the Sioux would not sell. In 1876, United States soldiers marched in to take the land.

Lieutenant Colonel George Custer led some of the soldiers. Two of the chiefs leading the Sioux were Sitting Bull and Crazy Horse. Custer attacked the Sioux and their Cheyenne allies at the Little Bighorn River. His soldiers were quickly surrounded by 2,500 Indians. In the battle that followed, Custer and all his soldiers were killed.

After the Battle of the Little Bighorn, the government sent more soldiers into the Black

Hills. The Sioux were made to return to their reservation, which was now much smaller than had been promised.

In 1890 a terrible massacre took place at Wounded Knee Creek in South Dakota. Some 300 Sioux were killed. It was the last battle between the Sioux and the army.

 Why did Custer attack the Sioux?

THE NEZ PERCES

The United States government used force against other Indian tribes, including the Nez Perces (NES PER•suhz). The Nez Perces lived on the Columbia plateau in Oregon. In 1877

the government told the tribe it had to move to a small reservation in Idaho. The Nez Perce leader, Chief Joseph, said no.

During the summer of 1877, Chief Joseph and a group of 800 men, women, and children tried to escape to Canada. They traveled for 15 weeks through the present-day states of Idaho, Montana, and Wyoming. Less than 40 miles (64 km) from the Canadian border, the group was caught by United States soldiers. Telling his people to give up, Chief Joseph said,

❝I am tired of fighting. Our chiefs are killed. . . . It is cold and we have no blankets. The little children are freezing to

INDIAN LANDS LOST

CANADA

BLACKFOOT
NEZ PERCE
CROW
SIOUX
CHIPPEWA
PAIUTE
SIOUX
PAWNEE
POTAWATOMI
SAUK AND FOX
UTE
UTE
CHUMASH
HOPI
KIOWA
CHEROKEE
CATAWBA
CHEROKEE
APACHE
COMANCHE
CHICKASAW
CREEK
CREEK
SEMINOLE
IROQUOIS
SUSQUEHANNOCK

PACIFIC OCEAN
ATLANTIC OCEAN
MEXICO
Gulf of Mexico

0 200 400 Miles
0 200 400 Kilometers
Albers Equal-Area Projection

Lake Superior
Lake Michigan
Lake Huron
Lake Erie
Lake Ontario

120°W
40°N
40°N
70°W
30°N
30°N
80°W
90°W

Legend:
- Before 1784
- 1784–1810
- 1811–1850
- 1851–1870
- 1871–1890
- Never formally ceded
- Present-day border

MOVEMENT This map shows when Indian lands were lost to the United States government. Some lands were bought through treaties. Others were taken. Some lands were never formally ceded, or officially given up.
■ In what direction were lands lost over time? How does this relate to the movement of settlers?

death. . . . My heart is sick and sad. From where the sun now stands, I will fight no more forever. "

 Why did Chief Joseph surrender?

THE APACHES

By 1880 almost all the American Indians in the United States had been made to move onto reservations. Among the last to give up were the Apaches (uh•PACH•eez), led by a chief named Geronimo. The Apaches fought one of the longest of the wars between Native Americans and the United States government.

The war began in the 1850s when miners and settlers started moving into the Apache lands of present-day New Mexico and Arizona. Fear and hate grew as both sides attacked each other. In 1877 the government made the Apaches move to the San Carlos Reservation in Arizona.

On the hot, dry reservation land, it was hard to grow food. Food that the government gave to the reservation was often spoiled. In 1881 the government heard about a planned rebellion, so soldiers were sent onto the reservation. Afraid that the army would attack, Geronimo and about 75 people went to the Sierra Madre of Mexico. From these mountains, they attacked Arizona settlers.

For the next five years the Indians escaped capture. At last, in 1886, an Apache scout working for the army led the soldiers to Geronimo's hiding place. Geronimo told the soldiers, "Once I moved about like the wind. Now I surrender to you and that is all."

Geronimo's surrender ended years of war between the Indians and the government. Although there was still some fighting, most Indians had been made to leave their lands and move onto reservations. The Indians' traditional way of life had come to an end.

 Why did the Apaches not want to live on the reservation?

Geronimo's Apache name, Goyaale, means "the smart one."

LESSON 4 REVIEW

Check Understanding

1. **Recall the Facts**   What was the most important resource for the Plains Indians?
2. **Focus on the Main Idea**   How did Native Americans in the late 1800s work to keep their ways of life?

Think Critically

3. **Personally Speaking**   How do you think you might feel if you were made to change your way of life?
4. **Think More About It**   What means other than force might the government have used to end the conflict with the Plains Indians? Explain your answer.

Show What You Know

Time Line Activity   With a partner, draw and illustrate a time line for the major events in this lesson. Display your time line in the classroom.

CONNECT MAIN IDEAS

Use this organizer to show that you understand how the chapter's main ideas are connected. Copy the organizer onto a separate sheet of paper. Then complete it by writing two or three sentences that summarize the main idea of each lesson.

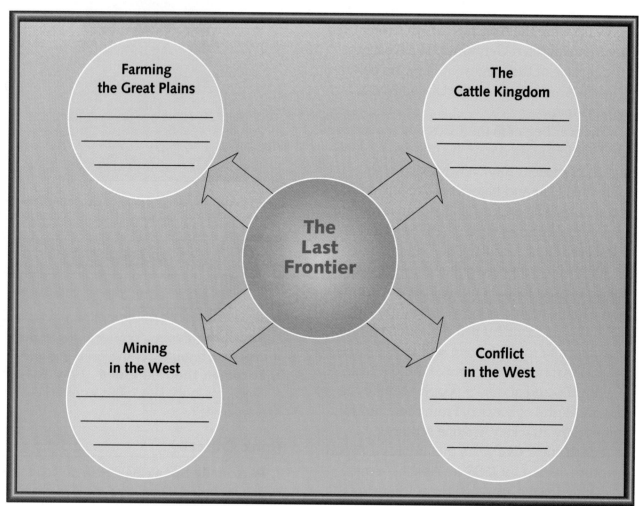

Farming the Great Plains

_____

_____

_____

The Cattle Kingdom

_____

_____

The Last Frontier

Mining in the West

_____

_____

_____

Conflict in the West

_____

_____

_____

WRITE MORE ABOUT IT

1. **Write an Advertisement**   To attract Easterners to the Great Plains, the railroads placed advertisements in newspapers offering free land to settlers. Write one of these advertisements. Your advertisement should describe the benefits of living in the Great Plains region and encourage people to move there.

2. **Write a Conversation**   Write a conversation that could have taken place between Chief Joseph and other leaders of the Nez Perces as they tried to escape to Canada in 1877. The conversation should describe the Indians' experiences as they fled from the U. S. Army soldiers.

USE VOCABULARY

Write a term from this list to complete each of the sentences that follow.

homesteader   reservation
open range   vaquero
prospector   vigilance

1. A _____ was a person who settled government land.

2. The government allowed ranchers on the Great Plains to use the land as _____.

3. A _____ was a Mexican cowhand.

4. A _____ searched for gold, silver, and other mineral resources.

5. _____ means "watching over someone or something."

6. When gold was discovered on the Sioux _____, the United States government tried to buy the land back from the Sioux.

CHECK UNDERSTANDING

1. Why did the railroad owners want more settlement on the Great Plains?

2. Why did many bonanza farms on the Great Plains go out of business?

3. How did settlers on the Great Plains use sod?

4. Who invented a stronger plow that helped farmers cut through the thick sod?

5. How were railroads important to early "cow towns"?

6. What caused the range wars?

7. Who brought law and order to mining towns?

8. What was the Plain Indians' most important resource?

9. Who led United States soldiers into the Battle of Little Bighorn? What caused this battle?

THINK CRITICALLY

1. **Past to Present** Farmers on the Great Plains continue to face problems. What do you think some of these problems are? How do you think farmers are working to solve them?

2. **Personally Speaking** Would you rather have been a homesteader, a cowhand, or a prospector? Explain your answer.

3. **Explore Viewpoints** Geronimo said, "Once I moved about like the wind." How might this statement help explain why Geronimo and his people fought so long and hard against the United States government?

APPLY SKILLS

How to Read a Climograph Use the climographs on page 489 to answer these questions.

1. Which city has more equal amounts of precipitation throughout the year?

2. Which city has warmer average temperatures in January?

3. What generalization can be made about the temperatures in June, July, and August for both cities?

READ MORE ABOUT IT

A Boy Becomes a Man at Wounded Knee by Ted Wood with Wanbli Numpa Afraid of Hawk. Walker. An Oglala Lakota boy describes the ride taken with his father and grandfather to observe the 100th anniversary of the tragedy at Wounded Knee.

Cowboys, Indians, and Gunfighters: The Story of the Cattle Kingdom by Albert Marrin. Atheneum. This book tells the story of the cattle industry.

The Forgotten Heroes: The Story of the Buffalo Soldiers by Clinton Cox. Scholastic. This nonfiction book tells the little-known story of the African American soldiers who served in the West.

General Information Concerning

PATENTS

U.S. DEPARTMENT OF COMMERCE
Patent and Trademark Office

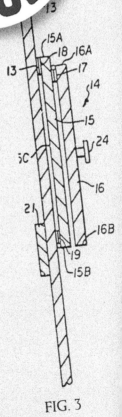

FIG. 3

JEANIE LOW, INVENTOR

Most inventions begin with a problem that needs to be solved. Thomas Edison was looking for a safe way to light people's homes when he invented the electric lightbulb. Granville T. Woods invented his air brake to make stopping a train safer. In the same way, Jeanie Low of Houston, Texas, was looking for a better step stool for young children when she invented the Kiddie Stool in 1992.

"When I was in kindergarten, I couldn't reach the bathroom sink," Low explains. "We had a plastic stool, but it got caught in the door and broke. I wanted to make a stool that folded up onto the door of the cabinet under the sink."

She first tried to make a fold-up stool using wire, but that did not work. A later design using wood was more successful. Like other inventors, Low applied for a patent, a government document saying that only the inventor has the right to make or sell his or her invention. On March 10, 1992, the United States government gave her patent number 5,094,515, making Jeanie Low the youngest female ever to receive a United States patent. Jeanie Low was 11 years old!

Patent drawi

THINK AND APPLY

Think about a problem in your school or home that might be solved with an invention. With a partner, brainstorm ideas for inventions that could make your lives easier or more enjoyable. Share your ideas with the class.

BUILDING CITIZENSHIP

FIG. 2

12
5C
10
13
19
10

13

23

9

21

15B

13
20
22
19

KIDDIE STOOL

* JEANIE

PATENT APPLICATION TRANSMITTAL LETTER   Docket Number (Optional)

To the Commissioner of Patents and Trademarks:
Transmitted herewith for filing under 35 U.S.C. 111 and 37 CFR 1.53 is the patent application of

_____ entitled _____

Enclosed are:
☐ _____ pages of written description, claims and abstract.
☐ _____ sheets of drawings.
☐ an assignment of the invention to _____
☐ executed declaration of the inventors

STORY CLOTH

Study the pictures shown in this story cloth to help you review the events you read about in Unit 8.

Summarize the Main Ideas

1. After the Civil War, American industry grew and changed. The first transcontinental railroad was completed in 1869.

2. Inventions helped industry grow. A new, less expensive way was found for making steel. Some inventions, such as the light bulb, would change everyday life.

3. During the late 1800s, millions of immigrants came to the United States hoping to find better lives.

4. Offers of free and low-cost land brought many settlers to the Great Plains.

5. Ranchers on the Great Plains raised cattle. Cowhands worked hard, especially on cattle drives and roundups.

6. Miners rushed to the West to find gold and other metals. The life in mining towns was rough, and booms sometimes led to busts.

7. Indians on the Great Plains fought for their homelands against United States soldiers. But by about 1890, most Indians in the United States had been forced onto reservations.

Write a Newspaper Article   Imagine that you are a newspaper reporter covering one of the events shown in this story cloth. Write an article describing the event for your newspaper.

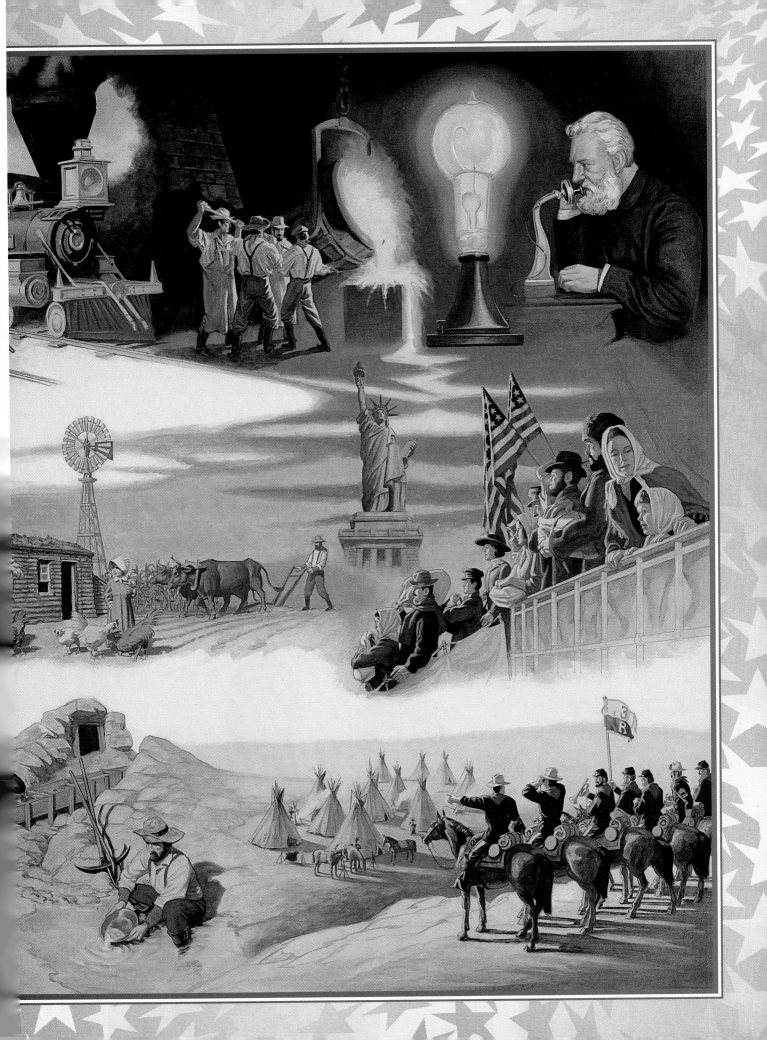

COOPERATIVE LEARNING WORKSHOP

Remember
- Share your ideas.
- Cooperate with others to plan your work.
- Take responsibility for your work.
- Show your group's work to the class.
- Discuss what you learned by working together.

Activity 1
Hold a Debate

Hold a debate that might have taken place between workers and business owners during the early 1900s. The topic should be whether labor unions are needed. To prepare for the debate, work in a group. Each group should research the concerns of business owners and the problems and working conditions of workers. Then the class should decide which groups will represent workers and which groups will represent business owners. During the debate, group members should take turns speaking.

Activity 2
Paint a Mural

Work together to paint a mural that shows how cities were changing in the early 1900s. Show both the problems that cities faced and how cities came to stand for all that was good in America. Display the mural in your classroom, and point to scenes as you talk to your class about changing city life in the early 1900s.

Activity 3
Make a Diorama

Work together to make a diorama that shows a homestead on the Great Plains or an early mining camp. Include a scene that shows how the people lived and the kinds of work they did. Display your diorama where classmates can see it, and answer any questions they may have.

Activity 4
Make a Class Book

Make a class book that shows how the Plains Indians struggled to keep their ways of life alive. Work in a group to research one Indian tribe that lived on the Great Plains. Then write a group report that tells how that tribe's traditions changed or were lost as greater numbers of settlers moved west. Cut out pictures from magazines to illustrate your report, or draw your own pictures. Add your group's report to the reports of other groups to make a class book. A committee can design a cover for the book.

USE VOCABULARY

Write the term that correctly matches each definition.

free enterprise	prospector
monopoly	sod
naturalization	stock

1. the freedom of businesses to offer for sale many kinds of goods and services

2. a share of a business

3. almost complete control of an industry

4. the process through which immigrants could become citizens

5. soil in which thick grass grows

6. a person who searches for gold, silver, and other mineral resources

CHECK UNDERSTANDING

1. Where did new industrial cities develop in the late 1800s?

2. How did workers try to improve their working conditions in the late 1800s?

3. How did James Oliver's plow help farmers living on the Great Plains?

4. Why was it important for ranchers to get their cattle to northern cities?

5. Why did Geronimo and his people refuse to stay on a reservation?

THINK CRITICALLY

1. **Past to Present** How are industries in the United States today like industries in the early 1900s? How are they different?

2. **Think More About It** Why do you think immigrants often moved to neighborhoods made up of other immigrants from the same country?

3. **Personally Speaking** Suppose you were a worker in the late 1800s. How might you feel about government leaders who thought that government should leave factory owners and their businesses alone? Explain your answer.

4. **Cause and Effect** What effect did the American Federation of Labor have on the treatment of American workers by business leaders?

APPLY GEOGRAPHY SKILLS

How to Use a Time Zone Map
Suppose you live in Nevada and want to visit a friend in Utah. It takes one hour to reach your friend's house by car. Use the map below to answer the questions.

1. By what time should you leave Nevada to reach your friend's house at 1:00 P.M.?

2. By what time should you leave Utah to be home at 9:00 P.M.?

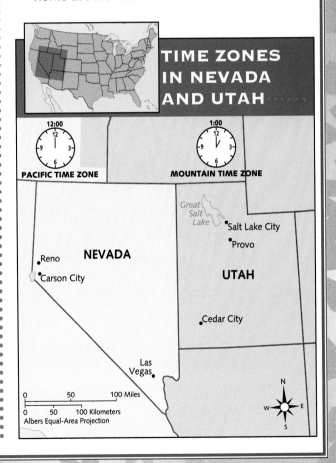

TIME ZONES IN NEVADA AND UTAH

12:00 PACIFIC TIME ZONE
1:00 MOUNTAIN TIME ZONE

Great Salt Lake
• Salt Lake City
• Provo

• Reno
NEVADA
• Carson City

UTAH

• Cedar City

Las Vegas •

0   50   100 Miles
0   50   100 Kilometers
Albers Equal-Area Projection

UNIT 9

BECOMING a WORLD POWER

1880

1890

1900

1910

1898
The Spanish-American War

1901
Theodore Roosevelt becomes President

1909
NAACP founded

1914
Panama Canal opens

*B*y the end of the 1890s, the United States had entered a new time in its history. Until then the nation had worked mostly to develop its own resources, away from the rest of the world. Now the United States was looking beyond its national borders. It was ready to become a world leader.

◄ Navy battleships return home after the American victory in the Spanish-American War.

1920

1930

1940

1950

1918
World War I ends

1920
The Jazz Age begins

1929
The Great Depression begins

1941
The United States enters World War II

1945
World War II ends

The United Nations is organized

1917
The United States enters World War I

1933
Franklin Roosevelt becomes President

SET the SCENE
with Literature

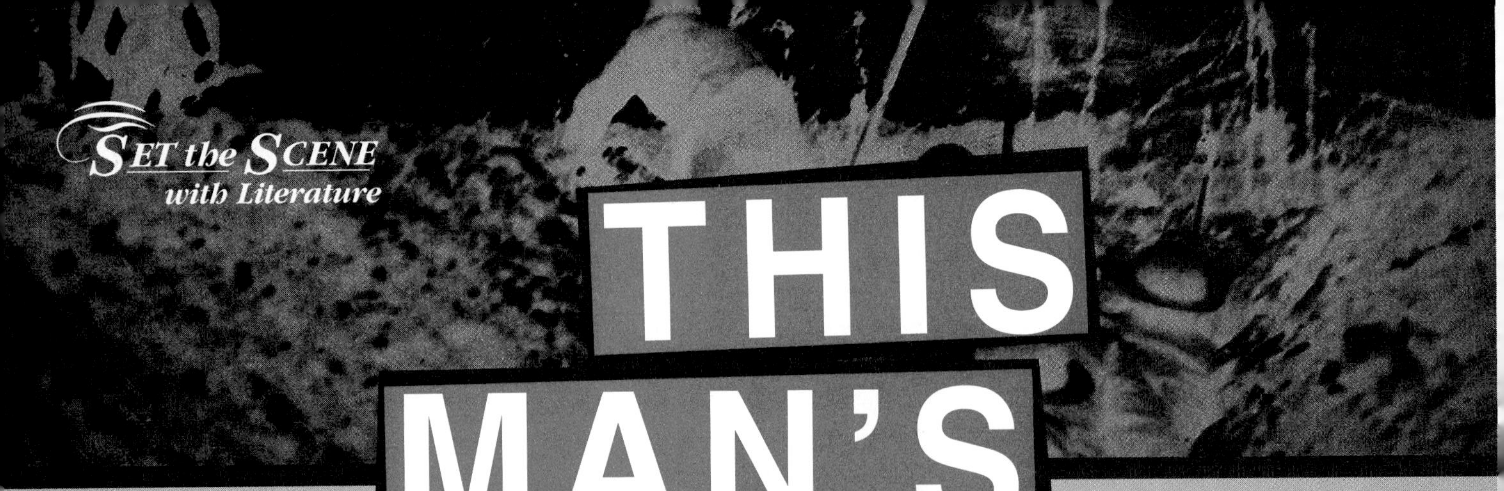

THIS MAN'S WAR

BY CHARLES F. MINDER

When the United States took part in events in other parts of the world, it was more than a government taking action. Individual Americans had an important part in each story. In the first half of the twentieth century, the United States fought in two world wars. More than 4 million American soldiers fought in the first war, which the United States entered against Germany in 1917. Read now from a letter written by one of those young soldiers to his mother. In it Charles Minder, from New York, describes how he felt about fighting in a war.

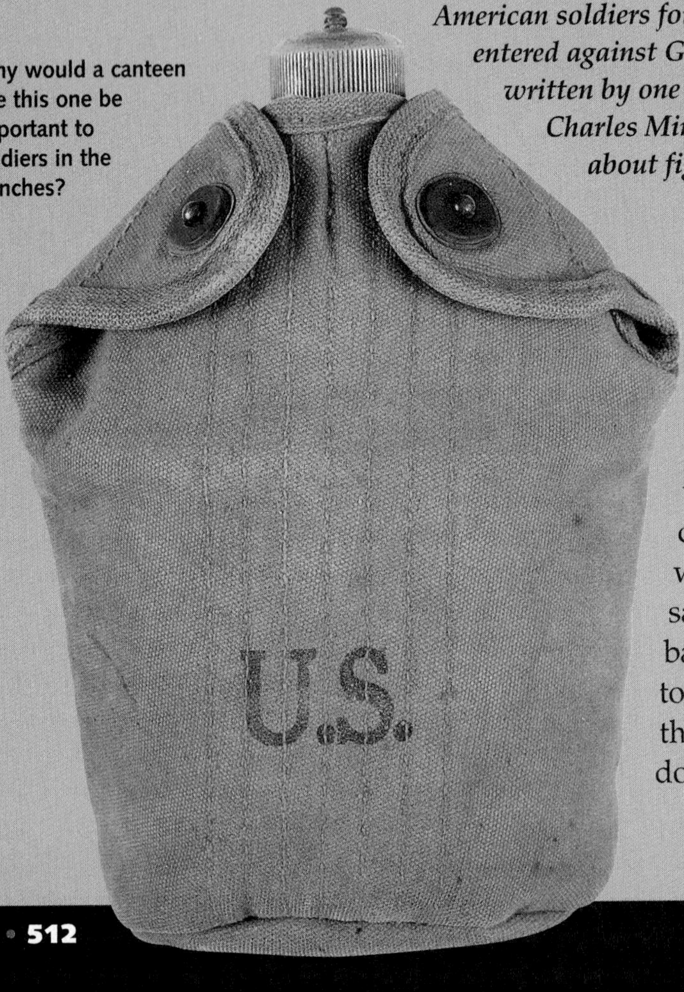

Why would a canteen like this one be important to soldiers in the trenches?

Thursday, August 15, 1918

Dear Mother,

. . . I felt a couple of bullets cut the long grass over my head. If I told you I wasn't scared, I would be a liar. I felt like a dumb animal cornered and that my end was near. As soon as it stopped a little, I said, "Come on, men!" and led the way back. It was starting to get light and we had to make the top of the hill and get back into the town, or we would be out of luck. We double-timed[1] up the hill gladly, with all our

[1] **double-timed:** moved quickly

equipment. Just near the top, we passed a well, and the bullets started to pick up the dirt all around us.

Some German machine gunner had spotted us. We all knelt on the other side of the well and, one by one, managed to crawl just a little farther, where we got behind a cement wall. It was almost daylight. . . . I looked at my watch and it was five o'clock. We were all dead tired and fell asleep and didn't wake up until nine this morning. We were hungry and opened up a couple of cans of corned-beef and hardtack[2] and, with some water in our canteens, that was our breakfast.

We saw some signs showing we were in a town called Fismes[3]. It sure had been wrecked by artillery[4] fire. I don't remember seeing one house that wasn't hit, and all being deserted, it was a very mysterious looking town. Marching back thru the town, we saw hundreds of dead Germans and Americans lying where they fell. It was the most gruesome sight I have seen yet, and made me realize more than ever, how ridiculous and unnecessary this business of war is.

I figured that the rest of the company must have returned to the next town over, Villersavoye, where we started out from yesterday afternoon. I was right, and when we got back there at noon today, they were all

surprised to see me and my squad. They thought that we had been killed last night.

Three of the men in my squad, who were with me last night, went to the hospital this afternoon, Purcell, Kujawa, and Stadler. My squad is shot to pieces, yet we are going back again tonight, when it gets dark, to where we started for yesterday.

We could smell some very beautiful lilacs last night while we were on the way up and took deep whiffs of their perfume in the dark, thinking that there was a lilac bush near by. We found out today that the smell was gas. Our Captain and Lieutenant Krell were gassed, and a lot of men in the other two platoons. My throat is raw and my eyes have been watering all afternoon, but outside of that I am all right.

We just had a good meal at four o'clock, and everybody has been resting and cleaning up this afternoon, as we go up again tonight to relieve the other machine-gun company that is in the line. I found out this afternoon that the place where we were last night is called the "Valley of Death." It is such a terrible position, because the Germans are on top of the hill on the other side and can shoot down on top of us and across the valley into the town of Fismes. It is one hot spot. So it looks like we are in for a little excitement. As soon as it gets dark, we start, so will close, Mother Dear. I wish I was home now.

Charles

---

[2] **hardtack:** biscuits baked hard to last a long time
[3] **Fismes:** (FEEM)
[4] **artillery:** large guns on wheels

CHAPTER 17

The United States and the World

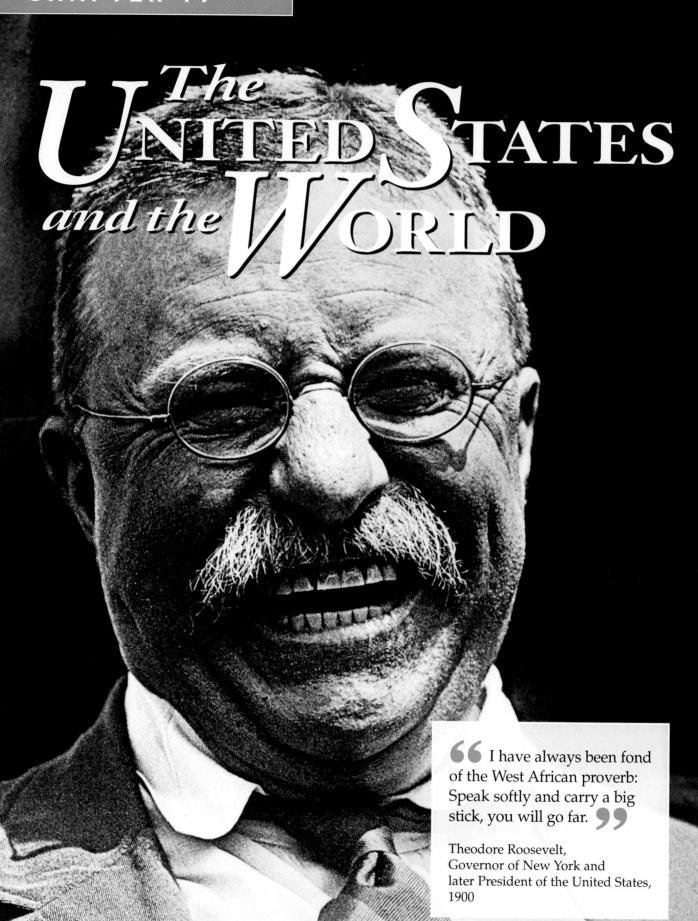

❝ I have always been fond of the West African proverb: Speak softly and carry a big stick, you will go far. ❞

Theodore Roosevelt, Governor of New York and later President of the United States, 1900

BUILDING *an* EMPIRE

*L*nk to Our World

Why might a country today decide to take a more active part in what is going on in the world?

Focus on the Main Idea
Read to find out why the United States decided at the end of the 1800s to add to its territory and power around the world.

Preview Vocabulary
imperialism
armistice

By the late 1800s the United States led the world in industry and agriculture. Like many European nations at that time, the United States wanted to stretch its borders and set up colonies. Many Americans were ready to find new frontiers, now that the western frontier had been settled. American leaders also felt that new lands would bring new sources of raw materials and new markets for the nation's goods. The time seemed right for the United States to become a world power.

ALASKA

In 1867 the United States bought Alaska from Russia for $7.2 million—about two cents an acre. Most Americans knew little about Alaska or its peoples. Many thought it was foolish of the United States to buy a piece of land so far north. "Polar Bear Garden," some called it.

Then, in 1896, prospectors found gold in the Klondike region. The Klondike was in Canada's Yukon Territory, near its border with Alaska. The discovery started a gold rush like the one in California in 1849. From 1897 to 1899 more than 100,000 people raced to Alaska hoping to get rich. Some did find gold. But conditions were harsh, and thousands died.

Alaska did bring new wealth to the United States. The land was full of natural resources, such as fish, timber, coal, and copper. Because buying Alaska turned out to be so profitable, many Americans soon thought the United States should try to get more new lands across the seas.

What caused people to become interested in Alaska?

THE HAWAIIAN ISLANDS

The Hawaiian Islands are about 2,400 miles (3,862 km) southwest of California, in the Pacific Ocean. Polynesian people in the Pacific migrated to Hawaii by the eighth century, and the islands were ruled by Polynesian kings and queens. By the 1800s many Americans had settled there.

Among the first Americans to arrive in Hawaii were Christian missionaries. They began to settle in the islands about 1820. Soon after, American business people started cattle ranches and sugar plantations there. By the 1870s American missionaries and sugar planters controlled much of the land and trade in Hawaii.

In 1887 the Hawaiian king, Kalakaua (kah•lah•KAH•ooh•ah), tried to keep the Americans from taking over the islands. The Americans then decided to take authority away from the king. They wanted the United States to annex Hawaii. The Americans made Kalakaua sign a new constitution that left the Hawaiian monarchy without authority.

In 1893 the new Hawaiian ruler, Queen Liliuokalani (li•lee•uh•woh•kuh•LAH•nee),

....

Lydia Liliuokalani (right) became queen of Hawaii in 1891 after her brother, King Kalakaua, died. Queen Lil', as she was called, wrote the well-known song "Aloha Oe," or "Farewell to Thee." The hibiscus (hy•BIS•kuhs) (below) is one of many beautiful flowers found in Hawaii.

tried to bring back the monarchy's authority. Liliuokalani promised to make "Hawaii for Hawaiians" once again. But the Americans made her give up her throne. They took over the government and set up a republic. In 1898 Congress decided to make Hawaii a territory of the United States.

 How did Hawaii become a territory of the United States?

WAR WITH SPAIN

After the United States took control of Alaska and Hawaii, some people accused the country's leaders of **imperialism**, or empire building. This brought the nation into conflict with European

Nearly one-fourth of the United States soldiers who fought in Cuba were African Americans. The soldiers in this photograph served in the United States Cavalry. Any soldier who had fought in the war could have a medal like the one shown here (right).

nations that had also spread beyond their borders—especially Spain.

By the end of the 1800s, Cuba and Puerto Rico were Spain's two remaining colonies in the Western Hemisphere. Many Cubans wanted independence from Spain. Twice, in 1868 and in 1895, they had rebelled against Spanish rule, but the rebellions failed.

Many Americans supported the Cubans' fight for independence, including Americans who had moved there to start businesses. Newspapers in the United States were full of stories about Spain's harsh rule of the island. As fighting continued, President William McKinley sent the battleship *Maine* to Havana, Cuba, to protect the lives and property of Americans living there. On February 15, 1898, the *Maine* exploded in Havana harbor. More than 200 sailors were killed. It was not clear why the ship blew up. The United States, however, blamed Spain.

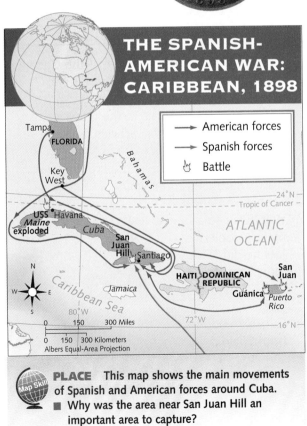

THE SPANISH-AMERICAN WAR: CARIBBEAN, 1898

→ American forces
→ Spanish forces
🔥 Battle

PLACE This map shows the main movements of Spanish and American forces around Cuba.
■ Why was the area near San Juan Hill an important area to capture?

"Remember the *Maine!*" Americans cried, calling for action. On April 25, the United States declared war on Spain.

The first battles of the Spanish-American War were not fought in Cuba. They were fought halfway around the world. Less than two weeks after war was declared, the United States Navy was sent to the Philippine Islands. Led by Commodore George Dewey, the navy destroyed the Spanish fleet and captured Manila Bay.

In the United States many thousands of Americans volunteered to fight in the war. The army grew from about 30,000 soldiers to more than 274,000. Among those who volunteered was Theodore Roosevelt, who had been assistant secretary of the navy. He had quit his job to form a fighting company made up mostly of cowhands and ranchers. In Cuba, the Rough Riders, as they were called, took part in the Battle of San Juan Hill and the siege of Santiago. The siege ended on July 17, 1898, and the Spanish in Santiago soon signed an armistice. An **armistice** is an agreement to stop fighting.

The Spanish-American War lasted less than four months. More than 5,000 American soldiers died, most from diseases such as malaria and yellow fever. In spite of the losses, the United States became a stronger world power. Under the peace treaty, Spain agreed to give the United States control of Cuba, Puerto Rico, Guam, and the Philippine Islands. Puerto Rico and Guam remain territories of the United States today.

 Why did the United States go to war with Spain?

THEODORE ROOSEVELT

Theodore Roosevelt returned from Cuba well known and well liked. He was soon elected governor of New York. Two years later he was Vice President, serving under President William McKinley. On September 6, 1901, President McKinley was shot in Buffalo, New York, by a person who was against the government. McKinley died eight days later, and Roosevelt became President.

Roosevelt was a man of action. He believed that the United States should actively use its power to shape events in the world. He believed that what happened in the rest of the world affected the United States.

When Russia and Japan were at war with each other in 1904 and 1905, President Roosevelt helped the two nations work out peace terms. Because of his work, Roosevelt became the first American to receive the Nobel Peace Prize. The Nobel Peace Prize is awarded each year to a person or an organization that helps bring peace to the world.

Who?

José Martí
1853–1895

José Martí (mar•TEE), a leader of the Cuban revolution, is a national hero for Cuban people today. He was a writer who spoke out against Spanish rule in the late 1800s. Many of Martí's poems, articles, and speeches were printed in newspapers in the United States. They helped tell the Cubans' story. Martí died three years before the Spanish-American War. Even so, many people feel he did more than any other Cuban leader to win Cuba's freedom from Spain.

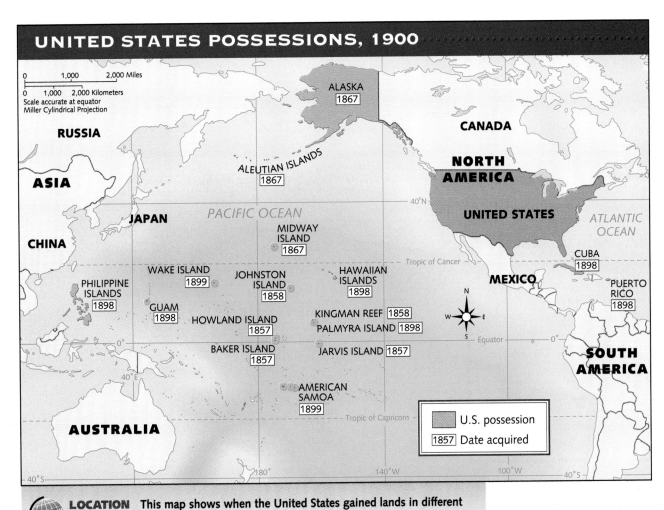

UNITED STATES POSSESSIONS, 1900

ALASKA 1867

ALEUTIAN ISLANDS 1867

RUSSIA

ASIA

JAPAN

CHINA

PACIFIC OCEAN

MIDWAY ISLAND 1867

WAKE ISLAND 1899

JOHNSTON ISLAND 1858

HAWAIIAN ISLANDS 1898

PHILIPPINE ISLANDS 1898

GUAM 1898

HOWLAND ISLAND 1857

KINGMAN REEF 1858

PALMYRA ISLAND 1898

BAKER ISLAND 1857

JARVIS ISLAND 1857

AMERICAN SAMOA 1899

AUSTRALIA

CANADA

NORTH AMERICA

UNITED STATES

ATLANTIC OCEAN

MEXICO

CUBA 1898

PUERTO RICO 1898

SOUTH AMERICA

Tropic of Cancer

Equator

Tropic of Capricorn

U.S. possession

1857 Date acquired

Scale accurate at equator
Miller Cylindrical Projection

LOCATION This map shows when the United States gained lands in different places around the world.
■ When did the United States acquire the lands that would become the state of Alaska? When did it acquire the lands that would become the state of Hawaii?

In 1907 President Roosevelt, the peace-maker, decided to remind other countries that he was also the leader of a powerful military force. He sent a fleet of warships, painted a dazzling white, on a world cruise. According to Roosevelt, the Great White Fleet showed the world that now "the Pacific was as much our home as the Atlantic."

Why did Roosevelt believe the United States should use its power in the world?

THE PANAMA CANAL

Among President Roosevelt's goals was to build a canal in Panama, located in Central America. The canal would link the Atlantic and Pacific oceans. This, in turn, would link American territories in the Atlantic with those in the Pacific. "I wish to see the United States the dominant power on the shores of the Pacific Ocean," Roosevelt said.

For years people had talked about building a canal in Panama. It would cut across the isthmus that joined North America and South America. A French company had tried to build such a canal in the 1880s but had given up because of the thick jungle and the diseases that killed many of the workers.

In 1902 Congress voted to build the canal. But the Isthmus of Panama did not belong to the United States. It belonged to Colombia. The United States offered Colombia $10 million for the right to build the canal. But Colombia put off deciding whether to sell.

THE PANAMA CANAL

THE CANAL ZONE

Caribbean Sea

PANAMA

CANAL ZONE

Gatun Lake

Panama Canal

PANAMA

Gulf of Panama

0   5   10 Miles
0   5   10 Kilometers

NORTH AMERICA

PACIFIC OCEAN

San Francisco

New York City

ATLANTIC OCEAN

5,200 miles (8,368 km)

Caribbean Sea

Panama Canal

Gulf of Panama

Equator

13,000 miles (20,921 km)

SOUTH AMERICA

0   750   1,500 Miles
0   750   1,500 Kilometers
Azimuthal Equal-Area Projection

MOVEMENT The Panama Canal provides an important shortcut for voyages between the Atlantic and Pacific oceans.
■ By how many miles did the canal shorten a voyage between New York City and San Francisco?

Roosevelt then spread the word that he would welcome a revolution in Panama to end Colombian rule. Roosevelt sent the United States Navy to protect the isthmus. If a revolution began, the navy was to keep Colombian troops from landing on shore. Within three months such a revolution took place, and the people of Panama formed a new nation. Panama's new leaders then gave the United States the right to build the canal. The United States would control the canal and a zone 5 miles (8 km) wide on each side of it.

Work on the canal began in 1904. Huge earth-moving machines began to cut down the trees and thick growth of jungle. Engineers designed huge canal locks to help ships move through the waterway.

Unlike the French workers who had first tried to build the canal, American workers were able to stay healthy. Doctors now knew that malaria and yellow fever, the diseases that had stopped the French, were carried by mosquitoes. They learned to control the mosquitoes by draining the swamps where the insects lived.

Building the canal took ten years. In 1906 Roosevelt visited the canal site. It was the first time a President had left the United States while in office. The first ship passed through the Panama Canal on August 15, 1914. Today the canal helps move people and goods around the world.

Why did the United States want to build the Panama Canal?

This photo shows the building of the Gatun (guh•TOON) Locks at the Panama Canal. These locks, near the Atlantic Ocean, are about 4,000 feet (1,219 m) long and can lift ships from the Atlantic about 85 feet (26 m).

LESSON 1 REVIEW

Check Understanding

1. **Recall the Facts**   What territories did the United States gain in the 1800s?

2. **Focus on the Main Idea**   Why did the United States decide to add to its territory and power around the world?

Think Critically

3. **Explore Viewpoints**   What do you think Queen Liliuokalani meant by the phrase, "Hawaii for Hawaiians"?

4. **Past to Present**   Do you think the Panama Canal is as important today as it was when it opened? Why or why not?

Show What You Know

Globe Activity   Work with a partner to trace water routes around the world. Use your finger to follow the routes a ship might follow from the east coast to the west coast of the United States before and after the opening of the Panama Canal.

Compare Map Projections

Why Is This Skill Important?

Because the Earth is round and maps are flat, no map can represent the Earth's shape exactly. Only a globe, which is round, can do that. To show the round Earth on a flat piece of paper, mapmakers must change the shape of the globe, splitting or stretching it to make it flat. As a result, every map has errors, or **distortions**.

Over the years, mapmakers have found different ways of showing the Earth on flat paper. These different views are called **projections**. All map projections have distortions, but different kinds of projections have different kinds of distortions. Identifying areas on a map that are distorted will help you understand how maps can best be used.

Understand the Process

Both Map A and Map B show the same area of the Earth, but they are different projections. Map A is an equal-area projection. Equal-area projections show the sizes of regions in correct

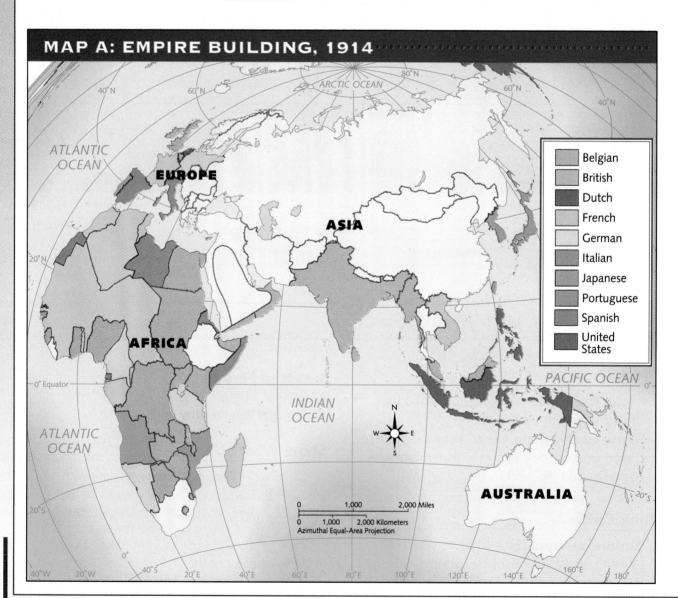

MAP A: EMPIRE BUILDING, 1914

Legend:
- Belgian
- British
- Dutch
- French
- German
- Italian
- Japanese
- Portuguese
- Spanish
- United States

Azimuthal Equal-Area Projection

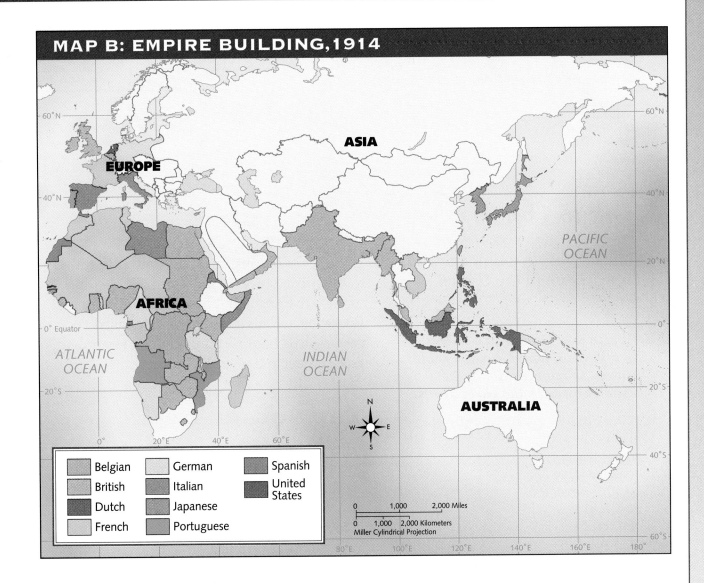

MAP B: EMPIRE BUILDING, 1914

Legend:
- Belgian
- British
- Dutch
- French
- German
- Italian
- Japanese
- Portuguese
- Spanish
- United States

0   1,000   2,000 Miles
0   1,000   2,000 Kilometers
Miller Cylindrical Projection

relation to one another, but they distort shapes. There are many different kinds of equal-area projections. The azimuthal (a•zuh•MUH•thuhl) equal-area projection on Map A is just one kind. Another is the Albers equal-area projection.

Map B is a conformal projection. Notice that the meridians are all an equal distance apart. On a globe the meridians get closer together as they near the poles. Also notice on Map B that the parallels closer to the poles are farther apart. On a globe the parallels are all equal distances apart. Conformal projections show directions correctly. But they distort sizes, especially of places near the poles. The Miller cylindrical is just one example of a conformal projection. Another is the Mercator (mer•KAY•ter) projection.

1. On which parts of Maps A and B do the shapes of the land areas appear to be the same?

2. On which map does Africa appear to be larger? On which map is the size of Africa the most accurate?

3. On which map do the meridians get closer together toward the poles?

4. On which map does the space between the parallels get larger toward the poles?

Think and Apply

Write a paragraph about the advantages and disadvantages of using equal-area and conformal projections. Compare your ideas with those of your classmates.

LESSON 2 PROGRESSIVES —and— REFORM

Link to Our World

How do people today work to improve life in the United States?

Focus on the Main Idea
As you read, look for ways people worked to improve life in the United States in the early 1900s.

Preview Vocabulary
progressive
commission
conservation
merit system
political boss
civil rights

Theodore Roosevelt brought the same energy he showed as a Rough Rider to the office of President.

President Theodore Roosevelt used the authority of his office in many ways. He added to American power in the world. He also worked to bring about needed reform at home. Roosevelt and his supporters were called progressives because they wanted to improve government and make life better.

THE SQUARE DEAL

Roosevelt believed it was the job of the federal government to help people as much as possible. He called his program the Square Deal. That meant he wanted everyone to be treated fairly.

To make sure that people could get fair treatment, Roosevelt wanted the federal government to make rules for businesses. He set up or strengthened special committees called commissions. One of these was the Interstate Commerce Commission. Part of its job was to study railroad fares. When the commission decided fares were too high, railroad owners were told to lower them.

Roosevelt asked Congress to give the government authority to see that foods and medicines were safe. In 1906 Congress passed the Pure Food and Drug Act. It said that all foods and medicines had to meet government safety standards. Congress also passed the Meat Inspection Act. It said that inspectors would go to all plants that packaged meat to make sure the meat was safe.

Roosevelt also was interested in conservation. Conservation is a way to protect the environment by keeping resources from being wasted or destroyed. Roosevelt set aside millions of acres of land in many parts of the country as wilderness areas and national parks. Among these were the Grand Canyon, Mesa Verde, and Glacier national parks.

 What was the Square Deal?

STATE AND CITY REFORMS

Progressives also worked in state governments. In Wisconsin, Governor Robert La Follette did for his state what Roosevelt was doing for the nation. La Follette made so many reforms that Roosevelt called Wisconsin a "laboratory of democracy."

Elected officials in many states had been giving government jobs to people who did favors for them. To keep this from happening in Wisconsin, La Follette started a **merit system** to make sure that people were qualified for their jobs. Each person applying for a government job was given a test. The person with the highest score got the job.

La Follette wanted to help workers. He asked the state legislature to pass a law saying that a workday must be no more than ten hours. A second law was passed listing jobs for which children could not be hired. A third law said that the state would pay workers who were hurt on their jobs. To provide the money to do this, factory owners were asked to make payments to the state.

People in other states called what La Follette was doing the Wisconsin Idea. Many states copied his changes. By 1918, 20 of the 48 states had passed progressive laws.

Many progressive reforms affected city government, which was often run by political bosses. Some city leaders—especially mayors—were called **political bosses** because they controlled the city government. Most bosses had dishonest people working

The explorer and writer John Muir helped persuade Congress to establish Yosemite (yoh•SEH•muh•tee) National Park in 1890. Muir (right) met there with Theodore Roosevelt in 1903.

for them. Some of these people gave money to voters so they would vote for the boss. Or, they counted the votes of people who were not citizens or of people who had died. In this way, bosses were elected to office again and again.

One of the best-known political bosses was William Tweed. Boss Tweed, as he was called, ran New York City for years and robbed it of millions of dollars. He protected himself by controlling the city police department.

Progressives wanted to break boss rule. One way to do this was to change the form of city government. To keep one person—the mayor—from having all the authority, some city governments set up commissions made up of several people. In the commission form of government, each person took care of one part of government, such as police, fire, or water services. Before long, more than 400 cities had set up commission governments.

 What reforms were made by states and cities?

Who?

W. E. B. Du Bois (standing at far right) is shown here in the office of the NAACP magazine called *Crisis*.

W. E. B. Du Bois
1868–1963

William Edward Burghardt Du Bois, better known as W. E. B. Du Bois, was proud of being black. "Beauty is black," he said. He wanted all African Americans to be proud of their African heritage. Du Bois was educated at Fisk University and at Harvard. A teacher and a writer, he devoted his career to improving life for African Americans. In his later years, Du Bois believed that prejudice in the United States would never be broken down. He left the United States in 1961 and spent the rest of his life in the African country of Ghana (GAH•nuh).

CIVIL RIGHTS

Progressive leaders showed what governments could do to make life better for many of the nation's people. However, they did little about the problems of prejudice. So African American leaders used progressive ideas to help deal with the problem.

One of the best-known African American leaders of this time was W. E. B. Du Bois (doo•BOYS). In 1909 Du Bois and other progressive leaders formed the National Association for the Advancement of Colored People (NAACP). The NAACP took steps to end violence against African Americans. Members of the NAACP worked to change state laws that did not give full civil rights to African Americans. **Civil rights** are the rights of citizens to equal treatment.

Another group that worked for equal rights was founded in 1910. The National Urban League worked to find jobs and homes for African Americans living in cities.

✓ *How did people try to fight prejudice in the early 1900s?*

LESSON 2 REVIEW

Check Understanding

1. **Recall the Facts**   Who were the leading progressives in the United States in the early 1900s?
2. **Focus on the Main Idea**   How did the progressives work to improve life in the United States?

Think Critically

3. **Think More About It**   How were the reforms of the Wisconsin Idea examples of progressive thinking?
4. **Past to Present**   How do people work for civil rights today?

Show What You Know

Simulation Activity   Imagine that you are a progressive reformer from the early 1900s. Think about one of the problems you read about in this lesson. State your view about the problem to the class.

The GREAT WAR

Link to Our World

Why do people today sometimes decide to take part in other people's disagreements?

Focus on the Main Idea
Read to learn why the leaders of the United States decided to enter World War I.

Preview Vocabulary
**alliance
military draft
no-man's-land
isolation**

This 1917 poster of "Uncle Sam" was used to bring in more soldiers for the wartime army.

I WANT YOU FOR U.S. ARMY
NEAREST RECRUITING STATION

The United States entered the twentieth century as a strong nation. When conflict among the nations of Europe exploded into war in 1914, the United States hoped to stay out of the fighting. In time, however, the nation's leaders decided to enter what was then known as the Great War. Later it would be called World War I.

DANGEROUS ALLIANCES

On one side in the war were the Allied Powers, or Allies—including Russia, France, Britain, and Italy. On the other side were the Central Powers—Germany, Austria-Hungary, the Ottoman Empire, and Bulgaria.

The European countries had formed these **alliances**, or partnerships, to protect themselves. In each alliance the members promised to help one another if they were attacked by another country. They hoped that this would prevent war. But it had the opposite effect.

Serbia, a country in southern Europe, bordered Austria-Hungary. Many Serbs lived in the southern part of Austria-Hungary and longed to be a part of their Serbian homeland. On June 28, 1914, a Serb rebel killed two members of Austria-Hungary's royal family in the city of Sarajevo (sar•uh•YAY•voh). Austria-Hungary soon declared war on Serbia. Bound by alliances, the European nations were drawn one by one into the conflict.

At first the United States did not join an alliance. President Woodrow Wilson asked Americans to be "impartial in thought as well as in action." He and many other Americans wanted the country to be neutral in the war.

But Americans were soon drawn into the conflict. Prowling the seas were German submarines, called *Unterseeboots*, or U-boats. On May 7, 1915, a U-boat sank the British passenger ship *Lusitania*. Among the dead were 128 Americans. People in the United States were angry. Some began to believe the United States should enter the war on the side of the Allies. But President Wilson still hoped to keep the United States neutral. In 1916 he was again elected President. His campaign slogan was, "He kept us out of war."

 Which countries were the Allies and which were the Central Powers?

NEUTRALITY ENDS

In early 1917, German leaders said that U-boats would attack all ships in British waters. U-boats then sank three American merchant ships, killing many Americans aboard. President Wilson had finally had enough. On April 2, 1917, he asked Congress to declare war on Germany, saying, "The world must be made safe for democracy." Four days later, the United States joined the Allied Powers.

The United States was not ready for war. Its army was small, and it did not have many weapons. To raise a larger army, Congress passed the Selective Service Act. The new law provided for a military draft, a way of bringing people into the army. All men between the ages of 18 and 45 had to sign up with a draft board. Soldiers were then chosen from the list of names.

Many Americans thought the draft was a good idea. They felt that it would bring together soldiers of different backgrounds. However, many Native Americans, Mexican Americans, African Americans, and immigrants faced the same prejudices in the military as they did at home. They were kept

The *Lusitania*, shown here in port, was a passenger ship. Before the ship was attacked, a warning (right) was printed in newspapers. It said that the German government might destroy British ships and that passengers traveled at their own risk.

OCEAN STEAMSHIPS.

CUNARD

EUROPE VIA LIVERPOOL
LUSITANIA
Fastest and Largest Steamer now in Atlantic Service Sails SATURDAY, MAY 1, 10 A. M.
Transylvania, Fri., May 7, 5 P.M.
Orduña, - - Tues., May 18, 10 A.M.
Tuscania, - - Fri., May 21, 5 P.M.
LUSITANIA, Sat., May 29, 10 A.M.
Transylvania, Fri., June 4, 5 P.M.

Gibraltar—Genoa—Naples—Piraeus
S.S. Carpathia, Thur., May 13, Noon

NOTICE!

TRAVELLERS intending to embark on the Atlantic voyage are reminded that a state of war exists between Germany and her allies and Great Britain and her allies; that the zone of war includes the waters adjacent to the British Isles; that, in accordance with formal notice given by the Imperial German Government, vessels flying the flag of Great Britain, or of any of her allies, are liable to destruction in those waters and that travellers sailing in the war zone on ships of Great Britain or her allies do so at their own risk.

IMPERIAL GERMAN EMBASSY
WASHINGTON, D. C., APRIL 22, 1915.

Allies

Central Powers

Neutral countries

Major battle

ICELAND (Denmark)

SWEDEN

NORWAY

RUSSIA

Moscow

North Sea

DENMARK

IRELAND (Great Britain)

GREAT BRITAIN

London

NETHERLANDS

BELGIUM

Berlin

Tannenberg

GERMANY

ATLANTIC OCEAN

Paris

Versailles

Château-Thierry

Argonne Forest

LUXEMBOURG

SWITZERLAND

Vienna

AUSTRIA-HUNGARY

FRANCE

ITALY

Caporetto

Lisbon

Madrid

Corsica

Rome

MONTENEGRO

ALBANIA

Sarajevo

SERBIA

ROMANIA

BULGARIA

Black Sea

Caspian Sea

PORTUGAL

SPAIN

Sardinia

GREECE

Constantinople

Gallipoli

OTTOMAN EMPIRE

ASIA

AFRICA

MOROCCO (France)

ALGERIA (France)

TUNISIA (France)

Sicily

Mediterranean Sea

Crete

Cyprus

REGIONS This map shows regions controlled by Central, Allied, and neutral countries in Europe during World War I.

■ What problems do you think Germany had because of Allies on both its eastern and western borders?

in separate units and given only certain jobs. Yet all American soldiers, no matter what their background, faced the same dangers.

What was the purpose of the draft?

NEW WEAPONS

When American soldiers arrived in Europe during the summer of 1917, many were sent to France, where most of the fighting took place. There, most soldiers fought each other from trenches,

or ditches, dug in the ground. The trenches were separated by a **no-man's-land**. This was land not held by either side but filled with barbed wire and land mines, or bombs buried in the ground.

Soldiers in the trenches also faced terrible new weapons. The Germans had developed a machine gun that fired hundreds of bullets each minute. Against the machine gun, the British brought in the tank. Tanks could cross the no-man's-land, crushing the barbed wire. Machine gun bullets could not go through the tank walls. Against the tank, the Germans used poison gas. Poison gas was the most feared of the new weapons. It killed soldiers—even

Soldiers wore gas masks as protection from poison gas.

those in tanks—by cutting off their breathing. While battles raged on the ground, dozens of airplane pilots fought overhead in air battles called dogfights.

During the summer of 1918, the war went on with neither side gaining much ground. The number of Americans in the trenches grew from 27,000 in early June to 500,000 by the end of August. Before the war ended, about 53,000 Americans were killed. Another 230,000 were wounded. In all more than 8 million people from countries around the world died in the war.

 What new weapons were used in the war?

WOMEN IN THE WAR

The United States government did not let women fight in the war. Instead, many

Before the war, the suffrage movement had been successful in some states. But not until after the war did women nationwide gain the right to vote.

women took over jobs left by men going to war. Some became mechanics and farm workers. Others became police officers. Some women made weapons. Some went to Europe as nurses and ambulance drivers. Thousands more joined the army and the navy as clerks and telegraph operators.

Katherine Stinson of San Antonio, Texas, wanted to become a fighter pilot in the war. Stinson started flying in 1910, and she and her mother opened a flying school in 1913. The army, however, would not let her fly in battle. So she flew across the United States, raising money for the Red Cross. Then she went to Europe as an ambulance driver.

When?

1917

While World War I was taking place in Europe, revolutions were taking place in other parts of the world. In 1910 Francisco Madero led a revolution in Mexico against President Porfirio Díaz, who ruled as a dictator. Several leaders fought for power in Mexico in the years that followed. In 1917 a new constitution was written. It is the basis of government in Mexico today.

A revolution also took place in Russia, where life for many was hard. In 1917 a group of revolutionaries led by Vladimir Ilyich Lenin took control. Russia's monarch, Nicholas II, was killed. Life became even worse when harsh new rulers came to power.

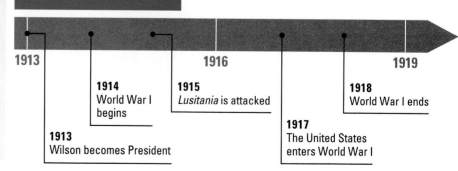

WORLD WAR I

1913

1913
Wilson becomes President

1914
World War I begins

1915
Lusitania is attacked

1916

1917
The United States enters World War I

1918
World War I ends

1919

Women's war work helped bring one very important change after the war. The Nineteenth Amendment to the Constitution was passed in 1920. It gave women the right to vote. President Wilson supported women's rights because of their wartime help. Carrie Chapman Catt, a women's suffrage leader, later called the Nineteenth Amendment "the greatest thing that came out of the war."

 How did women help in wartime?

THE WAR ENDS

Americans made an important difference in the Great War. Soldiers gave military help. Shiploads of American wheat, canned foods, and guns helped supply the Allied armies. Working together, the Allies began to push back the German army. On November 11, 1918, the Germans gave up. On that day they signed an armistice that ended the fighting.

The Great War was over, and American soldiers came home. Meanwhile, leaders of the Allies gathered to make peace terms. During these talks President Wilson described his idea for a League of Nations, to which all nations could belong. Wilson hoped the organization would help find peaceful ways to solve problems among nations.

The Treaty of Versailles (ver•SY), which had ended the war, set up the League of Nations, but the United States did not join. The United States Senate must vote to approve treaties. It voted not to approve this treaty because it did not want to belong to the League of Nations. Many senators believed that the United States should stay out of other countries' problems. They felt that the nation should return to a policy of **isolation**, remaining separate from other countries, as it had before the 1890s.

 What was the League of Nations?

 **SSON 3 REVIEW**

Check Understanding

1. **Recall the Facts** Why did European countries form alliances in the early 1900s?
2. **Focus on the Main Idea** Why did the leaders of the United States decide to enter World War I?

Think Critically

3. **Think More About It** Could the United States have avoided entering the war? Explain.
4. **Past to Present** How does the United States use its power to affect what happens in the world today?

Show What You Know

 Journal-Writing Activity
Imagine that you are a soldier in a trench in 1918. Write a journal entry that describes what you see and hear. You may wish to reread the literature selection that opened this unit before you begin. Share your work with a family member.

The peace treaty that ended World War I was signed in the Hall of Mirrors in France's Versailles Palace.

Recognize Propaganda

Why Is This Skill Important?

Propaganda is information or ideas designed to help or harm a cause. It is used by people to persuade others to share their views. Being able to recognize propaganda will help you make thoughtful and informed decisions.

Remember What You Have Read

Each side in a war often uses propaganda to help win support for its cause. Think about what you have read about World War I. The United States remained neutral during the early years of the war. Then, after German U-boats began to sink American ships, the United States joined the Allied Powers and declared war on Germany.

One week after war was declared, President Wilson set up the Committee on Public Information, headed by George Creel. Creel's job was to "sell the war to the American people." To do this, Creel hired artists and writers to wage a propaganda campaign in support of the war. The committee printed millions of leaflets and posters praising American soldiers for fighting for democracy. At the same time, they accused the German government of carrying out terrible crimes in their effort to take over the world.

The German government waged a propaganda campaign of its own during the war. German soldiers dropped leaflets like the one on page 533 from airplanes or hot-air balloons. The leaflets were dropped near where American troops were stationed. Some leaflets were packed in artillery shells and shot across the trenches to the Americans.

Understand the Process

Read the leaflet on page 533. Then use the following questions as a guide to help you think about this primary-source document.

1. To whom is the leaflet addressed?
2. What points are being made by the writer?
3. What arguments are being used to make these points?
4. What facts does the writer use? What opinions does the writer give?
5. If you were a German American soldier, do you think you would believe these arguments? Why or why not?

Think and Apply

Draw a poster that could have been used to build support in the United States for the Allied Powers in World War I. Your poster should focus on the idea of "making the world safe for democracy."

Much of the German propaganda was directed at American soldiers, like these soldiers in France.

To the American soldiers of German descent.

You say in your loose leaf that you serve in an honorable way in the U. S. Army. Do you think it honorable to fight the country that has given birth to your fathers or forefathers? Do you think it honorable to fall upon any country after it has heroically defended itself for four years against a coalition of peoples tenfold its superior in numbers? Look at the map and compare that tiny little spot representing Germany with the vast territories assigned to Russia, England and the United States, to mention only the biggest of Germany's adversaries, and you cannot remain in doubt that the heroism is entirely on Germany's side. We are fighting for every thing dear to us, for our homes, our very existence. What are you fighting for, why did you come over here, fourthousand miles away from your own home? Did Germany do you any harm, did it ever threaten you? Your leaders are Misleaders, they have lied to you that we were slaves of a tyrant, and you are guilty of gross ignorance if you believe one word of it. Everybody knowing anything about human nature and the history of European nations will tell you that slaves can never stand up against the whole world of fierce enemies, only free man fighting for their hapiness in life will endure so many years of fighting against the most colossal odds that ever a nation encountered. An everlasting shame that twenty millions of German-Americans could not prevent that man Wilson, who never was a genuine American but rather an English subject in disguise, to raise his hand against their mother country! Read Washington's Farewell Adress and imagine what he would have to say of the total collapse of real Americanism in our days. His golden words to his fellow citizens to only mind their own business have been thrown to the winds by the present administration. Go and repent ere it is too late, we shall welcome every lost sheep that finds its way back to its herd. There is more freedom in Germany indeed than in the land of Dictator Wilson. We do not try to deceive you, we do not promise you a farm, but we assure you that every honest man willing to work has infinitely better chances in Germany where we do not suffer corrupt politicians, deceiving land speculators, nor cheating contractors. Lay down your gun, your innermost soul is not in this fight. Come over to us, you will not regret it.

CONNECT MAIN IDEAS

Use this organizer to show that you understand how the chapter's main ideas are connected. Copy the organizer onto a separate sheet of paper. Then complete it by writing a sentence or two about each place, event, or idea.

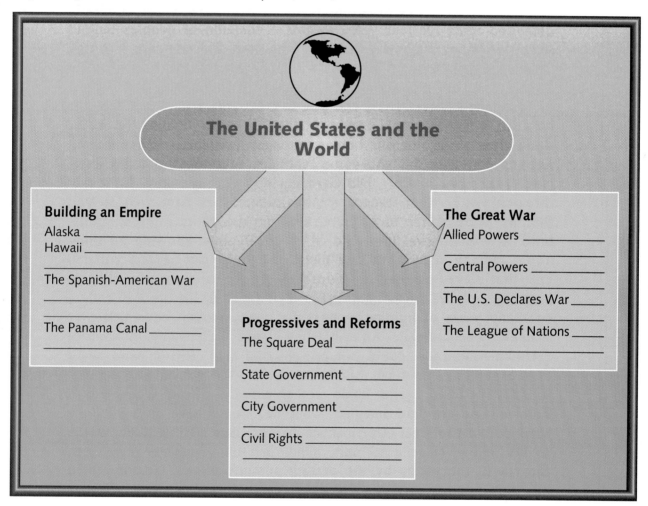

The United States and the World

Building an Empire
Alaska _____
Hawaii _____
_____
The Spanish-American War
_____
_____
The Panama Canal _____
_____

Progressives and Reforms
The Square Deal _____
_____
State Government _____
_____
City Government _____
_____
Civil Rights _____
_____

The Great War
Allied Powers _____
_____
Central Powers _____
_____
The U.S. Declares War _____
_____
The League of Nations _____
_____

WRITE MORE ABOUT IT

1. **Write a Letter** Imagine that you are living in the Hawaiian Islands during the late 1800s. Write a letter to a friend on the mainland. Describe why some people want the United States to annex Hawaii and why others do not. Tell how you feel about Americans gaining control of Hawaii.

2. **Write a Newspaper Article** Imagine that you are a newspaper reporter covering the fighting in Europe during World War I. Write a short newspaper article in which you describe the terrible fighting in no-man's-land. Tell how tanks and machine guns are affecting the fighting.

USE VOCABULARY

Write the term that correctly matches each definition. Then use each term in a complete sentence.

alliance   imperialism
armistice   isolation
civil rights   military draft
conservation   progressive

1. empire building

2. an agreement to stop fighting

3. a supporter of President Roosevelt who wanted to improve government and make life better

4. a way to protect the environment by keeping resources from being wasted or destroyed

5. the rights of citizens to equal treatment

6. a partnership

7. a way of bringing people into the army

8. remaining separate from other countries

CHECK UNDERSTANDING

1. What two territories became a permanent part of the United States as a result of the Spanish-American War?

2. How was President Roosevelt able to get permission from Panama to build a canal in that country?

3. How did a merit system keep elected officials from giving government jobs to people who did favors for them?

4. Why were the NAACP and the Urban League important to African Americans?

5. What alliance of countries won World War I? What alliance was defeated?

6. Why did Congress vote not to join the League of Nations?

THINK CRITICALLY

1. **Think More About It**   Why do you think the Germans decided to attack all ships in British waters, even American ships?

2. **Cause and Effect**   What effect did the passage of the Nineteenth Amendment have on women in the United States?

3. **Personally Speaking**   Some people think that the United States should not get involved in the problems of other countries. What do you think the United States should do when problems happen in other places?

APPLY SKILLS

How to Compare Map Projections Write the term that correctly matches each definition.

conformal   equal-area

1. a projection that shows the sizes of regions in correct relation to one another but distorts shapes

2. a projection that shows directions correctly but distorts sizes of places, especially near the poles

How to Recognize Propaganda   Choose an issue that concerns you. Create a leaflet to "sell concern about this issue to others." You may use propaganda to support your cause. As you create your leaflet, think about who you are addressing and what points you want to make.

READ MORE ABOUT IT

First World War by John Pimlott. Franklin Watts. This book is part of a popular series entitled *Conflict in the Twentieth Century*.

Theodore Roosevelt by Zachary Kent. Childrens Press. This biography highlights events in the life of the twenty-sixth President of the United States.

CHAPTER 18

GOOD TIMES and BAD

66 Time and place have had their say. So you will have to know something about the time and place where I came from, in order that you may interpret the . . . directions of my life. 99

Zora Neale Hurston, writer and anthropologist, in her 1942 book *Dust Tracks on a Road*

The ROARING TWENTIES

LESSON 1

After the serious days of World War I, the 1920s—often called the Roaring Twenties—brought good times to many Americans. It was a time when people were eager for change and enjoyment.

THE BOOM ECONOMY

When the United States entered World War I in 1917, the economy changed greatly. Factories began producing weapons and other war supplies. When the war was over, factories started to make new products. Now they made vacuum cleaners, washing machines, radios, and other appliances for the home. In the 1920s Americans bought more of these **consumer goods**—the name given to products made for personal use—than at any time before in the country's history.

Americans learned about consumer goods through advertisements in newspapers and magazines and on the radio. Business owners used advertisements in the hopes of making people want to buy their goods.

It was hard for many people to pay for goods all at once, so **installment buying** became common. This plan allows a buyer to take home a product after paying only a part of the selling price. The buyer then makes an installment, or payment, each month until the full price is paid.

While business boomed, agriculture slumped. Farmers had produced large amounts of food during World War I. The end of the war meant the end of high wartime demand. Farmers now had too many crops and no one to buy them.

 What led to a boom in the economy in the 1920s?

THE AUTOMOBILE

One reason for the boom of the 1920s was the growth of new industries. One of the most important of these was the automobile industry.

The first successful gasoline-powered automobile, or car, was built in the 1890s. By the time the United States entered World War I, automobile companies were producing about 1 million cars a year. By 1923 they were making more than 3 million a year.

Leading the auto industry was a Michigan man named Henry Ford. Ford had found a way to produce cars less expensively. The Ford Motor Company's system of mass production used a moving **assembly line**. Instead of being built one at a time, Ford's cars were assembled, or put together, as they were moved past a line of workers. Each worker did only one task, such as putting in headlights or seats. The assembly line cut the amount of time it took to make a car from about 12 hours to less than 2 hours. Ford passed on the savings to his customers. By 1925 a person could buy a new Ford car for about $260.

The automobile created a need for other new industries. The need for tires led to the growth of the rubber industry. The need for gasoline led to the growth of the oil industry. Gas stations were built, and more roads were paved. The United States was becoming a nation on wheels.

 How did Henry Ford change the automobile industry?

AVIATION

Air transportation, or **aviation**, also became an important industry in the 1920s. The first flight had been made in 1903 at Kitty Hawk, North Carolina, by brothers Orville and Wilbur Wright. Over the years, the airplane

LEARNING FROM GRAPHS
As a young man Henry Ford (right) worked as a machinist. His idea of producing cars on an assembly line (below) helped increase sales of automobiles.
■ About how many cars were sold in 1920? in 1929?

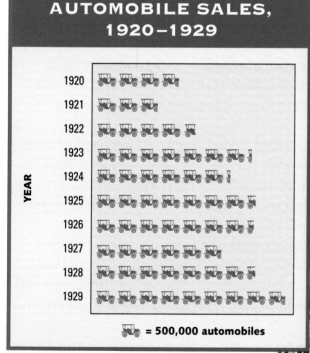

AUTOMOBILE SALES, 1920–1929

YEAR

1920
1921
1922
1923
1924
1925
1926
1927
1928
1929

🚗 = 500,000 automobiles

The Wright brothers' *Flyer* (above) takes off on the first powered flight. Charles Lindbergh (right) stands next to the famous plane that he flew across the Atlantic.

was improved. It was used in World War I, but after the war not many people traveled by plane. By 1927 that began to change.

On May 20, 1927, Charles Lindbergh, an airmail pilot, took off from New York in a small plane named the *Spirit of St. Louis*. His goal was to be the first person to fly alone across the Atlantic Ocean. If he did, he would win a $25,000 prize. Fighting off sleep, Lindbergh kept to his course over the open ocean. "My back is stiff; my shoulders ache; my eyes smart," he wrote in his journal.

It seemed impossible for Lindbergh to go on, but he did. He landed in Paris, France, about 34 hours after leaving New York. As news of his flight spread, Charles Lindbergh became a hero all over the world.

Lindbergh's flight helped make people more interested in air travel, and soon commercial airlines were making flights. A **commercial industry** is one run to make a profit. Between 1926 and 1930 the number of people traveling by plane grew from about 6,000 to about 400,000.

 **Who was Charles Lindbergh?**

ENTERTAINMENT

Many Americans heard the news of Lindbergh's flight on the radio. The first commercial radio stations began broadcasting in the 1920s. Detroit's WWJ and Pittsburgh's KDKA went on the air in 1920. By 1929 more than 800 stations were reaching about 10 million families.

Radio made possible an audience of millions of people at one time. Listening to the radio, Americans could follow sports around the country. In 1926, millions listened as Gene Tunney beat Jack Dempsey in a ten-round boxing match. Yankee fans cheered when Babe Ruth hit his sixtieth home run during the 1927 baseball season.

Over their radios Americans could also hear a new kind of music called jazz. **Jazz** grew out of the African American musical heritage. This heritage was made up of music brought from West Africa and spirituals sung by enslaved people in the United States. Jazz was so popular among both black and white Americans that some have called the 1920s the Jazz Age.

Movies were another new form of entertainment enjoyed by many people in the 1920s. The movie business, which was based in Hollywood, California, first turned out silent films. By 1927 the movies had sound.

D. W. Griffith, a film director, saw a bright future for talking pictures. He predicted,

66 Talkies, squeakies, moanies, songies, squawkies. . . . But whatever you call them, I'm absolutely serious in what I have to say about them. Just give them ten years to develop and you're going to see the greatest artistic medium the world has known. 99

 What new forms of entertainment were popular in the 1920s?

THE HARLEM RENAISSANCE

In the 1920s the New York City neighborhood of Harlem became a center of artistic development for African Americans. So many writers, musicians, and artists lived in Harlem that this period is now known as the Harlem Renaissance. The French word *renaissance* (REH•nuh•sahns) means "rebirth." It is

In the 1920s, families would gather around the radio (above) to listen to sports events, comedy shows, or music. A popular dance during the 1920s was the Charleston. These people (right) are dancing in front of the St. Louis, Missouri, city hall in 1925.

During the Harlem Renaissance, Langston Hughes (left) wrote poems about African American life. Louis Armstrong (seated at piano) made records with his group, the Hot Five.

used to mean a time of new interest and activity in the arts.

Among the best-known Harlem writers was poet Langston Hughes. He described Harlem during the 1920s as a magnet for African Americans from across the country. Young writers such as Claude McKay, Countee Cullen, and Zora Neale Hurston came to Harlem to share their work and encourage one another. Many of these artists and writers painted and wrote about what it was like to be black in the United States.

Large audiences of both black and white Americans came to Harlem to hear trumpeter Louis Armstrong, singer Billie Holiday, and bandleader Duke Ellington. They also came to see actors such as Paul Robeson.

✓ What was the Harlem Renaissance?

LESSON 1 REVIEW

Check Understanding

1. **Recall the Facts** What new industries helped the economy grow in the 1920s?
2. **Focus on the Main Idea** Why were the 1920s described as the Roaring Twenties?

Think Critically

3. **Explore Viewpoints** How do you think the viewpoints of farmers in the 1920s differed from those of people living in cities?
4. **Personally Speaking** Charles Lindbergh set for himself the goal of being the first person to fly alone across the Atlantic Ocean. Why is it a good idea for people to set goals?

Show What You Know

Poster Activity Review what you learned in this lesson about consumer goods, advertisements, and installment buying. Choose a product that was popular during the 1920s and make an advertisement poster that might make people want to buy the product. Display your advertisement in the classroom.

The GREAT DEPRESSION
AND THE NEW DEAL

Link to Our World

How does the federal government today help people who are out of work?

Focus on the Main Idea
Read to learn what the federal government did to help Americans who were out of work during the Great Depression.

Preview Vocabulary
stock market
depression
bureaucracy
unemployment
minimum wage
hydroelectric dam

During the Great Depression some people without jobs sold apples on the street to make money.

Many Americans thought that the good times of the 1920s would go on forever. President Herbert Hoover, elected in 1928, shared that hope. He had gained fame for his efforts to help poor and hungry people in Europe after World War I. He saw a much happier picture in the United States in 1928. "We in America today are nearer to the final triumph over poverty than ever before in the history of any land," he said. Little did he know how quickly that would change.

THE GOOD TIMES END

In the 1920s thousands of Americans pinned their hopes on a rich future by investing in the stock market. The **stock market** is a place where people can buy and sell stocks, or shares of businesses. If more people want to buy than sell a certain stock, the price of shares goes up. If more people want to sell than buy, the price goes down.

During the 1920s the prices on one stock market, the New York Stock Exchange, kept going higher. By 1929 some stocks were being sold at prices three times higher than they were sold for in 1920. People began to borrow money to buy stocks. "How can you lose?" they asked. Before long they learned the answer.

On October 24, 1929, thousands of investors wanted to sell stocks instead of buy them. They all wanted to turn their stocks into cash. With many sellers and few buyers, prices fell fast. On October 29, 1929, prices on the stock market crashed. Nearly everyone lost money.

On the day of the stock market crash, people gathered on New York City's Wall Street, where stocks are traded. Stock certificates like this one (right) had lost much of their value.

The crash of the stock market ended the good times of the Roaring Twenties. It was the beginning of hard times that are now called the Great Depression. During a **depression** there is little money and little economic growth.

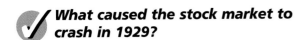

What caused the stock market to crash in 1929?

THE GREAT DEPRESSION

Most people who had invested in the stock market lost their money. Banks that had loaned too much money had to close. When banks closed, people lost their savings.

Because people had little money, they bought few goods. Manufacturers could not sell what they had made. Factory workers then lost their jobs because the factory owners could not pay their wages. When workers lost their jobs, they could not pay what they owed to banks or businesses. So banks and businesses began to fail.

During the Great Depression, poverty and hardship affected almost every American. President Hoover tried to encourage everyone. "Prosperity," he said, "is just around the corner." But it was not. Times got worse.

By 1932 one of every four American workers was without a job. People were starving. Hungry people stood in line for bread or for free meals at soup kitchens. Those who were homeless spent the night in public shelters or out on the streets. Entire families often had to live in shacks made of scraps of wood, tin, and tar paper.

One woman, a teenager during the Great Depression, remembers being sent by her mother to wait in line for free soup.

66 If you happened to be one of the first ones in line, you didn't get anything but the water on top. So we'd ask the

guy that was putting the soup into the buckets—everybody had to bring their own bucket to get the soup—he'd dip the greasy watery stuff off the top. So we'd ask him to please dip down to get some meat and potatoes from the bottom of the kettle. But he wouldn't do it. **"**

 What hardships did the Great Depression cause for many Americans?

FRANKLIN ROOSEVELT AND THE NEW DEAL

In the summer of 1932, the Democratic party chose Franklin Delano Roosevelt as its Presidential candidate. Roosevelt was a cheerful, likable person. He was married to Eleanor Roosevelt, a niece of Theodore Roosevelt. Franklin Roosevelt told the Democrats, "I pledge you, I pledge myself to a new deal for the American people." The words became the name for his plan to end the Great Depression—the New Deal. In November 1932 the American people elected Roosevelt President.

President Roosevelt believed that to end the depression, the federal government needed to take bold, new action. On his inauguration day, Roosevelt told the American people, "The only thing we have to fear is fear itself." He gave people hope that everything would be all right—that the government would do something to help. "This nation asks for action, and action now," he said.

In his speech Roosevelt called on Congress to act quickly. It did. Between March 9 and June 16, 1933, Congress passed many of Roosevelt's plans. During this time, later known as "The 100 Days," more new laws were passed than at any other time since the founding of the nation.

LEARNING FROM GRAPHS This bar graph shows the number of companies that went out of business during the Great Depression. The line graph shows the number of people who lost their jobs.

■ Compare the trends shown on these graphs. Are the trends similar? Why?

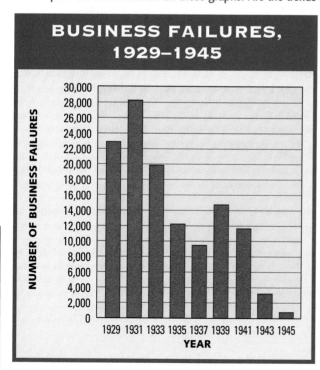

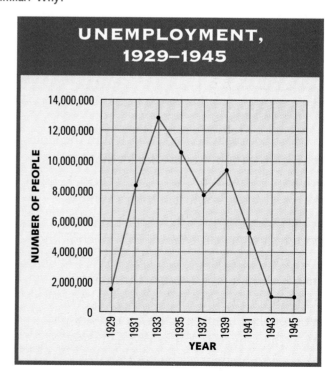

This photograph from 1930 (right) shows a breadline at St. Peter's Mission in New York City. Without money to pay for food, many people went hungry.

The New Deal gave the federal government more authority. It also made it larger. The growing number of government workers formed a **bureaucracy**—the many workers and groups that are needed to run government programs.

 What was Franklin Roosevelt's plan to end the Great Depression?

Who?

Franklin Delano Roosevelt 1882–1945

In 1921, eleven years before he won election as President, Franklin Roosevelt became ill with polio. The disease left him unable to walk. The year before, Roosevelt had been the Democratic candidate for Vice President. Polio forced him to leave politics for a time. But through hard work and the encouragement of his family, he recovered and learned to walk with the help of leg braces. In 1928 Roosevelt was elected governor of New York. In 1932 he was elected President of the United States. Roosevelt was reelected three more times, making him the only President to have been elected to four terms in office.

GOVERNMENT PROGRAMS

The New Deal's goal was to get people back to work. To help do that, it created a number of programs that were nicknamed Roosevelt's Alphabet Soup. The Civilian Conservation Corps, or CCC, hired young people to plant trees and care for the national parks. The Works Progress Administration, or WPA, hired workers to build roads, airports, and public buildings such as schools, libraries, and post offices. The WPA also hired writers and artists to record life in the Great Depression in words, paintings, and photographs.

Even with these government programs, **unemployment**, or the number of people without jobs, stayed high. But at least unemployment did not get worse.

The government helped workers who had jobs by supporting labor unions. There had often been strikes and conflicts over the rights of workers to organize unions. New laws gave workers the right to form unions and the right to a **minimum wage**, the lowest pay a worker can receive by law.

Workers were also helped by the Social Security Act. It was one of the most important programs of the New Deal. Social Security provides income to workers after they have retired. In addition, it gives help to children of workers who have no means of support. Money for the program comes from taxes on workers' earnings.

The federal government also started huge building projects that gave work to thousands of people. Among these projects was the building of **hydroelectric dams**. These dams use the water they store to produce electricity. The government sold the electricity at low rates to users. The dams helped economic development in the regions where they were built.

In 1933 Congress created the Tennessee Valley Authority, or TVA. TVA workers built hydroelectric dams and locks on the Tennessee River. Also during the New Deal, workers built the Hoover Dam on the Colorado River, helping to develop southern California and Arizona. The Grand Coulee and Bonneville dams on the Columbia River helped development in eastern Washington and Oregon.

During the Great Depression, artists like the ones in this photograph were hired by the WPA to paint pictures of American life.

✓ **What was Roosevelt's Alphabet Soup?**

LESSON 2 REVIEW

Check Understanding

1. **Recall the Facts** What was the New Deal?
2. **Focus on the Main Idea** How did the federal government help solve some of the problems of the Great Depression?

Think Critically

3. **Think More About It** How did the 1920s compare with the 1930s? Use the pictures in this chapter to help you.
4. **Personally Speaking** Some people have said that the most valuable thing people lost during the Great Depression was hope. What do you think that means?

Show What You Know

Newspaper Activity Have a family member help you look at the stock market report in the newspaper. Choose one stock and follow it for a week. Every day record the stock's closing price. Decide whether you would have lost or made money on the stock if you had invested in it that week. Compare your results with those of your classmates.

Children of the Dust Bowl

by Jerry Stanley

Farm families did not share in the good times of the 1920s. Crop and livestock prices dropped so low that farmers could not make a profit. When they could not pay off loans to the banks, they lost their farms. By the time of the New Deal, many farm families faced the same poverty and hardship as city families. The New Deal helped farmers by giving them loans so they would not lose their farms. But many farmers soon faced a new problem.

A drought came to the Great Plains early in the 1930s. Where healthy crops had grown, dry land blew away in the strong winds. Dust storms turned day into night. The western Great Plains became known as the Dust Bowl. The Oklahoma Panhandle had the worst time. As you read the following account of life in the Dust Bowl, think about how the "Okies," the people of Oklahoma, learned to live in hard times.

To escape the Dust Bowl, many families left Oklahoma to start new lives in California. But life was hard there, too. Some people who went to California, like this Okie mother and her two children, lived in squatter camps made up of tents and shacks.

Then when it seemed that things couldn't get any worse, they did. The year was 1936. It hadn't rained more than a few drops in the Panhandle for five straight years. One day the wind started to blow, and every day it blew harder and harder, as if nature were playing a cruel joke on the Okies. The wind blew the dry soil into the air, and every morning the sun rose only to disappear behind a sky of red dirt and dust. The wind knocked open doors, shattered windows, and leveled barns.

It became known as the Great Dust Bowl, and it was centered in the Panhandle near Goodwell, Oklahoma. From there it stretched to the western half of Kansas, the eastern half of Colorado, the northeastern portion of New Mexico, and northern Texas. In these areas, especially in the Panhandle, the dry winds howled for four long years, from 1936 to 1940. Frequently the wind blew more than fifty miles an hour, carrying away the topsoil and leaving only hard red clay, which made farming impossible.

In the flatlands of the Panhandle people could see the dust storms coming from twenty to thirty miles away. The winds made the sky "boil red, blood red," said Horace Ray Conley of Foss, Oklahoma. "You could see the northers[1] coming," he recalled. "It carried that old red dirt, and the whole sky

_____

[1]**norther:** windstorm blowing from the north

would be red. They were mean clouds, ugly clouds." As a child, Horace walked to school backward to keep the dirt from scraping him in the face. He remembered he was often let out of school to go to the family storm cellar where he would be safe.

As the clouds rose and roiled[2] each day, thousands of birds and rabbits raced in front of the approaching storms. That was the signal to the Okies to hurry before it was too late. They had to herd their cows into the barn quickly, tie down farm equipment and whatever supplies they had outside, then run for cover. Cracks around windows and doors were taped or stuffed with wet towels, but it was impossible to escape the dust. At night families slept with wet washcloths or sponges over their faces to filter out the dust, but in the morning they would find their pillows and blankets caked with dirt, their tongues and teeth coated with grit.

Every morning the house had to be cleaned. Everett Buckland of Waynocka said, "If you didn't sweep the dust out right quick between storms, you'd end up scooping it out with a shovel." And every morning someone had to go check the animals. The fierce gales buried chickens, pigs, dogs, and occasionally cattle. Children were assigned the task of cleaning the nostrils of cows two or three times a day. . . .

The Dust Bowl killed people who stayed out too long without shelter. Roland Hoeme of Hooker almost lost his grandmother to

---

[2]**roiled:** stirred up

An Oklahoma farmer and his son raising the height of a fence to keep it from being buried by drifts of blowing soil.

March 1936: A dust storm rises over the Texas Panhandle. Horace Ray Conley of Foss, Oklahoma, said storms like these made the sky "boil red, blood red."

one storm. "I remember my grandmother hanging on to a fence post," he said. "The wind was blowin' so hard she looked like a pennant in a breeze." However, more people died from "dust pneumonia"—when the dust caused severe damage to the lungs. Bessie Zentz of Goodwell summed up the nightmare experienced by the "Dust Bowlers," as they came to be called: "The dust storms scared us to pieces," Bessie said. "It was dark as the middle of the night, and it stayed that way all day."

The storms ended any hope of farming in the Panhandle. The Okies planted mulberry trees for windbreaks and plowed furrows deep in the ground to help keep the soil in place. But the wind blasted the seeds from the furrows and whipped the crops from the earth. . . .

The Okies were broke, they were without land, and they were hungry. And still the wind blew day and night, scraping all life from the earth. It's little wonder that Okies named this period in their lives the Dirty Thirties.

To end the conditions of the Dust Bowl, President Franklin Roosevelt started a conservation program as part of the New Deal. The goal was to stop the dust storms and save the land. An important part of the program was planting rows of large trees to break the sweep of the wind. In time, better plowing methods, more rainfall, and the new windbreaks ended the terrible dust.

Literature Review

1. What did people do to make it through the Dust Bowl days in Oklahoma?
2. How do you think you would have felt about living in the Dust Bowl?
3. Many people left Oklahoma to escape the Dust Bowl, but many stayed through all the hardships. With a partner, role-play a conversation between a person who is staying and a person who is leaving. Make sure the conversation gives the reasons for each person's decision. Present your conversation to the class.

WORLD WAR II

Link to Our World

What might cause conflict between countries today?

Focus on the Main Idea
As you read, look for the reasons that caused the United States and countries in Europe and Asia to go to war in the 1930s and 1940s.

Preview Vocabulary
concentration camp
civilian
rationing
relocation camp

The United States was not the only country to suffer an economic depression in the 1930s. Depression was, in fact, worldwide. Many Europeans, still rebuilding after the Great War, had a hard time finding jobs to support their families. In some places in Asia, countries were running out of the resources needed to make their economies grow. Strong leaders in both Europe and Asia promised to solve their countries' problems by force. Another war was on its way. This second world war, or World War II, would be even worse than the first.

THE RISE OF DICTATORS

After World War I the Allies expected Germany to pay for the costs of the war. But Germany did not have the money to do so. Its economy had been destroyed by the war and the depression.

During the 1920s a German leader named Adolf Hitler tried to convince people that Germany had not been treated fairly after World War I. He believed that the Germans who were blond and blue-eyed were the "true Germans" and were better than all other Germans and other peoples of the world. He made life especially difficult for Germany's Jews, whom he blamed for many of Germany's problems.

Hitler became the leader of a political party in Germany called the National Socialists, or Nazis. The Nazi party grew in power and set up an army. Its soldiers, who called themselves storm troopers, attacked Jewish people and others who were against Hitler. Soon the Nazis began to round up people who did not agree with them. They put these people in prisons called **concentration camps**.

Dictators used force against Jews and other people whom they labeled as enemies.

In 1933 the Nazi party took control of the German government, and representative government in Germany came to an end. Hitler ruled as a dictator, an all-powerful ruler. He had no respect for people's rights. Hitler rebuilt Germany's economy by preparing for another war. Factories produced tanks, guns, and other war supplies. Hitler dreamed that Germany would rule the world.

Bad economic conditions led to the rise of dictators in other countries of Europe. Joseph Stalin ruled the Soviet Union, which had become a dictatorship after the Russian Revolution in 1917. Francisco Franco ruled Spain. In Italy Benito Mussolini (buh•NEE•toh moo•suh•LEE•nee) came to power. He wanted Italy to regain the power and glory it had when it was the center of the Roman Empire in ancient times.

In Asia, dictators also ruled Japan. The emperor, Hirohito, had little authority after military officers took control of the government. Trade and industry were growing, but Japan did not have all the resources it needed. The military leaders planned to get oil, rubber, and iron for Japan by conquering other countries in Asia and the Pacific.

 In what countries did dictators rule after World War I?

THE WAR BEGINS

In 1931 Japan invaded Manchuria, in Asia. In 1935 Italy took over the African country of Ethiopia. In 1937 Japan started a war against China. In 1938 Germany moved into Austria and Czechoslovakia. Other countries, among them the United States, watched in horror but did little to stop the fighting.

Then, on September 1, 1939, Germany invaded Poland. German forces attacked with tanks on land and planes in the air. They destroyed cities, roads, and communication lines. Leaders in Britain and France had finally had enough. They declared war on Germany on September 3, 1939. World War II had begun.

The British and French armies were not able to stop the Germans from taking over most of Europe. By 1940 German troops had conquered the Netherlands, Belgium, Luxembourg, Denmark, Norway, and most of France. German bombers attacked British cities, but Britain fought on.

In the United States many people felt that their country should stay out of the war. President Franklin Roosevelt had promised, "As long as it remains in my power to prevent, there will be no blackout of peace in the United States." Nevertheless, Roosevelt felt that the country should be ready in case it was attacked. The United States started

making tanks, bombers, and other war supplies. It also began to send equipment and supplies to help Britain.

In 1940 Japanese troops invaded French Indochina, which is now made up of the countries of Laos, Cambodia, and Vietnam. American leaders feared that Japan would soon threaten the Philippines and other places in the Pacific. They were right.

 **When did World War II begin?**

THE UNITED STATES ENTERS THE WAR

At dawn on Sunday, December 7, 1941, it was warm and partly cloudy over the Hawaiian Islands. At 7:55 A.M. the roar of Japanese planes shattered the early morning calm. The planes broke through the clouds and dropped bombs on Pearl Harbor. Pearl Harbor is an American naval base in the Hawaiian Islands. World War II had come to the United States.

German soldiers invaded Poland in 1939 and marched through Paris (left) in 1940. What do you suppose Americans of that time were thinking when they read headlines about the war?

During the attack on Pearl Harbor, 19 American warships were sunk or disabled. Three others were damaged. The Japanese hoped that by the time the United States rebuilt its forces, Japan would have taken over more lands in Asia and the Pacific.

Where?

Pearl Harbor

Pearl Harbor is one of the largest natural harbors in the world. It is located on the Hawaiian island of Oahu (oh•AH•hoo) and lies west of downtown Honolulu, the capital of Hawaii. The United States began using Pearl Harbor as a coal station for its steamships in 1887. The navy started using it as a base in 1902. The surprise attack on Pearl Harbor by Japanese forces led the United States to enter World War II. Today the U.S.S. *Arizona* Memorial stands above one of the ships sunk in the attack.

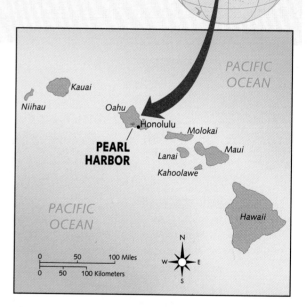

In less than two hours, the attack was over. Much of the United States' Pacific fleet lay sunk or burning in the harbor. At nearby Hickam Airfield, more than 140 planes were damaged or destroyed. More than 2,000 sailors and soldiers and 68 civilians were killed. A **civilian** is a person who is not in the military.

The day after the attack, President Roosevelt spoke to Congress:

66 Yesterday, December 7, 1941—a date which will live in infamy—the United States of America was suddenly and deliberately attacked by naval and air forces of the Empire of Japan. . . . I ask that the Congress declare that since the . . . attack by Japan . . . a state of war has existed between the United States and the Japanese Empire. 99

Congress declared war on Japan the same day. Three days later, when Japan's allies,

Germany and Italy, declared war on the United States, Congress recognized a state of war with them, too. Those countries were known as the Axis Powers. The United States joined Britain and the Soviet Union. They were called the Allies.

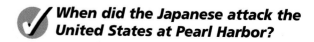 **When did the Japanese attack the United States at Pearl Harbor?**

AMERICANS AT WAR

After the bombing at Pearl Harbor, the United States began to produce more airplanes, tanks, and other war supplies. This work gave many people jobs. Now instead of not enough jobs, there were not enough workers. World War II ended the Great Depression in the United States.

As in World War I, women took over many jobs in factories, fields, and offices. Other women served in the armed forces. They made maps, drove ambulances, and worked as clerks or nurses. Some women, trained as pilots, flew airplanes from factories to airfields in Europe and the Pacific.

The demands of fighting a war led to further growth in the federal government's authority. To produce war supplies and feed thousands of soldiers, the government took control of defense businesses, setting prices and wages.

New government rules also called for **rationing**, or limiting, what Americans could buy, so that more supplies could be sent overseas. Government coupons were needed for such goods as butter, sugar, meat, home-heating oil, and gasoline. Each citizen had a coupon book for each kind of item. It was impossible to buy these goods without coupons.

 What did the government do to produce war supplies and feed its soldiers?

PROBLEMS FOR JAPANESE AMERICANS

War with Japan led to terrible problems for Japanese Americans. Some United States military officials believed that Japanese Americans would help Japan invade the United States.

In February 1942 President Roosevelt ordered the army to put about 110,000 Japanese Americans in **relocation camps**. These were camps that were like prisons.

LEARNING FROM GRAPHS
- By 1950, about how many American women were working outside the home?

WOMEN IN THE LABOR FORCE, 1900–1950

Japanese Americans who were being relocated, like this family, wore identification tags. Some identification tags looked like the one shown below.

WAR RELOCATION AUTHORITY

JAMES
KAWAMINAMI

14967

Barbed wire fenced people in. Soldiers with guns guarded the camps to keep people from leaving.

Even though most Japanese Americans were loyal United States citizens, they had to sell their homes, businesses, and belongings. They were moved to relocation camps in California, Arizona, Wyoming, Utah, Arkansas, and Idaho.

"Our home was one room in a large army-style barracks, measuring 20 by 25 feet," remembers one woman. "The only furnishings were an iron pot-belly stove and cots." Another woman recalls, "Can you imagine the despair and utter desolation of all of us? Everybody was weeping, youngsters hanging onto parents, fear and terror all around."

While their families and friends were in the relocation camps, more than 17,000 Japanese Americans served in the army. Japanese Americans formed the 442nd Combat Team. It received more service awards than any other unit its size in World War II.

✓ **Why did President Roosevelt order the army to put Japanese Americans in relocation camps?**

LESSON 4 REVIEW

Check Understanding

1. **Recall the Facts**   What countries were ruled by dictators in the 1930s?
2. **Focus on the Main Idea**   What caused different countries to take part in World War II?

Think Critically

3. **Think More About It**   How did World War II change life for many Americans?
4. **Personally Speaking**   How do you think you might feel as an American citizen if you were forced to live in a relocation camp?

Show What You Know

Interviewing Activity   Talk to people who are old enough to remember the attack on Pearl Harbor. Ask them when they first heard the news and how they felt. Write down your findings and report them to the class.

FIGHTING the WAR

Link to Our World

How do events that happened in the past affect today's world?

Focus on the Main Idea
Read to learn how World War II affected countries around the world.

Preview Vocabulary
front   cold war
D day
Holocaust
island-hopping
communism
free world

World War II was a new kind of war. Soldiers did not fight from trenches, as they had in World War I. Instead, they moved quickly by tank, ship, and airplane. Bombs dropped in air raids destroyed factories, hospitals, and homes and killed hundreds of thousands of civilians. The war was fought over an area much larger than that of any other war—almost half the world. It was fought on two major **fronts**, or battle lines. The first was in Africa and Europe. The second was in the Pacific. Victory on both fronts would be needed to win the war.

WAR IN AFRICA AND EUROPE

The first step in the Allies' battle plan in Europe was to gain control of the Mediterranean Sea. To do this, the Allies had to fight the Germans and Italians in North Africa and then invade Italy. The Allies won North Africa in May 1943 and then started pushing north through Italy. In September the Italian government surrendered. However, heavy fighting went on until June 1944, when the Americans captured Rome.

While the Allies were fighting in Italy, they were planning another invasion of Europe. On June 6, 1944, the date known as **D day**, the Allies worked together in the largest water-to-land invasion in history.

American General Dwight D. Eisenhower led the invasion. On the morning of June 6, he told his troops,

A "dog tag" was worn by soldiers for identification.

66 You are about to embark upon a great crusade. . . . The hopes and prayers of liberty-loving people everywhere go with you. 99

On D day American, British, and Canadian troops crossed the English Channel. They landed on the beaches of Normandy, in France, where the Germans met them with heavy gunfire. "Everything was confusion," remembers one soldier. "Shells were coming in all the time; boats burning, vehicles with nowhere to go bogging down, getting hit; supplies getting wet; boats trying to come in all the time, some hitting mines, exploding."

But the D day invasion was successful. The Allies broke through the German lines and began moving inland from the west, pushing back the enemy. At the same time, the Soviets were pushing back the German armies from the east. In May 1945, Allied troops met near Berlin, the German capital. There they learned that Hitler had killed himself.

Berlin fell to the Soviets on May 2, 1945, and the German military leaders asked to surrender. On May 8, the Allies accepted the surrender. This day was called V-E Day, or Victory in Europe Day. It marked the end of the war in Europe.

✓ **What happened on D day?**

THE HOLOCAUST

Only when the war was over in Europe did people understand what Hitler and the Nazis had done. Allied soldiers found the Nazis' concentration camps. The Allies learned that more than 12 million men, women, and children had been murdered in these camps. One of the largest of the death camps was at Auschwitz (OWSH•vits), in Poland.

The Nazis killed people for their religious or political beliefs. People who were ill or disabled and could not work were also killed. The largest group of victims were Jews, the people Hitler had blamed for Germany's problems.

During the war more than 6 million people were murdered on Hitler's orders because they were Jews. This terrible mass murder of

General Eisenhower talks with his troops (above right) before they leave for the D day invasion. On D day, 600 warships and 4,000 landing craft carried 176,000 soldiers across the English Channel.

Prisoners in concentration camps suffered horribly. The Nazis forced Jews to wear a yellow Star of David to make them stand out.

European Jews came to be known as the **Holocaust** (HOH•luh•kawst). Hitler had called it the "final solution to the Jewish question." It was a deliberate attempt to destroy an entire people.

 **What was Hitler's "final solution"?**

WAR IN THE PACIFIC

In the Pacific, Allied leaders planned to defeat the Japanese by forcing them back from the lands and islands they had conquered. Allied leaders decided on a plan of **island-hopping**. This meant that Allied troops would take back the islands one at a time until they reached Tokyo. At the same time, the Allies would bomb Japan from the air.

Battles on the islands of Iwo Jima (EE•woh JEE•muh) and Okinawa (oh•kuh•NAH•wah) showed island-hopping to be a costly plan. At Iwo Jima, an island 750 miles (1,207 km) from Tokyo, Japan's capital, more than 4,000 American soldiers lost their lives. More than

20,000 Japanese soldiers died. At Okinawa, 350 miles (563 km) from Tokyo, 11,000 Americans died. The Japanese lost more than 100,000 people. As the Allies came closer to Tokyo, the losses became greater.

By early April 1945 victory in the Pacific seemed near. But President Franklin Roosevelt did not live to see the end of the war. He died on April 12, 1945. Vice President Harry S. Truman became President.

After he became President, Truman learned that Roosevelt had agreed to the development of the most powerful bomb the world had ever known—the atom bomb. By the summer of 1945, this new weapon was ready. President Truman made the difficult decision to drop the atom bomb on Japan. He wanted to end the war quickly and save American lives.

On August 6, 1945, the American bomber *Enola Gay* flew over the industrial city of Hiroshima (hir•uh•SHEE•muh), Japan. A single bomb dropped. There was a flash like an exploding sun. Then a mushroom-shaped cloud rose from the city. The bomb flattened a huge area of Hiroshima and killed more than 75,000 people, mostly civilians.

As terrible as the atom bomb was, Japan did not surrender. On August 9 the United States dropped a second bomb, this time on Nagasaki (nah•guh•SAH•kee). Only then did Japan agree to surrender. On August 15, Americans celebrated V-J Day, or Victory over Japan Day.

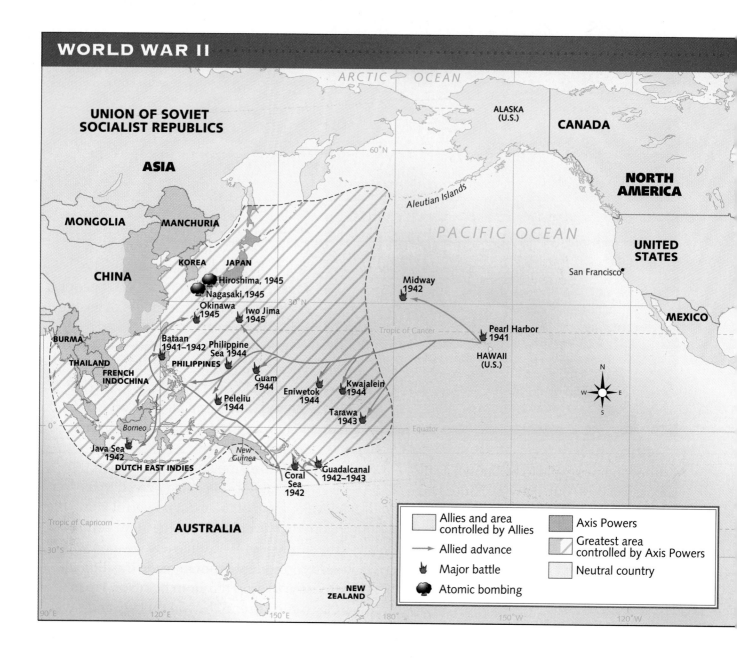

World War II was finally over. More than 321,000 American soldiers had died in the fighting.

✓ Why did Japan surrender to the United States?

A CHANGED WORLD

As after World War I, world leaders after World War II turned to the idea of an organization of nations. This time the United States supported the idea. In April 1945, delegates from 50 countries met in San Francisco to form the United Nations, or UN. The purpose of the UN is to keep world peace and promote cooperation among nations.

The United States came out of World War II as the strongest nation in the world. Americans used this strength to help other nations rebuild. Yet even as the war was ending and plans for peace were being made, new conflicts were beginning.

The United States and the Soviet Union were allies during World War II. After the war this quickly changed. The Soviet Union set up communist governments in the eastern European countries it had invaded

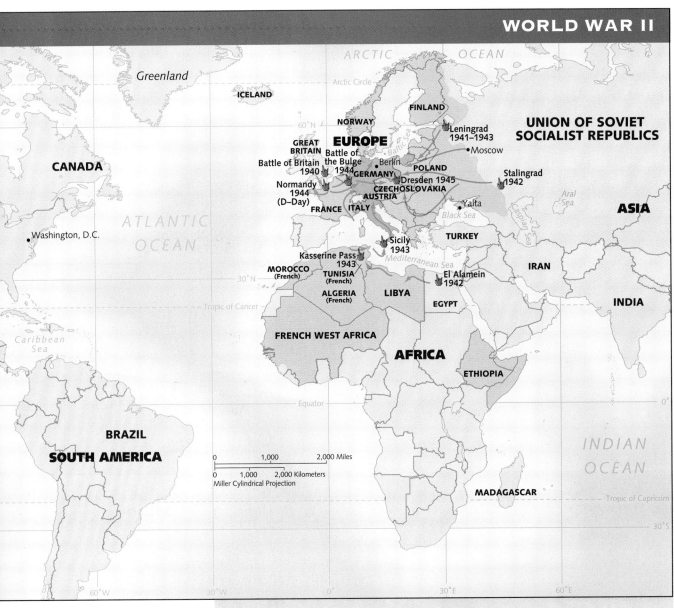

ARCTIC OCEAN

Greenland

ICELAND

Arctic Circle

60°N

FINLAND

NORWAY

EUROPE

UNION OF SOVIET SOCIALIST REPUBLICS

CANADA

GREAT BRITAIN

Battle of the Bulge 1944

Battle of Britain 1940

Leningrad 1941–1943

•Moscow

POLAND

Berlin

GERMANY

Dresden 1945

Stalingrad 1942

Normandy 1944 (D–Day)

CZECHOSLOVAKIA

AUSTRIA

FRANCE ITALY

•Yalta

Aral Sea

ASIA

ATLANTIC OCEAN

Washington, D.C.

Black Sea

Caspian Sea

Sicily 1943

Mediterranean Sea

TURKEY

IRAN

Kasserine Pass 1943

MOROCCO (French)

TUNISIA (French)

El Alamein 1942

30°N

INDIA

ALGERIA (French)

LIBYA

EGYPT

Tropic of Cancer

Caribbean Sea

FRENCH WEST AFRICA

AFRICA

BRAZIL

SOUTH AMERICA

0   1,000   2,000 Miles
0   1,000   2,000 Kilometers
Miller Cylindrical Projection

ETHIOPIA

Equator

INDIAN OCEAN

MADAGASCAR

Tropic of Capricorn

30°S

60°W   30°W   0°   30°E   60°E

LOCATION During the war, almost the whole world was divided between the Allies and the Axis Powers.

■ How do you think the location of the United States was helpful to the country in the war?

during the war. **Communism** is a social and economic system in which all land and industries are owned by the government. Individuals have few rights and little freedom.

The United States saw the spread of communism as a threat to freedom. It began to help countries fight communism by giving them military and economic help. In the fight against communism, the United States and its allies were known as the **free world**.

Hostility, or unfriendliness, developed between the free world and the communist nations. This hostility became known as the Cold War. A **cold war** is fought with propaganda and money rather than with soldiers and weapons. For much of the second half of the 1900s, the Cold War shaped world events.

How did the United States help fight communism?

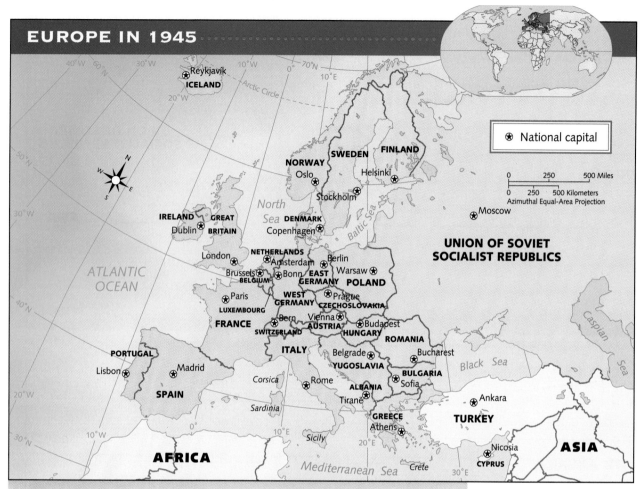

EUROPE IN 1945

National capital ⊛

0   250   500 Miles
0   250   500 Kilometers
Azimuthal Equal-Area Projection

 PLACE The war had changed Europe in ways that would affect the world for years to come.
■ What does this map show about changes that took place in Germany after World War II?

LESSON 5 REVIEW

Check Understanding

1. **Recall the Facts** Who led the D day invasion? When did it take place?

2. **Focus on the Main Idea** In what ways did World War II affect countries around the world?

Think Critically

3. **Think More About It** How were the reasons for fighting in World War I different from those in World War II?

4. **Cause and Effect** How did differences between the United States and the Soviet Union cause problems after World War II?

Show What You Know

Writing Activity Imagine that you are an Allied soldier who has helped free the people in a Nazi concentration camp. Use the picture in this lesson to write a letter home that describes what you saw there. Share your letter with a family member.

Read Parallel Time Lines

Why Is This Skill Important?

When there are many events happening at about the same time, it is difficult to put them in order. It even can be difficult to show them on one time line. Parallel time lines can help. Parallel time lines are two or more time lines that show the same period of time. Parallel time lines can also show events that happened in different places.

Understand the Process

The parallel time lines on this page show events that took place in 1945, the final year of World War II. Time Line A shows the important events that took place in Europe. Time Line B shows the important events that took place in the Pacific. You can use these parallel time lines to compare when different events happened.

1. Which event took place first, V-E Day or V-J Day?

2. Why do you think the label *Truman becomes President* is on both time lines?

3. Did the United States drop the atom bomb on Hiroshima before or after Soviet troops surrounded Berlin?

4. What was happening in Europe while the Battle of Iwo Jima was being fought?

Think and Apply

Create parallel time lines of events that have happened in your lifetime. Use one time line to show the important events in your life, beginning with the year you were born and ending with the present year. Use the other time line to show important events that have taken place in the United States during these same years.

WORLD WAR II, 1945

TIME LINE A: THE WAR IN EUROPE

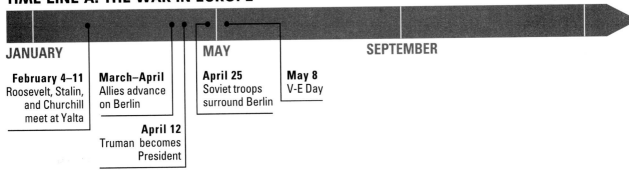

JANUARY   MAY   SEPTEMBER

February 4–11 Roosevelt, Stalin, and Churchill meet at Yalta

March–April Allies advance on Berlin

April 12 Truman becomes President

April 25 Soviet troops surround Berlin

May 8 V-E Day

TIME LINE B: THE WAR IN THE PACIFIC

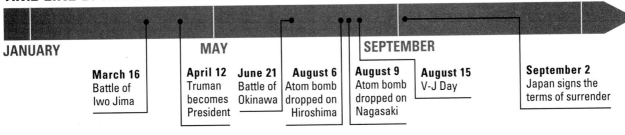

JANUARY   MAY   SEPTEMBER

March 16 Battle of Iwo Jima

April 12 Truman becomes President

June 21 Battle of Okinawa

August 6 Atom bomb dropped on Hiroshima

August 9 Atom bomb dropped on Nagasaki

August 15 V-J Day

September 2 Japan signs the terms of surrender

CONNECT MAIN IDEAS

Use the organizer to show that you understand how the chapter's main ideas are connected. Copy the organizer onto a separate sheet of paper. Then complete it by writing one or two sentences to summarize each idea or event.

The Roaring Twenties
_____
_____
_____

The Great Depression
_____
_____
_____

The Rise of Dictators
_____
_____
_____

The New Deal
_____
_____
_____

Good Times and Bad

The Atom Bomb
_____
_____
_____

Pearl Harbor
_____
_____
_____

The United Nations
_____
_____
_____

The Cold War
_____
_____
_____

WRITE MORE ABOUT IT

1. **Write a Want Ad**   Write a want ad that describes a job on one of Henry Ford's assembly lines.

2. **Write a Diary Entry**   Imagine that you are living in the 1920s. Write a diary entry about the day your family got its first automobile.

Describe what it was like to ride in an automobile for the first time.

3. **Write a Short Story**   Write a short story about going shopping with your family during World War II. Tell how the war has affected the way you shop and what you can buy.

USE VOCABULARY

For each group of terms, write a sentence or two explaining how the terms are related.

1. consumer goods, installment buying

2. assembly line, commercial industry

3. stock market, depression, unemployment

4. civilian, rationing

5. front, D day, island-hopping

6. communism, free world, cold war

CHECK UNDERSTANDING

1. How was Henry Ford able to produce cars less expensively?

2. How did jazz develop?

3. Why did Harlem attract so many people in the 1920s?

4. Why did many banks close during the Great Depression?

5. How did the WPA and other New Deal programs help workers?

6. How did hydroelectric dams help economic development?

7. What event caused the United States to enter the fighting in World War II?

8. Who were the largest group of victims in the Holocaust?

9. What did the leaders of the United States see as a threat to freedom following World War II?

THINK CRITICALLY

1. **Personally Speaking** Installment buying in the 1920s led to the present-day use of credit cards. How do you think credit cards can help people? What problems can they cause?

2. **Think More About It** How would your life be different if the automobile had never been invented?

3. **Past to Present** A law passed during the Great Depression gave workers the right to a minimum wage. What is the minimum wage today? How does the minimum wage continue to protect workers?

4. **Cause and Effect** What effects did relocation have on the lives of Japanese Americans during World War II?

APPLY SKILLS

How to Read Parallel Time Lines Use the parallel time line on page 563 to answer the questions.

1. What happened on April 12, 1945?

2. Which happened first, the Battle of Okinawa or the meeting at Yalta?

3. How many days after the first atom bomb was dropped on Hiroshima was one dropped on Nagasaki?

READ MORE ABOUT IT

Baseball Saved Us by Ken Mochizuki. Lee & Low. Japanese Americans in a relocation camp build a baseball field so that they can play ball.

The Buck Stops Here: A Biography of Harry Truman by Morrie Greenberg. Dillon. This book tells about President Truman's life.

Ida Early Comes Over the Mountain by Robert Burch. Viking. Things are never quite the same after the unpredictable Ida becomes the housekeeper for a family during the Great Depression.

Navajo Code Talkers by Nathan Aaseng. Walker. This book describes how Navajo Indians developed a secret code that was used by the United States during World War II.

MAKING SOCIAL STUDIES
RELEVANT

WAR and Children

Two great wars in the first half of the twentieth century touched the lives of many young people around the world. In Europe, Africa, and Asia—where most of the fighting took place—many children saw their homes destroyed and their family members killed or injured.

These wars also affected children in the United States. Many young people had family members or friends who went to other countries to fight in the wars, and many of these people were killed or wounded. For more than 30,000 Japanese American children, World War II caused fear and hardships. Along with their parents, they were forced to leave their homes and move to relocation camps.

It is hard for children in the United States today to imagine the life of a child during World War I or World War II. But wars continue to be fought in some parts of the world, and many children are deeply affected by them.

Zlata Filipovic was 10 years old in 1992 when she began keeping a diary about the war being fought in her country of Bosnia and Herzegovina in eastern Europe. Zlata described "the worst day ever" for her in Sarajevo, the city where she lived.

"The shooting started around noon. Mommy and I moved into the hall. Daddy was in his office under our apartment, at the time. We told him on the intercom to run quickly to the downstairs lobby where we'd meet him. . . . The gunfire was getting worse, . . . so we ran down to our cellar.

We listened to the pounding shells, the shooting, the thundering noise overhead. We even heard planes. At one moment I realized that this awful cellar was the only place that could save our lives. . . . It was the only way we could defend ourselves against all this terrible shooting. We heard glass shattering in our street. Horrible. I put my fingers in my ears to block out the terrible sounds."

Somalia

Southwest Asia

THINK AND APPLY

Think about the wars that are being fought around the world today. In the library, look for books or magazine articles that tell about children who lived through wars in different times. Compare what war is like for children today with what it was like for children at other times in history. Share your findings with family members.

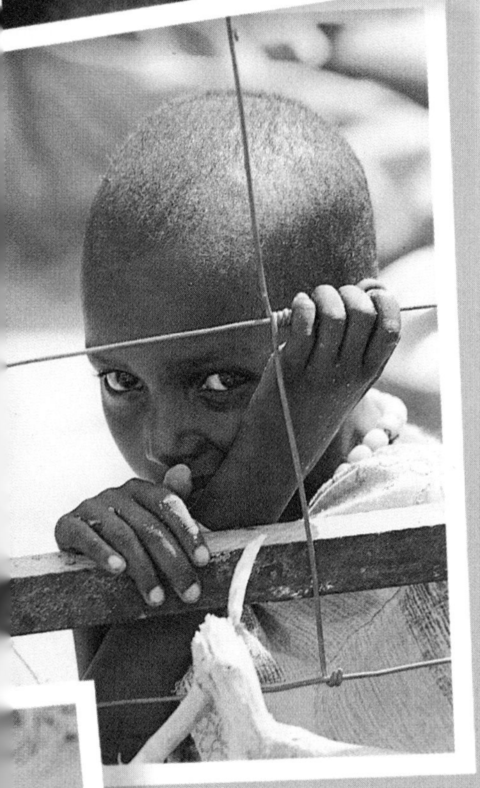

BUILDING CITIZENSHIP

Bosnia

Afghanistan

Vietnam

STORY CLOTH

Study the pictures shown in this story cloth to help you review the events you read about in Unit 9.

Summarize the Main Ideas

1. By 1900 the United States had become a world power. It had gained new territories after the Spanish-American War, in which Theodore Roosevelt's Rough Riders became famous.

2. The Panama Canal helped link American possessions in the Atlantic and the Pacific.

3. In 1917 the United States entered World War I. Soldiers fought from trenches and faced terrible new weapons.

4. After the war, women nationwide gained the right to vote. During the Roaring Twenties, the economy boomed and many people enjoyed good times.

5. The stock market crash of 1929 started the Great Depression. Businesses failed, and people stood in line for free food. Franklin Roosevelt's New Deal helped get people back to work.

6. Drought on the Great Plains brought still more suffering.

7. Worldwide depression helped lead to the rise of dictators and the start of World War II. The United States entered the war in 1941, when Pearl Harbor was attacked.

8. After the war, the United Nations was formed to help keep world peace. But the spread of communism led to the Cold War.

Write Newspaper Headlines   For each of the events shown in this story cloth, write a headline that might have appeared in newspapers of the time.

COOPERATIVE LEARNING WORKSHOP

Remember

- Share your ideas.
- Cooperate with others to plan your work.
- Take responsibility for your work.
- Show your group's work to the class.
- Discuss what you learned by working together.

Activity 1
Draw a Map

Work together to draw a map of the Panama Canal. Maps in your textbook and in encyclopedias and atlases can help you. Label the canal's major locks and the nearby cities and bodies of water. Then use your map as you tell classmates about how the canal came to be built and why it was important to the United States.

Activity 2
Make a Conservation Collage

Like Theodore Roosevelt, many people today are interested in conservation. Work in a group to make a collage that shows how people can conserve natural resources. Use reference books and other books from the library to get ideas about conservation. Then cut out pictures and words from newspapers and magazines to match the ideas you want to show. Arrange the pictures and words on posterboard, and

paste them into place. Give your collage a title before you display it in your classroom.

Activity 3
Give a Talk

Work together to research the Roaring Twenties. Find out about the ways in which life during that decade was similar to and different from life today. When your research is complete, give a short talk to your class. Describe the ways that people dressed and styled their hair. Tell about popular dance steps and the music that people listened to. If possible, play recordings of music from the 1920s and show pictures of people from that time.

Activity 4
Invite Guest Speakers

Work in a group to invite guest speakers to your class. With your teacher's help, choose a date and time for the speakers to come. Then write a letter to a seniors' group in your community, inviting five or six members to talk to your class about life during the Great Depression.

USE VOCABULARY

Use each term in a sentence that will help explain its meaning.

1. merit system
2. aviation
3. jazz
4. bureaucracy
5. unemployment
6. minimum wage
7. hydroelectric dam
8. concentration camp

CHECK UNDERSTANDING

1. What part did the battleship *Maine* play in the Spanish-American War?

2. How is the Panama Canal important to world trade?

3. How did Theodore Roosevelt promote the conservation of natural resources?

4. How did transportation and communication change in the 1920s?

5. How did the Great Depression affect Americans?

6. What ended World War II in the Pacific?

THINK CRITICALLY

1. **Past to Present**   How do alliances among countries affect the world today?

2. **Cause and Effect**   What caused hostility to develop between the United States and the Soviet Union following World War II?

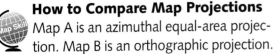

APPLY GEOGRAPHY SKILLS

How to Compare Map Projections Map A is an azimuthal equal-area projection. Map B is an orthographic projection. Use these maps to answer the questions.

1. On which map does the United States look larger?

2. On which map can you more clearly see the North Pole?

3. Which map shows parts of both the Eastern and Western Hemispheres?

4. What are the advantages and disadvantages of each map?

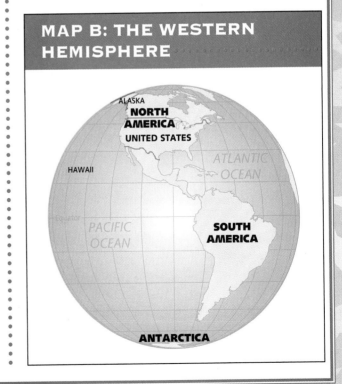

MAP A: THE NORTH POLE

MAP B: THE WESTERN HEMISPHERE

UNIT 10

The AMERICAS TODAY

1945

1948
Berlin airlift

1950
Korean War
begins

1955

1955
Montgomery bus
boycott

1957
The Soviet Union
launches *Sputnik*

1962
Cuban
missile crisis

1965

1964
Congress
passes the Civil
Rights Act

1969
American
astronauts land
on the moon

*T*hroughout their history Americans have been challenged in many ways—socially, politically, and economically. The years after World War II created even more challenges for Americans. Their responsibilities as citizens of a world power demanded new attitudes and new approaches, whether in confronting the communist world or in exploring outer space. In facing these challenges, Americans helped shape the future of their free and democratic society.

← **The space shuttle *Discovery* takes off from Kennedy Space Center.**

1975

1985

1995

1975
Vietnam War ends

1982
Canada adopts a new constitution

1991
Breakup of the Soviet Union

1994
NAFTA takes effect

End of military rule in Haiti

1993
Puerto Rico votes to remain a U.S. commonwealth

Set the Scene with Literature

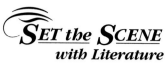

On the Pulse of Morning

by Maya Angelou

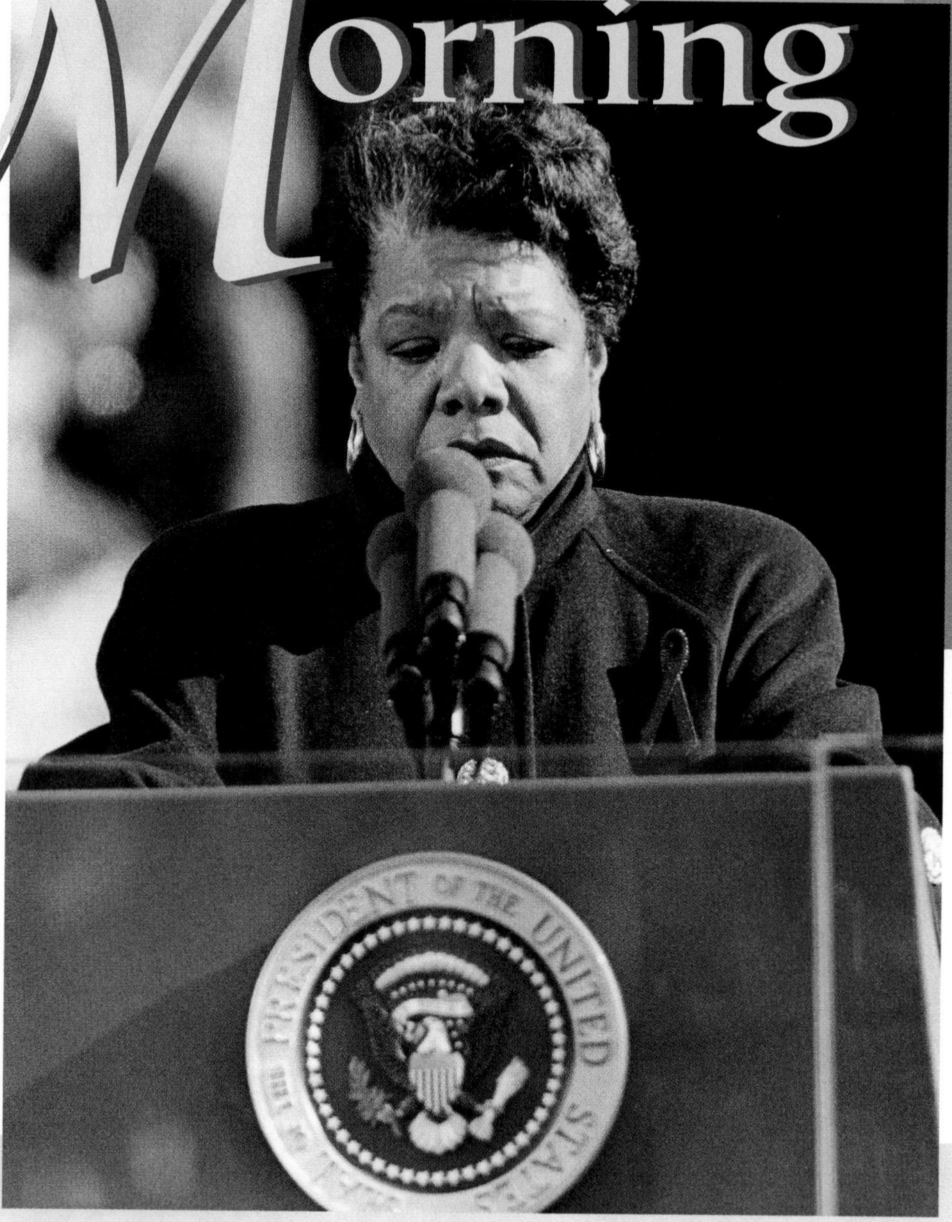

Maya Angelou (AN•juh•loh) wrote her poem "On the Pulse of Morning" for the inauguration of Bill Clinton as President of the United States. Clinton took the oath of office on January 20, 1993. In writing her poem, Angelou wanted to show that she loved her country despite its problems. She also wanted to celebrate the past while speaking hopefully about the future. As you read the poem, think about the problems and hopes many Americans had in the years after World War II.

Lift up your eyes
Upon this day breaking for you.
Give birth again
To the dream.

Women, children, men,
Take it into the palms of your hands,
Mold it into the shape of your most
Private need. Sculpt it into
The image of your most public self.
Lift up your hearts.
Each new hour holds new chances
For a new beginning.
Do not be wedded forever
To fear, yoked eternally
To brutishness.

The horizon leans forward,
Offering you space
To place new steps of change.
Here, on the pulse of this fine day,
You may have the courage
To look up and out and upon me,
The Rock, the River, the Tree, your country.
No less to Midas than the mendicant.
No less to you now than the mastodon then.

Here, on the pulse of this new day,
You may have the grace to look up and out
And into your sister's eyes,
And into your brother's face,
Your country,
And say simply
Very simply
With hope—
Good morning.

CHAPTER 19

The UNITED STATES
IN THE COLD WAR YEARS

> 66 I have a dream that my four little children will one day live in a nation where they will not be judged by the color of their skin but by the content of their character. 99
>
> Martin Luther King, Jr., in a speech at the Lincoln Memorial in Washington, D.C., on August 28, 1963

THE COLD WAR BEGINS

LESSON 1

Link to Our World

What can happen when powerful friends become enemies?

Focus on the Main Idea
Read to find out what happened when two World War II Allies, the United States and the Soviet Union, became enemies after the war.

Preview Vocabulary
superpower
airlift
missile
arms race

In the years after World War II, the United States and the Soviet Union became the world's most powerful nations. They were called the **superpowers** because of the important roles they played in world events. The two superpowers were very different from one another, and there were many conflicts between them. These conflicts were fought mostly with words and economic weapons. Even so, the threat of a real war was always present. These years, from 1945 to 1991, have become known as the Cold War years. They were a frightening time for many people.

THE BERLIN CRISIS

At the end of World War II, the victorious Allies divided Germany into four parts. Each major Ally took charge of one part. The United States, Britain, and France worked together to build a strong West Germany out of their parts. The Soviet Union held East Germany and formed a communist country there. Under this system, the government took over land and businesses. The people had little freedom.

Germany's capital city, Berlin, was in East Germany. It was divided into four parts, too. But the Soviet Union would not let the Western Allies send supplies to the area the Allies controlled, which made up the city of West Berlin. The Soviets blocked highway, rail, and water routes so that no food or fuel could get into the city. They hoped to drive the Western Allies out of West Berlin.

To get around the blockade, the Allies started the Berlin airlift in 1948. An **airlift** is a system of bringing in supplies

EUROPE AND THE COLD WAR

Communist country
Noncommunist country
— **Iron curtain**

0 — 250 — 500 Miles
0 — 250 — 500 Kilometers
Azimuthal Equal-Area Projection

NORWAY
SWEDEN
FINLAND
IRELAND
GREAT BRITAIN
DENMARK
ATLANTIC OCEAN
North Sea
Baltic Sea
NETHERLANDS
BRITISH ZONE
SOVIET ZONE
Berlin
EAST GERMANY
POLAND
BELGIUM
FRENCH ZONE
WEST GERMANY
LUXEMBOURG
CZECHOSLOVAKIA
FRANCE
AMERICAN ZONE
SWITZERLAND
AUSTRIA
HUNGARY
ROMANIA
PORTUGAL
SPAIN
ITALY
YUGOSLAVIA
BULGARIA
ALBANIA
GREECE
Black Sea
UNION OF SOVIET SOCIALIST REPUBLICS
TURKEY
Mediterranean Sea
AFRICA
ASIA

DIVISION OF BERLIN

FRENCH SECTOR
BRITISH SECTOR
West Berlin
AMERICAN SECTOR
East Berlin
SOVIET SECTOR

0 — 6 — 12 Miles
0 — 6 — 12 Kilometers

REGIONS Communist countries were said to be "behind the Iron Curtain," keeping them apart from other countries.
■ Which European countries were behind the Iron Curtain?

by airplane. For eleven months American and British pilots made more than 272,000 flights over East Germany to West Berlin. They carried more than two million tons of food and supplies to the people of West Berlin. Finally the Soviets opened the land routes from West Germany.

After the blockade ended, many people tried to leave East Berlin to get away from communist rule. In 1961 the East German government, with Soviet help, built a fence to keep people from leaving. Then East Germany took down the fence and put up a concrete wall with barbed wire on the top. The Berlin Wall, as it came to be known, was

An East German worker building the Berlin Wall

guarded by soldiers ready to shoot anyone who tried to cross it. The wall was an alarming symbol of the Cold War. It stood for the division between the free world and the communist countries.

 How did the Western Allies solve the problem of getting supplies to West Berlin?

THE KOREAN WAR

Just as Germany was divided after World War II, Korea—which had been conquered by Japan in 1910—was divided into two parts. The Soviet Union supported North Korea, and the United States supported South Korea. In 1948 North Korea formed a communist government and South Korea formed a republic.

In 1950 the North Korean army, which had been trained and equipped by the Soviet Union, invaded South Korea. North Korea wanted to make all of Korea communist. North Korea was also helped by China, which had become communist in 1949.

United States President Harry S. Truman quickly sent American soldiers to support South Korea. The United Nations also sent troops to stop the invasion. About 15 countries were now fighting a new war—the Korean War.

So many American soldiers died in the fighting that the Korean War became a major issue in the 1952 election for President of the United States. Dwight D. Eisenhower, the famous World War II general, promised that if he was elected he would work to end the war. Soon after his election he kept his promise. In 1953 an armistice was signed to stop the fighting. North Korean troops had been pushed back into North Korea. South Korea was still an independent country.

 What were the results of the Korean War?

A DIVIDED KOREA

REGIONS At the end of World War II, Soviet troops in Korea were north of the 38th parallel, and American troops were south of it.
■ How much did the cease-fire line of 1953 change the earlier division?

THE MISSILE CRISIS

In 1961 John F. Kennedy took the oath as President of the United States. Kennedy was 43 years old and the youngest person ever elected President. His energy and enthusiasm made him especially popular with young people. Soon after he took office, however, Cold War problems began to take up much of his time.

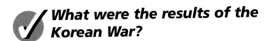

In October 1962 President Kennedy learned that the Soviet Union had built several launch sites for missiles in Cuba, just 90 miles (145 km) off the southern tip of Florida. A **missile** is a rocket that can carry a bomb thousands of miles. Fidel Castro had taken control of Cuba three years before. With the help of the Soviet Union, he had formed a communist government.

President Kennedy (seated at the center on the far side of the table) meets at the White House with his Cabinet during the Cuban missile crisis. Secretary of State Dean Rusk is seated at Kennedy's right. Secretary of Defense Robert McNamara is seated at Kennedy's left.

Worried that the Soviets would use these missiles to attack the United States, Kennedy ordered a blockade of the island nation. The United States Navy would stop Soviet ships that were carrying missiles from reaching Cuba. Americans worried as they listened to the news on radio and television. What if the ships refused to stop? Would there be a war?

Finally the Soviet Union agreed to stop sending missiles to Cuba and to remove all the missiles that were already there. The United States agreed to end the blockade.

Kennedy's success in handling the missile crisis increased his popularity. But he knew he would have to work hard to be elected President again. On November 22, 1963, the President and Jacqueline Kennedy, his wife, visited Dallas, Texas, to meet with supporters there. They were waving to the crowd as their car drove through the streets. Suddenly shots rang out. President Kennedy was killed. Hours after the assassination, Vice President Lyndon Baines Johnson took the oath of office as the new President.

✓ **Why did the United States take action when the Soviet Union set up missile bases in Cuba?**

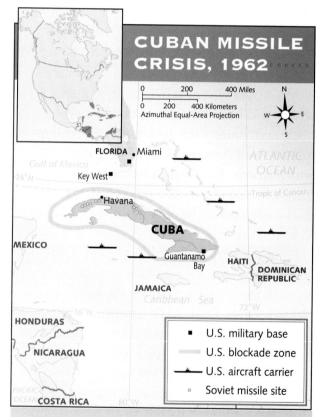

CUBA MISSILE CRISIS, 1962

0   200   400 Miles
0   200   400 Kilometers
Azimuthal Equal-Area Projection

FLORIDA • Miami
Gulf of Mexico
24°N   Key West ■
                              ATLANTIC OCEAN
                              Tropic of Cancer
• Havana
                    CUBA
MEXICO
              Guantanamo ■
                    Bay   HAITI
                                      DOMINICAN REPUBLIC
        JAMAICA
              Caribbean Sea   72°W
HONDURAS
    16°N
    NICARAGUA
                    ■ U.S. military base
PACIFIC   U.S. blockade zone
OCEAN   ⚓ U.S. aircraft carrier
COSTA RICA   80°W   ○ Soviet missile site

HUMAN-ENVIRONMENT INTERACTIONS
The United States blockaded Cuba during the missile crisis.
■ Why do you think aircraft carriers were placed where they were?

THE ARMS RACE

The Cold War triggered an **arms race** between the two superpowers. The United States and the Soviet Union each tried to build more weapons than the other. Leaders of each country believed that having more weapons—and the most powerful ones—would keep their country safe.

The arms race started with the atom bomb. The Soviet Union knew what atom bombs had done to the Japanese cities of Hiroshima and Nagasaki. It feared the power of the United States to destroy a whole city with one bomb. Soon the Soviet Union was building its own atom bombs.

After the Soviet Union had the atom bomb, however, the United States made an even more powerful bomb. Scientists said that the hydrogen bomb, or the H-bomb, was 1,000 times more powerful than the atom bombs dropped on Japan during World War II. Other atomic weapons were made, too. By the 1960s the superpowers had missiles that could carry bombs to targets halfway around the world.

Both the Americans and the Soviets lived in fear during the Cold War. Some Americans built special shelters below ground as protection in case of an attack. They stocked their shelters with flashlights, radios, first-aid kits,

During drills like this one, students were trained to prepare for a missile attack. How do you think the drills made them feel?

canned foods, water, and other supplies. At schools across the country, "duck-and-cover" drills were held to teach children to get under their desks if a missile attack came.

 What was each side's goal in the arms race?

LESSON 1 REVIEW

Check Understanding

1. **Recall the Facts**   What events contributed to Cold War tensions?
2. **Focus on the Main Idea**   How did relations between the United States and the Soviet Union change after World War II?

Think Critically

3. **Think More About It**   Why do you think a time of tensions is called a cold war?

4. **Personally Speaking**   How do you think people in the United States and people in the Soviet Union felt about each other during the Cold War?

Show What You Know

 **Letter-Writing Activity**
Imagine that you are living during the Cold War. Write a letter to President Kennedy telling him how you feel about the arms race.

One Giant Leap

**written and illustrated
by
Mary Ann Fraser**

The United States and the Soviet Union took the Cold War into space. In 1957 the Soviets surprised the United States by launching Sputnik (SPUT•nik). Sputnik was the world's first space satellite, an object sent by a rocket into an orbit around the Earth.

Because of Sputnik, the United States speeded up its own efforts to explore space. In 1958 Congress set up the National Aeronautics and Space Administration, or NASA, to develop the nation's space program. Then, in 1961, President John F. Kennedy set a goal for the United States. This was to put a person on the moon by the end of the 1960s.

In 1962 an American astronaut orbited the Earth. Then a series of explorations called the Apollo program prepared for a moon landing. In 1968 astronauts in Apollo 8 first circled the moon. By the next year NASA was ready to try a moon landing. On July 16, 1969, Apollo 11 blasted off from Cape Canaveral, Florida. On board were astronauts Neil Armstrong, Edwin Aldrin, Jr., and Michael Collins. NASA scientists at Mission Control in Houston, Texas, followed their flight closely. Now read the story of the first moon landing four days later.

July 20, 1969

As the sun rose in Houston, Mission Control gently woke the crew. "*Apollo 11*, *Apollo 11*—good morning from the Black Team."

Michael Collins replied, "Good morning, Houston . . . oh my, you guys wake up early."

The astronauts may not have been ready to wake up, but this was the day they had waited and trained for: landing day. After breakfast and a briefing from Mission Control, Aldrin and Armstrong put on their liquid-cooling under-garments. Grabbing hold of the handrails, they floated into *Eagle*. Collins remained behind so he could help his fellow astronauts if anything went wrong.

On *Apollo 11*'s thirteenth orbit, Collins pushed the switch to release the final latches. Gently the modules drifted apart to become two independent vehicles.

Houston broke through the static as *Eagle* soared from behind the moon. "Roger. How does it look?"

Armstrong was now controlling *Eagle*. He answered, "*Eagle* has wings."

One-and-a-half hours later tension mounted again as *Eagle* followed *Columbia* toward the back side of the moon to begin its descent. In less than 11 minutes Armstrong and Aldrin had to cross 300 miles of the moon's surface in *Eagle*, dropping in a long curve from 50,000 feet to touchdown.

Any equipment failure or miscalculation would mean turning back or certain disaster. If a leg on the lunar module came to rest on a boulder or slope and the module toppled over, *Eagle* would not be able to take off. The men would be stranded. Some scientists thought that the moon's windless surface had a dangerously deep coating of dust. They worried that the module or men would sink into this loose lunar soil.

Back on Earth, hundreds of journalists packed newsrooms while millions of TV viewers and radio listeners tuned in for word of the astronauts.

The people of Mission Control waited for the static on their headsets to clear.

Eagle swung around from behind the moon, heading for the landing site on the Sea of Tranquility. Armstrong's voice finally came through. "The burn was on time."

"Current altitude about 46,000 feet, continuing to descend," reported the flight controller in Houston.

Just then ground control lost direct communication with *Eagle*. All commands had to be relayed through Mike Collins in *Columbia*. Armstrong adjusted *Eagle*'s position in flight, and Mission Control tried again to communicate directly. "*Eagle*, Houston. You are go. Take it all at four minutes. Roger, you are go—you are go to continue power descent."

"Roger." Aldrin had heard the message and commented, "And the earth right out our front window."

Suddenly an alarm went off in the cabin. "Twelve-o-two—twelve-o-two!" shouted

Armstrong. "Give us the reading on the twelve-o-two program alarm."

The guidance computer was overloaded with data, but Mission Control decided *Eagle* should still proceed with landing. "Roger . . . we got—we're go on that alarm."

Armstrong peered through his small, triangular window. The computer was taking them to a stadium-size crater littered with ancient boulders, rock, and rubble. With the flip of a switch, Armstrong seized full manual control from the computer. Now he had to use all the flying skills he had learned as a pilot.

He adjusted the spacecraft's hovering position while Aldrin guided him. "Lights on. Forward. Good. Forty feet, down two and a half. Picking up some dust. Thirty feet, two and a half down. Faint shadow. Four forward. Four forward, drifting to the right a little." The rocket's firing was creating dust clouds, making it difficult to see.

Armstrong frantically searched for a site. Mission Control interrupted, "30 SECONDS!" Only 30 seconds of fuel for landing remained. Armstrong had to land immediately.

Slowly he lowered the craft. The blue light in the cockpit flashed. "Contact light," reported Aldrin. One of the three probes, like a feeler on a giant insect, had touched ground. "Okay, engine stop." They had landed four miles west of their original target, but still within the planned area.

"Houston, Tranquility Base here. The *Eagle* has landed, " said Armstrong.

"Roger, Tranquility, we copy you on the ground," replied Mission Control. "You've got a bunch of guys about to turn blue. We're breathing again. Thanks a lot."

Back on Earth people of all nationalities celebrated the moon landing. But while Americans Armstrong and Aldrin had been skillfully piloting their spacecraft toward the Sea of Tranquility, [the Soviet Union's unmanned] *Luna 15* had crashed into the moon's Sea of Crises at nearly 300 miles per hour.

For several seconds Aldrin and Armstrong, the first humans on the moon, waited for the dust to settle about their spacecraft. Slowly they got their first glimpse of an alien world that had not changed for millions of years.

Meanwhile Collins in *Columbia* orbited to the back side of the moon, totally on his own for the first time.

A billion people from all over the world anxiously waited for the first steps onto the moon. Aldrin and Armstrong were no longer being viewed as Americans, but as representatives of all humanity.

With the last snap of their helmets in place, Armstrong and Aldrin could see but could no longer hear, taste, smell, or feel anything outside their space suits. The suits were their only protection against the moon's extreme temperatures, which ranged from −247 to 212 degrees Fahrenheit. Any tear in the suit could be fatal.

With Aldrin guiding him, Armstrong carefully stepped down the nine rungs of the ladder toward the moon's airless, waterless surface.

"I'm at the foot of the ladder. . . . The surface appears very, very fine grained as you get close to it." Armstrong could see that *Eagle*'s landing pads had barely sunk into the lunar dust. The moon's surface seemed safe. "I'm going to step off the LM [lunar module] now."

Exactly 109 hours, 24 minutes and 15 seconds into the mission, Armstrong stepped off the landing pad and placed the first human footprint on the moon.

"That's one small step for man, one giant leap for mankind," he said.

He had meant to say, "one small step for a man," but in his excitement and nervousness he left out the *a*. A few moments later Aldrin joined him.

With those first prints in the lunar dust the people of Earth proved they could reach beyond their planet and touch the moon. Neil Armstrong,

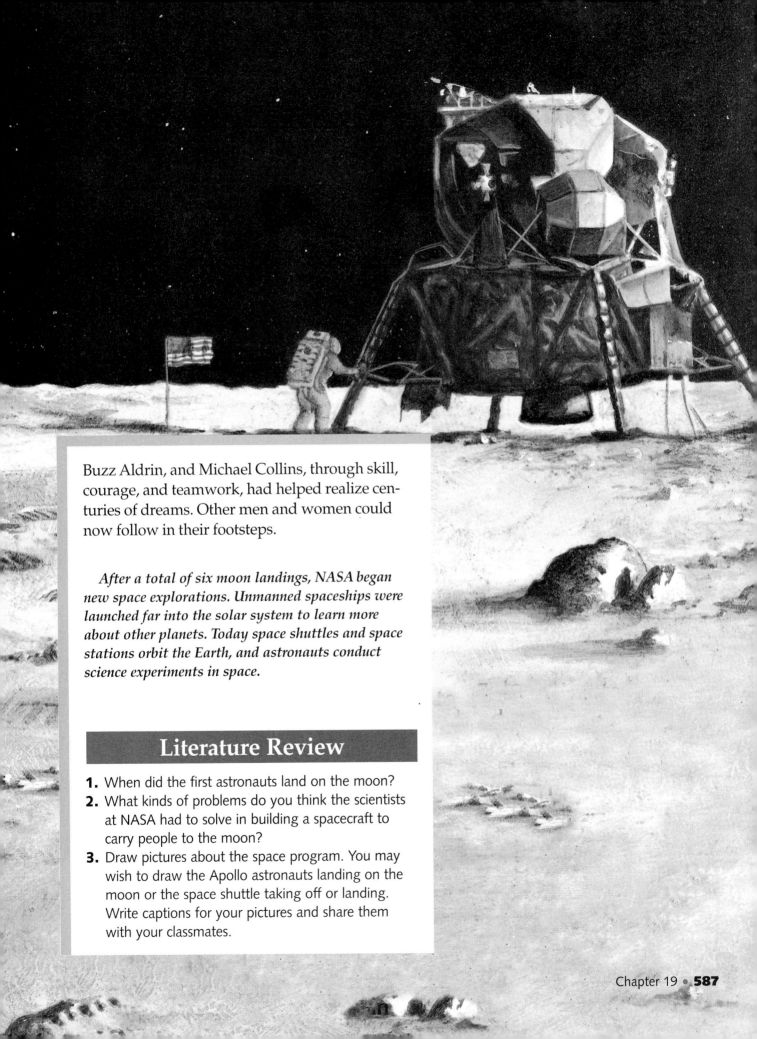

Buzz Aldrin, and Michael Collins, through skill, courage, and teamwork, had helped realize centuries of dreams. Other men and women could now follow in their footsteps.

After a total of six moon landings, NASA began new space explorations. Unmanned spaceships were launched far into the solar system to learn more about other planets. Today space shuttles and space stations orbit the Earth, and astronauts conduct science experiments in space.

Literature Review

1. When did the first astronauts land on the moon?

2. What kinds of problems do you think the scientists at NASA had to solve in building a spacecraft to carry people to the moon?

3. Draw pictures about the space program. You may wish to draw the Apollo astronauts landing on the moon or the space shuttle taking off or landing. Write captions for your pictures and share them with your classmates.

THE STRUGGLE FOR *EQUAL RIGHTS*

Link to Our World

How do people today work for change?

Focus on the Main Idea
Read to learn how people worked to change laws and win equal rights in the 1950s and 1960s.

Preview Vocabulary
nonviolence
integration

In the years after World War II, Americans hoped for real peace. Instead, they were in a cold war and an arms race with the Soviet Union. The struggle to bring peace to an uneasy world was not the only problem that Americans faced after World War II. People across the country continued to struggle for equal rights.

A COURT RULING

Seven-year-old Linda Brown of Topeka, Kansas, wanted to go to school with the other children in her neighborhood. She did not understand why state laws in Kansas said that black children and white children could not go to the same public schools. Federal laws supported this segregation, or separation of the races, as long as both black and white schools were equal. In most cases, however, they were not.

Thirteen African American families, among them Linda Brown's, decided to challenge these laws. The NAACP agreed to help them. One of its lawyers, Thurgood Marshall, presented the case before the Supreme Court. Marshall argued that separate schools could not provide an equal education.

In 1954 the Supreme Court made a decision that agreed with Thurgood Marshall. Chief Justice Earl Warren said, "In the field of education the doctrine of 'separate but equal' has no place." The Court ordered an end to segregation in public schools. However, many states were slow to carry out that order. Schools and other public places remained segregated.

These lawyers—(left to right) George Hayes, Thurgood Marshall, and James Nabrit—argued against school segregation. They are standing outside the Supreme Court Building just after the Court's decision.

 What did the Supreme Court say about segregation in public schools?

Rosa Parks (left) is fingerprinted after her arrest for not moving to the back of the bus. During the 1956 boycott in Montgomery, a bus (above) is almost empty.

THE MONTGOMERY BUS BOYCOTT

On December 1, 1955, Rosa Parks of Montgomery, Alabama, got on a bus and sat in the middle section. Under Alabama law, African Americans were supposed to sit in the back. They could sit in the middle section only if the seats were not needed for white passengers.

As the bus filled up, the bus driver told Rosa Parks to give up her seat to a white man. She refused. The bus driver called the police, and Parks was taken to jail.

Many African Americans were angry when they heard what had happened. They called a meeting and decided to do something that would let the bus company know how they felt. They thought this would be effective because the company's owners depended on the money spent by African Americans for bus fares. "Don't take the bus on Monday" was the word passed from person to person. A bus boycott began.

One of the leaders of the protest was Martin Luther King, Jr., a young minister in Montgomery. For more than a year King and other African Americans boycotted the buses. King said that by working together they could bring about change peacefully. At last the Supreme Court ruled that the bus company must end segregation on public buses.

Change using **nonviolence**, or peaceful ways, was important to King. He said that nonviolence would change people's minds and hearts. Violence would only make matters worse. So African Americans protested segregation in other public places—lunch counters, bus stations, schools, and other public buildings—in nonviolent ways.

The protesters often used songs to tell their goals. They sang,

66 We shall overcome,
We shall overcome,
We shall overcome someday.
Oh, deep in my heart, I do believe,
We shall overcome someday. 99

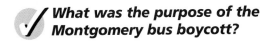

What was the purpose of the Montgomery bus boycott?

What?

Martin Luther King, Jr., Federal Holiday

Dr. Martin Luther King, Jr., was born on January 15, 1929, in Atlanta, Georgia. With the Montgomery bus boycott, he became a leader of the civil rights movement. He worked tirelessly for racial justice, despite many arrests and threats on his life. On April 4, 1968, King was shot and killed. Efforts to declare his birthday a federal holiday began in Congress four days later. In 1983 those efforts finally succeeded. President Ronald Reagan signed a law declaring the third Monday in January a federal holiday. The holiday was first observed on January 20, 1986. Today people celebrate the holiday with parades and other special events. They also use it as a time to think about how they can work to keep alive King's dream of equality, justice, and peace.

CIVIL RIGHTS MARCHES

Many African Americans looked on Martin Luther King, Jr., as their leader in the fight against segregation and for civil rights. In April 1963 King led a march in Birmingham, Alabama. The marchers wanted an end to all segregation. In its place they called for **integration**, or the bringing together of people of all races in education, jobs, and housing.

For eight days there were marches and arrests of the marchers by police. King was one of those taken to jail. While in jail he wrote, "We know through painful experience that freedom is never voluntarily given.... It must be demanded."

Later that year 250,000 people gathered for a march in Washington, D.C. The marchers were showing their support for a new civil rights law that President Kennedy had asked

Congress to pass. As they assembled in front of the Lincoln Memorial, Martin Luther King, Jr., spoke to them of his hopes. He said,

> **"**I have a dream that one day on the red hills of Georgia the sons of former slaves and the sons of former slave-owners will be able to sit down together at the table of brotherhood....**"**

In 1964 Congress passed the Civil Rights Act. The new law made segregation in public places illegal. It also said that people of all races should have equal job opportunities.

 What was the importance of the Civil Rights Act of 1964?

WORKING FOR CHANGE

In 1964 Martin Luther King, Jr., received the Nobel Peace Prize. He won the award for his use of nonviolent ways to bring about change. Not all African American leaders shared King's belief in nonviolent protests, however. One of them, Malcolm X, wanted change to happen faster.

Malcolm X was named Malcolm Little when he was born. He later changed his last name to X to stand for the African name his family had lost through slavery.

Proud of his African heritage, Malcolm X visited Egypt in 1964.

César Chávez (center) became a leader of labor organizations for farm workers.

Malcolm X was a follower of the Nation of Islam, or the Black Muslims. In his early speeches he called for a complete separation between white people and black people. Only in this way, he said, could African Americans truly be free. Malcolm X called for freedom to be brought about "by any means necessary." Later, after a trip to the Islamic holy city of Mecca, he talked less about separation and more about cooperation among groups.

Malcolm X had little time to act on his ideas. In February 1965 he was killed by an assassin. Then, in April 1968, Martin Luther King, Jr., also was assassinated.

Even though they had lost two important leaders, African Americans continued to work for change. Voting is one way that people bring about change. Knowing this, civil rights workers helped register African Americans to vote. By 1968 more than half of all eligible African Americans were registered voters.

 How were the views of Martin Luther King, Jr., and Malcolm X different?

MORE PEOPLE SEEK THEIR RIGHTS

Following the lead of the African American civil rights movement, some other groups of Americans began to organize for change. They, too, wanted equal rights under the law.

American Indians formed groups to work for the rights they had been guaranteed in earlier treaties with the federal government. Although the government had promised these rights, in many cases the treaties had not been followed. Groups such as the National Congress of American Indians, the National Tribal Chairman's Association, and the American Indian Movement (AIM) began to work for Indian rights. In 1975 the Indian Self-Determination Act was signed into law. For the first time Indian tribes were allowed to run their own businesses and health and education programs.

In the 1960s César Chávez organized a group that would become the United Farm Workers. Its members were mostly Mexican Americans. Like Martin Luther King, Jr., Chávez called for nonviolent action. In 1965 he called a strike of California grape pickers and started a nationwide boycott of grapes.

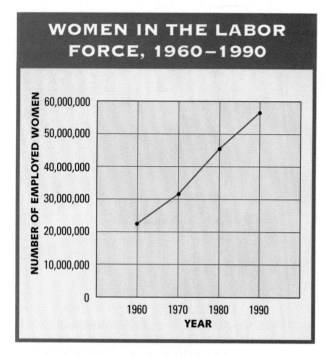

WOMEN IN THE LABOR FORCE, 1960–1990

NUMBER OF EMPLOYED WOMEN

60,000,000
50,000,000
40,000,000
30,000,000
20,000,000
10,000,000
0

1960 1970 1980 1990
YEAR

LEARNING FROM GRAPHS This graph shows how the number of women who worked outside the home increased from 1960 to 1990.

■ About how many more women were employed in 1990 than in 1960? About how many times as many were employed in 1990 as in 1960?

His goal was to win better wages and to improve working conditions. In 1970 Chávez reached agreement with the growers and helped the workers gain more rights.

 What did groups such as AIM and the United Farm Workers want to achieve?

THE WOMEN'S RIGHTS MOVEMENT

Although the Civil Rights Act of 1964 said that all people should have equal job opportunities, many jobs still were not open to women. When men and women did have the same kind of job, women were often paid less than men. As a result, in 1966 writer Betty Friedan and others started the National Organization for Women, or NOW.

NOW and other women's rights groups helped elect many women to public office.

They felt that in this way women would be better able to change unfair laws.

By the 1970s new laws had been passed saying that employers must treat men and women equally. No job could be open to men only or women only. As a result, more women began doing more kinds of work. Many began careers in the professions, such as law, medicine, and business. Some became astronauts, construction workers, and firefighters. Others became members of Congress or mayors of cities. In 1981 Sandra Day O'Connor became the first woman appointed to the United States Supreme Court. In 1984 Geraldine Ferraro became the first woman nominated for Vice President by a major political party.

 What rights had women gained by the 1970s?

LESSON 3 REVIEW

Check Understanding

1. **Recall the Facts**   Why did Martin Luther King, Jr., win the Nobel Peace Prize?
2. **Focus on the Main Idea**   How did people in the 1950s and 1960s work to change laws and win equal rights?

Think Critically

3. **Think More About It**   Why is it important for everyone to be treated equally?
4. **Past to Present**   What rights do people have today as a result of the struggles in the 1950s and 1960s?

Show What You Know

 **Simulation Activity**   Imagine that it is December 1, 1955, and you are on the bus with Rosa Parks. With a partner, role-play a conversation between you and a fellow passenger. Discuss what you both see and how you feel.

Act as a Responsible Citizen

Why Is This Skill Important?

Democratic nations depend on their citizens to act responsibly. Citizens must inform themselves, choose wise leaders, and take part in government. When a nation faces problems, its citizens may need to take action to solve those problems.

Remember What You Have Read

You have read about the struggle for civil rights in the United States during the 1950s and 1960s. Many citizens took part in the civil rights movement, which won important rights for

Martin Luther King, Jr., used his skills as a public speaker to help the civil rights movement. Here he addresses a huge crowd during the March on Washington.

African Americans. Martin Luther King, Jr., was a leader of this movement. His peaceful protests caught the attention of people around the world. King was not the only citizen to make a difference in the civil rights movement. Rosa Parks, who refused to give up her seat on a bus in Montgomery, Alabama, was one of hundreds of ordinary citizens to take part. Many risked their lives—and some were killed—as they worked to fight injustice.

Understand the Process

Acting as a responsible citizen is not always as difficult as it was during the struggle for civil rights. It can be as simple as becoming informed or voting. Almost always, however, it requires some special thought and action.

Here are some steps that civil rights workers followed to act as responsible citizens:

- They informed themselves about the problems of injustice in their country.
- They thought about what could be done to bring about change.
- They decided how to bring about change in a way that would be good for the whole country.
- Each person decided what contribution he or she could best make.
- People worked individually or with others to bring about change.

Think and Apply

Some acts of citizenship, such as voting, can be done only by adults. Others can be done by citizens of almost any age. The five steps above can help anyone know how to act as a responsible citizen. Apply the five steps as you decide on ways you and your classmates might act as responsible citizens of your community.

BUILDING CITIZENSHIP

War in Vietnam

AND PROTESTS AT HOME

Link to Our World

How can people's opinions affect the actions of their government?

Focus on the Main Idea
Read to find out how people's opinions brought about change during the times of President Johnson and President Nixon.

Preview Vocabulary
public opinion
hawk
dove
scandal
cease-fire

An American soldier signals to a helicopter in South Vietnam in 1967

While many groups were trying to win better treatment and equal rights, President Lyndon Johnson was working on government programs to make life better for all Americans. These programs were part of Johnson's dream—what he called the Great Society. Building on programs created under President Franklin Roosevelt during the New Deal, the Great Society programs included medical aid for older people and help with education, housing, and jobs for those who needed it.

Between 1965 and 1968 President Johnson was able to get Congress to pass many new laws. In three years he got more programs started than any other President except Franklin Roosevelt. Like Roosevelt, however, Johnson led the country during a time of war—the Vietnam War. Many people thought the Vietnam War was unnecessary and wrong.

THE VIETNAM WAR

Like Korea, Vietnam was divided into two countries after World War II. North Vietnam became a communist country, and South Vietnam became a republic. In the late 1950s the communists, called the Vietcong, tried to take over the South Vietnamese government. They were helped by North Vietnam. Between 1956 and 1962 the United States sent money, war supplies, and soldiers to help South Vietnam fight communism.

By the time Johnson became President in 1963, the Vietcong were winning the war. Then, in August 1964, it was reported that a North Vietnamese gunboat attacked a United States Navy ship in the Gulf of Tonkin near Vietnam. Johnson sent more soldiers to South Vietnam to prevent another attack. The soldiers also fought the Vietcong.

When troops failed to defeat the Vietcong quickly, the President ordered United States planes to bomb North Vietnam. He hoped this would stop the flow of supplies from North Vietnam to the Vietcong. The President also sent more troops to South Vietnam. By 1968 more than 500,000 United States soldiers were serving there.

The Vietnam War now was costing the United States billions of dollars each year. At the same time, President Johnson was starting many of his Great Society programs. Johnson said that the nation could afford both. As it turned out, he was wrong. To pay for both the Vietnam

President Lyndon B. Johnson had much on his mind in 1968. Here he is shown preparing for a major speech on Vietnam.

War and the programs of the Great Society, the government had to borrow a lot of money. This borrowing led to inflation. When there is inflation, goods and services become more expensive. People can buy less with the money they earn. A country's economy suffers.

 **How did the Vietnam War affect the economy of the United States?**

AMERICANS ARE DIVIDED

The Vietnam War divided American **public opinion**, or what people thought. Some people said the war was needed to stop the

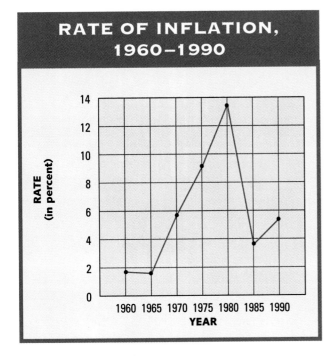

RATE OF INFLATION, 1960–1990

RATE (in percent)

YEAR

LEARNING FROM GRAPHS This graph shows how inflation increased during the 1960s and 1970s and then decreased during the 1980s.
■ How was the rate of inflation related to the country's changing role in the war?

A DIVIDED VIETNAM

0 100 200 Miles
0 100 200 Kilometers
Mercator Projection

CHINA

Hanoi

NORTH VIETNAM

BURMA

LAOS

Vientiane

Gulf of Tonkin

Hainan

Red River

HO CHI MINH TRAIL

Mekong River

THAILAND

Demilitarized Zone

Bangkok

CAMBODIA

SOUTH VIETNAM

Phnom Penh

Saigon

South China Sea

Gulf of Thailand

Mekong Delta

⊛ National capital

MOVEMENT The Ho Chi Minh Trail was a supply route from North Vietnam to South Vietnam. It was named for a communist leader in North Vietnam.
■ Why do you think the trail went through other countries?

spread of communism. Others said it was a civil war that should be settled by the Vietnamese.

These divisions were also seen in the government. Most government leaders were either hawks or doves. The **hawks** were people who supported the war at any cost. The **doves** were those who wanted the war to end at any cost.

As the number of Americans killed in Vietnam climbed into the thousands, more and more people began to oppose the war. All over the United States, protests and marches against the war took place. Some

young Americans resisted being drafted, or made to serve in the war. They burned their draft cards in protest. Some even moved out of the United States to avoid military service. Many of them went to Canada.

Because of the problems caused by the war, President Johnson decided not to run for reelection. In 1968 the American people elected a new President—Richard M. Nixon. Nixon tried to end the war by bombing North Vietnam even more than before. He also sent American soldiers into Cambodia, a country bordering Vietnam. Nixon's goal was to "bring an honorable end to the war." But the war did not end, and the protests against the war grew louder.

✓ **Why did people protest the Vietnam War?**

NIXON RESIGNS

In 1972 President Nixon was reelected. In his second term, however, the Watergate scandal ended his presidency. A **scandal** is an action that brings disgrace. During the election campaign, people working to help Nixon, who was a Republican, did some

President Nixon and his family say farewell to White House staff members at the time of the President's resignation.

What?

Veterans Day

To celebrate the signing of the armistice ending World War I, Armistice Day was first observed on November 11, 1919. In 1954 President Dwight D. Eisenhower changed the name of Armistice Day to Veterans Day. This day, "dedicated to world peace," honors all veterans of the United States armed forces. Today Veterans Day is still observed on November 11. People celebrate with parades and speeches that honor the service that members of the military have given their country. Many European nations still celebrate Armistice Day.

On April 30, 1975, the government of South Vietnam surrendered. North Vietnam gained control of the whole country. The unpopular war was over.

On Veterans Day in 1982, the Vietnam Veterans Memorial in Washington, D.C., was opened to visitors. It includes a wall of polished black granite. The wall lists the names of more than 58,000 American men and women who fought for their country and died or were reported missing in the Vietnam War.

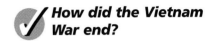

How did the Vietnam War end?

LESSON 4 REVIEW

Check Understanding

1. **Recall the Facts**   Which President was the first to resign from office?
2. **Focus on the Main Idea**   How did people's opinions bring about change during the times that Lyndon Johnson and Richard Nixon were President?

Think Critically

3. **Think More About It**   What might have happened if people had not protested against the Vietnam War?
4. **Past to Present**   Why do you think the Vietnam War is a painful memory for many Americans today?

Show What You Know

Art Activity   Write down your ideas about what different groups thought about the Vietnam War. Then make a mural that shows what these groups did to express how they felt about the conflict. Present your mural to the class.

---

things that were against the law. One thing they did was to break into an office of the Democratic party in the Watergate Hotel. Many people thought that President Nixon knew about these illegal acts and tried to cover them up.

Despite the scandal, President Nixon worked to end the Vietnam War. In 1969 he had begun a gradual withdrawal of American troops. But his plan to defeat the Vietcong by bombing North Vietnam harder failed. In January 1973 Nixon agreed to a **cease-fire**, or an end to the shooting and bombing. He also agreed to bring the remaining American soldiers back from Vietnam.

Finally, however, the Watergate scandal forced Nixon to step down. On August 9, 1974, he became the first President of the United States to resign. On that same day Vice President Gerald Ford became President.

Without help from the United States, South Vietnamese soldiers could not win the war.

HAWK
or
DOVE?

In this photo from 1970, United States soldiers patrol an area southwest of Saigon, near the Cambodian border.

Like most wars in United States history, the Vietnam War had strong supporters and emotional critics. The hawks—named for the fierce bird of prey—wanted the war to continue until victory was achieved. They believed that communism would spread to other countries unless the United States helped South Vietnam win the conflict. The doves—named for the traditional symbol of peace—wanted the war to end immediately. They believed people were dying needlessly in a conflict that South Vietnam could not win. Each side strongly believed that it was right and the other side was wrong. There seemed to be no possible compromise.

Can you tell a hawk from a dove? Read the following quotations, and decide what each speaker believed about the Vietnam War.

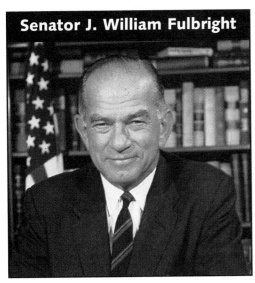

President Lyndon B. Johnson

❝Why are we in South Vietnam?

We are there because we have a promise to keep. Since 1954 every American President has offered support to the people of South Vietnam. We have helped to build, and we have helped to defend. Thus over many years we made a national pledge to help South Vietnam defend its independence. . . . To dishonor that pledge, to abandon this small and brave nation to its enemies, and to the terror that must follow, would be an unforgiving wrong.❞

Senator J. William Fulbright

❝We are in a war to 'defend freedom' in South Vietnam. . . . When we talk about the freedom of South Vietnam, we may be thinking about how our pride would be injured if we settled for less than we set out to achieve. We may be thinking about our reputation as a great power, as though a compromise settlement would shame us before the world, marking us as a second-rate people with flagging courage and determination. Such fears are nonsensical. They are unworthy of the richest, most powerful, most productive, and best educated people in the world.❞

COMPARE
VIEWPOINTS

1. Was President Johnson a hawk or a dove? How do you know?
2. What viewpoint about the war did Senator Fulbright hold? How do you know?
3. What reasons does each speaker give for continuing or ending the Vietnam War?
4. Do you think there is a compromise opinion on this issue? What would it be?

THINK
–AND–
APPLY

During most of the wars in our country's history, some Americans have been hawks while others have been doves. You read about the Sons and Daughters of Liberty and the Quaker pacifists during the American Revolution, for example. You read about the War Hawks during the War of 1812. Choose one of the wars you have studied in American history. Use encyclopedias and other references to identify people or groups who were hawks and those who were doves. Describe each group's point of view.

THE COLD WAR ENDS AND NEW
CHALLENGES BEGIN

Link to Our World

How do people help influence history?

Focus on the Main Idea
Read to learn how individuals helped bring the Cold War to an end.

Preview Vocabulary
arms control
détente
terrorism
hostage
deficit

Standing on the Great Wall of China are (center) President Nixon and Patricia Nixon, his wife.

Even with the Watergate scandal and his failure to end the Vietnam War, President Nixon accomplished many things. His most important achievement may have been reducing tensions between the free world and the communist nations. Nixon became the first American President to visit both China and the Soviet Union. Later, Cold War tensions would rise and fall and then nearly disappear.

NIXON VISITS CHINA AND THE SOVIET UNION

The United States cut ties with China after the Asian nation became a communist country in 1949. There was no trade, no exchange of ambassadors, no travel back and forth, and no communication.

In 1972 President Nixon accepted an invitation from China's leader, Mao Zedong (MOW zeh•DOONG), to go to China. As a result of Nixon's visit, the two nations agreed to trade with each other and to allow visits from each other's scientific and cultural groups.

Three months after visiting China, Nixon flew to Moscow to meet with Soviet leader Leonid Brezhnev (BREZH•nef). Nixon told Brezhnev, "There must be room in the world for two great nations with different systems to live together and work together."

As a result of this meeting, the United States and the Soviet Union agreed to increase trade with each other and work together on scientific and cultural projects. Most important, they agreed to **arms control**, or limiting the number of weapons that each nation could have. The agreement signed by Nixon and Brezhnev limited the number of

President Carter (center) earned worldwide praise for bringing about a peace agreement between two old enemies, Egypt and Israel. Carter is shown with President Sadat (suh•DAHT) of Egypt (left) and Prime Minister Begin (BAY•gin) of Israel (right). The peace treaty they signed was known as the Camp David Accords.

nuclear, or atomic, missiles on each side. This marked the beginning of a period of **détente** (day•TAHNT), or an easing of tensions, between the United States and the Soviet Union. But that did not last long.

 How did President Nixon ease tensions with China and the Soviet Union?

INCREASED TENSIONS

Southwest Asia, or the Middle East as Europeans and Americans have called the region, has long been a trouble spot. People there are divided by religious, cultural, and political differences. Some of the people have turned to **terrorism**, the use of violence to promote a cause. There have also been wars in the region. In 1948, 1956, 1967, and 1973, Israel fought wars with Egypt, Jordan, and Syria. In these wars, the United States took the side of Israel. The Soviet Union took the side of the Arab nations. In taking sides, the

United States and the Soviet Union increased Cold War tensions.

Then, in December 1979, Soviet troops invaded the country of Afghanistan (af•GA•nuh•stan) in Southwest Asia. The invasion moved Soviet troops much closer to the region's rich oil fields. President Jimmy Carter, who was elected in 1976, called the invasion a threat to world peace.

President Carter warned the Soviets to leave Afghanistan. When they did not, he cut back American trade with the Soviets and refused to agree to further arms control. He also said that American athletes would not take part in the 1980 Olympic games held in Moscow.

Afghan rebels fought fiercely against Soviet troops, making it difficult for the Soviets to control the country. After years of fighting, the Soviet Union finally began to withdraw its troops from Afghanistan in 1988.

Another problem in Southwest Asia proved to be even more troubling for President Carter. In 1979 a revolution took place in Iran. The shah, the country's leader, fled. Leaders of the revolution were angry at Americans because the United States had been friendly with the shah. To show their anger, the revolutionaries attacked the United States embassy at Tehran, Iran's capital. They captured 66 Americans and made them **hostages**, holding them as prisoners until the revolutionaries' demands were met. It seemed to many Americans that President Carter could do nothing to win their release. In 1980 he ran again for President but lost. On the day the new President, Ronald Reagan, took the oath of office, the Iranians finally released the hostages.

 What actions did Carter take when the Soviets invaded Afghanistan?

THE COLD WAR ENDS

In 1956, when the Soviet leader Nikita Khrushchev (krush•CHAWF) first learned about the destruction that hydrogen bombs could cause, he was so upset that he tossed and turned for nights, unable to sleep. "Then I became convinced," he said, "that we could never possibly use these weapons, and when I realized that I was able to sleep again."

Neither the Soviets nor the Americans used nuclear weapons during the Cold War. But throughout this period, both countries built more and more of them.

"Peace through strength" was Ronald Reagan's motto as he increased defense spending. Calling the Soviet Union "an evil empire," he said the Cold War was a "struggle between right and wrong, good and evil." Soviet leaders took a hard line, too, building more weapons and helping communist rebels all over the world.

Then a new leader took over the Soviet Union, and nothing was the same again. Mikhail Gorbachev (mee•kah•EEL gawr•buh•CHAWF) became leader of the Soviet Union in 1985.

When Gorbachev took over, President Reagan said he would welcome the chance to meet the new Soviet leader in the "cause of world peace." In April 1985 Gorbachev agreed to a meeting. He said that better relations between the United States and the Soviet Union were "extremely necessary—and possible."

The meeting between Reagan and Gorbachev in November 1985 marked the beginning of a real thaw in the Cold War. The President called it a "fresh start" in United States–Soviet relations. Soon the United States and the Soviet Union agreed to more treaties limiting nuclear missiles.

In the Soviet Union Gorbachev was already changing many of the old Soviet ways of doing things. He called for *perestroika* (pair•uh•STROY•kuh), or a "restructuring" of the Soviet government and economy. He also called for a new "openness," or *glasnost* (GLAZ•nohst). This would give the Soviet people more of the freedoms they wanted. Soviet citizens would be allowed to vote in free elections. They would be free to start their own businesses.

Reforms in the Soviet Union led to changes in many other communist nations. People in Poland, Czechoslovakia, and Hungary gained new freedoms. In communist East Germany, government leaders removed the armed guards from the Berlin Wall and

Soviet leader Gorbachev (left) and President Reagan (right) shake hands at their first meeting. They met each year from 1985 through 1988.

A man standing on the newly opened Berlin Wall makes a peace sign as East Germans flood into West Berlin.

A NEW WORLD ORDER

Talking about the idea of a world without the Cold War, President George Bush said,

66 Now we can see . . . the very real prospect of a new world order, a world in which freedom and respect for human rights find a home among all nations. 99

By "new world order," President Bush meant a world without the alliances and conflicts of the past. However, conflicts in the world have continued.

In 1990 the nation of Iraq, led by ruler Saddam Hussein (hoo•SAYN), invaded neighboring Kuwait (koo•WAYT), a major oil producer. When Iraq refused to withdraw, the allied forces of the United States, Britain, France, Egypt, and Saudi Arabia attacked. During Operation Desert Storm the Iraqis were pushed back, and Kuwait's rulers were returned to power.

In the meantime the end of communism in eastern Europe set off fighting in what was once the nation of Yugoslavia. The civil war there has taken hundreds of thousands of lives. In 1991 the Soviet Union itself broke up into independent countries. Many of these countries are fighting one another for power and the right to self-government.

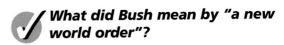 **What did Bush mean by "a new world order"?**

NEW CHALLENGES AT HOME

In 1995 President Bill Clinton gave the annual State of the Union Address. During this speech, the President said,

66 You know, tonight this is the first State of the Union Address ever delivered since the beginning of the Cold War when not a single Russian missile is pointed at the children of America. 99

opened its gates. In 1989 the German people tore down the Berlin Wall. The next year they reunited their country.

In 1989 the new President of the United States, George Bush, met Mikhail Gorbachev on a ship near Malta, a rocky island in the middle of the Mediterranean Sea. As a storm raged outside, the two men faced each other across a table. Years of mistrust between their countries made the outcome of the meeting uncertain. Neither one knew what to expect.

The leaders talked about the many changes taking place in Europe and the Soviet Union. At the end Gorbachev looked Bush in the eye. "I have heard you say that you want *perestroika* to succeed," he said, "but frankly I didn't know this. Now I know." The Cold War was finally ending.

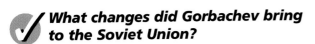 **What changes did Gorbachev bring to the Soviet Union?**

President Clinton held televised "town meetings" to listen to people's concerns and hear their views about the government.

With the end of the Cold War, however, the United States faces many new challenges. Among the most important are working for equality for all Americans, fighting crime, and caring for the environment.

Another important concern has to do with the economy. The United States has remained a military superpower. But many Americans believe it no longer is the economic superpower it once was. It still has the largest economy in the world, but it has economic problems. One reason is the government's budget **deficit**, or shortage. The government spends more money than it takes in each year in taxes and other income.

To pay its bills, the United States must borrow money. Each year, the government spends about 23 percent of its income just to pay the interest on the money it borrows to pay its debts. Some members of Congress have called for a balanced-budget amendment to the Constitution. This amendment would require the government to spend no more money than it takes in each year.

The United States is also challenged by an international trade deficit. It buys more goods from other countries than it sells. Inexpensive yet high quality imports from countries such as Japan, South Korea, and Taiwan are snapped up by American consumers. As a result, American businesses producing similar goods have suffered.

According to many economists, what is needed to be a world leader today is different from what was needed during the Cold War. World leadership, they say, is based more and more on economic strength. Many Americans

believe that one of the most important challenges today is for the United States to return to its role as an economic superpower.

 How has the budget deficit caused problems in the United States?

LESSON 5 REVIEW

Check Understanding

1. **Recall the Facts**   President Nixon's visits to what two countries led to a time of détente?
2. **Focus on the Main Idea**   How did individuals help bring an end to the Cold War?

Think Critically

3. **Think More About It**   What could have been some of the reasons Mao Zedong invited President Nixon to China?
4. **Cause and Effect**   How did the *glasnost* policies of the Soviet Union affect other communist nations?

Show What You Know

Picture-Essay Activity   Use information and pictures from current newspapers and magazines to make a picture essay titled *The World After the Cold War*. Share your picture essay with a partner, and discuss its meaning.

Understand Political Symbols

Why Is This Skill Important?

People often recognize sports teams, clubs, and other organizations by their symbols. The same is true for political parties, the President, Congress, the Supreme Court, and even voters. Being able to identify political symbols and what they stand for can help you better understand news reports, political cartoons, and other sources of information.

Recognizing Symbols

Two of the country's most famous political symbols are animals. The donkey represents the Democratic party. The elephant represents the Republican party. The donkey was probably first used to represent President Andrew Jackson, a Democrat, in the 1830s. Later the donkey became a symbol for the entire party. Cartoonist Thomas Nast introduced the elephant as a symbol of the Republican party in 1874. Both symbols are still used today.

One of the symbols for the national government is Uncle Sam—a white-haired man wearing a red, white, and blue hat and suit. The bald eagle and the Statue of Liberty are other symbols for our government. Buildings are often used as political symbols. The White House is a symbol for the President, and the United States Capitol is a symbol for Congress.

Understand the Process

When you see a political symbol, ask yourself these questions to help you understand its meaning:

- Do you recognize the symbol? Does it stand for the national government as a whole or only part of the national government? Does it stand for a person or a group that is involved in government, such as a political party?
- Where did you see the symbol? If it appeared in a newspaper or magazine, did the writer give you any clues about its meaning?
- Are there any captions or other words that help explain what the symbol means? A symbol labeled "The Halls of Justice," for example, might tell you that it stands for a court.

Think and Apply

Look through current news magazines or the editorial pages of newspapers. Find an example of a political symbol. Cut the example out and paste it to a sheet of paper. Below the symbol write a brief description of what the symbol stands for.

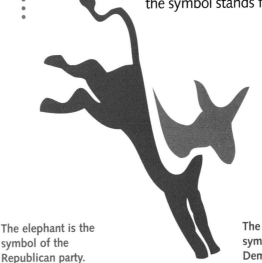

The elephant is the symbol of the Republican party.

The donkey is the symbol of the Democratic party.

CONNECT MAIN IDEAS

Use this organizer to show that you understand how the chapter's main ideas are connected. Copy the organizer onto a separate sheet of paper. Then complete it by writing the main idea of each lesson.

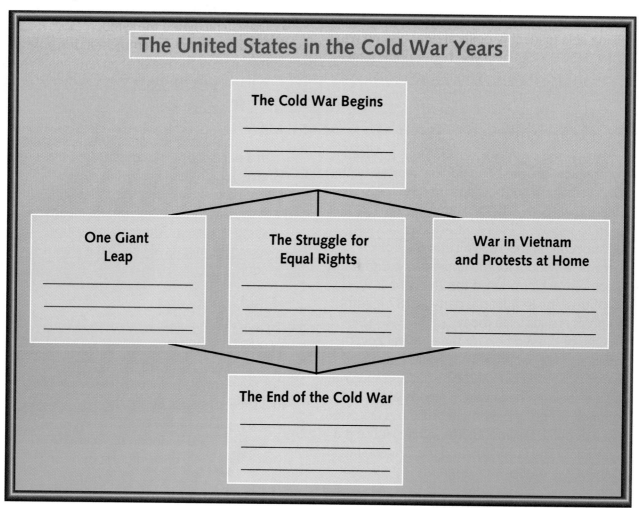

The United States in the Cold War Years

The Cold War Begins
_____
_____
_____

One Giant Leap
_____
_____
_____

The Struggle for Equal Rights
_____
_____
_____

War in Vietnam and Protests at Home
_____
_____
_____

The End of the Cold War
_____
_____
_____

WRITE MORE ABOUT IT

1. **Write a Radio News Report** Imagine that you are living in West Berlin during the Berlin Crisis. The radio station you work for has asked you to report on the conflict between the Soviet Union and the Allies. Write what you will say in your radio news report. Tell how the Allies are getting supplies to Berlin.

2. **Write Your Opinion** The three astronauts aboard *Apollo 11* faced many dangers during their long voyage to the moon, but they also made history. Write a paragraph or two telling why you would or would not have wanted to be an astronaut traveling on that historic flight.

USE VOCABULARY

Write a term from this list to complete each of the sentences that follow.

airlift   nonviolence
arms race   scandal
détente   superpower
integration   terrorism

1. The United States is a _____ because of the important role it plays in world events.

2. An _____ brought supplies to West Berlin after the Soviets blocked other routes into the city.

3. The _____ resulted because the United States and the Soviet Union each tried to build more weapons than the other.

4. Change using _____ was important to Martin Luther King, Jr.

5. The bringing together of all races in education, jobs, and housing is called _____.

6. A _____ ended the Nixon presidency.

7. In 1972 the United States and the Soviet Union began a period of _____, the easing of military tensions between countries.

8. _____ is the use of violence to get publicity for a cause.

CHECK UNDERSTANDING

1. Why did President Kennedy order a blockade of Cuba? What was the blockade's result?

2. How did a Supreme Court decision in 1954 change public schools?

3. How did the costs of the Great Society programs and the Vietnam War affect the economy of the United States?

4. How did President Carter help to ease tensions between Israel and Egypt?

5. What did President Bush mean by a "new world order"?

THINK CRITICALLY

1. **Cause and Effect** What event caused the Korean War?

2. **Explore Viewpoints** How were the views of Malcolm X different from the views of Martin Luther King, Jr.?

3. **Think More About It** In what ways has the women's rights movement changed the United States?

APPLY SKILLS

How to Act as a Responsible Citizen Think about a problem at your school. Then explain what you can do about the problem. List the steps you might follow to act as a responsible citizen.

How to Understand Political Symbols
Match each symbol to the person or thing it represents.

the Capitol   Uncle Sam
donkey   the White House
elephant

1. the Democratic party

2. the Republican party

3. the United States government

4. the President

5. the Congress

READ MORE ABOUT IT

Always to Remember: The Story of the Vietnam Veterans Memorial by Brent Ashabranner. Dodd, Mead. This book tells the story of the design and building of the Vietnam Veterans Memorial.

The Year They Walked: Rosa Parks and the Montgomery Bus Boycott by Beatrice Siegel. Four Winds. This book looks at the life of Rosa Parks and her part in the Montgomery bus boycott.

The WESTERN HEMISPHERE Today

> 66 With her friends in the United States she speaks English. . . . She dreams in both Spanish and English. 99

Kathleen Krull, describing 12-year-old Cinthya Guzman in *The Other Side: How Kids Live in a California Latino Neighborhood*

When Cinthya was eight years old, she moved with her family from Tijuana, Mexico, to the town of Chula Vista, California, near San Diego.

MEXICO TODAY

L ink to Our World

How might economic differences among people in a country cause problems?

Focus on the Main Idea
Read to learn how economic conditions have divided many of the people of Mexico.

Preview Vocabulary
metropolitan area
middle class
interest rate
free-trade agreement

The Republic of Mexico shares the North American continent with Canada and the United States. Mexico's lands are diverse—including coastal plains, rain forests, and mountains. These lands provide harvests of corn, wheat, and many other crops as well as natural resources such as silver, gold, and oil. All of these crops and resources have helped Mexico's economy in the past. In recent years, however, Mexico's economy has been troubled by many problems.

THE GROWTH OF CITIES AND THE MIDDLE CLASS

Seven out of every ten Mexicans live in urban areas. In the country's central and northern states, the urban population has boomed in recent years. Among the fastest-growing cities is Mexico City, in the central region.

Mexico City, ringed by volcanic mountains, stands on the site of the Aztec capital of Tenochtitlán. When the Aztecs built their capital in the 1300s, it was one of the world's largest cities. In the early 1500s the Spanish conquered the Aztecs and destroyed Tenochtitlán. In its place they built Mexico City to be the capital of the Spanish colony of New Spain.

Today Mexico City remains the nation's capital, or Federal District. Its population is the largest of all the cities in the world. More than 9 million people live within Mexico City. Almost 21 million people live in the metropolitan area. A **metropolitan area** is a city and all the suburbs and other population areas around it. The largest metropolitan area in the United States is New York City. It has about 20 million people.

Between 1940 and 1970 many factories were built in the northern region of Mexico. Cities there grew quickly. Hoping to find factory jobs, great numbers of people moved from rural areas to Monterrey, Ciudad Juárez (SEE•u•dahd HWAR•ays), Matamoros (mah•tah•MOH•rohs), and Tijuana (tee•WAH•nah).

As in the United States, the growth of manufacturing in Mexico led to the growth of a large **middle class**, an economic level between the poor and the wealthy. Shopkeepers, factory managers, lawyers, and other workers and their families make up the middle class. By the 1990s Mexico's middle class was one of the largest in all the countries of the Americas.

For many years most middle-class families in Mexico had enough money to buy the many new products manufactured in their country. Then, in 1994, Mexico's money suddenly became devalued. That is, the value of Mexico's money suddenly dropped. This caused prices to rise sharply. Some prices doubled. Others tripled. **Interest rates**, or the

Mexico City, like all large cities, has crowded streets at rush hour.

amounts that banks charge customers to borrow money, rose as high as 80 percent. Middle-class families found it very difficult to buy houses, cars, and most consumer products. The Mexicans called this economic disaster "the devaluation of 1994." The devaluation was caused by inflation and the Mexican government's need to pay its debts.

 How did the devaluation of 1994 affect Mexico's middle class?

Colorfully dressed dancers celebrate Cinco de Mayo in Austin, Texas.

What?

Cinco de Mayo

Cinco de Mayo, also known as Battle of Puebla Day, is a national holiday in Mexico. *Cinco de Mayo* means "the fifth of May" in Spanish. On May 5, 1862, the Mexican army fought the French army in the Mexican city of Puebla. The French were trying to take control of the Mexican government. Although the French army was much larger, the Mexican army won. Today the Mexican people and many Mexican Americans celebrate Cinco de Mayo with parades and fireworks. The holiday is important as a day to celebrate Mexican independence and national pride.

MEXICO

Tijuana
Nogales
Ciudad Juárez
Chihuahua
UNITED STATES
Gulf of California
Baja California
SIERRA MADRE OCCIDENTAL
SIERRA MADRE ORIENTAL
Río Grande
Torreón
Monterrey
Matamoros
Durango
Mazatlán
Zacatecas
Aguascalientes
León
Puerto Vallarta
Guadalajara
Mexico City ⊛
Cuernavaca
Puebla
Veracruz
Bay of Campeche
Gulf of Mexico
Mérida
Yucatán Peninsula
Caribbean Sea
BELIZE
Acapulco
Oaxaca
GUATEMALA
HONDURAS
EL SALVADOR
NICARAGUA
PACIFIC OCEAN

30°N, 25°N, Tropic of Cancer, 20°N, 15°N
115°W, 110°W, 105°W, 100°W, 95°W, 90°W, 85°W

0   150   300 Miles
0   150   300 Kilometers
Lambert Conformal Conic Projection

⊛   National capital

LOCATION   This map shows major cities in Mexico.
■ Which major cities are on a coast? Which are near the border with the United States?

REACTION TO NAFTA

Mexico's economy had caused problems for its people for many years. With the devaluation of 1994, the problems were made worse. People at all economic levels lost their jobs. Mexico's poor people, who make up 45 percent of the country's 90 million people, suffered the most. For them, even basic foods such as beans and eggs became luxuries.

Before the devaluation, the Mexican government had decided that one way the nation could make its economy stronger was to join the United States and Canada in signing the North American Free Trade Agreement, known as NAFTA. A **free-trade agreement** is a treaty in which countries agree to charge no tariffs, or taxes, on goods they buy from each

other and sell to each other. Such an agreement gives businesses in these countries the chance to compete more equally.

But the NAFTA agreement did not make everyone in Mexico happy. Among those who were angry that the Mexican government had joined NAFTA were many of the country's farmers. On January 1, 1994, the date NAFTA went into effect, about 2,000 poor farmers in the southern Mexican state of Chiapas (chee•AH•pahs) took control of several towns. Fighting between the farmers and Mexican soldiers soon broke out, and more than 100 people were killed.

Most of the farmers in Chiapas are of American Indian heritage. They make up half the population of the state. They are afraid that free trade will bring huge amounts of

This woman from Oaxaca (wuh•HAH•kuh), a state in southern Mexico, is baking tortillas. The living conditions of poor people in southern Mexico are much worse than those of middle-class Mexicans.

corn, soybeans, wheat, and other farm products to Mexico from the United States and Canada. These products would be sold more cheaply than the farmers of Chiapas could sell their crops. One leader of the farmers said, "The free-trade agreement is a death certificate for the Indian peoples of Mexico."

While many Mexicans in the rural southern states are against NAFTA, those in the more urban and industrial central and northern states support the free-trade agreement. Factory owners and other business people hope the agreement will help them sell more of their goods in the growing markets of the United States and Canada. They believe that this trade will bring jobs to Mexico and will strengthen the country's whole economy.

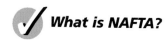 **What is NAFTA?**

LESSON 1 REVIEW

Check Understanding

1. **Recall the Facts** Which city in Mexico has the largest population?
2. **Focus on the Main Idea** How have economic conditions divided many of the people of Mexico?

Think Critically

3. **Cause and Effect** What effects did the devaluation of 1994 have on Mexico's middle class? What effects did it have on Mexico's poor people?

4. **Explore Viewpoints** How did farmers in southern Mexico view the NAFTA agreement? How did Mexico's business people view the agreement?

Show What You Know

 **Map Activity** Make a map that shows the states and major cities of Mexico. Add illustrations that show landforms and products. Discuss what you have learned about Mexico as you compare your map with those of classmates.

LEARN with LITERATURE

Focus on Civic Action

SAVE MY RAINFOREST

by Monica Zak

illustrations by Bengt-Arne Runnerström

English version by Nancy Schimmel

Omar Castillo lives in Mexico City, more than 800 miles (1,287 km) from the Selva Lacandona (SEL•vuh lah•kahn•DOH•nah), Mexico's last remaining rain forest. On the television news, Omar hears that the rain forest is in danger of being destroyed. He decides that he must try to do something to save the rain forest. With the help of his father, Omar sets out on foot to make a long, difficult journey that he will never forget.

Early one morning Omar and his father start walking. At first Omar is smiling and singing. On the road at last! And tonight, for the first time in his life, he will sleep in a tent.

For hours and hours they walk on the hot pavement. Finally, they leave the dirty yellow air of the city for the clear, clean air of the countryside. But Omar is too tired to notice. Then his feet begin to hurt. He goes a good ways before he says anything. When he does, his father stops and takes Omar's shoes off.

"You have blisters. I'll put a bandage on . . . there. Now we can get started again."

"But Papa, I'm too tired. I can't go on."

"I'm tired too," says his father, "but try to go a little farther. I'll buy us a cool drink at the next store." They find a fruit stand where a woman with long braids sells them tall glasses of pineapple drink.

She looks at them curiously and finally asks, "What does your banner say? I can't read."

Omar revives at once. "This side says 'Let's protect the rainforest' and the other side says 'Walk—Mexico City—Tuxtla Gutiérrez.'[1] Tuxtla's a long way south of here, but that's where we decided to go, to see the governor of the state of Chiapas, where the rainforest is. He is responsible for taking care of it. We need to tell him to save the rainforest so there will still be a rainforest in Mexico for us children when we grow up."

---

[1] **Tuxtla Gutiérrez:** (TOOST•lah goo•TYAIR•ehs)

"You must be sent from heaven!" she says.

Omar's father smiles. "No, he's just a regular kid. All kids have good ideas, but usually people don't listen to them. It never made any difference to me that they were destroying the rainforest and the animals, but when I thought about what my son said, I realized that he knew what he was talking about. That's why I decided to come with him."

Another day, the sun beats down through the thin mountain air. This time it is Omar's father who has blisters. He calls, "Must you walk so fast, Omar?"

After walking more than a week, they come down out of the mountains. They can see banana plantations now, and *mango* trees. They camp by the side of the road.

Omar lies in the tent and listens. The night before, he heard coyotes howling near the tent: ah-ooo, ah-ooo, ah-ooo. He was afraid. Now he listens to the murmuring leaves. *What if a snake should get into the tent? What if robbers attack us?* he thinks. An enormous truck rumbles past and shakes the tent. *What if the driver fell asleep and . . .*

"Omar, are you awake?" his father asks.

"Mm-hm," answers Omar. "I can't sleep."

"Well," says Omar's father, "we really had a tough day. Heat, no shade, and traffic. Now it's pleasant. We won't be cold tonight."

"No," says Omar, smiling. "Remember the first night in the tent? I thought it would be wonderful, camping, but then the rain started . . ."

"Yes," says his father, "and the water came in. At three in the morning! Remember how good that hot *pozole* tasted after we walked in the dark and cold?"

"Papa, how many more days do we have to walk?"

"I thought it would take fifteen or twenty days, but it will take much longer. I don't want to disappoint you, but I don't believe we can go on."

"But why?" asks Omar, astounded.

"We are running out of money."

They decide to keep going.

"We will have to beg for food," says Omar.

They go into a restaurant and Omar's father explains to the owner why they are walking. "We have no more money," Omar's

father says, "and my son is awfully hungry." The owner turns them out without giving them even a glass of water. But then a woman sitting outside a little hut motions them in, makes a fresh pot of coffee, and serves them coffee and bread. It goes like that. Some days people give them food, but often they have to walk the whole day without eating anything. Those days are hard.

When Omar sees boys playing soccer, he stops and watches with envy, but they never ask him to play. Sometimes there are things to look at in the road: a huge scorpion or snakes run over by cars. But more often,

walking is boring. Omar throws rocks at fenceposts, thinking *Why didn't I bring anything to play with?* Then somebody who hears he is going to the rainforest gives him a toy Tarzan. He passes the time pretending Tarzan is in the rainforest, swinging from vines.

People warn them not to take the shortest way to Tuxtla, the road that goes through poor villages. "They'll attack you and rob you. It's too dangerous!" But Omar and his father take that road anyway, because it is 125 miles shorter. At first they are a little afraid, but no one attacks them. In fact, women and children come out and give them oranges and *tortilla* chips. . . .

A few days later they stop in a little town to eat in a restaurant. An announcer comes on television to say there has been a terrible earthquake in Mexico City. They see a picture of a big pile of rubble and hear that it is the hospital where Omar's grandmother works! Omar starts to cry. His father has tears in his eyes. No one can reach Mexico City by telephone because the lines are out. Then a ham radio operator in the town promises he will help them get news.

After four days of waiting, the radio operator says, "Your *abuela* is alive, Omar. She wasn't in the hospital when the earthquake came. Your mother is well. She sends you kisses and says your house wasn't hurt at all. She wishes you a safe journey."

And now they can continue.

After thirty-nine days of walking, Omar and his father come to Tuxtla Gutiérrez. They have travelled 870 miles and they are tired. They have to wait the whole day outside the governor's office, but finally the moment comes that Omar has been hoping for.

His heart beats loudly as he faces the governor and says, "Save my rainforest and stop the hunting of the rainforest animals for the next twenty years." The governor pats Omar on the head and says there is nothing to worry about.

Omar still worries. *He is treating me like a kid,* he thinks. *He won't do anything.*

But Omar does get to see a rainforest. When Tuxtla was built, a piece of the rainforest was left as a park. At first, Omar is disappointed in the rainforest, too. There aren't lots of strange animals running around in plain sight. Just gigantic trees and a clean wet smell.

Omar stands quietly for a long time in the deep green light amid the huge trunks, listening to all the birds singing high above in the canopy of leaves. Then he knows that being in a real rainforest at last is worth the trouble of walking 870 miles.

Literature Review

1. Why did Omar and his father walk from Mexico City to Tuxtla Gutiérrez?
2. For what reasons might you take an action like Omar's?
3. In the years after his long journey, Omar Castillo continued to work with other children to save the rain forest. With a partner, brainstorm other environmental problems in the world today. Make a list of the actions you might take to help solve one of these problems.

How To

Use Population Maps

Why Is This Skill Important?

Like most other geographic information, population is shown on maps in many different ways. One way is with color. Another is with dots. A third way to show population is on a special kind of map called a cartogram. A **cartogram** is a map that shows information by changing the sizes of places. Knowing how to read different kinds of population maps can make it easier for you to find out where people live.

Understand the Process

Look at the key on the population map of Mexico. The key tells you that the colors on the map stand for different population densities. **Population density** is the number of people who live in 1 square mile or 1 square kilometer of land. On the map the color yellow stands for the least crowded areas. Red stands for the most crowded areas. Read the map key to find the areas in Mexico that have more than 250 people per square mile or more than 100 people per square kilometer. Is Mexico more crowded in the central part of the country or in the northern part?

The population of cities is also given on the population map of Mexico. Different-sized dots stand for cities with different population sizes. The largest dot on the map stands for a city with

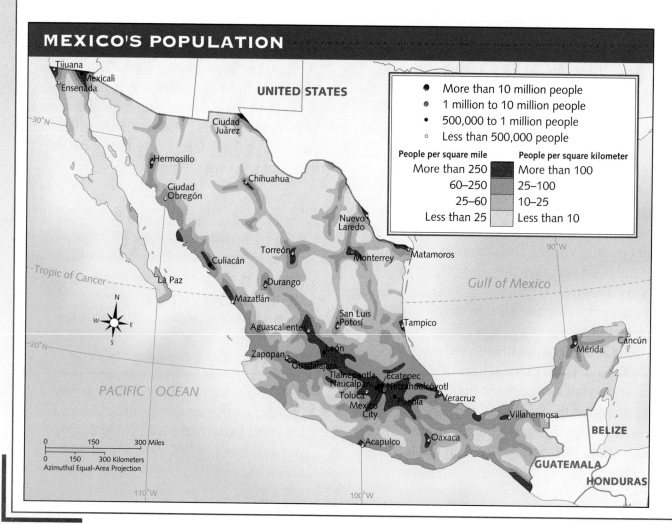

MEXICO'S POPULATION

- More than 10 million people
- 1 million to 10 million people
- 500,000 to 1 million people
- Less than 500,000 people

People per square mile	People per square kilometer
More than 250	More than 100
60–250	25–100
25–60	10–25
Less than 25	Less than 10

a population of more than 10 million people. The next-smaller dot stands for cities of 1 to 10 million people. These symbols do not give the exact populations of cities. But they do help you compare the sizes of cities. Find the dots for the cities of Guadalajara and Mérida. Which city has more people? Which city has fewer people, Monterrey or Puebla?

Now look at the cartogram of the Western Hemisphere. This cartogram also shows information about population, but in a much different way. On most maps, the size of a country is based on its land area. On a cartogram, however, the size of a country is based on its population instead of its land area.

A cartogram does not show the number of people who live in each country. But it does show how each country's population compares with that of another country. Countries with

larger populations are larger on a cartogram. Countries with smaller populations are smaller on a cartogram.

Find Canada and Mexico on a globe or map. You will notice that Canada has a larger land area than Mexico, so it is larger in size. Which of these two countries is larger on the cartogram below? What does the cartogram show about these countries?

Think and Apply

Study the population information given on the map on page 618 and on the cartogram below. Then show the same information by using charts, graphs, or tables. You might make a bar graph comparing the numbers of cities with different populations in Mexico or a table showing the five countries with the largest populations.

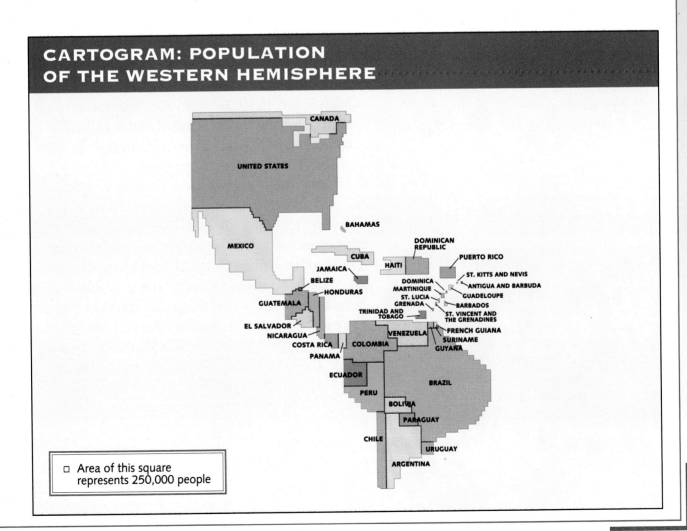

CARTOGRAM: POPULATION OF THE WESTERN HEMISPHERE

☐ Area of this square represents 250,000 people

DEMOCRACY
IN THE *Caribbean* AND IN —
Central America

LESSON 3

Link to Our World

How might political changes affect the way people live in a country?

Focus on the Main Idea
Read to find out how political changes have affected the way people live in the Caribbean and in Central America.

Preview Vocabulary
commonwealth
embargo
free election

Like the United States, many nations in the Caribbean and in Central America have a history of democracy. Costa Rica has a long democratic tradition. So does Puerto Rico, with its ties to the United States. In other places in the region, however, people continue to struggle for democracy.

PUERTO RICO

In 1898, after the Spanish-American War, the United States took control of Puerto Rico from Spain. In 1952 Puerto Rico became a kind of territory of the United States called a **commonwealth**. As citizens of a commonwealth, Puerto Ricans hold United States citizenship.

In 1993 the Puerto Rican people had to decide whether they wanted to change their political relationship with the United States. They had three choices. They could remain a commonwealth, declare independence, or become a state of the United States. Some Puerto Ricans who had lived in the United States said that statehood would be the best thing that could happen to Puerto Rico. Puerto Ricans who wanted their island to stay a commonwealth said they not only wanted to keep United States citizenship but also wanted Puerto Rico to keep its own identity. Puerto Ricans who wanted independence said they wanted Puerto Rico to be on its own.

In this important vote, more than 48 percent of the voters decided that Puerto Rico should remain a commonwealth. A close second in the voting was the choice of statehood, with 46 percent of the

Crowds of people wave Puerto Rican flags during a Puerto Rico Day parade in New York City.

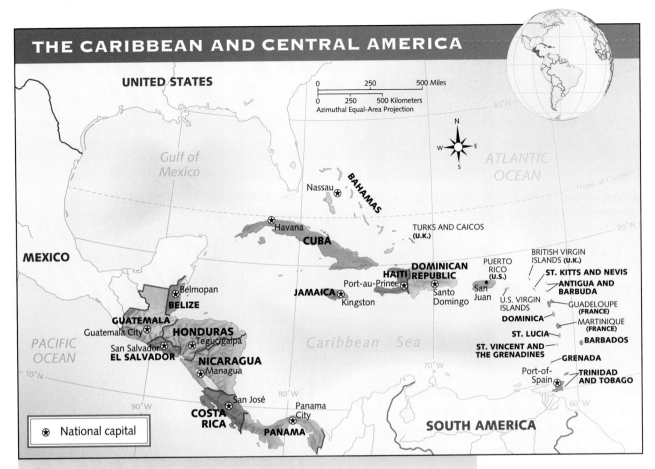

THE CARIBBEAN AND CENTRAL AMERICA

0   250   500 Miles
0   250   500 Kilometers
Azimuthal Equal-Area Projection

LOCATION Caribbean countries are on islands, and Central American countries are on the mainland.
■ Which countries are made up of more than one island?

vote. The vote showed that Puerto Ricans want to keep their special relationship with the United States.

✓ What is Puerto Rico's relationship with the United States?

CUBA

Like Puerto Rico, Cuba came under the control of the United States after the Spanish-American War. However, Cuba became independent soon after the war. Leaders of the newly independent Cuba wanted to build a strong economy. Political control soon fell into the hands of landowners and other wealthy Cubans.

Over the years, differences in the rights of the rich and the poor angered many of Cuba's farmers and workers. In 1959 a group of rebels led by Fidel Castro took over Cuba's government. They said their goal was to bring equal rights to all citizens and to solve many of Cuba's social and economic problems. To reach this goal, however, Castro made Cuba a communist nation. He has ruled Cuba as a dictator ever since.

Under communism, Cuba's government took over

Cuban leader Fidel Castro

Chapter 20 • **621**

Economic conditions in Cuba have gotten worse since the end of the Cold War, and supplies have been scarce. These Cubans are waiting in line to receive potatoes according to a rationing system. They receive an amount based on family size.

people's property and businesses. In 1962 the United States, which feared having a communist nation so close to its borders, set up an embargo against Cuba. During an **embargo** one country refuses to trade its goods with another country.

Cut off from the United States, Cuba came to depend on the Soviet Union for money and supplies. When the Cold War ended, however, the former Soviet Union was no longer able to support Cuba. Life in Cuba became very difficult. Many factories closed, and people lost their jobs. "If you don't have work," said one unemployed worker, "you can't even eat an orange any more."

Today many Cubans believe that the best hope for their nation is for the United States to lift its embargo. Many Cubans now living in the United States want their homeland to return to the free-enterprise system. Free enterprise, they say, will encourage people to start businesses that will create jobs. For this to happen, Cuba will need a democratic government that will allow free enterprise.

 What changes do some Cubans living in the United States want for their country?

HAITI

Haiti shares the island of Hispaniola with the Dominican Republic. Haiti is the second-oldest republic in the Western Hemisphere, after the United States. During the Haitian Revolution, which began in 1791, the people of the island rebelled against their French rulers. Haiti became an independent country in 1804.

For much of its history, however, Haiti has been ruled by dictators.

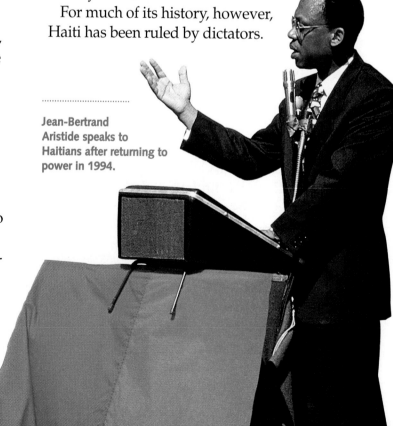

Jean-Bertrand Aristide speaks to Haitians after returning to power in 1994.

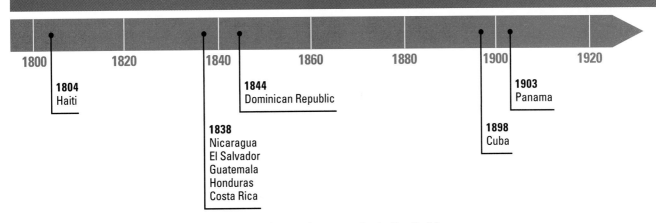

INDEPENDENCE IN THE CARIBBEAN AND CENTRAL AMERICA

1800   1820   1840   1860   1880   1900   1920

1804
Haiti

1844
Dominican Republic

1838
Nicaragua
El Salvador
Guatemala
Honduras
Costa Rica

1903
Panama

1898
Cuba

LEARNING FROM TIME LINES This time line shows when countries in the Caribbean and Central America became independent, after being controlled by other countries.
■ In what year did Cuba become independent from Spain?

In January 1988, Haitians chose new leaders by holding a **free election**—one in which there is a choice of candidates. It was the first free election held in Haiti in many years. But by June military leaders had overthrown the newly elected government and seized control of the country.

In 1990 a free election was held once again in Haiti. The people chose Jean-Bertrand Aristide (air•uh•STEED) as their president. But in 1991 his government, too, was overthrown by military leaders. He escaped to the United States.

The years of military rule in Haiti were harsh. Soldiers killed almost 4,000 of the country's 6 million people. Many Haitians wanted to go to the United States to escape the violence. Some risked death by traveling across the ocean in boats and on small rafts. When the Haitians arrived, however, the United States did not allow them to stay.

In 1994 the United States helped end military rule in Haiti by sending soldiers to Haiti. Soon President Aristide returned to office. He told his people,

66 Let us live in peace. All the guns must be silent. 99

Haiti still faces hard times, however. Its people are among the poorest in the Western Hemisphere, and its economic problems have yet to be solved.

 *What happened in Haiti in 1988?*

An American soldier talks with students at the Saint Anne Elementary School, in Port-au-Prince, Haiti, in 1994. During Operation Restore Democracy, American troops helped end years of violent rule by the Haitian military on the island nation.

NICARAGUA AND COSTA RICA

A dramatic change in government also took place in the Central American country of Nicaragua (nih•kah•RAH•gwah). In 1990, after years of civil war, voters elected Violeta Chamorro (vee•oh•LEY•tah chah•MAWR•oh) as Nicaragua's democratic president. Leaders in the United States were happy about Chamorro's victory. For many years the United States had helped democratic groups who wanted to end rule by Nicaraguan rebels known as Sandinistas. The United States had even placed an embargo against Nicaragua, as it had done against Cuba.

Years of fighting and natural disasters had hurt Nicaragua's economy. "War, hurricane, earthquake, tidal wave—Nicaragua has suffered all of that," explains one Nicaraguan citizen. "Now there is real hunger." With the election of Chamorro, the United States has lifted the embargo and has sent aid to help Nicaragua's economy and to strengthen the democratic government.

Unlike Nicaragua, neighboring Costa Rica has had a democratic government for many years. Its constitution was adopted in 1949.

One of Costa Rica's best known leaders is former president Oscar Arias Sánchez. President Arias won the 1987 Nobel Peace Prize for his leadership in creating a peace plan for Central America.

 In what year did rule by the Sandinistas in Nicaragua end?

Who?

Violeta Barrios de Chamorro
1929–

Violeta Chamorro was born in the Nicaraguan town of Rivas. After she married, she spent her early adult years raising her family. Chamorro's husband was a respected politician and the editor of a major newspaper. In 1978 the Nicaraguan dictator, Anastasio Somoza, ordered her husband killed. After his death, Chamorro ran the newspaper. She also served for a short time in the Sandinista government. From that time until her election as president in 1990, Chamorro spoke openly against the Sandinistas. Many people think that her bravery helped her win the presidential election.

LESSON 3 REVIEW

Check Understanding

1. **Recall the Facts** Why have some people left countries in the Caribbean and in Central America for the United States?
2. **Focus on the Main Idea** How have political changes in Caribbean and Central American countries affected citizens there?

Think Critically

3. **Explore Viewpoints** What different viewpoints did Puerto Ricans hold on the question of statehood?
4. **Cause and Effect** How did the end of the Cold War affect Cuba?

Show What You Know

 **Time Line Activity** Gather news articles on how democratic reforms have affected a country in the Caribbean or in Central America. Use these articles and other resources to create a time line of political events in the country you chose. Use your time line to teach a small group of classmates about political changes there.

CHALLENGES IN SOUTH AMERICA

LESSON 4

Link to Our World

How can problems in countries that seem far away affect the United States?

Focus on the Main Idea
As you read, think about how the problems of South America affect other parts of the world.

Preview Vocabulary
liberate
mestizo
deforestation

Native peoples lived in South America for thousands of years. Then, in the 1500s, Spain, Portugal, and other European countries began to build colonies there. European countries soon ruled most of the continent. By the mid-1800s most parts of South America had been **liberated**, or set free, from European rulers. Leaders of the independence movements included Simón Bolívar (see•MOHN boh•LEE•var) in Venezuela and José de San Martín (san mar•TEEN) in Argentina. Independence, however, did not solve all of the problems that many South American countries had faced as colonies.

NEW COUNTRIES WITH OLD PROBLEMS

Disagreements based on social class and economic level have long caused conflicts in South America. In many places, small groups of wealthy European landowners wanted to run South American countries after they were liberated. But much larger groups wanted an equal say in the new governments. These groups were American Indians, enslaved Africans, and **mestizos** (meh•STEE•zohz), people of mixed American Indian and European backgrounds.

New leaders promised to solve their countries' problems. But almost all of these leaders were military rulers supported by the European landowners. In the late 1800s and early 1900s, dictators ruled many South American countries. They did not solve the

Simón Bolívar began leading revolutions for independence in Caracas, Venezuela, his birthplace. He helped Venezuela, Bolivia, Colombia, Ecuador, and Peru gain independence from Spain.

Caribbean Sea

Barranquilla
Cartagena
Caracas
TRINIDAD AND TOBAGO

VENEZUELA
Medellín
Bogotá
Cali
COLOMBIA
Georgetown
Paramaribo
GUYANA
Cayenne
SURINAME
FRENCH GUIANA (FRANCE)

ATLANTIC OCEAN

Quito
ECUADOR
Guayaquil
Manaus
Belém
Leticia

Galapagos Islands (ECUADOR)

Equator

PERU
BRAZIL
Fortaleza
Natal
Recife

PACIFIC OCEAN

Lima
Cuzco
BOLIVIA
La Paz
Sucre
Salvador
Brasília

Belo Horizonte

PARAGUAY
Salta
Asunción
Rio de Janeiro
São Paulo
Curitiba

San Miguel de Tucumán

CHILE
Córdoba
Pôrto Alegre

Valparaíso
Rosario
Santiago
Mendoza
URUGUAY
Buenos Aires
Montevideo
ARGENTINA

Valdivia

Rio de la Plata

Tropic of Capricorn

Amazon River
São Francisco River
Paraguay River
Paraná River
Orinoco River
ANDES MOUNTAINS

N
W E
S

0   400   800 Miles
0   400   800 Kilometers
Modified Chambers Trimetric Projection

⊛ National capital

Strait of Magellan
Falkland Islands
Cape Horn

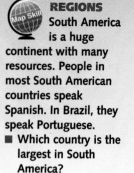

REGIONS
Map Skill
South America is a huge continent with many resources. People in most South American countries speak Spanish. In Brazil, they speak Portuguese.
■ Which country is the largest in South America?

problems of social and economic inequality that continue in many nations today.

 What problems have many countries in South America faced since independence?

NEW PROBLEMS FOR ALL COUNTRIES

Perhaps the greatest problem South Americans face today is how best to use the continent's vast resources. Thousands of square miles of rain forest have been cut down and burned to clear the land for

planting crops, raising cattle, and digging mines.

Clearing the forest land provides jobs for many people. But the burning has caused problems for the environment. Some scientists believe that it has led to a warming of the Earth. If average temperatures rise too high, the Earth's weather patterns could change. That might harm the plants and animals on which people everywhere depend.

In Brazil, **deforestation**, or the widespread cutting down of the forests, has left many American Indians homeless. Most of Brazil's Indians live in the thick rain forests of the country's Amazon River region. Because of deforestation many American Indians are struggling to keep their ways of life. "We must hold on to our land and culture," says Tikuna Indian leader Pedro Inácio Pinheiro. "We can never give these up."

Another problem in South America that affects other parts of the world is the production and sale of illegal drugs. In some areas of South America, especially in Bolivia and Colombia, farmers can earn more money by growing crops used to make harmful drugs than by producing other crops. People can make huge profits selling these illegal drugs in Europe and the United States. Conflicts have broken out between countries over stopping the trade in illegal drugs.

To build greater cooperation among countries of the Western Hemisphere, the Organization of American States, or OAS, was formed in 1948. Almost all the countries of South America, Central America, and the Caribbean, along with Mexico, Canada, and the United States, have joined. The chief purpose of the OAS is to settle disagreements among the member nations. The group also works to improve trade and understanding among the many peoples of the Americas.

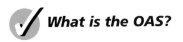 **What is the OAS?**

Check Understanding

1. **Recall the Facts**   What types of disagreements have caused conflicts all over South America?
2. **Focus on the Main Idea**   How have the problems of South America affected the United States and other parts of the world?

Think Critically

3. **Personally Speaking**   How do you think the history of South America is like the history of the United States? How do the histories seem different?
4. **Cause and Effect**   How has cutting down and burning the rain forests of South America affected other parts of the world?

Show What You Know

News-Writing Activity   With a partner, choose one country in South America. Work with your partner to prepare an article for a newsmagazine. The article should describe life in that country today. Focus on the important issues facing the people there. Compare your article with those written by your classmates.

The trees in this part of Brazil's Amazon rain forest have been burned to clear the land. Thousands of square miles of rain forest in Brazil are lost every year.

The PEOPLES of CANADA

Link to Our World

How might a nation protect the rights of all its citizens?

Focus on the Main Idea
As you read, find out how Canada has worked to protect the rights of its diverse groups of citizens.

Preview Vocabulary
province
separatist

Canada is the second-largest country in the world in area and covers almost half of North America. More than 28 million people live in this vast land. As in the United States, the first people in Canada were American Indians, who have lived there for thousands of years. In the 1500s the French arrived. In 1763, after Britain won the French and Indian War, Canada became a British colony. It remained a colony until 1867, when it was given limited independence. Not until 1982, when a new constitution was written, was Canada's independence complete.

THE CONSTITUTION OF 1982

The Constitution of 1982 is in many ways like the British constitution, which Canada had been using since 1867. But there is an important difference. Canada wanted to add a section called the Charter of Rights and Freedoms. This statement of rights is similar to the Bill of Rights in the United States Constitution.

The Canadian charter recognizes the rights of Canada's diverse peoples and promises to protect the country's multicultural heritage.

The charter allows both French and English to be used in public schools and in the courts. It also states that treaties with Indians in Canada will be upheld.

But not all Canadians in the nation's ten provinces and two territories were happy with the Constitution of 1982. The **provinces** are political regions much like states in the United States, but they have more authority. Each province has its own government and its own prime minister. A province can take many actions without the approval

The flag of Canada shows a maple leaf, a symbol of the country.

National capital

★ Provincial or territorial capital

National border

Provincial or territorial border

--- Proposed border

0 250 500 Miles

0 250 500 Kilometers
Azimuthal Equal-Area Projection

PLACE The Arctic Circle runs through the territories of Canada.
■ Why do you think most Canadians live in the provinces, which are farther south?

of the national government. Many leaders in the provinces worried that they would lose some of their authority under the new constitution.

There were also regional divisions in the country. People in the western provinces— Manitoba, Saskatchewan, Alberta, and British Columbia—felt they should have a greater say in the national government because the western provinces contain most of the country's natural resources. People in the eastern provinces—Ontario, Quebec, New Brunswick, Newfoundland, Nova Scotia, and Prince Edward Island—felt they should have more control because they have more people than the western provinces do.

> **Why were Canadian people divided over the country's Constitution of 1982?**

QUEBEC OPPOSES THE CONSTITUTION

Of all the provinces, Quebec has objected most to the Constitution of 1982. The reason for this can be found in the province's history.

Signs in Quebec, like this stop sign (below), are printed in both French and English. This cafe in Quebec City (right) reflects Quebec's French heritage.

Quebec was the oldest and most important part of the colony of New France, which was founded in the early 1600s. Even after the British took control of New France in 1763, French culture remained strong in Quebec. French families there have kept alive their language, laws, Catholic religion, and cultural traditions for hundreds of years. Today its French culture sets Quebec apart from Canada's other provinces. More than 83 percent of Quebec's people speak French. These French Canadians like to be called Québecois (kay•beh•KWAH).

While the other provinces have objected to the Constitution of 1982, only Quebec has refused to accept it. Many Québecois feel that the constitution does not recognize their special role in the founding of Canada. It does not give them the authority they have always had to veto national decisions. And it does not give them the right to use only French in schools, on public signs, and in the courts. Some Québecois even want to secede from Canada. Known as **separatists**, they want Quebec to become a separate, independent nation.

 Why have French Canadians in Quebec refused to accept the constitution?

KEY EVENTS IN CANADA'S HISTORY

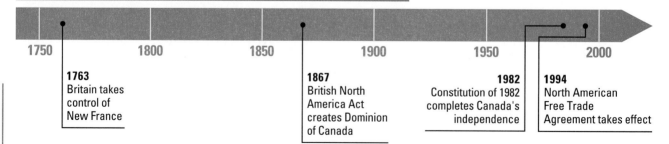

| 1750 | 1800 | 1850 | 1900 | 1950 | 2000 |

1763
Britain takes control of New France

1867
British North America Act creates Dominion of Canada

1982
Constitution of 1982 completes Canada's independence

1994
North American Free Trade Agreement takes effect

LEARNING FROM TIME LINES An important event in Canada's history took place when Parliament passed the British North America Act, making Canada a self-governing nation partly under British control.
■ When was this act passed? What type of nation was Canada called?

STANDING UP FOR NATIVE RIGHTS

Like the Québecois, the native peoples of Canada want greater protection for their cultures and their rights. Even with the Charter of Rights and Freedoms, which clearly states the rights of the Indians to keep their own land and to form their own governments, some American Indian groups feel these rights have been ignored.

In the summer of 1990, a violent conflict broke out in the town of Oka, in Quebec. Some people in Oka wanted to make a golf course larger, using part of a Mohawk burial ground. Mohawk men, women, and children put up a barrier to keep the builders away. Through their protests the Mohawks succeeded in stopping the construction on their land, but the deeper problem was not solved. "There is still great anger here," explains Mohawk artist Deborah Etienne. "The land is our identity, our life, and they wanted to take it away from us. . . . Our land claims are not settled. Nothing is resolved."

This Inuit family lives on Holman Island in the Northwest Territories. Native peoples make up a large part of the population in Canada's Arctic region.

In other cases, native groups have persuaded the Canadian government to take action. In 1984 the Canadian government gave the Cree and Naskapi (NAS•kuh•pee) peoples greater self-government. In 1992 the Inuits of Canada's Northern Territories won the right to form their own self-governing region. The territory, which the Inuits call Nunavut, meaning "our land," split from the Northern Territories. By these and similar actions, the Canadian government supports cultures in the Americas that are thousands of years old.

 What document lists the rights of the native peoples of Canada?

LESSON 5 REVIEW

Check Understanding

1. **Recall the Facts** What are some of the diverse groups that live in Canada?
2. **Focus on the Main Idea** How has Canada protected the rights of its diverse groups of citizens?

Think Critically

3. **Personally Speaking** What might happen if Quebec decides to secede from Canada? What do you think might happen if a large state like California broke away from the United States?
4. **Cause and Effect** What caused the Indian groups to take action to protect their rights? What have been the effects of their actions?

Show What You Know

Writing Activity Study maps and other resource materials that give information about the geography of Canada. Find the province in Canada that is most like the state in which you live. Then write two paragraphs comparing and contrasting the two places. Share your writing with a classmate.

REVIEW

ONNECT MAIN IDEAS

Use this organizer to show that you understand how the chapter's main ideas are connected. Copy the organizer onto a separate sheet of paper. Then complete it by writing the main idea of each lesson.

The Western Hemisphere Today

Mexico Today

_____
_____
_____
_____

The Peoples of Canada

_____
_____
_____
_____

Democracy in the Caribbean and in Central America

_____
_____
_____

Challenges in South America

_____
_____
_____

RITE MORE ABOUT IT

1. **Write a Poem** Omar and his father carried a banner that said, "Let's protect the rainforest." Write a poem about saving forests or conserving the environment.

2. **Write a Diary Entry** Imagine that you are living in Haiti in 1994. One morning you wake up and see American soldiers walking along the streets of your neighborhood. Write a diary entry telling what you think of having American troops in your country.

3. **Write a Postcard** Suppose that you are traveling through Canada on vacation. Write a postcard to a friend. Explain how Quebec is different from Canada's other provinces.

USE VOCABULARY

Write the term that correctly matches each definition. Then use each term in a complete sentence.

deforestation   liberate
embargo   metropolitan area
interest rate   province

1. a city and all the suburbs and other population areas around it

2. the amount that a bank charges customers to borrow money

3. the refusal of one country to trade its goods to another country

4. to set free

5. the widespread cutting down of forests

6. a political region of Canada

CHECK UNDERSTANDING

1. How did the devaluation of 1994 affect Mexico's middle class?

2. What is a free-trade agreement? What three nations signed NAFTA?

3. What did the Puerto Rican people decide about their political relationship with the United States in the 1993 election?

4. Why has life in Cuba become very difficult since the end of the Cold War?

5. What is the chief purpose of the OAS?

6. What is the Charter of Rights and Freedoms?

7. What do the separatists in Canada want?

THINK CRITICALLY

1. **Explore Viewpoints**   What viewpoint were the farmers in Chiapas expressing when they took control of several towns?

2. **Personally Speaking**   Omar walked 870 miles to be in a real rain forest. Describe a time when you had to work hard to do something. Was it worth all the hard work?

3. **Cause and Effect**   What effect did the election of Violeta Chamorro as president have on Nicaragua?

4. **Past to Present**   In the late 1800s and early 1900s, dictators ruled many South American countries. How does this fact affect the lives of the people who live there today?

5. **Think More About It**   How can cultural differences among people affect a nation's government?

APPLY SKILLS

 How to Use Population Maps   Use the population map on page 618 and the cartogram on page 619 to answer these questions.

1. Which city has more people, Monterrey or Tijuana?

2. In what part of Mexico is the population density the greatest?

3. Which country has more people, Costa Rica or Haiti?

READ MORE ABOUT IT

Canada by Pang Guek Cheng. Marshall Cavendish. This book looks at the many peoples of Canada and the country's rich resources.

Celebrating Earth Day: A Sourcebook of Activities and Experiments by Robert Gardner. Millbrook. This book has numerous ideas for learning about the Earth and ways to keep it healthy.

Goodbye USA—¡Hola Mexico! by Anne Elizabeth Bovaird. Barron's. Tom's mother teaches him a few Spanish words before he visits relatives in Mexico.

A VIEW FROM SPACE

"You get a marvelous view of the world from space," says space shuttle astronaut Fred Gregory. "The thing that impressed me was that you could see Houston, and then you'd see how really close Houston was to Mexico City, and how close Mexico City was to South America, to Africa, to Russia. Everything was right there. . . . You kind of wondered from above as you looked down and as you passed over what appeared to be city to city but was actually continent to continent, how there could be any problems at all down there, because everybody was everybody's neighbor."

People's views of our world today depend a lot on where they live. Many problems still cause conflict among neighbors on Earth. But in places around the world people are trying to work together to help solve those problems.

THINK AND APPLY

Think about a problem causing conflict in the world today. Find out how it could affect you and your school or community. Write a summary of the problem, describing its causes and effects. Tell about groups working to solve this problem. Share your summary with classmates.

STORY CLOTH

Study the pictures shown in this story cloth to help you review the events you read about in Unit 10.

Summarize the Main Ideas

1. The Cold War began after World War II. The Soviet Union cut off land routes to West Berlin in 1948, but an airlift brought in supplies.

2. War seemed near in 1962 when the Soviet Union sent missiles to Cuba. President Kennedy ordered a blockade of the island. Finally, Soviet leader Nikita Khrushchev agreed to remove the missiles.

3. In 1963 Martin Luther King, Jr. spoke for civil rights at a huge gathering in Washington, D.C.

4. The Soviet Union and the United States took the Cold War into space. The United States put the first person on the moon in 1969.

5. Americans were divided over the Vietnam War. After many deaths, the war ended in 1975.

6. Changes in the Soviet Union brought an end to the Cold War. In 1989 the Berlin Wall was torn down.

7. Today many of the countries in the Western Hemisphere face problems with their economies and governments. A major problem in South America is the clearing of rain forests.

8. Mexico, the United States, and Canada have signed the NAFTA agreement to remove tariffs on trade between these countries.

Choose an Event From this story cloth, choose the event that you think will have the most important effects in the future. Write a paragraph to explain your choice.

COOPERATIVE LEARNING WORKSHOP

Remember

- Share your ideas.
- Cooperate with others to plan your work.
- Take responsibility for your work.
- Show your group's work to the class.
- Discuss what you learned by working together.

Activity 1

Create a Space Travel Exhibit

Work in a group to research the future of space exploration. Find out what the United States and other countries are planning to do to explore space in the years to come. Create an exhibit that shows what you learned. In your exhibit, display posters, drawings, pictures of astronauts, books, magazines, photographs, and any other objects related to space exploration. Invite your classmates to visit the exhibit.

Activity 2

Prepare a Newscast

Work in a group to prepare a newscast that covers one of the following events: the Cuban missile crisis, the Montgomery bus boycott, the civil rights march in Washington, D.C., the Watergate scandal, Nixon's visit to China, or the 1985 Reagan and Gorbachev meeting. Each member of your group should have a job, such as researcher, writer, reporter, or set designer. When planning your newscast, include information that describes the changes that the event brought about. Present your newscast to your class.

Activity 3

Create a Hall of Fame

People from different ethnic groups and cultures have worked to bring about change in the United States. Your class should list 25 of these people to include in a Hall of Fame. They may be people that you read about in this unit or earlier units. The 25 names on the list should then be divided among small groups. Each group should make a poster for each person assigned to the group. The poster should include a drawing and a short biography of the person. Display all the posters together on a classroom wall or in a hallway.

SE VOCABULARY

Use each term in a sentence that will help explain its meaning.

1. nonviolence
2. public opinion
3. cease-fire
4. arms control
5. terrorism
6. metropolitan area
7. middle class
8. mestizo

 HECK UNDERSTANDING

1. Which President ordered a naval blockade during the Cuban missile crisis?

2. Who was the first person to set foot on the moon?

3. How did Martin Luther King, Jr., work to bring about change?

4. What organization was started by César Chávez? What was its purpose?

5. What was the Great Society?

6. How did Mikhail Gorbachev help change the Soviet Union?

7. How did the growth of manufacturing affect Mexico?

8. What are some important rights guaranteed under Canada's Constitution of 1982?

HINK CRITICALLY

1. **Past to Present** What might elected officials today learn from the Watergate scandal?

2. **Explore Viewpoints** Why do you think that Soviet leader Mikhail Gorbachev wanted better relations between the Soviet Union and the United States?

3. **Personally Speaking** Which United States President do you think made the greatest contributions to world peace? Explain your choice.

4. **Cause and Effect** What are the effects of cutting down and clearing the rain forest?

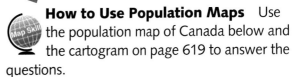 PPLY GEOGRAPHY SKILLS

How to Use Population Maps Use the population map of Canada below and the cartogram on page 619 to answer the questions.

1. Which Canadian city has a population greater than 1 million people?

2. Which city has more people, Calgary or Regina?

3. Which city has fewer people, Toronto or Ottawa?

4. In what part of Canada is the population density the greatest?

5. Which country has more people, Canada or Mexico?

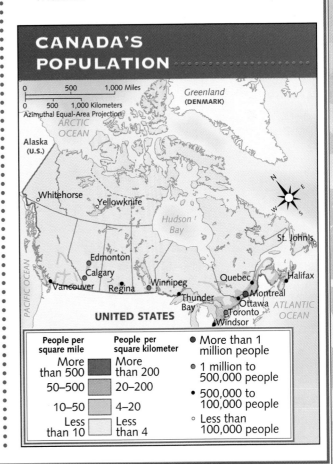

CANADA'S POPULATION

People per square mile	People per square kilometer	
More than 500	More than 200	● More than 1 million people
50–500	20–200	● 1 million to 500,000 people
10–50	4–20	● 500,000 to 100,000 people
Less than 10	Less than 4	○ Less than 100,000 people

FOR YOUR REFERENCE

CONTENTS

HOW TO GATHER AND REPORT INFORMATION

To write a report, make a poster, or do many other social studies projects, you may need information that is not in your textbook. You would need to gather this information from reference books, electronic references, or community resources. The following guide can help you in gathering information from many sources and in reporting what you find.

HOW TO USE REFERENCE TOOLS

Reference works are collections of facts. They include books and electronic resources, such as almanacs, atlases, dictionaries, and encyclopedias. In a library a reference book has an *R* or *REF* for *reference* on its spine along with the call number. Most reference books are for use only in the library. Many libraries also have electronic references on CD-ROM and the Internet.

WHEN TO USE AN ENCYCLOPEDIA

An encyclopedia is a good place to begin to look for information. An encyclopedia has articles on nearly every subject. The articles are in alphabetical order. Each gives basic facts about people, places, and events. Some electronic encyclopedias allow you to hear music and speeches and see short movies.

WHEN TO USE A DICTIONARY

A dictionary can give you information about words. Dictionaries explain word meanings and show the pronunciations of words. A dictionary is a good place to check the spelling of a word. Some dictionaries also include the origins of words and lists of foreign words, abbreviations, well-known people, and place names.

WHEN TO USE AN ATLAS

You can find information about places in an atlas. An atlas is a book of maps. Some atlases have road maps. Others have maps of countries around the world. There are atlases with maps that show crops, population, products, and many other things. Ask a librarian to help you find the kind of atlas you need.

WHEN TO USE AN ALMANAC

An almanac is a book or electronic resource of facts and figures. It shows information in tables and charts. However, the subjects are not in alphabetical order. You would need to use the index, which lists the subjects in alphabetical order. Most almanacs are brought up to date every year. So an almanac can give you the latest information.

How to Find Nonfiction Books

Nonfiction books give facts about real people and things. In a library, all nonfiction books are numbered and placed in order on the shelves. To find the nonfiction book you want, you need to know its call number. You can find this number by using a card file or a computer catalog, but you will need to know the book's title, author, or subject. Here are some sample entries for a book on American Indians.

INDIANS OF NORTH AMERICA. —————————— **Subject Card**

970.004   America's fascinating Indian heritage /
REA   [editor, James A. Maxwell]. -- Pleasantville,
            N.Y. : Reader's Digest Association, c1978.

            416 p. : ill. ; 29 cm.

            ISBN 0-89577-019-9

Maxwell, James A., 1912- ———————— **Author Card**

970.004   America's fascinating Indian heritage /
REA   [editor, James A. Maxwell]. -- Pleasantville,
            N.Y. : Reader's Digest Association, c1978.
E77.
            416 p. : ill. ; 29 cm.

            ISBN 0-89577-019-9

———————— **Title Card**

970.004   America's fascinating Indian heritage /
REA   [editor, James A. Maxwell]. -- Pleasantville,
            N.Y. : Reader's Digest Association, c1978.
E77
            416 p. : ill. ; 29 cm.

            At head of title: Reader's digest.
            Includes index.
            ISBN 0-89577-019-9

            1. Indians of North America.   I. Maxwell,
         James A., 1912- II. Title: Reader's digest.
         E77.A56   970'.004
                                               78-55614

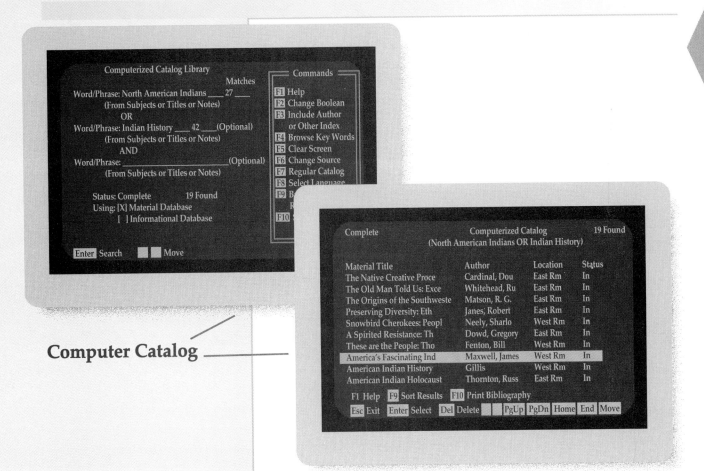

Computer Catalog

How to Find Periodicals

Libraries have special sections for periodicals—newspapers and magazines. Periodicals are good sources for the latest information and for topics not covered in books. New issues are usually displayed on a rack. Older issues are stored away, sometimes on film. Most libraries have an index that lists magazine articles by subject. The most widely used are the *Children's Magazine Guide* and the *Readers' Guide to Periodical Literature*.

The entries in these guides are in alphabetical order by subject and author, and sometimes by title. Abbreviations are used for many parts of an entry, such as the name of the magazine and the date of the issue. Here is a sample entry for an article on the Civil War.

Heading:
General topic you are researching

Title:
Title of the article

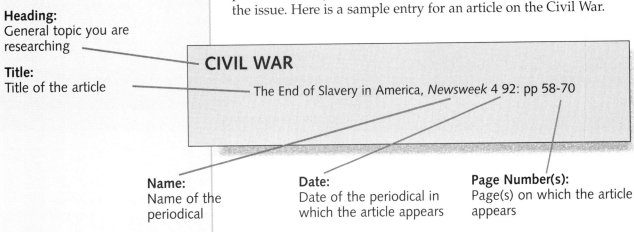

CIVIL WAR

The End of Slavery in America, *Newsweek* 4 92: pp 58-70

Name:
Name of the periodical

Date:
Date of the periodical in which the article appears

Page Number(s):
Page(s) on which the article appears

How to Conduct an Interview

Conducting interviews, or talking with people, is a good way to get facts and points of view.

Planning an Interview

1. Make a list of people to interview.

2. Call or write to each person to request an interview. When you contact the person, identify yourself and the purpose of the interview. Let the person know what you want to talk about.

3. Ask the person you will interview to set a time and place to meet.

Before the Interview

1. Read more about your topic, and, if possible, about the person. That way, you will be better able to talk with the person about your topic.

2. Make a list of questions to ask.

During the Interview

1. Listen carefully. Do not interrupt or argue with the person.

2. Take notes as you talk with the person, and write down his or her exact words.

3. If you want to use a tape recorder, first ask the person if you may do so.

After the Interview

1. Before you leave, thank the person you interviewed.

2. Follow up by writing a thank-you note.

How to Conduct a Survey

A good way to get information about the views of people in your community is to conduct a survey.

1. Identify your topic, and make a list a questions. Write them so that they can be answered with "yes" or "no" or with "for" or "against." You may also want to give a "no opinion" or "not sure" choice.

2. Make a tally sheet to use to record your responses.

3. Decide how many people you will ask and where you will conduct your survey.

4. During the survey, record your responses carefully on the tally sheet.

5. When you have finished your survey, count your responses, and write a summary statement or conclusion that your survey supports.

How to Write for Information

People in places far away can also give you information. You can write a letter to ask for information about a certain topic. When you write, be sure to do these things:

- Write neatly or use a word processor.
- Say who you are and why you are writing.
- Make your request specific and reasonable.
- Provide a self-addressed, stamped envelope for the answer.

You may or may not get a reply, but if you do, you may find that it was worth your time to write.

How to Write a Report

You may be asked to write a report on the information you have gathered. Most reports are from 300 to 500 words long.

Gather and Organize Your Information

Gather information about your topic from reference books, electronic references, or community resources. Then organize the information you have gathered.

- Take notes as you find information that you need for your report.
- Review your notes to make sure that you have all the information you want to include.
- Outline your information.
- Make sure the information is in the order in which you want to present it.

Draft Your Report

- Review your information. Decide whether you need more.
- Remember that the purpose of your report is to share information about your topic.
- Write a draft of your report. Put all your ideas on paper.

Revise

- Check that you have followed the order of your outline. Move sentences that seem out of place.
- Add any information that seems needed.
- Add quotations that show people's exact words.
- Reword sentences if too many follow the same pattern.

Proofread and Publish

- Check for errors.
- Make sure nothing has been left out.
- Write a clean copy of your report or use a word processor.

ALMANAC

FACTS ABOUT THE STATES

State	Year of Statehood	Population*	Area (sq. mi.)	Capital	Origin of State Name
Alabama	1819	4,361,000	51,609	Montgomery	Choctaw, *alba ayamule*, "one who clears land and gathers food from it"
Alaska	1959	663,000	586,412	Juneau	Aleut, *alayeska*, "great land"
Arizona	1912	4,223,000	113,909	Phoenix	Papago, *arizonac*, "place of the small spring"
Arkansas	1836	2,513,000	53,104	Little Rock	Quapaw, "the downstream people"
California	1850	33,364,000	158,693	Sacramento	Spanish, a fictional island
Colorado	1876	3,861,000	104,247	Denver	Spanish, "red land" or "red earth"
Connecticut	1788	3,268,000	5,009	Hartford	Mohican, *quinnitukqut*, "at the long tidal river"
Delaware	1787	736,000	2,057	Dover	Named for Lord de la Warr
Florida	1845	14,663,000	58,560	Tallahassee	Spanish, "filled with flowers"
Georgia	1788	7,324,000	58,876	Atlanta	Named for King George ll of England
Hawaii	1959	1,263,000	6,450	Honolulu	Polynesian, *hawaiki* or *owykee*, "homeland"
Idaho	1890	1,213,000	83,557	Boise	Shoshone, "light on the mountains"
Illinois	1818	11,989,000	56,400	Springfield	Algonquian, *iliniwek*, "men" or "warriors"
Indiana	1816	5,920,000	36,291	Indianapolis	*Indian + a,* = "land of the Indians"
Iowa	1846	2,893,000	56,290	Des Moines	Dakota, *ayuba*, "beautiful land"
Kansas	1861	2,652,000	82,264	Topeka	Sioux, "land of the south wind people"
Kentucky	1792	3,911,000	40,395	Frankfort	Cherokee, *Kentake*, "meadowland"
Louisiana	1812	4,404,000	48,523	Baton Rouge	Named for King Louis XIV of France
Maine	1820	1,236,000	33,215	Augusta	Named after a French province
Maryland	1788	5,180,000	10,577	Annapolis	Named for Henrietta Maria, Queen Consort of Charles I of England
Massachusetts	1788	5,959,000	8,257	Boston	Algonquian, "at the big hill" or "place of the big hill"
Michigan	1837	9,656,000	58,216	Lansing	Chippewa, *mica gama*, "big water"
Minnesota	1858	4,706,000	84,068	St. Paul	Dakota Sioux, "sky-blue water"
Mississippi	1817	2,700,000	47,716	Jackson	Chippewa, *mici sibi*, "big river"
Missouri	1821	5,347,000	69,686	Jefferson City	Algonquian, "muddy water" or "people of the big canoes"
Montana	1889	887,000	147,138	Helena	Spanish, "mountainous"
Nebraska	1867	1,670,000	77,227	Lincoln	Omaha, *ni-bthaska*, "river in the flatness"

State	Year of Statehood	Population*	Area (sq. mi.)	Capital	Origin of State Name
Nevada	1864	1,571,000	110,540	Carson City	Spanish, "snowy" or "snowed upon"
New Hampshire	1788	1,144,000	9,304	Concord	Named for Hampshire County, England
New Jersey	1787	8,015,000	7,836	Trenton	Named for the Isle of Jersey
New Mexico	1912	1,737,000	121,666	Santa Fe	Named by Spanish explorers from Mexico
New York	1788	18,198,000	49,576	Albany	Named after the Duke of York
North Carolina	1789	7,347,000	52,586	Raleigh	Named after King Charles II of England
North Dakota	1889	639,000	70,665	Bismarck	Sioux, *dakota*, "friend" or "ally"
Ohio	1803	11,318,000	41,222	Columbus	Iroquois, *oheo*, "beautiful, beautiful water"
Oklahoma	1907	3,313,000	69,919	Oklahoma City	Choctaw, "red people"
Oregon	1859	3,249,000	96,981	Salem	Algonquian, *wauregan*, "beautiful water"
Pennsylvania	1787	12,210,000	45,333	Harrisburg	*Penn + sylvania*, meaning "Penn's woods"
Rhode Island	1790	998,000	1,214	Providence	Dutch, "red-clay island"
South Carolina	1788	3,814,000	31,055	Columbia	Named after King Charles II of England
South Dakota	1889	750,000	77,047	Pierre	Sioux, *dakota*, "friend" or "ally"
Tennessee	1796	5,359,000	42,244	Nashville	Name of a Cherokee village
Texas	1845	19,180,000	267,338	Austin	Indian, *tejas*, "friend" or "ally"
Utah	1896	2,030,000	84,916	Salt Lake City	Ute, "land of the Ute"
Vermont	1791	584,000	9,609	Montpelier	French, *vert*, "green," and *mont*, "mountain"
Virginia	1788	6,814,000	40,817	Richmond	Named after Queen Elizabeth I of England
Washington	1889	5,735,000	68,192	Olympia	Named for George Washington
West Virginia	1863	1,832,000	24,181	Charleston	From the English-named state of Virginia
Wisconsin	1848	5,256,000	56,154	Madison	Possibly Algonquian, "grassy place" or "place of the beaver"
Wyoming	1890	501,000	97,914	Cheyenne	Algonquian, *mache-weaming*, "at the big flats"
District of Columbia		545,000	67		Named after Christopher Columbus

*These population figures are from the most recent available statistics.

FACTS ABOUT THE WESTERN HEMISPHERE

Country	Population*	Area (sq. mi.)	Capital	Origin of Country Name
North America				
Antigua and Barbuda	65,000	171	St. Johns	Named for the Church of Santa Maria la Antigua in Seville, Spain
Bahamas	273,000	5,382	Nassau	Spanish, *bajamar*, "shallow water"
Barbados	256,000	166	Bridgetown	Means "bearded"—probably referring to the beardlike vines early explorers found on its trees
Belize	209,000	8,867	Belmopan	Mayan, "muddy water"
Canada	28,114,000	3,849,674	Ottawa	Huron-Iroquois, *kanata*, "village" or "community"
Costa Rica	3,342,000	19,730	San José	Spanish, "rich coast"
Cuba	11,064,000	42,804	Havana	Origin unknown
Dominica	88,000	290	Roseau	Latin, *Dies Dominica*, "Day of the Lord"
Dominican Republic	7,826,000	18,704	Santo Domingo	Named after the capital city
El Salvador	5,753,000	8,124	San Salvador	Spanish, "the Savior"
Grenada	94,000	133	St. George's	Origin unknown
Guatemala	10,721,000	42,042	Guatemala City	Indian, "land of trees"
Haiti	6,491,000	10,695	Port-au-Prince	Indian, "land of mountains"
Honduras	5,315,000	43,277	Tegucigalpa	Spanish, "profundities"—probably referring to the depth of offshore waters
Jamaica	2,555,000	4,244	Kingston	Arawak, *xamayca*, "land of wood and water"
Mexico	92,202,000	756,066	Mexico City	Aztec, *mexliapan*, "lake of the moon"
Nicaragua	4,097,000	50,880	Managua	From Nicarao, the name of an Indian chief
Panama	2,630,000	29,157	Panama City	From an Indian village name

Country	Population*	Area (sq. mi.)	Capital	Origin of Country Name
St. Kitts (St. Christopher) —Nevis	41,000	104	Basseterre	Named by Christopher Columbus—St. Christopher, for a Catholic saint; Nevis, for a cloud-topped peak that looked like *las nieves*, "the snows"
St. Lucia	145,000	238	Castries	Named by Christopher Columbus for a Catholic saint
St. Vincent and the Grenadines	115,000	150	Kingstown	May have been named by Christopher Columbus for a Catholic saint
Trinidad and Tobago	1,328,000	1,980	Port-of-Spain	Trinidad, from the Spanish word for "trinity"; Tobago, named for tobacco because the island has the shape of an Indian smoking pipe
United States of America	260,714,000	3,787,318	Washington, D.C.	Named after the explorer Amerigo Vespucci

South America

Country	Population*	Area (sq. mi.)	Capital	Origin of Country Name
Argentina	33,913,000	1,073,518	Buenos Aires	Latin, *argentum*, "silver"
Bolivia	7,719,000	424,164	La Paz/Sucre	Named after Simón Bolívar, the famed liberator
Brazil	158,739,000	3,286,470	Brasília	Named after a native tree that the Portuguese called "bresel wood"
Chile	13,951,000	292,135	Santiago	Indian, *chilli*, "where the land ends"
Colombia	35,578,000	440,831	Bogotá	Named after Christopher Columbus
Ecuador	10,677,000	105,037	Quito	From the word *equator*, referring to the country's location
Guyana	729,000	83,044	Georgetown	Indian, "land of waters"
Paraguay	5,214,000	157,048	Asunción	Named after the Paraguay River, which flows through it
Peru	23,651,000	496,255	Lima	Quechua, "land of abundance"
Suriname	423,000	63,251	Paramaribo	From an Indian word, *surinen*
Uruguay	3,199,000	68,037	Montevideo	Named after the Uruguay River, which flows through it
Venezuela	20,562,000	352,144	Caracas	Spanish, "Little Venice"

*These population figures are from the most recent available statistics.

FACTS ABOUT THE
PRESIDENTS

Birthplace:
  *Westmoreland
  County, VA*
Home State: *VA*
Political Party: *None*
Age at
  Inauguration: *57*
Served: *1789–1797*
Vice President:
  John Adams

George Washington 1732–1799

Birthplace: *Braintree,
  MA*
Home State: *MA*
Political Party:
  Federalist
Age at
  Inauguration: *61*
Served: *1797–1801*
Vice President:
  Thomas Jefferson

John Adams   1735–1826

Birthplace: *Albemarle
  County, VA*
Home State: *VA*
Political Party:
  Democratic-Republican
Age at
  Inauguration: *57*
Served: *1801–1809*
Vice Presidents: *Aaron
  Burr, George Clinton*

Thomas Jefferson   1743–1826

Birthplace: *Port Conway,
  VA*
Home State: *VA*
Political Party:
  Democratic-Republican
Age at Inauguration: *57*
Served: *1809–1817*
Vice Presidents:
  *George Clinton,
  Elbridge Gerry*

James Madison   1751–1836

Birthplace:
  *Westmoreland
  County, VA*
Home State: *VA*
Political Party:
  Democratic-Republican
Age at Inauguration: *58*
Served: *1817–1825*
Vice President: *Daniel
  D. Tompkins*

James Monroe   1758–1831

Birthplace: *Braintree,
  MA*
Home State: *MA*
Political Party:
  Democratic-Republican
Age at Inauguration: *57*
Served: *1825–1829*
Vice President:
  John C. Calhoun

John Quincy Adams   1767–1848

Birthplace: *Waxhaw
  settlement, SC*
Home State: *TN*
Political Party:
  Democratic
Age at
  Inauguration: *61*
Served: *1829–1837*
Vice Presidents:
  *John C. Calhoun,
  Martin Van Buren*

Andrew Jackson   1767–1845

Birthplace:
  Kinderhook, NY
Home State: *NY*
Political Party:
  Democratic
Age at
  Inauguration: *54*
Served: *1837–1841*
Vice President:
  *Richard M.
  Johnson*

Martin Van Buren   1782–1862

Birthplace: *Berkeley, VA*
Home State: *OH*
Political Party: *Whig*
Age at Inauguration: *68*
Served: *1841*
Vice President: *John
  Tyler*

William H. Harrison   1773–1841

Birthplace:
  Greenway, VA
Home State: *VA*
Political Party: *Whig*
Age at
  Inauguration: *51*
Served: *1841–1845*
Vice President: *none*

John Tyler   1790–1862

Birthplace: *near
  Pineville, NC*
Home State: *TN*
Political Party:
  Democratic
Age at
  Inauguration: *49*
Served: *1845–1849*
Vice President:
  George M. Dallas

James K. Polk   1795–1849

Birthplace: *Orange
  County, VA*
Home State: *LA*
Political Party: *Whig*
Age at
  Inauguration: *64*
Served: *1849–1850*
Vice President:
  Millard Fillmore

Zachary Taylor   1784–1850

Birthplace: *Locke, NY*
Home State: *NY*
Political Party: *Whig*
Age at
    Inauguration: *50*
Served: *1850–1853*
Vice President: *none*

Millard Fillmore   1800–1874

Birthplace: *Hillsboro, NH*
Home State: *NH*
Political Party:
    Democratic
Age at
    Inauguration: *48*
Served: *1853–1857*
Vice President:
    William R. King

Franklin Pierce   1804–1869

Birthplace: *near Mercersburg, PA*
Home State: *PA*
Political Party:
    Democratic
Age at
    Inauguration: *65*
Served: *1857–1861*
Vice President: *John C. Breckinridge*

James Buchanan   1791–1868

Birthplace: *near Hodgenville, KY*
Home State: *IL*
Political Party:
    Republican
Age at
    Inauguration: *52*
Served: *1861–1865*
Vice Presidents:
    Hannibal Hamlin, Andrew Johnson

Abraham Lincoln   1809–1865

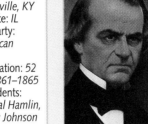

Birthplace: *Raleigh, NC*
Home State: *TN*
Political Party:
    National Union
Age at
    Inauguration: *56*
Served: *1865–1869*
Vice President: *none*

Andrew Johnson   1808–1875

Birthplace: *Point Pleasant, OH*
Home State: *IL*
Political Party:
    Republican
Age at
    Inauguration: *46*
Served: *1869–1877*
Vice Presidents:
    Schuyler Colfax, Henry Wilson

Ulysses S. Grant   1822–1885

Birthplace:
    Delaware, OH
Home State: *OH*
Political Party:
    Republican
Age at
    Inauguration: *54*
Served: *1877–1881*
Vice President:
    William A. Wheeler

Rutherford B. Hayes 1822–1893

Birthplace:
    Orange, OH
Home State: *OH*
Political Party:
    Republican
Age at
    Inauguration: *49*
Served: *1881*
Vice President:
    Chester A. Arthur

James A. Garfield   1831–1881

Birthplace:
    Fairfield, VT
Home State: *NY*
Political Party:
    Republican
Age at
    Inauguration: *51*
Served: *1881–1885*
Vice President: *none*

Chester A. Arthur   1829–1886

Birthplace: *Caldwell, NJ*
Home State: *NY*
Political Party:
    Democratic
Age at
    Inauguration: *47*
Served: *1885–1889*
Vice President:
    Thomas A. Hendricks

Grover Cleveland   1837–1908

Birthplace:
    North Bend, OH
Home State: *IN*
Political Party:
    Republican
Age at
    Inauguration: *55*
Served: *1889–1893*
Vice President:
    Levi P. Morton

Benjamin Harrison   1833–1901

Birthplace: *Caldwell, NJ*
Home State: *NY*
Political Party:
    Democratic
Age at
    Inauguration: *55*
Served: *1893–1897*
Vice President:
    Adlai E. Stevenson

Grover Cleveland   1837–1908

Birthplace: *Niles, OH*
Home State: *OH*
Political Party:
    Republican
Age at
    Inauguration: *54*
Served: *1897–1901*
Vice Presidents:
    Garret A. Hobart, Theodore Roosevelt

William McKinley   1843–1901

Birthplace: *New York, NY*
Home State: *NY*
Political Party:
    Republican
Age at
    Inauguration: *42*
Served: *1901–1909*
Vice President:
    Charles W. Fairbanks

Theodore Roosevelt 1858–1919

Birthplace:
    Cincinnati, OH
Home State: *OH*
Political Party:
    Republican
Age at
    Inauguration: *51*
Served: *1909–1913*
Vice President:
    James S. Sherman

William H. Taft   1857–1930

Birthplace: *Staunton, VA*
Home State: *NJ*
Political Party: *Democratic*
Age at Inauguration: *56*
Served: *1913–1921*
Vice President: *Thomas R. Marshall*

Woodrow Wilson   1856–1924

Birthplace: *near Blooming Grove, OH*
Home State: *OH*
Political Party: *Republican*
Age at Inauguration: *55*
Served: *1921–1923*
Vice President: *Calvin Coolidge*

Warren G. Harding 1865–1923

Birthplace: *Plymouth Notch, VT*
Home State: *MA*
Political Party: *Republican*
Age at Inauguration: *51*
Served: *1923–1929*
Vice President: *Charles G. Dawes*

Calvin Coolidge   1872–1933

Birthplace: *West Branch, IA*
Home State: *CA*
Political Party: *Republican*
Age at Inauguration: *54*
Served: *1929–1933*
Vice President: *Charles Curtis*

Herbert Hoover   1874–1964

Birthplace: *Hyde Park, NY*
Home State: *NY*
Political Party: *Democratic*
Age at Inauguration: *51*
Served: *1933–1945*
Vice Presidents: *John N. Garner, Henry A. Wallace, Harry S. Truman*

Franklin D. Roosevelt 1882–1945

Birthplace: *Lamar, MO*
Home State: *MO*
Political Party: *Democratic*
Age at Inauguration: *60*
Served: *1945–1953*
Vice President: *Alben W. Barkley*

Harry S. Truman   1884–1972

Birthplace: *Denison, TX*
Home State: *NY*
Political Party: *Republican*
Age at Inauguration: *62*
Served: *1953–1961*
Vice President: *Richard M. Nixon*

Dwight D. Eisenhower 1890–1969

Birthplace: *Brookline, MA*
Home State: *MA*
Political Party: *Democratic*
Age at Inauguration: *43*
Served: *1961–1963*
Vice President: *Lyndon B. Johnson*

John F. Kennedy   1917–1963

Birthplace: *near Stonewall, TX*
Home State: *TX*
Political Party: *Democratic*
Age at Inauguration: *55*
Served: *1963–1969*
Vice President: *Hubert H. Humphrey*

Lyndon B. Johnson 1908–1973

Birthplace: *Yorba Linda, CA*
Home State: *NY*
Political Party: *Republican*
Age at Inauguration: *56*
Served: *1969–1974*
Vice Presidents: *Spiro T. Agnew, Gerald R. Ford*

Richard M. Nixon   1913–1994

Birthplace: *Omaha, NE*
Home State: *MI*
Political Party: *Republican*
Age at Inauguration: *61*
Served: *1974–1977*
Vice President: *Nelson A. Rockefeller*

Gerald R. Ford   1913–

Birthplace: *Plains, GA*
Home State: *GA*
Political Party: *Democratic*
Age at Inauguration: *52*
Served: *1977–1981*
Vice President: *Walter F. Mondale*

Jimmy Carter   1924–

Birthplace: *Tampico, IL*
Home State: *CA*
Political Party: *Republican*
Age at Inauguration: *69*
Served: *1981–1989*
Vice President: *George H. W. Bush*

Ronald W. Reagan   1911–

Birthplace: *Milton, MA*
Home State: *TX*
Political Party: *Republican*
Age at Inauguration: *64*
Served: *1989–1993*
Vice President: *Dan Quayle*

George H. W. Bush 1924–

Birthplace: *Hope, AR*
Home State: *AR*
Political Party: *Democratic*
Age at Inauguration: *46*
Served: *1993–*
Vice President: *Albert Gore*

William Clinton   1946–

Home State refers to the state of residence when elected.

AMERICAN DOCUMENTS

THE DECLARATION OF INDEPENDENCE

In Congress, July 4, 1776.
The unanimous Declaration of the
thirteen United States of America,

When in the Course of human events it becomes necessary for one people to dissolve the political bands which have connected them with another, and to assume among the powers of the earth, the separate and equal station to which the Laws of Nature and of Nature's God entitle them, a decent respect to the opinions of mankind requires that they should declare the causes which impel them to the separation.

We hold these truths to be self-evident, that all men are created equal, that they are endowed by their Creator with certain unalienable Rights, that among these are Life, Liberty and the pursuit of Happiness.

That to secure these rights, Governments are instituted among Men, deriving their just powers from the consent of the governed,

That whenever any Form of Government becomes destructive of these ends, it is the Right of the People to alter or to abolish it, and to institute new Government, laying its foundation on such principles and organizing its powers in such form, as to them shall seem most likely to effect their Safety and Happiness. Prudence, indeed, will dictate that Governments long established should not be changed for light and transient causes; and accordingly all experience hath shown, that mankind are more disposed to suffer, while evils are sufferable, than to right themselves by abolishing the forms to which they are accustomed. But when a long train of abuses and usurpations, pursuing invariably the same Object evinces a design to reduce them under absolute Despotism, it is their right, it is their duty, to throw off such Government, and to provide new Guards for their future security.

Such has been the patient sufferance of these Colonies; and such is now the necessity which constrains them to alter their former Systems of Government. The history of the present King of Great Britain is a history of repeated injuries and usurpations, all having in direct object the establishment of an absolute Tyranny over these States. To prove this, let Facts be submitted to a candid world.

He has refused his Assent to Laws, the most wholesome and necessary for the public good.

He has forbidden his Governors to pass Laws of immediate and pressing importance, unless suspended in their operation till his Assent should be obtained; and when so suspended, he has utterly neglected to attend to them.

PREAMBLE
The Preamble tells why the Declaration was written. It states that the members of the Continental Congress believed the colonies had the right to break away from Britain and become a free nation.

STATEMENT OF RIGHTS
The opening part of the Declaration tells what rights the members of the Continental Congress believed that all people have. All people are equal and have the rights to life, liberty, and the pursuit of happiness. These rights cannot be taken away. When a government tries to take these rights away from the people, the people have the right to change the government or do away with it. The people can then form a new government that gives them these rights.

CHARGES AGAINST THE KING
The Declaration lists more than 25 charges against the king. He was mistreating the colonists, the Declaration says, in order to gain total control over the colonies.

The king rejected many laws passed by colonial legislatures.

The king made the colonial legislatures meet at unusual times and places.

The king and the king's governors often dissolved colonial legislatures for disobeying their orders.

The king stopped people from moving to the colonies and into the new western lands.

The king prevented the colonists from choosing their own judges. The king chose the judges, and they served only as long as the king was satisfied with them.

The king hired people to help collect taxes in the colonies.

The king appointed General Thomas Gage, commander of Britain's military forces in the Americas, as governor of Massachusetts.

The king expected the colonists to provide housing and supplies for the British soldiers in the colonies.

The king and Parliament demanded that colonists pay many taxes, even though the colonists did not agree to pay them.

Colonists were tried by British naval courts, which had no juries.

Colonists accused of treason were sent to Britain to be tried.

He has refused to pass other Laws for the accommodation of large districts of people, unless those people would relinquish the right of Representation in the Legislature, a right inestimable to them and formidable to tyrants only.

He has called together legislative bodies at places unusual, uncomfortable, and distant from the depository of their public Records, for the sole purpose of fatiguing them into compliance with his measures.

He has dissolved Representative Houses repeatedly, for opposing with manly firmness his invasions on the rights of the people.

He has refused for a long time, after such dissolutions, to cause others to be elected; whereby the Legislative powers, incapable of Annihilation, have returned to the People at large for their exercise; the State remaining in the mean time exposed to all the dangers of invasion from without, and convulsions within.

He has endeavored to prevent the population of these States; for that purpose obstructing the Laws for Naturalization of Foreigners; refusing to pass others to encourage their migrations hither, and raising the conditions of new Appropriations of Lands.

He has obstructed the Administration of Justice, by refusing his Assent to Laws for establishing Judiciary powers.

He has made Judges dependent on his Will alone, for the tenure of their offices, and the amount and payment of their salaries.

He has erected a multitude of New Offices, and sent hither swarms of Officers to harrass our people, and eat out their substance.

He has kept among us, in times of peace, Standing Armies without the Consent of our legislatures.

He has affected to render the Military independent of and superior to the Civil power.

He has combined with others to subject us to a jurisdiction foreign to our constitution, and unacknowledged by our laws; giving his Assent to their Acts of pretended Legislation:

For quartering large bodies of armed troops among us:

For protecting them, by a mock Trial, from punishment for any Murders which they should commit on the Inhabitants of these States:

For cutting off our Trade with all parts of the world:

For imposing Taxes on us without our Consent:

For depriving us in many cases, of the benefits of Trial by Jury:

For transporting us beyond Seas to be tried for pretended offences:

For abolishing the free System of English Laws in a neighboring Province, establishing therein an Arbitrary government, and enlarging its Boundaries so as to render it at once an example and fit instrument for introducing the same absolute rule into these Colonies:

For taking away our Charters, abolishing our most valuable Laws, and altering fundamentally the Forms of our Governments:

For suspending our own Legislatures, and declaring themselves invested with power to legislate for us in all cases whatsoever.

He has abdicated Government here, by declaring us out of his Protection and waging War against us.

He has plundered our seas, ravaged our Coasts, burnt our towns, and destroyed the lives of our people.

He is at this time transporting large Armies of foreign Mercenaries to complete the works of death, desolation and tyranny, already begun with circumstances of Cruelty & perfidy scarcely paralleled in the most barbarous ages, and totally unworthy the Head of a civilized nation.

He has constrained our fellow Citizens taken Captive on the high Seas to bear Arms against their Country, to become the executioners of their friends and Brethren, or to fall themselves by their Hands.

He has excited domestic insurrections amongst us, and has endeavored to bring on the inhabitants of our frontiers, the merciless Indian Savages, whose known rule of warfare, is an undistinguished destruction of all ages, sexes and conditions.

In every stage of these Oppressions We have Petitioned for Redress in the most humble terms: Our repeated Petitions have been answered only by repeated injury. A Prince, whose character is thus marked by every act which may define a Tyrant, is unfit to be the ruler of a free people.

Nor have We been wanting in attentions to our British brethren. We have warned them from time to time of attempts by their legislature to extend an unwarrantable jurisdiction over us. We have reminded them of the circumstances of our emigration and settlement here. We have appealed to their native justice and magnanimity, and we have conjured them by the ties of our common kindred to disavow these usurpations, which, would inevitably interrupt our connections and correspondence. They too have been deaf to the voice of justice and of consanguinity. We must, therefore, acquiesce in the necessity, which denounces our Separation, and hold them, as we hold the rest of mankind, Enemies in War, in Peace Friends.

We, therefore, the Representatives of the united States of America, in General Congress, Assembled, appealing to the Supreme Judge of the world for the rectitude of our intentions, do, in the Name, and by Authority of the good People of these Colonies, solemnly publish and declare, That these United Colonies are, and of Right ought to be Free and Independent States; that they are Absolved from all Allegiance to the British Crown, and that all political connection between them and the State of Great Britain, is and ought to be totally dissolved; and that as Free and Independent States, they have full Power to levy War, conclude Peace, contract Alliances, establish Commerce, and to do all other Acts and Things which Independent States may of right do.

The king allowed General Gage to take military action to enforce British laws in the colonies.

The king hired Hessian mercenaries and sent them to fight the colonists.

The king's governor in Virginia promised freedom to all enslaved people who joined the British forces. The British also planned to use Indians to fight the colonists.

The Declaration explained the efforts of the colonists to avoid separation from Britain. But the colonists said that the king had ignored their protests. Because of the many charges against the king, the writers of the Declaration concluded that he was not fit to rule free people.

A STATEMENT OF INDEPENDENCE
The writers declared that the colonies were now free and independent states. All ties with Britain were broken. As free and independent states, they had the right to make war and peace, to trade, and to do all the things free countries could do.

To support the Declaration, the signers promised one another their lives, their fortunes, and their honor.

And for the support of this Declaration, with a firm reliance on the protection of divine Providence, we mutually pledge to each other our Lives, our Fortunes and our sacred Honor.

John Hancock

NEW HAMPSHIRE

Josiah Bartlett
William Whipple
Matthew Thornton

MASSACHUSETTS

John Adams
Samuel Adams
Robert Treat Paine
Elbridge Gerry

NEW YORK

William Floyd
Philip Livingston
Francis Lewis
Lewis Morris

RHODE ISLAND

Stephen Hopkins
William Ellery

NEW JERSEY

Richard Stockton
John Witherspoon
Francis Hopkinson
John Hart
Abraham Clark

PENNSYLVANIA

Robert Morris
Benjamin Rush
Benjamin Franklin
John Morton
George Clymer
James Smith
George Taylor
James Wilson
George Ross

DELAWARE

Caesar Rodney
George Read
Thomas McKean

MARYLAND

Samuel Chase
William Paca
Thomas Stone
Charles Carroll of Carrollton

NORTH CAROLINA

William Hopper
Joseph Hewes
John Penn

VIRGINIA

George Wythe
Richard Henry Lee
Thomas Jefferson
Benjamin Harrison
Thomas Nelson, Jr.
Francis Lightfoot Lee
Carter Braxton

SOUTH CAROLINA

Edward Rutledge
Thomas Heyward, Jr.
Thomas Lynch, Jr.
Arthur Middleton

CONNECTICUT

Roger Sherman
Samuel Huntington
William Williams
Oliver Wolcott

GEORGIA

Button Gwinnett
Lyman Hall
George Walton

Members of the Continental Congress stated that copies of the Declaration should be sent to all Committees of Correspondence and to commanders of the troops and that it should be read in every state.

Resolved, That copies of the Declaration be sent to the several assemblies, conventions, and committees, or councils of safety, and to the several commanding officers of the continental troops; that it be proclaimed in each of the United States, at the head of the army.

THE CONSTITUTION OF
THE UNITED STATES OF AMERICA

PREAMBLE*

We the people of the United States, in order to form a more perfect Union, establish justice, insure domestic tranquillity, provide for the common defense, promote the general welfare, and secure the blessings of liberty to ourselves and our posterity, do ordain and establish this Constitution for the United States of America.

ARTICLE I
THE LEGISLATIVE BRANCH

SECTION 1. CONGRESS

All legislative powers herein granted shall be vested in a Congress of the United States, which shall consist of a Senate and House of Representatives.

SECTION 2. THE HOUSE OF REPRESENTATIVES

(1) The House of Representatives shall be composed of members chosen every second year by the people of the several states, and the electors in each state shall have the qualifications requisite for electors of the most numerous branch of the state legislature.

(2) No person shall be a Representative who shall not have attained to the age of twenty-five years, and been seven years a citizen of the United States, and who shall not, when elected, be an inhabitant of that state in which he shall be chosen.

(3) Representatives [*and direct taxes*]** shall be apportioned among the several states which may be included within this Union, according to their respective numbers [*which shall be determined by adding to the whole number of free persons, including those bound to service for a term of years, and excluding Indians not taxed, three-fifths of all other persons*]. The actual enumeration shall be made within three years after the first meeting of the Congress of the United States, and within every subsequent term of ten years, in such manner as they shall by law direct. The number of Representatives shall not exceed one for every 30,000, but each state shall have at least one Representative [*; and until such enumeration shall be made, the State of New Hampshire shall be entitled to choose three; Massachusetts eight; Rhode Island and Providence Plantations one; Connecticut five; New York six; New Jersey four; Pennsylvania eight; Delaware one; Maryland six; Virginia ten; North Carolina five; South Carolina five; and Georgia three*].

*Titles have been added to make the Constitution easier to read. They did not appear in the original document.
**The parts of the Constitution that no longer apply are printed in italics within brackets [ ]. These portions have been changed or set aside by later amendments.

PREAMBLE
The introduction to the Constitution states the purposes and principles for writing it. The writers wanted to set up a fairer form of government and to secure peace and freedom for themselves and for future generations.

CONGRESS
Congress has the authority to make laws. Congress is made up of two groups of lawmakers: the Senate and the House of Representatives.

(1) ELECTION AND TERM OF MEMBERS
Qualified voters are to elect members of the House of Representatives every two years. Each member of the House of Representatives must meet certain requirements.

(2) QUALIFICATIONS
Members of the House of Representatives must be at least 25 years old. They must have been citizens of the United States for at least seven years. They must live in the state that they will represent.

(3) DETERMINING APPORTIONMENT
The number of representatives a state may have depends on the number of people living in each state. Every ten years the federal government must take a census, or count, of the population in every state. Every state will have at least one representative.

(4) FILLING VACANCIES

If there is a vacancy in representation in Congress, the governor of the state involved must call a special election to fill it.

(5) SPECIAL AUTHORITY

The House of Representatives chooses a Speaker as its presiding officer. It also chooses other officers as appropriate. The House is the only government branch that may impeach, or charge, an official in the executive branch or a judge of the federal courts for failing to carry out his or her duties. These cases are tried in the Senate.

(1) NUMBER, TERM, AND SELECTION OF MEMBERS

Each state is represented by two senators. Until Amendment 17 was passed, state legislatures chose the senators for their states. Each senator serves a six-year term and has one vote in Congress.

(2) OVERLAPPING TERMS AND FILLING VACANCIES

One-third of the senators are elected every two years for a six-year term. This grouping allows at least two-thirds of the experienced senators to remain in the Senate after each election. Amendment 17 permits state governors to appoint a replacement to fill a vacancy until the next election is held.

(3) QUALIFICATIONS

Senators must be at least 30 years old. They must have been citizens of the United States for at least nine years. They must live in the state that they will represent.

(4) PRESIDENT OF THE SENATE

The Vice President acts as chief officer of the Senate but does not vote unless there is a tie.

(5) OTHER OFFICERS

The Senate chooses its other officers and a president pro tempore, who serves if the Vice President is not present or if the Vice President becomes President. *Pro tempore* is a Latin term meaning "for the time being."

(4) When vacancies happen in the representation from any state, the executive authority thereof shall issue writs of election to fill such vacancies.

(5) The House of Representatives shall choose their Speaker and other officers; and shall have the sole power of impeachment.

SECTION 3. THE SENATE

(1) The Senate of the United States shall be composed of two Senators from each state [*chosen by the legislature thereof*], for six years, and each Senator shall have one vote.

(2) [*Immediately after they shall be assembled in consequence of the first election, they shall be divided as equally as may be into three classes. The seats of the Senators of the first class shall be vacated at the expiration of the second year, of the second class at the expiration of the fourth year, and of the third class at the expiration of the sixth year, so that one-third may be chosen every second year; and if vacancies happen by resignation, or otherwise, during the recess of the legislature of any state, the executive thereof may make temporary appointments until the next meeting of the legislature, which shall then fill such vacancies.*]

(3) No person shall be a Senator who shall not have attained to the age of thirty years, and been nine years a citizen of the United States, and who shall not, when elected, be an inhabitant of that state for which he shall be chosen.

(4) The Vice President of the United States shall be President of the Senate, but shall have no vote, unless they be equally divided.

(5) The Senate shall choose their other officers, and also a President *pro tempore*, in the absence of the Vice President, or when he shall exercise the office of the President of the United States.

(6) The Senate shall have the sole power to try all impeachments. When sitting for that purpose, they shall be on oath or affirmation. When the President of the United States is tried, the Chief Justice shall preside; and no person shall be convicted without the concurrence of two-thirds of the members present.

(7) Judgment in cases of impeachment shall not extend further than to removal from office, and disqualification to hold and enjoy any office of honor, trust, or profit under the United States; but the party convicted shall nevertheless be liable and subject to indictment, trial, judgment and punishment, according to law.

SECTION 4. ELECTIONS AND MEETINGS

(1) The times, places, and manner of holding elections for senators and representatives shall be prescribed in each state by the legislature thereof; but the Congress may at any time by law make or alter such regulations, [*except as to the places of choosing Senators*].

(2) The Congress shall assemble at least once in every year, [*and such meeting shall be on the first Monday in December, unless they shall by law appoint a different day*].

SECTION 5. RULES OF PROCEDURE

(1) Each house shall be the judge of the elections, returns and qualifications of its own members, and a majority of each shall constitute a quorum to do business; but a smaller number may adjourn from day to day, and may be authorized to compel the attendance of absent members, in such manner and under such penalties as each house may provide.

(2) Each house may determine the rules of its proceedings, punish its members for disorderly behavior, and, with the concurrence of two-thirds, expel a member.

(3) Each house shall keep a journal of its proceedings, and from time to time publish the same, excepting such parts as may in their judgment require secrecy; and the yeas and nays of the members of either house on any question shall, at the desire of one-fifth of those present, be entered on the journal.

(6) IMPEACHMENT TRIALS
If the House of Representatives votes articles of impeachment, the Senate holds a trial. A two-thirds vote is required to convict a person who has been impeached.

(7) PENALTY FOR CONVICTION
If convicted in an impeachment case, an official is removed from office and may never hold office in the United States government again. The convicted person may also be tried in a regular court of law for any crimes.

(1) HOLDING ELECTIONS
Each state makes its own rules about electing senators and representatives. However, Congress may change these rules at any time. Today congressional elections are held on the Tuesday after the first Monday in November, during even-numbered years.

(2) MEETINGS
The Constitution requires Congress to meet at least once a year. That day is the first Monday in December, unless Congress sets a different day. Amendment 20 changed this date to January 3.

(1) ORGANIZATION
Each house of Congress may decide if its members have been elected fairly and are able to hold office. Each house may do business only when a quorum—a majority of its members—is present. By less than a majority vote, each house may compel absent members to attend.

(2) RULES
Each house may decide its own rules for doing business, punish its members, and expel a member from office if two-thirds of the members agree.

(3) JOURNAL
The Constitution requires each house to keep records of its activities and to publish these records from time to time. The House Journal and the Senate Journal are published at the end of each session. How each member voted must be recorded if one-fifth of the members ask for this to be done.

(4) ADJOURNMENT
While Congress is in session, neither house may take a recess for more than three days without the consent of the other.

(1) PAY AND PRIVILEGES
Members of Congress set their own salaries, which are to be paid by the federal government. Members cannot be arrested or sued for anything they say while Congress is in session. This privilege is called congressional immunity. Members of Congress may be arrested while Congress is in session only if they commit a crime.

(2) RESTRICTIONS
Members of Congress may not hold any other federal office while serving in Congress. A member may not resign from office and then take a government position created during that member's term of office or for which the pay has been increased during that member's term of office.

(1) MONEY-RAISING BILLS
All money-raising bills must be introduced first in the House of Representatives, but the Senate may suggest changes.

(2) HOW A BILL BECOMES A LAW
After a bill has been passed by both the House of Representatives and the Senate, it must be sent to the President. If the President approves and signs the bill, it becomes law. The President can also veto, or refuse to sign, the bill. Congress can override a veto by passing the bill again by a two-thirds majority. If the President does not act within ten days, two things may happen. If Congress is still in session, the bill becomes a law. If Congress ends its session within that same ten-day period, the bill does not become a law.

(3) ORDERS AND RESOLUTIONS
Congress can pass orders and resolutions, some of which have the same effect as a law. Congress may decide on its own when to end the session. Other such acts must be signed or vetoed by the President.

(4) Neither house, during the session of Congress, shall, without the consent of the other, adjourn for more than three days, nor to any other place than that in which the two houses shall be sitting.

SECTION 6. PRIVILEGES AND RESTRICTIONS
(1) The Senators and Representatives shall receive a compensation for their services, to be ascertained by law and paid out of the Treasury of the United States. They shall in all cases, except treason, felony, and breach of the peace, be privileged from arrest during their attendance at the session of their respective houses, and in going to and returning from the same; and for any speech or debate in either house, they shall not be questioned in any other place.

(2) No Senator or Representative shall, during the time for which he was elected, be appointed to any civil office under the authority of the United States, which shall have been created, or the emoluments whereof shall have been increased, during such time; and no person holding any office under the United States shall be a member of either house during his continuance in office.

SECTION 7. MAKING LAWS
(1) All bills for raising revenue shall originate in the House of Representatives; but the Senate may propose or concur with amendments as on other bills.

(2) Every bill which shall have passed the House of Representatives and the Senate shall, before it become a law, be presented to the President of the United States; if he approve, he shall sign it, but if not, he shall return it, with his objections, to that house in which it shall have originated, who shall enter the objections at large on their journal, and proceed to reconsider it. If after such reconsideration two-thirds of that house shall agree to pass the bill, it shall be sent, together with the objections, to the other house, by which it shall likewise be reconsidered, and, if approved by two-thirds of that house, it shall become a law. But in all such cases the votes of both houses shall be determined by yeas and nays, and the names of the persons voting for and against the bill shall be entered on the journal of each house respectively. If any bill shall not be returned by the President within ten days (Sundays excepted) after it shall have been presented to him, the same bill shall be a law, in like manner as if he had signed it, unless the Congress by their adjournment prevent its return, in which case it shall not be a law.

(3) Every order, resolution, or vote to which the concurrence of the Senate and House of Representatives may be necessary (except on a question of adjournment) shall be presented to the President of the United States; and before the same shall take effect, shall be approved by him, or being disapproved by him, shall be repassed by two-thirds of the Senate and House of Representatives, according to the rules and limitations prescribed in the case of a bill.

SECTION 8. POWERS DELEGATED TO CONGRESS

The Congress shall have power

(1) To lay and collect taxes, duties, imposts and excises, to pay the debts and provide for the common defense and general welfare of the United States; but all duties, imposts and excises shall be uniform throughout the United States;

(2) To borrow money on the credit of the United States;

(3) To regulate commerce with foreign nations, and among the several states [*and with the Indian tribes*];

(4) To establish a uniform rule of naturalization, and uniform laws on the subject of bankruptcies throughout the United States;

(5) To coin money, regulate the value thereof, and of foreign coin, and fix the standard of weights and measures;

(6) To provide for the punishment of counterfeiting the securities and current coin of the United States;

(7) To establish post offices and post roads;

(8) To promote the progress of science and useful arts by securing for limited times to authors and inventors the exclusive right to their respective writings and discoveries;

(9) To constitute tribunals inferior to the Supreme Court;

(10) To define and punish piracies and felonies committed on the high seas and offenses against the law of nations;

(1) TAXATION

Only Congress has the authority to raise money to pay debts, defend the United States, and provide services for its people by collecting taxes or tariffs on foreign goods. All taxes must be applied equally in all states.

(2) BORROWING MONEY

Congress may borrow money for national use. This is usually done by selling government bonds.

(3) COMMERCE

Congress can control trade with other countries and between states.

(4) NATURALIZATION AND BANKRUPTCY

Congress decides what requirements people from other countries must meet to become United States citizens. Congress can also pass laws to protect people who are bankrupt, or cannot pay their debts.

(5) COINS, WEIGHTS, AND MEASURES

Congress can print and coin money and decide its value. Congress also decides on the system of weights and measures to be used throughout the nation.

(6) COUNTERFEITING

Congress may pass laws to punish people who make fake money, bonds, or stamps.

(7) POSTAL SERVICE

Congress can build post offices and make rules about the postal system and the roads used for mail delivery.

(8) COPYRIGHTS AND PATENTS

Congress can issue patents and copyrights to inventors and authors to protect the ownership of their works.

(9) FEDERAL COURTS

Congress can establish a system of federal courts under the Supreme Court.

(10) CRIMES AT SEA

Congress can pass laws to punish people for crimes committed at sea. Congress may also punish United States citizens for breaking international law.

(11) DECLARING WAR
Only Congress can declare war.

(12) THE ARMY
Congress can establish an army, but it cannot vote enough money to support it for more than two years. This part of the Constitution was written to keep the army under civilian control.

(13) THE NAVY
Congress can establish a navy and vote enough money to support it for as long as necessary. No time limit was set because people thought the navy was less of a threat to people's liberty than the army was.

(14) MILITARY REGULATIONS
Congress makes the rules that guide and govern all the armed forces.

(15) THE MILITIA
Each state has its own militia, now known as the National Guard. The National Guard can be called into federal service by the President, as authorized by Congress, to enforce laws, to stop uprisings against the government, or to protect the people in case of floods, earthquakes, and other disasters.

(16) CONTROL OF THE MILITIA
Congress helps each state support the National Guard. Each state may appoint its own officers and train its own guard according to rules set by Congress.

(17) NATIONAL CAPITAL AND OTHER PROPERTY
Congress may pass laws to govern the nation's capital (Washington, D.C.) and any land owned by the government.

(18) OTHER NECESSARY LAWS
The Constitution allows Congress to make laws that are necessary to enforce the powers listed in Article I. This clause allows Congress to stretch its authority when new situations arise.

(11) To declare war, [*grant letters of marque and reprisal,*] and make rules concerning captures on land and water;

(12) To raise and support armies, but no appropriation of money to that use shall be for a longer term than two years;

(13) To provide and maintain a navy;

(14) To make rules for the government and regulation of the land and naval forces;

(15) To provide for calling forth the militia to execute the laws of the Union, suppress insurrections and repel invasions;

(16) To provide for organizing, arming, and disciplining the militia, and for governing such part of them as may be employed in the service of the United States, reserving to the states, respectively, the appointment of the officers, and the authority of training the militia according to the discipline prescribed by Congress;

(17) To exercise exclusive legislation in all cases whatsoever, over such district (not exceeding ten miles square) as may, by cession of particular states, and the acceptance of Congress, become the seat of government of the United States, and to exercise like authority over all places purchased by the consent of the legislature of the state in which the same shall be, for the erection of forts, magazines, arsenals, dock-yards, and other needful buildings; —and

(18) To make all laws which shall be necessary and proper for carrying into execution the foregoing powers, and all other powers vested by this Constitution in the government of the United States, or in any department or officer thereof.

SECTION 9. POWERS DENIED TO CONGRESS

(1) [*The migration or importation of such persons as any of the states now existing shall think proper to admit shall not be prohibited by the Congress prior to the year 1808; but a tax or duty may be imposed on such importation, not exceeding 10 dollars for each person.*]

(2) The privilege of the writ of habeas corpus shall not be suspended, unless when in cases of rebellion or invasion the public safety may require it.

(3) No bill of attainder or ex post facto law shall be passed.

(4) [*No capitation or other direct tax shall be laid, unless in proportion to the census or enumeration herein before directed to be taken.*]

(5) No tax or duty shall be laid on articles exported from any state.

(6) No preference shall be given by any regulation of commerce or revenue to the ports of one state over those of another; nor shall vessels bound to, or from, one state, be obliged to enter, clear, or pay duties in another.

(7) No money shall be drawn from the Treasury, but in consequence of appropriations made by law; and a regular statement and account of the receipts and expenditures of all public money shall be published from time to time.

---

(1) SLAVE TRADE
Some authority is not given to Congress. Congress could not prevent the slave trade until 1808, but it could put a tax of ten dollars on each slave brought into the United States. After 1808 when a law was passed to stop slaves from being brought into the United States, this section no longer applied.

(2) HABEAS CORPUS
A writ of habeas corpus is a privilege that entitles a person to a hearing before a judge. The judge must then decide if there is good reason for that person to have been arrested. If not, that person must be released. The government is not allowed to take this privilege away except during a national emergency, such as an invasion or a rebellion.

(3) SPECIAL LAWS
Congress cannot pass laws that impose punishment on a named individual or group, except in cases of treason. Article III sets limits to punishments for treason. Congress also cannot pass laws that punish a person for an action that was legal when it was done.

(4) DIRECT TAXES
Congress cannot set a direct tax on people, unless it is in proportion to the total population. Amendment 16, which provides for the income tax, is an exception.

(5) EXPORT TAXES
Congress cannot tax goods sent from one state to another or from a state to another country.

(6) PORTS
When making trade laws, Congress cannot favor one state over another. Congress cannot require ships from one state to pay a duty to enter another state.

(7) PUBLIC MONEY
The government cannot spend money from the treasury unless Congress passes a law allowing it to do so. A written record must be kept of all money spent by the government.

(8) TITLES OF NOBILITY AND GIFTS

The United States government cannot grant titles of nobility. Government officials cannot accept gifts from other countries without the permission of Congress. This clause was intended to prevent government officials from being bribed by other nations.

(1) COMPLETE RESTRICTIONS

The Constitution does not allow states to act as if they were individual countries. No state government may make a treaty with other countries. No state can print its own money.

(2) PARTIAL RESTRICTIONS

No state government can tax imported or exported goods without the consent of Congress. States may charge a fee to inspect these goods, but profits must be given to the United States Treasury.

(3) OTHER RESTRICTIONS

No state government may tax ships entering its ports unless Congress approves. No state may keep an army or navy during times of peace other than the National Guard. No state can enter into agreements called compacts with other states without the consent of Congress.

(1) TERM OF OFFICE

The President has the authority to carry out our nation's laws. The term of office for both the President and the Vice President is four years.

(2) THE ELECTORAL COLLEGE

This group of people is to be chosen by the voters of each state to elect the President and Vice President. The number of electors in each state is equal to the number of senators and representatives that state has in Congress.

(3) ELECTION PROCESS

This clause describes in detail how the electors were to choose the President and Vice President. In 1804 Amendment 12 changed the process for electing the President and the Vice President.

---

(8) No title of nobility shall be granted by the United States; and no person holding any office of profit or trust under them, shall, without the consent of the Congress, accept of any present, emolument, office, or title, of any kind whatever, from any king, prince, or foreign state.

SECTION 10. POWERS DENIED TO THE STATES

(1) No state shall enter into any treaty, alliance, or confederation; grant letters of marque and reprisal; coin money; emit bills of credit; make anything but gold and silver coin a tender in payment of debts; pass any bill of attainder, ex post facto law, or law impairing the obligation of contracts, or grant any title of nobility.

(2) No state shall, without the consent of the Congress, lay any imposts or duties on imports or exports, except what may be absolutely necessary for executing its inspection laws; and the net produce of all duties and imposts, laid by any state on imports or exports, shall be for the use of the Treasury of the United States; and all such laws shall be subject to the revision and control of the Congress.

(3) No state shall, without the consent of Congress, lay any duty of tonnage, keep troops, or ships of war in time of peace, enter into any agreement or compact with another state, or with a foreign power, or engage in war, unless actually invaded, or in such imminent danger as will not admit of delay.

ARTICLE II
THE EXECUTIVE BRANCH

SECTION 1. PRESIDENT AND VICE PRESIDENT

(1) The executive power shall be vested in a President of the United States of America. He shall hold his office during the term of four years, and together with the Vice President, chosen for the same term, be elected as follows:

(2) Each state shall appoint, in such manner as the legislature thereof may direct, a number of electors, equal to the whole number of Senators and Representatives to which the state may be entitled in the Congress; but no Senator or Representative, or person holding an office of trust or profit under the United States, shall be appointed an elector.

(3) [*The electors shall meet in their respective states, and vote by ballot for two persons, of whom one at least shall not be an inhabitant of the same state with themselves. And they shall make a list of all the persons voted for, and of the number of votes for each; which list they shall sign and certify, and transmit sealed to the seat of the government of the United States, directed to the president of the Senate. The president of the Senate shall, in the presence of the Senate and House of Representatives, open all the certificates, and the votes shall then be counted. The person having the greatest number of votes shall be the President, if such number be a majority of the whole number of electors*

appointed; and if there be more than one who have such majority, and have an equal number of votes, then the House of Representatives shall immediately choose by ballot one of them for President; and if no person have a majority, then from the five highest on the list the said House shall in like manner choose the President. But in choosing the President the votes shall be taken by states, the representation from each state having one vote: A quorum for this purpose shall consist of a member or members from two-thirds of the states, and a majority of all the states shall be necessary to a choice. In every case, after the choice of the President, the person having the greatest number of votes of the electors shall be the Vice President. But if there should remain two or more who have equal votes, the Senate shall choose from them by ballot the Vice President.]*

(4) The Congress may determine the time of choosing the electors, and the day on which they shall give their votes; which day shall be the same throughout the United States.

(5) No person except a natural-born citizen [*or a citizen of the United States, at the time of the adoption of this Constitution,*] shall be eligible to the office of the President; neither shall any person be eligible to that office who shall not have attained to the age of thirty-five years, and been fourteen years a resident within the United States.

(6) [*In case of the removal of the President from office, or of his death, resignation, or inability to discharge the powers and duties of the said office, the same shall devolve on the Vice President, and the Congress may by law provide for the case of removal, death, resignation or inability, both of the President and Vice President, declaring what officer shall then act as President, and such officer shall act accordingly, until the disability be removed, or a President shall be elected.*]

(7) The President shall, at stated times, receive for his services, a compensation, which shall neither be increased nor diminished during the period for which he shall have been elected, and he shall not receive within that period any other emolument from the United States, or any of them.

(8) Before he enter on the execution of his office, he shall take the following oath or affirmation:—"I do solemnly swear (or affirm) that I will faithfully execute the office of President of the United States, and will to the best of my ability, preserve, protect, and defend the Constitution of the United States."

SECTION 2. POWERS OF THE PRESIDENT
(1) The President shall be Commander in Chief of the Army and Navy of the United States, and of the militia of the several states, when called into the actual service of the United States; he may require the opinion, in writing, of the principal officer in each of the executive departments, upon any subject relating to the duties of their respective offices, and he shall have power to grant reprieves and pardons for offenses against the United States, except in cases of impeachment.

(4) TIME OF ELECTIONS
Congress decides the day the electors are to be elected and the day they are to vote.

(5) QUALIFICATIONS
The President must be at least 35 years old, be a citizen of the United States by birth, and have been living in the United States for fourteen years or more.

(6) VACANCIES
If the President dies, resigns, or is removed from office, the Vice President becomes President.

(7) SALARY
The President receives a salary that cannot be raised or lowered during a term of office. The President may not be paid any additional salary by the federal government or any state or local government. Today the President's salary is $200,000 a year plus expenses such as housing, travel, and entertainment.

(8) OATH OF OFFICE
Before taking office, the President must promise to perform the duties faithfully and to protect the country's form of government. Usually the Chief Justice of the Supreme Court administers the oath of office.

(1) THE PRESIDENT'S LEADERSHIP
The President is the commander of the nation's armed forces and of the National Guard when it is in service of the nation. All government officials of the executive branch must report their actions to the President when asked. The President can excuse people from punishment for crimes committed.

(2) TREATIES AND APPOINTMENTS

The President has the authority to make treaties, but they must be approved by a two-thirds vote of the Senate. The President appoints justices to the Supreme Court, ambassadors to other countries, and other federal officials with the Senate's approval.

(3) FILLING VACANCIES

If a government official's position becomes vacant when Congress is not in session, the President can make a temporary appointment.

DUTIES

The President must report to Congress on the condition of the country. This report is now presented in the annual State of the Union message.

IMPEACHMENT

The President, the Vice President, or any government official will be removed from office if impeached, or accused, and then found guilty of treason, bribery, or other serious crimes. The Constitution protects government officials from being impeached for unimportant reasons.

FEDERAL COURTS

The authority to decide legal cases is granted to a Supreme Court and to a system of lower courts established by Congress. The Supreme Court is the highest court in the land. Justices and judges are in their offices for life, subject to good behavior.

(1) GENERAL AUTHORITY

Federal courts have the authority to decide cases that arise under the Constitution, laws, and treaties of the United States. They also have the authority to settle disagreements among states and among citizens of different states, and between a state and a citizen of another state.

(2) SUPREME COURT

The Supreme Court can decide certain cases being tried for the first time. It can review cases that have already been tried in a lower court if the decision has been appealed, or questioned, by one side.

(2) He shall have power, by and with the advice and consent of the Senate, to make treaties, provided two-thirds of the senators present concur; and he shall nominate, and by and with the advice and consent of the Senate, shall appoint ambassadors, other public ministers and consuls, judges of the Supreme Court, and all other officers of the United States, whose appointments are not herein otherwise provided for, and which shall be established by law; but the Congress may by law vest the appointment of such inferior officers, as they think proper, in the President alone, in the courts of law, or in the heads of departments.

(3) The President shall have power to fill up all vacancies that may happen during the recess of the Senate, by granting commissions which shall expire at the end of their next session.

SECTION 3. DUTIES OF THE PRESIDENT

He shall from time to time give to the Congress information of the state of the Union, and recommend to their consideration such measures as he shall judge necessary and expedient; he may, on extraordinary occasions, convene both houses, or either of them, and in case of disagreement between them, with respect to the time of adjournment, he may adjourn them to such time as he shall think proper; he shall receive ambassadors and other public ministers; he shall take care that the laws be faithfully executed, and shall commission all the officers of the United States.

SECTION 4. IMPEACHMENT

The President, Vice President and all civil officers of the United States, shall be removed from office on impeachment for, and conviction of, treason, bribery, or other high crimes and misdemeanors.

ARTICLE III
THE JUDICIAL BRANCH

SECTION 1. FEDERAL COURTS

The judicial power of the United States shall be vested in one Supreme Court, and in such inferior courts as the Congress may from time to time ordain and establish. The judges, both of the supreme and inferior courts, shall hold their offices during good behavior, and shall, at stated times, receive for their services a compensation, which shall not be diminished during their continuance in office.

SECTION 2. AUTHORITY OF THE FEDERAL COURTS

(1) The judicial power shall extend to all cases, in law and equity, arising under this Constitution, the laws of the United States, and treaties made or which shall be made, under their authority; to all cases affecting ambassadors, other public ministers and consuls; to all cases of admiralty and maritime jurisdiction; to controversies to which the United States shall be a party; to controversies between two or more states; [between a state and citizens of another state;] between citizens of different states; —between citizens of the same state claiming lands under grants of different states, [and between a state or the citizens thereof, and foreign states, citizens, or subjects.]

(2) In all cases affecting ambassadors, other public ministers and consuls, and those in which a state shall be party, the Supreme Court shall have original jurisdiction. In all the other cases before mentioned, the Supreme Court shall have appellate jurisdiction, both as to law and fact, with such exceptions, and under such regulations as the Congress shall make.

(3) The trial of all crimes, except in cases of impeachment, shall be by jury; and such trial shall be held in the state where the said crimes shall have been committed; but when not committed within any state, the trial shall be at such place or places as the Congress may by law have directed.

SECTION 3. TREASON

(1) Treason against the United States shall consist only in levying war against them, or in adhering to their enemies, giving them aid and comfort. No person shall be convicted of treason unless on the testimony of two witnesses to the same overt act, or on confession in open court.

(2) The Congress shall have power to declare the punishment of treason, but no attainder of treason shall work corruption of blood, or forfeiture except during the life of the person attainted.

ARTICLE IV
RELATIONS AMONG STATES

SECTION 1. OFFICIAL RECORDS

Full faith and credit shall be given in each state to the public acts, records, and judicial proceedings of every other state. And the Congress may by general laws prescribe the manner in which such acts, records, and proceedings shall be proved, and the effect thereof.

SECTION 2. PRIVILEGES OF THE CITIZENS

(1) The citizens of each state shall be entitled to all privileges and immunities of citizens in the several states.

(2) A person charged in any state with treason, felony, or other crime, who shall flee from justice, and be found in another state, shall on demand of the executive authority of the state from which he fled, be delivered up, to be removed to the state having jurisdiction of the crime.

[(3) No person held to service or labor in one state, under the laws thereof, escaping into another, shall in consequence of any law or regulation therein, be discharged from such service or labor, but shall be delivered up on claim of the party to whom such service or labor may be due.]

---

(3) TRIAL BY JURY
The Constitution guarantees a trial by jury for every person charged with a federal crime. Amendments 5, 6, and 7 extend and clarify people's right to a trial by jury.

(1) DEFINITION OF TREASON
Acts that may be considered treason are making war against the United States or helping its enemies. A person cannot be convicted of attempting to overthrow the government unless there are two witnesses to the act or the person confesses in court to treason.

(2) PUNISHMENT FOR TREASON
Congress can decide the punishment for treason, within certain limits.

OFFICIAL RECORDS
Each state must honor the official records and judicial decisions of other states.

(1) PRIVILEGES
A citizen moving from one state to another has the same rights as other citizens living in that person's new state of residence. In some cases, such as voting, people may be required to live in their new state for a certain length of time before obtaining the same privileges as citizens there.

(2) EXTRADITION
At the governor's request, a person who is charged with a crime and who tries to escape justice by crossing into another state may be returned to the state in which the crime was committed.

(3) FUGITIVE SLAVES
The original Constitution required that runaway slaves be returned to their owners. Amendment 13 abolished slavery, eliminating the need for this clause.

(1) ADMISSION OF NEW STATES
Congress has the authority to admit new states to the Union. All new states have the same rights as existing states.

(2) FEDERAL PROPERTY
The Constitution allows Congress to make or change laws governing federal property. This applies to territories and federally owned land within states, such as national parks.

GUARANTEES TO THE STATES
The federal government guarantees that every state have a republican form of government. The United States must also protect the states against invasion and help the states deal with rebellion or local violence.

AMENDING THE CONSTITUTION
Changes to the Constitution may be proposed by a two-thirds vote of both the House of Representatives and the Senate or by a national convention called by Congress when asked by two-thirds of the states. For an amendment to become law, the legislatures or conventions in three-fourths of the states must approve it.

(1) PUBLIC DEBT
Any debt owed by the United States before the Constitution went into effect was to be honored.

(2) FEDERAL SUPREMACY
This clause declares that the Constitution and federal laws are the highest in the nation. Whenever a state law and a federal law are found to disagree, the federal law must be obeyed so long as it is Constitutional.

(3) OATHS OF OFFICE
All federal and state officials must promise to follow and enforce the Constitution. These officials, however, cannot be required to follow a particular religion or satisfy any religious test.

SECTION 3. NEW STATES AND TERRITORIES
(1) New states may be admitted by the Congress into this Union; but no new state shall be formed or erected within the jurisdiction of any other state; nor any state be formed by the junction of two or more states, or parts of states, without the consent of the legislatures of the states concerned as well as of the Congress.

(2) The Congress shall have power to dispose of and make all needful rules and regulations respecting the territory or other property belonging to the United States; and nothing in this Constitution shall be so construed as to prejudice any claims of the United States, or of any particular state.

SECTION 4. GUARANTEES TO THE STATES
The United States shall guarantee to every state in this Union a republican form of government, and shall protect each of them against invasion; and on application of the legislature, or of the executive (when the legislature cannot be convened) against domestic violence.

ARTICLE V
AMENDING THE CONSTITUTION
The Congress, whenever two-thirds of both houses shall deem it necessary, shall propose amendments to this Constitution, or, on the application of the legislatures of two-thirds of the several states, shall call a convention for proposing amendments, which, in either case, shall be valid to all intents and purposes, as part of this Constitution, when ratified by the legislatures of three-fourths of the several states, or by conventions in three-fourths thereof, as the one or the other mode of ratification may be proposed by the Congress; provided that [*no amendment which may be made prior to the year 1808 shall in any manner affect the first and fourth clauses in the Ninth Section of the First Article; and that*] no state, without its consent, shall be deprived of its equal suffrage in the Senate.

ARTICLE VI
GENERAL PROVISIONS
(1) All debts contracted and engagements entered into, before the adoption of this Constitution, shall be as valid against the United States under this Constitution, as under the Confederation.

(2) This Constitution, and the laws of the United States which shall be made in pursuance thereof, and all treaties made, or which shall be made, under the authority of the United States, shall be the supreme law of the land; and the judges in every state shall be bound thereby, anything in the Constitution or laws of any state to the contrary notwithstanding.

(3) The Senators and Representatives before mentioned, and the members of the several state legislatures, and all executive and judicial officers, both of the United States and of the several states, shall be bound by oath or affirmation, to support this Constitution; but no religious test shall ever be required as a qualification to any office or public trust under the United States.

ARTICLE VII
RATIFICATION

The ratification of the conventions of nine states, shall be sufficient for the establishment of this Constitution between the states so ratifying the same.

Done in convention by the unanimous consent of the states present the seventeenth day of September in the year of our Lord one thousand seven hundred and eighty seven and of the independence of the United States of America the Twelfth. In witness whereof we have hereunto subscribed our names.
George Washington—President and deputy from Virginia

DELAWARE
George Read
Gunning Bedford, Jr.
John Dickinson
Richard Bassett
Jacob Broom

MARYLAND
James McHenry
Daniel of St. Thomas Jenifer
Daniel Carroll

VIRGINIA
John Blair
James Madison, Jr.

NORTH CAROLINA
William Blount
Richard Dobbs Spaight
Hugh Williamson

SOUTH CAROLINA
John Rutledge
Charles Cotesworth Pinckney
Charles Pinckney
Pierce Butler

GEORGIA
William Few
Abraham Baldwin

NEW HAMPSHIRE
John Langdon
Nicholas Gilman

MASSACHUSETTS
Nathaniel Gorham
Rufus King

CONNECTICUT
William Samuel Johnson
Roger Sherman

NEW YORK
Alexander Hamilton

NEW JERSEY
William Livingston
David Brearley
William Paterson
Jonathan Dayton

PENNSYLVANIA
Benjamin Franklin
Thomas Mifflin
Robert Morris
George Clymer
Thomas FitzSimons
Jared Ingersoll
James Wilson
Gouverneur Morris

ATTEST: William Jackson, secretary

RATIFICATION
In order for the Constitution to become law, 9 of the 13 states had to approve it. Special conventions were held for this purpose. The process took nine months to complete.

BASIC FREEDOMS
The Constitution guarantees our five basic freedoms of expression. It provides for the freedoms of religion, speech, the press, peaceable assembly, and petition for redress of grievances.

WEAPONS AND THE MILITIA
This amendment was included to prevent the federal government from taking away guns used by state militias.

HOUSING SOLDIERS
The federal government cannot force people to house soldiers in their homes during peacetime. However, Congress may pass laws allowing this during wartime.

SEARCHES AND SEIZURES
This amendment protects people's privacy and safety. Subject to certain exceptions, a law officer cannot search a person or a person's home and belongings unless a judge has issued a valid search warrant. There must be good reason for the search. The warrant must describe the place to be searched and the people or things to be seized, or taken.

RIGHTS OF ACCUSED PERSONS
If a person is accused of a crime that is punishable by death or that is very serious, a grand jury must decide if there is enough evidence to hold a trial. People cannot be tried twice for the same crime, nor can they be forced to testify against themselves. No person shall be fined, jailed, or executed by the government unless the person has been given a fair trial. The government cannot take a person's property for public use unless fair payment is made.

RIGHT TO A FAIR TRIAL
A person accused of a crime has the right to a public trial by an impartial jury, locally chosen. The trial must be held within a reasonable amount of time. The accused person must be told of all charges and have the right to see, hear, and question any

AMENDMENT 1 (1791)***
BASIC FREEDOMS

Congress shall make no law respecting an establishment of religion, or prohibiting the free exercise thereof; or abridging the freedom of speech, or of the press; or the right of the people peaceably to assemble, and to petition the government for a redress of grievances.

AMENDMENT 2 (1791)
WEAPONS AND THE MILITIA

A well-regulated militia, being necessary to the security of a free state, the right of the people to keep and bear arms shall not be infringed.

AMENDMENT 3 (1791)
HOUSING SOLDIERS

No soldier shall, in time of peace, be quartered in any house, without the consent of the owner; nor in time of war, but in a manner to be prescribed by law.

AMENDMENT 4 (1791)
SEARCHES AND SEIZURES

The right of the people to be secure in their persons, houses, papers, and effects, against unreasonable searches and seizures, shall not be violated; and no warrants shall issue but upon probable cause, supported by oath or affirmation, and particularly describing the place to be searched, and the persons or things to be seized.

AMENDMENT 5 (1791)
RIGHTS OF ACCUSED PERSONS

No person shall be held to answer for a capital, or otherwise infamous crime, unless on a presentment or indictment of a grand jury, except in cases arising in the land or naval forces, or in the militia, when in actual service in time of war or public danger; nor shall any person be subject for the same offense to be twice put in jeopardy of life or limb; nor shall be compelled in any criminal case to be a witness against himself; nor be deprived of life, liberty, or property, without due process of law; nor shall private property be taken for public use without just compensation.

AMENDMENT 6 (1791)
RIGHT TO A FAIR TRIAL

In all criminal prosecutions, the accused shall enjoy the right to a speedy and public trial, by an impartial jury of the state and district wherein the crime shall have been committed, which district shall have been previously ascertained by law, and to be informed of the nature and cause of the accusation; to be confronted with the witnesses against him; to have compulsory process for

***The date beside each amendment is the year that the amendment was ratified and became part of the Constitution.

obtaining witnesses in his favor, and to have the assistance of counsel for his defense.

witnesses. The federal government must provide a lawyer free of charge to a person who is accused of a serious crime and who is unable to pay for legal services.

AMENDMENT 7 (1791)
JURY TRIAL IN CIVIL CASES

In suits at common law, where the value in controversy shall exceed 20 dollars, the right of trial by jury shall be preserved, and no fact tried by a jury shall be otherwise re-examined in any court of the United States, than according to the rules of the common law.

JURY TRIAL IN CIVIL CASES
In most federal civil cases involving more than 20 dollars, a jury trial is guaranteed. Civil cases are those disputes between two or more people over money, property, personal injury, or legal rights. Usually civil cases are not tried in federal courts unless much larger sums of money are involved or unless federal courts are given the authority to decide a certain type of case.

AMENDMENT 8 (1791)
BAIL AND PUNISHMENT

Excessive bail shall not be required, nor excessive fines imposed, nor cruel and unusual punishments inflicted.

BAIL AND PUNISHMENT
Courts cannot treat people accused of crimes harshly or punish them in unusual or cruel ways. Bail is money put up as a guarantee that an accused person will appear for trial. In certain cases bail can be denied altogether.

AMENDMENT 9 (1791)
RIGHTS OF THE PEOPLE

The enumeration in the Constitution, of certain rights, shall not be construed to deny or disparage others retained by the people.

RIGHTS OF THE PEOPLE
The federal government must respect all natural rights, whether or not they are listed in the Constitution.

AMENDMENT 10 (1791)
POWERS OF THE STATES AND THE PEOPLE

The powers not delegated to the United States by the Constitution, nor prohibited by it to the states, are reserved to the states respectively, or to the people.

POWERS OF THE STATES AND THE PEOPLE
Any rights not clearly given to the federal government or denied to the states belong to the states or to the people.

AMENDMENT 11 (1798)
SUITS AGAINST STATES

The judicial power of the United States shall not be construed to extend to any suit in law or equity, commenced or prosecuted against one of the United States or citizens of another state, or by citizens or subjects of any foreign state.

SUITS AGAINST STATES
A citizen of one state cannot sue another state in federal court.

ELECTION OF PRESIDENT AND VICE PRESIDENT

This amendment replaces the part of Article II, Section 1, that originally explained the process of electing the President and Vice President. Amendment 12 was an important step in the development of the two-party system. It allows a party to nominate its own candidates.

AMENDMENT 12 (1804)
ELECTION OF PRESIDENT AND VICE PRESIDENT

The electors shall meet in their respective states, and vote by ballot for President and Vice President, one of whom, at least, shall not be an inhabitant of the same state with themselves; they shall name in their ballots the person voted for as President, and in distinct ballots the person voted for as Vice President, and they shall make distinct lists of all persons voted for as President, and of all persons voted for as Vice President, and of the number of votes for each, which lists they shall sign and certify, and transmit, sealed, to the seat of government of the United States, directed to the President of the Senate; the President of the Senate shall, in the presence of the Senate and House of Representatives, open all the certificates, and the votes shall then be counted; the person having the greatest number of votes for President shall be the President, if such a number be a majority of the whole number of electors appointed; and if no person have such majority, then from the persons having the highest numbers not exceeding three on the list of those voted for as President, the House of Representatives shall choose immediately, by ballot, the President. But in choosing the President, the votes shall be taken by states, the representation from each state having one vote; a quorum for this purpose shall consist of a member or members from two thirds of the states, and a majority of all the states shall be necessary to a choice. [*And if the House of Representatives shall not choose a President whenever the right of choice shall devolve upon them, before the fourth day of March next following, then the Vice President shall act as President, as in the case of the death or other constitutional disability of the President.*] The person having the greatest number of votes as Vice President, shall be the Vice President, if such number be a majority of the whole number of electors appointed, and if no person have a majority, then, from the two highest numbers on the list the Senate shall choose the Vice President; a quorum for the purpose shall consist of two thirds of the whole number of Senators, and a majority of the whole number shall be necessary to a choice. But no person constitutionally ineligible to the office of President shall be eligible to that of Vice President of the United States.

END OF SLAVERY

People cannot be forced to work against their will unless they have been tried for and convicted of a crime for which this means of punishment is ordered. Congress may enforce this by law.

AMENDMENT 13 (1865)
END OF SLAVERY

SECTION 1. ABOLITION

Neither slavery nor involuntary servitude, except as a punishment for crime whereof the party shall have been duly convicted, shall exist within the United States, or any place subject to their jurisdiction.

SECTION 2. ENFORCEMENT

Congress shall have power to enforce this article by appropriate legislation.

CITIZENSHIP

All persons born or naturalized in the United States are citizens of the United States and of the state in which they live. State governments may not deny any citizen the full rights of citizenship. This amendment also guarantees due process of law. According to due process of law, no state may take away the rights of a citizen. All citizens must be protected equally under law.

AMENDMENT 14 (1868)
RIGHTS OF CITIZENS

SECTION 1. CITIZENSHIP

All persons born or naturalized in the United States and subject to the jurisdiction thereof, are citizens of the United States and of the state wherein they reside. No state shall make or enforce any law which shall abridge the privileges or immunities of citizens of the United States, nor shall any state deprive any person of life, liberty, or property, without due process of law; nor deny to any person within its jurisdiction the equal protection of the laws.

SECTION 2. NUMBER OF REPRESENTATIVES

Representatives shall be apportioned among the several states according to their respective numbers, counting the whole number of persons in each state, [*excluding Indians not taxed*]. But when the right to vote at any election for the choice of electors for President and Vice President of the United States, representatives in Congress, the executive and judicial officers of a state, or the members of the legislature thereof, is denied to any of the [*male*] inhabitants of such state, being [*twenty-one years of age and*] citizens of the United States, or in any way abridged, except for participation in rebellion or other crime, the basis of representation therein shall be reduced in the proportion which the number of such [*male*] citizens shall bear to the whole number of [*male*] citizens [*twenty-one years of age*] in such state.

SECTION 3. PENALTY FOR REBELLION

No person shall be a Senator or Representative in Congress, or elector of President and Vice President, or hold any office, civil or military, under the United States, or under any state, who, having previously taken an oath, as a member of Congress, or as an officer of the United States, or as a member of any state legislature, or as an executive or judicial officer of any state, to support the Constitution of the United States, shall have engaged in insurrection or rebellion against the same, or given aid or comfort to the enemies thereof. But Congress may, by a vote of two thirds of each house, remove such disability.

SECTION 4. GOVERNMENT DEBT

The validity of the public debt of the United States, authorized by law, including debts incurred for payment of pensions and bounties for services in suppressing insurrection or rebellion, shall not be questioned. But neither the United States nor any state shall assume or pay any debt or obligation incurred in aid of insurrection or rebellion against the United States, [*or any claim for the loss or emancipation of any slave;*] but all such debts, obligations, and claims shall be held illegal and void.

SECTION 5. ENFORCEMENT

The Congress shall have power to enforce, by appropriate legislation, the provisions of this article.

AMENDMENT 15 (1870)
VOTING RIGHTS

SECTION 1. RIGHT TO VOTE

The right of citizens of the United States to vote shall not be denied or abridged by the United States or by any state on account of race, color, or previous condition of servitude.

SECTION 2. ENFORCEMENT

The Congress shall have power to enforce this article by appropriate legislation.

AMENDMENT 16 (1913)
INCOME TAX

The Congress shall have power to lay and collect taxes on incomes, from whatever source derived, without apportionment among the several states, and without regard to any census or enumeration.

NUMBER OF REPRESENTATIVES
Each state's representation in Congress is based on its total population. Any state denying eligible citizens the right to vote will have its representation in Congress decreased. This clause abolished the Three-fifths Compromise in Article I, Section 2. Later amendments granted women the right to vote and lowered the voting age to 18.

PENALTY FOR REBELLION
No person who has rebelled against the United States may hold federal office. This clause was originally added to punish the leaders of the Confederacy for failing to support the Constitution of the United States.

GOVERNMENT DEBT
The federal government is responsible for all public debts. It is not responsible, however, for Confederate debts or for debts that result from any rebellion against the United States.

ENFORCEMENT
Congress may enforce these provisions by law.

RIGHT TO VOTE
No state may prevent a citizen from voting simply because of race or color or condition of previous servitude. This amendment was designed to extend voting rights to former slaves. Congress may enforce this by law.

INCOME TAX
Congress has the power to collect taxes on its citizens based on their personal incomes rather than on the number of people living in a state.

DIRECT ELECTION OF SENATORS
Originally, state legislatures elected senators. This amendment allows the people of each state to elect their own senators directly. The idea is to make senators more responsible to the people they represent.

PROHIBITION
This amendment made it illegal to make, sell, or transport liquor within the United States or to transport it out of the United States or its territories. Amendment 18 was the first to include a time limit for approval. If not ratified within seven years, it would be repealed, or canceled. Many later amendments have included similar time limits.

WOMEN'S VOTING RIGHTS
This amendment granted women the right to vote.

TERMS OF OFFICE
The terms of the President and the Vice President begin on January 20, in the year following their election. Members of Congress take office on January 3. Before this amendment newly elected members of Congress did not begin their terms until March 4. This meant that those who had run for reelection and been defeated remained in office for four months.

AMENDMENT 17 (1913)
DIRECT ELECTION OF SENATORS

SECTION 1. METHOD OF ELECTION
The Senate of the United States shall be composed of two Senators from each state, elected by the people thereof, for six years; and each Senator shall have one vote. The electors in each state shall have the qualifications requisite for electors of the most numerous branch of the state legislatures.

SECTION 2. VACANCIES
When vacancies happen in the representation of any state in the Senate, the executive authority of such state shall issue writs of election to fill such vacancies: *Provided*, that the legislature of any state may empower the executive thereof to make temporary appointments until the people fill the vacancies by election as the legislature may direct.

SECTION 3. EXCEPTION
[*This amendment shall not be so construed as to affect the election or term of any Senator chosen before it becomes valid as part of the Constitution.*]

AMENDMENT 18 (1919)
BAN ON ALCOHOLIC DRINKS

SECTION 1. PROHIBITION
[*After one year from the ratification of this article the manufacture, sale, or transportation of intoxicating liquors within, the importation thereof into, or the exportation thereof from the United States and all territory subject to the jurisdiction thereof for beverage purposes is hereby prohibited.*]

SECTION 2. ENFORCEMENT
[*The Congress and the several states shall have concurrent power to enforce this article by appropriate legislation.*]

SECTION 3. RATIFICATION
[*This article shall be inoperative unless it shall have been ratified as an amendment to the Constitution by the legislatures of the several states as provided in the Constitution, within seven years from the date of the submission hereof to the states by the Congress.*]

AMENDMENT 19 (1920)
WOMEN'S VOTING RIGHTS

SECTION 1. RIGHT TO VOTE
The right of citizens of the United States to vote shall not be denied or abridged by the United States or by any state on account of sex.

SECTION 2. ENFORCEMENT
Congress shall have power to enforce this article by appropriate legislation.

AMENDMENT 20 (1933)
TERMS OF OFFICE

SECTION 1. BEGINNING OF TERMS
The terms of the President and Vice President shall end at noon on the 20th day of January, and the terms of Senators and Representatives at noon on the 3rd day of January, of the years in which such terms would have ended if this article had not been ratified; and the terms of their successors shall then begin.

SECTION 2. SESSIONS OF CONGRESS

The Congress shall assemble at least once in every year, and such meeting shall begin at noon on the 3rd day of January, unless they shall by law appoint a different day.

SECTION 3. PRESIDENTIAL SUCCESSION

If, at the time fixed for the beginning of the term of the President, the President-elect shall have died, the Vice President-elect shall become President. If a President shall not have been chosen before the time fixed for the beginning of his term, or if the President-elect shall have failed to qualify, then the Vice President-elect shall act as President until a President shall have qualified; and the Congress may by law provide for the case wherein neither a President-elect nor a Vice President-elect shall have qualified, declaring who shall then act as President, or the manner in which one who is to act shall be selected and such person shall act accordingly until a President or Vice President shall be qualified.

SECTION 4. ELECTIONS DECIDED BY CONGRESS

The Congress may by law provide for the case of the death of any of the persons from whom the House of Representatives may choose a President whenever the right of choice shall have devolved upon them, and for the case of the death of any of the persons from whom the Senate may choose a Vice President whenever the right of choice shall have devolved upon them.

SECTION 5. EFFECTIVE DATE

[*Sections 1 and 2 shall take effect on the 15th day of October following the ratification of this article.*]

SECTION 6. RATIFICATION

[*This article shall be inoperative unless it shall have been ratified as an amendment to the Constitution by the legislatures of three fourths of the several states within seven years from the date of its submission.*]

AMENDMENT 21 (1933)
END OF PROHIBITION

SECTION 1. REPEAL OF AMENDMENT 18

The eighteenth article of amendment to the Constitution of the United States is hereby repealed.

SECTION 2. STATE LAWS

The transportation or importation into any state, territory, or possession of the United States for delivery or use therein of intoxicating liquors, in violation of the laws thereof, is hereby prohibited.

SECTION 3. RATIFICATION

[*This article shall be inoperative unless it shall have been ratified as an amendment to the Constitution by conventions in the several states, as provided in the Constitution within seven years from the date of the submission hereof to the states by Congress.*]

TWO-TERM LIMIT FOR PRESIDENTS

A President may not serve more than two full terms in office. Any President who serves less than two years of a previous President's term may be elected for two more terms.

PRESIDENTIAL ELECTORS FOR DISTRICT OF COLUMBIA

This amendment grants three electoral votes to the national capital.

BAN ON POLL TAXES

No United States citizen may be prevented from voting in a federal election because of failing to pay a tax to vote. Poll taxes had been used in some states to prevent African Americans from voting.

PRESIDENTIAL VACANCY

If the President resigns from or dies while in office, the Vice President becomes President.

AMENDMENT 22 (1951)
TWO-TERM LIMIT FOR PRESIDENTS

SECTION 1. TWO-TERM LIMIT

No person shall be elected to the office of the President more than twice, and no person who has held the office of President, or acted as President, for more than two years of a term to which some other person was elected President shall be elected to the office of the President more than once. [*But this article shall not apply to any person holding the office of President when this article was proposed by the Congress, and shall not prevent any person who may be holding the office of President, or acting as President, during the term within which this article becomes operative from holding the office of President, or acting as President, during the remainder of such term.*]

SECTION 2. RATIFICATION

[*This article shall be inoperative unless it shall have been ratified as an amendment to the Constitution by the legislatures of three-fourths of the several states within seven years from the date of its submission to the states by the Congress.*]

AMENDMENT 23 (1961)
PRESIDENTIAL ELECTORS FOR DISTRICT OF COLUMBIA

SECTION 1. NUMBER OF ELECTORS

The District constituting the seat of Government of the United States shall appoint in such manner as Congress may direct:

A number of electors of President and Vice President equal to the whole number of Senators and Representatives in Congress to which the District would be entitled if it were a state, but in no event more than the least populous state; they shall be in addition to those appointed by the states, but they shall be considered, for the purposes of the election of President and Vice President, to be electors appointed by a state, and they shall meet in the District and perform such duties as provided by the twelfth article of amendment.

SECTION 2. ENFORCEMENT

The Congress shall have power to enforce this article by appropriate legislation.

AMENDMENT 24 (1964)
BAN ON POLL TAXES

SECTION 1. POLL TAX ILLEGAL

The right of citizens of the United States to vote in any primary or other election for President or Vice President, for electors for President or Vice President, or for Senator or Representative in Congress, shall not be denied or abridged by the United States or any state by reason of failure to pay any poll tax or other tax.

SECTION 2. ENFORCEMENT

The Congress shall have power to enforce this article by appropriate legislation.

AMENDMENT 25 (1967)
PRESIDENTIAL SUCCESSION

SECTION 1. PRESIDENTIAL VACANCY

In case of the removal of the President from office or of his death or resignation, the Vice President shall become President.

SECTION 2. VICE PRESIDENTIAL VACANCY

Whenever there is a vacancy in the office of the Vice President, the President shall nominate a Vice President who shall take the office upon confirmation by a majority vote of both houses of Congress.

SECTION 3. PRESIDENTIAL DISABILITY

Whenever the President transmits to the President pro tempore of the Senate and the Speaker of the House of Representatives his written declaration that he is unable to discharge the powers and duties of his office, and until he transmits to them a written declaration to the contrary, such powers and duties shall be discharged by the Vice President as Acting President.

SECTION 4. DETERMINING PRESIDENTIAL DISABILITY

Whenever the Vice President and a majority of either the principal officers of the executive departments or of such other body as Congress may by law provide, transmit to the President pro tempore of the Senate and the Speaker of the House of Representatives their written declaration that the President is unable to discharge the powers and duties of his office, the Vice President shall immediately assume the powers and duties of the office as Acting President.

Thereafter, when the President transmits to the President pro tempore of the Senate and the Speaker of the House of Representatives his written declaration that no inability exists, he shall resume the powers and duties of his office unless the Vice President and a majority of either the principal officers of the executive department or of such other body as Congress may by law provide, transmit within four days to the President pro tempore of the Senate and the Speaker of the House of Representatives their written declaration that the President is unable to discharge the powers and duties of his office. Thereupon Congress shall decide the issue, assembling within 48 hours for that purpose if not in session. If the Congress, within 21 days after receipt of the latter written declaration, or, if Congress is not in session, within 21 days after Congress is required to assemble, determines by two-thirds vote of both houses that the President is unable to discharge the powers and duties of his office, the Vice President shall continue to discharge the same as Acting President; otherwise the President shall resume the powers and duties of his office.

AMENDMENT 26 (1971)
VOTING AGE

SECTION 1. RIGHT TO VOTE

The right of citizens of the United States, who are 18 years of age or older, to vote shall not be denied or abridged by the United States or any state on account of age.

SECTION 2. ENFORCEMENT

The Congress shall have the power to enforce this article by appropriate legislation.

AMENDMENT 27 (1992)
CONGRESSIONAL PAY

No law, varying the compensation for the services of the Senators and Representatives, shall take effect, until an election of Representatives shall have intervened.

VICE PRESIDENTIAL VACANCY
If the office of the Vice President becomes open, the President names someone to assume that office as long as both houses of Congress approve by a majority vote.

PRESIDENTIAL DISABILITY
This section explains in detail what happens if the President cannot continue in office because of sickness or any other reason. The Vice President takes over as acting President until the President is able to resume office.

DETERMINING PRESIDENTIAL DISABILITY
If the Vice President and a majority of the Cabinet inform the Speaker of the House and the president pro tempore of the Senate that the President cannot carry out his or her duties, the Vice President can then serve as acting President. To regain the office, the President has to inform the Speaker and the president pro tempore in writing that he or she is again able to serve. But, if the Vice President and a majority of the Cabinet disagree and inform the Speaker and the president pro tempore that the President is still unable to serve, then Congress decides who will hold the office of President.

VOTING AGE
All citizens 18 years or older have the right to vote. Formerly, the voting age was 21.

CONGRESSIONAL PAY
A law raising or lowering the salaries for members of Congress cannot be passed for that session of Congress.

The Star-Spangled Banner

"The Star-Spangled Banner" was written by Francis Scott Key and adopted as the national anthem in March 1931. The army and navy had recognized it as such long before Congress approved it.

During the War of 1812, Francis Scott Key spent a night aboard a British warship in the Chesapeake Bay while trying to arrange for the release of an American prisoner. The battle raged throughout the night, while the Americans were held on the ship. The next morning, when the smoke from the cannons finally cleared, Francis Scott Key was thrilled to see the American flag still waving proudly above Fort McHenry. It symbolized the victory of the Americans.

There are four verses to the National Anthem. In these four verses, Key wrote about how he felt when he saw the flag still waving over Fort McHenry. He wrote that the flag was a symbol of the freedom for which the people had fought so hard. Key also told about the pride he had in his country and the great hopes he had for the future of the United States.

(1)

Oh, say can you see by the dawn's early light
What so proudly we hail'd at the twilight's last gleaming,
Whose broad stripes and bright stars through the perilous fight
O'er the ramparts we watch'd were so gallantly streaming?
And the rockets' red glare, the bombs bursting in air,
Gave proof through the night that our flag was still there.
Oh, say does that star-spangled banner yet wave
O'er the land of the free and the home of the brave?

(2)

On the shore dimly seen through the mist of the deep,
Where the foe's haughty host in dread silence reposes,
What is that which the breeze, o'er the towering steep,
As it fitfully blows, half conceals, half discloses?
Now it catches the gleam of the morning's first beam,
In full glory reflected now shines in the stream.
'Tis the star-spangled banner, oh, long may it wave
O'er the land of the free and the home of the brave!

(3)

And where is that band who so vauntingly swore
That the havoc of war and the battle's confusion
A home and a country should leave us no more?
Their blood has wash'd out their foul footsteps' pollution.
No refuge could save the hireling and slave
From the terror of flight or the gloom of the grave,
And the star-spangled banner in triumph doth wave
O'er the land of the free and the home of the brave.

(4)

Oh, thus be it ever when freemen shall stand
Between their lov'd home and the war's desolation!
Blest with vict'ry and peace may the heav'n-rescued land
Praise the power that hath made and preserv'd us a nation!
Then conquer we must, when our cause it is just,
And this be our motto, "In God is our Trust,"
And the star-spangled banner in triumph shall wave
O'er the land of the free and the home of the brave.

THE PLEDGE OF ALLEGIANCE

I pledge allegiance to the Flag
of the United States of America,
and to the Republic
for which it stands,
one Nation under God, indivisible,
with liberty and justice for all.

The flag is a symbol of the United States of America. The Pledge of Allegiance says that the people of the United States promise to stand up for the flag, their country, and the basic beliefs of freedom and fairness upon which the country was established.

BIOGRAPHICAL DICTIONARY

The Biographical Dictionary lists many of the important people introduced in this book. The page number tells where the main discussion of each person starts. See the Index for other page references.

BIOGRAPHICAL DICTIONARY

A

Adams, Abigail *1744–1818* Patriot who wrote about women's rights to John Adams, her husband. p. 242

Adams, John *1735–1826* 2nd U.S. President and one writer of the Declaration of Independence. p. 310

Adams, Samuel *1722–1803* American Revolutionary leader who set up a Committee of Correspondence in Boston and was a leader of the Sons of Liberty. p. 222

Addams, Jane *1860–1935* American reformer who brought the idea of settlement houses from Britain to the United States. With Ellen Gates Starr, she founded Hull House in Chicago. p. 476

Anderson, Robert *1805–1871* Union commander of Fort Sumter who was forced to surrender to the Confederacy. p. 406

Anthony, Susan B. *1820–1906* Women's suffrage leader who worked to enable women to have the same rights as men. p. 371

Aristide, Jean-Bertrand (air•uh•STEED, ZHAHN bair•TRAHN) *1953–* Freely elected president of Haiti who was overthrown in 1991 but was returned to office in 1994. p. 623

Armstrong, Louis *1900–1971* Noted jazz trumpeter who played in Harlem during the Harlem Renaissance. p. 541

Arnold, Benedict *1741–1801* Continental army officer who became a traitor and worked for the British army. p. 251

Atahuallpa (ah•tah•WAHL•pah) *1502?–1533* Inca ruler who was killed in the Spanish conquest of the Incas. p. 125

Attucks, Crispus *1723–1770* Patriot and former slave who was killed during the Boston Massacre. p. 221

Austin, Moses *1761–1821* American pioneer who wanted to start a colony of Americans in Texas. p. 359

Austin, Stephen F. *1793–1836* Moses Austin's son. He carried out his father's dream of starting an American colony in Texas. p. 359

B

Balboa, Vasco Núñez de (bal•BOH•uh, NOON•yes day) *1475–1519* Explorer who in 1513 became the first European to reach the western coast of the Americas—proving to Europeans that the Americas were separate from Asia. p. 116

Banneker, Benjamin *1731–1806* African who helped survey the land for the new capital of the United States. p. 311

Barrett, Janie Porter *1865–1948* African American teacher who founded a settlement house in Hampton, Virginia. p. 477

Barton, Clara *1821–1912* Civil War nurse and founder of the American Red Cross. p. 419

Bessemer, Henry *1813–1898* British inventor of a way to make steel more easily and cheaply than before. p. 454

Bienville, Jean Baptiste Le Moyne, Sieur de (bee•EN•vil) *1680–1768* French explorer who—with his brother, Pierre Le Moyne, Sieur de Iberville—started an early settlement at the mouth of the Mississippi River. p. 167

Bolívar, Simón (boh•LEE•var, see•MOHN) *1783–1830* Leader of independence movements in Bolivia, Colombia, Ecuador, Peru, and Venezuela. p. 625

Bonaparte, Napoleon (BOH•nuh•part, nuh•POH•lee•uhn) *1769–1821* French leader who sold all of the Louisiana region to the United States. p. 332

Boone, Daniel *1734–1820* American pioneer who was one of the first to cross the Appalachians. p. 327

Brezhnev, Leonid (BREZH•nef) *1906–1982* Leader of the Soviet Union from 1964 until his death. President Nixon's 1972 visit with him in the Soviet Union led to arms control and began a period of détente. p. 600

Brown, John *1800–1859* American abolitionist who seized a weapons storehouse to help slaves rebel. He was caught and hanged. p. 396

Brown, Linda *1943–* African American student whose family was among a group that challenged public-school segregation. p. 588

Brown, Moses *1742–1827* Textile pioneer who built the first textile mill in the United States, using Samuel Slater's plans. p. 349

Burgoyne, John (buhr•GOYN) *1722–1792* British general who lost a battle to the Continental army on October 17, 1777, at Saratoga, New York. p. 250

Burnet, David G. *1788–1870* 1st president of the Republic of Texas, when it was formed in 1836. p. 361

Bush, George *1924–* 41st U.S. President. He was President at the end of the Cold War and during Operation Desert Storm. p. 602

Byrd, William *1674–1744* Early Virginia planter who kept a diary of his daily life. p. 189

C

Cabeza de Vaca, Alvar Núñez (kah•BAY•sah day VAH•kuh) *1490?–1560?* Spanish explorer who went to Mexico City and told stories of the Seven Cities of Gold. p. 128

Caboto, Giovanni *1450?–1499?* Italian explorer who in 1497 sailed from England and landed in what is now Newfoundland, though he thought he had landed in Asia. The English called him John Cabot. p. 114

Calhoun, John C. *1782–1850* Vice President under John Quincy Adams and Andrew Jackson. He was a strong believer in states' rights. p. 356

Calvert, Cecilius *1605–1675* First proprietor of the Maryland colony. p. 170

Cameahwait (kah•MEE•ah•wayt) *1800s* Chief of the Shoshones during the Lewis and Clark expedition. He was Sacagawea's brother. p. 334

Carnegie, Andrew *1835–1919* Steel entrepreneur who bought other kinds of companies to supply his steel business. p. 455

Carter, Jimmy *1924–* 39th U.S. President. He brought about a peace agreement between Israel and Egypt. p. 601

Cartier, Jacques (kar•TYAY, ZHAHK) *1491–1557* French explorer who sailed up the St. Lawrence River and began a fur-trading business with the Hurons. p. 135

Castro, Fidel *1926–* Leader who took over Cuba in 1959 and made it a communist nation. p. 621

Cavelier, René-Robert (ka•vuhl•YAY) *See* La Salle.

Chamorro, Violeta (chuh•MAWR•oh, vee•oh•LET•uh) *1929–* Nicaragua's democratic president, elected in 1990, after years of communist rule. p. 624

Champlain, Samuel de (sham•PLAYN) *1567?–1635* French explorer who founded the first settlement at Quebec. p. 136

Charles I, *1600–1649* British king who chartered the colony of Maryland. p. 170

Chávez, César *1927–1993* Labor leader and organizer of the United Farm Workers. p. 591

Clark, William *1770–1838* American explorer who aided Lewis in an expedition through the Louisiana Purchase. p. 333

Clay, Henry *1777–1852* Representative from Kentucky who worked for compromises on the slavery issue. p. 400

Clinton, William *1946–* 42nd U.S. President. p. 602

Clinton, George *1739–1812* American politician who helped form the Democratic-Republican party. p. 309

Cody, William (Buffalo Bill) *1846–1917* Cowhand known for shooting many buffalo. p. 498

Columbus, Christopher *1451–1506* Italian-born Spanish explorer who in 1492 sailed west from Spain and thought he had reached Asia but had actually reached islands near the Americas, lands that were unknown to Europeans. p. 99

Cornish, Samuel *1795–1858* African who in 1827 helped John Russwurm found an abolitionist newspaper called *Freedom's Journal.* p. 370

Cornwallis, Charles *1738–1805* British general who surrendered at the Battle of Yorktown, resulting in victory for the Americans in the Revolutionary War. p. 251

Coronado, Francisco Vásquez de (kawr•oh•NAH•doh) *1510?–1554* Spanish explorer who led an expedition from Mexico City into what is now the southwestern United States in search of the Seven Cities of Gold. p. 129

Cortés, Hernando (kawr•TEZ) *1485–1547* Spanish conquistador who conquered the Aztec Empire. p. 123

Crazy Horse *1842?–1877* Sioux leader who fought against General George Custer. p. 499

Custer, George *1839–1876* U.S. army general who led an attack against Sioux and Cheyenne Indians. Custer and all of his men were killed in that battle. p. 499

D

da Gama, Vasco (dah GA•muh) *1460?–1524* Portuguese navigator who sailed from Europe around the southern tip of Africa and on to Asia in 1497–1498. p. 107

Davis, Jefferson *1808–1889* Mississippi senator who became president of the Confederacy. p. 406

Dawes, William *1745–1799* American who, along with Paul Revere, warned the Patriots that the British were marching toward Concord. p. 225

de Soto, Hernando (day SOH•toh) *1496?–1542* Spanish explorer who led an expedition into what is today the southeastern United States. p. 129

Dekanawida (deh•kahn•uh•WIH•duh) *1500s* Legendary Iroquois holy man who called for an end to the fighting among the Iroquois, a view that led to the formation of the Iroquois League. p. 76

Dewey, George *1837–1917* American naval commander who destroyed the Spanish fleet and captured Manila Bay in the Spanish-American War. p. 518

Dias, Bartholomeu (DEE•ahsh) *1450?–1500* Portuguese navigator who in 1488 became the first European to sail around the southern tip of Africa. p. 107

Dickinson, John *1732–1808* Member of the Continental Congress who wrote most of the Articles of Confederation, adopted in 1781. p. 267

Douglas, Stephen A. *1813–1861* American legislator who wrote the Kansas-Nebraska Act and debated Lincoln in a race for a Senate seat from Illinois. p. 403

Douglass, Frederick *1817–1895* Abolitionist speaker and writer who had escaped from slavery. p. 370

Drake, Francis *1543–1596* English explorer who sailed around the world. p. 139

Du Bois, W.E.B. *1868–1963* Progressive African American who helped form the National Association for the Advancement of Colored People (NAACP). p. 526

E

Eisenhower, Dwight D. *1890–1969* 34th U.S. President and, earlier, American general who led the D day invasion. p. 557

Elizabeth I *1533–1603* Queen of England during the middle to late 1500s. p. 139

Ellicott, Andrew *1754–1820* American surveyor who helped survey land for the new United States capital. p. 311

Ellington, Edward Kennedy (Duke) *1899–1974* Big Band leader who played in Harlem clubs. p. 541

Equiano, Olaudah (ek•wee•AHN•oh, OHL•uh•dah) *1750–1797* African who was kidnapped from his village and sold into slavery. He later wrote a book describing his experiences. p. 188

Eriksson, Leif (AIR•ik•suhn, LAYV) *?–1020?* Viking explorer who sailed from Greenland to North America in the A.D. 1000s. p. 100

Estéban (ehs•TAY•bahn) *1500–1539* African explorer who went with Cabeza de Vaca to Mexico City and told stories of the Seven Cities of Gold. Estéban was killed on a later expedition, the purpose of which was to find out whether or not the stories were true. p. 128

F

Farragut, Jorge (FAIR•uh•guht) *1755–1817* Spanish-born man who fought in the Continental army and also the navy. p. 250

Ferdinand II *1452–1516* King of Spain who—with Queen Isabella, his wife—sent Christopher Columbus on his voyage to find a western route to Asia. p. 108

Ford, Gerald *1913–* 38th U.S. President. The Vietnam War ended during his term. p. 597

Ford, Henry *1863–1947* American automobile manufacturer who mass–produced cars at low cost by using assembly lines. p. 538

Forten, James *1766–1842* Free African in Philadelphia who ran a busy sail factory and became wealthy. p. 399

Franklin, Benjamin *1706–1790* American leader who was sent to Britain to ask Parliament for representation. He was a writer of the Declaration of Independence, a delegate to the Constitutional Convention, and a respected scientist and business leader. p. 219

Friedan, Betty *1921–* Writer who helped set up the National Organization for Women to work for women's rights. p. 592

Frontenac, Louis de Buade, Count de (FRAHN•tuh•nak) *1622–1698* French leader who was appointed governor-general of New France by King Louis XIV. p. 165

G

Gage, Thomas *1721–1787* Head of the British army in North America and colonial governor of Massachusetts. p. 224

Gálvez, Bernardo de (GAHL•ves) *1746–1786* Spanish governor of Louisiana who sent supplies to the Patriots in the Revolutionary War and led his own soldiers in taking a British fort in Florida. p. 250

Garrison, William Lloyd *1805–1879* American abolitionist who started the newspaper called the *Liberator*. p. 370

Gates, Horatio *1728–1806* American general who defeated the British in 1777, at Saratoga, New York. p. 250

George III *1738–1820* King of England during the Revolutionary War. p. 231

Geronimo *1829–1909* Apache chief who fought one of the longest wars between Native Americans and the United States government. p. 501

Glidden, Joseph *1813–1906* Inventor of barbed wire. p. 493

Gompers, Samuel *1850–1924* Early labor union leader who formed the American Federation of Labor. p. 461

Gorbachev, Mikhail (gawr•buh•CHAWF, myik•uh•EEL) *1931–* Leader of the Soviet Union from 1985 to 1991. He improved relations with the United States and expanded freedom in the Soviet Union. p. 601

Grant, Ulysses S. *1822–1885* 18th U.S. President and, earlier, commander of the Union army in the Civil War. p. 426

H

Hallidie, Andrew S. *1836–1900* American who invented the cable car. p. 478

Hamilton, Alexander *1755–1804* American leader in calling for the Constitutional Convention and winning support for it. He favored a strong national government. pp. 300, 309

Hancock, John *1737–1793* Leader of the Sons of Liberty in the Massachusetts colony. p. 225

Harrison, William Henry *1773–1841* 9th U.S. President. Earlier he directed U.S. forces against the Indians at the Battle of Tippecanoe and was a commander in the War of 1812. p. 337

Henry *1394–1460* Henry the Navigator, prince of Portugal, who set up the first European school for training sailors in navigation. p. 106

Henry, Patrick *1736–1799* American colonist who spoke out in the Virginia legislature against paying British taxes. His views became widely known, and Loyalists accused him of treason. p. 217

Hiawatha (hy•uh•WAH•thuh), *1500s* Onondaga chief who persuaded other Iroquois tribes to form the Iroquois League. p. 76

Hirohito *1901–1989* Emperor of Japan from 1926 until his death. p. 552

Hitler, Adolf *1889–1945* Nazi dictator of Germany. His actions led to World War II and the killing of millions of people. p. 551

Holiday, Billie *1915–1959* Great jazz singer who sang in Harlem during the Harlem Renaissance. p. 541

Hooker, Thomas *1586–1647* Minister who helped form the Connecticut colony. His democratic ideas were adopted in the Fundamental Orders. p. 171

Hoover, Herbert *1874–1964* 31st U.S. President. When the Depression began, he thought that the economy was healthy and conditions would improve. p. 542

Houston, Sam *1793–1863* President of the Republic of Texas and, later, governor of the state of Texas. p. 361

Hudson, Henry *?–1611* Explorer who sailed up the Hudson River, giving the Dutch a claim to the area. p. 137

Hughes, Langston *1902–1967* Poet and one of the best-known Harlem writers. p. 541

Hurston, Zora Neale *1903–1960* Novelist and one of the best-known Harlem writers. p. 536

Hutchinson, Anne *1591–1643* English-born woman who left Massachusetts because of her religious beliefs. She settled near Providence, which joined with other settlements to form the Rhode Island colony. p. 172

I

Iberville, Pierre Le Moyne, Sieur de (ee•ber•VEEL) *1661–1706* French explorer who—with his brother, Jean Baptiste Le Moyne, Sieur de Bienville—started an early settlement at the mouth of the Mississippi River. p. 167

Isabella I *1451–1504* Queen of Spain who—with King Ferdinand, her husband—sent Columbus on his voyage to find a western route to Asia. p. 108

J

Jackson, Andrew *1767–1845* 7th U.S. President and, earlier, commander who won the final battle in the War of 1812.

As President he favored a strong union and ordered the removal of Indians from their lands. p. 355

James I *1566–1625* King of England in the early 1600s. The James River and Jamestown were named after him. p. 141

Jay, John *1745–1829* American leader who wrote letters to newspapers, defending the Constitution. He became the first chief justice of the Supreme Court. pp. 300, 307

Jefferson, Thomas *1743–1826* 3rd U.S. President and the main writer of the Declaration of Independence. p. 237

Jenney, William *1832–1907* American engineer who developed the use of steel frames to build tall buildings. p. 477

John I *1357–1433* King of Portugal during a time of great exploration. Father of Prince Henry, who set up a school of navigation. p. 106

Johnson, Andrew *1808–1875* 17th U.S. President. Differences with Congress about Reconstruction led to his being impeached, though he was found not guilty. p. 437

Johnson, Lyndon B. *1908–1973* 36th U.S. President. He started Great Society programs and expanded the Vietnam War. p. 594

Joliet, Louis (zhohl•YAY, loo•EE) *1645–1700* French fur trader who explored lakes and rivers for France, with Marquette and five others. p. 166

Joseph *1840–1904* Nez Perce chief who tried to lead his people to Canada after they were told to move onto a reservation. p. 500

K

Kalakaua (kah•lah•KAH•ooh•ah), *1836–1891* Hawaiian king who tried but failed to keep Americans from taking over the Hawaiian Islands. p. 516

Kalb, Johann, Baron de *1721–1780* German soldier who helped the Patriots in the Revolutionary War. p. 248

Kennedy, John F. *1917–1963* 35th U.S. President. He made the Soviet Union remove its missiles from Cuba. pp. 579, 580

King, Martin Luther, Jr. *1929–1968* African American civil rights leader who worked for integration in nonviolent ways. He won the Nobel Peace Prize in 1964. pp. 589, 590

King, Richard *1825–1885* Rancher in South Texas who founded the country's largest ranch. p. 491

Knox, Henry *1750–1806* Secretary of War in the first government under the Constitution. p. 308

Kosciuszko, Thaddeus (kawsh•CHUSH•koh) *1746–1817* Polish officer who helped the Patriots in the Revolutionary War. He later returned to Poland and led a revolution there. p. 248

Kublai Khan (KOO•bluh KAHN) *1215–1294* Ruler of China who was visited by Marco Polo. p. 103

L

Lafayette, Marquis de (lah•fee•ET) *1757–1834* French noble who fought with the Americans in the Revolutionary War. p. 250

La Follette, Robert *1855–1925* Wisconsin governor who began many reforms in his state, including a merit system for government jobs. p. 525

Lafon, Thomy *1810–1893* Free African who made a fortune from businesses in New Orleans. p. 399

La Salle, René-Robert Cavelier, Sieur de (luh•SAL) *1643–1687* French explorer who found the mouth of the Mississippi River and claimed the whole Mississippi Valley for France. p. 167

Las Casas, Bartolomé de (lahs KAH•sahs, bar•toh•luh•MAY day) *1474–1566* Spanish missionary who spent much of his life trying to help native peoples in the Americas. p. 132

Law, John *1671–1729* Scottish banker who was appointed proprietor of the Louisiana region in 1712. p. 168

Le Moyne, Jean Baptiste (luh•MWAHN, ZHAHN ba•TEEST) *See* Bienville.

Le Moyne, Pierre (luh•MWAHN) *See* Iberville.

Lee, Richard Henry *1732–1794* American Revolutionary leader who said to the Continental Congress that the colonies should cut off all ties with Britain and become independent. p. 236

Lee, Robert E. *1807–1870* United States army colonel who gave up his post and became commander of the Confederate army in the Civil War. p. 416

L'Enfant, Pierre Charles *1754–1825* French engineer who planned the buildings and streets of the new capital of the United States. p. 311

Lewis, Meriwether *1774–1809* American explorer chosen by Thomas Jefferson to be a pathfinder in the territory of the Louisiana Purchase. p. 333

Liliuokalani (li•lee•uh•woh•kuh•LAH•nee) *1838–1917* Hawaiian queen who tried but failed to bring back the Hawaiian monarchy's authority. p. 516

Lincoln, Abraham *1809–1865* 16th U.S. President, leader of the Union in the Civil War, and signer of the Emancipation Proclamation. pp. 403, 405, 420, 427, 430

Lindbergh, Charles *1902–1974* Airplane pilot who was the first to fly nonstop between the United States and Europe. p. 539

Livingston, Robert R. *1746–1813* One of the writers of the Declaration of Independence. *p. 237*

Lowell, Francis Cabot *1775–1817* Textile pioneer who set up an American mill in which several processes were completed under one roof. p. 350

Lucas, Eliza *1722?–1793* South Carolina settler who experimented with indigo plants. She gave away seeds, and indigo then became an important cash crop. p. 175

M

Madison, Dolley *1768–1849* James Madison's wife and First Lady during the War of 1812. p. 339

Madison, James *1751–1836* 4th U.S. President. He was a leader in calling for the Constitutional Convention, writing the Constitution, and winning support for it. p. 272

Magellan, Ferdinand (muh•JEH•luhn) *1480?–1521* Portuguese explorer who in 1519 led a fleet of ships from Spain westward to Asia. He died on the voyage, but one of the ships made it back to Spain, completing the first trip around the world. p. 117

Malcolm X *1925–1965* African American leader who disagreed with Martin Luther King's views on nonviolence and integration. p. 591

Mann, Horace *1796–1859* American school reformer in the first half of the 1800s. p. 368

Mao Zedong (MOW zeh•DOONG) *1893–1976* Leader of China from 1949 until his death. President Nixon's 1972 visit with him in China led to trade and cultural exchange with the United States. p. 600

Marquette, Jacques (mar•KET, ZHAHK) *1637–1675* Catholic missionary who knew several Indian languages. He explored lakes and rivers with Joliet for France. p. 166

Marshall, Thurgood *1908–1993* NAACP lawyer who argued the school segregation case that the Supreme Court ruled on in 1954 and, later, was the first African American to serve on the Supreme Court. p. 588

Martí, José (mar•TEE) *1853–1895* Cuban leader who did much to win Cuban independence from Spain. p. 518

Mason, George *1725–1792* Virginia delegate to the Constitutional Convention who argued to have slave trading stopped. p. 282

McCormick, Cyrus *1809–1884* Inventor of a reaping machine for harvesting wheat. p. 487

McCoy, Joseph *1837–1915* Cattle trader who arranged to move large herds by using stockyards near railroad tracks. p. 490

McKinley, William *1843–1901* 25th U.S. President. The Spanish-American War was fought during his term. p. 517

Menéndez de Avilés, Pedro (muh•NEN•duhs day ah•vuh•LAYS) *1519–1574* Spanish leader of settlers in St. Augustine, Florida, the first permanent European settlement in what is now the United States. p. 159

Mongoulacha (mahn•goo•LAY•chah) *1700s* Indian leader who helped Bienville and Iberville. p. 167

Monroe, James *1758–1831* 5th U.S. President. He established the Monroe Doctrine, which said that the United States would stop any European nation from expanding its American empire. p. 340

Morris, Gouverneur (guh•vuh•NIR) *1752–1816* American leader who worked out each sentence of the United States Constitution. p. 275

Motecuhzoma (maw•tay•kwah•SOH•mah) *1466–1520* King of the Aztecs when they were conquered by the Spanish. He has also been known as Montezuma. p. 123

Mott, Lucretia *1793–1880* American reformer who, with Elizabeth Cady Stanton, organized the first convention for women's rights. p. 371

Mussolini, Benito (moo•suh•LEE•nee, buh•NEE•toh) *1883–1945* Dictator of Italy from 1925 until 1943. p. 552

N

Nixon, Richard M. *1913–1994* 37th U.S. President. He tried to end the Vietnam War, he reduced tensions with communist nations, and he resigned the presidency because of the Watergate scandal. pp. 596, 600

Niza, Marcos de (NEE•sah) *1495–1558* Spanish priest who was sent with Estéban to confirm stories of the Seven Cities of Gold. When he returned to Mexico City, he said he had seen a golden city. p. 128

O

O'Connor, Sandra Day *1930–* First woman to be appointed to the United States Supreme Court. p. 592

Oglethorpe, James *1696–1785* English settler who was given a charter to settle Georgia. He wanted to bring in debtors from England to help settle it. p. 175

Otis, James *1725–1783* Massachusetts colonist who spoke out against British taxes and called for "no taxation without representation." p. 216

P

Paine, Thomas *1737–1809* Author of a widely read pamphlet called *Common Sense,* in which he attacked King George III and called for a revolution to make the colonies independent. p. 236

Parks, Rosa *1913–* African American woman whose refusal to give up her seat on a Montgomery, Alabama, bus started a year-long bus boycott. p. 589

Penn, William *1644–1718* Proprietor of Pennsylvania under a charter from King Charles II of Britain. Penn was a Quaker who made Pennsylvania a refuge for settlers who wanted religious freedom. p. 173

Perry, Oliver Hazard *1785–1819* American naval commander who won an important battle in the War of 1812. p. 339

Pickett, Bill *1870–1932* Cowhand who was the first African American elected to the Cowboy Hall of Fame. p. 492

Pike, Zebulon *1779–1813* American who led an expedition down the Arkansas River to explore the southwestern part of the Louisiana Purchase. p. 334

Pizarro, Francisco (pee•ZAR•oh) *1475?–1541* Spanish conquistador who conquered the Inca Empire. p. 125

Pocahontas (poh•kuh•HAHN•tuhs) *1595–1617* Indian chief Powhatan's daughter. p. 142

Polk, James K. *1795–1849* 11th U.S. President. He gained land for the United States by setting a northern boundary and fighting a war with Mexico. pp. 362, 364

Polo, Marco *1254–1324* Explorer from Venice who spent many years in Asia in the late 1200s. He wrote a book about his travels that gave Europeans information about Asia. p. 103

Ponce de León, Juan (PAHN•say day lay•OHN) *1460–1521* Spanish explorer who landed on the North American mainland in 1513, in what is now Florida. p. 127

Powhatan (pow•uh•TAN) *1550?–1618* Chief of a federation of Indian tribes that lived in the Virginia territory. Pocahontas was his daughter. p. 142

Pulaski, Casimir (puh•LAS•kee) *1747–1779* Polish noble who came to the British colonies to help the Patriots in the Revolutionary War. p. 248

R

Raleigh, Walter (RAH•lee) *1554–1618* English explorer who used his own money to set up England's first colony in North America, on Roanoke Island near North Carolina. p. 140

Randolph, Edmund *1753–1813* Virginia delegate to the Constitutional Convention who thought the number of representatives a state would have in Congress should be based on the population of the state. p. 279

Read, George *1733–1798* Delaware delegate to the Constitutional Convention who thought the states should be done away with in favor of a strong national government. p. 278

Reagan, Ronald *1911–* 40th U.S. President. His meetings with Soviet leader Gorbachev led to a thaw in the Cold War, including advances in arms control. p. 601

Red Cloud, *1822–1909* Sioux chief who led his people on a three-year fight to keep miners and army troops off a road through Sioux land. p. 499

Revere, Paul *1735–1818* American who warned the Patriots that the British were marching toward Concord, where Patriot weapons were stored. p. 225

Riis, Jacob (REES) *1849–1914* Reformer and writer who described the living conditions of the poor in New York City. p. 475

Robeson, Paul *1898–1976* African American actor and singer who performed in Harlem and outside the United States. p. 541

Rockefeller, John D. *1839–1937* American oil entrepreneur who consolidated many refineries into the Standard Oil Company. p. 455

Roosevelt, Franklin Delano *1882–1945* 32nd U.S. President. He began New Deal programs to help the nation out of the Depression, and he was the nation's leader during World War II. p. 544

Roosevelt, Theodore *1858–1919* 26th U.S. President. He showed the world America's strength, made it possible to build the Panama Canal, and worked for progressive reforms and conservation. pp. 518, 524

Russwurm, John *1799–1851* African who in 1827 helped Samuel Cornish found an abolitionist newspaper called *Freedom's Journal.* p. 370

Rutledge, John *1739–1800* Delegate to the Constitutional Convention, South Carolina governor, and Supreme Court Justice. p. 282

S

Sacagawea (sak•uh•juh•WEE•uh) *1786–1812* Shoshone woman who acted as an interpreter for the Lewis and Clark expedition. p. 334

Salem, Peter *1750?–1816* African who fought with the Minutemen at Concord and at the Battle of Bunker Hill. p. 243

Samoset *1590?–1653?* Indian chief who spoke English and who helped the settlers at Plymouth. *p. 143*

San Martín, José de (san mar•TEEN) *1778–1850* Leader of an independence movement in Argentina. p. 625

Santa Anna, Antonio López de *1794–1876* Dictator of Mexico who defeated Texans at the Alamo. p. 360

Scott, Dred *1795?–1858* Enslaved African who took his case for freedom to the Supreme Court and lost. p. 402

Scott, Winfield *1786–1866* American general in the war with Mexico. p. 364

Serra, Junípero *1713–1784* Spanish missionary who helped build a string of missions in California. p. 162

Shays, Daniel *1747?–1825* Leader of Shays's Rebellion, which showed the weakness of the government under the Articles of Confederation. p. 269

Sherman, Roger *1721–1793* One of the writers of the Declaration of Independence. Connecticut delegate to the Constitutional Convention who worked out the compromise in which Congress would have two houses—one based on state population and one with two members from each state. pp. 237, 280

Sherman, William Tecumseh *1820–1891* Union general who, after defeating Atlanta, led the March to the Sea, on which his troops caused great destruction. p. 428

Sitting Bull *1831–1890* Sioux leader who fought against General George Custer. p. 499

Slater, Samuel *1768–1835* Textile pioneer who helped bring the Industrial Revolution to the United States by providing plans for a new spinning machine. p. 349

Slocumb, Mary *1700s* North Carolina colonist who fought in the Revolutionary War. p. 242

Smith, John *1580–1631* English explorer who, as leader of the Jamestown settlement, saved its people from starvation. p. 141

Smith, Joseph *1805–1844* Mormon leader who settled his people in Illinois and was killed there. p. 363

Spalding, Eliza *1807–1851* American missionary and pioneer in the Oregon country. p. 362

Spalding, Henry *1803–1874* American missionary and pioneer in the Oregon country. p. 362

Sprague, Frank *1857–1934* American inventor who built the trolley car, an electric streetcar. p. 478

Squanto *See* Tisquantum.

Stalin, Joseph *1879–1953* Dictator of the Soviet Union from 1929 until his death. p. 552

Stanton, Elizabeth Cady *1815–1902* American reformer who, with Lucretia Mott, organized the first convention for women's rights. p. 371

Starr, Ellen Gates *1860–1940* Reformer who, with Jane Addams, founded Hull House in Chicago. p. 476

Steuben, Friedrich, Baron von (STOO•buhn), *1730–1794* German soldier who helped train Patriot troops in the Revolutionary War. p. 248

Stinson, Katherine *1891–1977* American pilot who wanted to become a fighter pilot in World War I but was not allowed to fly in battle. p. 530

Stowe, Harriet Beecher *1811–1896* American abolitionist who in 1852 wrote the book *Uncle Tom's Cabin.* p. 370

Sutter, John *1803–1880* American pioneer who owned the sawmill where gold was discovered, leading to the California gold rush. p. 365

T

Taney, Roger B. (TAW•nee) *1777–1864* Supreme Court Chief Justice who wrote the ruling against Dred Scott. p. 402

Tascalusa (tus•kah•LOO•sah) *1500s* Leader of the Mobile people when they battled with Spanish troops led by Hernando de Soto. p. 130

Tecumseh (tuh•KUM•suh) *1768–1813* Shawnee leader of Indians in the Northwest Territory. He wanted to form a strong Indian confederation. p. 336

Tenskwatawa (ten•SKWAHT•uh•wah) *1768–1834* Shawnee leader known as the Prophet. He worked with his brother Tecumseh and led the Indians at the Battle of Tippecanoe in 1811. p. 336

Tisquantum *1585?–1622* Native American who spoke English and who helped the Plymouth colony. p. 143

Tonti, Henri de (TOHN•tee, ahn•REE duh) *1650–1704* French explorer with La Salle. p. 167

Toussaint-Louverture, Pierre (TOO•san LOO•ver•tur) *1743–1803* Haitian revolutionary and general who took over the government of St. Domingue from France and became the ruler of Haiti. p. 332

Truman, Harry S. *1884–1972* 33rd U.S. President. He sent American soldiers to support South Korea in 1950. p. 579

Truth, Sojourner *1797?–1883* Abolitionist and former slave who became a leading preacher against slavery. p. 370

Tubman, Harriet *1820–1913* Abolitionist and former slave who became a conductor on the Underground Railroad. She led more than 300 slaves to freedom. p. 398

Turner, Nat *1800–1831* Enslaved African who led a rebellion against slavery. More than 100 slaves were killed, and Turner was caught and hanged. p. 396

Tweed, William (Boss) *1823–1878* New York City political boss who robbed the city of millions of dollars. p. 525

V

Vanderbilt, Cornelius *1843–1899* American railroad owner during the railroad boom of the late 1800s. p. 454

Vespucci, Amerigo (veh•SPOO•chee, uh•MAIR•ih•goh) *1454–1512* Italian explorer who made several voyages from Europe to what many people thought was Asia. He determined that he had landed on another continent, which was later called America in his honor. p. 114

W

Wald, Lillian *1867–1940* Reformer who started the Henry Street Settlement in New York City. p. 477

Waldseemüller, Martin (VAHLT•zay•mool•er) *1470–1518?* German cartographer who published a map in 1507 that first showed a continent named America. p. 116

Warren, Earl *1891–1974* Chief Justice of the Supreme Court who wrote the 1954 decision against school segregation. p. 588

Warren, Mercy Otis *1728–1814* Massachusetts colonist who spoke out against new British taxes on goods. p. 216

Washington, George *1732–1799* 1st U.S. President, leader of the Continental army during the Revolutionary War, and president of the Constitutional Convention. pp. 231, 307

Westinghouse, George *1846–1914* American inventor who designed an air brake for stopping trains. p. 454

Wheatley, Phillis *1753?–1784* American poet who wrote poems that praised the Revolution. p. 241

White, John *?–1593?* English painter and cartographer who led the second group that settled on Roanoke Island. p. 140

Whitman, Marcus *1802–1847* American missionary and pioneer in the Oregon country. p. 362

Whitman, Narcissa *1808–1847* American missionary and pioneer in the Oregon country. p. 362

Whitney, Eli *1765–1825* American inventor most famous for his invention of the cotton gin and his idea of interchangeable parts, which made mass production possible. pp. 350, 391

Williams, Roger *1603?–1683* Founder of Providence in what is now Rhode Island. He had been forced to leave Massachusetts because of his views. p. 172

Wilson, James *1742–1798* Pennsylvania delegate to the Constitutional Convention who argued for a single chief executive elected by an electoral college. p. 286

Wilson, Woodrow *1856–1924* 28th U.S. President. He brought the country into World War I after trying to stay neutral. He favored the League of Nations, but the Senate rejected U.S. membership in the league. p. 528

Woods, Granville T. *1856–1910* African American who improved the air brake and developed a telegraph system for trains. p. 454

Wright, Orville *1871–1948* Pioneer in American aviation who—with his brother, Wilbur—made and flew the first successful airplane, at Kitty Hawk, North Carolina. p. 538

Wright, Wilbur *1867–1912* Pioneer in American aviation who—with his brother, Orville—made and flew the first successful airplane, at Kitty Hawk, North Carolina. p. 538

Y

York *1800s* Enslaved African whose hunting and fishing skills contributed to the Lewis and Clark expedition. p. 333

Young, Brigham *1801–1877* Mormon leader who came after Joseph Smith. He moved his people west to the Great Salt Lake valley. p. 363

GAZETTEER

The Gazetteer is a geographical dictionary that will help you locate places discussed in this book. The page number tells where each place appears on a map.

A

Abilene A city in central Kansas on the Smoky Hill River; a major railroad town. (39°N, 97°W) p. 484

Acadia Original name of Nova Scotia, Canada; once a part of New France. p. 165

Acapulco A seaport in Guerrero state, Mexico, on the Pacific Ocean. (17°N, 100°W) p. 611

Adena (uh•DEE•nuh) An ancient settlement of the Mound Builders; located in southern Ohio. (40°N, 81°W) p. 54

Alamo A mission in San Antonio, Texas; used as a fort during the Texas Revolution. p. 361

Albany The capital of New York. (43°N, 74°W) p. 174

Albemarle Sound (AL•buh•mahrl) An inlet of the Atlantic Ocean; located in northeastern North Carolina. p. 140

Alberta One of Canada's ten provinces; bordered by the Northwest Territories, Saskatchewan, the United States, and British Columbia. p. 629

Alcatraz Island A rocky island in San Francisco Bay, California; formerly a U.S. penitentiary, closed in 1963. p. 468

Aleutian Islands (uh•LOO•shuhn) A chain of islands extending west from the Alaska Peninsula. p. 519

Allegheny River (a•luh•GAY•nee) A river in the northeastern United States, joining the Monongahela River at Pittsburgh, Pennsylvania, to form the Ohio River. p. 76

Altamaha River (AWL•tuh•muh•haw) A river that begins in southeastern Georgia and flows into the Atlantic Ocean. p. 175

Amazon River The longest river in South America, flowing from the Andes Mountains, across Brazil, and into the Atlantic Ocean. p. 125

American Samoa (suh•MOH•uh) A United States territory in the Pacific Ocean. p. 519

Anastasia Island (an•uh•STAY•zhuh) An island off the coast of St. Johns County in northeastern Florida, south of St. Augustine. p. 160

Andes Mountains (AN•deez) The mountains extending along the west coast of South America; the longest chain of mountains in the world. p. 125

Angel Island An island in San Francisco Bay, California. p. 468

Annapolis The capital of Maryland; located on Chesapeake Bay; home of the United States Naval Academy. (39°N, 76°W) p. 175

Antietam (an•TEE•tuhm) A creek in north-central Maryland; site of a major battle of the Civil War. (39°N, 77°W) p. 429

Antigua An island in the eastern part of the Leeward Islands, in the eastern West Indies. p. 621

Appalachian Mountains (a•puh•LAY•chuhn) A large chain of mountains that extends in the United States from Maine to northern Georgia and central Alabama. p. 170

Argentina A country in southern South America. p. 626

Arkansas River A tributary of the Mississippi River, beginning in central Colorado and ending in Desha County, Arkansas. p. 54

Asunción A city in South America, located on the eastern bank of the Paraguay River where the Paraguay and Pilcomayo rivers join. (25°S, 57°W) p. 626

Athabasca River A south tributary of the Mackenzie River in Alberta, western central Canada; flows northeast and then north into Lake Athabaska. p. 629

Atlanta Georgia's capital and largest city. (33°N, 84°W) p. 353

Attu Island (A•too) A rocky island in the Near Islands, the most westerly of the Aleutian Islands; located in southwestern Alaska.

Augusta A city located in eastern Georgia on the Savannah River. (33°N, 82°W) p. 175

Aztec A city in the northwestern corner of New Mexico. (36°N, 108°W) p. 93

B

Baffin Bay A large inlet of the Atlantic Ocean between western Greenland and eastern Baffin Island; connects with the Atlantic Ocean by the Davis Strait. p. 629

Baffin Island Land partially in the Arctic Circle west of Greenland; once known as Helluland. p. 100

Bahama Islands Independent state comprising a chain of islands, cays, and reefs lying southeast of Florida and north of Cuba. p. 124

Baja Peninsula A peninsula extending south-southeast between the Pacific Ocean and the Gulf of California, in northwestern Mexico. p. 611

Baltimore A major seaport in Maryland; located on the Patapsco River at Chesapeake Bay. (39°N, 77°W) p. 175

Banks Island An island in western Franklin district, Northwest Territories, Canada. p. 629

Barbados An island in the Lesser Antilles, West Indies; located east of the central Windward Islands. p. 621

Barbuda A flat coral island in the eastern West Indies. p. 621

Baxter Springs A city in the southeastern corner of Kansas. (37°N, 94°W) p. 492

Beaufort Sea A sea that is northeast of Alaska, northwest of Canada, and west of Banks Island in the Arctic Archipelago. p. 629

Bedloe's Island Now called Liberty Island; a small island in Upper New York Bay; the Statue of Liberty is located there. p. 468

Belém A seaport city in northern Brazil, on the Pará River. (1°S, 48°W) p. 626

Belize (bay•LEEZ) A country in Central America. p. 611

Belmopan A town in Central America; capital of Belize. (17°N, 88°W) p. 621

Belo Horizonte A city in eastern Brazil. (20°S, 44°W) p. 626

Bennington A village in the southwestern corner of Vermont. (43°N, 73°W) p. 249

Bering Strait A narrow water passage separating Asia from North America. p. 38

Beringia (bair•IN•gee•uh) An ancient land bridge that once connected Asia and North America. p. 38

Big Hole A national battlefield in southwestern Montana; site of the battle on August 9, 1877, between U.S. troops and Nez Perce Indians under Chief Joseph. p. 499

Birmingham A large city in Alabama; located near iron and coal deposits. (33°N, 86°W) p. 330

Black Hills A group of mountains in South Dakota; its highest peak, more than 7,000 feet (2,134 m), is the highest point in the Plains states. p. 497

Block House Located in northeastern Tennessee. (35°N, 84°W) p. 328

Bogotá A city in South America located on the plateau of the Andes; capital of Colombia. (4°N, 74°W) p. 626

Boise (BOY•zee) Idaho's capital and largest city. (44°N, 116°W) p. 497

Bolivia A country in west-central South America. p. 626

Bonampak An ancient settlement of the Mayan civilization; located in the eastern Yucatán Peninsula. p. 82

Boonesborough (BOONZ•ber•uh) A town in east-central Kentucky; now called Boonesboro; site of a fort founded by Daniel Boone. (38°N, 84°W) p. 328

Boston The capital and largest city of Massachusetts; settled by the Puritans in 1630. (42°N, 71°W) p. 172

Boston Harbor The western section of Massachusetts Bay; located in eastern Massachusetts; the city of Boston is located at its western end. p. 225

Brainerd A town in southeastern Tennessee. (35°N, 85°W) p. 357

Brandywine A battlefield on Brandywine Creek in Pennsylvania, northwest of Wilmington; site of a battle on September 11, 1777, in which the British defeated the Americans. p. 249

Brasília A city in South America on the Paraná River; capital of Brazil. (15°S, 48°W) p. 626

Brazil The largest country in South America; located in the northeastern part of the continent. p. 626

Brazos River (BRAH•zohs) A river in central Texas; formed by the junction of the Salt Fork and Double Mountain Fork rivers in northern Texas; flows southeast into the Gulf of Mexico. p. 361

British Columbia One of Canada's ten provinces; located on the west coast of Canada and bordered by the Yukon Territory, the Northwest Territories, Alberta, the United States, and the Pacific Ocean. p. 629

Brookline A town in eastern Massachusetts; west-southwest of Boston. (42°N, 71°W) p. 225

Brooklyn A borough forming part of New York City; located in the state of New York. p. 468

Brooks Island An island off the coast of California, in San Francisco Bay. p. 468

Buenos Aires The capital of Argentina. (34°S, 58°W) p. 626

Buffalo A city in western New York; located on the Niagara River at Lake Erie. (43°N, 79°W) p. 330

Bull Run A stream in northeastern Virginia, flowing into the Potomac River; site of two major battles in the Civil War. p. 429

Butte (BYOOT) A city in southwestern Montana; located on the plateau of the Rocky Mountains. (46°N, 112°W) p. 497

C

Cahokia (kuh•HOH•kee•uh) An ancient settlement of the Mound Builders; located near East St. Louis, Illinois. p. 54

Cajamarca (kah•hah•MAR•kah) A city on the Cajamarca River, northwest of Lima, Peru. p. 125

Calgary A city in southern Alberta, Canada; located on the Bow River. (51°N, 114°W) p. 629

Cambridge A city in northeastern Massachusetts; located near Boston. (42°N, 71°W) p. 225

Camden A city in northern central South Carolina, near the Wateree River. (34°N, 81°W) p. 249

Campbelltown A city in south-central North Carolina, on the Cape Fear River. p. 175

Canada The country located to the north of the United States; Canada and the United States share the longest undefended border in the world. p. 364

Canal Zone A strip of territory in Panama. p. 520

Canary Islands An island group in the Atlantic Ocean off the northwest coast of Africa. p. 113

Canyon de Chelly (duh SHAY) A national monument in northeastern Arizona. p. 499

Cape Cod A cape in southeastern Massachusetts; located between Cape Cod Bay and the Atlantic Ocean; Pilgrims sailing on the *Mayflower* landed here. (42°N, 70°W) p. 172

Cape Fear A cape in southeastern North Carolina. (34°N, 78°W) p. 175

Cape Fear River A river in central and southeastern North Carolina; formed by the Deep and Haw rivers; flows southeast into the Atlantic Ocean at eastern Brunswick County. p. 175

Cape Hatteras (HA•tuh•ruhs) A cape on Hatteras Island southeast of Dare County, North Carolina. (35°N, 75°W) p. 175

Cape Horn A cape on the southern tip of South America, on Horn Island; named by Dutch explorers. p. 626

Cape of Good Hope The southernmost tip of Africa, on the Atlantic Ocean. (34°S, 18°E) p. 117

Cape Verde Islands (VERD) Islands off the west coast of Africa. (16°N, 24°W) p. 113

Caracas A city in northern Venezuela; capital of Venezuela. (10°N, 67°W) p. 626

Carson City The capital of Nevada. (39°N, 119°W) p. 509

Cartagena A seaport on the northwestern coast of Colombia. (10°N, 75°W) p. 626

Cascade Range A mountain range in the western United States; extends north from California to Oregon and Washington; Mt. Rainier is its highest peak. p. 366

Cayenne A city on the northwestern coast of Cayenne Island; capital of French Guiana. (5°N, 52°W) p. 626

Cemetery Hill A hill where much of the fighting of the first two days of the Battle of Gettysburg took place; located in Gettysburg, Pennsylvania, at the end of Cemetery Ridge. p. 432

Cemetery Ridge A low ridge in Pennsylvania; located south of Gettysburg. p. 432

Chachapoyas (chah•chah•POH•yahs) An industrial center in northern Peru, northeast of Trujillo. (6°S, 78°W) p. 125

Chaco Canyon (CHAH•koh) An ancient settlement of the Anasazi; located in northwestern New Mexico. p. 54

Chancellorsville (CHAN•slerz•vil) A city in Virginia, just west of Fredericksburg; site of a Civil War battle in 1863. p. 429

Chapultepec (chah•POOL•teh•pek) An ancient settlement of the Aztec civilization; located in south-central Mexico, slightly west of Tenochtitlán. p. 82

Charles River A river in eastern Massachusetts; separates Boston from Cambridge; flows into Boston Bay. p. 225

Charleston A city in South Carolina; a major port on the Atlantic Ocean; once called Charles Towne. (33°N, 80°W) p. 175

Charleston Harbor An inlet of water in eastern South Carolina near the city of Charleston. p. 407

Charlestown A city in Massachusetts; located on Boston Harbor between the mouths of the Charles and Mystic rivers. p. 225

Charlotte The largest city in North Carolina. (35°N, 81°W) p. 249

Charlottetown The capital of Prince Edward Island, Canada; located in the central part of the island, on Hillsborough Bay. (46°N, 63°W) p. 629

Chattanooga (cha•tuh•NOO•guh) An industrial city on the Tennessee River in southeastern Tennessee. p. 353

Chattooga Village Located in northwestern Georgia. p. 357

Cherokee Nation (CHAIR•uh•kee) An American Indian nation located in present-day northern Georgia, eastern

Alabama, southern Tennessee, and western North Carolina. p. 357

Chesapeake Bay A bay of the Atlantic Ocean; surrounded by Virginia and Maryland. p. 144

Cheyenne (shy•AN) The capital of Wyoming. (41°N, 105°W) p. 492

Chicago A city in Illinois; third-largest city in the United States. (42°N, 88°W) p. 330

Chickamauga (chik•uh•MAW•guh) A city in northwestern Georgia; site of a Civil War battle in 1863. p. 429

Chihuahua A city in northern Mexico. (28°N, 106°W) p. 611

Chile A country in southwestern South America. p. 626

Cholula (choh•LOO•lah) An ancient settlement of the Aztec civilization, located in south-central Mexico, to the southeast of Tenochtitlán. (19°N, 98°W) p. 82

Churchill River A river located in central Canada; flows east across Saskatchewan and north Manitoba and then turns northeast into Hudson Bay at Churchill. p. 629

Cincinnati A large city in southern Ohio. (39N°, 85°W) p. 353

Ciudad Juárez A city in Chihuahua state, in northern Mexico. (31°N, 106°W) p. 611

Cleveland The largest city in Ohio; located at the mouth of the Cuyahoga River on Lake Erie. (41°N, 82°W) p. 330

Cold Harbor A city in east-central Virginia, north of the Chickahominy River; site of two battles of the Civil War. p. 429

Colombia A country in northwestern South America. p. 626

Colorado River A river in the southwestern United States; its basin extends from the Rocky Mountains to the Sierra Nevada; flows into the Gulf of California. p. 54

Columbia River A river that begins in the Rocky Mountains in Canada, forms the Washington-Oregon border, and supplies much of that area's waterpower. p. 366

Columbus The capital of Ohio. (40°N, 83°W) p. 353

Compostela (kahm•poh•STEH•lah) A city in Mexico; founded in 1535. (21°N, 105°W) p. 128

Comstock Lode A mining area near Virginia City, Nevada, that once supplied half the silver output of the United States. p. 497

Concord A town in Massachusetts near Boston; site of a famous battle of the American Revolution. (42°N, 71°W) p. 225

Concord River A river in northeastern Massachusetts; formed by the junction of the Sudbury and Assabet rivers; flows north into the Merrimack River at Lowell. p. 225

Connecticut River The longest river in New England; begins in New Hampshire, flows south through Massachusetts and Connecticut, and empties into Long Island Sound. p. 170

Copán (koh•PAHN) An ancient settlement of the Mayan civilization; located in the southern Yucatán Peninsula in present-day Honduras. (15°N, 89°W) p. 82

Costa Rica A republic in southern Central America. (10°N, 84°W) p. 621

Cowpens A town in northwestern South Carolina; just north of the town is the site of a Revolutionary War battle in which the Americans defeated the British in 1781. (35°N, 82°W) p. 249

Coxcatlán An ancient settlement of the Aztec civilization; located in south-central Mexico, to the south of the town of Cholula. p. 82

Cozumel (koh•zooh•MEL) An island in the Caribbean Sea; located east of the Yucatán Peninsula; part of Mexico. p. 82

Crab Orchard An ancient settlement of the Mound Builders; located in southern Illinois. p. 54

Cuba An island country in the Caribbean; the largest and westernmost island of the West Indies. (22°N, 79°W) p. 124

Cuernavaca A town in southern central Mexico; capital of Morelos state. (19°N, 99°W) p. 611

Culp's Hill A hill where much of the fighting of the first two days of the Battle of Gettysburg took place; located in Pennsylvania at the end of Cemetery Ridge. p. 432

Cumberland A city in northwestern Maryland, on the Potomac River. (40°N, 79°W)

Cumberland Gap A pass through the Appalachian Mountains; located in Tennessee; Daniel Boone traveled through this gap into Kentucky. p. 328

Cumberland River A river in southern Kentucky and northern Tennessee. p. 249

Cuzco (KOOS•koh) A large South American city during the 1400s. (13°S, 72°W) p. 101

D

Dahlonega (duh•LAHN•uh•guh) A city in northern Georgia. (35° N, 84 °W) p. 357

Dallas An industrial city in northeastern Texas; located on the Trinity River. (38°N, 97°W) p. 330

Davis Strait A strait between southwestern Greenland and eastern Baffin Island; connects Baffin Bay with the Atlantic Ocean. p. 629

Dawson A city in the Yukon Territory, Canada; located on the right bank of the Yukon River, near the joining of the Yukon and Klondike rivers. (64°N, 139°W) p. 629

Deadwood A city in western South Dakota; located in Deadwood Gulch in the northern Black Hills. (44°N, 104°W) p. 497

Deerfield A town in northwestern Massachusetts; one of the oldest towns in the Connecticut River valley. (43°N, 73°W) p. 172

Delaware Bay A bay of the Atlantic Ocean; located between New Jersey and Delaware. p. 174

Delaware River A river in the northeastern United States; begins in southern New York and flows into the Atlantic Ocean at Delaware Bay. p. 76

Denver Colorado's capital and largest city. (40°N, 105°W) p. 484

Des Moines (dih•MOYN) Iowa's capital and largest city. (42°N, 94°W) p. 165

Detroit The largest city in Michigan; located on the Detroit River; center of the U.S. automobile industry. (42°N, 83°W) p. 165

Dickson An ancient settlement of the Mound Builders; located in what is now central Illinois. p. 54

Dodge City A city in southern Kansas; located on the Arkansas River; once a major railroad center on the Santa Fe Trail. (38°N, 100°W) p. 492

Dominica An island and a republic in the West Indies; located in the center of the Lesser Antilles between Guadeloupe and Martinique; used to be a self-governing state in association with Great Britain. p. 621

Dominican Republic A country in the West Indies, occupying the eastern part of the island of Hispaniola. p. 517

Dover (DE) A commercial city in Delaware; located south of Wilmington. (39°N, 76°W) p. 174

Dover (NH) A city in southeastern New Hampshire. (43°N, 71°W) p. 172

Durango A city in northwestern central Mexico. (24°N, 104°W) p. 611

E

East River A strait connecting Long Island Sound and New York Bay. p. 468

Ecuador A country in the northwestern part of South America. p. 626

Edenton (EE•duhn•tuhn) A town in northeastern North Carolina, on the Albemarle Sound near the mouth of the Chowan River. (36°N, 77°W) p. 175

Edmonton The capital of Alberta, Canada; located in the south-central part of the province on both banks of the north Saskatchewan River. (53°N, 113°W) p. 629

El Paso A city at the western tip of Texas; located on the Rio Grande. (32°N, 106°W) p. 162

El Salvador A republic in Central America. p. 611

Ellesmere Island (ELZ•mir) The most northern of Canada's Arctic Islands. p. 629

Ellis Island An island in Upper New York Bay; located southwest of Manhattan. (40°N, 74°W) p. 468

Ellsworth A city in central Kansas. p. 492

Emerald Mound An ancient settlement of the Mound Builders; located in southwestern Mississippi. p. 54

Erie Canal The longest canal in the world; connects Troy (on the Hudson River) with Buffalo (on Lake Erie). p. 353

F

Fairbanks A city in central Alaska. (65°N, 148°W) p. 497

Falkland Islands A British colony in the Atlantic Ocean; located east of the Strait of Magellan. p. 626

Falmouth A town in southwest Maine, north of Portland. (44°N, 70°W) p. 172

Finger Lakes Located in west-central New York; near Seneca Falls.

Fort Atkinson A fort in southern Kansas. p. 366

Fort Boise (BOY•zee) Located in eastern Oregon on the Snake River. p. 366

Fort Bridger A village in southwestern Wyoming; nearby is the site of a trading post built in 1843 by James Bridger, as a station on the Oregon Trail. p. 366

Fort Crèvecoeur (KREEV•KUR) A fort built by La Salle on the Illinois River in 1680. p. 166

Fort Crown Point Located in northeastern New York on the shore of Lake Champlain. p. 211

Fort Cumberland Located in northeastern West Virginia on its border with Maryland. p. 211

Fort Dearborn A fort built in 1803; eventually became part of Chicago, Illinois. p. 338

Fort Donelson A fort located in northwestern Tennessee; captured by General Ulysses S. Grant during the Civil War. p. 429

Fort Duquesne (doo•KAYN) A French fort on the site of modern Pittsburgh, Pennsylvania; captured by the British in 1758 and renamed Fort Pitt. p. 211

Fort Edward A village in eastern New York on the Hudson River. (43°N, 74°W) p. 211

Fort Frontenac (FRAHNT•uhn•ak) A French fort on the site of modern Kingston, Ontario, in Canada; captured by the British in 1758. p. 166

Fort Gibson A fort in northeastern Oklahoma. (36°N, 95°W) p. 381

Fort Hall Once a fort at a junction on the Oregon Trail; located on the Snake River, north of Pocatello in southeastern Idaho. p. 366

Fort Laramie A fort in southeastern Wyoming. p. 366

Fort Ligonier (lig•uh•NIR) Located in southern Pennsylvania near the Ohio River. p. 211

Fort Louisbourg Located in eastern Canada on the coast of the Atlantic Ocean. p. 211

Fort Mackinac (MA•kuh•naw) Located on the tip of northern Michigan. p. 338

Fort Mandan A fort in the north-central United States on the Missouri River. p. 332

Fort McHenry A fort in Baltimore, Maryland; established in 1725. p. 338

Fort Miamis A French fort in North America, on the eastern shore of Lake Michigan and on the border between Michigan and Indiana. p. 166

Fort Necessity A fort in southwestern Pennsylvania on its border with West Virginia. p. 211

Fort Niagara A fort at the mouth of the Niagara River in New York; captured by the British in 1813 and returned to the United States in 1815. p. 166

Fort Oswego Located in western New York on the coast of Lake Ontario. p. 211

Fort Sumter A fort on an island in the harbor of Charleston, South Carolina; the first Civil War battle took place there. p. 407

Fort Ticonderoga (ty•kahn•der•OH•gah) A historic fort on Lake Champlain, in New York; site of important battles in the American Revolution. p. 211

Fort Vancouver Once a fort; now the city of Vancouver; located in Washington on the Columbia River. (45°N, 122°W) p. 366

Fort Walla Walla A fort in southeastern Washington. p. 366

Fort William Henry A fort in eastern New York. p. 211

Fort Worth A city in northern Texas on the Trinity River. (33°N, 97°W) p. 492

Fortaleza A city and port in northeastern Brazil. (3°S, 38°W) p. 626

Fox River Located in southeast and central Wisconsin; flows southwest, nearing the Wisconsin River, then into Green Bay. p. 166

Franklin A city in northern central Missouri on the Missouri River. (39°N, 93°W) p. 353

Fraser River A river that begins in the Rocky Mountains in Canada and empties into the Pacific Ocean near Vancouver, British Columbia. p. 629

Fredericksburg A city in northeastern Virginia on the Rappahannock River. (38°N, 77°W) p. 175

Fredericton The capital of New Brunswick, Canada; located in the southwestern part of the province. (46°N, 66°W) p. 629

French Guiana An overseas department of France, in north-central South America. p. 626

Frenchtown A town in eastern Michigan; site of a battle in the War of 1812. (42°N, 83°W) p. 338

Frobisher Bay An inlet extending to the northwest in southeastern Baffin Island, Northwest Territories.

G

Gander A town located in northeastern Newfoundland. (49°N, 54°W) p. 629

Gatun Lake (gah•TOON) A lake in Panama; Gatun Dam forms the lake. p. 520

Georgetown A city in South America located at the mouth of the Demerara River; capital of Guyana. (6°N, 58°W) p. 626

Georgian Bay A bay located in eastern Lake Huron, along the southwestern coast of Ontario. p. 76

Germantown A residential section of Philadelphia, Pennsylvania, on Wissahickon Creek; site of a battle during the American Revolution. (40°N, 75°W) p. 249

Gettysburg A town in Pennsylvania; site of a Civil War battle in 1863. (40°N, 77°W) p. 429

Golconda (gahl•KAHN•duh) A city in the southeastern corner of Illinois. (37°N, 88°W) p. 381

Gonzales (gohn•ZAH•lays) A city in south-central Texas; scene of the first battle of the Texas Revolution. (30°N, 97°W) p. 361

Governors Island An island in New York Bay near the mouth of the East River. p. 468

Great Basin One of the driest parts of the United States; located in Nevada, Utah, California, Idaho, Wyoming, and Oregon; includes the Great Salt Lake Desert, the Mojave Desert, and Death Valley. p. 366

Great Bear Lake A lake located in northwestern central Mackenzie district, Northwest Territories, Canada. p. 629

Great Lakes The largest group of freshwater lakes in the world; located in north-central North America. p. 338

Great Plains The western part of the Interior Plains. p. 366

Great Salt Lake The largest lake in the Great Basin; located in Utah. p. 366

Great Slave Lake A lake located in southern Mackenzie district, Northwest Territories, Canada. p. 629

Greenland The largest island on Earth; located in the northern Atlantic Ocean, east of Canada. p. 38

Grenada An island in the West Indies; the southernmost of the Windward Islands. p. 621

Groton (GRAH•tuhn) A town in southeastern Connecticut; located on Long Island Sound at the mouth of the Thames River; Fort Griswold is located there. (41°N, 72°W) p. 172

Guadalajara A city in western central Mexico; capital of Jalisco state. (20°N, 103°W) p. 611

Guadalupe (gwah•dah•LOO•pay) An archaeological site located in northwestern New Mexico. p. 93

Guam (GWAHM) U.S. territory in the Pacific Ocean; largest of the Mariana Islands. p. 519

Guánica (GWAHN•ih•kah) A town in southwestern Puerto Rico, on the Guánica Harbor. (18°N, 67°W) p. 517

Guantánamo Bay (gwahn•TAH•nah•moh) A bay on the southeastern coast of Oriente province; located in eastern Cuba. p. 580

Guatemala A republic in Central America. p. 611

Guatemala City A city in Central America; capital of Guatemala (the republic); largest city in Central America. (14°N, 90°W) p. 621

Guayaquil A seaport in southwestern Ecuador; capital of Guayas province. (2°S, 80°W) p. 626

Guilford Courthouse (GIL•ferd) Located in north-central North Carolina, near Greensboro; site of a Revolutionary War battle in 1781. p. 249

Gulf of California A part of the Pacific Ocean in northwestern Mexico. p. 611

Gulf of Mexico A body of water off the southeast coast of North America; surrounded by the United States, Cuba, and Mexico. p. 54

Gulf of St. Lawrence A deep gulf of the Atlantic Ocean, off the east coast of Canada, between Newfoundland and the Canadian mainland. p. 136

Guntersville A town in northeastern Alabama on the Tennessee River. (34°N, 86°W) p. 357

Guyana A country in north-central South America. p. 626

H

Haiti A country in the West Indies, occupying the western part of the island of Hispaniola. p. 517

Halifax The capital of the province of Nova Scotia, Canada; a major port on the Atlantic Ocean; remains free of ice all year. (44°N, 63°W) p. 629

Harrodsburg A city in central Kentucky. p. 328

Hartford The capital of Connecticut. (42°N, 73°W) p. 172

Havana The capital of Cuba. (23°N, 82°W) p. 128

Hawaiian Islands A chain of volcanic and coral islands; located in the north-central Pacific Ocean. p. 519

Hawikuh (hah•wee•KOO) A city in New Mexico. p. 128

Helena The capital of Montana. (47°N, 112°W) p. 497

Hispaniola (ees•pah•NYOH•lah) An island in the West Indies made up of Haiti and the Dominican Republic; located in the Caribbean Sea between Cuba and Puerto Rico. p. 124

Honduras (ohn•DUR•ahs) A republic in Central America. p. 580

Honolulu (hah•nuhl•OO•loo) Hawaii's capital and largest city. (21°N, 158°W) p. 554

Hopewell An ancient settlement of the Mound Builders; located in southern Ohio. (18°N, 94°W) p. 54

Horseshoe Bend A national military park in eastern Alabama; established in 1959; site of a battle between General Andrew Jackson's forces and the Creek Indian Confederacy, March 27, 1814. p. 338

Houston The largest city in Texas; third-largest port in the United States; leading industrial center in Texas. (30°N, 95°W) p. 330

Hudson Bay A bay in Canada surrounded by the Northwest Territories, Manitoba, Ontario, and Quebec; connects with the Atlantic Ocean through the Hudson Strait. p. 165

Hudson River A river in the northeastern United States beginning in upper New York and flowing into the Atlantic Ocean; named for the explorer Henry Hudson. p. 76

Hudson Strait A strait between southern Baffin Island and northern Quebec, in northeastern Canada; connects the Atlantic Ocean with Hudson Bay. p. 629

I

Iceland An island country in the northern Atlantic Ocean, between Greenland and Norway. p. 560

Illinois River A river in Illinois; flows southwest into the Mississippi River. p. 166

Independence A city in western Missouri; the starting point of the Oregon Trail. (39°N, 94°W) p. 366

Indianapolis Indiana's capital and largest city. (39°N, 86°W) p. 353

Isthmus of Panama (IHS•muhs) A narrow strip of land that connects North America and South America. p. 117

J

Jacksonville A city in northeastern Florida; located near the mouth of the St. Johns River. (30°N, 82°W) p. 330

Jamaica (juh•MAY•kuh) An island country in the West Indies, south of Cuba. p. 124

James River A river in central Virginia; begins where the Jackson and Cowpasture rivers join; flows into Chesapeake Bay. p. 144

Jamestown The first permanent English settlement in the Americas; located on the shore of the James River. (37°N, 76°W) p. 144

Juneau (JOO•noh) The capital of Alaska. (58°N, 134°W) p. 497

K

Kahoolawe (kah•hoh•uh•LAY•vay) One of the eight main islands of Hawaii; located west of Maui. p. 554

Kansas City The largest city in Missouri; located on the Missouri River on the Kansas-Missouri border. (39°N, 95°W) p. 457

Kaskaskia (ka•SKAS•kee•uh) A village in southwestern Illinois, near the junction of the Kaskaskia and Mississippi rivers. (38°N, 90°W) p. 249

Kauai (KOW•eye) The fourth-largest of the eight main islands of Hawaii. p. 554

Kennebec River (KEH•nih•bek) A river in west-central and southern Maine; flows south from Moosehead Lake to the Atlantic Ocean. p. 172

Kennesaw Mountain (KEH•nuh•saw) An isolated peak in northwestern Georgia, near Atlanta; site of a Civil War battle in 1864. p. 429

Kentucky River A river in north-central Kentucky; flows northwest into the Ohio River. p. 328

Key West A city in southwestern Florida, on Key West island. (25°N, 82°W) p. 517

Kings Mountain A ridge in northern South Carolina and southern North Carolina; the part in South Carolina is the site of a Revolutionary War battle in which the Americans defeated the British on October 7, 1780. p. 249

Kingston A commercial seaport in the West Indies; capital of Jamaica. (18°N, 76°W) p. 621

Klondike An area in the Yukon Territory, Canada; gold was discovered there in 1896. p. 497

L

La Paz A city in South America; capital of Bolivia. (16°S, 68°W) p. 626

La Venta An ancient settlement of the Olmecs; located in southern Mexico. p. 54

Labrador The northeastern tip of North America; once known as Markland. p. 100

Labrador City A city located in western Newfoundland. (53°N, 67°W) p. 629

Lake Athabasca A lake located in northeastern Alberta and northwestern Saskatchewan. p. 629

Lake Champlain (sham•PLAYN) A lake between New York and Vermont. p. 76

Lake Erie The fourth largest of the Great Lakes; borders Canada and the United States. p. 76

Lake Huron The second largest of the Great Lakes; borders Canada and the United States. p. 28

Lake Michigan The third largest of the Great Lakes; borders Michigan, Illinois, Indiana, and Wisconsin. p. 28

Lake Ontario The smallest of the Great Lakes; borders Canada and the United States. p. 76

Lake Superior The largest of the Great Lakes; borders Canada and the United States. p. 28

Lake Texcoco (tes•KOH•koh) A lake in present-day Mexico City; the ancient Aztec civilization built their capital, Tenochtitlán, on islands in the lake. p. 82

Lake Titicaca (tih•tih•KAH•kah) The highest navigable lake in the world; located on the border between Peru and Bolivia. p. 125

Lake Winnipeg A lake located in Manitoba. p. 629

Lanai (luh•NY) An island in central Hawaii; a major pineapple-producing area. p. 554

Lancaster A city in southeastern Pennsylvania. (40°N, 76°W) p. 174

Las Vegas A city in the southeastern corner of Nevada. p. 509

Lava Beds A national monument located in northern California; made of lava and ice caves; battleground of the Modoc Wars in 1873. p. 499

Leadville (LED•vil) A town in Colorado. (39°N, 106°W) p. 497

Leticia A town in southeastern Colombia, on the Amazon River. (4°S, 70°W) p. 626

Lexington A town near Boston, Massachusetts; first battle of the American Revolution took place there. (42°N, 71°W) p. 225

Lima (LEE•mah) The capital of Peru; located on the Rimac River. (12°S, 77°W) p. 125

Little Bighorn River A river in southern Montana; site of a fierce battle between Sioux and Cheyenne Indians and U.S. Army soldiers led by General George Armstrong Custer. p. 499

Little Round Top A hill in Pennsylvania at the end of Cemetery Ridge. p. 432

Long Island An island located east of New York City and south of Connecticut; lies between Long Island Sound and the Atlantic Ocean. p. 174

Los Adaes A city in eastern Texas. p. 162

Los Angeles The largest city in California; second-largest city in the United States. (34°N, 118°W) p. 366

Louisville (LOO•ih•vil) The largest city in Kentucky; located on the Ohio River. (38°N, 86°W) p. 330

M

Machu Picchu (mah•choo•PEE•choo) The site of an ancient Inca city on a mountain in the Andes, northwest of Cuzco, Peru. p. 125

Mackenzie River A river located in western Mackenzie district, Northwest Territories, Canada; flows north-northwest into Mackenzie Bay; second-longest river in North America. p. 629

Macon (MAY•kuhn) A city in central Georgia; located on the Ocmulgee River, southeast of Atlanta. (33°N, 84°W) p. 353

Managua A city in Central America; capital of Nicaragua; located on the south shore of Lake Managua. (12°N, 86°W) p. 621

Manaus A city located in western Brazil on the left bank of Rio Negro. (3°S, 60°W) p. 626

Manhattan An island at the north end of New York Bay; surrounded by the Spuyten Duyvil Creek, the Harlem River, the East River, New York Bay, and the Hudson River. p. 468

Manitoba (ma•nuh•TOH•buh) A province in central Canada; bordered by Hudson Bay, Ontario, the United States, and Saskatchewan; located on the Interior Plains of Canada. p. 629

Massachusetts Bay An inlet of the Atlantic Ocean on the east coast of Massachusetts; extends from Cape Ann to Cape Cod. p. 172

Matamoros (mah•tah•MOH•rohs) A town in Coahuila state, northeastern Mexico. (26°N, 97°W) p. 611

Maui (MOW•ee) The second-largest island in Hawaii. p. 554

Maumee River (maw•MEE) Located in Indiana and Ohio; formed by the junction of the St. Joseph and St. Marys rivers in northeastern Indiana; flows east and then northeast into Lake Erie. p. 249

Mazatlán A seaport in Sinaloa state, western Mexico; largest Mexican seaport on the Pacific coast. (23°N, 106°W) p. 611

Meadowcroft The site of an archaeological dig in southwestern Pennsylvania. p. 42

Medford A city in northeastern Massachusetts, north of Boston. (42°N, 71°W) p. 225

Memphis A city in the southwestern corner of Tennessee, on the Mississippi River. (35°N, 90°W) p. 353

Mendoza A city located southeast of Aconcagua in Argentina. (33°S, 69°W) p. 626

Menotomy Located in northeastern Massachusetts. p. 225

Mérida A city in southeastern Mexico; capital of Yucatán state. (21°N, 89°W) p. 611

Merrimack River A river in southern New Hampshire and northeastern Massachusetts; formed by the junction of the Pemigewasset and Winnipesaukee rivers at Franklin, New Hampshire. p. 172

Mesa Verde (MAY•suh VAIR•day) An ancient settlement of the Anasazi; located in southwestern Colorado. p. 54

Mexico The country to the south of the United States; one of the most mountainous countries in the world. p. 162

Mexico City The capital of Mexico; located on the southern edge of the Central Plateau; has an elevation of about 7,000 feet (2134 m). (19°N, 99°W) p. 162

Miami A city in southeastern Florida, on Biscayne Bay. (25°N, 80°W) p. 580

Midway Island A United States territory in the Pacific Ocean. p. 519

Milwaukee The largest city in Wisconsin; located on Lake Michigan. (43°N, 88°W) p. 330

Minneapolis The largest city in Minnesota; located on the Mississippi River; twin city with St. Paul. (45°N, 93°W) p. 457

Mississippi River The largest river in the United States; its source is Lake Itasca, Minnesota; flows into the Gulf of Mexico. p. 54

Missouri River A tributary of the Mississippi River, beginning in Montana and ending at St. Louis, Missouri. p. 54

Mobile (moh•BEEL) A seaport in Alabama; located at the mouth of the Mobile River. (31°N, 88°W) p. 457

Mobile Bay An inlet of the Gulf of Mexico; the site of a Civil War naval battle in 1864. p. 429

Mohawk River A tributary of the Hudson River, beginning in central New York. p. 76

Molokai (mah•luh•KY) An island in Hawaii. p. 554

Monongahela River (muh•nahn•guh•HEE•luh) A river in northern West Virginia and southwestern Pennsylvania; flows north across the Pennsylvania border and at Pittsburgh joins with the Allegheny River to form the Ohio River.

Monte Albán (mahn•tee ahl•BAHN) An ancient settlement of the Aztec civilization; located in south-central Mexico, to the south of Coxcatlán. p. 82

Monterrey A city in northeastern Mexico; capital of Nuevo León state. (25°N, 100°W) p. 611

Montevideo A seaport city located in the southern part of the north shore of La Plata estuary; capital of Uruguay. (35°S, 56°W) p. 626

Montgomery The capital of Alabama. (32°N, 86°W) p. 353

Montreal The largest city in Canada; located in the province of Quebec, in the St. Lawrence lowlands. (45°N, 73°W) p. 136

Morristown A town in northern New Jersey, west-northwest of Newark. (41°N, 74°W) p. 174

Moundville An ancient settlement of the Mound Builders; located in what is now central Alabama. (33°N, 87°W) p. 54

Mount Vernon The home and burial place of George Washington; located in Fairfax County, Virginia, on the Potomac River, below Washington, D.C. p. 311

Murfreesboro A city in central Tennessee on the West Fork of the Stone River. (36°N, 86°W) p. 381

Mystic River A short river rising in the Mystic Lakes; located in northeastern Massachusetts; flows southeast into Boston Harbor north of Charlestown. p. 225

N

Nashville The capital of Tennessee. (36°N, 87°W) p. 330

Nassau A city on the northeastern coast of New Providence Island; capital of the Bahama Islands. (25°N, 77°W) p. 621

Natal A seaport city in northeastern Brazil. (5°S, 35°W) p. 626

Natchez A city in southwestern Mississippi on the Mississippi River. (32°N, 91°W) p. 353

Nauvoo (naw•VOO) A city in western Illinois on the Mississippi River. (41°N, 91°W) p. 366

Nazca An Indian civilization on the central coast of Peru. p. 125

New Bern A city and port in southeastern North Carolina. (35°N, 77°W) p. 175

New Brunswick One of Canada's ten provinces; bordered by Quebec, the Gulf of St. Lawrence, Northumberland Strait, the Bay of Fundy, the United States, and Nova Scotia. p. 629

New Echota (ih•KOHT•uh) An Indian town in northwestern Georgia; chosen as the capital of the Cherokee Nation in 1819. (34°N, 85°W) p. 357

New Guinea (GIH•nee) An island of the eastern Malay Archipelago; located in the western Pacific Ocean, north of Australia; second-largest island in the world. p. 560

New Haven A city in southern Connecticut on New Haven Harbor. (41°N, 73°W) p. 172

New London A city in southeastern Connecticut on Long Island Sound at the mouth of the Thames River. (41°N, 72°W) p. 194

New Orleans The largest city in Louisiana; a major port located between the Mississippi River and Lake Pontchartrain. (30°N, 90°W) p. 165

New River A river in southwestern Virginia and southern West Virginia; flows north across Virginia and into south-central West Virginia. p. 328

New Ulm (UHLM) A city in southern Minnesota on the Minnesota River. (44°N, 94°W) p. 499

New York City The largest city in the United States; located in southeastern New York at the mouth of the Hudson River. (41°N, 74°W) p. 174

Newark A port in northeastern New Jersey on the Passaic River and Newark Bay. (41°N, 74°W) p. 174

Newfoundland (NOO•fuhn•luhnd) One of Canada's ten provinces; among the earliest Viking settlements in North America, once known as Vinland. p. 100

Newport A city on the southern end of Rhode Island; located at the mouth of Narragansett Bay. (41°N, 71°W) p. 172

Newton A city in south-central Kansas. (38°N, 97°W) p. 492

Niihau (NEE•how) An island in northwestern Hawaii. p. 554

Nogales A town in Sonora state, in northwestern Mexico. (31°N, 111°W) p. 611

Nome A city on the southern side of the Seward Peninsula; located in western Alaska. (65°N, 165°W) p. 497

Norfolk (NAWR•fawk) A city in southeastern Virginia; located on the Elizabeth River. (37°N, 76°W) p. 175

North Pole The northernmost point on the Earth. p. 571

Northwest Territories One of Canada's two territories; located in northern Canada. p. 629

Nova Scotia (noh•vuh•SKOH•shuh) One of Canada's ten provinces; located on a peninsula. p. 136

Nueces River (noo•AY•says) A river in southern Texas; flows into Nueces Bay, which is at the head of Corpus Christi Bay. p. 361

O

Oahu (oh•AH•hoo) The third-largest of eight main islands of Hawaii; Honolulu is located there. p. 554

Oaxaca (wuh•HAH•kuh) A city and state in southern Mexico. (17°N, 96°W) p. 611

Ocmulgee (ohk•MUHL•gee) An ancient settlement of the Mound Builders; located in central Georgia. p. 54

Ocmulgee River (ohk•MUHL•gee) A river in central Georgia; formed by the junction of the Yellow and South rivers, flows south and southeast to join the Oconee River and then forms the Altamaha River. p. 175

Ogallala (oh•guh•LAHL•uh) A city in western Nebraska on the South Platte River. (41°N, 102°W) p. 492

Ohio River A tributary of the Mississippi River beginning in Pittsburgh, Pennsylvania, and ending at Cairo, Illinois. p. 54

Oka A town located in southeastern Quebec, on the St. Lawrence River. (45°N, 74°W) p. 629

Omaha The largest city in Nebraska; located on the Missouri River. (41°N, 96°W) p. 366

Ontario (ahn•TAIR•ee•oh) One of Canada's ten provinces; located between Quebec and Manitoba. p. 629

Orinoco River A river in Venezuela; flows west then north forming a section of the Colombia-Venezuela boundary, then turns east in central Venezuela and empties through a wide delta into the Atlantic Ocean. p. 626

Ottawa (AH•tuh•wuh) The capital of Canada; located in Ontario on the St. Lawrence Lowlands. (45°N, 75°W) p. 629

P

Palenque (pah•LENG•kay) An ancient settlement of the Mayan civilization; located just west of the Yucatán Peninsula. (17°N, 92°W) p. 82

Palmyra Island (pal•MY•ruh) One of the northernmost of the Line Islands; located in the central Pacific Ocean. p. 519

Palo Duro Canyon A canyon on the Red River; located in northwestern Texas; contains a state park. p. 499

Panama The southernmost country in Central America. (9°N, 79°W) p. 125

Panama Canal A canal across the Isthmus of Panama; extends from the Caribbean Sea to the Gulf of Panama. p. 520

Panama City A city in Central America; capital of the Republic of Panama. (9°N, 79°W) p. 621

Paraguay A country in south-central South America. p. 626

Paraguay River A river in south-central South America; empties into the Paraná at the southwestern corner of Paraguay. p. 626

Paramaribo A seaport city located on the Suriname River; capital of Suriname. (5°N, 55°W) p. 626

Paraná River A river in southeast-central South America; formed by the joining of the Rio Grande and the Paranaíba River in south-central Brazil. p. 626

Peace River A river in western Canada; flows east across border of Alberta, turns northeast and joins the Slave River just north of its outlet from Lake Athabaska. p. 629

Pearl Harbor An inlet on the southern coast of Oahu, Hawaii; the Japanese attacked an American naval base there on December 7, 1941. p. 554

Pecos River (PAY•kohs) A river in eastern New Mexico and western Texas; empties into the Rio Grande. p. 492

Pee Dee River A river in North Carolina and South Carolina; forms where the Yadkin and Uharie rivers meet and empties into Winyah Bay. p. 175

Perryville A city in east-central Kentucky; site of a battle in the Civil War. (38°N, 85°W) p. 429

Perth Amboy A port city; located in central New Jersey on Raritan Bay at the mouth of the Raritan River. (40°N, 74°W) p. 174

Peru A country in northwestern South America. p. 626

Petersburg A city in southeastern Virginia. (37°N, 77°W) p. 429

Philadelphia A city in southeastern Pennsylvania; located where the Delaware and Schuylkill rivers meet; major U.S. port. (40°N, 75°W) p. 174

Philippine Islands A group of more than 7,000 islands off the coast of Southeast Asia, making up the country of the Philippines. p. 117

Phoenix Arizona's capital and largest city. (34°N, 112°W) p. 486

Pikes Peak A mountain peak in the Rocky Mountains; named for Zebulon Pike. p. 332

Pittsburgh The second-largest city in Pennsylvania; the Allegheny and Monongahela rivers meet there to form the Ohio River. (40°N, 80°W) p. 330

Platte River (PLAT) A river in central Nebraska; flows east into the Missouri River below Omaha. p. 366

Plattsburg A city in the northeastern corner of New York, on the western shore of Lake Champlain. (45°N, 73°W) p. 338

Plymouth A town on Plymouth Bay in Massachusetts; site of the first settlement built by the Pilgrims who sailed on the *Mayflower*. (42°N, 71°W) p. 144

Port Royal A town in western Nova Scotia, Canada; name changed to Annapolis Royal in honor of Queen Anne. p. 136

Port-au-Prince A seaport located in Hispaniola Island, in the West Indies, on the southeastern shore of the Gulf of Gonave; capital of Haiti. (18°N, 72°W) p. 621

Portland (ME) A seaport city in southwestern Maine. (44°N, 70°W) p. 330

Portland (OR) Oregon's largest city. (46°N, 123°W) p. 484

Pôrto Alegre A seaport city in southern Brazil; located on an inlet at the northern end of Lagoa dos Patos. p. 626

Port-of-Spain A seaport in the northwestern part of the island of Trinidad on the Gulf of Paria; capital of Trinidad and Tobago. (10°N, 61°W) p. 621

Portsmouth (NH) A seaport city in southeastern New Hampshire. (43°N, 71°W) p. 172

Portsmouth (RI) A town in southeastern Rhode Island; located on the Sakonnet River. (41°N, 71°W) p. 172

Potomac River (puh•TOH•muhk) A river on the Coastal Plain of the United States; begins in West Virginia and flows into Chesapeake Bay; Washington, D.C., is located on this river. p. 170

Potosí (poh•toh•SEE) One of the highest cities in the world; a major industrial center in Bolivia. (19°S, 65°W) p. 125

Prince Edward Island One of Canada's ten provinces; located in the Gulf of St. Lawrence. p. 629

Princeton A borough in west-central New Jersey, northnortheast of Trenton. (40°N, 75W) p. 249

Promontory Point The point in northwestern Utah where the tracks of the Union Pacific and Central Pacific railroads met in 1869, completing the first transcontinental railroad in the United States.

Providence Rhode Island's capital and largest city. (42°N, 71°W) p. 172

Puebla A city in southeastern central Mexico. (19°N, 98°W) p. 611

Pueblo (PWEH•bloh) A city in Colorado. p. 492

Pueblo Bonito (PWEH•bloh boh•NEE•toh) Largest of the prehistoric pueblo ruins; located in Chaco Canyon National Monument, New Mexico. p. 93

Puerto Rico A commonwealth of the United States; an island about 1,000 miles (1,609 km) southeast of Florida. p. 128

Puerto Vallarta A coastal town in Jalisco state, in west-central Mexico. (20°N, 105°W) p. 611

Put-in-Bay A bay in South Bass Island, Lake Erie, in Ohio; the scene of Commodore Perry's victory over the British fleet on September 10, 1813. p. 338

Pyramid Lake A lake in northwestern Nevada. (40°N, 119°W) p. 499

Q

Quebec (kwih•BEK) The capital of the province of Quebec, in Canada; located on the north side of the St. Lawrence River; the first successful French settlement in the Americas; established in 1608. (46°N, 71°W) p. 136

Quito (KEE•toh) A city in South America; lies almost on the equator, just southeast of the volcano Pichincha; capital of Ecuador. (0°, 78°W) p. 626

R

Raleigh (RAW•lee) The capital of North Carolina. (36°N, 79°W) p. 353

Recife A seaport located in eastern Brazil at the mouth of the Capibaribe River, near Point Plata. (8°S, 35°W) p. 626

Red Clay A town located in southeastern Tennessee. p. 357

Red River A tributary of the Mississippi River; rises in eastern New Mexico, flows across Louisiana and into the Mississippi River; forms much of the Texas-Oklahoma border. p. 332

Regina (rih•JY•nuh) The capital of Saskatchewan, Canada; located in the southern part of the province. (50°N, 104°W) p. 629

Resolute A town located in the Parry Islands. (74°N, 95°W) p. 629

Richmond The capital of Virginia; located on the Fall Line of the James River. (38°N, 77°W) p. 175

Rio Balsas A river in southern Mexico. p. 82

Rio de Janeiro A commercial seaport in southeastern Brazil on the southwest shore of Guanabara Bay. (23°S, 43°W) p. 626

Rio de la Plata A river on the southeastern coast of South America. p. 626

Rio Grande A river in southwestern North America; it begins in Colorado and flows into the Gulf of Mexico; the river forms the border between Texas and Mexico. p. 54

Rio Usumacinta (oo•sooh•mah•SIN•tah) A river in the southern Yucatán Peninsula; borders Mexico and Guatemala. p. 82

Roanoke Island (ROH•uh•nohk) An island near the coast of North Carolina; the site of the lost colony. p. 140

Roanoke River (ROH•uh•nohk) A river in southern Virginia and northeastern North Carolina; flows east and southeast across the North Carolina border and continues southeast into Albemarle Sound. p. 170

Rochester (RAH•ches•ter) A port city located in western New York. (43°N, 78°W) p. 371

Rocky Mountains A range of mountains covering much of the United States and Canada and extending from Alaska to New Mexico; these mountains divide rivers that flow east from those that flow west. p. 366

Roxbury A residential district in southern Boston, Massachusetts; formerly a city, but became part of Boston in 1868; founded in 1630. (42°N, 71°W) p. 225

S

Sabine River (sah•BEEN) A river in Texas. p. 361

Sacramento The capital of California. (39°N, 121°W) p. 366

Sacramento River A river in California. p. 366

Salem A city in northeastern Massachusetts. (43°N, 71°W) p. 172

Salisbury (SAWLZ•behr•ee) A city in central North Carolina. (36°N, 80°W) p. 276

Salmon An ancient Anasazi settlement; located on the San Juan River. (45°N, 114°W) p. 93

Salt Lake City Utah's capital and largest city; located on the Jordan River. (41°N, 112°W) p. 366

Salvador A seaport city in eastern Brazil, located on All Saints Bay. (13°S, 38°W) p. 626

San Antonio A city in south-central Texas; located on the San Antonio River; the Alamo is located there. (29N°, 99°W) p. 361

San Antonio River A river in southern Texas; flows southeast and empties into San Antonio Bay. p. 361

San Diego A large city on the coast of southern California. (33°N, 117°W) p. 162

San Francisco The largest city in northern California; located on San Francisco Bay. (38°N, 123°W) p. 162

San Francisco Bay A part of the Pacific Ocean; San Francisco is located on this large bay in northern California. p. 468

San Jacinto (jah•SIN•toh) Located in eastern Texas; a battle was fought near the mouth of the San Jacinto River on April 21, 1836, in which the Americans under General Sam Houston defeated the Mexicans under General Santa Anna. (31°N, 95°W) p. 361

San José A city in Central America; capital of Costa Rica. (10°N, 84°W) p. 621

San Juan (san WAHN) Puerto Rico's capital and largest city. (18°N, 66°W) p. 517

San Juan Hill (san WAHN) A hill near Santiago de Cuba, in eastern Cuba; captured by Cuban and American troops during the Spanish-American War in 1898. p. 517

San Juan River (san WAHN) A river in Colorado, New Mexico, and Utah; flows southwest across the Colorado–New Mexico border, bends west and then northwest across southwestern Colorado, flows into Utah, and then empties into the Colorado River. p. 93

San Lorenzo An ancient settlement of the Olmecs; located in southern Mexico. p. 54

San Salvador One of the islands in the Bahamas; located in the Atlantic Ocean; Christopher Columbus landed there in 1492. p. 113

Santa Fe (san•tah FAY) The capital of New Mexico. (36°N, 106°W) p. 163

Santee River A river in southeast-central South Carolina; formed by the junction of the Congaree and Wateree rivers; flows southeast into the Atlantic Ocean. p. 175

Santiago (san•tee•AH•goh) A seaport on the southern coast of Cuba; second largest city in Cuba. (20°N, 75°W) p. 517

Santo Domingo A city and the capital of the Dominican Republic. (18°N, 70°W) p. 621

São Francisco River A river in eastern Brazil; flows north, northeast, and east into the Atlantic Ocean south of Maceió. p. 626

São Paulo A city in southeastern Brazil; capital of São Paulo state. p. 626

Saratoga A village on the west bank of the Hudson River in eastern New York; site of a Revolutionary War battle; now called Schuylerville. (43°N, 74°W) p. 249

Saskatchewan (suh•SKA•chuh•wahn) One of Canada's ten provinces; located between Alberta and Manitoba. p. 629

Saskatchewan River A river located in southwestern and south-central Canada; flows from the Rocky Mountains east into north Lake Winnipeg. p. 629

Sault Sainte Marie A city in southern Ontario, Canada; located at the falls on St. Mary's River. (46°N, 84°W) p. 629

Savannah The oldest city in Georgia; located at the mouth of the Savannah River. (32°N, 81°W) p. 175

Savannah River A river that forms the border between Georgia and South Carolina; flows into the Atlantic Ocean at Savannah, Georgia. p. 170

Schenectady (skuh•NEK•tuh•dee) A city in New York; located on the Mohawk River, northwest of Albany. (43°N, 74°W) p. 174

Seattle The largest city in Washington State; located on Puget Sound. (48°N, 122°W) p. 484

Sedalia (suh•DAYL•yuh) A city in west-central Missouri. (39°N, 93°W) p. 492

Seminary Ridge A ridge in Pennsylvania, near Gettysburg. p. 432

Seneca Falls (SEN•uh•kuh) A town located in west-central New York on the Seneca River. (43°N, 77°W) p. 371

Serpent Mound An ancient settlement of the Mound Builders; located in present-day southern Ohio. p. 54

Shiloh (SHY•loh) Located in southwestern Tennessee; site of a Civil War battle in 1862. (35°N, 88°W) p. 429

Sierra Madre Occidental (see•EH•rah mah•dray ahk•sih•den•TAHL) A mountain range in western Mexico, running parallel to the Pacific coast. p. 128

Sierra Nevada The mountain range in eastern California that runs parallel to the Coast Ranges. p. 366

Silver City A town in southwestern New Mexico. (33°N, 108°W) p. 497

Snake River A river that begins in the Rocky Mountains and flows west into the Pacific Ocean; part of the Oregon Trail ran along this river. p. 366

South Pass A pass in southwestern Wyoming; crosses the Continental Divide; part of the Oregon Trail. p. 366

South Pole The southernmost point on the Earth. p. 112

Spiro An ancient settlement of the Mound Builders; located in eastern Oklahoma. (35°N, 94°W) p. 54

Spokane (spoh•KAN) A city in eastern Washington on the falls of the Spokane River. (48°N, 117°W) p. 497

Spring Place A town located in northwestern Georgia. p. 357

Springfield (MA) A city in southwestern Massachusetts; located on the Connecticut River, north of the Connecticut-Massachusetts border. (42°N, 73°W) p. 172

Springfield (MO) A city in southwestern Missouri. (37°N, 93°W) p. 381

St. Augustine (AW•guh•steen) A city in Florida on the Atlantic Ocean; the oldest city founded by Europeans in the United States. (30°N, 81°W) p. 128

St. Croix (KROY) A city in Maine; located west of Port Royal. p. 136

St. Ignace (IG•nuhs) A city in Mackinac County, on the southeastern side of Michigan's upper peninsula. (46°N, 84°W) p. 166

St. John's A city on the southeastern coast of Canada, on the Atlantic Ocean; the capital of Newfoundland. (47°N, 52°W) p. 629

St. Joseph A city in northwestern Missouri on the Missouri River. (39°N, 95°W) p. 492

St. Lawrence River A river in northeastern North America; begins at Lake Ontario and flows into the Atlantic Ocean; forms part of the border between the United States and Canada. p. 54

St. Louis The second-largest city in Missouri; a major Mississippi River port; known as the Gateway to the West. (38°N, 90°W) p. 165

St. Lucia An island and an independent state of the Windward Islands; located in the eastern West Indies, south of Martinique and north of St. Vincent. p. 621

St. Marys A village in southern Maryland. (38°N, 76°W) p. 175

St. Paul The capital of Minnesota. (45°N, 93°W) p. 457

Strait of Magellan (mah•JEH•lahn) The narrow waterway between the southern tip of South America and Tierra del Fuego; links the Atlantic Ocean with the Pacific Ocean. p. 117

Sucre A city in South America. (19°S, 65°W) p. 626

Sudbury River A river in western Massachusetts; connects with the Concord River. p. 225

Suriname A country in north-central South America. p. 626

Susquehanna River (suhs•kwuh•HA•nuh) A river in Maryland, Pennsylvania, and central New York; rises in Otsego Lake, New York, and empties into the northern Chesapeake Bay. p. 170

T

Tampa A city in western Florida; located on the northeastern end of Tampa Bay. (28°N, 82°W) p. 486

Tegucigalpa A city in Central America; capital of Honduras. (14°N, 87°W) p. 621

Tennessee River A tributary of the Mississippi River; begins in eastern Tennessee and flows into the Ohio River in Kentucky. p. 249

Tenochtitlán (tay•nohch•teet•LAHN) An ancient settlement of the Aztec civilization; became the major center of Aztec trade and culture; located at the site of present-day Mexico City. (19°N, 99°W) p. 82

Thunder Bay A city in southwestern Ontario, Canada; located on the shore of Lake Superior. (48°N, 89°W) p. 629

Tiahuanaco (tee•ah•wah•NAH•koh) A site of prehistoric ruins in western Bolivia. p. 125

Tijuana A town in Baja California Norte, northwestern Mexico. (32°N, 117°W) p. 611

Tikal (tih•KAHL) An ancient settlement of the Mayan civilization; located in the central Yucatán Peninsula. (17°N, 89°W) p. 82

Toledo (tuh•LEE•doh) An industrial city and port; located in northwestern Ohio on the Maumee River at the southwest corner of Lake Erie. (42°N, 84°W) p. 353

Tombstone A city in the southeastern corner of Arizona; formerly a mining center widely known for its rich mines. (32°N, 110°W) p. 497

Toronto The capital of the province of Ontario, in Canada; located near the northwestern end of Lake Ontario; third-largest city in Canada. (43°N, 79°W) p. 629

Treasure Island An artificial island in San Francisco Bay; today a naval base. p. 468

Trenton The capital of New Jersey; site of an important battle in the American Revolution. (40°N, 75°W) p. 249

Tres Zapotes (TRAYS sah•POHT•ehs) An ancient settlement of the Olmecs; located in southern Mexico. (18°N, 95°W) p. 54

Trinidad and Tobago An independent state made up of the islands of Trinidad and Tobago; located in the Atlantic Ocean off the northeastern coast of Venezuela. p. 621

Tucson (too•SAHN) A city in southeastern Arizona; located on the Santa Cruz River. (32°N, 111°W) p. 162

Tucumán A city in northern Argentina. (26°S, 66°W) p. 626

Tula An ancient settlement of the Aztec civilization; located in south-central Mexico, north of Tenochtitlán. (23°N, 99°W) p. 82

Tumbes (TOOM•bays) A city in Peru on the Tumbes River, northwest of Lima, near the Peru-Ecuador border. (3°S, 80°W) p. 125

Turkeytown A town in eastern Alabama. (34°N, 86°W) p. 357

Turtle Mound An ancient settlement of the Mound Builders; located on the east coast of Florida. p. 54

U

Uranium City A city located in northwestern Saskatchewan, on the shore of Lake Athabaska. (59°N, 108°W) p. 629

Uruguay A country in southeastern South America. p. 626

Uxmal (oosh•MAHL) An ancient settlement of the Mayan civilization; located in the northern Yucatán Peninsula. (20°N, 89°W) p. 82

V

Valdivia A city located in the Los Lagos region in southern central Chile, on the Valdivia River. (39°S, 73°W) p. 626

Valparaíso A seaport located in Chile, west-northwest of Santiago on the Bay of Valparaíso; capital of Valparaíso. (33°S, 71°W) p. 626

Vancouver Canada's eighth-largest city; located where the north arm of the Fraser River empties into the Pacific Ocean. (49°N, 123°W) p. 629

Vancouver Island An island off the southwest coast of British Columbia, Canada. p. 629

Vandalia (van•DAYL•yuh) A city in south-central Illinois. (39°N, 89°W) p. 353

Venezuela A country in northwestern South America. p. 626

Veracruz (veh•rah•KROOZ) A seaport in Veracruz state, in eastern Mexico; located on the Gulf of Mexico. (19°N, 96°W) p. 124

Vicksburg A city in western Mississippi; located on the Mississippi River; site of an important Civil War battle. (32°N, 91°W) p. 429

Victoria The capital of British Columbia, Canada; located on southeastern Vancouver Island. (48°N, 123°W) p. 629

Victoria Island The third-largest of Canada's Arctic Islands. p. 629

Vincennes (vihn•SENZ) A town in southwest Indiana; oldest town in Indiana. (39°N, 88°W) p. 165

Virginia City A village in western Nevada. (39°N, 119°W) p. 497

W

Wabash River A river in Indiana and Illinois; rises in western Ohio, flows west and southwest across Indiana to form part of the Indiana-Illinois border, and then empties into the Ohio River in southwestern Indiana. p. 249

Wake Island A United States territory in the Pacific Ocean. p. 519

Washington, D.C. The capital of the United States; located on the Potomac River in a special district that is not part of any state. (39°N, 77°W) p. 311

West Indies The islands stretching from Florida in North America to Venezuela in South America. p. 183

West Point A United States military post; located in southeastern New York on the west bank of the Hudson River, just southeast of Storm King and Crow's Nest mountains. p. 249

Whitehorse The capital of the Yukon Territory, Canada; located on the south bank of the Yukon River. (60°N, 135°W) p. 629

Whitman's Mission A mission in southeastern Washington; site of an Indian mission and school established in 1836 by Marcus Whitman and his wife; named a national monument in 1936 and became a national historic site in 1963. p. 366

Williamsburg A city in southeastern Virginia; located on a peninsula between the James and York rivers. (37°N, 77°W) p. 175

Wilmington A city in northern Delaware; located where the Delaware and Christina rivers meet Brandywine Creek. (40°N, 76W) p. 174

Winchester A city in northern Virginia. (39°N, 78°W) p. 276

Windsor A city in southeastern Ontario, Canada, on the Detroit river. (42°N, 83°W) p. 629

Winnipeg The capital of the province of Manitoba, in Canada; located on the Red River; fourth-largest city in Canada. (50°N, 97°W) p. 629

Wisconsin River A river that flows south through central Wisconsin, turns west, and then enters the Mississippi River on the border between Crawford and Grant counties. p. 166

Y

Yadkin River A river in central North Carolina; flows east, turns south, and then joins the Uharie River to form the Pee Dee River. p. 328

Yagul An ancient settlement of the Aztec civilization; located in south-central Mexico to the south of Monte Albán. p. 82

Yellowknife A town in southern Mackenzie district, Canada; located on the northwestern shore of Great Slave Lake at the mouth of the Yellowknife River; capital of the Northwest Territories. (62°N, 114°W) p. 629

Yellowstone River A river in northwestern Wyoming and southern and eastern Montana; flows north through Yellowstone Lake and Yellowstone National Park, continues north across the Montana border, and then flows east and northeast to the Missouri River on the Montana–North Dakota border. p. 366

Yorktown A small town in Virginia; located on Chesapeake Bay; the last major battle of the Revolutionary War was fought here in 1781. (37°N, 76°W) p. 249

Yucatán Peninsula (yoo•kah•TAN) A peninsula in southeastern Mexico and northern Central America. p. 54

Yukon River A river that begins in the southwestern Yukon Territory, Canada, flows through Alaska, and empties into the Bering Sea. p. 629

Yukon Territory One of Canada's two territories; bordered by the Arctic Ocean, the Northwest Territories, British Columbia, and Alaska. p. 629

GLOSSARY

The Glossary contains important social studies words and their definitions. Each word is respelled as it would be in a dictionary. When you see this mark ´ after a syllable, pronounce that syllable with more force than the other syllables. The page number at the end of the definition tells where to find the word in your book.

add, āce, câre, pälm; end, ēqual; it, īce; odd, ōpen, ôrder; tŏŏk, pōol; up, bûrn; yōō as u in fuse; oil; pout; ə as a in above, e in sicken, i in possible, o in melon, u in circus; check; ring; thin; this; zh as in vision

A

abolish (ə•bol´ish) To end. p. 369

abolitionist (ab•ə•lish´ə•nist) A person who wants to abolish slavery. p. 370

absolute location (ab´sə•lōot lō•kā´shən) Exact location on Earth. p. 26

adobe (ä•dō´bä) A kind of sandy clay that can be dried into bricks. p. 56

agent (ā´jənt) A person who does business for other people. p. 137

agriculture (ag´rə•kul•chər) Farming. p. 49

airlift (âr´lift) A system of delivering supplies by airplane. p. 577

allegiance (ə•lē´jəns) Loyalty. p. 236

alliance (ə•lī´əns) Partnership. p. 527

ally (al´ī) A friend, especially in time of war. p. 210

ambassador (am•ba´sə•dər) A representative from one country to another. p. 268

amendment (ə•mend´mənt) An addition or change to the Constitution. p. 304

analyzing (an´əl•īz•ing) A thinking process in which you break something down into its parts and look closely at how those parts connect with each other. p. 24

annex (ə•neks´) To add on. p. 340

Anti-Federalist (an´tī•fed´ər•əl•ist) A citizen who was against ratification of the Constitution. p. 299

apprentice (ə•pren´tis) A person who learns a trade by moving in with the family of a skilled worker and working for several years. p. 184

archaeologist (är•kē•ol´ə•jist) A scientist who studies the cultures of people from long ago. p. 39

arid (âr´əd) Very dry. p. 66

armada (är•mä´dä) A fleet of warships. p. 140

armistice (är´mə•stis) An agreement to stop fighting. p. 518

arms control (ärmz kən•trōl´) A limit to the number of weapons nations can have. p. 600

arms race (ärmz rās) Competition between countries for the most bombs and the most powerful weapons. p. 581

artifact (är´tə•fakt) An object that early people left behind. p. 40

assassination (ə•sas•ə•nā´shən) The murder of a political leader such as a President. p. 430

assembly line (ə•sem´blē līn) A system of mass production in which parts of a product, such as a car, are put together as they move past a line of workers. p. 538

auction (ôk´shən) A public sale. p. 188

authority (ə•thôr´ə•tē) Control over someone or something. p. 212

aviation (ā•vē•ā´shən) Air transportation. p. 538

B

band (band) A small group of people who work together to do things, such as hunting. p. 38

barbed wire (bärbd wīr) A wire with sharp points or barbs along it. p. 494

barrio (bär´rē•ō) A neighborhood of people from Mexico. p. 467

barter (bär´tər) To trade with people by exchanging goods. p. 64

bill (bil) An idea for a new law. p. 280

Bill of Rights (bil uv rīts) A list of rights added to the Constitution as the first ten amendments. p. 304

blockade (blo•kād´) To use warships to prevent other ships from entering or leaving a harbor. p. 223

bonanza farm (bə•nan´zə färm) A large farm on the Great Plains in which people from the East invested money. p. 486

boom (bōom) A time of quick economic growth. p. 496

border state (bôr´dər stāt) A state between the North and the South that allowed slavery but did not secede from the Union during the Civil War. p. 415

borderlands (bôr´dər•landz) Areas of land on or near the borders of two adjoining countries, colonies, or regions. p. 159

boycott (boi´kot) A refusal to buy goods or services. p. 219

broker (brō´kər) A person who is paid to buy and sell goods for someone else. p. 187

buffer (bu´fər) An area of land that serves as a barrier. p. 159

bureaucracy (byŏŏ•rok´rə•sē) The many workers and groups needed to run government programs. p. 545

bust (bust) A time of quick economic decline. p. 496

C

Cabinet (kab´nit) The group made up of the President's most important advisers. p. 308

campaign (kam•pān´) A race for office. p. 310

canal (kə•nal´) A human-made waterway. p. 352

capital resource (kap´ə•təl rē´sôrs) Money to run a business. p. 454

cardinal direction (kär´də•nəl də•rek´shən) One of the main directions: north, south, east, or west. p. 42

carpetbagger (kär´pit•bag•ər) A Northerner who went south after the Civil War to help with Reconstruction or to make money through buying land or opening businesses. p. 439

cartogram (kär´tə•gram) A map that shows information by changing the sizes of places. p. 618

cartographer (kär•tog´rə•fər) A person who makes maps. p. 101

GLOSSARY

cash crop (kash krop) A crop that people raise to sell rather than to use themselves. p. 169

cease-fire (sēs•fīr´) An end to shooting and bombing. p. 597

census (sen´səs) A population count. p. 285

century (sen´shə•rē) A period of 100 years. p. 51

ceremony (ser´ə•mō•nē) A service or ritual performed for a special purpose, such as for a religion. p. 67

charter (chär´tər) A document giving a person or group official approval to take a certain action. p. 169

checks and balances (cheks and bal´ən•siz) A system that gives each branch of government different powers so that each branch can check on the others. p. 287

chronology (krə•nä´lə•jē) A record of events in the order in which they happened. p. 23

citizen (sit´ə•zən) A member of a town, state, or country. p. 19

city-state (sit´ē•stāt) A city that has its own ruler and government. p. 80

civil rights (siv´əl rīts) The rights of citizens to equal treatment. p. 526

civil war (siv´əl wôr) A war between people of the same country. p. 125

civilian (sə•vil´yən) A person who is not in the military. p. 554

civilization (siv•ə•lə•zā´shən) A culture that has well-developed forms of government, religion, and learning. p. 52

claim (klām) To declare that you or your country owns something. p. 129

clan (klan) A group of families that are related to one another. p. 63

class (klas) A group of people treated with more or less respect, depending on the group's place in society. p. 80

classify (kla´sə•fī) To sort by topic. p. 177

climograph (klī´mə•graf) A graph that shows the average monthly temperature and the average monthly precipitation for a place. p. 488

cold war (kōld wôr) A war fought with propaganda and money rather than with soldiers and weapons. p. 561

colonist (kol´ə•nist) A person who lives in a colony. p. 131

colony (kol´ə•nē) A settlement ruled by another country. p. 131

commercial industry (kə•mûr´shəl in´dəs•trē) An industry run to make a profit. p. 539

commission (kə•mi´shən) A special committee. p. 524

Committee of Correspondence (kə•mi´tē uv kôr•ə•spän´dəns) A type of committee set up in all of the colonies to quickly share information about taxes and other issues by writing letters. p. 222

common (kom´ən) An open area where sheep and cattle grazed. p. 181

commonwealth (kom´ən•welth) A part of a country whose people have the rights of citizens of the mother country but that functions mostly independently. p. 620

communism (kom´yə•niz•əm) A social and economic system in which all industries, land, and businesses are owned by a government. p. 561

compact (kom´pakt) An agreement. p. 143

compass (kum´pəs) A device with a needle that always points north. A compass is used to find a direction. p. 105

compass rose (kum´pəs rōz) A direction marker on a map. p. 29

compromise (kom´prə•mīz) To give up something in order to reach an agreement. p. 278

concentration camp (kon•sən•trā´shən kamp) A guarded camp where prisoners are held. p. 551

conclusion (kən•kloo´zhən) A decision or idea reached by thoughtful study. p. 115

Conestoga (kä•nə•stō´gə) A very large covered wagon used by farmers and western settlers. p. 182

Confederacy (kən•fe´də•rə•sē) The Confederate States of America, a new country that was formed by Southern states that seceded from the Union after Abraham Lincoln was elected President in 1860. p. 406

confederation (kən•fe•də•rā´shən) A loosely united group of governments. p. 76

congress (kon´grəs) A meeting of representatives who have the authority to make decisions. p. 220

conquistador (kon•kēs´tə•dôr) Any of the Spanish conquerors in the Americas during the early 1500s. p. 124

consequence (kon´sə•kewns) The result of an action. p. 223

conservation (kon•sər•vā´shən) Keeping resources and the environment from being wasted or destroyed. p. 524

consolidate (kən•sä´lə•dāt) To join one business with another. p. 455

constitution (kon•stə•too´shən) A plan for governing. p. 267

consumer good (kən•soo´mər good) A product made for personal use. p. 537

Continental (kän•tən•en´təl) A soldier in the first colonial army, which was headed by George Washington. p. 233

Continental Congress (kän•tən•en´təl kong´rəs) A meeting of representatives of the British colonies. p. 225

convention (kən•ven´shən) An important meeting. p. 273

corporation (kôr•pə•rā´shən) A business that sells shares of stock to investors. p. 454

cotton gin (kot´ən jin) A machine that removes the seeds from cotton fibers. p. 391

council (koun´səl) A group that makes laws. p. 76

county (koun´tē) A large part of a colony or, in the United States today, a part of a state. A county has its own local government. p. 183

county seat (koun´tē sēt) The main town for a county or, in the United States today, the city where the government of a county is located. p. 183

cultural diffusion (kul´chər•əl di•fyoo´zhən) The spread of a culture from one place to another. p. 53

cultural region (kul´chər•əl rē´jən) An area where peoples share some ways of life. p. 61

culture (kul´chər) A way of life. p. 39

D

D day (dē dā) June 6, 1944, the day the World War II Allies worked together in the largest water-to-land invasion in history. p. 557

debate (di•bāt´) To argue opposite sides of an issue. p. 280

debtor (det´ər) A person who owes money. p. 176

decade (dek´ād) A period of 10 years. p. 51

declaration (dek•lə•rā´shən) An official statement. p. 237

deficit (def´ə•sit) A budget shortage caused by spending more money than is earned. p. 604

deforestation (dē•fôr•ə•stā´shən) The widespread cutting down of forests. p. 626

delegate (del´ə•git) A representative. p. 273

democracy (di•mok´rə•sē) A government in which the people take part. p. 210

depression (di•presh´ən) A period of time in which there is little money and little economic growth. p. 543

desertion (di•zûr´shən) Running away from duties, such as military duties. p. 130

détente (dā•tänt´) The easing of military tensions between countries. p. 601

dictator (dik´tā•tər) A leader who has total authority. p. 360

distortion (di•stôr´shən) An error on a map. p. 522

diversity (də•vûr´sə•tē) Differences, such as those among different peoples. p. 61

doctrine (däk´trən) A government plan of action or statement of policy. p. 340

dove (duv) A person who supports an end to the fighting of a war. p. 596

drought (drout) A long period of dry weather. p. 57

due process of law (do͞o präs´ses uv lô) The right to a fair, public trial. p. 305

dugout (dug´out) A boat made from a hollowed-out log. p. 63

E

earthwork (ûrth´wərk) A mound, or hill of earth, that people built. p. 54

economy (i•kon´ə•mē) The way people use resources to meet their needs. p. 30

electoral college (i•lek´tə•rəl kä´lij) A group of electors chosen by citizens to vote for the President. p. 286

elevation (el•ə•vā´shən) The height of land. p. 366

Emancipation Proclamation (i•man•sə•pā´shən prok•lə•mā´shən) The Presidential order of 1863 that freed enslaved people in the Confederate states. p. 419

embargo (im•bär´gō) A refusal by one country to trade its goods with another country. p. 622

emperor (em´pər•ər) The ruler of an empire. p. 83

empire (em´pīr) A government in which one ruler governs many lands and peoples. p. 83

encounter (in•koun´tər) A meeting, such as one between peoples who have never met before. p. 100

encroach (in•krōch´) To move onto without asking permission. p. 242

enlist (in•list´) To join. p. 234

entrepreneur (än•trə•prə•nûr´) A person who sets up a new business, taking a chance on making or losing money. p. 455

equality (i•kwä´•lə•tē) The same rights for all people. p. 370

evidence (e´və•dəns) Proof. p. 40

executive branch (ig•zek´yə•tiv branch) The branch of government that sees that the laws are carried out. p. 284

expedition (ek•spə•dish´ən) A journey made for a special reason. p. 117

exploration (ek•splə•rā´shən) Searching a new place to learn more about it. p. 101

export (eks´pôrt) A product sent from one country to another to be sold. p. 184

extinct (ik•stingkt´) No longer living, like a kind of animal that has died out. p. 48

F

fact (fakt) A statement that can be proved true. p. 119

farm produce (färm prō´do͞os) Grains, fruits, and vegetables that farmers can trade for goods and services. p. 182

federal system (fed´ər•əl sis´təm) A governing system in which the states share the authority to govern with the national government. p. 278

Federalist (fed´ər•ə•list) A citizen who was in favor of ratifying the Constitution. p. 299

federation (fe•də•rā´shən) An organization made up of many member groups. p. 462

forty-niner (fôrt´ē•nī´nər) A gold seeker who went to California in 1849. p. 365

free election (frē i•lek´shən) An election in which there is a choice of candidates. p. 623

free enterprise (frē en´tər•prīz) An economic system in which businesses are free to offer for sale many kinds of goods and services. p. 453

free state (frē stāt) A state that did not allow slavery. p. 400

free world (frē wûrld) The United States and its allies who worked together to fight communism. p. 561

free-trade agreement (frē•trād ə•grē´mənt) A treaty in which countries agree to charge no tariffs, or taxes, on goods they buy from and sell to each other. p. 611

front (frunt) A battle line. p. 557

frontier (frun•tir´) The western border of settlement. p. 192

Fundamental Orders (fun•də•ment´əl ôr´dərz) The first written system of government in North America. It was adopted in Connecticut. p. 172

G

generalization (jen´ər•əl•ə•zā´shən) A summary statement based on facts. p. 194

Gettysburg Address (get´ēz•bûrg ə•dres´) A short speech given by Abraham Lincoln in 1863 at the dedication of a Gettysburg cemetery. p. 427

glacier (glā´shər) A huge sheet of ice. p. 38

grant (grant) A gift of money to be used for a special purpose. p. 127

grid (grid) On a map, the north-south and east-west lines that cross each other to form a pattern of squares. p. 29

grievance (grē´vəns) A complaint. p. 238

H

hacienda (ä•sē•en´dä) A large estate. p. 161

hawk (hôk) A person who supports the fighting of a war. p. 596

historical empathy (hi•stôr´i•kəl em´pə•thē) Understanding the actions and feelings of people from other times and other places. p. 24

hogan (hō´gən) A cone-shaped house built by covering a log frame with mud or grass. p. 69

Holocaust (hol´ə•kôst) The murder of more than six million Jews in concentration camps during World War II. p. 559

homesteader (hōm´sted´ər) A person who settled government land between 1862 and 1900. p. 483

hostage (hos´tij) A person held as a prisoner by a terrorist until demands are met. p. 601

human features (hyōō´mən fē´chərz) Buildings, bridges, farms, roads, and people themselves. p. 27

human resource (hyōō´mən rē´sôrs) A person. p. 460

human rights (hyōō´mən rīts) Basic freedoms all people should have. p. 305

hydroelectric dam (hī•drō•i•lek´trik dam) A dam that uses stored water to generate electricity. p. 546

I

immigrant (im´ə•grənt) A person who comes to live in a country from another country. p. 174

impeach (im•pēch´) To accuse an official of wrongdoing. p. 286

imperialism (im•pir´ē•ə•liz•əm) Empire building. p. 516

import (im´pôrt) A product brought into a country from another country, to be sold. p. 182

impressment (im•pres´mənt) Forcing workers to work for a government. p. 338

indentured servant (in•den´chərd sûr´vənt) A person who agrees to work for another person without pay for a certain length of time. p. 187

independence (in•di•pen´dəns) Freedom to govern on one's own. p. 236

indigo (in´də•gō) A plant from which blue dye is made. p. 175

Industrial Revolution (in•dus´trē•əl rev•ə•lōō´shən) A time during the late 1700s and early 1800s when new inventions changed the way people lived, worked, and traveled. p. 349

inflation (in•flā´shən) An economic condition in which it takes more and more money to buy the same goods. p. 269

inset map (in´set map) A small map within a larger map. p. 29

installment buying (in•stôl´mənt bī´ing) Paying a small part of the purchase price for an item, taking it home, and paying the remaining cost on a schedule. p. 537

integration (in•tə•grā´shən) Allowing people of all races to live and work together as equals. p. 590

interchangeable parts (in•tər•chān´jə•bəl pärts) Identical parts made by machine so that if one part breaks, a new one can be installed. p. 350

interest rate (in´tə•rəst rāt) The amount that a bank charges customers to borrow money. p. 610

intermediate direction (in•ter•mē´dē•ət də•rek´shən) One of the in-between directions: northeast, northwest, southeast, or southwest. p. 42

interpreter (in•tûr´prə•tər) A person who translates from one language to another. p. 144

invest (in•vest´) To buy a share of a business in the hope of making a profit. p. 454

Iroquois League (ir´ə•kwoi lēg) A group of Iroquois tribes that decided to work together peacefully. p. 76

island-hopping (ī´lənd•hä´ping) The process of the Allies capturing island after island as they advanced toward Japan. p. 559

isolation (ī•sə•lā´shən) Remaining separate from other countries. p. 531

isthmus (is´məs) A narrow strip of land that connects two larger land areas. p. 116

J

jazz (jaz) A kind of music that grew out of the African American musical heritage. p. 539

judicial branch (jōō•dish´əl branch) The branch of government that settles disputes about the meaning of the laws. p. 284

jury (jûr´ē) A group of citizens who decide a case in court. p. 305

justice (jus´təs) A judge who serves on the Supreme Court. p. 286

K

kachina (kä•chē´nə) One of the spirits that are important in the religion of the Hopis and other Pueblo peoples. p. 67

kiva (kē´və) An underground room where the Anasazi held religious services. p. 57

knoll (nōl) A small, round hill. p. 100

L

labor union (lā´bər yōōn´yən) A group of workers who take action to protect their interests. p. 461

legend (lej´ənd) A story handed down over time, often to explain the past. p. 76

legislative branch (lej´is•lā•tiv branch) The branch of government that makes the laws. p. 284

legislature (lej´is•lā•chər) The lawmaking branch of a colony, a state government, or the national government. p. 210

liberate (li´bə•rāt) To set free. p. 625

liberty (lib´ər•tē) Freedom. p. 218

lines of latitude (līnz uv la´tə•tōōd) East-west lines on a map or globe that are always the same distance apart. Also called parallels. p. 112

lines of longitude (līnz uv lon´jə•tōōd) North-south lines on a map or globe that run from pole to pole. Also called meridians. p. 112

locomotive (lō•kə•mō´tiv) A railroad engine. p. 354

long drive (lông drīv) A cattle drive in which Texas ranchers drove herds of cattle north to be sold in northern markets. p. 491

longhouse (lông´hous) A long wooden house in which several Indian families lived together. p. 76

Loyalist (loi´ə•list) A colonist who supported the British monarch and laws. p. 217

M

mainland (mān´land) The main part of a continent, rather than an island near the continent. p. 127

maize (māz) Corn. p. 50

majority (mə•jôr´ə•tē) The greater part of a whole. p. 284

manifest destiny (ma´nə•fest des´tə•nē) The belief that the certain future of the United States was to stretch from the Atlantic Ocean to the Pacific Ocean. p. 359

map key (map kē) A part of a map that explains the symbols used. Also called a legend. p. 28

map scale (map skāl) A part of a map that gives a comparison of distance on the map with distance in the real world. p. 29

map title (map tī´təl) Words on a map that describe the subject of the map. p. 28

mass production (mas prə•duk´shən) A way to produce large amounts of goods at one time. p. 350

massacre (mas´ə•kər) The killing of people who cannot defend themselves. p. 221

Mayflower Compact (mā´flou•ər kom´pakt) An agreement by those on the *Mayflower* to make and obey laws for their colony. This was the first self-rule by American colonists. p. 143

mercenary (mûr´sə•ner•ē) A hired soldier. p. 233

meridians (mə•rid´ē•ənz) North-south lines on a map or globe that run from pole to pole. Also called lines of longitude. p. 112

merit system (mer´ət sis´təm) A way of making sure that the most qualified people get government jobs. p. 525

mesa (mā´sä) A high, flat-topped hill. p. 56

mestizo (me•stē´zō) A person of mixed Native American and European background. p. 625

metropolitan area (met•rə•pol´ə•tən âr´ē•ə) A city and all the suburbs and other population areas around it. p. 609

middle class (mid´əl klas) An economic level between the poor and the wealthy. p. 610

migration (mī•grā´shən) A voluntary or forced movement of people from one place to another. p. 37

military draft (mil´ə•ter•ē draft) A way of bringing people into the military. p. 528

militia (mə•lish´ə) A volunteer army of a colony or state. p. 182

millennium (mə•le´nē•əm) A period of 1,000 years. p. 51

minimum wage (min´ə•məm wāj) The lowest pay a worker can receive by law. p. 545

Minutemen (min´it•men) Members of the Massachusetts colony militia who could quickly be ready to fight the British. p. 225

missile (mi´səl) A rocket that can carry a bomb thousands of miles. p. 580

mission (mish´ən) A small religious community founded by a church. p. 162

missionary (mish´ən•er•ē) A person who teaches his or her religion to others. p. 131

monarch (mä´nərk) A king or queen. p. 105

monopoly (mə•nop´ə•lē) To have almost complete control. p. 455

movement (mōōv´mənt) An effort by many people. p. 241

N

nationalism (nash´ən•əl•iz•əm) Pride in a country. p. 340

naturalization (na•chə•rə•lə•zā´shən) The process of becoming an American citizen by living in the country a certain number of years and then taking a test. p. 469

navigation (nav•ə•gā´shən) The study or act of planning and controlling the course of a ship. p. 106

negotiate (ni•gō´shē•āt) To talk with one another to work out an agreement. p. 253

neutral (nōō´trəl) Not taking a side in a conflict. p. 240

noble (nō´bəl) A person from an upper-class family. p. 81

nomad (nō´mad) A wanderer who has no settled home. p. 38

no-man's-land (nō´manz•land) In a war, land that is not held by either side but is filled with obstacles such as barbed wire and land mines. p. 529

nonviolence (nän•vī´ə•ləns) The use of peaceful ways to bring about change. p. 589

Northwest Passage (nôrth•west´ pas´ij) A water route that explorers wanted to find so that traders could go through North America to Asia. p. 135

olive branch (ä´liv branch) A symbol of peace. p. 231

open range (ō´pən rānj) The huge grassland area of the Great Plains where cattle were allowed to roam and graze. p. 491

opinion (ə•pin´yən) A statement that tells what a person thinks or believes. p. 119

opportunity cost (ä•pər•tōō´nə•tē kôst) The cost of giving up one thing to get another. p. 277

oral history (ôr´əl his´tə•rē) Accounts that tell the experiences of people who did not have a written language or who did not write down what happened. p. 23

ordinance (ôr´də•nəns) A law or a set of laws. p. 271

origin story (ôr´ə•jən stôr´ē) A story that tells of people's beliefs about the world and their place in it. p. 40

override (ō´və•rīd) To cancel. p. 287

overseer (o´vər•sē•ər) A person who was hired to watch slaves to see that they did their work. p. 395

P

pacifist (pa´sə•fist) A believer in a peaceful settlement of a conflict. p. 241

parallels (par´ə•lelz) East-west lines on a map or globe that are always the same distance apart. Also called lines of latitude. p. 112

Parliament (pär´lə•mənt) The part of the British government in which members make laws for the British people. p. 209

pathfinder (path´fīn•dər) Someone who finds a way through an unknown region. p. 333

Patriot (pā´trē•ət) A colonist who was against British rule. p. 225

patriotism (pā´trē•ə•ti•zəm) Love of one's country. p. 306

permanent (pûr´mə•nənt) Long-lasting. p. 159

perspective (pər•spek´tiv) Point of view. p. 24

petition (pə•tish´ən) A signed request for action. p. 218

physical features (fiz´i•kəl fē´chərz) Landforms, bodies of water, climate, soil, plant and animal life, and other natural resources. p. 27

pilgrim (pil´grəm) A person who makes a journey for a religious reason. p. 142

pioneer (pī•ə•nir´) A person who first settles a new place. p. 327

pit house (pit hous) A house built partly over a hole dug in the earth so that some of its rooms are under the ground. p. 63

plantation (plan•tā´shən) A large farm. p. 131

planter (plan´tər) A plantation owner. p. 186

political boss (pə•li´ti•kəl bôs) An elected official—especially a mayor—who has many dishonest employees and who is able to control the government. p. 525

political cartoon (pə•li´ti•kəl kär•tōōn´) A cartoon that expresses opinions about politics or government. p. 235

political party (pə•li´ti•kəl pär´tē) A group of people involved in government who try to get others to agree with their ideas and who choose leaders who share the party's points of view. p. 309

population density (pop•yə•lā´shən den´sə•tē) The number of people who live in 1 square mile or 1 square kilometer of land. p. 618

portage (pôr´tij) The carrying of canoes and supplies around waterfalls and rapids or overland between waterways. p. 165

potlatch (pot´lach) A type of American Indian feast at which the hosts give away valuable gifts. p. 64

Preamble (prē´am•bəl) The introduction to the Constitution. p. 275

prediction (pri•dik´shən) A forecast of what will most likely happen next based on what has happened before. p. 341

prejudice (prej´ŏŏ•dis) A feeling that some people have against others, often based on race or culture. p. 465

presidio (prā•sē´dē•ō) A fort. p. 159

primary source (prī´mer•ē sôrs) A record made by people who saw or took part in an event. p. 22

prime meridian (prīm mə•rid´ē•ən) The meridian marked 0°. It runs north and south through Greenwich, England. p. 112

profit (prof´it) In a business, money that is left over after everything has been paid for. p. 140

progressive (prə•gre´siv) A person who wants to improve government and make life better. p. 524

projection (prə•jek´shən) One of many different ways to show the round Earth on flat paper. p. 522

propaganda (prä•pə•gan´də) Information or ideas designed and distributed to help or harm a cause. p. 532

proprietary colony (prə•prī´ə•ter•ē kol´ə•nē) A colony that was ruled by one or more proprietors appointed by a monarch. p. 168

proprietor (prə•prī´ə•tər) An owner. p. 168

prospector (prä´spek•tər) A person who searches for gold, silver, and other mineral resources. p. 495

province (prov´ins) A political region in Canada that is much like an American state. p. 628

public opinion (pub´lik ə•pin´yən) What people think. p. 595

public school (pub´lik skōōl) A school paid for by taxes and open to all children. p. 368

pueblo (pweb´lō) A group of adobe houses that the Anasazi and other Pueblo peoples lived in. p. 56

purchase (pur´chəs) To buy. p. 332

Puritan (pyûr´ə•tən) A member of the Church of England who wanted to "purify" its practices. p. 171

pyramid (pir´ə•mid) A building with three or more triangle-shaped sides that slant toward a point at the top. p. 52

quarter (kwôr´tər) To provide housing. p. 223

range war (rānj wôr) A fight between farmers and ranchers during the late 1800s. p. 494

ratify (rat´ə•fī) To agree to something and thus make it a law. p. 297

rationing (rash´ə•ning) Limiting what people can buy. p. 555

Reconstruction (rē•kən•struk´shən) A time of rebuilding the country after the Civil War. p. 436

refinery (ri•fī´nər•ē) A factory where crude oil is made into marketable products. p. 455

reform (ri•fôrm´) A change for the better. p. 368

refuge (ref´yōōj) A safe place. p. 170

regiment (rej´ə•mənt) A troop of soldiers. p. 243

region (rē´jən) An area on Earth whose features make it different from other areas. p. 27

regulate (reg´yə•lāt) To control by law. p. 464

relative location (re´lə•tiv lō•kā´shən) What a place is near or what is around it. p. 26

relief (ri•lēf´) Differences in height of an area of land. p. 366

religion (ri•lij´ən) Beliefs about God or gods. p. 50

relocation camp (rē•lō•kā´shən kamp) Prisonlike camps in which Japanese Americans were held after the bombing of Pearl Harbor. p. 555

repeal (ri•pēl´) To undo a law or tax. p. 220

representation (re•prē•zen•tā´shən) Acting or speaking on behalf of someone or something. p. 217

republic (ri•pub´lik) A form of government in which people elect representatives to run a country. p. 268

reservation (rez•ər•vā´shən) An area of land set aside by the government for American Indians. p. 499

resist (ri•zist´) To act against. p. 396

revolution (rev•əl•ōō´shən) A sudden, complete change of government. p. 236

right (rīt) A freedom. p. 225

royal colony (roi´əl kol´ə•nē) A colony controlled by a monarch. p. 164

ruling (rōō´ling) A decision. p. 358

rumor (rōō´mər) A story that has been told but has not been proved. p. 128

saga (sä´gə) An adventure story about the brave deeds of people long ago. p. 99

scalawag (skal´ə•wag) A person who supported something for his or her own gain. p. 438

scandal (skan´dəl) An action that brings disgrace. p. 596

scarce (skers) Not plentiful. p. 160

scurvy (skûr´vē) A sickness caused by not getting enough Vitamin C, which is found in fresh fruit and vegetables. p. 118

secede (si•sēd´) To leave the Union. p. 357

secondary source (sek´ən•dâr•ē sôrs) A record of an event, written by someone who was not there at the time. p. 22

sectionalism (sek´shə•nəl•izm) Regional loyalty. p. 356

segregation (seg•rə•gā´shən) Separation. p. 439

self-government (self•guv´ərn•mənt) A system of government in which people make their own laws. p. 209

self-sufficient (self•sə•fish´ənt) Self-supporting. p. 161

separation of powers (se•pə•rā´shən uv pou´erz) The division of the national government into three branches instead of having one all-powerful branch. p. 284

separatist (se´pə•rə•tist) A person who wants to become or remain separate from a government or group. p. 630

settlement house (set´əl•mənt hous) A community center where people can learn new skills. p. 476

shaman (shä´mən) A religious leader and healer. p. 70

sharecropping (shâr´krop•ing) A system of working the land, in which the worker was paid with a "share" of the crop. p. 436

siege (sēj) A long-lasting attack. p. 250

skyscraper (skī´skrā•pər) A tall steel-frame building. p. 477

slave code (slāv kōd) A law that shaped the day-to-day lives of enslaved people. p. 395

slave state (slāv stāt) A state that allowed slavery. p. 400

slavery (slā´vər•ē) The practice of holding people against their will and making them carry out orders. p. 81

sod (sod) Soil in which thick grass grows. p. 484

specialize (spesh´əl•īz) To work at only one kind of job. p. 50

spiritual (spir´i•chə•wəl) A religious song based on the Bible. p. 396

states' rights (stāts rīts) The idea that individual states could have final authority over the national government. p. 356

stock (stok) A share in a company or business. p. 454

stock market (stok mär´kit) A place where people can buy and sell stocks, or shares in businesses. p. 542

strike (strīk) To stop work in protest of conditions. p. 461

suffrage (suf´rij) The right to vote. p. 371

superpower (soō´pər•pou•ər) A very powerful nation with an important role in world events. p. 577

surplus (sûr´plus) More than is needed. p. 50

T

tariff (tar´if) A tax on goods brought into a country. p. 216

tax (taks) Money that is paid by people to support the work of government. p. 211

technology (tek•nol´ə•jē) The use of scientific knowledge or tools to make or do something. p. 47

temple (tem´pəl) A place of worship. p. 52

tenement (ten´ə•mənt) A poorly built apartment house. p. 468

tepee (tē´pē) A cone-shaped tent made of poles covered with animal skins. p. 71

territory (ter´ə•tôr•ē) Land that belongs to a national government but is not a state. p. 270

terrorism (ter´ə•riz•əm) The use of violence to promote a cause. p. 601

textile mill (teks´tīl mil) A factory where fibers such as cotton and wool are woven into cloth. p. 349

theory (thē´ə•rē) A possible explanation for something. p. 39

time line (tīm līn) A diagram that shows the events that took place during a certain period of time. p. 51

time zone (tīm zōn) A region in which a single time is used. p. 458

totem pole (tō´tem pōl) A wooden post that is carved with shapes of people and animals. p. 65

town meeting (toun mē´ting) A meeting in which male landowners in the New England colonies could take part in government. Today in the New England states, all the citizens of a town can take part in town meetings. p. 181

township (toun´ship) A square of land in the Northwest Territory that measured six miles per side. Today a township is a kind of local government. p. 271

trade network (trād net´wərk) A system in which trade takes place between certain groups of people. p. 137

trade-off (trād´ôf) What you have to give up buying or doing in order to buy or do something else. p. 277

transcontinental railroad (trans•kon•tə•nen´təl rāl´rōd) A railroad that links a continent, like one that links the Atlantic and Pacific coasts of the United States. p. 453

transport (trans•pôrt´) To carry. p. 352

treason (trē´zən) Working against one's own government. p. 218

treaty (trē´tē) An agreement between countries. p. 252

trend (trend) A pattern of change over time. p. 394

triangle trade route (trī´ang•gəl trād rōot) A shipping route that included Britain, the British colonies, and Africa. p. 184

tribe (trīb) A group of people with a shared culture and land. p. 50

tributary (trib´yə•ter•ē) A river or stream that feeds a larger river. p. 167

tribute (trib´yōōt) Payments that a ruler demands from his or her people. p. 84

U

unconstitutional (ən•kän•stə•tōō´shə•nəl) Going against the Constitution. p. 287

Underground Railroad (un´dər•ground rāl´rōd) A system of escape routes for enslaved people, leading to free land. p. 398

unemployment (un•im•ploi´mənt) The number of people without jobs. p. 545

Union (yōōn´yən) The United States of America. p. 282

V

vaquero (bä•kä´rō) A Mexican cowhand. p. 493

veto (vē´tō) To reject a proposal passed by a legislature. p. 286

vigilance (vi´jə•ləns) Watching over something or someone. p. 497

INDEX

Page references for illustrations are set in italic type. An italic m indicates a map. Page references set in boldface type indicate the pages on which vocabulary terms are defined.

Abilene, Kansas   *Bald eagle*

For permission to reprint copyrighted material, grateful acknowledgment is made to the following sources:

Carmen Lara D. del Barco: From an untitled poem in *La Poesia Quechua* by Jesús Lara. First edition published by Imprenta Universitaria, Cochabamba, Bolivia, 1947. Second and third editions published by Fondo de Cultura Economica, Mexico, D. F. , 1947, 1979.

Beacon Press: From "Flowers and Songs of Sorrow" in *The Broken Spears* by Miguel Leon-Portilla. Text copyright © 1962, 1990 by Miguel Leon-Portilla

Children's Book Press: From *The People Shall Continue* by Simon Ortiz. Text © 1977 by Children's Book Press; revised edition text © 1988 by Children's Book Press.

Crown Publishers, Inc.: From *Children of the Dust Bowl: The True Story of the School at Weedpatch Camp* by Jerry Stanley, cover photograph by Russell Lee. Text copyright © 1992 by Jerry Stanley. Cover photograph courtesy of the Library of Congress.

Farrar, Straus & Giroux, Inc.: "Prayer" and "House Blessing"from *In the Trail of the Wind,* edited by John Bierhorst. Published by Farrar, Straus & Giroux, Inc., 1971.

Harcourt Brace & Company: From *1787* by Joan Anderson. Text copyright © 1987 by Joan Anderson. From a quotation by Fred Gregory in *Black Stars in Orbit: NASA's African American Astronauts* by Khephra Burns and William Miles. Text copyright © 1995 by Khephra Burns and William Miles. From *Guns for General Washington: A Story of the American Revolution* by Seymour Reit. Text copyright © 1990 by Seymour Reit.

HarperCollins Publishers: The Great Migration by Jacob Lawrence. Text copyright © 1993 by The Museum of Modern Art, New York, and The Phillips Collection.

Holiday House, Inc.: From *Cassie's Journey: Going West in the 1860's* by Brett Harvey, illustrated by Deborah Kogan Ray. Text copyright © 1988 by Brett Harvey; illustrations copyright © 1988 by Deborah Kogan.

Henry Holt and Company: From *One Giant Leap* by Mary Ann Fraser. Copyright © 1993 by Mary Ann Fraser. "The Americas in 1492" from *The World in 1492* by Jean Fritz, Katherine Paterson, Patricia and Fredrick McKissack, Margaret Mahy and Jamake Highwater. Text copyright © 1992 by The Native Land Foundation.

Houghton Mifflin Company: From *The Pueblo* by Charlotte and David Yue. Copyright © 1986 by Charlotte and David Yue.

Lincoln Cathedral Library, Lincoln, England: From the 1630 handbill *Proportion of Provisions.*

McGraw-Hill, Inc.: From book #60660 *The Log of Christopher Columbus* by Robert H. Fuson. Text copyright 1987 by Robert H. Fuson. Original English language edition published by International Marine Publishing Company, Camden, ME.

Glenn Morris: From "Breaking the Bering Strait Barrier" by Glenn Morris. Originally published in *Indian Country Today,* October 27, 1993.

The Newborn Group: Cover illustrations by Teresa Fasolino from *1787* by Joan Anderson.

Pantheon Books, a division of Random House, Inc.: From *Hard Times: An Oral History of the Great Depression* by Studs Terkel. Text copyright © 1970 by Studs Terkel.

G. P. Putnam's Sons: From *Shh! We're Writing the Constitution* by Jean Fritz, illustrated by Tomie dePaola. Text copyright © 1987 by Jean Fritz; illustrations copyright © 1987 by Tomie dePaola. From *Stonewall* by Jean Fritz. Text copyright © 1979 by Jean Fritz. From *1492: The Year of the New World* by Piero Ventura. Text copyright © 1991, 1992 by Arnoldo Mondadori Editore S. p. A., Milano.

Random House, Inc.: From "On the Pulse of Morning" in *On the Pulse of Morning* by Maya Angelou. Text copyright © 1993 by Maya Angelou. From *The Story of Thomas Alva Edison* by Margaret Cousins. Text copyright © 1965 by Margaret Cousins; text copyright renewed 1993 by Margaret Cousins and Random House, Inc.

Scholastic Inc.: From *By the Dawn's Early Light* by Steven Kroll, illustrated by Dan Andreasen. Text copyright © 1994 by Steven Kroll; illustrations copyright © 1994 by Dan Andreasen.

Simon & Schuster Books for Young Readers, a division of Simon & Schuster: From "The Wilderness Is Tamed" in *Away Goes Sally* by Elizabeth Coatsworth. Text copyright 1934 by Macmillan Publishing Company; copyright renewed © 1962 by Elizabeth Coatsworth Beston.

Viking Penguin, a division of Penguin Books USA Inc.: From *Zlata's Diary: A Child's Life in Sarajevo* by Zlata Filipovic. Translation copyright © 1994 by Fixot et editions Robert Laffont.

Volcano Press, Inc.: From *Save My Rainforest* by Monica Zak, illustrated by Bengt-Arne Runnerström, English version by Nancy Schimmel. Text © 1987 by Monica Zak; English language text © 1992 by Volcano Press, Inc. Originally published in Sweden under the title *Rädda Min Djungel* by Bokförlaget Opal, 1989.

Walker and Company, 435 Hudson St., New York, NY 10014: From *I, Columbus: My Journal 1492-1493,* edited by Peter and Connie Roop, illustrated by Peter E. Hanson. Illustrations copyright © 1990 by Peter E. Hanson.

Frederick Warne Books, a division of Penguin Books USA Inc.: From *Greenhorn on the Frontier* by Ann Finlayson. Text copyright © 1974 by Ann Finlayson.

Albert Whitman & Company: From *Samuel's Choice* by Richard Berleth, illustrated by James Watling. Text copyright © 1990 by Richard J. Berleth; illustrations copyright © 1990 by James Watling.

ILLUSTRATION CREDITS:

Jeff Barson, pp. 564–565; Kevin Beilfuss, pp. 420–421; Randy Berrett, pp. 506–507; Chris Costello, pp. 63, 68, 69, 77; Judith Degraffenreid, pp. 200—201; John Edens, pp. 47, 65; Kim Fujiwara, pp. 96–97; Steve Gardner, pp. 150–151; Dave Henderson, pp. 90–91, 258–259, 463–463, 636–637; Uldis Klavins, pp. 206–207, 378–379; Bill Maughan, pp. 318–319; Pronto Design & Production, Inc., pp. 277, 279, 285, 287, 312; Tom Newsom, p. 410; Victor Valla, p. 116, 161, 182 top, 187, 350, 362 top left

COVER CREDIT:

Keith Gold & Associates

All maps by GeoSystems

PHOTO CREDITS:

Key: Page positions are shown in abbreviated form as follows: (t)-top, (b)-bottom, (l)-left, (r)-right, (c)-center, (bg)-background, (fg)-foreground

iii, Werner Forman/Art Resource, NY; iv(t), Michal Heron/Woodfin Camp; iv(b), Scala/Art Resource, NY; v(t), Detail, Photo Archives, Denver Museum of Natural History. All rights reserved; v(b), The Santa Barbara Mission; vi(t), Detroit Institute of Arts Founders Society; vi(b), The Boston Atheneum; vii(t), Bequest of Winslow Warren. Courtesy, Museum of Fine Arts, Boston; vii(b), New York State Historical Association, Cooperstown; viii(t), Superstock; viii(b), Stanley B. Burns MD and the Burns Archive; ix(t), Archives Division - Texas State Library; ix(b), Detail, National Portrait Gallery, Smithsonian Institution/Art Resource, NY; x(t), Courtesy of The Library of Congress; x(b), UPI/Bettmann; xi(t), The Denver Public Library, Western History Department; xi(b), Theodore Roosevelt Collection Harvard College Library; xii(t), Print Courtesy Stetson Kennedy; xii(b), Flip & Debra Schulke/Black Star; xiii, David Hautzig; A1, David Wagner/Phototake; 18, Dennie Cody/FPG International; 20, Architect of the Capitol; 21, Harcourt Brace & Company/Terry D. Sinclair; 22(t), Bettmann; 22(c), Harcourt Brace & Company/Victoria Bowen; 22(b), The Granger Collection, New York; 23(t), Harcourt Brace & Company/Victoria Bowen; 23(b), National Park Service/Edison National Historic Site; 24(l), H. Armstrong Roberts; 24(r), Harcourt Brace & Company/Terry D. Sinclair; 25, Harcourt Brace & Company/Victoria Bowen; 26-27, Harcourt Brace & Company/Victoria Bowen; 30(t), Harcourt Brace & Company/Victoria Bowen; 30(c), Steve Whalen/Nawrocki Stock Photo; 31 Harcourt Brace & Company/Terry D. Sinclair. 30(b), Bob Daemmrich; 32(bl), 1973(3) Courtesy Department of Library Services, American Museum of Natural History; 32(br), Photo Researchers; 32-33, Courtesy of Abell-Hanger Foundation and Permian Basin Petroleum Museum, Midland, Texas, where painting is on display. © 1973, Abell Hanger Foundation; 33(bl), Object from the Smithsonian National Museum of Natural History, Photographed by Mark Gulezian; 33(br), Werner Forman/Art Resource, NY; 34,1428(3), Courtesy Department of Library Services American Museum of Natural History; 35(l), Photo by Rod Hook, Courtesy of the Wheelwright Museum of The American Indian, No. P21-#14; 35(r), 3837(4), Courtesy Department of Library Services, American Museum of Natural History; 36, Werner Forman/Art Resource, NY; 38, Tom Bean/The Stock Market; 39, Mercyhurst Archaeological Institute; 40(t), Dr. Thomas D. Dillehay, Department of Anthropology, The University of Kentucky; 40(b), Mercyhurst Archeological Institute; 41(l), Amerind Foundation, Inc., Dragoon, Arizona; 41(r), National Museum of American Art, Washington DC/Art Resource, NY; 44, John Maier, Jr/JB Pictures; 45(t), Tom Wolff/St. Remy Press; 45(b), Jerry Jacka; 46, Tom McHugh/Photo Researchers; 48(t), 4950(3), Courtesy Department of Library Services, American Museum of Natural History; 48(b), 1973(3) Courtesy Department of Library Services American Museum of Natural History; 49, Courtesy of the National Museum of the American Indian Smithsonian Institution (slide #S3242); 50(t), Vera Lentz; 50(b), Object from the Smithsonian National Museum of Natural History, Photographed by Mark Gulezian; 52, Michel Zebe; 53, Felipe Davalos/National Geographic Image Collection; 55(l), Photograph © The Detroit Institute of Arts, National Park Service, Hopewell Culture National Historical Park, Chillicothe, Ohio. © Dirk Bakker, Photographer; 55(r), Comstock; 56-57, Jerry Jacka; 57(c), Amerind Foundation, Dragoon, AZ-Robin Starcliff, Inc.; 57(r), Object from the Smithsonian National Museum of Natural History, photo by Mark Gulezian; 60, Michal Heron/Woodfin Camp; 63, Courtesy of the Thomas Burke Memorial Washington State Museum Catalog #2-3844, photo by Eduarado Calderon; 64, 4075(2), Courtesy Department of Library Services, American Museum of Natural History; 67(l), John L. Doyle; 67(r), John Cancalosi/Stock Boston; 70, Jerry Jacka; 71, National Museum of the American Indian, New York City; 72-73, National Museum of American Art, Washington DC/Art Resource, NY; 73(r), Patterson Graphics, Dayton, Ohio; 74, Courtesy of the National Museum of the American Indian Smithsonian Institution (slide #S2600); 75, "Iroquois Bone Comb," Herbert Bigford, Sr. Collection, Longyear Museum of Anthropology/Colgate University; 78(l), Peabody Museum-Harvard University, photograph by Hillel Burger; 78(r), Rare Books & Manuscripts Division, The New York Public Library, Astor, Lenox, and Tilden Foundations; 80, The Metropolitan Museum of Art, Gift of Eugene and Ina Schnell, 1989(1989.110); 81(l), Michel Zebe; 81(r), Dimitri Kessel, Life © TIME, Inc.; 82, Justin Kerr; 83, Michel Zebe; 84, Bob Schalkwijk; 85, Michel Zebe; 88(l), First Light; 88(r), Paul Grebliunas/Tony Stone Images; 88-89(bg), Harcourt Brace & Company/Victoria Bowen; 89(t), Jed Share/First Light; 89(bl), Harald Sund/The Image Bank; 89(br), Peter Hendrie/The Image Bank; 89(lc), Steve Dunwell/The Image Bank; 89(rc), Art Brewer/Tony Stone Images; 92, Harcourt Brace & Company; 94(bc), Loren McIntyre; 94(bl), ET Archive; 94(br), Dr. David Dye, University of Memphis; 94-95, Rijksmuseum, Amsterdam; 95(bl), Michael Holford; 95(br), From the Collection of The Minnesota Historical Society; 98, Scala/Art Resource, NY; 99, Werner Forman/Art Resource, NY; 100, Werner Forman/Art Resource, NY; 102, The New York Public Library Map Division Astor, Lenox and Tilden Foundations; 103, Giraudon/Art Resource, NY; 104(t), Collection of the National Palace Museum, Taipei, Taiwan, Republic of China; 104(b), Biblioteque National, Paris; 105, Michael Holford; 106(l), Biblioteque Nationale; 106(r), Nationalbibliotek; 108-111(bg), RGS33895 Europe and Mediterranean: "Portolan of Frederici d' Ancore," 1497, from Vicomte de Santarem's "Atlas of Mappaemundi and Portolans," pub. 1842-53 Royal Geographical Society, London/Bridgeman Art Library, London; 114, ZIN41924 Selection of Arab and European Astrolabes from 14th to 16th century, copper Museum of the History of Science, Osford/Bridgeman Art Library, London; 115, The New York Public Library, Map Division; 118, AKG London; 119, The Bettmann Archive; 122, Detail, Photo Archives, Denver Museum of Natural History. All rights reserved; 123, Scala/Art Resource; 124, 1412(5) Courtesy Department of Library Services, American Museum of Natural History; 125, Detail, Collection of the J. Paul Getty Museum, Malibu, California; 126(bg), Loren McIntyre; 126(fg), ET Archive; 127, Sallet helmet, probably Spanish, steel second half of the fifteenth century. Photo by Don Eaton, Courtesy of the Higgins Armory Museum, Worcester, Massachusetts; 129(t), Dr. David H. Dye, University of Memphis; 129(b), Courtesy of The Library of Congress; 131, © 1986 Mel Fisher/Maritime Heritage Society, Key West, FL. Photo by Scott Nierling; 132(l), Archivo Fotographico Sevilla; 132(r), Courtesy of The Hispanic Society of America, New York; 133, Werner Forman/Art Resource, NY; 134, National Maritime Museum, London; 135, American Beaver by J.J. Audubon(detail). Taken from plate XLVI Vivb., Quadrupeds of North America. Missouri Historical Society, St. Louis; 137(l), The Surveyor: Portrait of Captain John Henry Lefroy, © 1845-55, attributed to Paul Kane. Glenbow Collection, Calgary, Canada; 137(r), From the Collection of the Minnesota Historical Society; 138(tl), The Minnesota Historical Society #67.230.177; 138(bl), The Minnesota Historical Society; 138(r), The Granger Collection, New York; 139, BAL1648 Elizabeth I, Armada portrait by Anonymous Private Collection/Bridgeman Art Library, London; 141(tl), The Library of Virginia; 141(tr), A.H. Robins, photo by Don Eiler; 141(bl), BAL10692 Town of Pomeiooc, Virginia(w/c) by White, John(fl.c.1570-93)British Museum, London/Bridgeman Art Library, London; 143, Courtesy of the Pilgrim Society, Plymouth Massachusetts; 148(fg), Harcourt Brace & Company/Victoria Bowen; 148-149(bg), Michael Melford/The Image Bank; 149(fg), Harcourt Brace & Company/Victoria Bowen; 152, Harcourt Brace & Company/Terry D. Sinclair; 154(bl), Julius Fekete/The Stock Market; 154-155 ,I.N. Phelps Stokes collection, Miriam & Ira D. Wallach Division of Art, Prints, and Photographs. The New York Public Library, Astor, Lenox, and Tilden Foundation; 155(bl), Courtesy, Winterthur Museum; 155(br), National Geographic Image Collection; 156(t), Rare Books & Manuscripts Division, The New York Public Library Astor, Lenox and Tilden Foundations; 156(b), Courtesy of The Pilgrim Society, Plymouth, Massachusetts; 157(t), Courtesy of the Pilgrim Society, Plymouth, Massachusetts; 157(c), Walter Meayers Edsards/National Geographic Image Collection; 157(b), Courtesy of The Pilgrim Society; 158, The Santa Barbara Mission; 160, Steve Vidler/Leo De Wys; 163, George H.H. Huey; 164, Stretched beaver pelt. Collection of Massachusetts Division of Fisheries and Wildlife, Photo by Mark Sexton; 167(l), Courtesy of The Adirondack Museum, photo by James Swedberg; 167(r), Manfred Gottschalk/Tom Stack & Associates; 168, The Historic New Orleans Collection, Accession No. 1991.60; 169, Science and Technology Section Science, Industry & Business Library. The New York Public Library, Astor Lenox and Tilden Foundations; 171(t), Worcester Art Museum, Worcester, Massachusetts, Gift of Mr. and Mrs. Albert Rice; 171(b), Courtesy of The Pilgrim Society, Plymouth, Massachusetts; 172, The Bettmann Archive; 173(t), Culver Pictures; 173(b), Culver Pictures; 174(bg), Detail, Giraudon/Art Resource, New York; 174(fg), The Historical Society of Pennsylvania; 176(l), Methodist Collection of Drew University, Photographed by George Goodwin; 176(r), Courtesy of Oglethorpe University; 180 Detroit Institute of Arts Founders Society.182, Smithsonian Institution, Division of Transportation; 184, Colonial Williamsburg Foundation ; 186, Garry D. MacMichael/Photo Researchers; 188(l), Chicago Historical Society #X 1354; 188(c), Courtesy, American Antiquarian Society; 188(r), EX 17082 Negro Portrait: Olaudah Equiano by English School,(18th century) Royal Albert Memorial Museum, Exeter/Bridgeman Art Library, London; 189, The Metropolitan Museum of Art, Gift of Edgar William and Bernice Chrysler Garbisch, 1963.(63.201.3); 191(fg), W.J. Bennett(inventor) George Harvey(artist) Spring #2: Burning Fallen Trees in a Girdled Clearing - Western Scene Yale University Art Gallery, The Mabel Brady Garvan Collection.; 191-193(bg), Tom & Pat Leeson; 192, National Geographic Image Collection; 193(l), Smithsonian Institution, Division of Agriculture, Neg. #34769; 193(r), Smithsonian Institution, Domestic Life Division, Neg. #LIA-83-30016-9; 198-199(bg), Ken Biggs/Tony Stone Images; 199(l,fg), Joseph Pobereskin/Tony Stone Images; 199(r,fg), Jon Ortner/Tony Stone Images; 202, Harcourt Brace & Company/Terry D. Sinclair; 204(bl), Courtesy of Massachusetts Historical Society; 204(br), Peabody Essex Museum, Salem, Massachusetts; 204-205, The Historical Society of Pennsylvania; 204-205(bg) Harcourt Brace & Company/Victoria Bowen; 205(bl), Smithsonian Institution, Division of Political History, Neg. #83-4689; 205(bc), Courtesy of G. Gedney Godwin, Inc.; 205(br), Ed Wheele/The Stock Market; 208, The Boston Atheneum; 210, Courtesy of the Library Of Congress; 212, Dan McCoy/Rainbow; 214, James L. Stanfield/National Geographic Image Collection; 215, Courtesy of the Massachusetts Historical Society; 216, Peabody Essex Museum, Salem, Mass. Photo By Mark Sexton; 217(tl, bl, c), Courtesy of Massachusetts Historical Society; 218,Virginia Historical Society, Richmond, VA; 220(l), The Historical Society of Pennsylvania; 220(r), The Bucks County Historical Society; 221(l), The Metropolitan Museum of Art, Gift of Mrs. Russell Sage, 1909.(10.125.103); 221(r), Stock Montage; 222, Paul Rocheleau; 223(t), Deposited by the City of Boston. Courtesy, Museum of Fine Arts, Boston; 223(b), Daughters of the American Revolution Museum, Washington, DC; 224, The Paul Revere Life Insurance Company, Worcester, Massachusetts; 225, Courtesy of the Concord Museum, Concord, Massachusetts, photograph by Chip Fanelli; 226, Gift of Joseph W. Revere, William B. Revere, and Edward H.R. Revere Courtesy, Museum of Fine Arts, Boston; 227,Colonial Williamsburg Foundation; 230, Bequest of Winslow Warren. Courtesy, Museum of Fine Arts, Boston; 232, The Historical Society of Pennsylvania; 233(t), A detail , Charles Willson Peale. George Washington at the Battle of Princeton, Yale University Art Gallery, Gift of the Associates in Fine Arts and Mrs. Henry B. Loomis in memory of Henry Bradford Loomis , B.A. 1875; 233(b), Courtesy of Massachusetts Historical Society; 234, Delaware Art Museum, Howard Pile Collection; 235, American Philosophical Society; 236, Detail, Thomas Paine, John Wesley Jarvis, Gift of Marian B. Maurice © Board of Trustees, National Gallery of Art, Washington; 237(tr), The Bettmann Archive;

237(tl), Artwork from Wood River Gallery, Mill Valley, CA; 237(b), Smithsonian Institution, Division of Political History, Neg. #83-4689; 238, A detail - John Trumbull, The Declaration of Independence, 4 July 1776 Yale University Art Gallery, Trumbull collection; 239, Ed Wheele/The Stock Market; 240, Ted Spiegel; 241(t), Fraunces Tavern Museum, New York City; 241(b), The Granger Collection, New York; 242, William T. Ranney Marion Crossing the Peedee, oil on canvas, 1850, accession number 1983.126, Amon Carter Museum, Fort Worth, Texas; 248, Ted Spiegel; 250, The Pennsylvania Capitol Preservation Committee/Hunt Commercial Photography; 252, A detail, John Trumbull The Surrender of Lord Cornwallis at Yorktown, 19 October 1781 Yale University Art Gallery, Trumbull collection.; 256-257, Reuters/Bettmann; 260 Harcourt Brace & Company; 262(bl), Michael Bryant/Woodfin Camp; 262(br), Smithsonian Institution, Division of Political History, Neg. #81-5397; 262-263, Architect of the United States Capitol, Washington, DC; 263(bl), Independence National Historical Park Collection; 263(br), Sally Anderson Bruce; 266, New York State Historical Association, Cooperstown; 267, The Historical Society of Pennsylvania; 268, Cranbrook Institute of Science; 269(l), The Bettmann Archive; 269(r), Courtesy, American Antiquarian Society.; 271, Smithsonian Institution, Division of Political History, Neg. #81-5397; 272, The Commonwealth of Massachusetts, State House, Boston; 274,The Historical Society of Pennsylvania; 275(l), Independence National Historical Park Collection; 275(r), Independence National Historical Park Collection; 278, Courtesy of The National Archives; 280(l), The Library of Virginia; 280(c), Princeton University, Bequest of William Paterson, grandson of the subject in 1899; 280(r), Emmet Collection, Rare Books and Manuscripts Division, The New York Public Library, Astor, Lenox and Tilden Foundations; 281,"Residence and Slave Quarters of Mulberry Plantation" by Thomas Coram, The Gibbes Museum of Art, Charleston, SC; 283, Ralph Earl Roger Sherman(1721-1793), M.A.(Hon.) 1786 Yale University Art Gallery Gift of Roger Sherman White, B.A. 1899, L.L.B 1902; 284, Courtesy of the U.S. Senate Collection; 286, Wally McNamee/Woodfin Camp ; 290, Michael Bryant/Woodfin Camp; 296 Superstock; 298(l), Michael Bryant/Woodfin Camp; 298(r), Michael Bryant/Woodfin Camp; 300(t), Collection of The New York Historical Society; 300(b), The Bettmann Archive; 302(l), Colonial Williamsburg Foundation; 302(r), The White House Historical Association; 303(l), Courtesy of the Library of Congress; 303(l,inset), Courtesy of the Library of Congress; 303(r), Courtesy of the Library Of Congress; 303(r,inset), The Granger Collection, New York; 304, The Smithsonian Institution, National Numismatic Collection.; 305, North Wind Picture Archives; 306, Smithsonian Institution, Division of Textiles, Neg. #75-15211; 307, Smithsonian Institution, Division of Political History, Neg. #80-3963; 308(l), Mr. and Mrs. John Harney; 308(r), Sally Anderson-Bruce; 309, Sally Anderson-Bruce; 310(l), Independence National Historical Park Collection; 310(r), Independence National Historical Park Collection; 311, Maryland Historical Society, Baltimore; 313, Eric P. Newman Numismatic Education Society; 316-317(bg) Harcourt Brace & Company; 316-317(fg), Harcourt Brace & Company/Victoria Bowen; 320 Harcourt Brace & Company; 322(bl), Reynolda House Museum of American Art, Winston-Salem, North Carolina; 322(br), Culver Pictures; 322-323, The National Cowboy Hall of Fame and Western Heritage Center, Oklahoma City, Oklahoma; 322-323(bg), Image © 1996 PhotoDisc, Inc.; 323(bl), Lee Boltin; 323(br), Gill C. Kenny/The Image Bank; 326, Stanley B. Burns MD and the Burns Archive; 327, Smithsonian Institution, Division of Social History, Neg. #94-146; 328,George Caleb Bingham, Daniel Boone Escorting Settlers through the Cumberland Gap, 1851-52, detail. Oil on canvas, 36 1/2 X 50 1/4". Washington University Gallery of Art, St. Louis.; 329, Reynolda House Museum of American Art, Winston-Salem, North Carolina; 331, Collection of the New York Historical Society; 332, The Bettmann Archive; 333(tl), Library, The Academy of Natural Sciences of Philadelphia; 333(bl), Peabody Museum - Harvard University, Photograph by Hillel Burger; 333(r), Charles Russell"Lewis and Clark on the Lower Columbia", gouache, watercolor and graphite on paper 1905, Amon Carter Museum, Fort Worth, Texas; 334, Courtesy of the Montana Historical Society; 335(l), Courtesy, Independence National Historical Park; 335(r), Gerry Addison/Stock Boston; 337(l), The Field Museum Photo by: John Weinstein; 337(r), Computer Generated Image Courtesy of Pathways Productions, Inc. All rights reserved ©1994.; 339(l), The Granger Collection, New York; 339(r), Collection of the New York Historical Society; 340, Courtesy U.S. Naval Academy Museum; 341, The Bettmann Archive; 343, Lee Boltin; 348, Archives Division - Texas State Library; 350(l), Smithsonian Institution, National Museum of American Art, Registrar's office Neg. #P-64260-A; 350(tr), Slater Mill Historic Site Pawtucket, Rhode Island; 350(br), Smithsonian Institution, Division of Engineering, Neg. #86-9625; 351(l), Museum of American Textile History; 351(r), Progress for Cotton, No. 4 Carding, detail Yale University Art Gallery The Mabel Brady Garvan Collection; 354, The Granger Collection, New York; 355, The Smithsonian Institution; 357, Philadelphia Museum of Art: Given by Miss William Adger; 358, "Choctaw Removal" Valjean Hessing, The Philbrook Museum of Art, Tulsa, Oklahoma; 359, Archives Division - Texas State Library; 360, Friends of The Governor's Mansion, Austin, Texas; 362(t), Courtesy of The National Archives; 362(b), Courtesy of the San Joaquin County Historical Society, Lodi, CA; 363, "Winter Quarters" C.C.A. Christensen, © Courtesy Museum of Art, Brigham Young University. All rights reserved.; 365, California State Library; 367 The Kansas State Historical Society, Topeka, Kansas. 368, The Bettmann Archive; 369(l), Book cover slide of "Uncle Tom's Cabin," by Harriet Beecher Stowe. Courtesy of the Charles L. Blockson Afro-American Collection, Temple University.; 369(frame), Harcourt Brace & Company Photo; 369(r), The Harriet Beecher Stowe Center, Hartford, CT; 370, State Archives of Michigan; 371, The Bettmann Archive; 372, The Bettmann Archive; 376-377(bg), The Bettmann Archive; 377(t), Courtesy of the Library of Congress; 377(b), Stock Montage, Inc.; 380, Harcourt Brace & Company/Terry D. Sinclair; 382(b), Smithsonian Institution, Division of Textiles, Neg. #73-11287; 382-383, Anne S.K. Brown Military Collection, Brown University Library; 383(bl), Lincoln Library and Museum, Fort Wayne, Indiana; 383(bl,frame), Harcourt Brace & Company Photo; 383(br), From The Civil War: Forward To Richmond Photograph by Larry Cantrell©1983 Time-Life Books, Inc.; 384, Chris Nelson Collection; 385(frames), Harcourt Brace & Company Photo; 385(l), Valentine Museum, Richmond, Virginia; 385(r), The Bettmann Archive; 386-387, Anne S.K. Brown Military Collection, Brown University Library; 387(b), Eleanor S. Brockenbrough Library The Museum of the Confederacy Richmond, Virginia photograph by Katherine Wetzel; 388, Detail, National Portrait Gallery, Smithsonian Institution/Art Resource, NY; 390(t), From the Collection of the Public Library of Cincinnati and Hamilton County; 390(b), Courtesy of The Library of Congress; 391, The Granger Collection, New York; 392(l), Smithsonian Institution, Division of Textiles, Neg. #73-11287; 392(r), Mary Evans Picture Library; 393(t), Courtesy of The Library of Congress; 393(b), The Bettmann Archive; 395, Courtesy of the Charleston Museum, Charleston, South Carolina; 396, "Last Sale of Slaves on the Courthouse Steps" by Thomas Satterwhite Noble, 1860. Oil on canvas. Missouri Historical Society, St. Louis, MO #1939.003.0001; 397(l), The Brooklyn Museum; 397(r), The Granger Collection, New York; 398, The Bettmann Archive; 400, The Metropolitan Museum of Art, Gift of I.N. Phelps Stokes, Edward S. Hawes, Alice Mary Hawes, Marion Augusta Hawes, 1937; 402(l), "Dred Scott" oil on canvas by Louis Schultze, 1881 #1897.009.0001, The MissourI Historical Society, St. Louis, MO ; 402(r), Courtesy of The Library of Congress; 403, Sophia Smith Collection Smith College, Northampton MA ; 404, Courtesy of the Illinois State Historical Library; 405, Museum of Political Life, University of Hartford; 406(t), Stock Montage; 406(b), Museum of American Political Life, University of Hartford West Hartford, CT; 407, National Archives; 409(bg), From the Photo Collection of the Architect of the US Capitol; 409(l), The Granger Collection, New York; 409(r), National Portrait Gallery, Washington, DC/Art Resource, New York; 411(t), Photri, Inc.; 411(b), The Granger Collection, New York; 414, Courtesy of The Library of Congress; 416(t), The Museum of the Confederacy, Richmond, VA. Photo by Larry Sherer. TLB 2713: from Echoes of Glory: Arms & Equipment of the Confederacy © 1991 Time-Life Books, Inc.; 416(c),NMAH, Smithsonian, TLB 2717 from Echoes of Glory: Arms & Equipment of the Union, photographed by Larry Sherer © 1991 Time-Life Books, Inc.; 416(b), Obtained from Washington and Lee Univeristy; 419(l), The National Archives; 419(r), Massachusetts Commandery Military Order of the Loyal Legion and the US Army Military History Institute ; 420-421(t), The Granger Collection, New York; 421, The Bettmann Archive; 421(frame), Harcourt Brace and Company photo; 422, The Bettmann Archive; 423, The Architect of the Capitol; 424, Massachusetts Commandery Military Order of the Loyal Legion and the US Army Military History Institute, photographed by Jim Enos; 425, Peter Newark; 425(frame), Harcourt Brace & Company photo; 426, Chicago Historical Society ; 427(t), National Archives; 427(b), Salamander Books; 430, Tom Lovell © National Geographic Society; 431, Stanley B. Burns, MD and the Burns Archive; 435, Courtesy Houston Metropolitan Research Center, Houston Public Library; 436, Cook Collection, Valentine Museum; 437, The Metropolitan Museum of Art, Morris K. Jesup Fund, 1940.(40.40); 438(l), Courtesy of The Library of Congress; 438(r), Courtesy of The Library of Congress; 439, Courtesy of The Library Of Congress; 442-443, UPI/Bettmann; 446 Harcourt Brace & Company; 448(bl), Stanford University Museum of Art AAA Gift of David Hewes; 448(br), Michael Freeman; 448-449(t), Andrew Smith Galleries, Inc., Santa Fe, New Mexico/KEA; 448-449(b), David Bassett/Tony Stone Images; 449(bl), Comstock; 449(br), Jon Ortner/Tony Stone Images; 450, Michael Freeman; 451, From the Collections of Henry Frot Museum & Greenfield Village; 452, UPI/Bettmann; 453, Stanford University Museum of Art AAA Gift of David Hewes; 454, Smithsonian Institution, Division of Electricity, Neg. # 27-979; 455 ,From William J. Gaughan, Archives of Industrial Society, University of Pittsburgh; 456(l), The Bettmann Archive; 456(r), The Bettmann Archive; 458(l), The Granger Collection, New York; 458(r), Culver Pictures; 460, Courtesy of The Library of Congress; 461, The Bettmann Archive; 463, Brown Brothers; 464, UPI/Bettmann; 465, Courtesy of the Musuem of Chinese in the Americas; 466, The Institute of Texan Cultures, San Antonio, Texas; 467, Brown Brothers; 469, Calumet Regional Archives, Indiana University Northwest; 470, The Phillips Collection, Washington, D.C.; 471(t), The Phillips Collection, Washington, D.C.; 471(b), Lawrence, Jacob. "They also worked on the railroads."Panel 38 from The Migration Series.(1940-41; text and title revised by the artist, 1993). Tempera on gesso on composition board, 12x18"(30.5 x 45.7 cm). The Museum of Modern Art, New York. Gift of Mrs. David M. Levy. Photograph ©1995 The Museum of Modern Art, New York; 472, Lawrence, Jacob. "The Migration gained in momentum." Panel 18 from The Migration Series.(1940-41; text and title revised by the artist, 1993). Tempera on gesso on composition boarad, 18x12"(45.7x30.5 cm). The Museum of Modern Art, New York. Gift of Mrs. David M. Levy. Photograph ©1995 The Museum of Modern Art, New York.; 473(t), Lawrence, Jacob. "But living conditions were better in the North." Panel 44 from The Migration Series.(1940-41; text and title revised by the artist, 1993) Tempera on gesso on composition board, 12x18"(30.5x45.7 cm). The Museum of Modern Art, New York. Gift of Mrs. David M. Levy. Photograph ©1995 The Museum of Modern Art, New York.; 473(b), The Phillips Collection, Washington, D.C.; 474, Lawrence, Jacob. "In the North the Negro had better educational facilities." Panel 58 from The Migration Series.(1940-41; text and title revised by the artist, 1993). Tempera on gesso on composition board, 12x18"(30.5x45.7 cm). The Museum of Modern Art, New York. Gift of Mrs. Davaid M. Levy. Photograph ©1995 The Museum of Modern Art, New York.; 475, Steven Mays/The Encyclopedia of Collectibles, for Time-Life Books, Courtesy of Rebus, Inc., New York, N.Y.; 476, Detail "Baxter Street Court, 22 Baxter Street" The Jacob A. Riis Collection, #108 The Museum of The City Of New York; 477(t), Brown Brothers; 477(b), The Bettmann Archive; 477(b,inset), The Bettmann Archive; 478, Detail "Trolley Car, Brooklyn Trolley Car Strike, 1899" The Museum of the City Of New York, The Byron Collection; 479(l), Stock Montage; 479(r), University of Illinois at Chicago the University Library Jane Addams Memorial Collection; 482, The Denver Public Library, Western History Department; 483,"Missouri is Free" Advertising card for Hannibal and St. Joseph Railroad, ca 1867. Advertising #60A, The Missouri Historical Society, St. Louis, MO; 485,Nebraska State Historical Society; 486, Grant Heilman; 487, The Bettmann Archive; 488, Grant Heilman Photography; 490, Steven Mays/The Encyclopedia of Collectibles, for Time-Life Books, Courtesy of Rebus, Inc., New York, N.Y.; 491, Frederic Remington(1861-1909) "American Stampede" oil on canvas #0127.2329 from the Collection of Gilcrease Museum, Tulsa.; 492, UPI/Bettmann; 493, Wyoming Division of Cultural Resources; 494(l), Stephen Ogilvy; 494(r), Smithsonian Institution, Division of Political History, Neg. #94-186; 495, Gill C. Kenny/The Image Bank; 496(t), Michael Friedman; 496(b), California State Library Neg. #: 912; 498, North Wind Picture Archive; 500 , Catalogue no. 358879, Department of Anthropology, Smithsonian Institution; 501, Culver Pictures; 504(l), Courtesy of the US Patent Office; 504(r), Courtesy of Jeanie Low; 504-505(bg), David Jeffrey/The Image Bank; 504-505(bg, c), Courtesy of Jeanie Low; 505(t), Courtesy of Jeanie Low; 505(b), Courtesy of the US Patent Office; 508, Harcourt Brace & Company/Terry D. Sinclair; 510(bl), Ted Spiegel; 510(br), Museum of American Political Life, University of Hartford, West Hartford, CT; 510-511(t), Fred Pansing "The Naval Parade", 1898 oil on canvas, 42.10 x 19.12 cm Museum of the City of New York, 31.94.7; 510-511(b), Image © 1996 PhotoDisc, Inc.; 511(bl), ET Archive; 511(bc), Clint Eley/The Image Bank; 511(br), Private Collection; 512(b), Ted Spiegel; 512-513, Archive Photos; 514, Theodore Roosevelt Collection Harvard College Library; 516(l), Gary Buss/FPG International; 516(r), Culver Pictures; 517(t), The National Archives; 517(b), Ted Spiegel; 518, Brown Brothers; 520-521, The Bettmann Archive; 524, Museum of American Political Life, University of Hartford, West Hartford, CT; 525, Culver Pictures; 526, The Bettmann Archive; 527, Artwork from Wood River Gallery, Mill Valley, California; 528(l), Culver Pictures; 528(r), Culver Pictures; 529, The Bettmann Archive; 530, FPG International; 531, National Portrait Gallery, Smithsonian Institution/Art Resource, NY; 532, UPI/Bettmann; 533, Courtesy of The Library of Congress; 536 Print Courtesy Stetson Kennedy; 538(t), Culver Pictures; 538(b), From the collections of Henry Ford Museum & Greenfield Village; 539(t), The Granger Collection, New York; 539(b), The Bettmann Archive; 540(t), The Bettmann Archive; 540(b), Missouri Historical Society, St. Louis, MO; 541(t), The Bettman Archive; 541(b), The Bettmann Archive; 542, The Bettmann Archive; 543(t), UPI/Bettmann; 543(b), New York Stock Exchange Archives; 545(t), The Bettmann Archvie; 545(b), UPI/Bettmann; 546, San Francisco History Room, San Francisco Public Library; 547, Courtesy of the Library of Congress; 547-550(bg), Barry Rowland/Tony Stone Images; 548, Dorthea Lange Courtesy of the Library of Congress; 549, Arthur Rothstein, Courtesy of the Library of Congress; 550, Arthur Rothstein, Courtesy of the Library of Congress; 552, UPI/Bettmann Newsphotos; 553(l), The Bettmann Archive; 553(r), Culver Pictures; 554, UPI/Bettmann; 555, Courtesy of The Library of Congress; 556(l), Courtesy of the Japanese American Museum; 556(r), AP/Wide World Photos; 557, Private Collection; 558(t), UPI/Bettmann; 558(b), The Bettmann Archive; 559(l), Culver Pictures; 559(r), Yellow Star, Germany, 1930's. Printed cotton. Gift of Moriah Artcraft Judaica, Photograph by Greg Staley, Courtesy of B'nai B'rith Klutznick National Jewish museum; 566(b), Steve McCurry/Magnum Photos; 566-567(bg), Bruce Stoddard/FPG International; 566-567(bg,c), Harcourt Brace & Company; 567(t), Joanna B. Pinneo/Aurora; 567(lc), AP/Wide Worlld Photos; 567(rc), Alexandra Boulat/Sipa Press; 567(b), Winfield I Parks/National Geographic Image Collection; 570, Harcourt Brace & Company/Terry D. Sinclair; 572(bl), UPI/Bettmann; 572(br), Dan Weiner, Courtesy of Sandra Weiner; 572-573(t), Roger Ressmeyer/Corbis; 572-573(b), NASA; 573(bl), UPI/Bettmann; 573(br), John Brooks/Gamma Liaison; 574, Reuters/Bettmann; 575, National Museum of American Art, Washington DC/Art Resource, NY; 576, Flip & Debra Schulke/Black Star; 578, UPI/Bettmann; 580, UPI/Bettmann; 581, UPI/Bettmann; 588, UPI/Bettmann; 589(l), AP/Wide World Photos; 589(r), Dan Weiner, Courtesy of Sandra Weiner; 590, John Lounois/Black Star; 591, Bob Fitch/Black Star; 593, UPI/Bettmann; 594, UPI/Bettmann; 595, UPI/Bettmann Newsphotos; 596, Mark Godfrey; 597, UPI/Bettmann Newsphotos; 598, UPI/Bettmann; 599(t), Archive Photos; 599(b), UPI/Bettmann; 600, UPI/Bettmann; 601, Dennis Brack/Black Star; 602, UPI/Bettmann; 603, AP/Wide World Photos; 604, AP/Wide World Photos; 605(l), Courtesy of the Republican National Committee; 605(r), Courtesy of the Democratic National Committee; 608, David Hautzig; 610(t), Anthony Suau/Gamma Liaison; 610(b), Bob Daemmrich; 612, Florence Parker/Archive Photos; 620, Comstock; 621, Tom Haley/Sipa Press; 622(t), Cindy Karp/Black Star; 622(b), Chantal Regnault/Gamma Liaison; 623, Alon Reininger/Contact Press; 624, Bill Gentile/Sipa Press; 625, The Bettmann Archive; 627, Claus Mayer/Black Star; 628, John Brooks/Gamma Liaison; 630(l), Ron Watts/First Light; 630(r), Lee Foster/FPG International; 631, First Light; 638, Harcourt Brace & Company; Facing R1, Dennis Hallinan/FPG International; R1(t), Comstock; R1(b), Hartmann-Dewitt/Comstock; R41(bg), Henryk Kaiser/Stock Imagery; R12 Row 1(l), National Portrait Gallery; R12 Row 1(c), National Portrait Gallery; R12 Row 1(r), Bettmann; R12 Row 2(l), National Portrait Gallery; R12 Row 2(c), National Portrait Gallery; R12 Row 2(r), National Portrait Gallery; R12 Row 3(l), The Granger Collection, New York; R12 Row 3(c), National Portrait Gallery; R12 Row 3(r), National Portrait Gallery; R12 Row 4(l), National Portrait Gallery; R12 Row 4(c), National Portrait Gallery; R12 Row 4(r), The Granger Collection, New York; R13 Row 1(l), The Granger Collection, New York; R13 Row 1(c), Bettmann; R13 Row 1(r), National Portrait Gallery; R13 Row 2(l), New York Historical Society; R13 Row 2(c), The Granger Collection, New York; R13 Row 2(r), The Granger Collection, New York; R13 Row 3(l), National Portrait Gallery; R13 Row 3(c), National Portrait Gallery; R13 Row 3(r), National Portrait Gallery; R13 Row 4(l), The Granger Collection, New York; R13 Row 5(l), National Portrait Gallery; R13 Row 5(c), The Granger Collection, New York; R13 Row 5(r), Bettmann; R14 Row 1(l), National Portrait Gallery; R14 Row 1(c), National Portrait Gallery; R14 Row 1(r), The Granger Collection, New York; R14 Row 2(l), The Granger Collection, New York; R14 Row 2(c), The Granger Collection, New York; R14 Row 2(r), National Portrait Gallery; R14 Row 3(c), The Granger Collection, New York; R14 Row 4(l), The Granger Collection, New York; R14 Row 4(c), National Portrait Gallery; R14 Row 5(l), Wide World Photos; R13 Row 4(c), White House Historical Association; R14 Row 3(l), Eisenhower Library; R14 Row 3(r), Wide World Photos; R14 Row 4(r), White House Historical Association; R14 Row 5(c), David Valdez/The White House; R14 Row 5(r), The White House; R41(fg), Harcourt Brace & Company/P&F Communications.

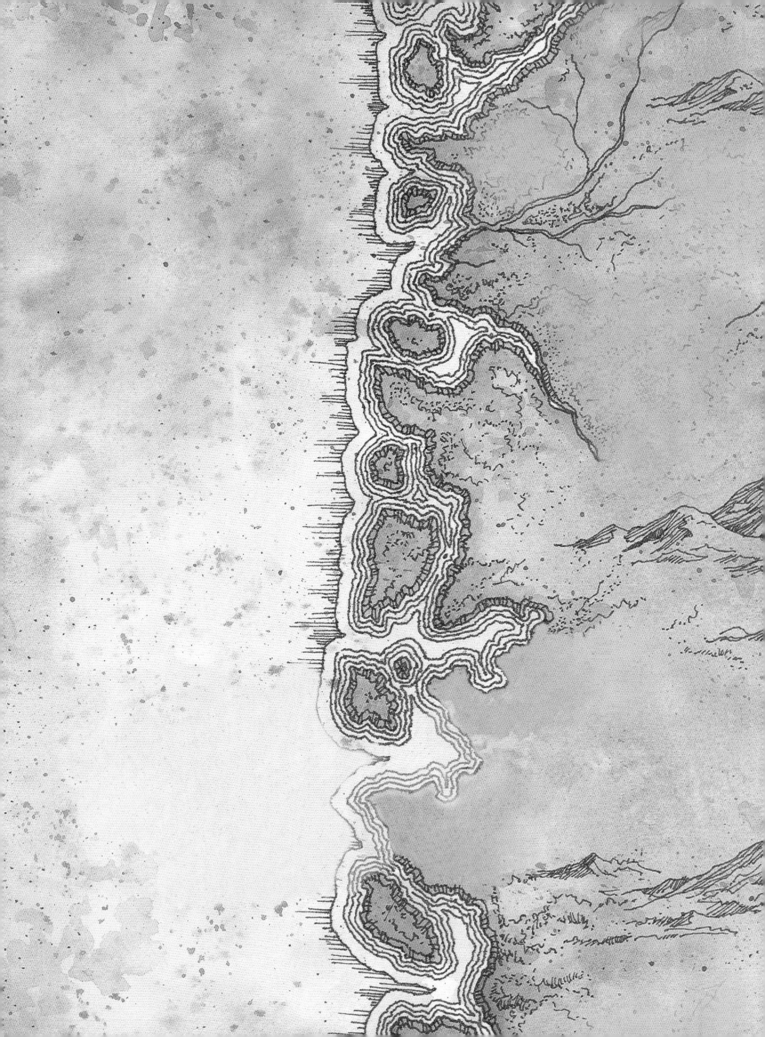